Consumer Credit in the United States

Consumer Credit in the United States

A Sociological Perspective from the 19th Century to the Present

Donncha Marron

palgrave
macmillan

CONSUMER CREDIT IN THE UNITED STATES

An earlier version of chapter 7 appeared as an article in Volume 36 of *Economy & Society* entitled "Lending by numbers: credit scoring and the constitution of risk within the United States." I am very grateful to the two anonymous referees for useful advice and criticisms.

Illustrations in chapters 10 and 11 are Copyright © Fair Isaac Corporation. Used with permission. Fair Isaac, FICO, myFICO, the Fair Isaac logos, and the Fair Isaac product and service names are trademarks or registered trademarks of Fair Isaac Corporation.

First published in 2009 by
PALGRAVE MACMILLAN®
in the United States—a division of St. Martin's Press LLC,
175 Fifth Avenue, New York, NY 10010.

Where this book is distributed in the UK, Europe and the rest of the world, this is by Palgrave Macmillan, a division of Macmillan Publishers Limited, registered in England, company number 785998, of Houndmills, Basingstoke, Hampshire RG21 6XS.

Palgrave Macmillan is the global academic imprint of the above companies and has companies and representatives throughout the world.

Palgrave® and Macmillan® are registered trademarks in the United States, the United Kingdom, Europe and other countries.

ISBN: 978–0–230–61518–2

Library of Congress Cataloging-in-Publication Data

Marron, Donncha.
    Consumer credit in the United States : a sociological perspective from the 19th century to the present / Donncha Marron.
        p. cm.
    Includes bibliographical references and index.
    ISBN 978–0–230–61518–2
    1. Consumer credit—Social aspects—United States. 2. Consumer credit—United States. I. Title.

HG3756.U54M27 2009
332.7′43—dc22   2009013907

First edition: December 2009

10 9 8 7 6 5 4 3 2 1

Printed in the United States of America.

For my parents, Sean and Mary Marron

Contents

Figures

Acknowledgments

I would like to thank Harvie Ferguson, Bridget Fowler, Donald McKenzie, Stuart Waiton, and Stephen Vertigans for thoughtful comments, advice, and help at various stages of this project. I am also grateful for the assistance and considerable patience of Sam Hasey and Julia Cohen at Palgrave. Eternal thanks are due to Catherine Corbett who helped proof earlier drafts of the material and for her considerable help and support throughout many stages of this project.

Most especially, I'd like to express my gratitude to Gerda Reith who oversaw the entire duration of the dissertation upon which this book is based. Her experience, good humor, insight, and breadth of sociological knowledge were utterly invaluable in helping me cohere my ideas and commit them to paper. She also never let a "poor student" pay for lunch.

This book originally started out as a doctoral dissertation in the Department of Sociology, Anthropology and Applied Social Sciences at the University of Glasgow. Generous funding was provided by the Faculty of Law, Business and Social Sciences at the university and I am extremely grateful to them for seeing value in the initial proposal. Particular credit [sic] is due to the Interlibrary Loans Department of Glasgow University Library who unfailingly hunted down all texts, regardless of how obscure or difficult to obtain.

Introduction

Beautiful credit! The foundation of modern society. Who shall say that this is not the golden age of mutual trust, of unlimited reliance upon human promises? That is a peculiar condition of society which enables a whole nation to instantly recognize point and meaning in the familiar newspaper anecdote, which puts into the mouth of a distinguished speculator in lands and mines this remark: "I wasn't worth a cent two years ago, and now I owe two millions of dollars."

— Mark Twain, *The Gilded Age*

"A Peculiar Condition of Society"

Perhaps one of the most overcited quotes in English literature whenever the topic of debt is mentioned is in Hamlet when the pompous Polonius sternly cautions his son Laertes to "neither a borrower nor a lender be." Aside from the words of the bard, Gelpi and Labruyère note some seventy proverbs that enjoin the receiver against the perils of lending and indebtedness, from the American "a bad loan is like a broken mirror" to the rather ambiguous Persian injunction that "debts are husbands to men" (2000: 177–8). Beyond such homely wisdom, debt and credit, borrowing and lending, have proven extremely problematic activities that since the dawn of humanity have attracted the active intervention of the social body to frame its occurrence and course. The Code of Hammurabi, the first written corpus of laws etched on a two meter high stele, regulated the form and substance of credit agreements throughout the duration of the Babylonian empire from 1800 B.C. It bound maximum interest rates, required that loans of any kind had to be drawn up in the presence of a public official, specified in detail the process of pledging collateral for loans, permitted servitude for debt up to a maximum of three years, and mandated that repayment was null and void in the event that the lender violated any of the code's terms (Homer, 1963: 25–31; Gelpi and Labruyère, 2000: 3–4).

In ancient Greece from the seventh century B.C., in the wake of a new wave of commercialization, the influential political and economic reforms of Solon, and the emerging preeminence of Athens, the great philosophers elaborated a theoretical condemnation of interest. Plato rejected commercialism as a degrading detraction from affairs of state while Aristotle's analysis of money concluded that both interest and profits from trade were illegitimate by virtue of the fact that money was unproductive, a barren means of exchange rather than a productive capital that could not be held to "naturally" attract a return. Only agriculture was held by Aristotle to be the true source of wealth. Despite this elitist intellectual opposition, however, credit remained an integral part in trading, manufacturing, agriculture, and state affairs in Greece (Gelpi and Labruyère, 2000: 4–8).

In early Christianity, the doctrine of usury was articulated to outlaw virtually all forms of lending (Burton, 2008: 8–9). Whereas the "Deuteronomic double standard" had allowed the charging of usury to strangers but not to one's brother, the new universalistic Christian church held this distinction to be unconscionable (Nelson, 1969: 3–28). Even as European trade and commerce recovered in the eleventh and twelfth centuries, the doctrine of usury "weighted heavily on the consciences of political and Church leaders and of merchants and bankers" and fundamentally shaped the progress of economic affairs until the Reformation (Homer, 1963: 71). At the same time though, a new theory of interest, as opposed to usury, was elaborated, which articulated the reasonableness of a charge upon money, not for its use but as a form of compensation in the event of delayed repayment. This was soon extended to cover the administrative cost of making loans, to defray the opportunity cost of the money loaned as well as for compensating the risk of lost principal (Homer, 1963: 73–4; Gelpi and Labruyère, 2000: 34–7).

In the fourteenth century, the church attempted to alleviate problems of poverty through the raising of money and provision of interest-free loans while, in the century that followed, charitable pawnshops known as *montes pietatis* became established by church and municipal authorities around Italy to alleviate the suffering contrived by extortionate pawnbrokers (Homer, 1963: 78–9; Hudson, 1982: 25–7; Gelpi and Labruyère, 2000: 42–5). In 1515, the Lateran Council finally legitimized the charging of interest on such transactions on the basis of it being a compensation for administrative expense. In the sixteenth century, with the promulgation of the Reformation and Luther's declaration that a Christian man "was free, under no obligation to observe dead Mosaic ordinances" (Nelson, 1969: 29), usury now took the form, not of a complete prohibition on interest taking, but of interest that was excessive or exploitative. With the rise of modernity, the Catholic Church was losing control of its monopoly over time upon which the traditional concept of usury had been founded (Adam, 2004: 125–6). Within Britain, as Hoppit (1990) shows, the expansion of public, commercial, and personal forms of indebtedness within the tumultuous period between the late seventeenth and early eighteenth centuries sparked ongoing, vigorous debates on the ethics, morality, and practicality of borrowing in all its forms, from the corruption inherent in the emerging permanent national debt to the extortionate rates of interest charged by pawnbrokers and Jewish moneylenders.

Although loans have always been made for personal use, consumption as a particularly distinctive domain arose only with the emergence of wage labor and the separation of home life from workplace under capitalism. In doing so, it came to represent a site integral for the reproduction of labor and of capital itself yet, at the same time, denoting a sphere characterized by the threat of devourment and destruction of productive potential (Reith, 2005: 230). It is the conflation of this ambivalent sphere with the particular characteristics of credit that, perhaps, serves to inject consumer credit with the profoundly problematic cultural understanding it has endured since its inception, a contradiction most clearly evident within the United States. The New World has represented, on the one hand, a young dynamic society, progressive and industrialized, free from the constraints of its colonial forbears. Toward the end of the nineteenth century, it also became one of the most resolutely consumerized, with novel developments in retailing, commercial distribution, and advertising, as well as consumer credit, promulgating and feeding on the longings and desires of individuals as consumers. On the other hand, the Puritan legacy of industry, frugality, asceticism, and service, secularly exemplified by Benjamin Franklin has long been held as the core element at the cultural heart of the United States. Still to this day, long after Jeremy Bentham's "In Defence of Usury" had won the argument for the ending of usury ceilings in Britain by 1859, most individual states in the United States continue to impose some form of interest or usury ceiling in credit contracts. It is for these reasons that the United States provides the specific historical context for this book.

Myths of Consumer Credit

In his extraordinary contribution to our understanding of the development of consumer credit within the United States, cultural historian Lendol Calder (2002) argues that two polar "myths" have driven the conceptualization of consumer credit. On the one hand, the myth of credit as the "great democratizer" presents credit as being a social equalizer, of promoting higher standards of living among the masses and allowing all to enjoy the realization of their consumerist desires. While president of Princeton University, Woodrow Wilson remarked in 1903 that the automobile would bring socialism to America as everyone would want one but not everyone could afford one. On the contrary, it was the commercial organization of credit installment plans that was to accomplish this task of individualized personal fulfillment. In the early decades of the twentieth century, economists such as Edwin R.A. Seligman (1927), and Evans Clark (1930) gave intellectual respectability to this myth, reframing foundational concepts such as "production" and "consumption," "luxuries" and "necessities" to show that consumer installment selling was socially beneficial. In the postwar era, commercial economist Clyde Phelps (1954, 1955) presented installment credit as being an essential component in the dynamic of a rising standard of living, fruitfully straddling the two pillars of mass production and mass consumption. More recently the redoubtable Alan Greenspan as chairman of the Federal Reserve linked the growth and distribution of American prosperity to a flexible, competitive, technologically intensive consumer credit marketplace, cautioning a role for government regulation only in creating a level playing field where individual initiative is respected.[1] Today, many economists are relatively cautious about the development of consumer credit yet trust to innovation and freedom of individuals and markets to ensure optimal outcomes (for example, Bostic, 2002; Maki, 2002).

The other perhaps more culturally potent myth surrounding consumer credit has been the "myth of lost economic virtue." Calder (1999) notes how the so-called under-consumptionists of the Great Depression saw it as a necessary period of retrenchment in compensation for the economic growth supplied by the "borrowed" wealth of consumer installment credit (see also Brinkley, 1995). Decades later, in the late 1950s, the likes of Galbraith (1958) linked the development of consumer credit to the creation of a new host of "needs of the second class," contrived by the advertising and sales industry to fabricate demand for goods not "needed" by individuals. Within this spirit, through a muckraking exposé of the consumer credit industry, Hillel Black (1962) attacked the mindless hedonism of consumers nourished by new forms of credit, especially among those who could least afford it. He also excoriated the heedless profit mongering of financial institutions and retailers, the calculated invasiveness of credit bureaus and bill collectors, the luring of children into debt as a "normal" practice, and the particular exploitation of the poor. For Black, it is not credit itself that is the problem so much as its development as a rapacious industry within itself, combined with the development of a new class of indigent debtor, new forms of "on-the-cuff" living and the growing pervasiveness of an "economic immaturity" where debt outweighs savings. In this witches' brew of commercial and consumer greed, immorality, deception, and diminished competition were perceived to flourish, not least serving the propaganda aims of America's Cold War enemy.

Undeniably, the most prominent and thoughtful exponent of this myth of lost virtue has been Daniel Bell's *The Cultural Contradictions of Capitalism* first published in 1975. Following Weber's argument that thought, conduct, and social structure are interlinked and are characterized in developed Western societies by instrumental rationality, Bell (1996) argues that the twentieth century has seen a massive divergence in the character of the social structure and culture with the former adhering to bourgeois precepts of efficiency, functionality, and best means to given ends while the latter has, in essence, become autonomous from the social structure, typified by ever-greater anti-rationalism and subjectivism. Bourgeois authority has been challenged and undermined and its puritan culture deemed old-fashioned and arcane to the point of indefensibility. Accordingly, for Bell, social position and cultural styles no longer correspond. Increases in discretionary income, greater education, and social permissiveness have disjointed the correspondence of social position to cultural style as people become free to select their own cultural tastes and lifestyle, aided by the percolation of the lifestyles of the elite to the many via mass media forms.

The rise of mass consumption and the incorporation of more social groups in the consumption of so-called luxuries is, for him, the key to understanding why culture has changed. This change, he suggests, can be derived back to certain specific innovations in the techno-economic structure: the application of electricity, the development of assembly line production, the rise of segmented marketing, new means of transportation and communications and finally, the emergence of installment credit, which Bell thinks so radically undermines the so-called Protestant fear of debt. The final factor is summed succinctly in Bell's belief that "the trick of installment selling was to avoid the word 'debt' and to emphasize the word 'credit'" (1996: 69). The cumulative effect of these developments is that work and the concomitant accumulation of wealth as reward remain, no longer, the primary social values as emulative consumption and display come to dominate the cultural order. Ultimately the social structure, and capitalism itself, becomes gradually weakened as the motivational system upon which it is built gives way to new forms of hedonism. Therefore, as it would seem, the rise of consumer credit within capitalism exists as one of the contributory factors that is leading to a diminishment of the puritan ethic and an increase in wanton consumption within a process that is fundamentally damaging to the underlining cultural basis that makes capitalism possible.

More recently, David Tucker's (1991) *The Decline of Thrift in America* has argued along similar lines that the growth of personal indebtedness was part of a grand shift in national mindset stemming from the beginning of the twentieth century but gathering particular form in the aftermath of World War II. This cultural change, "from saving to spending," however, exists not merely at the level of the individual but is reflected at the level of state macroeconomic management as well, from the popularity of Keynesian deficit interventionism to the "supply-side" economics of Reagan. Even the Monetarist School of the 1980s, which advocated government retrenchment for stable prices, higher growth and the promotion of entrepreneurialism, ignored the need for the fostering of traditional moral virtues upon which, Tucker claims, economic survival and development rely.

In the 1960s, sociologist David Caplovitz (1968) saw an inextricable link between the development of a new affluent society and the increasing use of credit. However, he perceived this not merely as an outgrowth of economic development or new consumer culture but as the long-term outcome of the changing occupational structure characterized by the growth of a new, salaried middle class. Whereas, he argued, the wealth of the older ascetic entrepreneurial middle class was grounded on capital, investment, and profit engaged within the market, the new white collar class employed in the vast bureaucratic edifices of mass society was characterized by job security, salaried stability, and a predictable trajectory of occupational advancement. It was this latter factor, in particular he argued, that would provide the higher future income needed to bridge the pressing consumerist needs of the present among a class that was increasingly consumer conscious.[2]

The few contemporary social scientists who have explicitly examined consumer credit have tended to concentrate on the thesis of an evaporating cultural heritage played out against wider societal dislocation. In a self-conscious examination of the fate of the contemporary American middle class, Sullivan, Warren, and Westbrook (1989, 2000), Williams (2004), and Karger (2005) link current economic prosperity to the expansion of consumer debt and position a causal link between rising bankruptcy rates and the changing social conditions of the middle class. For them, the profound social dislocations and widened economic inequality since the 1970s, particularly through the depredations of Reaganomics and the rise of globalization, have undermined the economic position of the middle class already racked by rising divorce and remarriage rates, lack of medical insurance, and the increased burden of homeownership. While increasing equity, rising homeownership rates across all population segments have driven up levels of personal debt, increasing vulnerability and recourse to bankruptcy. In this mix too are seen the exacerbating effects of rising material expectations, the lure of marketing and "a change of attitude among Americans over the past twenty years or so that permits this unprecedented accumulation of debt" (Sullivan et al., 2000: 25). The consumer credit market itself is seen to exacerbate the situation by offering home equity loans that exploit rising property prices to allow consumers to finance spending and consolidate accumulated personal debt. The rising burden of personal debt thus serves as both a dynamic cause and effect of the imperilment of the American middle class.

To the pot of cultural and economic changes, George Ritzer (1995) adds the proliferating technological form of the credit card as a temptation to imprudence, appearing in the minds of individuals, as he sees it, at a greater, more abstract remove from the tangible value of cash. Through this mechanistic relationship, credit card companies' profit-seeking business practices, aggressive marketing campaigns, and promotion of expensive services such as ATM cash advances are held to have seduced legions of consumers into a state of crippling indebtedness to which consumers themselves contribute through their "unrestrained consumption" and "compulsive" tendencies (Ritzer, 1995: 68). Schor (1998), too, posits a fundamental link between rising indebtedness, the insatiability of escalating emulative consumer wants, and the proliferation of expensive forms of plastic credit that seemingly erode the link between getting and spending. She reprovingly cites one psychology experiment where participants exhibited an "almost Pavlovian" response to spending more after being exposed to some subtly positioned MasterCard logos (1998: 73).

For Robert Manning, consumer credit represents an "erosion of the traditional cognitive connect, or fiscal equilibrium between household income and consumption decisions" (2000: 105). Through a nuanced historical account, he traces the dissolution of this link between "getting and spending" to the end of the nineteenth century and the emergence of a new consumerist culture built around the stimulation of a desire rooted in imaginative consciousness. Although battered further in the twentieth century the economic excesses of the roaring twenties, the cultural brake of the Depression and the calculated postwar solidity of social life sustained by a new welfarist federal state preserved the essential integrity of this cultural ethic until the 1970s. However, again, the financial onslaught of profit hungry institutions, the "psychological optimism of affluence" and the egotistical consumerism that was to follow were key components in finally dissolving the threads of the old "cognitive connect." Like Sullivan et al. and Williams, he sees the relentless increase in debt over the 1980s as a product of the remorseless marketing of credit card debt within a context where the unyielding desire for the symbols of middle class consumption (higher "spending") clashed with the reality of material uncertainties caused by polarizing wealth, corporate downsizings, unemployment, and rising rates of divorce (lower "getting"). Manning, like Tucker, does not point the finger solely at the consumer but identifies the rise also of corporate and government thriftlessness, forming what he sees as a grand "triangle of debt" elevating the contemporary national economy at the cost of future prosperity (2000: 31–65).

Rethinking Consumer Credit

Yet, not all concerned analysts have approached the development of consumer credit forms within these explanatory conventions. In his commentary on James Mill, Marx ([1844a] 1975) himself took the development of credit to be a logical extension in the progress of the system of money under capitalist relations. A credit relation, for Marx, was fundamentally still a money transaction, with value being displaced from its inscription within paper or metal to its incision within the very being of the human subject. Even in benevolent, non-usurious lending from a rich man to a poor one, the financial return with interest is grounded in the very human essence of the borrower and all his potential, as well as the implicit force guaranteed by law. In borrowing between relatively equal economic actors, credit too represents money elevated to an ideal form; value forsakes its physical incarnation and comes to reside in the social being of the borrower and the form of relations between individuals. However, although seeming to bring a new intimacy to human relations, credit simultaneously alienates them in profound ways for, in such a transaction, the worth of an individual comes to be morally assessed not in human terms but in economic ones. It provides, fundamentally, a new means of accumulation for those in possession of capital and a new mode of degradation for those without, fostering mutual deception and deceit and a new level of estrangement among individuals under capitalism. Credit, then, is not the symptom of a breakdown in capitalism but rather the manifestation of a new strengthened phase.

Writing in the 1970s, Jean Baudrillard (1998) updated this position in his analysis of consumption. Contemporary consumption, he posited, was not hedonistic or anomic but, counterintuitive, a field increasingly penetrated by the rationalizing logic of capitalism. Rather than a mode of instant gratification, he suggests that the development of credit represents a "regime of enforced saving," a new variant of Puritanism that disciplines individuals in their new crucial role as consumers, albeit under the guise of self-fulfillment, in much the same way that factory bosses once regulated labor. More recently, analyzing the development of consumer credit within America up until the 1950s, Calder (1999) describes how individuals' flows of income became regularized by their removal from individual control and their subjection to legal-bureaucratic processes to which individuals willingly, and gladly, came to subject themselves. Puritan self-denial, self-restraint, and self-control in accumulating resources, he argues, were subsumed by budget plan restraint characterized by the external fetter and control of the contractual obligations of sale. Yet, what Calder fails to elaborate on, as Baudrillard does, is that contemporary consumer credit, at least, is not experienced as a field of repression or enforced control. On the contrary, its use is fundamentally acted upon and experienced as the essence of freedom, albeit a freedom that is always governed.

Outline of the Argument

It seems that sociology has often fallen into a position of treating consumer credit en masse as a thing, a novel manifestation of amorality, of capitalist greed and exploitation, of social fragmentation, and (middle class) cultural dissolution.[3] What I attempt within this book is to present a sociological alternative where credit is treated as a social process rather than as a symptom of something else; a dynamic field that, as Lendol Calder shows, has a history and genealogy stretching back to at least the nineteenth century. In a sense, as we will see, credit has always been seen as a problem in need of a solution; at the same time, often being presented as a solution to an array of other problems.

The central argument can be stated as follows: in our complex, late modern societies, the economic prerogatives of capitalism have become tied to the continuous generation, satisfaction, and regeneration of consumer wants and desires while the individual's sense of self and sociability have become indelibly linked to the self-realizing possibilities of marketed forms of consumption and credit. At the same time, the use of credit has become closely monitored and regulated from outside *and* inside the individual through governing processes that act upon and through the individual's means and capacity for self-constraint. In addressing what I believe to be this fundamental and underanalyzed condition, I avoid a retracing of the means by which consumer credit is conceived as a universal pathway toward an all-embracing economic citizenship for all. Neither do I attempt to measure the degree to which our so-called consumer societies have somehow lost an older, simpler cultural economic virtue where what was consumed was conditioned only by the resources that one possessed. More broadly, it is also too soon to say what the effects of the 2008 "credit crunch" in wholesale bank lending and the subsequent economic recession will have on consumer credit. It should perhaps be noted, though, that after precipitous falls post-1929 and the onset of the Great Depression, consumer credit levels did gradually recover their former levels during the 1930s.

The ambition of my argument is, on one level, quite modest. Eschewing "grand theory," it hopes to show in the messy reality of consumer credit provision the changing ways in which consumers are governed within consumer credit transactions. Yet, at the same time, such a modest ambition requires a broad scale and scope of analysis. In this regard, it is influenced by the legacy of Foucault and informed by the emergence of a "governmentalist" approach to the analysis of power implicated within social relations. Governmentality emphasizes the continuous inventiveness and resourcefulness of authorities, whether individuals, institutions, or diverse actors acting under the power rubric of the state, toward understanding and framing the actions of others, economic processes, or the course of perceived problems and issues.

The scope of this book encompasses the specific historical contexts of consumption and the role of consumers, where needs, wants, and desires for goods engender satisfaction, pleasure, and meaning for individuals. It connects with the ways capitalist enterprise has come to embrace consumer lending as a source of profit—whether directly, by specialist lenders offering credit, or in the form of retailers facilitating deferred payment as a means of enhancing sales. Here, the shifting, changing technologies within which the freedom of credit consumers is addressed and acted upon is presented as being particularly important, involving as we will see, the deployment of such elements as form filling, legal contracts, the systematic organization of time, bureaucratic tabulation, information sharing, and systematic modes of assessment that invoke the power of expertise and wider material technologies. Finally, the government of credit is shown to be bound, in a more conventional sense, to the political rationalities and programs of the liberal state. These conceive of credit provision and legislatively shape and direct it in historically contingent ways—such an intervention proving crucial for framing the legal possibilities of the lending process.

What I wish the reader to take away at the end of the book is an understanding of the degree to which consumer credit has become a nexus point in late modern societies, a key lynchpin interlinking processes of identity formation through consumption and the continuous creation of profit and reproduction of capital. It is also a site of conflicting political significance perceived to be in need of state intervention, whether to nurture and encourage "economic enterprise," promote "financial inclusion," or protect the rights of a generic constituency of "consumer." At this stage, the reader can perhaps guess why the United States was chosen as the area of enquiry for this book: it was, of course, where consumer credit was born and where it has developed to the greatest degree. However, such advancement has not only been achieved in dollar terms, of debt outstanding, but by other indices too: the sheer volume and range of credit contracts American households possess; the dependency upon a sophisticated credit reporting network; the complexity, advancement, and coverage of the credit scoring systems used by creditors; the American polity's array of specialist, continuously updated and revised legislation; and the degree to which its citizens have come to conceive of and act upon themselves as consumers in need of credit. Yet, the areas examined and the arguments raised have a wider salience for all Western societies and, increasingly, the successfully developing countries of South America and Asia that have embraced a consumer "buy now, pay later" ethic either serviced by domestic capital or imported from the United States.

The complexity and detail of material examined in this book does not preclude the discernment and identification of those wide-scale changes that have occurred within and through the field of consumer credit. As consumer goods came to play an increasing role in the mediation of social life during the first half of the twentieth century, consumer credit grew in scale and form to attract mainstream finance capital. Despite a recurrent social fear about "consumer debt," credit generally came to be seen as something positive, if not essential, to social life and individual freedom. The state, in general, moved from a strategy of repression through usury interest rate caps to one of protection and management in the interest of promoting a wider social well-being. By the 1920s and 1930s, the conditional sale installment credit form represented the paradigmatic form of credit. With it, lenders channeled credit to consumers through carefully calibrated bureau-legal processes that served to discipline and regulate credit use and repayments to prevent losses due to non-repayment. This corresponds to the highpoint of what Burton (2008) calls the "old economy of credit."

Since the 1960s and 1970s, against the backdrop of a realignment of political endeavor, the forsaken possibilities of collective action and belief, and the fragmentation of social life, a "new economy of credit" has emerged. Its paradigmatic form, it is suggested here, is the credit card—a personalized, mobile resource to be drawn upon by individuals in the increasingly autonomous, market-derived living of their lives. For its part, the state's regulation of credit has shifted on the basis of its perceived responsibility to promote this "enterprising" mode of life. Lenders, who now have become tasked with governing whole populations of credit consumers, have become progressively more reliant upon large-scale risk technologies, the unimpeded constitution and circulation of data about individual ability to make choices as well as the reflexive, self-governing capabilities of consumers themselves.

* * *

In chapters 1–3, through a sociological examination of historical studies analyzing the development of emergent forms of credit in the nineteenth and twentieth centuries, we will attempt to trace the socio-genesis of consumer lending and the formation of new modalities for its government. We will explore how out of the fiery cauldron of industrialization, immigration, and urbanization of the mid-nineteenth century, new forms of lender began to proliferate to meet the borrowing needs of a new urban workforce. Mirroring the growth of labor with wages as its primary means of subsistence, emergent salary lenders began to make loans less on the security of tangible capital that defined traditional pawnbroking and increasingly around the abstract conception of future wages. On this basis, these creditors deployed new means for acting upon the actions of borrowers, locking them within habitual temporal practices, relying upon their embedded position within the community as well as fabricating a web of legal artifice and subterfuge to insist upon repayment through a legal framework where such lending was almost certain to be illegal under the strict state usury laws of the time.

In the latter half of the nineteenth century, the middle class and elites, deriving from a moral evangelical Christian tradition, became increasingly concerned by the apparent fragmentation of society propelled by industrialization and the rise of anomic urban landscapes deprived of a coherent system of moral regulation. The so-called loan shark menace of the salary lenders encapsulated this sense of dissolution as the elite resolved to act through the setting up of remedial loan lenders inspired by the historical European tradition of low cost, religious, or municipally run pawnbrokers. As the new century dawned, a nascent social scientific sensibility within the spirit of Progressivism began to empirically analyze the problem, giving a new weight and density to the phenomenon under scrutiny. Its evocative studies and efforts prompted and promoted new imaginative forms of state intervention beyond the failures of philanthropy, an intervention that would radically alter the terms and possibilities of personal borrowing.

Historically, the installment selling of goods as a form of credit attracted significantly less authoritative attention than that of cash borrowing. Increasingly developed by retailers within the nineteenth century to promote the sale of consumer goods including manufactured furniture, pianos, and sets of encyclopedia to the new middle classes, it existed outside the ambit of the usury laws with little coercive regulation of borrower repayment. Later, more downscale installment selling among cheap furniture stores and its extension to the marketing of the new sewing machine to women prompted a generalized anxiousness about indebtedness, loss of independence and exploitation, a synecdoche for an insecure patriarchal middle class deeply uneasy at the increasing commercial and social flux of the nineteenth century.

Yet, as we will see, credit found new respectable conduits in the development of department stores and national mail order businesses. The expansion of installment selling by mail order provides an interesting case study in the development of credit. Just at the new department store form conjured imaginative longings in urban dwellers, catalog merchants brought the pleasures of image and desire to increasing swathes of a still predominantly rural nation. In the new century, it was installment selling mail order firms, which faced with the demands and difficulties of governing consumers at a physical remove, attempted to inscribe a conception of their field of subjects through increasingly detailed and refined application forms and questionnaires, tools that represented the world "out there" in the credit offices of these retailers.

By the 1920s, the development of the mass-produced automobile embodied new, profound shifts in American society. Personal transit shrank the boundaries of time and space while the built environment itself—housing, work, and leisure—became molded to the possibilities of automotive transport. Its manufacture wrought and perfected changes to new production and working conditions while the car itself became the ultimate symbol of a new form of consumption. The car proved equally instrumental in the development of mass personal finance in the twentieth century as new, specialized intermediaries harnessed mainstream financial capital for the profitable exploitation of consumer desire and the giant industrial manufacturers, particularly General Motors, funneled valuable capital to ensure a continuous ready demand for the products streaming from their assembly lines. Yet, in its early stage, car ownership remained a largely middle class phenomenon, with credit being engaged in a new temporal, legal bureaucratic matrix that disciplined excited, consuming desire to ensure prompt, regular repayment.

* * *

In chapters 4–6, we pick up our analysis in the shifting discourses and ethics of debt circulating around the emerging system of mass consumer credit. Increasingly, personal debt was justified as "productive," an essential element in the facilitation of a mass consumption being imbricated within the American way as a necessary corollary to mass production. Crucially, with the legacy of the New Deal and the growth in the reach and scope of the federal state, such mass credit became an object of regulation—as part of the new grand regulation of the banking sector and more directly, through the imposition of wartime controls by the Federal Reserve, which made consumer credit a calculable mechanism in the service of the national interest. Yet, just as the postwar affluent society came under sustained attack from cultural critics as well as a capitalist vanguard of organizational theorists, advertisers, and marketers, a revolutionary form of credit began to take root as the emblem of a new consumerism—the credit card. As we will examine through an analysis of its institutional development and the particular ways through which it has become marketed today, the credit card has come to embody a personalized, malleable credit resource to be drawn upon by consumers in the fulfillment of their wants and desires; a form of credit that, as I will demonstrate, has become sculpted to, and an essential part of, the formation of contemporary consumer lifestyles.

Within the shifting context of the later twentieth century, disillusionment with mass society and disaffection with New Deal welfarism and economic interventionism were met with the rise of new, individualizing political rationalities of neoliberalism. Responding to this, credit market deregulation and liberalization have become key political strategies for freeing the field of choices available to the consumer. Yet, as we shall see, this does not imply that the state has not continued to intervene heavily within credit markets. Through an analysis of the work of legal scholars, behavioral economists, and others, we will explore how the so-called

Truth in Lending Act 1968 represented a new legislative template for the government of credit that sought, not to direct the functioning of the market as in the past, but to shape the autonomy of consumers. It attempted to lay out the ways consumers were advertised to and the format of the legal credit contracts they signed up to in order that they might be better informed, more rational, and more suitably equipped as consumers. Ultimately, it attempted (unsuccessfully it has been argued) to program consumers to be the kinds of individual economic actors political authorities imagined they should be.

The expansion of the market for credit, characterized by diffuseness and the broad reach of personal choice, took place against the development of new regulatory mechanisms by lenders. As we will examine, the growth of an electronically mediated industry of credit reporting came to systematize the identity of all consumers via a virtual "credit identity," inscribing the exercise of their credit choices in such a way that provided lenders the possibility of acting upon them for profitable ends. At the same time, it also opened up new ways for credit consumers to conceive of themselves in relation to the fulfillment of their consuming ambitions. To these ends, we will draw upon an array of material including privacy-rights analysts, information sharing advocates, relevant legislative initiatives, and recent theoretical literature on the sociology of surveillance.

* * *

In chapters 7–8 we examine in detail the development of credit scoring technologies by institutional lenders, in conjunction with statisticians and operations researchers, which emerged most notably in the 1970s and 1980s for the regulation of consumer borrowers. Drawing together an analysis of technical papers and other sources on credit scoring and informed by recent sociological and criminological theory on the constitution and deployment of risk as a technology, chapter 7 traces the emergence of such governing mechanisms in the development of a national market for consumer credit and the emergence of the population as the key locus of analysis for lenders. As we shall see, such technologies interlinked with particular concerns of the state to make credit available as a universal right of every citizen contingent only on their ability to police their own desires and choices and, more broadly, to direct and manage the course of their own lives. The risk-based assessments constituted in an expert-legitimated credit scoring system proved an attractive mechanism. Risk allowed market entitlement to be emptied of the old moral baggage attached to sanctioning decisions made on the basis of class, race, and gender; instead, a new morality predicated individual market freedom on the basis of "objective," statistical relations discerned within populations of consumers.

As will be demonstrated, credit scoring systems gradually became knitted within the institutional fabric of consumer lenders, presented by its expert advocates as distinct from, fairer, more controllable and more efficient than lender sanctioning systems pejoratively referred to as being based on "judgmental" decision making. Yet, today, credit scoring represents anything but a homogeneous, unified progressive technology. Its experts continuously grapple with systematic uncertainties, "risks," that are perceived to impair its effective attribution of consumers as risks. They also formulate alternative, competing approaches and epistemologies for the creation of scoring models that seem to have their own endemic advantages and difficulties, models that offer only situational rather than paradigmatic superiority. Notwithstanding, risk as a technology has filtered into more and more areas within consumer lending, its strategic advantages in governing a multitude of consumers increasingly leading to the conception of individuals as risks in a host of new, diffuse ways. The tactical government of risk has altered too in recent years, with individuals constituted as risks being acted upon in new ways emphasizing the scope of individual responsibility.

While credit markets are inclusionary and expansionary in their quest for higher revenues and profits, the attribution of risk by lenders serves ultimately to exclude. It would seem that the constitution of individuals as relative risks always presupposes those who will be "too risky" to profitably engage. Those representing an excessive likelihood of failure, be it because of their seemingly inadequate job, income, neighborhood, history of credit use, and performance will tend to be marginalized by lenders, ignored, denied the general benefits of choice within the mainstream credit market. Yet, even here the market intervenes to fill the vacuum of need and desire, want, and desperation nurtured by the oxygen of credit. As we will examine through an analysis of a range of social scientific empirical studies, newly ascendant payday lenders, pawnbrokers, and rent to own retailers offer an ersatz alternative to credit cards and personal loans for the poor and the marginalized, but in ways that make no pretence that such consumers can or are in a position to govern themselves. They generate coercive practices redolent of their nineteenth-century forebears, compelling a regime of repayments that exact the considerable price of triple-figure interest rates for the privilege of their borrowing services. These fringe borrowers represent the obverse of the self-determining neoliberal ideal; poor and marginalized, they lack the material and systemic potential for free choice, a lack invoked by economists as being irrational but subjectable to educative intervention.

* * *

In chapters 9–11, we examine recent developments in the government of consumer credit, in particular, new forms that emphasize the individual's responsibility to reflexively govern themselves. This will involve a case-study of Fair Isaac Corporation and their development of an Internet-based service that allows consumers to purchase and manage their attributed credit score under a particular type of generic credit scoring system known as FICO®.

In the last several years, consumers have increasingly become concerned with managing their own credit conduct in light of this FICO risk attribution, and credit scores more generally. Through an analysis of key documentary material, consumer advice leaflets and informational brochures, we will attempt to demonstrate how a technology deployed for governing a population in terms of risk has become reoriented as a technology for subjective self-government under conditions of uncertainty. Whereas the deployment of risk by lenders in credit scoring engenders a calculated probability of default for the management of financial losses, the adoption of risk as an identity by consumers induces them to pursue certain actions in using credit for the purposes of optimizing their ongoing credit use. Risk in this sense allows the consumer to manage the uncertainty they experience in relation to future credit consumption, not by rendering it calculable, but by permitting them to contain it through the operation of a strict regimen of the self.

Following this, we will investigate how the opportunity for this form of self-government has been marketed as a commodity for the personal management of credit consumption. To this end, we will draw upon an analysis of the publicity material and marketing campaign of Fair Isaac for its new suite of consumer focused products as well as other related data sources including press releases and company magazine articles. It will be argued that consumers are persuaded to deploy these facilities in order to manage prudentially the uncertainty related to their consumption choices and resources, pervasive uncertainties that are held to threaten the individual consumer's ability to sustain an ongoing ability to use credit. Yet, not only are consumers directed in certain specific ways to be responsible for their own consumer choices, they must also be responsible for ensuring their credit identities are free from errors and discrepancies intrinsic to the system itself.

CHAPTER 1

Fishing for Sharks and Governing Small Loans

Within the United States, borrowing money and buying goods and services over time was an intrinsic part of agricultural and commercial life from colonial times; indeed as Calder (1999) points out, cash represented a relatively scarce resource in the eighteenth and early nineteenth centuries and much trade was secured on the basis of credit and barter. Yet within the context of an industrializing, increasingly urbanized but as Robert Wiebe (1967) terms it, an acutely "distended" social context, new forms of personalized credit in the form of cash borrowing and new goods purchased in temporal increments increasingly began to implant and penetrate the consumption practices of the emerging working and middle classes.

Chapters 1 and 2 set out to explore the disparate genealogy of consumer credit from the nineteenth century, in particular, its inextricable relationship to the development of consumption and how individuals, in different ways, have been understood as consumers of credit. A running theme throughout is the historically different ways that the shifting field of consumer credit was understood to be in need of "government." Drawing on Foucault's (1983, 1991) definition of government as "the conduct of conduct," I attempt to elucidate how creditors have attempted to manage the financial uncertainty of repayment by consumers and how the state, regional or federal, has undertaken to regulate both lenders and consumers in order to promote wider objectives of stability and well-being. The concept of government, though, is not merely a synonym for control or manipulation but captures, at different levels, the relative autonomy of lenders and consumers to act within a field of possibilities but yet whose freedom to do so has been programmatically shaped and molded in historically specific ways.

Pawnbroking or a Visit to "My Uncle"

Within urban centers from the seventeenth century, pawnbrokers played a crucial role in providing the means of material survival for the working classes. In terms of its history, pawnbroking has a long lineage stretching back to medieval times where, despite church hostility, Italian merchant families such as the Lombards supplied pawning services to sections of the aristocracy, often to finance military campaigns. From the fifteenth century onward, charitable pawnshops known as *mons pietatis* were organized in northern Italy by a Franciscan religious order that lent sums of money at low interest to small artisans and struggling tradesmen, financed by church taxation, grants and donations—this form of lending later spreading in modified form to Germany, France, and Belgium (Hudson, 1982: 25–7).

Within Britain, specialized pawnbroking to the masses was as Hudson remarks, "a child of the industrial revolution." Up to the latter half of the seventeenth century, the idea of a pawnbroker had been indistinguishable from that of banker or goldsmith. However, with the rapid urbanization of a new mercantile economy, pawnbroking increasingly developed as a specialized enterprise servicing the laboring poor, providing a means for individuals to secure small sums of money by pledging a wide array of goods such as clothing, furniture, and work tools. A series of acts from the middle of the eighteenth century regulated its operations, specifying compulsory registration of pawnshops and exemption from general usury limits, that is, maximum interest rates that could be charged. As Tebbutt details, with bare subsistence incomes and pronounced material insecurity, especially given the irregularity of employment, the pawnbroker (sardonically referred to as "My Uncle") provided a critical means for "bridging the gap" of survival, particularly in the wake of such buffeting events as illness, lay off, or bereavement (1983: 12–4). Given such small margins, these acute events often forced individuals into unending cycles of pledging and redemption as pay days and rent days came and went. Therefore, chronic poverty and material uncertainty made pawnshops an often integral part of working class habitus that conceived of goods purchased as potentially pawnable assets and consigned saving as an unconscionable luxury—"insecurity of income and the physical conditions of life thus combined to produce a distinct outlook of which pawning was an integral part" (p. 19).

Within these conditions, pawnbroking endured much social opprobrium, its practitioners often associated with the practice of an immoral trade operating in direct contravention of puritan values of thrift. Pledgers themselves were labeled feckless and improvident, the inability to live within one's means bundled with other perceived working class habits such as drunkenness to illustrate the inherently flawed capacity of the poor to live up to the demands of self-restraint and reason (cf. Valverde, 1996).

However, the characteristic mode of British liberalism never endorsed the charitable or municipal pawnshops, the *mons pietatis*, which were popular in many European countries. Despite the middle class's profound disdain for the act of pawning, it was held to at least compel self-reliance on the part of the borrower, accommodating individual weakness and mandating responsibility on the part of the improvident for their own conditions. Ultimately, it helped to avoid a bigger evil—the burden of the poor upon the ratepayer (Tebbutt, 1983).

Within the United States, pawnbroking traces a history from the earliest colonial settlements but, as in Britain, its more widespread dissemination in the nineteenth century depended upon the development of densely populated urban centers that arose with industrialization (Patterson, 1899: 256). Although, as we saw, recourse to the pawnshop was a product of the vicissitudes and marginality of industrial life, nevertheless as Patterson describes it, the cycle of pledging and redemption followed weekly patterns that mirrored the payment of wages and the periodic nature of household expenses, most importantly, rent. Monthly patterns reflected the often seasonal nature of employment and variable need for goods—for example, the warmer weather of the summer months led to an upsurge in the pledging of winter clothing to be redeemed later in the year (1899: 273–80). In the records of a famous New York pawnshop, Simpson's, for 1 April 1935, a whole panoply of items offered as pledges is recorded, from a silver and gold watch to a piece of cashmere, corsets, a telescope, even a lace (Simpson, Simpson, and Samuels, 1954: 29).

The terms of pawnbroking were governed by a patchwork of state and municipal laws that varied in scope and intensity depending on the geographical concentration of urban areas, such disparate governance reflecting the fragmented, relatively unintegrated nature of the wider American nation (Patterson, 1899; Levine, 1913; Raby, 1924). However, most of the state statutes regulating pawnbroking provided for interest rates that were above individual state usury ceilings to permit legal pawnbroking but perceived sufficiently low so as to prevent the grievous exploitation of the borrower. Pawnbrokers too were free to levy additional fixed charges for "inspection," "insurance," and "storage" that inflated the real interest rates paid by borrowers. Pawning was thus constituted as a distinctive type of borrowing, which despite the predominant cultural stigmatization of personal indebtedness, was recognized legally as a necessary evil. However, the problems that the disparate pawnbroking regulations of this early period attempted to counter were not only the condition of the pawner but the challenge posed to the law by theft facilitated by pawnbroking (Oeltjen, 1991: 68; Caskey, 1994: 20). Within America's enlarged cities, the growing flux and anonymity of social life was reflected in the concern that valuable and untraceable goods could so easily be converted into cash and sold on by the pawnbroker at public auction. The trade seemed to provide a ready outlet for the proceeds of larceny, perhaps even with the complicity of the pawnbroker themselves (Levine, 1913; Raby, 1924). The enforcement of licensing, registration, and bonding of pawnbrokers was "to afford some assurance that those who are permitted to conduct the business are persons of good character and responsibility and not likely to act in wilful collusion with thieves" (Raby, 1924: 5).

The specification of systematic ticket receipts for articles pledged sought to impose a traceability within the pledging transaction. Similarly, requirements that individual items pledged be registered with police authorities, sometimes even including a physical description of the pledger, existed as a means for producing a web of visibility by which individual municipalities and states could locate all pawn transactions. The main aim here was to minimize broader threats to private property. Even the limitation of opening hours was seen as an effective means of ensuring that "burglars or highwaymen who operate in the dead of night shall not have the opportunity to dispose of their loot as quickly as it is obtained" (Raby, 1924: 6). Both pledgers and pawnbrokers were thus viewed within a miasma of immorality and illegality, the regulation of which manifested a broader concern of the elites for the problems of social life in America's industrial cities.

Chains of Lenders, Borrowers in Chains

Distinctive changes took place in consumer lending between the 1870s and 1880s. According to Robinson and Nugent, advertisements began to appear in newspapers that offered money on furniture loans but "without removal," creating a distinctively new form of lending based not on the physical pledge of goods but on the pledge of the good's legal title, a form of credit that became known as *chattel lending*. "By this time the pawnbroker seems to have been superseded entirely in the field of furniture loans by the chattel mortgage lender" (1935: 40). In the advertisements that Robinson and Nugent analyzed, sums of money between $200 and $500 were offered on the security of such items as furniture, pianos, and diamonds, amounts that were almost certainly aimed at relatively affluent sections of the population. With the rise of chattel lending for significant sums, advertisements also increasingly emphasized confidentiality and discretion within the transaction. This, of course, was now enabled by the more abstract nature of the lender's claim over the collateral. Increasingly, borrowing was becoming more feasible for the middle classes who were able to evade the logistical difficulty of transporting pledges, maintain the use within their homes of the goods with which they sought to relay their social status, and assure themselves that their borrowing was safely hidden behind the scenes.

During the 1880s and 1890s a more separate branch of lending developed, secured on the basis of wage assignment, that is, on a legal title to the future wages of the borrower. This quickly grew to become the most popular form of lending (Robinson and Nugent, 1935; Haller and Alviti, 1977; Shergold, 1978). Such *salary lending* represented a further abstraction in the nature of the security of the loan, divorced from a specific good and relocated instead onto the future income flows of the borrower. With the spread of wage labor under industrial capitalism, personal lending became, for the first time, a direct corollary of the worker's sole major asset—intangible unearned future income—rather than a specific volume of tangible capital pledged as security. Initially, such lending depended on the lender being able to reliably identify the occupation and means of the borrower. In consequence, loans tended to be channeled toward city employees or the employees of firms whose payroll records the lender could illegally gain access through bribery. According to Haller and Alviti (1977), borrowers from salary lenders were married, almost by definition steadily employed regular employees such as clerical civil servants, insurance clerks, and railroad workers. Calder argues that, where pawnbrokers tended to concentrate on the lower end of the borrower market, working class individuals living a marginal existence, salary lenders serviced those sections of the middle class whose incomes did not quite match up to their middle-class consuming ambitions (1999: 52). However, Haller and Alviti demonstrate that salary loans were sought for relatively exceptional circumstances that did not necessarily distinguish them from the pawnbroker; for example in addition to "holiday" and "Christmas" money, loans were sought to finance a house move, to pay a rent advance, or to finance medical treatment (1977: 128).

Borrowers were attracted through the use of advertising in daily newspapers and also, far more commonly, through the distribution of notices and handbills. Customers were also funneled by friends and acquaintances offered commissions by lenders to direct trade toward them. Lenders themselves tended to locate their offices within city centers close to concentrated areas of employment, particularly the railroads, and near financial districts where they assumed officious sounding titles to impart a veneer of legitimacy to their operations. However, such offices were located very discretely in secluded, plainly furnished upstairs premises, which it is suggested, helped them avoid the attentions of law enforcement officials and provided for little in the way of lost capital if the office were raided and closed down.

With the shift toward more abstract forms of security in legal title and even more so in terms of unearned future salary, the actions of the borrower became of increasing concern to the lender. Consequentially, the focus on the value of the collateral by the lender was displaced by a heightened concern to more intensively govern the repayment actions of the individual borrower through the medium of time (see Robinson and Nugent, 1935; Nugent, 1941; Haller and Alviti, 1977; Shergold, 1978):

1. In advance, the individual filled out lengthy forms specifying personal information such as address, occupation, payday, relatives and neighbors, property, and other credit obligations. As well as assessing this information for its accuracy themselves, the lender typically consulted with the payroll clerk at the borrower's employer to verify the individual's personal background and wage rate. The individual might also be required to furnish the names of two guarantors who would supposedly be responsible for the debt in the event of nonrepayment.

2. During the course of repayment, the principal and interest outstanding might be amalgamated and repayment sought in weekly or monthly amounts. More common though was the "extension-plan" where the full-loan repayment fell due after a month but which could be rolled over for a period of up to six months on payment of the interest portion of the loan. Both of these strategies closely governed the repayment actions of the borrower, but toward different ends. Whereas the former was aimed at allowing the individual to sequentially pay down the loan in a calculable way, the latter tended to keep the borrower in debt in such a manner that they would be obliged to pay interest for as long as possible without making inroads into paying off the principal. The lender thus bound the borrower to their repayment obligation through fixing them to a particular physical and social location and locking the repayment schedule to the wages of the individual, often contriving to "farm" the client into an ongoing profitable state of indebtedness.

3. Finally, in the aftermath of default, the creditor could formally apply to garnish, or legally appropriate, a portion of the borrower's ongoing wages. Or, for a chattel loan, exercise their legal title over the security in the possession of the borrower and seek a court order to claim it. However, these were really options of last resort with less formal methods being preferred to coerce payment based on the social stigma of debt.

The lender thus governed the timeliness of repayments less by formal legal mechanisms of contract than by the social stigma within which indebtedness was held, for both chattel and salary lenders essentially operated outside the law, charging interest rates that were in excess of what was permissible under state usury ceilings of around 6 percent per year. With the former case, interest was charged at around 10 percent per month for amounts under $50, declining slightly for larger amounts. For salary lenders, around double the chattel rate was the norm. Repayment terms varied by lender and tended to be set on a flexible basis depending on the needs of the individual applicant; commonly, loans were agreed for the period of a month with the option to extend this term up to six months after which the loan could be repeatedly renewed on payment of an extra charge (Robinson and Nugent, 1935: 56–9).

In spite of the illegality of these activities, the business developed rapidly from the 1880s through relatively lax enforcement (Wassam, 1908: 41–2; Robinson and Nugent, 1935: 45–7; Nugent, 1941: 5–6). An increased pace and breadth of press advertising reflected the increasing concentration of lending in specific cities while a significant expansion in the scope of individual lenders occurred with the development of office chains across the country. The first to follow this path was Frank J. Mackey, a chattel lender whose firm would later go on to be the mainstream Household Finance Corporation. However, more striking were the chains formed by salary lenders such as John Mulholland and the notorious Daniel H. Tolman, reflecting the scale of demand for this form of lending despite the higher interest rates it charged. Mulholland, from his beginnings in Kansas City, invested both the profits of his firm and the proceeds of a private stock issue to operate over one hundred offices nationwide. Similarly, Tolman extended his operations to sixty-three cities in both the United States and Canada, developing such innovations as the employment of women in his branches to defuse irate male customers. Later, in 1913, he was imprisoned for usury by a New York court (Grant, 1992: 83–4).

As a commercial practice, chattel and salary lending of the late nineteenth century operated in an uncertain place between artifice and reality. Such lenders worked outside the law and yet conducted their business by way of legal form filling and contracts through which the individual committed their property or earnings against the value of a loan. This is despite the fact that such an agreement would have proven almost impossible to enforce in the courts. They engaged in expensive print advertising, located in financial districts and proclaimed the size of their loan capital, and sometimes the scope and respectability of their operations. In contrast, the actual practice of lending was carried out in cramped dingy surrounds that might at any moment have been raided by the police. They were also one of the first exponents of the national chain store method that would prove essential to the operation of consumer-oriented enterprises into the twentieth century and yet such a method was essential for lenders to grow if they were to avoid unwanted legal attention in any one location. Despite this expansion but given its dubious legal status, small loan lending remained a relatively uncapitalized industry. In other words, it was financed by individual lenders themselves through whatever capital they could personally raise between themselves, partners, and acquaintances and through the ongoing generation of profits from invested lending activities rather than from an influx of conventional commercial capital (Robinson and Nugent, 1935: 62).

As American cities attracted increasing numbers of workers from the rural hinterlands and new immigrants from the Eastern and Southern European continent for manual labor (Jones, 1992)—industrial laborers who were cut off from the land and reliant on the continuity of their wages for survival—personal small loan lending grew in its reach and scale of operations to service their needs. It became increasingly commercially organized and profitable but yet outside the formal sanction of the law. It provided a resource for individuals that both filled specific needs and wants when income was inadequate but yet depended on the regularity and continuity of wages for repayment and profit. The fact that the industry was able to expand as it did suggests, significantly, both its necessity for urban workers as well as its capacity to produce a profitable investment through the effective temporal and bureaucratic regulation of these borrowers.

Tailing the Shark: Philanthropic Lending

During the first half of the nineteenth century, the specter of the industrial poor presented a stark challenge to liberal government. Classical liberalism had conceived of the economy and wider civil society as natural domains where free subjects acted in their own interests and whose natural dynamism and impulse the state must carefully uphold and defend (Foucault, 1991). Yet poverty, fostered by those very economic processes on an industrial scale, had not only failed to disappear but had grown. It became entrenched within the urban cores of Western societies, its presence contrasting with the growing wealth and refinement of a bourgeois elite, its proliferation suggestive of a willful opposition and threat to that elite's supremacy (Katz, 1996). Now it seemed, not only was labor insufficient to depauperize the population, the labor process itself was now seen to be threatening social disorder and mass demoralization (Procacci, 1991; Dean, 1991; Harrison, 1997). As Donzelot (1980) demonstrates, the problem for government was how it could actively resolve this problem of an entrenched pauperism without inflating the role of the liberal state to such an extent that it violated its self-imposed commandment to limit its own activities. Associated with this, there was also the problem of how to effectively govern the wider working classes that accumulated within cities; how to infuse them with a sense of responsibility for their own condition, to nurture and foster them in a positive fashion.

One early mechanism of intervention, according to Donzelot, was philanthropy. This was pursued not merely as a simple private intervention within the problems of the poor but a deliberate strategy of charting a course between economic affairs and the delimited sphere of the state. In the United States, the final third of the nineteenth century saw the proliferation of the *Charity Organization Society* as a diffuse voluntary response by the middle class to the "moral decay and social disintegration of the masses" (Boyer, 1978: 144; see also Katz, 1996; Recchiuti, 2007). Although the problems of poverty were held to be endemic to character, it was felt that adherence to the habits of the puritan ethic—work, discipline, order, punctuality—could habituate the poor and the immigrant to the reality of industrial modernity (Ewen, 1985: 78; Gutman, 1973). With the spread of small loan lending toward the end of the nineteenth century, recognition became accorded to the plight of the small borrower and the expense of borrowing. The problem was not that such individuals were outside the labor process; on the contrary, borrowing, by definition, was dependent on the ability of workers both to earn and freely dispose of their wages (Nugent, 1941). The specific problem, as it became articulated, was that workers had become reliant upon the chattel or salary lender; that in response to certain pressures they had temporarily borrowed money but, in doing so, had become systematically trapped in a cycle of indebtedness, servicing ever greater interest payments without being able to repay the original amount. It was from such a position of lost independence that they sank ever more fully into poverty (Wassam, 1908: 11–13; Ham, 1909: 10–11).

To combat this emergent problem, charitable efforts were marshaled, generally by local religious groups through fundraising efforts, which lent on the basis of nominal or no interest. However, these enterprises were unstable, requiring frequent fundraising to supply capital and the sustained efforts of the benevolently inclined to keep them going (Robinson and Nugent, 1935; Shergold, 1978). More profound, though, to the government of small loan lending were the philanthropic *remedial loan societies* that were set up in various cities across the United States from 1859, the most famous of which was the Provident Loan Society of New York (Patterson, 1899; Nugent, 1932). The Provident was opened in New York in 1894 by banker James Speyer who attempted to import the idea of municipal pawnshops, the *mons pietatis*, he had seen at work in Europe. It was operated by a voluntary board of trustees that oversaw all the terms of the Provident's operation and attracted the membership and funding of America's economic elite, including the likes of J.P. Morgan, Gustav H. Schwab, and Cornelius Vanderbilt. However, what distinguished the Provident was the commercial nature of its philanthropically intended investment. It was commercially financed through tradable bonds and instruments known as *certificates of contribution*, which at the discretion of the board were interest bearing up to a defined limit. Its lending form was that of a pawnbroker, offering cash in exchange for pledges of goods of variable sizes, but at interest rates significantly below those charged by conventional, small loan rivals.

The Provident along with other remedial organizations that established themselves across the country in the latter half of the nineteenth century, lending relatively small sums on the basis of pledges and chattel loans, represent a philanthropic strategy. This articulated for the first time the problem of small loan lending as a distinctly social problem in need of remedy. Its mushrooming growth indicated that individual state responses of repression through unfeasibly low usury ceilings, which limited the interest that could be charged, were ineffective. At the same time, its spread and intensification demonstrated its necessity among working class and some middle-class households for surviving the exigencies of an industrial urban life beset by the unforeseen and the unexpected, whether illness, eviction or lay off. As the century drew to a close, indebtedness to the small loan lender was now seen less as a matter of personal character failing on the part of the supposedly autonomous borrower than as a complex symptom or product of the social environment within which they were located (cf. Boyer, 1978: 198–9). Small loan lenders, though, were increasingly characterized as "loan sharks" who encapsulated this distorted environment, ensnaring and entrapping individuals faced with legitimate financial emergency into a degraded and destructive state of indebtedness, often with the connivance of corrupt police, courts, municipal public servants, and payroll employees:

> How can men be so reckless as to borrow from these agencies that are everywhere known as sharks, leeches and remorseless extortioners? It is clear that these concerns cater to a need that is in some part real and unavoidable, that the majority of borrowers have been overtaken by sudden emergencies which under their standard of living cannot be met out of income. To such, an easy and quick means of relief seems acceptable at any price, especially if no other and more reasonable source of assistance is at hand. (Ham, 1912: 1)

As such, small loan borrowers were seen as being vulnerable rather than culpable. They were victims of their own material deprivation, perhaps also their "short-sightedness" and "gullibility" (Nugent, 1941: 3), or their unwarranted "improvidence and extravagance" (Ham, 1911 cited in Calder, 1999: 129) that, in turn, made them ripe for exploitation in the rapacious lending practices of the sharks.

The Provident and its kind represented a bourgeois response to the material difficulties of poverty, tracing an independent line between both the perceived natural workings of the market and the administrative ambit of individual states and municipalities. Although it invoked private capital and even potentially offered a financial return on investment, the latter was of secondary importance, for both the investor and board, to the primary goal of maximizing the number of small loans it could offer. At the same time, commercial capital and a relatively formal organizational structure allowed it to be a sustainable enterprise, to continue to act in a predictable and calculable fashion for its philanthropic purposes without serving as a drain upon the pocketbooks of its wealthy benefactors. Commercial capital also allowed the Provident and others attain scale that would make it possible for them to provide effective competition to other small loan lenders.

On the other side of the liberal coin, remedial lending existed outside the ambit of authorities, both in terms of its financing and administrative organization. Indeed, the only action required of individual states was that they pass whatever requisite "enabling" legislation was required to permit such enterprises to exist (Robinson and Nugent, 1935: 83). In many ways, small loan lending served perfectly the philanthropic ideal of promoting autonomy within the population toward which it was targeted; those whom were to be helped were not being made subject to charity or handouts and thus would not be fostered into a condition of ongoing dependence inimical to liberalism. On the contrary, the act of borrowing would help them to sustain their own independence, allowing them to meet demands upon their resources through the mortgaging of their future wages upon which they would pay a "fair" rate of interest. However, remedial lenders were by their nature paternalistic, concerned not only with supplying funds on the basis of what was thought to be a reasonable price but, as Ham relates, with a specific regard as to whether the loan would be a "good thing" for the borrower (1909: 37). The remedial institution also offered the possibility of remoralizing the individual borrower by encouraging them to become savers, inculcating the ethic of thrift to preserve them from future indebtedness and promote their autonomy (see Donzelot, 1980):

> Among the many services rendered the public by The Economy [a remedial lender based in Cleveland, Ohio] is its Savings Department, in which 5% is paid on certificates of deposit. The borrower is encouraged to form the savings habit, and many of our depositors are those who were once borrowers, a fact that emphasizes the perfect understanding existing between The Economy and its patrons. (Ham, 1912: 3)

In terms of a response to the perceived loan shark "evil," remedial lending can be seen as an attempt to counter existing lenders by targeting the same elements of the population, paralleling their operations and imitating their mechanisms. It did so, however, under a philanthropic spirit that sought to relieve the difficulties of the poor for what was held to be their best interests and the interests of the common good rather than exploiting them for profit. It sought to eradicate, or at least limit the problem, by means of the market, charging a sustainable rate of interest sufficiently below that inflicted by the "sharks" in order to competitively drive them out of business. This strategy aimed to rid urban centers of a debilitating institutional menace that was held to have corrupted the wider social environment, substituting in its place a benevolent, "enlightened" alternative that would properly assist the needy and steer them back to a state of financial self-reliance and moral propriety. The market though was not the end but the means, not an autonomous domain for the realization of profit and the reproduction of capital but a technically expedient mechanism invoked to alleviate this newly distinctive social danger.

Taming the Shark: Expertise, the State, and the Small Loan Laws

By the turn of the century, the small loan issue became increasingly subject to philanthropic interest. In 1907, the Russell Sage Foundation was founded with the express purpose of improving the "social and living conditions" of American citizens; toward these ends it engaged researchers of the nascent social sciences in the professional study of those conditions through which it hoped to direct its ameliorative efforts. Among its early targets included low-income housing, urban planning, social work, and labor reform but it was in the arena of small lending that it established its early reputation (Glenn, Brandt, and Andrews, 1947; Anderson, 2005). It enlisted two graduate students of Columbia University who carried out research on the issue of consumer borrowing—Clarence Wassam (1908) on the salary-lending business and Arthur Ham (1909) on the chattel loan business.

The employment of two research fellows suggests a new departure in systematic philanthropic intervention centered on the importance of expertise in the production of knowledge about, and articulation of, social problems. Expertise, according to Miller and Rose, represents the "social authority ascribed to particular agents and forms of judgment on the basis of their claims to possess specialized truths and rare powers" (1990: 2). As such, it helps square the circle of liberalism, of the need to regulate without unduly interfering within those areas that the state sought to govern. Through exercising a monopoly over a specific area of knowledge, expertise represents an ally with which the state could act through, and in concert with, to achieve its aims. In relation to the issue of small loan lending, the deployment of a social scientific expertise by the Russell Sage Foundation helped rationalize and augment their influence over the phenomenon. It became constituted through the fieldwork of Ham and Wassam as a "real" social problem with empirically discernable effects and subjectable to dispassionate, scientific consideration with which to inform a calculated intervention. The relatively closed and rarefied nature of such knowledge could thus ordain their articulated strategies special significance and legitimacy with regard to the problem.

In the wake of the publication of his research, Ham became engaged in what were termed the "campaigns" or "crusades" against the loan sharks: giving speeches, writing newspaper columns, and even composing a screenplay that impassionedly cited the illegal practices of the industry; petitioning papers not to carry such advertising; offering advice and legal referral to victims who wrote to him as well as attempting to persuade employers not to accept the garnishment of a defaulter's wages (Glenn et al., 1947; Carruthers, Guinnane, and Lee, 2005: 5–6). Such a campaign seems to have had much in common with the morally charged temperance and sexual purity campaigns that, as Hunt (1999) demonstrates, became more prolific within American cities after the Civil War. Indeed, both attracted the favorable attentions and funding of the capitalist elite, while on a pejorative level the association of urban problems, like prostitution with disease and plague, resonated with the small lender's moniker as a shark infesting urban waters. Here was a creature primordially attracted to the metaphorical blood seeping from the wounds of the indigent. Just as with the seediness of the saloon and the lasciviousness of the prostitute, the loan shark's perceived role as irresistible seducer and preying, vicious atavistic menace embodied the seeming fluidity, disorder, and danger that the established but insecure middle classes felt toward urban life in the closing decade of the nineteenth century (cf. Hunt, 1999: 128). The response of such campaigns were therefore "urgent expressions of the self-assertion of upper and middle classes, who both feared the consequences of rampant urbanism and yet were committed to accelerated economic development which caused precisely the social problems that they feared" (p. 131).

Arthur Ham accepted, however, that campaigning alone was insufficient to combat the problem of loansharking given how expansive and ingrained it had become (1909: 8). To understand why, the small loan lending problem has to be set within the context of the Progressive movement within the United States. Progressivism was a contradictory endeavor, lacking any fixed coherence or sense of purpose as a political movement (Filene, 1970). Yet, as historians have argued, it is more apt, rather, to conceive of it as a disparate, shifting alliance of middle-class reformers and moral campaigners who gathered force through the 1900s. They did not view urban space or capitalism itself as being inherently negative; what motivated their challenge to rethinking the purposes of government was the sheer scale and scope of change wrought by the Gilded Age with its extensive industrialization and urbanization: the destruction of competition and the excessive centralization of economic power and wealth within the hands of the industrial plutocrats; the misery of labor and urban living conditions; the open conflict and bloody suppression provoked by unionized labor in the Pullman, Haymarket, and Homestead strikes of the 1880s and 1890s; the political and cultural upheaval produced by a "third wave" of new immigrants from Eastern and Southern Europe; and the corruption of the polity by the party machine, commercial monopoly interests and city boss garnering the votes of immigrants in exchange for the granting of favors (Hofstadter, 1955; Wiebe, 1967; Buenker, 1977; Boyer, 1978; Chambers, 1980; Jones, 1992; Katz, 1996; Foote, 2003; Recchiuti 2007). Within its rhetoric of attacking economic and political interests, the solution that Progressivism embodied was the extension of technologies of administrative control through the paradigm of "organization." This could ensure collective fairness while preserving the essential aspect of individual and market freedom (Hofstadter, 1955; Hamilton and Sutton, 1989). In one of the most enduringly successful initiatives from the era, state legislatures, increasingly displacing the courts in the molding of law, overlaid the antagonism of employer worker liability claims with the enactment of the first risk-based workman's compensation schemes. These provided automatic compensation to workers for work-related accidents (Lubove, 1967; Weinstein, 1967; Recchiuti 2007; see also Defert, 1991).

Similarly, the creation of diverse organizations from voluntary settlement houses, the National Consumers League to new federal regulatory agencies such as the Federal Trade Commission were aimed at conciliation and rational planning between individuals, now increasingly understood as "consumers," and enterprises without recourse to heavy-handed state intervention (Cohen, 2001); as Hamilton and Sutton remark, "their task was to be administrative in nature rather than law making and law enforcing: they were to maintain the 'natural' social order of society" (1989: 32). Intrinsic, too, to Progressivism was science and the formation of enclosed boundaries of expertise devoted to selfless service, objectivity, and efficiency (Burnham, 1977: 20; Recchiuti 2007: 17–18), which were both applied to and elaborated within the "social" problems being encountered. In its broadest sense, science provided a rational claim to truth; it was a privileged, objective knowledge that stood above the claims and contestation of politics but instead could be applied by its elitist promulgators to the nonpartisan resolution of urban problems (O'Connor, 2001: 25–6). However, the new social science that gathered momentum rejected the old voluntarism of independent autonomous actors and embraced systems of explanation rooted in diverse, contradictory modes of explanation such as heredity, environment, culture, stimulus-response, and the subconscious—explanations unified by the fact that they "seldom located causation close to the surface of events or in the conscious, willing minds of individuals" (Haskell, 2000: 251).

The moralizing campaigns against urban vices such as prostitution or drinking were not opposed to a sober, rational Progressivism but were actually a significant dimension of its wider reforming impulse (Boyer, 1978; Chambers, 1980). All Progressive reforms, as such, were moral if not implicitly religious in intent, connecting the unbearable laboring and living conditions of the working masses with the proliferation of drunkenness and urban vice. Similarly, antisaloon and antiprostitution organizations came to rely increasingly on the objectivity-claiming instruments of statistics and sociological study to ground their cause and formulate their strategic purpose. It was within this framework that the Russell Sage studies, although committed to philanthropic remedial lending and the crusades to drive out the "sharks," recognized that:

1. Demand for small loans was extensive but which existing legal lending institutions could or would not satisfy, in the process, creating a large black market of illegal lenders.
2. Small loan lending was profitable, could still be profitable at rates significantly lower than those charged among illegal lenders but was simply not feasible at the usury limits of most states.
3. Usury ceilings were easily evadable and, iatrogenically, not only did not keep down costs for small borrowers but harmed them by contributing to higher interest rates within the black market.
4. Most crucially, not only were more remedial lenders required but legislation was needed to permit a profit-making small loan business industry to be established.

(see Robinson and Nugent, 1935: 87–8)

According to Burnham (1977), one of the features that distinguished late nineteenth-century reforms from their Progressive incarnations was the rather sudden shift from "negative" reportage to "positive" conceptualization. Rather than merely criticizing institutional interests or exposing the misery of poverty, the new mindset of the Progressives sought to imagine and conceive of an ameliorated future. Therefore, although Arthur Ham and the Russell Sage Foundation were intimately involved in remedial lending, it was felt ultimately to be failing in its purpose to drive the loan sharks out of business and philanthropically prop up the desperate borrower. In a strategic shift, their attention thus turned to the politicization of the small loan problem, not to eliminate and supplant the sharks, but to calculably control the legal conditions under which they acted. The ambition became one of taming the sharks thus widening the scope of the paternalistic protection of borrowers. Not legal repression or philanthropy but only the careful organization of the economic was held to be sufficient to solve this now manifestly "social" problem (Neifeld, 1941).

Given the highly decentralized and divided structure of the United States political and legal administration, usury limits nominally limiting small loan lending were enshrined in law by individual states and so would have to be amended on a state-by-state basis. As Carruthers et al. (2005) demonstrate, the wider problem of a lack of legal harmonization between states began to be tackled from the late 1880s when the National Conference of Commissioners on Uniform State Laws, an organization composed of practicing professional lawyers, advocated legislative templates or "model laws" for enactment by individual states. This was to serve the purpose of promoting interstate trade and commerce. Later, this organizing endeavor was one of the main forces behind the setting up of the short-lived National Bar Association in 1888 (Brockman, 1966). Within this vein, Ham began to formulate the basic features of a model law that states could draw upon in legislating for small loan lending (Nugent, 1933; Robinson and Nugent, 1935; Anderson, 2005, Carruthers et al, 2005). Its general terms were that a lender could charge a maximum interest rate of 2 to 3 percent per month, which Ham "scientifically" determined through the careful analysis of a remedial lender's operations, to be the optimum interest rate for small loan lending (as opposed to the typical 6 percent per year that most states recorded). To do so, however, they would have to be licensed, to submit a bond, be subject to legal supervision by a state regulator, and would be prohibited from charging any additional fees or charges to clients to surreptitiously inflate the mandated interest rate. In addition, the model law detailed specific penalties to deter legal breaches by those registered. Following some legislative action by states from 1911 on the small loan question, New Jersey enacted the Egan Act in 1914, for the first time incorporating all the provisions sought by Ham.

In passing the Egan Act, the New Jersey legislature specifically sought the advice and assistance of Ham and Russell Sage in the drafting of the legislation, signifying again the importance of expertise to the process of government (Robinson and Nugent, 1935: 103). Based on their reputation, their accumulated knowledge, their documented analysis, and social scientific credentials, the employment of Ham and his Russell Sage division by state authorities produced an alliance. The former could realize their ambitions of combating the loan shark problem through liberalizing usury ceilings while the latter could intervene to secure the common welfare, aiding sizeable elements of the working classes entrenched in expensive debt. In consequence, a potential political threat was diffused through social amelioration while such intervention was justified by the state of the basis of having an access to "truth."

Lenders generally opposed regulatory efforts and in 1916 formed themselves into a national organization to do so—the American Association of Small Loan Brokers (AASLB). Crucially though, such opposition was grounded on the basis of the allowable maximum interest rates they could charge, not by questioning the oversight principle of regulation itself. Only the smallest, highest charging lenders rejected any move toward regulation (Calder, 1999: 133). Later that year, the shift in the mode of government from the loan shark crusade to small loan regulation climaxed in the compromise of a maximum chargeable interest rate between Russell Sage and the AASLB and their alliance to formulate a Uniform Small Loan Law (USLL) and advocate for its state-by-state enactment. By 1923, eighteen states in total had passed equivalent small loan laws.

This Progressive shift toward legislative change signaled a significant shift in how the small loan problem was to be regulated. The relative failure of remedial lending demonstrated that attempting to repel the loan shark by philanthropic measures had failed just as certainly as repression of borrowing through usury limits had. Now reformers acted through rather than against lenders, replacing a strategy of supplanting from without with one of acting upon from within. In creating an exception to usury ceilings for personal loans, the loan shark could potentially become legitimized, the menace eradicated not by eliminating it but by turning it into something else: a tolerable, even necessary enterprise. The Progressive era liberal state thus acted on the basis of collective intent by recalibrating the legislative margins, transforming the small loan from a social problem into a private transaction within the economy. Now newly freed, the small loan lender would be subject to that arena's autonomous laws of competition, accumulation, and rational self-interest. Such intervention also acted upon the freedom of individuals and families themselves; in legalizing higher rates to promote competition, capital influx and thus, ostensibly, lower rates for the borrower, the state sought to advance the self-sufficiency of individuals and promote family autonomy in borrowing decisions. They could now be freed from the repressiveness of "usurious" interest. Rather than seeking to act upon the conduct of borrowers directly through the institution of remedial lending, they would be acted upon more obliquely but with far greater effectiveness through the government of how small loan lenders governed them. To some extent, then, the state recognized the self-governing capacities of workers. It recognized not only that they needed to borrow but that they could exhibit the stability and capacity to enter into their own contracts with lenders as legal subjects, plotting their own decisions of how much to borrow and how to structure their repayments.

Yet the state did not trust to simply hand over the problem to the economy for once enshrined as a social problem in need of state intervention, it could not simply be disengaged. The state came to govern small lending from a distance through the expertise of the Russell Sage Foundation. The enactment of the Uniform Small Loan Laws, as well as legitimizing lenders, simultaneously created a new kind of regulatory system. It raised such credit forms from the margins and the darkness where it had been crudely consigned by law but where it had bred and multiplied in new urban conditions, both reflecting and embodying the flux and turmoil of industrialization, and coaxed it into the light of legality. Now its growth and development could be dispassionately assessed and accounted for. Individual states licensed lenders through oversight departments or officials, whether dedicated or part of a wider financial regulatory apparatus, licensing fees even disbursing the costs of administration back onto lenders themselves. The specification of systematic record keeping along with the requirement for regular auditing thus constituted the supervisory office as a calculating center, which could penetrate, tabulate, and analyze such lending while simultaneously providing for legal enforcement. Maximum loan amounts and "scientifically fair" interest limits defined the boundaries of what could and could not be charged, financial bonds helped secure the lender's adherence to the terms of the legislation, while the practice of wage assignments was carefully specified with the requirement of notification to employer and spouse. Ultimately, punitive fines and penalties enforced the state's will.

This new regime, then, represented not merely the government of lenders but of lending itself, and thus of borrowers as participants. The terms of the law carefully inscribed how borrowing was to be undertaken by the individual—they would not be free simply to contract at any rate of interest for any amount, nor could they dispose of their wages as they saw fit outside of the domain of the family or the employment contract. Their transaction, no longer anonymous, would be itemized with all others, agglomerated and channeled to the requisite authorities for review where its economic significance would be accounted for and future policy adjusted accordingly (see, for example, Robinson and Stearns, 1930). The gradual institution of the Uniform Small Loan Law by states thus freed defined forms of personal borrowing and lending but simultaneously crafted a channel that continuously shaped the course that such transactions could take in the interests of a wider social harmony.

* * *

Pawnbroking represents one of the earliest, most institutionalized, forms of personal lending and images of the three balls, furtive or feckless pledgers, and shelves of goods stacked in gloomy surrounds soak much of the imagination of early industrial life. Around the mid-nineteenth century, however, as industrialization began to take hold within America's urban centers, new forms of borrowing developed around the pledge of future salary and the legal title of possessions. Secured by abstract title rather than material possession, these small lenders attempted to govern the uncertainty of repayment, the possibility of financial loss and the opportunity for profit through an assessment of the borrower's fixedness within their neighborhood, the contrivance of legal claim, the strict temporal regulation of repayments, and the coercive threat of revelation to neighbors and employers. Despite, and in some ways because of, the illegality of such lending where interest was charged typically well in excess of legislative state ceilings, some successful lenders developed into chains of small offices throughout America's major cities.

In the flux and turmoil of industrialization and the discovery of "poverty" as a social problem ineradicable by the market, the phenomenon of small loan borrowing became understood as a financial and moral burden upon workers and their families. In response, elites promulgated the philanthropic solution of remedial lending to competitively eliminate the threat that small loan lending seemed to represent by providing a cheaper source of funds that would both aid the needy and provide for the possibility of their remoralization through the inculcation of thrifty habits. Within the context of Progressivism, a disparate response at the turn of the century to the fragmentation and disorder of urban industrial life, a new social scientific expertise developed in relation to the problem of small loan lending. Although vilifying lenders as exploitative loan sharks, leading crusades to have them eliminated and championing alternative benevolent forms of borrowing such as credit unions and the remedials, these experts also recognized the intrinsic limitations of these alternatives. What they strategized instead, at the start of the new century, was a new proposed role for states in legalizing and licensing commercial small lending, simultaneously providing for the needs of workers and governing the terms under which such lending took place.

CHAPTER 2

Consuming by Installments: The Rise of Retail Credit

Within this chapter, we will examine the development of retail installment credit in the nineteenth century and the ways in which it manifests a significantly different history to the practices of small loans that we have already looked at. Fundamentally, retail credit was not understood by American courts to be a credit transaction in the same way that cash borrowing and pawnbroking were. It was developed by small retailers as a way of boosting sales to consumers and defending market share, with many department stores and the main catalog merchants initially shunning it as a disreputable practice. This parallels how commercial small loan providers were dismissed as contemptible usurers and their customers feckless or vulnerable. And just like the small loan business, this aloofness was not to be maintained. We will see how borrowers were governed by sellers, not only through the rigorous organization of time and money payments but also through the assessed will of the borrower.

The increasing popularity of installment selling toward the end of the nineteenth century, however, rendered it an object of middle-class disdain and anxiety, a stigma that would not be repealed until the mass marketing of the automobile in the first decades of the twentieth century. At the same time that installment credit was suffering such opprobrium, charge accounts began to develop within the very finest of retail establishment for an elite stratum of consumer. What such distinctions reveal, of course, is the stratified nature of credit in terms of how it was deployed and, most significantly, the ways in which its class, race, and gendered consumers were understood to be in need of different kinds of government.

The Will to Consume: The Rise of Retail Installment Lending

The selling of goods on time payments, or on the "installment plan," demonstrates a different genealogy within the nineteenth century to that of cash lending. In fact, as Lynn argues, the originator of installment lending was actually the American state itself through the Harrison Act of 1800, which sold off vast tracts of public land to farmers in exchange for a 25 percent down payment with the rest falling due in three increments up to four years after the sale (1957: 415). More germanely, the first cooperative Building and Loan association set up in Philadelphia in 1831 to aid families of relatively modest means to afford their own homes pioneered the concept of the self-amortizing "sinking-loan fund." This was a loan paid-off by a borrower in multiple payments, including fees, over a fixed time span (Jackson, 1985: 130). Within rural America, as Lynn demonstrates, the sale of new motorized farm equipment such as threshers and reapers on installments began to be advertised in farming periodicals from around the 1850s, heralding a labor saving, productivity enhancing industrial revolution on the farm.

It is generally held that installment selling of consumer goods within the United States began in 1807 with the large New York furniture firm of Cowperthwait and Sons, spreading to rival firms and other cities to form what has been termed a "high grade" installment business around mid-century, focused mainly on prosperous wage and salary earners and small businessmen (Mussey, 1903; Seligman, 1927; Nugent, 1939). In addition to furniture, sales of pianos also became mediated through the mechanism of the installment contract around the 1850s. The purchase of a piano, at the time costing around $1,000, represented a particularly sizeable investment and was aimed at more affluent families. As Seligman notes, terms were stricter with a one-third down payment required with the rest payable in relatively large monthly installments over two or three years.

Seligman contends that such credit opened up a consuming space in between those who could afford such purchases outright and so had no necessity for credit and those that were excluded and so had no recourse to it. The latter, whose latent danger was manifested by such symptoms as their class, race, and residential neighborhood, were regarded as being unreliable. This was not simply because of their meager resources but, more fundamentally, because they were "financially irresponsible" (1927: 15). The working classes were thus regarded as being unable to fulfill the terms of their credit contract because of a strongly moralistic understanding of their character. If liberalism depends upon the self-governing capacities of individuals to manage their freedom, to exert a "self-despotism" over their own actions, desires, and wants as Valverde (1996) terms it, such capacities were not conceived to be equally present or instilled across the population but to be naturalized along class, race, and gender divides (1997: 262). Just as differences in nineteenth-century inebriety treatment programs that Valverde (1997, 1998) discusses embodied and entrenched assumptions of differential subjectivity, so too did installment merchants approach borrowers on the basis of how such individuals were understood to govern themselves.

As profit-oriented businessmen, high-grade furniture sellers recognized the facility that credit could offer toward expanding their sales, allowing certain classes who would otherwise be unable to purchase their wares to do so. To these ends, the concept of character provided a means to mediate the potential for loss due to nonrepayment. This provided a way for distinguishing between those who were sufficiently "self-despotic" to control and rationally manage their freedom and those who were seen to be unable to keep to contractual repayment terms agreed because of an innate ill-potentiality to govern their "nature." For Seligman, "owing to the great care in the selection of the purchasers, losses from dishonesty are comparatively uncommon, the default being generally due to unforeseen contingencies" (1927: 15–16, see also Mussey, 1903: 13). So even when nonrepayment did occur, it was interpreted as being not the result of an inability to self-rule but rather the outcome of unfortunate circumstances that could not be directly attributed to the moral qualities of the individual. The treatment of such high-grade customers was "exceedingly liberal" and even in the event of default, as both Mussey and Seligman suggest, such retailers were loathe to foreclose on the goods, refraining from doing so only after the possibility of repayment seemed lost and often only repossessing furniture to the value of the portion of credit outstanding. Even allowing for these authors' possibly sanguine analyses, such a credit agreement appeared more as a gentleman's agreement relying on and assuming a moral fortitude and resolve on the part of customers rather than on a contract providing recourse to a coercive legal remedy. Installment credit was not conceived as a form of borrowing and thus was not subject to statutory usury restrictions; rather, it was adjudged through a succession of court judgments as a form of deferred payment that was contractually agreed to by the parties concerned (Berger, 1935).

In contrast to the state's inhibition of personal borrowing through the mechanism of law, installment buying existed legally as a private accommodation that lay outside the scope of detailed regulation, an economic transaction marshaled solely by means of the will of the parties concerned. Although dismissed as a convenient legal fiction by Berger (see also Crowther Committee, 1971), such a genealogy reveals the differential understanding that underlay installment buying. In contrast to pawning or cash borrowing, it was not a morally charged practice of desperation, dependence, or profligacy at work among lower elements of the population, which a liberal state had a duty to regulate for the collective good; rather, it was a self-governing contractual agreement freely entered into by middle-class participants, which a liberal state had no warrant to interfere within.

The freedom of the purchaser-borrower, however, was not something that was merely taken for granted but, rather, represented an aspect that was actively constituted within the context of the transaction. As Nugent (1939) suggests, this type of credit differed from the kinds of "open-book" credit that had gone before where customers accumulated an account that they paid off at periodic intervals. In contrast, installment credit was a formal agreement for the purchase of a single item under which the seller maintained legal title to the good until the final payment. Although the item being sold represented a significant purchase, the length of the agreement mandated relatively small payments over a period of up to eighteen months. In addition, a minimum 10 percent cash deposit was required in advance (1939: 54–5). Therefore, although a certain strata of the middle class were deemed sufficiently self-governing to be trusted with "high-grade" credit, the actions of such borrowers were enmeshed within a structured framework of external constraints regulating the exercise of their free conduct. A deposit required that a certain sum be accumulated in advance and be put toward the purchase cost. The individual's payments were set out and agreed in advance conditioned by a strict timing regimen that would determine when the borrower was to pay and how much. The payments themselves were sufficiently small to ensure that they did not prove onerous and thus endanger the agreement but yet were balanced against a bounded contractual period that was short enough to prevent distraction of the borrower's responsibilities and the excessive locking up of the seller's working capital. Finally, through the legal mechanism of the conditional sales contract, the seller maintained ownership over the good until the end and could, whether or not reluctantly, exert this right at any stage that the borrower failed to adhere to what was required of him. The free self-governing liberal subject defined by the successful pursuit of self-despotism was a precondition for the emerging "reputable" installment sellers of the mid-nineteenth century but alone it was insufficient; it was to be accompanied by an intersecting system of external despotism that, once sanctioned by the signing of a contract, would brace the will of the subject with a required upfront prepayment, the enforced habitual routine of installment payments, and the grim threat of repossession.

In the case of these early furniture and piano retailers, the extent to which credit was offered was strictly limited—at this time, not every wage earner but only individuals who demonstrated themselves to be of requisite character, capable of exerting the close self-discipline required of freedom, could gain admittance to the status expressing goods available on installments. Thus, the mid-century beginnings of formalized systems of credit for relatively expensive household goods reflect the shift of capital under American industrialization, with certain forms of consumption becoming bound up in both affirming and constituting new emergent strains of middle-class salaried employee, dependent upon but also defining the expression of freedom within the realm of consumption.

A New Consumerism

The post–Civil War reconstruction period saw the United States experiencing a sharp increase in investment, industrialization and capitalist concentration and growth as it entered the so-called Gilded Age (Trescott, 1963; Porter, 1973). The continent became bound for the first time by new transport and communications infrastructures, including the Northern Pacific Railway and a national telegraph network (Thompson, 1947; Stover, 1961; Dwyer, 2000; Verstraete, 2002). This material unity was mirrored in the mobilization of a new elite generation through a higher education, centered on the prestigious East Coast universities, now increasingly oriented toward formalized business education (Chambers, 1980; Hall, 1982). An increasingly national market was coming to displace dispersed, self-sufficient "island communities." The nation's major cities, themselves swelling in size with influxes of rural migrants and foreign immigrants, increasingly began to serve as commercial hubs radiating outward in their regional control of finance, farm production, and the products of industry (Hays, 1957; Wiebe, 1967). Within these cities themselves, a new downtown emerged that Nye represents as the "physical expression of concentrated energy use" (1998: 173). Electricity animated the new trolleybuses and subways that propelled individuals in and around newly constructed skyscrapers made possible by powered lifts, ventilation systems, and telephone networks. Within this context, a new structure of centralized consumer retailing began to take shape: in Lears's (1994) words, the peddler became "reformed," stabilized within the form of the department store.

Beginning in 1846 with the opening of A.T. Stewart's Marble Palace, department stores such as Macy's and Marshall Field's began to emerge in the 1860s and 1870s as large retailers selling multiple lines of goods (Hendrickson, 1979: 60–149; Leach, 1993; see also Miller, 1981; Rappaport 2000). Three key organizing principles underlay how this new type of firm operated (Strasser, 1989: 204–6). Rather than the traditional price bargaining system between buyer and seller that had been predominant, such stores sold goods on the basis of fixed single prices. These were set according to a continuous calculated profit-oriented analysis of stock turnover as opposed to being the outcome of incremental, transaction-specific bargaining between buyer and seller. As their name suggests, such stores were departmentalized into units selling specific lines of goods that were then analyzed by a centralized administration, which assessed the sales effectiveness of individual employees as well as the profitability engendered by the department as a whole (see also Benson, 1986; Walsh and Jeacle, 2003). These firms combined new merchandising and distribution approaches with economic weight and the integration of manufacturing to change how consumption was organized and related to the individual.

It was not simply the rationalization of retailing that fostered changes in consumption; goods themselves became related to the individual in new ways. The fixed price system nurtured individuals into a new role as consumers, engaging them not as active participants within acts of purchase but as passive democratic participants of an experience "where consumers are an audience to be entertained by commodities, where selling is mingled with amusement, where arousal of free-floating desire is as important as immediate purchase of particular items" (Williams, 1982: 67). From around the 1880s to the end of the century, department stores began to condition a new aesthetic to the sale of their goods. They used new electric light to illuminate the increasing diversity of wares and services; created seductively arranged, often fantastical window and exotically thematic shop displays; and arranged space to foster a new intimacy between customers and goods, including separating and rendering invisible the manufacturing and clerical labor that underlied the "dream worlds" being created upon the shop floor (Leach, 1993).

Department store shopping, though, remained an urban phenomenon, attracting only those within a relatively easy urban commute. The second main thrust in the concentration of consumption was the development of the mail order firms from the 1870s, particularly the two Chicago giants Montgomery Ward and Sears, Roebuck & Co., who fostered an enhanced, nationalized spirit of consumption in isolated rural areas beyond the confines of the peddler and the general store (Emmet and Jeuck, 1950; Boorstin, 1973; Hendrickson, 1979: 205–3; Lears 1989; Blanke, 2000: 184–215). It was not by chance that both were located in this city for Chicago served as the major hub in the development of the national railway infrastructure, the location allowing these firms to effectively distribute their wares over most parts of the country. It was Montgomery Ward himself who, building upon his experience as a traveling salesman, pioneered the mail order concept, setting up his company in 1872 with the support of the Grange farmers' organization and the promise to reduce prices by eliminating the "middle man" and "selling only for cash."

The catalog was the crucial element in mail order, the site that allowed the seller to present the goods available for purchase. Initially small in size with the emphasis on written description and simple woodcut illustrations, the end of the century saw ever multiplying circulation and new innovations such as linotype and color printing, which expanded the scope for a realistic visual projection of the product being sold. Crucial to the development of mail order was a scheme known as rural free delivery (RFD), which initially emerged in the 1890s to guarantee a reliable postal delivery system to farm addresses. More broadly, like the roll out of the railway and the telegraph, RFD integrated territory by separating out time and space in the formation of a national marketplace. "For the rural American, the change was crucial. Now he was lifted out of the narrow community of those he saw and knew, and put in continual touch with a larger world of persons and events and things read about but unheard and unseen" (Boorstin, 1973: 133).

Neither department stores nor mail order firms remained unchallenged as they expanded their arc to define new patterns of consumption. Reflecting wider anxieties about consumer affluence (Horowitz, 1985; Barton, 1989; Lears, 1989), the 1890s saw the emergence of an antidepartment store crusade composed of unions, small merchants, women's groups, and some politicians who rallied against the exploitative and competition-threatening power wielded by such enterprises (Leach, 1993). Similarly, local traders being threatened with extinction by nationally oriented mail order companies petitioned for restrictive state legislation and attempted to form systematic boycotts to limit the scope of these outside rivals whom they accused of draining money from the country to the capitalist elite of the city. Some even went so far as to organize community book burnings of catalogs (Cohn, 1940: 510–17; Smalley and Sturdivant, 1973: 51; Hendrickson, 1979: 212–17). Neither type of campaign, though, could ultimately restrain the new national commercial tide that consumption was attaining.

"Gullible, Ignorant, and Illiterate": Installment Credit and Deficient Wills

Within this post–Civil War period, credit itself began to undergo a rapid expansion in terms of its geographic spread, the merchandising lines within which it was offered and the types of people who used it (Seligman, 1927; Nugent, 1939; Calder, 1999). Whereas before, it was exclusively for the financing of significant durable items of consumption like furniture and pianos, by the 1870s, its use extended to such relatively ephemeral household items as bedding, dishes, and kitchenware as well as for the purchase of suits, coats, and dresses on such terms as one-fifth down payment and eight weekly installments. With the cheapening of sewing machine production and competition between agents, installment terms became pervasively liberalized so that by the 1870s a machine could be had for as little as $1 down and 50 cents a week (Nugent, 1939: 67). The types of individuals using such credit also shifted to encompass Blacks, immigrants, and the "proletariat" of Midwest cities so that the class distinction that had maintained the technique of installment credit as a tool of a rising or aspiring middle class dissolved. In Seligman's blunt language, installment credit became extended to a "lower grade" of both commodity and purchaser (1927: 19). Such a shift was associated with rising numbers of urban workers and immigrants with materially limited incomes who were disjointed from home and land as sites of production and cut adrift within a new, fluid urban milieu (Nugent 1938: 43–4). Attempting to accumulate both household furnishings and express new forms of consumption, installment credit provided the possibility of their attainment by exploiting the relative regularity of wages—an extended sequence of interminably fractional payments mirroring the (hopefully) interminable cycle of the fixed weekly pay packet (Calder, 1999).

In their analysis of the Spiegel Company of Chicago, an installment merchandiser that began to supply furniture on installments to working class families in the 1890s, Smalley and Sturdivant suggest that:

> Although expensive, such a selling technique enabled families to acquire necessary goods out of income by making frequent small instalments. Certainly many such families would not have been able to exert the necessary self-discipline to accumulate the money for full payment of many goods in the absence of a semi-forced savings scheme. (1973: 26)

This shows, albeit retrospectively, the transformation of understanding that the spread of installment credit encapsulated. As we saw previously, the early availability of installment credit had been associated with the demonstration of character, the facility of a class fraction that was believed able to exert a strict self-government over itself and could thus be largely trusted with expensive household goods on a sequence of deferred payments. However, with its spread down the social scale, the marketing of such credit became seen as an instrument of material necessity. Now its fulfillment by the individual stemmed not just from the contractual nature of the agreement but the repetitive sequencing of payments constituting a despotic mechanism substituting for, rather than supporting, the self-government of the individual. As social investigator Henry Mussey described it, "[t]heir methods are copied after those of the large dealers, but necessarily involve more severity, because they deal with a less responsible class of customers, and are themselves of a lower grade of business training and ethics" (1903: 15).

The arrival and growth of department stores also had an important, albeit indirect, effect on installment selling. These stores themselves did not offer such credit—in fact, they prized themselves on their cash only policies—but their competitive commercial strength forced many single-line retailers into offering installment terms. Such credit also allowed individuals to attain a higher standard of consumption, particularly for clothing. With the increasing preponderance of mass produced clothes and in new urban milieus beset by flux and shifting, uncertain social relations and class identities, credit allowed increasing numbers to adopt the exterior aspects of a higher social class within a context that increasingly grounded judgment on appearance (Calder, 1999: 169–71; see also Boorstin, 1973; Horowitz, 1985).

The consequences of this expansion of installment credit beyond a specific middle-class stratum to more and more members of the working class were that it was increasingly rendered as culturally illegitimate for the former, probably by virtue of its association with working class consumption. As Veblen ([1899] 1925) and Bourdieu (1984) famously showed, both goods and the taste for goods correspond with the expression of fundamental social status differences and that the distinctive power of both goods and taste declines in line with the ability of lower classes to appropriate them. We might translate this to late nineteenth-century America so that the mode of financing mediating the possibility of appropriating the distinctive potentialities of goods, too, came to represent a particular type of stylistic possibility as much as the goods to which it gave purchase. As installment credit widened the consuming possibilities of lower classes, appropriating in some measure the symbolic value of items formerly reserved for middle-class consumption, cash buying was reserved as a distinguishing practice of middle-class consumption being catered for at new department store emporia. These retailers combined the presentation of spectacle with a brusque refusal to entertain the possibility of installment credit.

It was not simply, though, that such credit lost an intrinsic power of distinction for the middle class; rather that, in doing so, it became associated with a degradation and inhibition of freedom. At the end of the nineteenth century certain marginal forms of consumption (and by implication consumer) were understood to be unproductive and irrational in direct contravention of the liberal injunction to self-control (Hilton, 2004). By the 1890s, as Nugent (1939) attests, installment selling "attracted a largely disreputable fringe" that pushed prices up, reduced down payments, and extended contract times. Such a dismantling of regulatory buttresses was matched by the increased use of punitive sanctions such as the deployment of liens over other household goods as well as the aggressive pursuit of wage garnishment.

Among such groups as Blacks and non-English speaking immigrants, this hardening "liberalization" of credit was exacerbated by outright fraud, the impecunious threat of imprisonment and even bodily violence. At the turn of the century, for instance, social investigator Henry Mussey (1903) analyzed a flourishing "fake installment business" in New York City where unscrupulous vendors, targeting immigrants in particular, sold worthless or highly overpriced merchandise on installments and surreptitiously altered contracts to defraud unfortunate borrowers. If, as Wightman (1996) suggests, the classical liberal contract is defined as the formal meeting of two wills, then Nugent's description of immigrants and minorities as being typified by "gullibility, ignorance and illiteracy" indicates how deficient their will was understood to be. To a greater or lesser extent then, certain marginalized sections of an industrialized, urban population were understood to be nonrational; lacking the capacity for self-control that characterized the free liberal subject, they were perceived as being unable to act in their own self-interest when entering into credit transactions. As weak parties to an unequal exchange, they were thus seen as vulnerable to manipulation through the self-interest of others, a form of exploitation that they were incapable of resisting because of their inability to recognize and defend their own interest.

Thus, at the turn of the century, most working-class users of installment credit were understood to lack the capacity for freedom, materially, through inferior resources but also in their competence to regulate themselves, to exert their will to bear the responsibilities of freedom. They were therefore fated to manifest their degraded will in such credit use—the more deficient the capacity for freedom, the greater the coercion experienced and the more disreputable installment credit became. In general, by avoiding or hiding installment credit use, the middle class sought to distinguish itself, not merely because such credit was excessively common symbolically but because it had become inextricably associated with a morally constituted incapacity for self-government. It was the obverse of this through which the middle class understood and defined its own freedom (Valverde, 1996).

Department Stores and Charge Accounts

Despite the social contempt with which installment credit was held from the 1880s, other forms of credit began to circulate within the consumption practices of more affluent classes toward the end of that century. Within burgeoning department stores, characterized significantly by their "prolific middle classness" (Leach, 1993: 20), charge accounts were offered to wealthy customers in order to encourage a specifically "high class clientele" (Jeacle and Walsh, 2002: 740). As the latter authors note, such individuals often exploited such facilities by accumulating charges and delaying payment for several months upon which, in general, no interest was charged. The distinction between such charge accounts and the stigmatized working class forms of installment credit reveals the different forms of government that underlay each and the different understandings of the subjects involved. Charge accounts were an extension of the older forms of open book credit that had been common between retail merchants and their customers; they were trust-based "promises to pay" rather than legally enforceable contractual obligations. However, unlike open book credit, they were not bound within dense communal relations but presumed a high degree of self-regulation on the part of the customer. In contrast to installment payments, charge accounts were paid off as and when the individual client saw fit. No mechanical regimen regulated the repayments and neither could the retailer seek to legally reclaim the goods in the event of default—on the contrary, everything rested on the individual's desire to clear their account. Of course, the motivation for credit was understood by department store management not as a "necessity," a means of bridging the purchase of goods in the present through the calculable, regulated allotment of the future; on the contrary, it was seen as a "convenience," a mechanism of streamlining the purchase of goods in the present by extending its boundaries by means of the perceived strength of will of the individual.

These forms of credit, though, did not remain the preserve of an elite. As Leach notes, by the end of the 1890s, department stores began to actively market their charge services to less affluent strata than before—soliciting existing charge customers to recommend friends and acquaintances to join.[1] As Calder suggests, department stores implemented such a shift as they increasingly felt the pressure of competition from supposedly lower class installment retailers while the increasing administrative rationalization of its operations made such a strategy bureaucratically possible (1999: 71–2). Soon, some stores began issuing numbered metal coins to be proffered by customers to identify themselves when charging purchases (Leach, 1993: 125).

With this proliferation of credit, charge accounts even gave way to installment-like credit plans; for instance in 1900, Wanamaker's department store began to sell pianos on an installment-like "contract basis" that obliged monthly payments, although no down payment was required (Leach, 1993: 127). The most notable exception was Macy's in New York that persistently prided itself on a cash-only policy, ostensibly presented as a strategy to keep prices low. In 1902, as an alternative strategy to the charge plan, it opened a dedicated facility that allowed regular customers to deposit cash against which purchases could be conveniently charged and to which interest and annual bonuses were paid by the store. However, although such debit sales exhibited moderate growth as a proportion of total sales over the succeeding years, its proportion was less than a fifth of comparable charge sales in other stores (Hower, 1943: 341–4).

The loosening of department store credit policy, though, called into question the presupposition of the freedom of the consumer. Particularly given the association of department stores with feminized consumption, Leach draws attention to the proliferation of turn of the century court cases involving upper and middle-class women accumulating debts on charge accounts that their husbands were unable to pay.[2] At this time, as Zukin notes, "women were continually accused of being too weak to withstand the temptations of choice; they were charged with spending money beyond their means, abusing their husband's charge accounts and shoplifting. Kleptomania was considered to be the middle class woman's disease" (2004: 16). Zukin's association of desire, credit, and kleptomania brings into relief how women were perceived. Like immigrants or the working class, the middle-class woman was seen to be intrinsically lacking in will, deficient in her ability to control the irrational sensuous passions of her own nature and thus exceedingly vulnerable to the almost sexual stimulation conjured by new arenas of consumption (Abelson, 1989; Spiekermann, 1999). Shopping, thieving, and credit abuse were thus closely related constructions of the same underlying condition attributed to middle-class, homebound women—the Janus-faced inability to resist both their own irrational selves and the quality of the potent consuming temptations to which they were exposed. The end result, then, was a supposed compulsion to steal or rack up charges that their husbands struggled to contend with.

Mail Order Installment Credit

The development of "low grade" installment credit, however, did not remain confined to urban centers. In 1904 the Spiegel home furnishings retailer of Chicago, founded in 1893 and which concentrated on selling household goods on installments to lower middle-class and working-class families, began to develop a mail order business concentrated initially on a geographical area within a hundred miles of Chicago (Smalley and Sturdivant, 1973). Following the mass retailing lead of mail order houses Montgomery Ward and Sears, it produced a catalog detailing a limited array of furniture goods and disseminated it to addresses acquired through mailing lists, freely available town directories and the bribing of postmasters. Crucially, unlike its larger rivals that mirrored department stores in stridently refusing to engage in installment selling, Spiegel offered all such goods on installments with the cost of such credit built into an inflated purchase price. Whereas Sears declared even as late as 1910 that "Our only terms are for cash; we do not sell on installments or extend credit" (Cohn, 1940: 524), the early slogan adopted by its smaller rival—"We Trust the People—Everywhere"—demonstrates the supposed democratizing intentions of making both consumption and credit freely available on a uniform basis to wider sections of a dispersed population. Indeed, as Smalley and Sturdivant note, given how credit was so bound up within Spiegel's mail retailing strategy, the management placed particular emphasis on credit as a "respectable" practice for the new "great army of salary-earners" whose comforts should not be limited by an insistence on cash (1973: 48). In a letter to reluctant customers, credit was even identified by the firm with the buying habits of the wealthy classes, which was now available to people of more modest means but who were declared to be of equal honesty and responsibility.

Although repayment on credit for furniture was felt to be reasonably secure on the basis that the accumulation of furniture was an indicator of permanence, stability and personal responsibility—"good character"—the conditional sales contract provided the possibility of a more coercive regulation through repossession. However, the entry of the company into the installment selling of clothing, and the consequential eclipsing of the possibility of repossession of items sold in such a way, generated greater fears about security, which were seen by certain sections of management to be endemic to "the dirty rag business" (Smalley and Sturdivant, 1973: 63). In other words, without the possibility of resorting to despotic forms of regulation through acting to repossess the good and reserve any payments that had been made, individuals might be less relied upon to exert the self-despotism necessary to maintain their repayments.

With the widening physical distance between consumers and the central retailer implied by mail order and its branching out into new areas of merchandising, Spiegel increasingly developed itself as a "centre of calculation" across a national market, governing consumers through the notion of character. This could not, of course, be attained at first hand, through a proximate assessment; instead an array of circuits were marshaled that connected the retailing apparatus with each individual and potential customer, funneling relevant information back to the firm's administrative credit office. As Rose and Miller (1992) argue, processes of governance, acting upon distant events, deploy mechanisms of accumulating information that both enable and legitimize it. At first, local lawyers and bankers residing within the individual's community were harnessed as sources of information on credit applicants; later, specialized local agents came to be used as well as references submitted by the applicant. However, from 1917 onward, individuals themselves became increasingly employed in the firm's government of them through the widening scope of the application form. The answers to an array of such questions as occupation, earnings, address, age, marital status, and race were increasingly correlated with a perceived degree of self-regulation in repaying credit and were relied upon by the firm in determining the creditworthy character of the customer.

* * *

From the mid-nineteenth century, the installment selling of consumer goods demonstrated a different set of governing practices to cash borrowing—most particularly, charges for its use were not interpreted by the courts to be a form of interest and so were not subject to typical state usury restrictions. In the antebellum years, the practice of installment selling developed among certain furniture and piano retailers who governed the uncertainty of repayment through the use of down payments, the reservation of legal title and the temporal discipline of small incremental payments. But they also relied upon the strength of will of the individual consumers who were accepted—the potentiality for such self-government being assessed and determined along class, race, and gender lines. Credit thus became part of the consuming practices of elements of the middle class who were attempting to assuage desire but yet were unable to do so without recourse to such credit. In the final turbulent decades of the century, as installment credit became increasingly used by workers, immigrants, and Black minorities, it also became pervasively stigmatized, associated through narratives of skullduggery and exploitation, the exhibition of deficient will and an absence of freedom. From this the middle classes carefully distanced themselves at the same time that many of them, paradoxically, began to embrace the credit possibilities of retailer-based charge accounts. As we shall see in the next chapter, such social prohibitions on installment credit could not resist the rise of that most revolutionary of newly mass-produced consumer goods—the automobile.

CHAPTER 3

Assembling the Automobile, Reassembling Thrift

I t seems almost a cliché to mention the importance of the mass-produced, mass-owned automobile to the development of American society in the twentieth century. The very shape and form of American streets, cities, and highways have been bound to its proliferating ownership (St. Clair, 1986; McShane, 1994). Ling (1990) links its development early in the new century to that of the Progressivism with its organizing impulse to incorporate rural "island communities" and ease the menace of urban overcrowding; yet, so too did the car provide a means of privacy, escape, and freedom in an increasingly organized world. In this latter, Belasco (1997) demonstrates how the car became a central feature of the new leisure pursuit of itinerant autocamping as middle-class families sought a return to older times characterized by independence, closeness to nature, and family solidarity—ultimately spawning the birth of the motel industry in the twentieth century. Particularly in rural areas, as Berger (1979) shows, growing car ownership among farming households, reaching 30.7 percent as early as 1920, altered the field of possibilities of family life and the structure of previously isolated communities, particularly with respect to religion, education, and healthcare.

The proliferation and mainstream mass commercialization of consumer credit within the United States during the twentieth century is inextricably related to the development of mass ownership of assembly line manufactured automobiles. Just as the automobile seems to encapsulate something of the essence of the "coming of age" of American consumerism and culture more broadly, such mass ownership was only made possible through new mechanisms of financing such ownership. Ford's perfecting of mass production had to be met by what Clark (1930) calls new agencies and institutions of "mass finance" to put the fruits of such production within the realm of consumption. What is often regarded as the spark is the peculiar seasonality of capital intensive automobile production and the effect that this had on the need for credit facilities (Olney, 1991). Put simply, production had to be level to minimize costs while people tended to buy cars seasonally, thus forcing an excessive production of cars at certain times of the year. However, it wasn't manufacturers that bore the costly burden of storing this inventory, but rather, the car dealerships who were tied to specific manufacturers. As Olney suggests, demand for dealerships far exceeded supply thereby putting the manufacturer in a relative position of power vis-á-vis the dealer and able to dictate terms favorable to it, including passing the burden of storage on to the dealer on a cash-on-demand basis. For the dealer, an external source of financing was clearly required if it was to avoid its stock of working capital being tied up in warehousing cars for months at a time. This, though, was not forthcoming from the traditional commercial banking sector that saw cars as, by and large, unnecessary expenses and dealers as bad risks given the power of manufacturers to cancel dealership agreements without notice.

What emerged as a solution was the finance company, either contracted or owned by manufacturers, to fund such an inventory build-up on behalf of the dealerships. Dealers essentially sold their stock, at a discount, to such companies, which then authorized dealers to accept future customer payment for the cars on their behalf. These companies essentially acted as intermediaries between banks and dealers by contracting capital from the former and supplying it to the latter in order for them to finance the inventory purchasing of cars from manufacturers. Within Olney's economistic analysis, the emergence of specialized finance companies was not a response to an increasing demand by consumers but was, rather, fundamentally related to their role as "production smoothing devices," from which they only later branched out to promote credit to consumers.

It would seem one-dimensional, however, to declare, as Olney does, that finance companies emerged simply as a response to production bottlenecks and the desire of manufacturers to maintain control over dealers. The historical practice of commercial firms borrowing using amounts owed to them, and not just stock, as collateral has had a long lineage within the United States, with such financing becoming applied to consumer forms of debt around 1905 (Seligman, 1927: 33–5). In fact, it was through the "industrial" or "Morris" banks, one of the first commercialized agencies of consumer lending, that credit for automobile purchases first became available in 1910, even before the mass production of automobiles had really taken off. In 1913, the Weaver Company became the first finance company to purchase the debts of car dealers followed by Guaranty Securities Company in 1915, which began a similar practice for Willys-Overland dealers in Ohio before quickly expanding both nationally and to other makes of car (GM's future president Alfred Sloan was one of its directors at this time).

By 1917, there were six finance companies specializing in automobile finance or who had added it to their business activities. As Seligman's more balanced account relates: "the desire of the automobile user to be provided with a somewhat easier method of payment, and the interests of the automobile manufacturer to secure a larger as well as an even, uninterrupted flow of output, conspired to bring about the introduction of the installment method" (1927: 30). By 1922, there were 1,000 companies trading in automobile financing, rising to 1,600 by 1925, although the vast majority of trade was concentrated in a handful of major companies (Clark, 1930: 21; Plummer and Young, 1940: 33–5). The source of this financing came mainly from short-term borrowing at commercial banks although the large national companies would eventually come to offer their debt as an investment on the open market. Yet, the question remains as to how or why people were being increasingly implicated within the consumption of the automobile, and why they were submitting themselves to a regime of indebtedness to do so. As we have seen, the instrument of the installment plan was not itself new, its deployment as a technology to mediate consumption stretches back far into the nineteenth century. Nevertheless, the automobile saved installment credit from the cultural disrepute into which it had fallen, in particular, its strong association with working class consumption. As such, the automobile represented a good whose function and symbolic qualities relegitimized the use of installment purchasing by the middle class.

Consuming Desire

The nature of commercial organization within the United States shifted dramatically up to the 1920s and beyond as the promotion, facilitation, and quality of consumption increasingly became central to the calculations of capitalist enterprise. What Wiebe (1967) calls the "distended" society of the late nineteenth century, where industrialization had progressed without a correspondingly coherent sense of integrated organization, began to give way to new forms of productivity and economic consolidation through commercial mergers, the proliferation of new forms of mass merchandising through chain stores, the growth in size, scale, and scope of department stores, and the professionalization of consumer industries through the formalization of knowledge in such areas as retailing, merchandising, sales, and specific areas of service provision. Banks, too, were drawn into a new role within this maelstrom of change, shifting from their role as commodity brokers to permanent financiers of a system of consuming desire (Leach, 1993). Building upon and developing the industrial mass production that took shape during the nineteenth century, new means of nationally oriented mass distribution, most notably the chain-store method, were predicated on the emergence of a mass consumer market (Bowlby, 2001). Advertising became the language, or as Marchand (1985) calls it, the "lubricant" of this anonymous sphere (see also Ewen, 1976), appealing to an emerging mass audience at the level of the subjective and playing on the idea of a perpetual state of yearning and desire; with retail purchasing still perceived to be the role of the "female," the mass audience itself was feminized, perceived, and constituted through advertising and marketing as being inherently subject to caprice and emotionality. Even the very notions of what constituted individuality and character were also becoming transformed with the emergence of organized capitalism, the lengthening chains of social interdependency and the growth of consumer "abundance" (Lears, 1989; Stearns 1999; Susman 2003; Sandage 2006; Mennell 2007).

Into the twentieth century, the nature of production itself was shifting to encompass consumer "need"—as Cross details, from 1900 to 1930, discretionary spending increased while the number of hours in the working week declined (2000: 17–18). Yet, the vanguard of a new capitalism, the Ford Motor Company, was coming to epitomize a relationship between labor and capital that was increasingly organized and instrumentally rational with little care for the novelty of ephemeral desire. With the establishment of the Highland Park plant in 1910, new lines of bureaucratic administration and centralized planning were drawn out across the factory; capital-intensive assembly belt methods combined with unskilled, usually immigrant workers enmeshed in an extensive, precise division of labor; and men, machines and materials were progressively allotted in calculated, rational workflows within the production process. Even workers' homes were subject to the managerial scrutiny of Ford's "Sociological Department" on the look out for thriftless or ill-disciplined family habits (Meyer, 1981, 1989; Gartman, 1986; Ling, 1990; Bachelor, 1994; Brinkley, 2004).

Even the celebrated profit sharing "five dollar day" policy instituted in January 1914 was part of a conscious strategy to integrate labor within the new heavy industrial production methods that the Ford name has become inextricably associated with. It riveted workers in their place within the new organized, "solid" capital-intensive industrial system, literally by reducing the incidence of staff turnover, strategically by countering unionization but more fundamentally by ensuring the adherence of labor to a hierarchical, top-down order that increasingly deprived it of initiative and creativity (Bauman, 2000: 57–8). Despite contemporary misconceptions, such a raising of wages was not an immediate ploy to transform workers into consumers, or at least not consumers of automobiles. As Cohen notes in her study of Chicago workers, even by the 1920s automobile ownership among this labor segment stood at only 3 percent (1990: 103). These workers, in contrast, persisted in buying traditional items like furniture and smaller consumer items like phonographs on credit or, more commonly, saved their surplus income and paid cash for their purchases. Despite the "easy payments" facility offered by auto installment credit, the market for installment credit was more or less limited to the relatively affluent and the middle classes (p. 104).

Fordism, therefore, represents an incomplete model for articulating and understanding the new forms that capitalism was taking with the elevation of mass consumption (Meyer, 1989: 81–3). Although pioneering the capital intensive assembly line with its super-scientific management of labor, Ford was wedded to the idea of the single perfected product of the Model T that was standardized, uniform, and would eliminate competition through low marginal prices (Ling, 1990; Tedlow, 1990). Consumer demand was not a factor to be analyzed, to be accounted for, to be problematized and systematically assembled as an independent element within the broader production endeavor. It was held simply as a corollary of the factory process and the utilitarian features of the product. By making production leaner and more efficient, prices could be reduced and more Model Ts would be bought.

Alfred Sloan, vice president at General Motors from 1918 and committed like Ford to mass production, mapped out an alternative vision that positioned the consumer at the heart of production. He conceived and realized a line of progressively priced products of different grades that would segment the market and through which each model would be changed annually to embody the latest style and fashion. Whereas Henry Ford held the critical feature of his Model T to be unchanging simplicity, Sloan drew a deliberate parallel between automobile marketing and the regenerative novelty of consumerist fashion declaring "it is not too much to say that the 'laws' of the Paris dressmakers have come to be a factor in the automobile industry—and woe to the company which ignores them." Furthermore, he strategized on "the degree to which styling changes should be made in any one model run.... The changes in the new model should be so novel and attractive as to creative demand for the new value and, so to speak, create a certain amount of dissatisfaction with past models as compared with the new one...." ([1963] 1980: 265).

Fordism of the 1910s thus encapsulates a type of capitalism that acted as a key locus for twentieth-century consumption but which, by the 1920s, was already becoming obsolete. Henry Ford himself, perhaps, represents the last of the nineteenth-century entrepreneur industrialists not only in his sole concern for the "need" rather than the "desire" of car ownership, which included the elimination of advertising but also the virtual sabotaging of his own organizational management structure and his drive in 1916 to sole ownership and all-encompassing control of the company (Tedlow, 1990: 161). Within itself, the austerity of the Model T, its simplicity and steadfast resistance to style, its trumping of value and durability as opposed to stylistic innovation represented the commodified incarnation of traditional Puritan values (McShane, 1994: 135). The Fordist devotion to the fixed, the unalterable, and the permanent stands in contrast to the elevation of consumer desire as a "social good" impelled by the continuous cycle of dissatisfaction within the minds of consumers, an inexorable cycle driven by a new internalized spirit that Campbell (1983, 1987, 1995a, 1995b) calls "modern illusory hedonism." As automobile ownership became increasingly pervasive among American households, the profits of capital came increasingly to depend on a new rationalization of the totality of consumer needs (Baudrillard 1998). Firstly, through the creation of a graduated product line, General Motors created a system of distinct symbolic differences that corresponded to the different dispositions of different classes. As Bourdieu (1984) explains, such dispositions are formed not only by the material conditions of class but by their dynamic ranking in relation to one another, a ranking formed through the cultural dialectic of identification and distinction. In creating different cars to suit different pockets, containing different performances, features, styling, and accessories, each such product was ranked by the degree of banality and distinction it projected, in turn, "naturally" corresponding and appealing to the objectively inscribed taste of a specific class. Secondly, the company tapped into the illusory hedonism of modern consumption, promoting the annual model change that both exploited and deepened the dissatisfaction that individuals felt toward the car that they already possessed. This infused the latest model with the gleam of novelty through new styling and features that stimulated the imaginative longing of consumers for the promise of new pleasures not yet encountered.

Installing Consumer Discipline

The conflict of an outmoded productivism of Ford and the progressive consumerism of General Motors extended also to the field of installment credit and the contrasting formations of the General Motors Acceptance Corporation (GMAC) and the Ford "Weekly Purchase Plan." GMAC, a wholly owned but independent subsidiary of General Motors, was created in 1919 to ensure stability in productive output by aiding dealers in stocking inventory and directly financing consumer installment purchasing (Sloan, [1963] 1980: 305).

Sloan saw installment purchasing as an integral element in selling something more than the basic transportation represented by the Model T. As car ownership expanded, the used car market grew to service the need of getting from "A to B," the technical attributes of the car improved (most notably, the closed body) and the annual model policy took hold, installment credit was to be instrumental in selling not cars as fixed objects but in servicing a demand for "progress in new cars, for comfort, convenience, power, and style" ([1963] 1980: 163). From the outset then, installment credit allowed GM to draw desire into the sphere of production. Profits were connected less with a rational need for transportation and more with such amorphous, aesthetic qualities as style and comfort that the company believed the consumer, or certain types of consumer, wished to experience. By 1925, GMAC was by far the largest of the national finance companies, developing through an overall expansion of sales of GM cars but also contributing to an ever greater proportion of such sales (Seligman, 1927; Clark, 1930).

Facing declining sales due to intense competition from rival manufacturers pursuing the increased sales inherent through installment plans, the Ford Company instituted the Ford Weekly Purchasing Plan in 1923. This called on consumers to commit to a new Ford purchase by saving the cost, in five-dollar weekly increments, within a specially designated and administered interest-bearing account (Nevins and Hill, 1957: 268–9; Calder, 1999: 195–9). Like Macy's "Deposit Account" strategy mentioned in the last chapter, the prepayment plan was designed to both encourage consumers to be thrifty and self-disciplined as well as obviating the perceived administrative and default losses inherent to the provision of installment credit facilities. The plan, though, was a spectacular and embarrassing failure. Eighteen months after its launch, of the 400,000 that had signed up, only 131,000 continued their investment to purchase—the equivalent of around one month's sales. The purchase plan clearly embodied older Puritan values that had long been instilled within workers. Saving was a key means by which independence and sovereignty could be assured, the mechanism through which the individual worker and their family could be made self-reliant and self-governing under liberalism (c.f. Donzelot, 1980). However, within a context that increasingly targeted consumption and the continuous regeneration of desire, saving became a distinctly inadequate medium for its satisfaction.

The period between the spurring of imaginative longing for the possibilities of new forms of consumption, and its resolution in acquisition, represents what Campbell (1987) calls a "happy hiatus." Here the possibility of perfected experience injects goods with their greatest pleasurable potential before the inevitable dissolution of such perfection encountered by the goods in their "real" state. Fundamentally, as Campbell explains, puritanism and modern consumerism are two sides of the same coin, embodying the separation of individual feeling from action, the autonomous manipulation of emotion within the individual in anticipation of a future to come. The commercial development of installment credit, though, released the possibility of immediate purchase and instant gratification of consuming desire while the fate of Ford's purchase savings plan indicates that the gap between accumulation and actual purchase was an hiatus too far to bridge for too many consumers. Within this qualitatively new period of consumption, with higher wages in a bureaucratic/machine-organized world and a host of new and continuously surfacing objects playing on the imaginations of consumers through new forms and media of advertising, the scope of desire became widened and its pace multiplied. Even with the possibility of prompt gratification of specific wants, the experience of wanting now came to exist as a general state to which the consumer was permanently exposed (1987: 92–3).

In many ways, installment credit represents a systematic effort by capitalism to fulfill the goals of desire, but also to discipline and mold that desire—what Calder (1999) calls the "regulation of abundance." This follows Baudrillard's position that, while credit operates under a semblance of hedonism, it produces a rationalizing effect over the actions of individuals, allowing them to be incorporated as calculating consumers where otherwise they would remain outside the limits of profitable consumption. It is worth recalling here Simmel's (1978) argument that the space separating a subject and an object of desire must be sufficiently distant to permit those objects to be desired, to be imaginatively and abstractly dwelt upon and understood within the consciousness of the individual beyond the purely sensory. Nevertheless, such objects cannot be too distant from individuals, otherwise desire collapses or is dissolved to nothing more than a "vague wish" as the possibility of possession appears too far fetched. Objects that reside within these so-called upper and lower limits, although experienced as resistant to the subject, are within sufficient scope of the actions of the subject for such resistance to be overcome.

The systematization and extension of installment credit thus delicately recalibrated the distance between the desiring consumer and the mass produced automobile. Although the assembly line helped lower production costs and thus price, it was the technology of the installment plan, borrowed from the merchandising success of older consumer goods such as the piano but newly infused with specialized finance capital, which transformed the automobile from a vague wish into a realizable object of desire. Simultaneously, consumer involvement in such installment credit agreements involved a submission to a regimen of discipline, which tightly governed the actions of those consumers. Desire, stimulated by a new array of consumer choice, became specifically regulated by the binding of time and money flows within the installment plan:

- Despite being a form of borrowing, an initial payment amounting to around one-third of the purchase price had to be saved and offered in advance as a down payment.
- The sequential, step-by-step liquidation of debt characterizing this form of credit amalgamated principal and interest elements into a

fixed number of simple, all-inclusive predictable payments set out in advance for the life of the agreement.

• Missed payments became potentially manageable. Given the break down of repayments, the missing of one payment rather than whole principal meant that the credit agreement did not necessarily break down. The lender could potentially renegotiate the credit agreement, especially near the latter stages. The missing of payments in early stages, on the other hand, provided early warning indication of difficulties on the part of the debtor and the goods could be repossessed quickly before the continued onset of costly depreciation.

• The legal characterization of the contract as a conditional sale ensured that the good could be repossessed and the down payment and monthly payments already made remained the property of the creditor.

It is perhaps no coincidence that the formalized installment plan governing credit consumption at this time seems to resonate with the characteristic mode of production of the assembly line. Both sought to govern complex new domains of consumption and production respectively through a detailed arrangement of time and space that impelled individual action into a repetitive array of simplified tasks dictated to the individual from above.

To briefly summarize the events of the 1920s, the scope and scale of credit increasingly came to bridge the hiatus between consuming desire and fulfillment. Between 1919 and 1929, the amount of total outstanding consumer installment debt at finance companies increased from $0.72 billion to $2.95 billion before plummeting with the onset of the Great Depression (see fig. 3.1). It was not until the onset of a war economy at the end of the 1930s that rates recovered to something like their previous highs.

In the financing of automobile purchase, increased competition led to an extension of repayment times and a lowering of required down payments that helped to propel new car sales from 1.3 million to 3.2 million over the 1920s (Olney, 1991: 96). As advanced industrial production brought new goods such as mechanical refrigerators, radios, phonographs, washing machines as well as cars to the market in what Olney has termed a "durable goods revolution," new and existing finance companies deployed installment credit to locate these consumerist items within the boundaries of desire for broader swathes of the population (Seligman, 1927; Clark, 1930; Ayres, 1938). These new goods were met by the process of home electrification that spread from 10 percent of households in 1905 to around 75 percent by the end of the 1920s (Nye, 1998: 171). Installment selling also increasingly penetrated into other retail spaces including the department store as well as being more widely adopted by the national mail order companies Sears and Montgomery Ward (Cohn, 1940: 524–36; Emmet and Jeuck, 1950; Leach, 1993; Calder, 1999; Blanke, 2000).

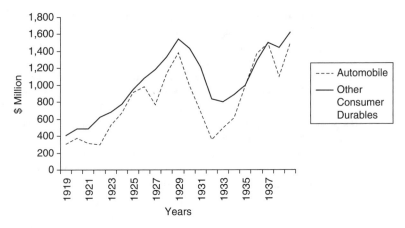

Figure 3.1 Outstanding U.S. consumer installment debt, 1919–1939.
Source: Reproduced from Olney, 1991: 93–4.

Until the 1930s, as Olney (1999, 2002) demonstrates, the "conditional sale" contract form underpinning the structure of the installment contract was heavily punitive toward consumer indiscipline. Any monthly payment defaulted could result in the finance company repossessing the car to which they held title until the end of the credit period as well as their retaining of the initial down payment made and whatever number of payments had been completed. As Seligman shows, in the early development of such firms, the use of the conditional sale form, the specification of a one-third down payment and a six to twelve month contract period were carefully calculated contrivances to maximize revenues. They played upon what were understood to be the incentives of consumers toward repayment or default. In many ways installment credit presupposed but also sought to nurture an economizing, entrepreneurial mentality—by setting out a legal framework to govern credit consumption, individuals freely entering into such contracts could be relied upon to defend and respond to their own material interests as consumers for the benefit of the creditor. Later during the Great Depression of the 1930s, as loss rates on merchandise and mortgage loans jumped markedly, Olney cites such constraints as being the reason why losses on installment credit were maintained at around 1–2 percent (1999: 325). Freedom to engage credit to bring about a resolution of consuming desire was thus predicated on particular institutional forms that both permitted and regulated the path through which that freedom was to be realized.

It would be superficial, however, to contrast a traditional Puritanism dependent upon resolute self-restraint and self-government to a neo-Puritanism where individuals seem unable to exert self-government in the face of consuming desire and will is submitted to the external government of bureau-legal processes. As Olney (1999) details, the early development of installment selling was regulated legally under case law as opposed to legislation. In other words, neither the federal nor individual states sought to intervene to cohesively govern this form of credit; rather, its form developed on the basis of contracts freely entered into by individuals and the challenges and contestations they provoked in the courts under contract law. The conditional sales contract form that such credit took implied that it was not perceived, at least legally, as borrowing and so did not come under the ambit of state usury laws. Interest charges were merely the extra cost imposed for the "convenience" of purchasing a good over time. In contrast to small loan lending, the subjective will of individuals was to be the primary basis through which such forms of credit was to be governed—not coincidentally then was installment selling of cars concentrated upon middle-class consumers (Seligman, 1927; Cohen, 1990), those whom it was believed could be relied upon to discipline their own freedom. Nevertheless, it should be noted that in a limited number of cases, borrowing was drawn upon from newly legitimate small loan lenders in order to pay the balance on installment debts, including for cars (Robinson and Stearns, 1930: 123). An early form of debt consolidation, cash could be borrowed from Peter the salary lender to pay Paul the financier.

Calder invokes the term "regulated abundance" to describe how individuals' flows of income are regularized by their removal from individual control and their subjection to legal-bureaucratic processes so that individuals willingly come to subject themselves, and their actions, to external forces. From his perspective, puritan self-denial, self-restraint and self-control in accumulating resources are subsumed by a neo-Puritan budget plan restraint characterized by the external fetter and control of the contractual obligations of sale that require payment. Rather prosaically, it is argued that people need the external regulation of installment-type credit as they would otherwise not be able to save in the conventional way for relatively expensive durable goods and would end up frittering away household resources upon less important but more easily acquired nondurable goods.

Attempting to refute Daniel Bell's argument that consumer credit embodies a disjuncture between an increasingly hedonistic cultural realm and a productive system crucially dependent upon values of discipline, self-restraint, and deferred gratification, Calder observes that consumer credit embodies, in many ways, a continuation of older Puritan values. In engaging in installment purchasing, individuals must be strict in their own personal finances and disciplined money managers within a context where this necessity is imposed upon them. The implications of this line of argument, however, are that people are seen as being in awe of an infinite array of consumption possibilities and have no option but to spend, to take advantage of emergent credit facilities for durable goods that they cannot otherwise afford and thus more or less voluntarily bow to the environmental-institutional constraints inherent to installment credit. From this perspective, credit actively reigns in and channels the compulsive and impulsive desires of consumers (cf. Starr, 2007: 215; for a rational-choice treatment of this phenomenon see Schelling, 1980; Dresser, 1982; Elster, 1984). Yet, even with the liberalization of credit conditions for automobiles during the 1920s with lower down payments, longer repayment terms and lower rates of interest—an ostensible weakening of the external regulation governing installment buying—such credit use expanded among the middle classes and defaults, according to Olney's (1991) evidence, remained low.

What is elided by Calder's argument is that the development of mass finance installment credit among the middle class recognized and acted upon the capacity for self-constraint within individuals (cf. Elias, 1994; Stearns, 1999). The emerging white collar middle class lived in relatively stable and regularized social environments. Within these, they were financially equipped to make repayments, were sufficiently foresighted to assess their current income, future income and other necessary expenditures in order to dispassionately imagine, in advance, the necessity of making weekly or monthly repayments until the term of their agreement expired. In expressing their will through a formal contract, individuals were expected to rationally weigh up, in advance and over time, the benefits and costs of such an agreement. They were also expected to exhibit self-control in terms of their behavior and engage in not so much deferred gratification as managed gratification. This involved subordinating short-term impulses to expend resources on other attainable goods for the immediately accessible, longer-term gains of the good for which the credit agreement was contracted. Of course the actions of individuals, in their increasingly prominent role as consumers, were being shaped by external constraints. Yet these constraints could not impose self-discipline; this could only emanate from individuals consciously imagining in advance how they would act in order to adhere to the terms of the agreement to which they had freely contracted. In essence then, individuals had to be instilled with and assume the capacity, the will, to be subjected to an institutionally created repayment system within an increasingly more complex, "organized" and interdependent society.

Reinventing Thrift

Benjamin Franklin, through the publication of "Poor Richard's Almanack," had sought to encourage what Weber ([1930] 1976) has called a particular spirit of capitalism. Shorn of an explicit puritan ideology, this offered a moralized ethic for the living of one's life that frowned upon personal indebtedness as a threat to independence and self-sufficiency (Lasch, 1979; Tucker, 1991). Under industrialism, as Horowitz (1985) indicates, the bourgeois habit of thrift was used as a basis for promoting industrious and disciplined habits among a growing, often immigrant, urban labor force. In classical political economy the promotion of such a virtuous personal conduct was linked up to a wider economic well-being. Adam Smith ([1776] 1910), in *The Wealth of Nations*, emphasized how lending for production allowed capital to be employed in its own reproduction with profit from which the lender could be reimbursed. On the contrary, lending for immediate consumption engendered the "unproductive" dissolution of wealth while repayment and interest presented a drain upon future alternate revenues. "The man who borrows in order to spend will soon be ruined, and he who lends to him will generally have occasion to repent of his folly" (p. 313). Similarly for John Stuart Mill (1888), while credit did not represent the creation of wealth, the activity of banking allowed idle savings to be efficiently placed in the care of the "industrial talent of the country" who could turn it to productive use and increase public wealth. However, in the hands of "unproductive" consumers, even though it may be repaid, credit served as a dissipation of public wealth measurable in the lost opportunity to create value.

Such precepts through which economic expertise both discerned and helped constitute the idea of the "economy" as a vibrant, independent sphere changed into the twentieth century. As the formation of capitalism altered through innovative modes of organization, the production of new forms and types of goods and the bedding-in of a national market, economic discourses began to shift. In the same decade that consumer installment credit was becoming legitimated on a wider commercial scale, the economist H.G. Moulton (1918) argued against the prevailing orthodoxy of economics by presenting evidence that under a complex industrial society capital formation depends not on a simple "thrifty impulse." Rather, savings must be made available for both productive investment and sufficient consumer demand. In doing so he excoriated his expert profession for its persistent adherence to outdated assumptions and moralized posturing, "the economist thus aspires to be more than a pure scientist; he is also a preacher of the gospel of individual economic salvation. The chief difficulty here is that in preaching so ardently we have usually forgotten to be scientific" (p. 864).

In the 1920s the economist Edwin Seligman (1927) of Columbia University, working on behalf of General Motors, published his landmark *The Economics of Installment Selling*. Through an analysis of credit, he attempted to deconstruct the entire economic dualism of the "production" and "consumption" of wealth into the all-encompassing neutral term of *utilization*, which itself could be "creative," "neutral," "wasteful," or "destructive." In contrast to classical economics, he reasoned that credit for consumption was not inherently degrading to wealth and neither was credit for production self-evidently beneficial; the social usefulness of credit depended, rather, on the specific purposes to which it was put. Evans Clark, of the policy research Twentieth-Century Fund, even suggested that modern business was increasingly conceiving of consumers "as business men or women in their own right," who had to be constantly replenished with liquid capital in order to enable them to continue making purchases and thus sustain the markets that were being built around them (1930: 3).

German economist Ferdynand Zweig (1934) emphasized, too, the productivity-raising impetus that installment credit had provided to the post–World War I American economy, raising the quality of working class consumption by assisting the purchase of durable goods and stimulating mass consumption into a virtuous tandem with mass production. Such credit even served, he believed, as a form of income redistribution through which the savings of the "well-to-do classes" could be channeled to increase the share of income and consumption possibilities of the working class. In a simple but telling metaphor of this new elision of the productive and the consumptive in lending, Rolf Nugent imagined a consumer thinking of not "going into debt" so much as "expanding both sides of his balance sheet" through having the simultaneous use of the objects for which he was paying for through credit (Nugent, 1938: 44).

Within the banking industry of the 1920s, such a discursive shift in the conceptualization of thrift connected with the programmatic language of scientific management and, more broadly, the shift of capitalist enterprise toward large scale organization (Roe, 1965). Rather than being abandoned, thrift was revised and rearticulated from what was understood as a blind, unthinking saving to the efficient, planned management of resources: "[t]he thrifty man in the age of scientific management did not skimp or hoard; rather, he planned and controlled the *use* of his financial resources. The family budget allotted amounts computed with exact precision to subsistence, pleasures, investment and, above all, saving" (p. 625). Despite conservatism within the industry, the Economic Policy Commission of the American Bankers Association accepted the possibility of installment selling as a normal "ingredient" within the economy, once such credit was neither subject to individual "abuse" nor posed a wider economic danger. To these ends, as Roe discerns, particular emphasis was given to the collation of statistics and the creation of a "scientific formula" that would calculably regulate applicant acceptance, down payment amount and loan period. Installment credit could thus be subject to effective direction and management in order to maximize its productive potential and minimize any detrimental effects.

As well as plotting the increase in the volume, proportion and prominence of advertising for credit terms by goods retailers during the 1920s, Murphy (1995) also analyzes the particular way that such advertising came to project the use of credit. Rather than simply selling the goods concerned, she argues that the advertising of the period also attempted to sell the idea of credit itself, employing modalities of language that represented it to individuals as a restrained, frugal, and thrifty practice. The five modalities she notes are the:

- favorable comparison of weekly installments with the rhythmical habit of savings
- declaration of the dignity of particular credit plans, even how it might result in savings
- presentation of the easy affordability of installment payments that would present "no strain on your income"
- elevation of the productive usefulness of having immediate access to a good and the convenience of paying while using
- indication of tailored credit repayments to suit the income and savings of the individual

William H. Whyte would note a few decades later in the advertising of credit that "[f]ew talents are more commercially sought today than the knack of describing departures from the Protestant Ethic as reaffirmations of it" (1956: 17). So it was that in the opening decades of the twentieth century thrift proved too durable a virtue of self-government to be abandoned; it provided rather a plastic, chameleonic one that could be remolded and retinted to fit a new capitalism whose profitability depended on the stimulation of consumer desire. An older bourgeois thrift of frugality and asceticism, part of a calculating and instrumental capitalist spirit became subsumed into a twentieth-century thrift of middle-class consumption. This was equally, if not more, calculating and instrumental in its exhorting of "income management." It now emphasized, however, the productivism, utility—and the need to discipline—the fulfillment of consumption.

* * *

Into the twentieth century, with new forms of industrial and capitalist organization and an increasing focus on the national market, the constant unbound regeneration of consumer desire increasingly took primacy in the calculations of capital. Particularly in the development of the mass, assembly line produced automobile, installment credit became relegitimized for the realization of desire, with mainstream finance capital of the 1920s increasingly being directed toward the personalized financing of, firstly, automobiles and soon a whole host of new consumer goods for a growing mass market. Installment credit therefore came to provide a medium for the satisfaction of desire, locating increasing numbers of goods within the boundaries of possibility for more individuals. At the same time, such credit provoked a disciplining and regulation of that desire through bureaucratic-legal constraints, working through the capacity of those individuals to regulate their own conduct. In conjunction with the development of mass financing, the idea of thrift became articulated by bankers, economists, and advertisers in new ways that incorporated consumer credit as a productive endeavor, an essential economic activity and as a normal component of a disciplined consumer's budget.

CHAPTER 4

Mass Credit, Mass Society, and Their Discontents

The early decades of the twentieth century saw the United States become an economically centralized nation oriented around the systematic production of fulfillment for consuming desire, a desire experienced by individuals who were increasingly understood as a mass of "consumers." Crucially, the development of new forms of mass credit financed by specialized external finance capital helped foster and nurture this circling trail of production and consumption by providing a medium that made possible the simultaneous realization and disciplining of consuming desire.

Within this context, new discourses began to circulate which legitimized the new forms that consumption and credit were taking, building upon earlier justifications put forward in the late nineteenth century (Horowitz 1985; Barton 1989). Edwin Seligman (1927) challenged the age-old distinctions of production and consumption, the "woeful poverty of economic analysis" that supported the cultural virtue of thrift as well as the understanding of luxury as inherently corruptive. Such a discursive shift, though, did not proceed smoothly or without challenge. During the 1920s and 1930s, board members of the nation's Federal Reserve maintained a strict opposition to installment credit that in diverse ways they condemned as self-indulgent and immoral, destabilizing to commercial banks, commercially deceptive to business, and an aggravating cause of the Great Depression itself (Kubik, 1996). However, in the post–World War II consumer boom, with reconversion from war to consumer commodity production, the political rationality of Keynesianism held out the responsibilities of the state to be the facilitation of economic growth through the encouragement of mass consumption (Cohen, 2003). In a virtuous spiral, the continuous pursuit of mass commodity ownership provided for high employment, wages, and productive output in the enhancement of collective social well-being, a process that the state sought to foster through a policy of economic interventionism.

Clyde Phelps (1954), an academic economist and proselytizer for credit, argued that the American standard of living was the greatest and fastest growing in the world and installment credit was essential to its maintenance. To these ends, he presented credit use as a phenomenon not of poverty or wealth but of that "great mass" of middle income groups who "needed" the enjoyment and convenience of those goods whose purchase was made possible by credit. Although credit involved "going into debt," he reasoned that this was offset by the equity that consumers built up in the goods that they purchased, a wealth dignified with such productivist terms as "consumer plant," "equipment," and "household capital formation." As with Seligman, production and consumption were not conceived as a dualism but as indisassociable factors in which the perpetuation of individual well-being was symbiotically bound to the continuation of a collective economic and social security. Within this conceptualization of production and consumption the individual and collective consumer credit was seen to form a key locus point, particularly from 1950 when consumer capital expenditure was calculated as outstripping its equivalent "producer" form for the first time (Shay, 1965: 370–1). Ultimately, as Phelps wrote, "installment buying has played an important part in raising living standards by helping to facilitate the rise and expansion of great new industries, creating millions of jobs, and by assisting in making possible through the economies of mass production lower prices and improved quality of consumers' durable goods" (1954: 28–9).

In the new century, materializing this changing discourse, commercial banks forsook their historical disdain for consumer lending and increasingly engaged it as a profitable avenue of activity. This occurred obliquely, as we have seen, through the capitalization of sales finance companies for installment lending but also more directly through the facilitation of loans to consumers. The Depression was ultimately to prove a watershed moment in the conception of consumer credit provision for, as the banking system veered on a state of collapse with innumerable bank closures, only thirty-nine consumer sales finance companies were forced to close between 1925 and 1933, with less than half involving financial losses to creditors (Plummer and Young, 1940: 66–7).

In 1928, National City Bank opened the first personal loan department in New York servicing city employees, clerks, stenographers, and other office workers with cash credit at interest rates of around 12 percent per year, seen at the time as a massive blow against the travails of the salary lenders. By the end of 1930, it was facilitating double the number of personal loans of all other banks in the country combined (Clark, 1930: 74–5; Grant,

1992: 306–11). Throughout the 1930s, despite the pressures of the Depression and the skepticism of the Federal Reserve, the numbers of banks offering loans expanded from around 85 before 1925 to over 1,222 in 1938, with banks by that time offering over $196 million in such credit. When sales finance companies are added, the total number of banks servicing consumers directly and indirectly was 1,500 with total credit outstanding amounting to $500 million (Chapman, 1940: 21–46). Commenting on the postwar era, Robert Shay (1965) could claim that the combined economic weight of consumer installment credit had become "strategic" to the growth of employment and national productivity by virtue of its sheer economic weight in financing consumer durable "investment" (Shay, 1965: 379).

Consumer Credit and State Regulation, Part 1: Defending Collective Welfare

The Great Depression in the United States encouraged two significant regulatory initiatives in relation to a banking industry, which it was believed, by overextending itself through ruinous competition and inflexibility, had helped precipitate the speculative bubble that had such disastrous consequences on the American economy (Nocera, 1994; Dymski and Veitch, 1996; Brand, 2002). The McFadden-Pepper Act of 1927 pressed responsibility onto states to regulate the banks within their borders while also prohibiting banks from operating branches outside of their home state, thus preventing behemothian regional banks from destroying their smaller counterparts. This was later reinforced in 1956 by the Bank Holding Company Act, which prevented the operation of multiple banks in multiple states by a single parent holding company. The Glass-Steagall Act of 1933, on the other hand, placed severe limitations on banks from engaging in multiple business activities and also created the Federal Deposit Insurance Corporation to federally insure the savings of bank depositors.

This regulatory bulwark not only governed the wider scope of bank activities but also served to regulate the narrower form of consumer credit practices. Although seemingly paradoxical in today's context, these statutory initiatives were part of the welfarist New Deal political rationality that shaped the post-Depression space of rule. This conceived of the economy and society as dynamic totalities that could, theoretically, be governed through rational, calculated planning, thus ensuring economic and social progress without the comprising of individual autonomy and excessive state intervention (Rose, 1999b: 127–8). These initiatives did not merely mean a new role for the American federal state but tilted the balance of legislative authority away from the political heterogeneity of individual states to the homogeneity of the nation as a whole. Indeed, by the 1930s in the wake of the New Deal, the consumer-as-citizen was held to be both the counterweight of production and shorthand for the general public interest (Cohen, 2001; Jacobs, 2001) while, within ascendant Keynesian thought, consumption was heralded as the driving force of economic activity (Brinkley, 1995).

The New Deal federal state, however, served not only to limit the scope and reach of bank market activities but, in one element at least, actively fostered the business of consumer lending. The Federal Housing Administration (FHA), which had been set up to administer the insurance of residential home mortgage loans and thus encourage lenders back into the business of making them, included a provision under Title I of its enabling legislation, the National Housing Act of 1934, for the insurance of home improvement loans for "repair and modernization" (Coppock, 1940). The socialization of risk that the FHA provided, in addition to the stated aims of reducing unemployment and costs and reinvigorating market flows helped acclimatize lenders to the profitable opportunities inherent in consumer lending in an environment where they were secured against the unknown hazards of financial loss (Chapman, 1940: 23; Coppock, 1940: 3; Calder, 1999: 282–3).[1] Another New Deal measure, the Electric Home and Farm Authority, sought to encourage the development of rural electrification by providing subsidized, long-term consumer installment finance through dealerships for household electrical appliances, mainly refrigerators but also ranges, water heaters, washing machines, and radios (Coppock, 1940: 115–18). Thus, in the interest of collective welfare based on promulgating employment and social stability, the diffuse New Deal state itself intervened to provide fiscal and administrative direction and support to marketized consumer credit.

During the mid-decades of the century, a highly direct macro regulation of consumer credit was undertaken during times of perceived crisis. In the formation of the "war economy" in the 1940s, the Federal Reserve was empowered under Regulation W to set minimum down payments and maximum loan periods for all types of consumer credit, including installment and store charge accounts, in order to dampen the threat of inflation and facilitate conversion to war production (Cole, 1988; Schreft, 1990). This was repeated in 1948 in an effort to combat postwar inflation and again in 1950 during the onset of the Korean War. Although consumer credit was conceived as a market mechanism for the facilitation of consumer desire, the use of term controls established the Federal Reserve as a calculating center from which it could temporally calibrate the opportunities of such desire. By periodically adjusting the contractual terms that creditors could offer to individual consumers across a diverse space of lending, it sought to defend and promote the wider collective economic security of the nation. Just as the controlled promulgation of mass consumption and credit were inextricably bound to economic growth and social harmony, during times of crisis its deliberate curbing by the state was deemed equally essential in order to curtail the corrosive menace of price inflation and, during war, to redirect the economy as a whole toward the defense of sovereignty.

At the state level, as we have seen, installment selling had remained outside the scope of both small loan legislation and statutory usury control due to the preponderance of court judgments that rejected the concept of installment charges as a form of interest. By the 1930s, however, the introduction of several bills and acts sought to enforce some measure of control over installment selling in order to remedy the perceived inequality of bargaining power understood to be inherent to that form of contract (Greene, 1935; Reuss, 1935). By the 1950s, 12 states had passed some form of installment selling regulation (Mors, 1950). The perceived abuses that legislation was designed to counter were: firstly, deceptive computation that presented interest in an artificially low manner and the use of "widely varying and frequently incomprehensible formulas" to calculate interest, both of which were thought to impede the consumer from rationally deciding between credit offers; secondly, the nondisclosure of contractual terms and the incentivizing of retailers by finance companies that unduly encouraged individuals to take on credit they could not afford; thirdly, wage assignments and coercive provisions for nonrepayment that provided for unfair leverage over the buyer's actions by the finance company (Cavers, 1935; Reuss, 1935; Foster, 1938; Mors, 1943, 1950). In response, the various bills that were introduced formulated a concept of consumer disclosure whereby any installment contract would be required to clearly state the cash price of the item, the down payment amount, the unpaid balance, additional charges, the contract duration, and the specific installment amounts that were to be paid. Some also required a formal licensing of dealers and finance companies and the submission of regular reports to a central supervisory authority.

Unlike the Uniform Small Loan Law, constituted on the basis of personal borrowing as a social problem stemming from the widespread exploitation of borrower indebtedness, the creation of legislation to regulate installment borrowing was predicated on its conception as a form of "consumer protection." It was invoked not as a response to the specter of urban industrial poverty afflicting labor but to the effective problem of how consumers could "shop intelligently": "patently the need is for a uniform, accurate, outspoken method of statement, universally applied whenever installment credit is granted" (Foster and Foster, 1935: 190).[2] Rather than a subject who was understood as being both materially and morally vulnerable, the installment buyer was a hampered consumer whose will was not dissolute in itself but merely weaker relative to the dealer and finance company, which could command considerable administrative, legal, and financial resources. By their form, rather than their quality, such individuals were understood to be impeded in the free exercise of rational choice and the free recognition of the consequences of their actions. Thus, the installment legislation passed was based on obviating this inequality, not by regulating the form of operation as the USLL did but by dictating the formula of the contract within which terms were freely agreed. The state did not fix maximum amounts or legal monthly rates of interest; rather it sought to induce transparency into the transaction in such a way that the individual could readily compare market alternatives, between different installment offers or using installment credit at all, and pursue their own rational self-interest as a consumer.

Mid-century, at multiple layers of the American polity, these new banking laws, provisions, temporal terms controls, and installment selling regulatory initiatives problematized, in a general sense, the market as being potentially destructive and dangerous to the well-being of society. Although the pursuit of individualized self-interest was a crucial function of the market, its exigencies and externalities were rationalized by the state (and states) in diffuse ways as being in need of a calculating and deliberative intervention. The problem became how to both dampen its self-destructive tendencies and boost its activities where these were seen to be in need of intervention. The autonomy of the market—of banks, finance companies, retail lenders, and consumers—was penetrated while leaving them as formally autonomous actors, the present and future pursuit of individual self-interest anchored within a framework of ongoing collective welfare.

With the implementation of banking laws, market subsidization, and the temporary injunction of terms controls, this collective welfare was "society" in its broadest sense, the organic tissues of the nation that had been so wrenched through the economic turmoil of a Depression believed to have been compounded by the suicidal competitive activities of the banking sector (Brand, 2002). With respect to installment selling regulations, on the other hand, this welfare was a generalized constituency of credit consumers, a distinctive, newly concrete collective constituency in danger of being subjugated by the growing economic power of finance companies whose sheer size was held to warp the fabric of competition.

Conformity and Mass Society

In the middle part of the twentieth century, mass consumption and production had become the binary pillars supporting the weight of the collective well-being of the nation. The superiority of this "American way" was concretized by the fulfillment of such consumer desires for: the latest automobile model hot off the assembly lines of Detroit; a new Levittstown home, the mass-produced prefabricated housing constructed for the young postwar generation in the new growing suburbs of the major cities; a television, the new entertainment that bound the individual into a mass audience for the national broadcasters; and the assorted household goods from washing machines to fridge-freezers that Richard Nixon was so sure "lightened the burden" of the housewife (Gans, 1967; May, 1988; Baldassare, 1992; Cross, 2000; Cohen, 2001, 2003; Jacobs 2001).

Mass consumption, though, was predicated on mass production, the bureaucratic effectiveness of the organization, the careful calibration of labor through group relations psychology and the regulated physics of workflow systems that ensured optimal output and maximal return on capital and high wages for a workforce that formed a continuing layer of demand (Rose, 1999a). The state itself fostered a welfarist system that bound society in a web of solidarity through such diffuse programs as state-enacted workman's compensation laws of the 1910s (see chapter 1), the development of social security in the 1930s (Miron and Weil, 1997), and the formation of the Federal Housing Administration to administer homeowner mortgage insurance for the middle class and provide financial guarantees for the construction of multifamily housing for those on low incomes. With a national system of mortgage insurance, the state sought to directly penetrate the housing market through the administration and funding of a scheme that conjoined the subjective desires of the individual for suburban space to the protection of mortgage providers and, more indirectly, the stimulation of the home construction industry (Jackson, 1985; Caves, 1989; Carliner, 1998).

In the immediate postwar period, the development of the Employment Act of 1946 was premised on the Keynesian belief that the labor market was too crucial to be left to vagaries of capital; the state thus charged itself with the responsibility of guaranteeing full employment through the provision of appropriate fiscal expenditure (Santoni, 1986; De Long, 1996, 1998). As Klausen (2002) shows, the goals of the act enjoyed cross-party political support; with a widely held belief that demobilization would lead to deflation and economic recession, it was conceived that only the pursuit of full employment through what Weir and Skocpol (1985) have called "commercial Keynesiansim" could prevent the inevitable onset of social dislocation.

By mid-century, mass consumption was seen to be the natural corollary of economic growth—mass production with stable full-employment and high wages fed mass consumption in a benevolent cycle that constantly pushed forward the limits of the American standard of living (Cohen, 2003; Horowitz, 2004). Over this virtuous circle stood the state, exerting its fiscal and administrative powers to act as a "guarantor of progress" for all, dispelling hostilities and binding the individual, the economy, and society through mechanisms of solidarity (Achenbaum, 1986; cf. Donzelot, 1991). As Christopher Lasch (1979) suggests, the postwar decade, characterized by the extended reach of the welfare state and the concentrated strength of American capitalism, had seemingly dissolved the dangers of poverty and gross inequality while bequeathing an unprecedented affluence across broader reaches of the population. Yet, within this ordering of society, a wide range of social critics saw considerable danger in "the decline of individualism and the menace of conformity." These critics, from a diversity of political positions, persistently sought to inveigh from the wings on the dangers of the so-called mass society.

Erich Fromm (1942) suggested that the "mass" conditions of twentieth-century industrial life, of centralized capital, vast cities, complex markets, and media bombardment, had alienated the individual and destroyed the possibility of individual freedom. In order to escape their sense of isolation and powerlessness, the modern individual had renounced their true individuality and had essentially ceased "to be himself." Directly comparing its effects to those of hypnosis, he argued that the modern individual had become nothing more than an "automaton"; the expression of any supposed individuality was merely the reflexive regurgitation of wider culture, the effluent of an unthinking subjection of the self to society. For the critical theorists such as Adorno and Horkheimer (1972) and Marcuse (1964), culture had been systematically and wholly penetrated by a scientifically organized capitalism rendering it staid, homogeneous, and unchanging, exploiting and dulling workers outside the working day as much as in it. The pleasure of consuming desire, in particular, represented a set of "false" needs imposed upon the indoctrinated and manipulated masses so penetrated by the distorted form of society that they were unable to recognize and reconcile their "true" objective needs.

Among the more popular variants of this thesis was Vance Packard's (1957) muckraking *The Hidden Persuaders* that sought to penetrate what he saw as the carefully calculated manipulation of a witless mass audience by a cynical advertising industry armed with the latest subliminal techniques. In a more academic vein, Galbraith (1958) criticized what he saw as the excessive devotion of energies of the new "affluent society" toward satisfying the overproductiveness of industry, the "needs" for which had to be contrived by a burgeoning advertising industry. Such a fixation upon the private, he argued, distracted attention and resources away from the nurturing of a viable public infrastructure within which inequality could be alleviated and a more broadly conceived, more meaningful quality of life improved. Sociologists and other theorists also examined the implications of mass society on the individual's sense of self. William H. Whyte (1957) elaborated on the fall of the traditional individual, governed by the tenets of the Protestant ethic and the rise of what he termed "Organization Man" living in the "packaged villages" of suburbia whose social ethic compels his affinity and aspiration of belonging to the group. In a similar vein, David Riesman and his collaborators (1950) interpreted this as the decline of an "inner-directed" character-type, propelled by a strong internalized moral code, and the subsequent postwar development of an "other-directed" personality motivated by the compulsion to fit in and be liked.

Identity and Consuming Self-Fulfillment

Yet within the United States from the 1960s, just as these diverse critiques gathered force, the constitution of the mass consumer-led market that had been assembled from the end of the nineteenth century, began to fragment (see Marglin and Schor, 1990). Examining the case of consumer markets, Ewen and Ewen argue:

A broad, relatively undifferentiated approach to marketing had spurred economic growth during the 1920s and then, impressively, in the 1950s. By the end of the 1960s, however, that growth had begun to stagnate. Even more alarming was the conspicuous emergence of local and subcultural forms of expression. Many of these explored the possibility of a mode of life, and of a material culture, that looked beyond the gargantuan system of production, distribution, and merchandising that had defined the American Way of Life since the 1920s. (Ewen and Ewen, 1992)

In response to languishing profits and perceived market saturation, against a wider backdrop of macroeconomic decline, marketers and advertisers increasingly began to tailor the mediation of consuming desire within the framework of cultural identity. Intersecting with the rise of Black and feminist identity politics and the youth subculture movements, goods were increasingly imbued with symbolic qualities that appeared to resonate with such specific concerns, offering in turn a target-marketed set of values and meanings to be desired and appropriated to help give material form to the expression of a "meaningful" sense of self (Ewen and Ewen, 1992; Frank, 1997; Miller and Rose, 1997; Turow, 1997; Cohen, 2003).

In recent years, prominent European sociologists have been to the fore in attempting to understand the wider importance of the concepts of identity and lifestyle (Giddens, 1991; Beck, 1992: 127–38; Beck, Giddens, and Lash, 1994; Beck, Bonss, and Lau, 2003: 21–6; Bauman, 1988, 1997, 1998a, 2000, 2007). Within conditions of what is variously termed *high, late,* or *liquid* modernity, characterized by the dynamism and fluidness of social relations, the idea of the self as a reflexive project comes to the fore as the overriding mission of individuals. They are to attempt to weave a personalized narrative for themselves, to interlink their actions, choices, and experiences in a deliberate and more or less coherent fashion so that "what the individual becomes is dependent on the reconstructive endeavors in which she or he engages" (Giddens 1991: 75). Self-actualization becomes the goal to strive for, if never to reach; the casting off of a perfidious self, which may have been imposed by the past. Individuals also face a world where their traditional sense of place has been swept away, along with the authority of cultural and political elites, the work ethic, the traditional bonds of class and a societal belief in politics and political institutions. The majority of the population are now "free" from these bonds but, in exchange, are tasked with the responsibility of aesthetic self-construction; they must delve into the market for symbolically redolent goods or quasi-therapeutic resources and continually fashion a personalized identity for the self (Rose, 1996b, 1999a).

Within this context, it is not what is chosen that is significant for there are no overarching guidelines determining relative values; it is rather the availability and scope of choice itself which becomes the meta-narrative of existence. Older bonds such as work remain, of course, but not so much as a source of identity than as a key facilitating element in one's ability to choose; work becomes, too, an aspect of identity to be judged aesthetically as any other commodity or service in its capacity to generate pleasurable experience and meaning and to be woven into a broader tapestry of self-fulfillment.

In analyzing the relationship between consumption, postmodernism and identity, Featherstone (2007) explores how contemporary experience has become relentlessly aestheticized, with advanced communications media "saturating the fabric of everyday life," from market commodities to cityscapes, with an unending flow of shifting and changing signs and images deconstructing the boundaries between high and popular culture. For him, the bohemian artistic lifestyle has become universalized—no longer do individuals unthinkingly adopt ways of living; living, rather, becomes an aestheticized experience: "the new heroes of consumer culture make lifestyle a life project and display their individuality and sense of style in the particularity of their assemblage of goods, clothes, practices, experiences, appearance and bodily dispositions they design together into a lifestyle" (2007: 84).

The effacement of boundaries between high and low culture, though, do not imply that class has faded in significance in terms of shaping and structuring consumption. Rather, as Bourdieu (1984) and Featherstone (2007) argue, new modes of hedonistic and expressive consumption are bound up in the historical formation of a new class of petite bourgeoisie. Whereas this class fraction had been traditionally concerned with a puritan "morality of duty," which promoted ascetic self-denial as the means toward social advancement, the "new petite bourgeoisie" takes the morality of pleasure as a duty. In popularizing a framework of living previously the preserve of the intelligentsia, they adopt a permanent learning mode to life; they search for self-expression and meaning in such fields as the cultivation of personal health and the care of the body, through a preoccupation with fostering communication and intimate relations with others, and the legitimation of new styles and modes of authentic living. Arguably, culture becomes less stratified around *what* is consumed than the way and manner of *how* it is consumed (Peterson and Kern, 1996).

Within contemporary American society, class and levels of cultural capital continue, albeit in subtle and nuanced ways, to be important in structuring and symbolically distinguishing the consuming practices of consumers (Holt, 1997). Those classes embodying high levels of cultural capital greatly value the taste for self-actualization and personalized narrative that may manifest in greater consumption of idealist products which emphasize "experience" over ostentatious material satisfaction. Experiential ethnic dining, for example, is preferred over a posh French restaurant, as is the consumption of "decommodified" commodities that purposefully disdain the mass market, for example local micro-brews. At the same time, though, lower classes with lower cultural capital tastes may not quite exhibit the same gravitation toward the pursuit of individualized, authentic lifestyles to which the higher strata are drawn (Holt, 1998).

* * *

Within the twentieth century, consuming desire became increasingly located as a necessary element of a mass production/mass consumption society, a virtuously interdependent binary that the state sought to regulate in the interests of unified economic and social welfare. As part of this interventionism, new forms of state-level installment selling laws were instituted from the 1930s to "protect" the installment consumer while, at a federal level, new banking laws were drawn up in the wake of the Great Depression to dampen the destructive tendencies of economic competition. Similarly, in the aftermath of the Second World War, consumer credit was temporarily targeted as a calculable conduit to ease wider price inflation and defend national sovereignty. Yet, by mid-century, the idea of mass-society began to fragment as polyvocal discourses gathered force, criticizing the rigid conformism and dehumanization of mass society while crises of market saturation and profitability hit consumer industries. Increasingly within consumption, in marketing, and in how individuals understood and acted upon themselves, individual identity, the quest for personal meaning and the fulfillment of a personalized lifestyle became all-encompassing ideals. In the next chapter we will explore how the credit card was born out of mass society but ultimately became embedded as the flexible mechanism for the attainment of these ideals, indeed, even taking these ideals unto itself.

CHAPTER 5

Plastic Credit, Plastic Lifestyles

In their new North American rebranding and marketing campaign launched in September 2005, Visa adopted the tag line "Life Takes Visa" and deployed resonant emotional imagery, from the everyday to the spectacular, to demonstrate the possibilities of consumer empowerment through the ubiquity of their credit card. But how did Visa and its ilk come to encapsulate the idea of consumer credit, providing for the possibility of "consumer empowerment" in the twenty-first century and, more importantly, what has been the significance of this process for American society and beyond? As we shall explore within this chapter, Visa, MasterCard, and the other plastic credit providers that we so take for granted today were born to the logic of mass society, of mass mail drops, mass markets, anonymity and homogeneous terms. Their later development, however, under deregulation and new entrants, segmented markets and expansionary ownership, accelerated their role as instruments of personalized, individualized consumer fulfillment. Today, against the wider backdrop of a "new economy of credit" (Burton, 2008), credit cards have come to be the sine qua non of contemporary consumerism. They embody an instantaneously deployable global payment instrument, an unconstrained, personalized credit resource, an object of aesthetic delight or ethical purpose, an access point for elevated consuming experiences and more. As we shall explore within this chapter, the consumer's plastic card has become emblematic of contemporary consumer credit and of the hegemony of consumption more generally.

New Way to Pay: The Birth of the Credit Card

From the end of the nineteenth century, as we have discussed earlier, charge accounts had been developed in department stores as instruments of convenience for an elite clientele, gradually becoming more widespread for customers of more modest resources into the new century. By the 1930s, the Wanamaker's department store of Philadelphia modified their charge account system to incorporate an element of balance carryover for up to four months. This was extended later into a fully rotating charge account by Filene's of Boston and Bloomingdale's of New York whereby customers could carry over unpaid balances from month-to-month. In the immediate postwar period, cooperative credit ventures took place when groups of large retailers pooled their individual charge accounts into a common system in which the individual credit consumer was identified by means of a "charga-plate" (Mandell, 1990: 34–5).

Department stores, however, were not the first retailers to embark on such a venture. As early as the 1920s, oil companies had issued "courtesy" cards to frequent customers that allowed them to charge gasoline purchases at any service station of that company to a common account to be paid-off monthly. Just prior to World War II Standard Oil bypassed the usual policy of issuing such cards to loyal, well-known customers of particular stations and engaged in a mass, unsolicited distribution of a quarter of a million cards (ibid: 19). Just as the purchase of the automobile played a crucial role in advancing the mass financing technique of the installment plan, its fuelling helped bequeath the development of a new mass financing of more ephemeral, more open-ended forms of consumption based around a mobile system of identity. By 1949, the creation of Diner's Club heralded the development of a new breed of Travel and Entertainment Card that would be joined within a decade by American Express and Carte Blanche (Mandell, 1990; Nocera, 1994). Although designed to be paid-off within a single monthly billing cycle, these companies represented the incursion of a new outside source of capital into consumer financing. In doing so, consumer credit became divorced both from particular sites and forms of consumption; it was no longer channeled and governed through individual retailers but through specialized large-scale centralized administrative organizations determining consumer accessibility through increasingly abstract, bureaucratic procedures.

At the end of the 1950s, the emergent charge cards were challenged by the setting up of revolving bank card systems (Mandell, 1990; Nocera, 1994; Manning, 2000; Chutkow, 2001). The first of these was California-based Bank of America, the then (and now) largest bank within the United States, and Chase Manhattan of New York. Bank-issued credit cards were distinct from other types of card payment form. They offered customers a means not only of purchasing a wide array of goods and services that were not restricted to particular retailers but of rolling-over balances from month-to-month. The arrival of the bank card extended the sophistication of the plastic credit pioneered by Diners Club and American Express by introducing an interest element on unpaid balances that could be pushed forward indefinitely. Balances were now dependent not simply upon the amounts charged by credit consumers but on the proportion of the balance paid (or unpaid) at the end of the monthly billing cycle.

Banks, however, faced a particular predicament that has been termed the "chicken and egg" dilemma (Nocera, 1994). This double-bind implied that customers would only take a card that was accepted as a means of payment at a relatively large number of retailers while retailers would only sign-up at a merchant for a particular type of card if there were sufficient numbers of customers in possession of it. Banks attempted to solve this by engaging in a policy of potential merchant-courting while pursuing a strategy of indiscriminate mass-mail solicitation to attract customers. The undifferentiated mass-mail drop thus characterized the early efforts of these banks that were attempting to both reach, and create, a mass market for a new credit form that depended upon mass deployment for its profitability. Unlike retailer-specific charge accounts developed to promote sales and, to a lesser extent, ongoing loyalty, the credit card's profits for banks stemmed from the interest and annual fees paid by customers. These also included the discount rates that retailers offered in order to operate as card merchants. The banks' concerns for profitability thus became directly mapped on to the maximization of possession and usership in the facilitation of consumption, and resonated more broadly with the Keynesian state's concerns for the nurturing of economic growth through the calculable fostering of mass consumption.

By the end of 1960, there were around forty independent credit card systems across the country (Evans and Schmalensee, 1999: 63), each system servicing a particular concentrated regional area. However, the extensiveness of Bank of America's branch network within California encouraged its early preeminence as a credit card provider with its BankAmericard brand, its branch network giving it access to a largely concentrated, relatively affluent population base (Mandell, 1990; Chutkow, 2001). The forging of a mass market through mass mailing proved, though, an attritional process. Nocera details with regard to the BankAmericard effort how heavy delinquency, default and fraud proved an onerous burden on operating costs that ran at some $20 million in real terms just fifteen months after its launch (1994: 29). In 1966, Bank of America spun off its credit card into a separate company, National BankAmericard Incorporated, which offered to franchise the card brand to willing banks beyond the state boundaries of California. Although customers and merchants were recruited by local banks, with settlements organized centrally, the credit card itself began to establish itself as a nationally recognized credit facility, a brand that could facilitate consumption anywhere across the United States. The credit card thus evolved as a mass-issued but personalized credit form that increasingly mediated the possibilities of consumption beyond the boundaries of form, time, and space.[1] Just as the BankAmericard spread to other states, a rival network was established by a group of East Coast banks, forming the Interbank Card Association who then purchased the rights to the "Master Charge" card brand.

In significant ways, the expansion of the credit card across the United States proved a significant impulse in undermining the regulatory capacities of the state. The post-Depression governance of the market through federal statute was constructed to dampen what were perceived as the excessively competitive actions of financial institutions by restricting them to individual state boundaries. However, the expansionist ambitions of Citibank to overtake Bank of America as the largest bank in America were dependent on it being able to operate not merely within the state of New York but across a broader national stage (Nocera, 1994; Manning, 2000; Millman, 2001). As Nocera rhetorically asks, "[b]ut how could a bank 'go national' and still remain within the letter of the law? That answer was credit cards. Just as the Chicago banks had once dropped credit cards in the Illinois suburbs to attract suburban customers, so could Citibank now use credit cards to try to attract customers all across the nation" (1994: 145). In 1977, taking advantage of BankAmericard's rebranding as the more aspirationally titled Visa, Citibank purchased extensive mailing lists and engaged in a program of mass mail solicitation. During this time it issued three million credit cards, not only within its own state but nationwide, in doing so becoming the largest issuer of credit cards in the country.

The Credit Card Matures

In the 1980s, new card brands entered the market to challenge the preeminent Visa and MasterCard. The Discover Card, offering lower interest rates, a percentage cash back to consumers and competitive discount rates to retailers, was established and distributed directly by long-standing mail order king Sears before being sold to money market firm Dean Witter. The venerable American Express, which had traditionally offered its product as a charge card aimed at the business and affluent user, marketed its Optima card that could be revolved month-to-month like a bank-issued card (Ritzer, 1995; Evans and Schmalensee, 1999; Klein, 1999). In the same decade, a new breed of bank like Capital One, Providian, MBNA, and First USA emerged and began to take root within the credit card market; known as "monolines," they specialized primarily or exclusively in the offering of credit cards. These new creditors innovated new credit scoring systems and sophisticated marketing techniques, including the teaser 0 percent balance-transfer facility, to attract new customers. They also tailored credit card features such as annual fees, credit limits, and additional services to profitably solicit and administer particular types of consumer, incorporating customer responses to further refine their marketing and account management techniques (Williams, 2004: 50). As Capital One's founder remarked, "we built an information-based company that can create an infinite number of products and put them through massive scientific testing to get down to a market of one, or mass customization" (Millman, 2001: 6). Credit cards, like the invocation of consumer desire more generally, were increasingly oriented toward, not a mass canvass of American consumers, but the inscription and cultivation of particular groups or types of individuals whose credit consumption choices were being conceived, and acted upon, as personalized, knowable expressions.

Of course, consumers will only carry cards if there are retailers willing to accept them. In the 1960s, the spread of credit card acceptance tended to be limited to smaller retail merchants, particularly in tourist areas, which did not operate their own independent credit system (Evans and Schmalensee, 1999: 130–6). By the mid-1980s, both MasterCard and Visa actively solicited acceptance from thirty high profile department stores such as Bloomingdales's and Macy's, which apart from the more prestigious American Express, had not accepted any credit cards up to that time. In the 1990s, the national card brands also began to penetrate into the supermarket chains, increasing their coverage from 5 percent in 1991 to 90 percent by the end of the decade (p. 132).

During the 1980s, the credit card organizations themselves began to become concerned with their consumer image and their market positions in relation to one another. As Klein (1999) shows, the 1983 Visa marketing campaign targeted professional working women, the DINK (double-income-no-kids) "super class" that was perceived to be emerging, and the affluent baby boom generation who were seen to be entering their peak earning years. The aspiration that enveloped the campaign was one that the company hoped would foster an "emotional bond" between the individual and their Visa card. Within television advertisements, transactions for various more or less mundane goods that become woven into an individual's or family's search for self-fulfillment are shown to be facilitated by use of their credit card. In magazine pictures, images of individuals enjoying fulfillment in unspoiled natural settings are overlaid with inspirational quotes that emphasize the infinite possibilities of discovery in the unfurling path of life. For Klein, the campaign was an attempt to locate Visa within the bounds of a personalized search for identity, to culturally associate their product, through the themes of individuality and choice, with the realization of individuals' personalized desires. In a sense, Visa was projected as a product capable of embodying the exercise of choice through consumption, the "visa" for giving voice to the quest for identity.

From the 1970s, the credit card has emerged as one of the key facilitating instruments of contemporary consumption. As can be seen in figure 5.1,

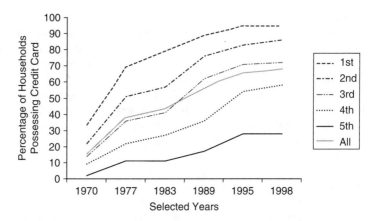

Figure 5.1 Prevalence of credit cards within United States by income quintiles, 1970–1998.
Source: Durkin, 2000.

possession among all American households increased from around one-sixth in 1970 to over two-thirds in 1998. Although continually stratified by income, card possession increased most markedly for the lowest income groups, from a low base rising fourteenfold to 28 percent while, in the same timeframe, becoming virtually ubiquitous among the economic elite (for consumer credit more generally see Bostic, 2002). As can be seen in figure 5.2, there has also been a shift in the balance of debt held by American consumers away from installment-type consumer loans to revolving credit facilities that characterize the credit card form. As Durkin (2000) suggests, such a shift reflects the preference of consumers for the convenience offered by "pre-arranged" lines of credit. In addition to increasing rates of credit card possession across the population, the proportion of cardholders carrying or revolving a balance forward has also increased, from 37 percent to 55 percent. It is noteworthy, though, that in the last 25 years, despite this increase in credit card debt, total overall consumer debt relative to income has remained static at just under 30 percent (Dynan and Kohn, 2007: 13).

Since the 1960s the credit card, embodying an open-ended, self-renewing credit agreement, has emerged as a generic form of credit. Disassociable from particular goods or retailers but encompassing the broader arena of consumption, it has come to represent a malleable, personalized resource in consumption practices. Through the credit card, individuals have come to exercise heightened levels of self-determination in terms of the credit that they engage. It becomes merged across goods purchased and across periods of time, assuming a quantified monetary form expressed and carried over time.

It is also divorced from the specific goods it finances, encompassing the continuous, ongoing process of consumption facilitated through the

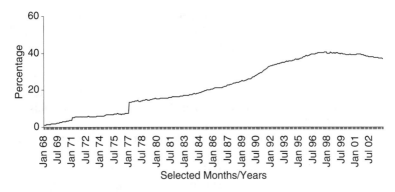

Figure 5.2 U.S. credit card debt as percentage of total consumer debt, 1968–2003.

Source: Federal Reserve Web site http://www.federalreserve.gov/releases/g19/hist/ in June 2006.

widening scope of such credit. In Daniel Klein's (1999) analysis of consumer credit and experiential consumption, he argues that the credit card has located whole new spheres of ephemeral consumption within the reach of credit financing including theme park tourism, telephone sex lines, psychic hot lines, themed hotel fantasy suites, each in their own way making marketed pleasure, meaning or affective, quasi-therapeutic advice more readily available for choosing. But the credit card has also become banal; no longer a status symbol within itself, it has come to represent just another means of representing and exchanging value—a new part of the nation's wider monetary system (Zelizer, 1994: 206). We now, of course, use credit cards to pay for such relatively unreflexive consumption choices as public transport and parking fines, property taxes and dental checkups.

Time, Money, and the Credit Consumer

The form of revolving credit represented by the credit card demonstrates a new conception of time that is characterized by its diffuseness and open-endedness in contrast to, as we have seen earlier, installment credit's tight apportionment of time. Although a strict structure is still maintained in terms of a monthly balance statement and the apportionment of annual interest, a more fluid structure is evident in terms of there being no fixed payment required beyond an agreed minimum and an upper chargeable credit limit, which itself is negotiable and subject to periodic review. The sub-units of time framing installment credit, as we saw in relation to automobile financing of the 1920s, were conceived as being discrete and self-contained, interlinked only in terms of being part of a broader series of steps toward final payment. The flow of funds in any one period were not inherently linked or affected by that in any other. Within this system of predictability and regularity, installment credit represented the discrete and defined nature of desire, which was fixed upon particular objects and governed through the incremental, regulatory nature of the contract as well as the will of the individual.

Under revolving credit, although time continues to be distinctly apportioned, these units are interlinked as balances carried over time, with the individual's particular actions in any period affecting future periods. As such, individuals must orient their own actions across a more complex formation of time where specific periods have consequences on others. This must be taken into account by consumers within a context where the strict, apportioned teleology of installment credit dissolves to a shifting, indefinitely time-bordered, personalized form embodying the continual consumption practices of the individual. There is no overall amount with which the agreement is concerned nor a fixed balance that remains to be paid; in their place, rather, are variable limits determined by the creditor's assessment of the ongoing creditworthiness of the consumer and constantly renewing, changing balances that build up or deplete down in tandem with the self-determined credit consumption of the individual.

In consequence, the tightly structured link between amounts of time and money inherent to the installment forms of credit we examined in chapter 3 gives way. Although an apportioned interest rate and balances are organized monthly, credit card agreements are characterized by the loose constraints of an upper maximum ceiling (which is, in fact, variable over time) and a minimum payment amount (which is usually calculated as a proportion of the overall balance). Within these terms, a free interplay takes place between time and money, shaped only by the credit user's desire and level of self-constraint in terms of the apportioning of income, expenditure, desire, and ability to repay. Over an indefinite time period, the individual sets the specific terms of credit use and repayment that are as infinitely variable in formation as the individual wishes them to be. In certain ways, credit cards embody an increasing dependence upon the self-governing capacities of consumers and, in consequence, time itself becomes deregulated. The relative absence of external constraints on individual action, in contrast to the characteristics of installment credit, actually requires an increasing need for self-constraint as to a consumer's momentary impulses, enhanced foresight as to the consequences of their actions and an ability to increasingly manage their own behavior, in an objective and instrumental way, over longer and more complexly interwoven periods of time. This is not to say that consumer failure, in terms of "overcommitment," poor financial management, or changed financial circumstances, is obviated (Rowlingson and Kempson, 1994). The fact remains, however, that credit card management, successful or otherwise, has become the individual's responsibility.

Commodified Credit and the Consuming Self

The 2005 Visa advertising campaign perhaps throws into relief something important about the contemporary development of the credit card. This campaign continued the aspirationalist theme of the 1983 one referred to earlier but in a manner that emphasized more the emotional bond between consumer and credit card; in the words of their advertising agency creative director Rob Schwartz, the company sought to increase its so-called share of heart to match its "share of wallet" in order to persuade consumers of Visa's potential to empower them to get "the most out of life":

> The credit card category is rife with conventions. Brands spend a lot of money to show that because they're big, you can trust them. But big isn't enough. We're leveraging Visa's size to empower life experiences. It's not about your credit card company being big, it's about how big life can be. (TBWA, 2005)

Rather than the narrativized interweaving of ostensible products and experiences or allusion to grand metaphors of freedom and self-fulfillment enabled by credit, the new campaign dwelt on both curious and spectacular experiences not necessarily consumerist within themselves but designed to resonate with the wider existential possibilities of the self. Reflecting this, the advertising messages produced sought to emphasize the "brand" rather than the "card." As such, the need was felt to persuade consumers, not to get and use credit, but to feel an ongoing affinity toward the one logo among the many present on the plastic that they do or may potentially carry in a cacophonically symbol-imbued credit card market. If, as Holt argues, the "semiotic potency" of marketed brands to give meaning to consumption is diluted the greater and more intensively they are marketed within the hyper conditions of postmodernity (1998: 21), then, as an alternative strategy of appeal, Visa sought to mask the actual market within which their credit card is offered for use.

The credit card does not simply represent an instrument for consumption practices or lifestyle generation through the expansion and facilitation of consumer choice (Bernthal, Crockett, and Rose, 2005) but has, within itself, come to embody the aspects of a consumable commodity.[2] Product characteristics such as interest rates, credit lines, fees, and special features like cash rebates, points, and payment protection insurance allow creditors to compete with one another for market share as "each issuer tries to get consumers to take its card, either in addition to or in place of cards from other issuers. Each issuer then tries to get consumers who have its card to charge more purchases on it and.... to carry greater balances" (Evans and Schmalensee, 1999: 210). Credit cards have thus become commodities within themselves, brands to be produced and marketed as though they were toothpaste or breakfast cereal. For instance, a 1999 survey of credit cards administered by market research firm J.D. Power carried out interviews with a sample of consumers to assess thirty-five "products" from seventeen of the largest credit card issuers, breaking responses down by market segment—"general/gold," "rewards," and "platinum"—and ranking them with a quantified score (Souccar, 1999). Consumers were assessed on their "satisfaction" with a particular card, their use of the card and their plans for future usage.

The development of reward programs on credit cards, whereby credits are accumulated over time by the user in proportion to the volume of their card purchases, provides a prudential means for credit consumers to customize and enhance the scope of choice that credit cards enable. The most widespread form of this are varied "points" schemes such as MBNA's "Goldpoints," "Worldpoints," and "Elite Rewards" that provide the consumer with a range of free goods and services, discounts, and benefits tiered according to the number of credits that have been accumulated by the individual through their card use. MBNA also offer affiliated reward schemes with specific retailers, airlines, and cruise lines to provide consumers with discounts and other benefits redeemable at those particular affiliates.

Credit card issuers also offer schemes involving cash rebates rather than redeemable points. For instance, MBNA's "Cash Back" card offers an immediate 1 percent credit on application for net purchases of $2,500 while its "Motley Fool" co-branded option offers a yearly check for 1 percent of the total volume charged to the card during the preceding twelve months.[3] Other credit card products also allow the credit user to divert such cash returns into the investment products of partner financial organizations, from federally insured savings accounts to investment products that provide a means of savings for a child's future college tuition fees.[4] Within contemporary consumption, it seems as though Weber's ([1930] 1976) Protestant ethic has obtained a curious new form. Whereas it had been based on the deferment of gratification toward the ends of accumulating wealth, this contemporary version, embodied in the accumulation of credit card points and rebates, is based on the continuous engagement of consumer gratification. It is through one's more intensive consumption of credit, the ongoing fulfillment rather than the suppression of want and desire, that greater advantage is presented as being accrued.

The dissolution of such tension, however, does not make such "saving" any less rational than before. If rationality is the ability to dispassionately calculate a means/end calculus over relatively extended periods of time, then it is the content of such rationality that has altered. In contrast with the Protestant ethic, it represents not an overarching orientation based on the sustained self-constraint of one's desire in order to maximize one's capital.

Instead, it is a self-governed choice to be made among a variety of marketed options in the interests of optimizing one's capacity to choose. To these ends, it is not the option of saving that is or is not chosen—for with credit card reward schemes, accumulation is automatic and contemporaneous to consumption—but the *type* of "savings." Ultimately what is chosen by the prudent and aware credit consumer will depend on their long-term ideals and desires. Perhaps they enjoy the vicarious pleasures of catalog browsing (Goldpoints can be accumulated for catalog purchases), embracing their Irish-American identity and traveling to the "old country" to trace their family lineage ("Aer Lingus Shamrock Rewards" can be accumulated for free flights) or possess an ethical concern for a "distant other" (Barnett et al., 2005) in the preservation of North America's wetland habitats (an ongoing donation to which will be made on their behalf by their use of a "Ducks Unlimited" affinity card). As a byproduct of their consumer hedonism, the credit card consumer might also choose to be a prudential subject, calculating and preparing for the future through choosing the card with generous payment protection insurance and the latest identity theft and fraud protection features. In the longer term, they might choose to save their cash rebate into an interest-accruing account or invest in the future opportunities of their children by accumulating a fund for college tuition.[5]

Meanwhile, the development of "affinity card" programs have made credit cards available as a more immediately distinctive element in the construction of a particular sense of self. The leading purveyor of affinity cards, the American bank MBNA, offers cards with affiliate ties to professional organizations, students, and alumni of particular universities, environmental causes, cultural organizations, charities, and sports. Not only is the card personalized with the insignia of the affiliate but the bank offers particular incentives such as donations on the consumer's behalf, discounts and brand-name merchandise. On the application form for the "Elvis Presley" card, for example, in addition to the more conventional incentives such as worldpoints and 0 percent interest on balance transfers and cash advances, potential consumers are offered Elvis-related collectibles, charitable donations, discounts, and free parking at Graceland.[6] The exercise of one's entire scope of consumption through a credit card thus becomes inflected with the tint of a taste or affiliation that the consumer desires to give further form to. In doing so the consumer may be rewarded with customized, preferential choices accruing only to them and others like them who have chosen to give expression to themselves in that distinctive fashion.[7]

With the proliferation of credit cards, the supposed "democratization of credit" across broader reaches of the population, creditors have come to produce new visible symbolic distinctions such as gold and platinum cards with more restrictive eligibility criteria based on income. These offer higher credit limits, often with a range of complementary additional services to suit the consumer. Credit cards thus act not only as a conduit in the formation of identity but serve to illuminate that identity directly through the creditor's careful calculation of its symbolic scarcity. However, it is not simply through their rarity that they attain value. Hierarchical cards do not simply represent the strata of the individual whose name is embossed, but in a more nuanced fashion, materially represent, to others and the self, the scale and scope of choice that individual enjoys through credit (cf. Bauman 1998a: 31).

With the possession of an exclusive credit card, though, consuming choice is not merely enhanced by the extensive credit limit that one is able to engage but by the shaping of exclusive conditions under which one's credit use is exercised. MBNA's elite "Quantum" card, in addition to offering lines of credit of up to one million dollars, produces a "frosty-looking, translucent" piece of plastic, which "looks more like an accessory than a credit card" (Lee, 2000: 11). A limited-edition version of American Express's competing "Centurion" card features a motif of an x-rayed, sequined, boot-clad leg produced by haute-couture fashion designer Alexander McQueen. This was unveiled at a celebrity London catwalk show as though it were the latest fashion season's offering.[8] The distinction of the symbolic properties of the physical card are not merely conferred by a quantitative rarity but by the appropriation of a culturally recognized high-fashion aesthetic that commodifies the plastic card possessed by the individual as an appropriable, rarefied style element within itself.

A rewards program offered by UBS Warburg for "high-net-worth" customers who have charged a sufficient volume to their cards, provides for such distinguished consuming experiences as a round of golf with a professional golfer and the opportunity to design one's own wine at a commercial vineyard (Creamer, 2006). More broadly, American Express offers its platinum card holders such privileges as free upgraded airline tickets on certain airlines, complimentary access to business class airport lounges, facilities such as free breakfasts and late checkouts at selected hotels and complimentary premium-club membership at car rental agencies to "bypass lines and paperwork, [and] go right to your waiting car."[9] Visa's premium "Signature" card allows card users to get dinner reservations at the most exclusive restaurants, even if they are fully booked.[10] The eminence of choice experienced through card purchases is elevated, not only by the quantity of credit that the individual consumer can command but the qualitative form such credit takes. For those whose scope of choice qualifies them, rarefied and distinguished consuming experiences become the reward for continued credit use while the potential pleasure generated by such credit use can be automatically multiplied or prolonged, or a delay in gratification eliminated, simply as of the qualified cardholder's right.

Yet, what is to be chosen? Many high-end credit cards also offer what is known as a "concierge" service, a customer service representative who can be contacted by telephone or email to procure advice, research, and assistance not only on one's card use but on anything that the card might be used to purchase. In the nineteenth century, Marx ([1844b] 1975) famously observed that under conditions of capitalist alienation, money, because it offers the universal property of being able to appropriate all objects, makes the qualities of those objects the possession of the individual who possesses money. In the twenty-first century, however, it is no longer simply the tangible amount of money that one possesses which gives form and weight to the subject under capitalist relations of production; now the same ends can be accomplished through the intangible quality of one's credit entitlements. The credit card concierge acts as a permanent counselor to the elite consumer; they offer the cardholder equipped with the financial means to choose, but bewildered by the possibilities or constrained by the boundaries of time and space, the wherewithal to give effect to his or her will to make the right choice (or neutralize the consequences of a choice that has been ill-made). For instance, advertising for the American Express platinum card rhetorically asks, "How Can a Platinum Card Concierge Help You?"[11] Here a concierge can arrange champagne and flowers for one's honeymooning child, source replacement passports, find a piece of jewelry one spotted on holiday in Greece, even organize for one's house to be painted (including selecting the color). Marx might have blushed.

Consumer Credit and State Regulation, Part 2: Autonomizing the Consumer

It is not simply, however, that the preoccupation with choice, the formation of identity and the fulfillment of a lifestyle are the mere outcomes of a totalizing shift from modernism to some variant of postmodernity. They connect in very specific ways, and provide new modalities for, new rationalities through which individuals are governed. As Miller and Rose suggest, the idea of consumer choice has been accorded a vital economic role within contemporary forms of government so that "economies are successful to the extent they can promote this, at one and the same time, proliferating and differentiating needs, producing products aligned to them and ensuring the purchasing capacity to enable acts of consumption to occur" (1990: 25).

As argued by governmentality theorists, the latter decades of the twentieth century in Western societies has seen "advanced" or "neo"-liberalism come to replace welfare-interventionism as the dominant political rationality of government. Just as welfarism sought to transcend the externalities of liberalism characterized by self-destructive economic competition, commercial monopoly and fragmenting social bonds, neoliberalism stemmed from a cross-political matrix of discourses that attacked the welfare state as a bureaucratic morass and the inflationary pressures produced by an active fiscal interventionism into the economy (Rose and Miller, 1992; Rose, 1993, 1996b, 1999b; Dean, 1999a; see also Maglin and Schor, 1990). Neoliberalism, as an assembly of ideas about how to govern, was not simply a reactivation of a classical liberalism. Liberalism had conceived of the economy as a quasi-naturalistic sphere endowed with its own immanent logic and dynamics derived from and fulfilling the essentialized and self-referential needs of the workers, producers, and consumers that participate within it. Against this, neoliberalism envisages the market as a spontaneous social order that emerges through the development of civilization, that is, the development of rules of learned conduct. Markets are not somehow fundamental and ahistorical but emerge through a process of institutional, economic, and cultural development (Burchell, 1993; Dean 1999a). Similarly, choice is not a product of autonomized, irreducible individual interest but is a human faculty that can be manipulated and made calculable through the context within which it is made. The neoliberal rationality of government is thus not about freeing people but about *making* people free. The programs it implements concern not simply "freeing" the market (although this is important in some respects) but about *enabling* a market mechanism to exist in a diversity of contexts.

Although government becomes stripped of its social functions, it does not mean that government does not seek to intervene; on the contrary, government is compelled to promote and sustain an environment conducive to a sense of "entrepreneurship" on the part of its citizens. Here, enterprise figures as a permanent ethical blueprint for the promotion of the autonomous choosing individual. Such individuals are to govern their own lives, to skillfully and judiciously deploy their resources over time in order to optimize their autonomous capacity to choose and thus calculably fashion a fulfilling and meaningful life for themselves (Miller and Rose, 1990; Rose, 1996b; O'Malley, 2004). To these ends, individuals are to be "enterprised," to have their environments acted upon in such a fashion so that they are empowered as choice-makers. In a sense, all individual action is reconceived as economic action—individuals are seen as calculating entrepreneurs of themselves who shape their own lives on a cost/benefit basis through the choices that they make.

In relation to consumer credit within the United States, new statutory initiatives from the 1970s have proved crucial in shaping the institutional context of consumer credit in a distinctly neoliberal way. These, it will be argued, have promoted the autonomy of individuals through setting the framework of possibilities for the exercise of their market choices. Two prominent examples have been the Equal Credit Opportunity Act 1974 and the Community Reinvestment Act 1977.

The Equal Credit Opportunity Act of 1974 (ECOA), as we will explore in more detail in chapter 7, was enacted to prohibit discrimination in credit decisions based on race, national origin, age, gender, and marital status. In essence, it attempted to program a unified field of consumers upon which credit sanctioning decisions would be decided on "objective" grounds of creditworthiness (Elliehausen and Durkin, 1989: 7–8). Of course, the act was not predicated on the fact that those of different races or ethnic origins, of different ages or genders were or are equally creditworthy or enjoy equal access to credit. However, by removing the explicit usage of such attributes and in sanctioning statistical risk systems which lay claim to objectivity through binding expertise and empirical derivation, unequal access to credit becomes explicable in terms of "really existing" differences in creditworthiness of different groups.

The Community Reinvestment Act (CRA) of 1977, which built upon the Home Mortgage Disclosure Act of 1975, attempted to broaden access to credit by acting upon the operations of lenders. Like the ECOA, the concerns that motivated the passing of the act related to the phenomenon of "redlining" where banks refused to make mortgage loans to those living in poor ethnic minority neighborhoods (Schill and Wachter, 1994: 224–5; Dymski, 1999: 37–8). Through the CRA, lenders are periodically examined and rated by the particular federal agency responsible for their supervision in terms of their provision of credit to the geographic communities within which they operate including explicitly defined "low and moderate income neighborhoods." The CRA rating attributed to the lender is then taken into account by those agencies when deliberating on applications for deposit facilities, mergers, and acquisitions by that lender. Thus the ostensibly free market for consumer financial services is penetrated by calculative systems of financial control and target setting, the resultant benchmarks and indices serving to shape its operation according to the programmatic aims of the state (cf. Power, 1997). However, as Peterson reports, the gap between idealized conception and programmatic reality has been wide with little or no regulatory sanctions being recorded against creditors who shirk their "reinvestment" responsibilities (2004: 103–4).

The Truth in Lending Act

In the latter half of the twentieth century, however, the main plank through which the state has governed consumer credit has been the Consumer Credit Protection Act, in particular, the first title that became known as the Truth in Lending Act (TILA). The act, which endured a tortuous eight year passage through the legislature before being passed into law in 1968, had three stated aims (Rubin, 1991). The first, betraying the discursive persistence of Keynesian economic management, was to help provide economic stability by encouraging the informed use of credit; the second was to empower consumers to shop around for the most advantageous credit terms; the third was to protect consumers from unfair and inaccurate billing. The activating mechanism deployed was that of disclosure, similar to the uniform installment sales laws that we examined in chapter 4. The concern, though, was not simply with protecting the consumer but actively privileging their position within the market. Essentially, creditors were required to calculate the annual percentage rate (APR) of every credit product they marketed, that is, the cost of the credit including interest and all incidental costs, in a standardized fashion and prominently display this charge so that consumers could compare and contrast the costs of different credit products available.

The terms of the act were intended not merely as a means of promoting a general transparency about prices within the market; rather, in a more amorphous fashion, its main purpose was perceived to lie in its effective fostering and improving of the cognitive, attitudinal, and behavioral processes of consumers in relation to the efficient shopping for, and use of, credit (Durkin and Elliehausen, 2002). From a cross-political perspective it was thought that consumer "behavior" could be programmed in a desirable fashion, persuaded rather than compelled to govern itself for the maximization of its own interest. This, in turn, would compel creditors to compete on equal terms thus increasing overall industry efficiency (Brandt and Day, 1974).

In contrast to older forms of regulation that directly regulated and channeled such economic transactions through the specification of interest limits, licensing requirements and oversight mechanisms, TILA embodied an attempt by the state to govern the transactions of consumer borrowing at a distance. In effect, it would act upon the self-governing propensities of consumers. Consumers were free to borrow, whenever and from whichever source these chose, but such self-interest could not be taken for granted. On the contrary, the state sought to render the exercise of choice a more efficient practice by attempting to enforce a homogenization of a particular set of conditions within the national market for consumer credit, thus prioritizing the role of the consumer. Through simplifying choice, the act of choosing could be made more efficient and so the consuming activities of individuals, involved in their personalized projects of consumption, could be enhanced and made more effective. As Rubin notes, disclosure has proven a popular technology within contemporary neoliberal governmental programs for acting upon the self-governing propensities of individuals. For instance, it forms the backbone of such related consumer protection statutes as the Fair Credit and Charge Card Disclosure Act of 1988 and the Truth in Savings Act of 1991 as well as the regulation of other diverse areas such as securities, consumer good quality, and the environment (1991: 234).

As a programmatic attempt to articulate a role for the state in the government of credit, TILA was subject to criticism for its ineffectiveness and its counterproductive outcomes. These allegedly left creditors vulnerable to legal challenges on the basis of what were understood to be spurious technicalities (Rubin, 1991: 236–8; cf. Rose and Miller 1992: 9–10). In a certain sense, consumers were seen to be excessively privileged by the terms of the act to the detriment of creditors. Yet, at the same time, consumers, too, were felt to be ill-served by an act whose provisions "were not telling them what they needed to know" (Rubin, 1991: 238). Numerous empirical studies suggested that, rather than streaming information toward the consumer in order for them to make the best possible choice, TILA soaked the consumer in a torrent of impenetrable disclosure terms that overwhelmed their ability to discern the "true" cost of credit and effectively compare the merits of different credit products (Jordan and Warren, 1966; Kripke, 1968; Brandt and Day, 1974; Davis, 1977). In particular, lower class consumers ill-equipped with the cultural capital to interrogate lengthy legal forms and whose use of credit was governed more significantly by availability rather than price, were seen to be more than relatively disadvantaged under the terms of the act (Kripke, 1969; Worden and Sullivan, 1987).

So, just as a dearth of information might starve the basis of entrepreneurial action, a state-enforced deluge could be cloying to it, not simplifying but, on the contrary, actively hindering the free exercise of choice. In response, as Peterson reports, TILA was amended five times, in 1970, 1974, 1976 (twice), and 1978 before being completely overhauled in 1980 by the Truth in Lending Simplification and Reform Act (2004: 126). This latter act served to eliminate many of the legal problems that beset creditors while streamlining certain consumer disclosure requirements. However, almost inevitably it seems, "[t]here is little evidence . . . that this present version has been any more effective in communicating information to consumers or in encouraging them to shop effectively for credit" (Rubin, 1991: 239). Like the fatalism of bringing a horse to water, no governing process can successfully enforce an economically rational consumer consciousness.

The Carter Controls

What was perhaps the last gasp of an active state intervention within the market for consumer credit occurred in 1980. Faced with the perceived wide-scale political, economic and social threats of rising double-digit inflation, the Carter administration triggered executive powers under the Credit Control Act of 1969. These equipped the Federal Reserve to reduce outstanding credit and thus ease upward pressure on prices in the interests of general economic stability (Schreft, 1990; Grant, 1992; Williams, 2004). As well as limiting the lending activities of financial institutions more generally, the new measures attracted particular attention in terms of specific mechanisms that sought to control the growth of consumer credit. Indeed, in his speech announcing this new measure, President Carter made specific reference to older notions of thrift in the American citizenry, arguing that instead of saving, consumers had become conditioned to take advantage of inflation in their use of credit; their pursuit of a consuming self-interest spiraled a problem that undermined the integrity of the American economy.[12]

Such credit controls, however, did not simply embody a reversion to a welfare-interventionist form of government. Firstly, the controls differed from their older wartime incarnations in that instead of directly dictating minimum down payments and loan amounts, much greater emphasis was placed on voluntary restraints and the specification of depositary requirements. This allowed financial institutions to pursue their own specific strategies to determine how credit growth would be restrained. Its mechanism of operation thus brought into play contemporary governmental "technologies of performance" that do not seek to dictate the form of economic activity but, rather, to set goals and delegate the process of their achievement to the free play of the market itself (see Dean, 1999a: 168–70). Secondly, despite the intention of raising the cost of credit extension to protect the economic domain, the controls incorporated specific exemptions for smaller creditors as well as loans that were used to finance automobiles, mobile homes, and mortgage loans. In fact, under the voluntary restraint element of the controls, loans to finance mortgages, car purchases, and inventory financing by automobile dealers were specifically encouraged rather than limited (Schreft, 1990: 36).

In reality, the activated terms of the Credit Control Act fell between two liberal stools in initiating state intervention for a common well-being yet specifying, in a neoliberal fashion, that consumer autonomy necessitated that certain sections of the market be beyond the scope of such an intervention. Mirroring the political discourse on the failures of the welfare state, much of the criticism that followed the initiative was the degree to which its restrictions "harmed" consumers, particularly the most hard-pressed and vulnerable who did not have access to alternative sources of financing. As consumers, they were being deprived of the self-realizing possibilities of choosing.

It was anticipated by the Federal Reserve that limiting the extension of consumer credit would actually have negligible effects on combating inflation, providing instead a "symbolic" component of action. As it turned out, applications for credit plummeted while retail sales as a whole slumped as the wider economy entered recession. Whether the regulatory controls "caused" the recession or not, lenders and businesses believed that they did, just as their abandonment a mere six months later was held to have contributed to an immediate economic recovery (Schreft, 1990). In part, by compromising the autonomy of consumers, restricting the scope of their credit and thus dampening down on consumer choice, the state had endangered, not secured, the basis of economic vitality. It was, though, not merely the particular formulation of controls that was held to have been deleterious but the very attempt at making any kind of wholesale, calculable intervention. As the vice chairman of the Federal Reserve, Frederick H. Schultz suggested at the time:

> We learned in 1980 that it is exceedingly difficult to assess in advance the impact of control on economic activity. When the Board enacted its program, we did not anticipate, and we had no reason to anticipate, the market impact it would have. Given the limited coverage of the program, it would have been expected to have had a moderate effect on aggregate demand; however, we did not reckon correctly the dimensions of the psychological impact of the program on borrowers and lenders. (cited in Schreft, 1990: 46)

It was not just that the actions of the state failed in this particular instance; the neoliberal view was that they were fated to fail for any attempt to regulate the economy en masse in any dimension was seen to set off a chaotic series of unintended, unforeseeable consequences. Located within and through the mindset of individuals, these spread out and infected other economic sectors until the whole arena of the economy itself becomes undermined. Like the cautionary tale of the sorcerer's apprentice, bedlam and disorder are supposedly the fruits of any well-meaning but overdetermining intervention to guide the economy beyond the autonomy and freedom of its participants. By 1982, the credit control powers granted to the president under the act were abolished and have not been reintroduced by Congress since.

*   *   *

It seems now that consumer credit has come of age with widespread ownership of credit cards. But this ubiquity only reveals the profound fragmentation of the credit card for, like a fingerprint of consumer culture, no two credit cards are the same. Different providers and systems are offered, different credit limits and APRs given, different monthly and minimum payments made, different colors, charities, and cumulative points schemes offered. Various added benefits are promoted while exclusive aesthetics are given and chosen. The contemporary credit card radiates fluidity, individuality, uniqueness. Yet, never has using a credit card become so mundane and everyday an exercise; no longer the novel accessory of the affluent traveling businessman, the credit card populates everyday life and any market transaction, from the grocery store to the doctor's surgery. Despite its lifestyle generating possibilities, the credit card is inevitably tied up in the wider world of everyday practices in which consumption is involved (cf. Warde, 2005).

As we saw in the latter part of the chapter, the emergence of new kinds of governing legislation—particularly the all-encompassing Truth in Lending Act—was designed to promote, defend, support, and buttress the credit choices of consumers, allowing them a mechanism for optimizing their self-interest. Or, at least that was the aim if not the result. But the credit card itself promotes, embodies, and relies upon a self-determined freedom of choice. In the following chapters, we will be examining key mechanisms through which this freedom is both constituted and realized.

Perhaps a word is due on the recent unprecedented interventions by the American federal state into the banking sector. In a whirlwind of events in 2008, the wholesale mortgage providers Fannie Mae and Freddie Mac were taken into effective public ownership while insurer AIG was nationalized to the tune of $85 billion. Most notably, the Emergency Economic Stabilization Act 2008 (EESA) made $700 billion available for capital injections and the purchase of stricken assets from financial institutions. Yet, this is not the active, purposive intervention by the American state within the banking sector that we outlined in the last chapter. Here the New Deal state deliberately curtailed bank competition, channeled money into schemes and directly administered systems of mortgage insurance, initiatives rationalized by a wider vision of common, calibrated welfare. In contrast, the EESA represents a reaction to crisis conditions rather than the promotion of an alternative way of governing. American political elites have simply pumped public money to free up liquidity and shore up confidence in the existing system rather than seeking to fundamentally alter the territory of government or dethrone the primacy of the market. What is hoped, it appears, is that the system will eventually, albeit chastened, return to something like its former self—even banker remuneration.

CHAPTER 6

Credit Reporting and Consumer Surveillance

During the course of the twentieth century, consumer credit expanded and intensified across the United States, incorporating specialized financial capital to create and invent new possibilities for the ongoing fulfillment of a continuously regenerated, increasingly heightened process of consumer desire. Credit, as a commercialized contractual agreement to pay for goods or repay money borrowed in the present against some temporal conception of the future, has always presented lenders with uncertainty: the possibility of profit from interest or other charges balanced against the threat or hazard of loss from nonrepayment, default or delinquency. Since the 1960s, as we have seen, most particularly with the entry of banks into direct consumer lending and the development of new forms of credit like the credit card, the process of lending and borrowing money becomes abstracted from specific sites of consumption. In doing so, it has increasingly come to rely upon the self-governing capacities of individuals, their potential to regulate and control both their use of, and their repayment to, a personalized, instantly deployable, temporally unbounded form of credit.

Lenders, however, do not merely rely upon the existence of such a capacity. On the contrary, consumers have become enmeshed within new bureaucratic inscription mechanisms, practices and commercial transactions of information sharing, circuits of computerization, processes of information storage, retrieval, and distribution between multiple lenders, service providers, collection agencies, and state institutions. A shifting "surveillant assemblage" (Haggerty and Ericson, 2000) has come into being within the domain of consumer credit. This figuration of practices not only provides a means for tracking and accounting for the actions of individual credit consumers, it has come to constitute them in particular ways. It gives them meaning and salience in a form that can be readily identified and acted upon by lenders and others for their particular ends. In doing so, this assemblage has come to constitute credit consumers as a collective and as individual subjects, its logic and procedures, its storage and circulation of data, its inventions and innovations giving them a particular density and substance. This has proven significant not only for lenders but also in how credit consumers have come to think about, and act upon, themselves.

A Brief History of the Credit Reporting Industry

The sharing of information on the abstract creditworthiness of individuals has its antecedents in nineteenth-century commercial trading. Up until the mid-nineteenth century American merchants relied upon their established personal, religious, and social ties with the other businessmen they dealt with in order to assess creditworthiness for deferred payment (Madison, 1974; Mennell, 2007: 108–10). As Max Weber pointed out, citing Benjamin Franklin, credit was essential to industry and reputation was essential in accessing credit. However, higher volumes of commercial activity across greater distances in the expanding and integrating markets of the nineteenth century presented businesses with a problem of distance. How were credit facilities to be advanced to far away, unknown buyers who might not pay? Around this problem emerged credit reporting firms such as the Mercantile Agency and R.G. Dun and their vast network of local investigators. These were established to provide written compiled reports of commercial creditworthiness in a context where the personal, embedded relationships of old governing access to credit had been torn asunder and the problem of identity was increasingly coming to the fore (Foulke, 1941; Sandage, 2006).

Despite the increased distance of commercial trade and the intervention of specialized third party reporting agencies, the formulation of written reports adhered to a localized, often significantly moral conceptualization of character in their assessments (Madison, 1974; Lears, 1989; Olegario, 2002; see also Susman 2003). This is no surprise given that these assessments were formulated by reporters—usually attorneys or postmasters—living within the locality. Although traits often held multiple meanings, aspects of character related to clients by credit reporting agencies can be seen to divide into three types. These were: *personal* details that included such markers as age, marital status, and ethnicity; *entrepreneurial/productivist* qualities such as approximate wealth, professional trade experience, entrepreneurial drive, and perseverance; and overtly *moral* attributes like honesty, punctuality, level of personal, and family extravagance or thrift, drinking, or gambling vices.

Consumer bureaus, like their commercial equivalents began to emerge at the beginning of the new century within the United States as well as other countries, reflecting the greater prominence of retail consumer credit (Westin and Baker, 1972; Cole, 1988). Initially comprised of lists of bad debts organized and shared between retailers on a nonprofit basis or organized by trade associations in large cities, they allowed each contributor to avoid advancing credit facilities to those who had defaulted elsewhere. Such people were interpreted as being of intrinsically flawed character and thus liable to repeat their actions. Within the United States from the 1920s and 1930s, ever greater numbers of consumer reporting agencies, increasingly organized on a commercial basis and now recording the general performance of all an individual consumer's accounts as well as particular incidences of default, began to establish themselves in smaller and smaller towns. This reflected the rapid diffusion of automobile installment finance and the progressive development of retail store installment and charge accounts at the time. From around one hundred bureaus in 1916, membership of the national association grew to around eight hundred in 1927 and double that by the mid-1950s, achieving collective coverage of all consumers by 1960 (Hunt, 2002: 9).

In 1965, Credit Data Corporation (CDC) was established and, in breaking with the traditional paper filing system that had gone before, began to exploit new computer and telecommunications technologies to provide the first form of electronic access to, and sharing of, consumer records within the wider California region as well as the major cities of the eastern seaboard (Rule, Caplovitz, and Barker, 1969; Westin and Baker, 1972; Guseva 2008: 25–6). This shift toward computerized, high-speed access of credit records intersected with the particular demands of the large-scale banks, now concentrating on high-volume consumer lending. These banks were increasingly concerned with assessing creditworthiness based on the statistical distribution of predefined characteristics across a population of borrowers rather than creditworthiness as an individuated, subjective phenomenon. This electronic mediation of data led to new ways of inscribing the information held in credit files. Closed-ended, numeric categories were deployed detailing the "objective" payment performance of the individual to previous creditors, incorporating such information as account types held, account status, and number and severity of delinquencies. These replaced such bureau formulated evaluative judgments as "good payer," "slow payer," and so on which had been traditionally inscribed.

CDC was bought out in 1968 by TRW, an automobile parts and military defense contractor and from the 1970s, considerable industry consolidation occurred as lenders began to focus nationally on the marketing of consumer credit. Ultimately, three credit bureaus, deploying fully automated electronic systems of information retrieval, agglomeration, and distribution have emerged as national repositories for consumer credit information. These are TRW, which later became Experian when it was bought out by

British conglomerate Great Universal Stores, Equifax (a long established bureau previously known as Retail Credit) and TransUnion, (the parent company of Union Tank Car Company, a railcar leasing firm, which in a corporate strategy of diversification, acquired the Credit Bureau of Cook County in 1969) (Westin and Baker, 1972). By the 1980s, each bureau had individually attained coverage of the national population of consumers. However, smaller bureaus, often in commercial affiliation with the three nationals, have remained servicing low-volume clients or particular niche markets such as medical service providers and insurers, landlords, and utility providers (Hunt, 2002: 12, 2006: 313–14).

Currently, around two million credit reports are issued each day to lenders and other parties such as landlords and insurance companies defined as having a "permissible purpose" under the federal Fair Credit Reporting Act. Lenders incorporate this information into sanctioning decisions as to whether to grant credit to an individual, what interest rates and other terms should be applied, or to adjust the terms of a preexisting credit account. Individually, each of the three national bureaus maintain files on around 200 million individual consumers encompassing approximately 1.5 billion credit agreements. Each bureau receives and updates their files with approximately 2 billion items of information each month from thousands of lenders and other organizations, processing the information in between one and seven days (Avery, Calem, and Canner, 2003: 49–51). Credit bureau records themselves are divided into files for individual consumers and each file into five relevant categories encompassing consumer identifying information, credit account details, public records, debt collection history, and a list of recent inquiries by other parties (Avery et al., 2003).

Inscribing the Field of Consumers

Since the 1980s, American consumer credit reporting has come to represent a unified infrastructure distributed across three commercial firms. In doing so, it has also come to function as a technology for inscribing the domain or space of what is to be governed (Foucault, 1990, 1991; Hacking, 1990; Miller and Rose, 1990, 1992). Bureaucratically shorn of moral judgment and qualitative assessments that marked an older conception of creditworthiness intimately associated with wider notions of character, the contemporary credit reporting structure reflects, and represents an amalgamation of, those micro bureaucratic technologies of inscription existing at the level of the individual credit grantor. Through these, the creditor governs the sanctioning and repayment of lines of credit through the deployment of a bureaucratic edifice of filing, tabulation, indexing, and quantitative credit control that replaces relatively personalized, character-based assessments and judgments. From the micro-locales of the lender, the establishment of credit reporting conduits and the formation of "calculating centers" in the databases of the national credit bureaus opens up the world of credit consumers as a reality, a reality instantiated and regenerated through the ongoing practices and commercial relationships between consumers, lenders, and bureaus. Accordingly, a space is formed through the countless recorded actions of a multitude of credit consumers, the institutional prerogatives of lenders, and other organizations, the capitalist strategizing of credit bureaus, and the possibilities and costs of data technologies; a domain with its own dynamism and intensity within which it becomes possible to assess and to intervene, to appraise and to govern.

Credit bureaus in their contemporary form caution that they record only "objective" information and seek to impart no evaluative judgment on those individuals whom they maintain records on: nobody is "good" nor "bad."[1] The development of such an objectivity within a developing credit market makes possible, and in turn is further strengthened by, the utilization of electronic technologies in recording, agglomerating, and distributing data. These technologies, necessary to the contemporary market of mass, high volume credit, depend for their efficiencies on the simple coding of information into yes/no binaries (for example, credit agreement fulfilled or unfulfilled), clearly defined limited categories (for example, types of credit agreement entered into), and quantitative scales (for example, number of times delinquent). However, such information is not merely a neutral recording mechanism—on the contrary, its framing embodies particular expectations and understandings of what is to be measured, and how that measurement is understood (Miller and Rose, 1990; Rose, 1999b). It presents each individual as an individual consumer abstracted from the social context of a household, a community, a social class, or ethnicity; individuals become linked only as the voluntary cosignatories to the same recorded loan. Each credit account opening and payment recorded, each collection and bankruptcy detailed inscribes an ostensible choice or sequence of choices that the individual has exercised, whether wisely or otherwise.

The production of credit information, objectivized in its formulation and construction, is essential to the systematized integration of credit reporting across the breadth of the national population. Simmel (1978) explained in relation to the emergence of the money economy that the standardized expression of value implied by modern money was essential to the facilitation of trade in foreign markets and as a means of integrating activities under an extended division of labor. Accordingly trust, based on shared meaning and understanding derived from the tightly structured interaction of smaller social groups, was being increasingly displaced. Similarly, the process of instantaneously tracing creditworthiness across more extensive areas of space supplants nuance-rich, qualitative assessments based on the slowly accumulated "tacit knowledge" of lender management (Rock,

1973; Leyshon and Thrift, 1999; Guseva, 2008). This is replaced, within the context of an increasingly specialized, narrowly functional relationship between borrowers and lenders, with a homogenized understanding of both the meaning of creditworthiness and individuals as being creditworthy.

As Rose (1999b) has argued in relation to the significance of numbers within government, the founding of a domain of objectivity is inherently related to social developments such as enhanced population mobility and the establishment of new large-scale markets. These create a meaning system residing not in the personalities of tightly bounded small social groupings but emanating from the wider intricacies of a dense web of interdependencies. In such a fashion, credit reporting has come to represent a reified conception of creditworthiness beyond the subjective, producing and reproducing the credit history of consumers not on their own terms, but only as a component of a wider constituted population. Contemporary lenders do not assess potential consumers as independent entities but as precisely identifiable elements of a wider body of some 200 million consumers. Counting the number of successful repayments made by an anonymous consumer on a precisely defined kind of credit agreement, over a definite period of time, with a tightly categorized kind of lender only produces an understanding of creditworthiness against the current and past actions of other consumers, the numbers and length of their repayments and delinquencies, and what array of loan types they use with what precisely categorized kinds of lender.

Surveillance and the Subject

In recent years, the development of computer and telecommunications mediated surveillance, of which contemporary credit reporting can be seen as part, has been understood by some social theorists to have strikingly novel consequences for the individual as a subject. In their influential article on evolving patterns of surveillance, Haggerty and Ericson (2000) argue that contemporary practices of surveillance mediated by technological networks represent amorphous assemblages. These capture individual bodies in particular relations of power, formatting, and capturing their information flows from dispersed centers thus rendering them as flows of data that can be instantaneously reassembled and scrutinized as required. Ultimately, a new "body" emerges, an electronic doppelganger representing the corporeal body above and beyond itself, which circulates in its place through an assortment of calculating centers for the determination of action about the individual.

Mark Poster (1990, 1996) takes up this theme of the reconfigured subject. For him, the "superpanopic" power of computerized databases to both instantaneously transfer and indefinitely preserve inscribed, personalized information not only leads to a disinterring of the divide between the public and the private—every private act, to pay a bill or forego child support payments instantly becoming a matter of public record—but decenters the formation of the subject from its "ideologically determined unity." In consequence, such modernist conceptions as public/private, consumption/production are rendered obsolete. Building on Foucault's elaboration of discourses and the constitution of subjects within relations of power, Poster suggests that the unprecedented potentiality of computer-mediated institutional databases to absorb, disseminate, and reconfigure the effects of notation leads to an interpellation, within its files and data fields, of the contemporary subject. As a result, the subject becomes objectified, dispersed, and exteriorized by the database.

Mass society and the sovereign individual subject thus become transformed, the former into banks of nebulous samples and markets, the latter into a "dividual," a perpetually reconfigurable assortment of elements derived from its circulation within these wider media (Deleuze, 1992: 5). Although coining the term *superpanopticon* to describe this process, Poster deliberately contrasts it to Foucault's conception of the panopticon as the perfected embodiment of an older disciplinary power—one that attempted to craft the individual as a subject, autonomous and capable of possessing a sense of self and of governing their own destiny. Taking this analysis to its postmodernist limit, Bogard (1996) suggests that these institutionally and technologically fabricated "designer identities" are more real than the real self. In enmeshing the actions of bodies within flows of information channeled and arranged by the system's parameters, imperious to the boundaries posed by time and space, contemporary surveillance has given, or is giving way to simulation, reality to hyper-reality. Whereas surveillance, according to Bogard, sought to uncover truth, to unmask what was real within a framework of imposing control upon subjects, simulated surveillance, paradoxically, both ensures perfect visibility and control while at the same time, disposing of that space of "reality" as something to be known.

Unlike that "avalanche of numbers," which made possible the modern nation-state (see Hacking, 1990; 1991), the credit reporting system does not empower a single calculating entity at its center. On the contrary, the calculating potential it engenders is dispersed back to those micro-locales from which it was drawn. Within this system, flows of data function not merely as instruments for surveilling credit consumers but as a commodified service that generates not only a governing potential for lenders but a profit stream for credit bureaus. Consumers are opened up and rendered visible for the purposes of individual creditors, operationalized through their autonomous choices to seek credit. Significantly, then, it is consumers themselves who implicate themselves within practices of credit reporting, whose continual conscious choices to seek and use credit voluntarily enmeshes their bodies within this surveillant assemblage. They are, as Poster notes, both the source and recorder of the data generated about them (1990: 93). Even if resistance to such practices is generated in the name of privacy, such privacy functions for the individual not as an absolute value but as Haggerty and Ericson term it, a "shifting space of negotiation" (2000: 616). The vast majority of Americans seek credit, desire its realizing potential and, in doing so, contractually submit themselves to its information-distributing infrastructure despite concerns of privacy invasion and suspicion as to the motives of such a system.

How any creditor will seek to act in order to govern consumers will be determined by its general objective of maximizing profitability—but how this is realized will depend on their individual commercial strategy, particularly within a specialized, diversified market. In the past, creditors avoided those whose lack of creditworthiness was implied by their character. But as creditworthiness has become functionally specific and relativized, it is no longer a fixed attribute of the individual but a shifting, variable *attribution* created within the specific context of a credit transaction. Although the credit reporting assemblage opens up a field of credit consumers, it offers only a potentiality rather than an impetus to intervention. As we shall examine in the next chapter, the emergence of a technologically mediated, relatively centralized credit reporting system has been concomitant to the proliferating deployment of statistical risk scoring technologies by lenders. It is this risk technology, typically unique to the firm and crafted from their own localized, inscribed empirical history, feeding upon the written application for credit and the customer's credit file, which evaluates the credit seeker and represents them as a risk. Not only that, but how the customer is to be governed in light of this constituted risk is dependent upon how the firm conceives its profitability—minimizing risk exposure or maximizing revenues, cross-subsidizing products to maximize customer acquisition, or marketing to risky yet potentially profitable "subprime" risk categories.

Putting forward his thesis of contemporary surveillance as a "panoptic sort," Oscar Gandy (1993), in part, posits contemporary surveillance practices as something of a continuation of older disciplinary practices now no longer constrained by the confines of space nor sight in their enforcement of norms. In this he draws a specific parallel between the colored epaulettes worn by the different classes of pupil of the École Militaire, as described by Foucault (1979: 181–2), which entitled them to differential categories of privilege and the multicolored American Express cards brandished by contemporary consumers enabling them with varying levels of consuming license. Gandy's analogy is, however, flawed. The categorization of the French pupils served as a mechanism of normalization, the worst could aspire to higher appanages while the best were motivated to avoid the ignominies of their lower ranked. Such a system thus served to homogenize the space of government, ultimately serving to disappear under its own logic. On the contrary, the color-coded cards that American Express offers are segmented categories that dissolve the "mass-ness" of the mass market into identifiable segments that permit its more profitable exploitation. This logic here is one of heterogeneity not homogeneity; it aspires not to uniformity but to customization, the rolling out of bespoke credit products precisely tailored to the characteristics of every single consumer.

There is no single gaze exercising an individualizing surveillance within contemporary credit consumption. As Deleuze (1992) describes it, such practices as exemplified by credit reporting are a form of modulation, with control affected not centrally or coercively but through a matrix of shifting "flows and transactions" between the individual subject and those activities through which he or she engages. Haggerty and Ericson (2000) deploy the descriptive adjective "rhizomatic" to explain this form that contemporary surveillance takes, one that is expansive and regenerative but spatially unfocused and hierarchically flattened. Its strength emanates not from its intensification of a unidirectional gaze upon the individual but by its incorporation and forging of new connections between the multitude of different circuits of technology and data within which individuals are ensconced through their everyday practices.[2]

Within credit reporting, changing and manipulable virtual identities or "data doubles" are created through information flows, abstracting key elements from individuals and rendering them as meaningful within specific practices. Far from being "innocent or innocuous virtual fictions," their existence and distribution do determine access to certain benefits in certain contexts (Lyon, 2003: 27). Yet, at least in this context, they do not abstract or dissolve the notion of a centered, autonomous subjectivity. On the contrary, within contemporary consumption, the centered, autonomous subject has never been stronger. Individuals are obliged to be free, to constitute a meaningful life for themselves through the deployment of their sovereign, autonomous choice within all those areas of life configured as "markets"—shopping, work, education. Far from being disparate and fragmentary, the individual subject is tasked with exercising this choice to actively forge an ongoing cohesive narrative within and through their life. Within consumption, credit has become established as a key mechanism for the fulfillment of desire, temporally reframing the possibilities of choice. Consequently, those who sustain an engagement with credit in the consumerist pursuit of a meaningful sense of self will be those who exhibit the longest, most richly detailed, most extensive virtual selves.

Thus, an abstract data double—what I term a *credit identity*—with the widest panorama and greatest resolution of detail does not deconstruct the unity and centeredness of the contemporary subject, at least not in the consumption of credit. On the contrary, it exists in articulation with the centered subject. On the one hand, it reflects the subject's ongoing labor to sustain itself, recording in its stylized "objective" way each credit choice and all exhibited capacity to uphold these choices in repayment; and on the other, it provides a central resource for future credit consumption, presenting itself as a report card of the individual's capacity to self-govern, a cumulative history taken as evidence by whatever lenders take a commercial interest in that consumer at any given time.

Rhizomatic surveillance technologies such as credit reporting can perhaps best be conceived as a means of securitizing the identity of consumers at access points to consumption (Rose, 1999b: 243). The presence of a credit bureau record and its content enable creditors, on their own terms, to determine who to sanction lines of credit to, for how much and for how long. As Bauman remarks:

> it is the credit and marketing companies which are the main movers and users behind the database, and what they seek is to make sure that the records confirm the "credibility" of the people on record—their reliability as clients and *choosers*, and that those incapable of choice are sifted out before damage is done or resources wasted; indeed, *being included* in the database is the prime condition of "creditworthiness" and so is the means of access to "the best game in town." (Bauman, 1998b: 50–1, emphasis in original)

Although Bauman is correct in noting that the existence of a credit record tends to be a precondition for entry to circuits of consumption, the detailing of delinquencies and defaults, referrals to collection agencies for unpaid debts and court judgments can serve as an agglomerated, overarching securitized identification of the individual's incapacity to govern themselves under the desires proffered by consumption. This may potentially serve as an exclusionary marker for lenders. It is not only paucity of detail, then, which may proclaim the failure of self-government.

Events in the American financial system since 2008, however, may call into question the individuated attribution of individual creditworthiness. C. Wright Mills (1959) famously drew a distinction between private troubles, the difficulties of everyday life that beset the individual and appear as personal problems, and public issues. Public issues arise when economic and political events pull back the veil rendering private troubles individually focused and expose the wider social and historical forces buffeting individual lives. With employment increasing and home foreclosures at record levels in 2009, it remains to be seen the extent to which the condition of creditworthiness as a purely individual state and the result of the individual's own actions will become rearticulated as a consequence of wider economic conditions. The desire of the Obama administration to suspend residential mortgage foreclosures is, perhaps, one recognition of this—particularly given the importance of homeownership as a cultural value. It seems doubtful, though, to what degree consumer debts could be similarly treated.

It might be suggested that the credit reporting assemblage actually serves as a two-way street in its relationship to credit consumption. With the free availability of credit under favorable economic conditions, credit reporting assists and nurtures the expansion and intensification of credit use and the overall vitality and diversity of the market (Cate, 2002). Nevertheless, the reverse may also be seen to be true. As economic conditions deteriorate swiftly and the relative free availability of credit declines due to unemployment and falling incomes, incurred consumer debt becomes more difficult to repay and sustain. In extensively and intensively detailing rising delinquencies and defaults across the American population, removed from the embeddedness of how and why, these individuals will inevitably experience a curtailment of credit choices. They will be increasingly deemed uncreditworthy within a context where the overall availability of credit is itself declining. Within a recessionary economy, credit reporting will reinforce and spiral a dearth of credit use.

Homo Economicus and Surveilling the Self

Within the United States, from 1960 to 1970, three congressional committees and five state legislatures held hearings into the practices of the credit reporting industry (Westin and Baker, 1972). Reflecting growing public concern, particularly the heightened speed and scope of data distribution in the wake of computerization, the committees focused on such issues as the content of reports, their accuracy and completeness, procedures for disputing information held and precautions taken by the industry against unlawful access. Although the debate is often approached within the conceptual domain of privacy, it is perhaps more interesting to consider it as one of "credit due process" as Westin and Baker remark. As argued earlier, with the rise in the preeminence of the consumer and the increased government of individual conduct through consumption, the supposed deregulation of the credit industry has implied, on the contrary, a reorientation of regulation in favor of fostering the autonomy of the consumer. Rule et al. (1969), analyzing the industry at the time, castigated the credit reporting process as one of intense secrecy, favoring the interests of business over those of the consumer. They called for greater transparency and oversight in the "public interest," but a public interest not built on solidarity but on collective individualized autonomy. They note, for example, that:

> The credit file may be an indispensable condition to enjoyment of the basic material trappings of life, including one's house, automobile, home furnishings and entertainment; yet if things function smoothly, as they

most often do, the existence of the file remains completely hidden. (1969: 162)

There is no sense here of a unified social framework, but rather, of individual self-interest ("one's house, one's automobile") enabled by a systematic credit reporting assemblage. What they criticize is not the existence or principle of credit reporting; on the contrary, such a system is a necessity for individual consumer self-realization (see Barron and Staten, 2001). What is at stake is its opacity and the potential negative consequences it may hold in store for some consumers—in effect, its inadequacy at sufficiently realizing consumer autonomy. In such a vein, Rule et al. (1969: 162–5) chart its flaws: its dissemination of erroneous information, its mishandling of information, its failure to reflect consumer dispute with the credit provider and its inability to adequately reflect up-to-date public information. In sum, what is derided is not the existence of such a system but its inadequacies, the degree to which the virtual identities it manufactures do not adequately reflect their corporeal counterparts. It therefore not only enables and empowers individualized consumption but can, potentially, be unreflective of consumption potential.

Arguing from a free market perspective, Dunkelberg, Johnson, and DeMagistris (1979), Klein and Richner (1992), and Klein (2001) defend the credit reporting industry from "misguided" government regulation (particularly of the European privacy variety). They argue, in effect, that the market has evolved an efficient means of objective and narrowly functional "institutionalized gossip" for securing the reputation of consumers in large, complex societies. It is this system that has allowed the modern consumer credit market to flourish and from which consumers benefit through greater and cheaper availability of credit. However, again, their analysis reveals a distinctly neoliberal framing for Klein and Richner's approach takes credit seeking actions as a narrow form of economic behavior. Rather than collective well-being being served by the pursuit of individuals' self-interest, they see the use of credit as a form of cost/benefit practice that requires the formation of an external institution imposing costs of reputation harm:

> When credit reporting is in place, consumers have an extra incentive to pay their bills. They are eager to keep their credit report clean, for otherwise they may lose the benefits of credit. . . . By enhancing accountability, credit bureaus help turn consumers into responsible individuals. (Klein and Richner, 1992: 395)

The liberal subject of interest is thus dethroned in favor of the neoliberal *homo economicus* as manipulable man (Gordon, 1991: 43). "His" fundamental, reductionist capacity to choose must be permanently worked upon through his environment in order to elicit forms of acceptable conduct beneficial to the collective interest. Interestingly, it seems the subject is not presumed to be moral but must be made so through credit reporting as a "precise and unintrusive means of social control" (Klein and Richner, 1992: 398). To paraphrase Adam Smith's famous words, it is not from the benevolence of Capital One, Bank of America, or Citibank that we can expect our credit card, nor is their regard for their own self-interest sufficient; rather, what is essential is the conduct shaping effects continuously imparted by an effective credit reporting mechanism that rewards the "good" consumer with future credit and punishes the malfaisant with refusal (Klein, 2001: 326). Yet despite their disdain for state interventionism, they implicitly support the legal right of American consumers to access their own credit record. Critically, responding to consumer complaints is seen not only to be a legal requirement—it is a managerial necessity. Only by the input generated by consumer queries can the reliability of credit reporting procedures be tested and the quality of its service improved.

In 1970, the Fair Credit Reporting Act (FCRA) was passed that provided for the rights of consumers in the following ways:

- The limitation of commercial dissemination of reports to individuals or companies with a legitimate "permissible purpose."
- To know if refusal of credit was based wholly or in part on the contents of a credit report and the details of the bureau that supplied the information.
- To access one's own credit report for a "reasonable fee" and for free in the event that the consumer was turned down for credit in light of the report.
- To dispute information perceived to be inaccurate or incomplete— the bureau must investigate the complaint with the lender who provided the information and report back to the consumer, amending the record where necessary.
- To have inaccurate, incomplete. or unverified information removed within a "reasonable" timeframe.
- In general, information must be deleted from the report after seven years, with the exception of bankruptcy information, which can be maintained for ten years.

(Camden, 1988; Jentzsch, 2001: 21–3;
Cate, 2002; Avery et al., 2003: 48–9)

Two subsequent amendments to the Fair Credit Reporting Act were introduced with the Consumer Credit Reporting Reform Act of 1996 (CCRRA) and the Fair and Accurate Credit Transactions Act of 2003 (FACTA). The first of these, the CCRRA, imposed new specific time limits of 30 days for responding to consumer requests, allowed consumers, for the first time, to query incorrect records directly with lenders in addition to credit bureaus, and specified new responsibilities on credit bureaus and lenders to distribute data amended in light of queries (Cate, 2002; Jentzsch, 2001: 24–7).

More recently FACTA, in emphasizing consumer rights to question accurate but fraudulent data included on their credit files by way of identity theft, has among other provisions: granted borrowers the right to a free annual credit report from the three majors bureaus, enhanced the disclosure of consumer rights, mandated the revelation of credit scores for a fee, imposed a new duty on lenders to inform consumers of "negative" items being reported, and required lenders to inform consumers when their credit terms were substantially less favorable than the most favorable terms available (FACTA, 2003; CFA, 2004).

Such programmatic attempts to intervene within credit reporting can be seen as an attempt to disrupt the particularized interest of creditors and bureaus that have created a system which is simultaneously both essential and potentially detrimental to the individualized interests of consumers. However, rather than impeding it, the implementation of the FCRA enhanced a credit reporting assemblage essential to the increased extensiveness and intensiveness of consumer credit use, a use more and more implicated in the facilitation of consumption practices. The expansion and agglomeration of the industry and its deployment of an advanced information retrieval, storage, and distribution apparatus was both enabled and propelled by higher volumes of credit, accessed at greater speed and across a more diverse range of products, encompassing more and more individuals within a more nationally homogenous market.

In creating objectivized, functionally specific credit identities of consumers emptied of localized meaning and prejudicial, normative content, practices of credit reporting helped "make up" such a field of consumers reality. The state, in problematizing the role of economic government as one in which national prosperity and well-being were to be enhanced by autonomizing and enterprising individuals within their consumption practices, acted through the FCRA to secure the basis of consumer self-government. The main thrust of the FCRA was the legislative assurance of consumer access to their own records generated through the credit reporting process—it preserved the surveillant assemblage underpinning the possibility of choice through consumption. At the same time, the act elevated the rights of the consumer and imposed a duty of care on bureaus and lenders above the conditions of the contractual transaction entered into by the individual. In establishing such a new right or freedom, however, its effect was to burden individuals with the responsibility of maintaining the accuracy of their credit identities. They were to become self-surveilling consumer subjects. Lenders and their affiliated agencies were not to be accountable for the errors that they had committed in forming virtual identities; on the contrary, individuals were to become responsible for themselves, with errors and the constituted effect of identity theft being circumscribed as random, uncertain events—like illness or unemployment—which the consumer was to be conditioned to prudentially manage on their own behalf.

With the establishment of technologies of inscription and the constitution of new domains, new ways are created for individuals to think about themselves (Rose and Miller, 1992; Miller and O'Leary, 1994; Rose, 1999b). Therefore, through the terms of legislation, individuals as consumers and credit users were to be governed to consider the "objective" content and possible consequences of their objectivized credit identity for their sustained access to credit and the consumption potential offered. They were to view their access to credit as a generalized function of their abilities to "responsibly" adhere to their repayment obligations on a multitude of dutifully recorded credit agreements, to accept negative but accurate information as the justified outcome and reflection of their own faulty choices or overzealousness in credit use, and to see inaccuracies as a systemic imposition, which they were obligated to challenge and remedy in the pursuit of maximizing their own consumption potential. Above all else, they were to avoid the consumer suicide of bankruptcy—the ultimate dissolution of one's self-governing potential in the eyes of lenders. The legislative shaping of credit reporting can be seen, therefore, as an extension of the self-governing remit of individuals into the management of their credit use, implanting within consumers a new legally sanctioned possibility and mechanism for conceptualizing, calculating and judging their own actions.

*　*　*

The free choosing capabilities of consumers are not merely an exogenous social phenomenon animating a new credit-dependent consumer capitalism; in significant ways, they became actively fabricated through the development of a national credit reporting system systematically inscribing the credit choices made by consumers. Credit reporting, as we have seen, is as old as the market for consumer credit itself and the forms it has taken have altered in articulation with the wider development of credit provision. Embodying the increased specialization, centralization, and fluidity of contemporary consumer credit, the credit reporting industry manifests a commercial, centrally organized form that enables informational organization and instantaneous data distribution between lenders and its agencies.

Within this disparate, shifting assemblage, the bureaucratic surveillance of individual consumers' credit choices has become heavily technologically mediated: on the one hand, extensively reflecting data from a wide array of lenders and other sources and, on the other, intensively mining a more finely grained detail on the credit obligations and repayment performances of individuals. For each and every consumer then, a dynamic informational projection, a cohesive securitized credit identity, reflects in continuous detail the scope of their actions in using credit. At the same time, it simultaneously conditions their possibilities of ongoing choice within the market for credit and, beyond, in the wider field of consumption.

Yet it is not only lenders and other providers who engage with this abstract credit identity—consumers themselves, codified by federal statute, have harnessed their consuming ambitions to a recognition of this means by which they are inscribed and assessed. Individual projects of consumption, dependent upon the means of credit, have become increasingly bound to a reflexive consciousness of the means by which their free choices are inscribed and regulated. Credit consumers are thus both the objects of surveillance and self-surveillance in their exercise of choice. The more intense their consumption, the more extensive their engagement in market credit, and the more profoundly they express their freedom as consuming subjects—the more they must be located within and made subject to a regime of informational regulation by lenders and themselves.

CHAPTER 7

Risk and Technologies of Credit Scoring

We have seen up to now that the development of consumerism and neoliberal government have situated individuals as entrepreneurs of the self, driven by a requirement to condition a life for themselves through the upholding of a capacity to choose; to extend and animate their lives as a subjectively directed narrative of consuming desires and wants. Consumer credit plays a (if not *the*) crucial mechanism of consuming fulfillment. Within this, an individual's unique credit identity—the abstract dynamic reflection of the individual's accumulated "choices" continuously produced within the credit reporting assemblage—represents and secures the ability of the consumer to consume. However, as we have seen, credit identities are "objectively" constituted, supposedly shorn of any overt normative or prejudicial marker. Credit bureau TransUnion presents it that:

> Creditors make credit decisions. Each creditor has their own formula for evaluating a credit application, and only the creditor can tell you why they made a decision. TransUnion does not grant or deny credit. Our role is to supply the creditor with the contents of the report, which they can review in order to assist them in making a sound decision.[1]

How then do creditors make their lending decisions within a market context increasingly dependent upon the sustained, self-governing abilities of the consumer? How is the permanently lurking threat of default to be systematically governed? Or, to put it more brusquely, how do contemporary creditors choose who is creditworthy and who is not?

In this chapter, I want to examine how a probabilistic conception of risk increasingly came to define what was meant by the creditworthiness. This is not something that was progressively achieved or represented a necessary logical follow-on from older conceptualizations of creditworthiness. Arising within the context of an ongoing expansion in the market for consumer credit, the conceiving of creditworthiness as risk evidences a discursive break, a new departure in managing consumers and their credit agreements that distinguishes it from older focal points such as character. Risk represents an abstract technology, or sets of technologies, operationalized within particular techniques and practices of statistical credit scoring that came to be applied by lenders, unevenly and in a relatively unplanned manner, to the problem of reducing losses due to the nonrepayment of credit loans. To these ends, the attribution of risk signifies a generalized means of understanding, of grasping the nature of credit consumers with respect to the future.

As Les Levidow (1994) notes, contemporary discussions about risk have a pronounced tendency to reify the concept. Within credit therefore, the conceptualization and technical production of someone as a "risk" naturalizes the potential harm of default as an inherent property of the individual. However, as Ewald (1990, 1991) suggests, there is no risk in reality but anything can be considered as a risk, depending on how one understands the circumstance. The production of consumer credit as a profit-making enterprise within an advanced capitalist economy represents the binding of time, the location of such transactions in relation to a sense of the future, which because of the complexity of social life, the relative disembeddedness of transactions from social relations and a heightened dependence upon the self-governing potential of individuals, is permeated with uncertainty. As capitalism is built upon instrumental rationality and the capacity for foresight, risk, as a probabilistic analysis of the recursiveness of events within complexity, brings the future contingency of default and financial loss within the boundaries of consideration in the present. It makes the uncertainty of the future knowable in specific ways and thus incorporable within the calculated objective of maximizing profit. Risk, thus, represents the relations between people and a way of thinking about the future contingency of those relations, finding form in particular settings for the attainment of particular ends.

In this chapter I want to examine the emergence of the question of the population within American consumer credit and how its role as a new locus of analysis was bound up in new forms of consumption and new media of mass credit in tandem with the development of a collectively oriented Keynesianism. From the 1970s, a technocratic, statistical expertise gradually became applied by lenders to the problem of regulating default within populations of borrowers, exposing consumers to new kinds of visibility and making them amenable, as risks, to new kinds of government. Later this novel form of intervention was given official sanction by the state through legislation as a means of guaranteeing equality of opportunity to the market according to the individual's capacity for self-government. This capacity, naturalized and cohered as "objective" risk, removed it from the terrain of politics and thus from the possibility of political challenge.

Yet, as I will attempt to show, the use of technologies to constitute default risk are themselves seen to be subject to "risks"—methodological, procedural, and temporal—which degrade their theoretical and practical facility for distinguishing between populations of "good" and "bad" credit consumers. Such technologies are thus subject to a constant process of reflexive reevaluation and regeneration by experts seeking to sustain and enhance the discriminating efficacy of the models they produce as well as the seductive offerings of competing epistemologies promising alternative, more effective ways of constituting individuals as risks.

At the same time, the successful proliferation of credit scoring technologies among consumer lenders in determining default risk has led to its colonization of other areas of contingent decision making within the operations of lenders, stretching and rearticulating the meaning of risk in temporally, spatially, and functionally novel ways. The construction of individuals as risks has also become interlinked in a new fashion, as a partial antecedent and predicate, with other circuits of risk woven to enframe the uncertainties experienced by lenders and other institutions trading entire portfolios of loans encompassing a multitude of consumers and credit agreements.

Not only is the technical constitution of risk unstable but how risk is deployed represents an historically variable condition. Within the shifting figuration of the American consumer credit industry in the 1980s and 1990s, it is argued that the modality of such risk has become disjointed away from strategies of hierarchized avoidance by lenders to ones of polysemous engagement, from the treatment of risk as a cost to its deployment as a profitable opportunity. To these ends two recent practices are explored: the development of "profit scoring" technologies that subsume default risk as a constituent variable within a broader consideration of the profitability of the consumer; and the use of "risk-based pricing," the individualized setting of interest rates and other terms according to the specific risk represented by a consumer.

Consumer Credit and the Emergence of the Population

It has been argued previously that the twentieth century increasingly saw the facilitation of installment and charge account credit lines at large department stores and mail-order firms who had previously offered cash-only terms as the profitable opportunities presented, competition and the legitimization of installment credit through automobile sales conspired to render them more widespread. Within department stores themselves, specialized credit offices came to be established, tasked with the specific responsibility of managing credit applications in a systematic and ordered fashion. Potential applicants were interviewed and assessments of creditworthiness made on the basis of the perceived physical demeanor of the applicant—how "shifty," "evasive," "seedy," or "flashy" they looked (Jeacle and Walsh, 2002: 743, see also Rock, 1973). Specialized staff also examined the applicant's local neighborhood and made judgments as to its reputability, cross-referencing with local retailers to incorporate their appraisal of the individual's standing within the locality. In addition, existing credit accounts were maintained with a regularly updated written narrative as to the customer's perceived wealth, income, and personal circumstances. These assessment procedures, concentrating on a localized, qualitative perception of the borrower's "character" grounded within the intimacy of personal relations and community, acted upon an understanding of the individual as a concrete subject with an autonomous capacity for action (see Castel, 1991). In doing so, the possibility of default seemed to reside as an immanent, intrinsically uncertain aspect of the individual. Examining their physical attributes, inquiring as to their local status, recording the narrativized observations of staff members represented a discrete, individualized search for symptoms of an eventuality of default and an attempt to intervene to prevent its occurrence through the denial of credit.

This system, though, gradually gave way to a more rationalized, bureaucratic set of procedures during the 1920s and 1930s (Jeacle and Walsh, 2002). New innovations in record administration: the unit file, a systematic, permanent customer identification scheme, a tabulated coding procedure for categorizing customers and innovations in accounting techniques opened up the debtor to the individualizing gaze of the lender. This rendered their credit use more visible and malleable through a systematization of facts and numbers within a customer's written dossier. Similarly, within the operations of national mail order firms such as Sears and Spiegel's, assessments to grant credit increasingly came to be made on the basis of a calculated appraisal of questionnaires returned by potential customers governed through a standardized set of credit terms coming under the regulation of a specialist credit manager. This replaced, as we have seen, the use of local attorneys and investigators to assess the socially embedded, locally articulated character of the individual (Emmet and Jeuck, 1950; Smalley and Sturdivant, 1973).

Simultaneously then, through a totalizing gaze, the collective body of borrowers was made visible as a dynamic entity within itself, with certain norms of repayment present across its breadth that could be discerned and made known and against which the individual could be made subject for the purposes of controlling costs. Increasingly, then, a body of borrowers cohered, its attributes, extended balances and repayment streams becoming autonomous, self-referential phenomena within the firm's accounts. In consequence, new ways of recording data and understanding transactions within the firm, in addition to the greater reach of credit rendered for lenders the agglomerated body of consumers as a coherent entity. This body demonstrated attributes as though they were intrinsic to it, independent from the actions of the individual consumers that composed it.

The 1950s and 1960s, as discussed previously, represent the birth of a new form of mass consumer credit with provision dislocated away from specific retailers and even types of goods to the diverse, borderless domain of everyday, generalized consumption itself. This, in turn, widened the scope and possibilities of consumer choice. In a very pragmatic way, these emerging credit card providers epitomized a new industry paradigm of managing consumers as a population rather than as individual subjects. First and foremost, rather than extra sales or loyalty, their profitability depended on a percentage of a high turnover of low value credit purchases, both in terms of interest payments paid by consumers and the discount fees paid by affiliated retailers. It was not isolated acts of consumption enabled by credit that engaged the calculations of these new lenders but the sustained use of credit in and of itself. In this regard, as we have seen, the task that most preoccupied them was establishing a wide customer base. Without this, merchants would not be attracted to join the scheme while, in turn, consumers would not be drawn into a system where few retailers were willing to accept their cards. In dealing with such a large body, the administration of accounts was abstracted from the heuristic processes and "tacit knowledge" (Leyshon and Thrift, 1999: 441) that had previously characterized retailer-specific credit accounts and dealt with bureaucratically by way of simple application forms with a limited number of tightly categorized variables on each individual customer (Mandell, 1990: 56). Within this agglomeration of a large customer base, individuals were no longer acted upon as subjects. They became instead an accretion of limited variables and attributes, bureaucratically accumulated over time and assessed with reference to the distribution of those attributes across the population of customers.

With the mid-century adoption of Keynesianism, mass consumption by the population came to dominate the governmental calculations of the American state in relation to the economy, a consumption increasingly mediated through plastic credit to ever finer levels of expenditure. At the same time, the growth of a profit-oriented, specialized consumer credit disembedded from the intricacies of personal relations and specific sites of consumption was becoming implicated in the facilitation of a generalized, ascendant mass consumption. The profit goals of these lenders, where revenues were generated as a particular percentage of the individual low value/high volume credit transactions they facilitated, became more directly mapped onto the total volume of consumers they could enlist and consumer credit they could generate. The economic exigencies of this new generic credit nurtured a bureaucratic administration of limited, categorical, quantified data such as occupation, neighborhood, balances, and repayment history. As a result, the breadth and color of detail on each customer, characterizing older credit forms, faded relative to a new depth and specificity of data on the whole population of such consumers.

Constructing Risk, Objectifying Equality, and the Ghost of Cause

In 1941, the first known formal application of a specific statistical "imaginary" to the problem of controlling the incidence of consumer credit default was carried out by David Durand on behalf of the National Bureau of Economic Research (Durand, 1941). The particular methodology he used, discriminant analysis, had been developed by the statistician Gary Fisher (1936) in order to determine population differences where the explicit differentiating quality was not visible—he succeeded in deducing different varieties of iris and origins of skulls by their physical measurements. In Durand's case, applying this abstract statistical technology, he analyzed a selected sample of historical loan accounts at a range of institutional creditors including commercial banks and a variety of specialized finance companies. What he demonstrated was that groups of "creditworthy" and "uncreditworthy" borrowers, defined in probabilistic terms as to whether they would or would not default on a specific credit agreement, could be adduced in advance from an analysis of certain attributes demonstrated by those individuals. Analyzing his case-study samples, he formulated numerical decision rules that could theoretically be applied to new applicants for credit (Durand, 1941: 83–91).

A series of scholarly exercises by other researchers followed at a variety of different types and scope of creditor, each attempting to formulate a particular "credit scoring" model using actual, historical credit data and retrospectively demonstrating how the model in question would have reduced, anywhere between 7 percent and 24 percent, the number of bad loans that were actually accepted at that creditor had it been in operation.[2] Within these academic exercises, the possibility of governing credit sanctioning decisions by risk was demonstrated through the construction of a model embodying certain understandings on the part of the statistician. These included the ascription of thresholds, the categorization of the application data, the definition as to what constituted default and how the length of the credit agreement was to be defined. Against an accumulation of actual historical data including application details and the performance of credit agreements during their lifespan, these derived models ascribed certain statistical relations between attributes and repayment outcomes, which when applied to individuals, produced a predictive, probabilistic statement as to the calculated likelihood, or "risk," of default.

As we have seen before, expertise operates a key role within "government" in its widest sense, the knowledge from which it derives its authority, grounded in neutrality, disinterestedness, and claims to efficacy as distinct from the argument and rhetoric of politics, becoming harnessed in various ways within its exercise. Thus statisticians and consultants, exerting title to a scientific and technical knowledge, became employed as experts in the construction of technical models for the identification of risk. Their claims as to the objectivity and efficiency they could provide promised lenders new possibilities for the governing of consumers. They created norms in terms of risk around which could be ordered the population of consumers, thereby opening up default across the population of consumers as something to be rendered calculable in the interests of profit. For lender management, scoring technologies came to provide a nexus threading together commercial considerations of the default costs threatened by individual consumers, the operational costs of the firm encompassing the whole field of customers and the standardization of credit sanctioning procedures engaged by the lender's credit sanctioning staff. Scoring and the process of constituting risk thus came to provide the lender with a new means of understanding and conjoining the government of individual consumers, its population of customers and its rank of employees (Lewis, 1992b).

From the 1950s, with economic governance by the state effected through the management, en masse, of the capacity of its citizens to consume, the ability to engage in consumption constituted a crucial manifestation of one's membership of society as a free individual. However in the 1960s and 1970s, marginalized groups such as Blacks and women, increasingly agitating for equality through the civil rights movement and second wave feminism, articulated specific demands for the end of discriminatory practices within consumer credit, which often curtailed the ability of these social groups to access credit (Hiltz 1971; Garrison 1976; Cohen 2003; Williams, 2004). After hearings held by the National Commission on Consumer Finance to investigate the discrimination experienced by mostly married women in applying for credit, the Equal Credit Opportunity Act of 1974 (with subsequent amendments) was enacted to outlaw discrimination in credit sanctioning based on the characteristics of gender, marital status, race, national origin, religion, or income source (ECOA, 1974; Anonymous, 1979; Hsia, 1979; Elliehausen and Durkin, 1989; Chandler, 2001). To this end, credit scoring was encoded in "Regulation B" of the act, explicitly delineating what could constitute a statistical model by defining it as one based on the analysis of key applicant attributes and default based on statistically representative sample groups—anything else was residually termed a *judgmental system*. The act effectively gave legislative recognition to scoring systems as being objective, scientific devices permitting a dispassionate, empirically derived account of creditworthiness and explicitly identified the role they could play in eliminating "subjective" discrimination and helping to bring about an enhanced mass consumer credit market that would discriminate only on merit.[3]

Through the objectivity produced in scoring, bound to a necessary consideration of consumers as risks within the context of a population, the act gave impetus to creditors to deploy statistical models as a means for defending against suits for unlawful discrimination in credit granting. The scientific-statistical-empirical framework of scoring thus allowed lenders to claim that all credit decisions were made in line with the "real" creditworthiness of the credit applicant and not some inherent discrimination or prejudice. In addition, with scoring objectified within a document-based bureaucratic system, the creditor could demonstrate irrefutably, through the presentation of the bureaucratic procedural audit trail through which the sanctioning decision was accomplished, that it was arrived at in a "legitimate" fashion (Bunn and Wright, 1991: 509; see also Campbell, Roberts, Rogers, 2008). Thus, in a certain sense, it is not just the "scientific statistical" nature of the scoring endeavor based on its consistency of application and correct weighting of predictive variables that forges the seeming objectivity needed for impartial sanctioning decisions. Important also are its rigorously documented nature and amenability to audit (Dawes, 1999; Bunn and Wright, 1991). As Rothstein, Huber, and Gaskell (2006: 93) remark, risk provides a "defensible procedural rationality" not only in terms of managing the objects that an organization is tasked with regulating but also the wider institutional threats that the organization experiences. Risk thus becomes not merely an expedient means of determining whether to grant credit, but of minimizing the legal threat of its decisions not to do so.

The multifarious judgments and subjective decisions that go into the creation of quantified risk systems and underlie every single determination of risk are, in Rose's (1999, 2002) words "blackboxed," rendered hidden and incontestable by the apparent simplicity of the single figure that is generated. Yet, as both Porter (1992, 1995) and Rose (1996, 1999) observe, reliance on the apparent objectivity of numbers occurs not when the institutions are strong but when they are weak, beset by challenges to their ability to govern. Therefore, by camouflaging its subjective design, considering individuals not as individuals but as arrays of categorized attributes, demonstrating a verifiable relationship between these variables and certain outcomes and creating a quantified probabilistic statement that can be demonstrably audited, the deployment of credit scoring creates individual creditworthiness as something that exists as though it were something real, independent of its measurement.[4]

The facility that credit scoring offers to the question of discrimination is the treatment of individuals, not as subjects, the bearers of particular aptitudes or moral qualities but as objects, agglomerations of particular quantifiable attributes. In doing so, scoring undercuts the coherent identity of being female or black within which oppression or marginalization is experienced. It displaces credit decisions onto an array of discrete characteristics or attributes seemingly innocent within themselves and seemingly individually predictive of repayment performance, independent of subjective will. Yet power divisions, inequalities, and exploitation are inherently bound within society; their worst excesses may be alleviated through legislation and the nurturing of credit scoring, however, within a system that individualizes responsibility for the opportunity to consume, their effects cannot be eliminated if a profitable, extensive system of consumer credit in its current form is to exist. One's position in the social structure does indeed predicate whether one has the ability to repay credit.[5]

Pete McCorkell, a representative of risk scoring design firm Fair Isaac, defends credit scoring against charges of discrimination against minorities by arguing that detractors are asking the wrong question (2002: 214). Although scoring results in higher reject rates for certain groups, he argues that this is because "income, property, education and employment" structural factors he sees as bearing upon an individual's capacity and propensity to default are not evenly distributed across society. In fact it would be irrational, he suggests, for an objective measurement of risk *not* to demonstrate systematic risk discrepancies under such conditions. However, it is "social" and "political" questions that such discrimination raises rather than "technical" ones. Whether some kind of "affirmative action" should be put in place to favor minority groups is a question that McCorkell reserves for political consideration, albeit one he admits to being unthinkable in the current political climate.[6]

Nevertheless, the production of objectivity through the elimination of the question of the subject and its re-situation across disparate, independent variables creates a counter problem, and source of dissent, in terms of a loss of a coherent sense of cause (Johnson, 1992: 21–4). Despite its disavowal of cause in practice and its concern simply with counting the calculable effects of default (Lewis, 1992a: 6–7; Thomas, 2000: 152), risk rests uneasily with how individuals experience the world as subjects. Dawes (1999), a researcher in the field of economic psychology, argues that individuals are more or less incapable of acting solely on the basis of objective probabilities, that there is always a need for a causal explanatory narrative to justify or explain relations between variables. Without such a narrative, a statistical relation will tend to be rejected or ignored, especially if there are alternative intuitive explanations or it clashes with prevailing cultural beliefs.

Concern with the effects of "brute-force empiricism" informed Capon's (1982) trenchant denunciation of scoring systems where he argued that credit decisions should be confined to variables that have an "explanatory" bearing on repayment outcomes rather then a "statistical" one. The treatment of individuals simply on the basis of statistical correlation, he believed, offended against cultural traditions of individual responsibility and due process. More recently sociologist George Ritzer (1995), in an extension of his famous neo-Weberian "McDonaldization" thesis, has criticized credit scoring systems for their degrading potential and their celebration of the virtues of calculability over human meaning and understanding. On a practical level, with rejected credit applicants being statutorily entitled to know the "reasons" for the refusal of their application, the implementation of a risk system is constrained by the degree to which it can be contextualized within an explicatory framework. Therefore, by law, it cannot be enough to say that there is an abstract statistical correlation between an attribute and likelihood of default—a refusal decision framed by credit scoring must be couched in terms that make it intuitively comprehensible to the applicant (Chandler, 2001: 47).[7]

Risky Risk

From the 1970s, particularly with the wider dissemination of the credit card among American consumers, the development of computing power for statistical modeling and the electronic storage of records, credit scoring technologies were progressively deployed by lenders so that the sanctioning of new credit to new consumers increasingly became framed within a discourse of risk. In 1990, 82 percent of banks had adopted credit scoring mechanisms (Rosenberg and Gleit, 1994: 606) while today the technology is seen to be virtually ubiquitous within the consumer credit industry (Makuch, 2001a: 3–4). Yet, analysts of credit scoring present this not as a straightforward, unhindered rational adoption by lenders—on the contrary, it is put forward as a narrative of the persuasive triumph of the unquestionable efficiency of risk scoring over the relative inefficiency of human "judgmental" decision making. On one level, this is presented as a straightforward quantitative superiority—for example, its discriminatory potential is estimated to be 20–30 percent better, thus increasing the number of profitable customers accepted and decreasing the number of costly defaulters (McCorkell, 2002: 213). Yet it is not only in elevated revenues and dampened costs that the use of risk is adjudged to prove its worth but in the wider efficiencies that it imparts to the lender's organizational operations. To these ends, credit scoring is deemed transparent, consistent, uniform, unbiased, less labor intensive, and automatable. In addition it is time-saving, thus lowering the attrition levels of lost customers experienced while also providing a close calculable management control over lending policy (see for example Lawrence, 1992: 76–7; Jennings, 2001; Makuch,

2001a: 3; Glassman and Wilkins, 1997: 54–5; Rosenberg and Gleit, 1994: 590; Leyshon and Thrift, 1999: 445; Avery et al., 2000: 523).

Scoring, though, had not only to face the problem of effectively constituting individuals as risks, it also had to "gain the acceptance of the credit community" (Lewis, 1992a: 19). In this account of the "mercurial outsider," statistical and operations research experts battled the regressive conservatism of lender managements, historically wedded to judgmental decision making as the traditional means of sanctioning credit, to convince them of the progressive potential that credit scoring offered (p. 10–11). For instance, on the website of score modeler Fair Isaac noting "milestones" in the company's history, one of the early events recorded in 1958 was when the company "sends letter to the 50 biggest American credit grantors, asking for the opportunity to explain a new concept: credit scoring. Only one replies" (Fair Isaac, 2006). Yet, that one reply from American Investment Corporation provided the humble launch pad for Fair Isaac to prove the irresistible benefits of credit scoring (Lawrence, 1992: 74). But, while a discourse of risk may have eventually triumphed over this managerial rearguardism to become the preeminent means of conceptualizing consumers in relation to default, the technologies through which risk itself is constituted are seen by experts to be subject to a permanent process of failure, contestation, and regeneration. The rivalrous claims of competing methodologies, or even epistemologies, of risk must also be contended with.

The conceptual and operational basis upon which scoring models are built and deployed is subject to a permanent reflexive analysis. This seeks not to dissolve the framework of statistical scoring methods but, on the contrary, to improve their potential discriminatory power in practice by rendering more accurately the predictive risk determinations of particular cases of default that they attempt to formulate. However, failure is endemic to the government of default through risk for the underlying ontological assumption is one of indeterminism and irreducible stochasticity; although certain regularities can be seen within the population, the future actions of any one individual are not only not known but are inherently *unknowable* (Knight, 1971; Hacking, 1990). The effectiveness of a credit scoring model can thus only be judged macroscopically on how well it distinguishes, at the level of the population of consumers and across numerous cases, the distinctive sub-groupings of "good" and "bad" consumers.

A credit scoring model's efficacy at distinguishing these sub-populations is seen itself to be subject to numerous "risks," which interfere in its effective constitution of default risk.

First, *methodological risks* attach to specific techniques used in the construction of models: discriminant analysis may be seen to suffer from the assumption of equal covariance and normal distribution within the population sample while logistic regression may be particularly prone to analytical difficulties if the sample size is insufficient (for example, Rosenberg and Gleit, 1994: 594; Lee and Jung, 2001).

Second, *procedural risks* attach to the specific construction of a model. Most critical here also is seen to be the problem of "sample bias" (for example Lewis, 1992a: 41–2; Glennon, 2001: 245–52; Hand, 2001). Credit scoring is based upon the bureaucratic archived repayment history of the creditor, which inscribes the collective against which any individual is deconstructed and assessed in terms of risk. However, by definition, that recorded history will only be composed of those consumers who were accepted in the past and thus is not representative of the whole range of applicants that the creditor will encounter in the future. Another issue is seen to be that of an excessively homogenous population (Avery et al., 2000). A large creditor deploying a scoring model across a large territory with an homogenous conception of population cannot take into account regional economic characteristics and thus evident regional sub-population differences. Therefore, while the model may be predictive overall, it records relatively inaccurate risk scores, that is, an inappropriate ranking for individuals between regions.

Third, *temporal risks* pose a threat to the integrity of a scoring model's risk determination (for example Glassman and Wilkins, 1997: 55; Hand and Henley, 1997: 525; Lee, 2001). Conceived as the problem of "population drift," the correlations calculated between variables used to make risk predictions are fixed within the model but change and alter over time "in the real world" of the population.

All these risks—methodological in terms of the statistical technique to be used to animate the empirical data, procedural in terms of the technical process of crafting the model and temporal, by virtue of the dynamism and naturalism of populations—are perceived to affect the ability of a formulated credit scoring model to distinguish groups of good and bad borrowers, deplete the accuracy of the risk assessment made at an individual level and degrade the efficiency of the lender at producing profit. At any given threshold, more costly defaulters will be accepted and more profitable consumers will be refused credit. In response, the experts who elucidate these risks simultaneously offer means for obviating them: by formulating new techniques to improve predictive accuracy, establishing benchmarks for deriving representative samples, detailing how multiple scorecards can be deployed to account for regional and population variations, suggesting "reject inference" techniques to estimate the probabilistic fates of historically rejected consumers and advocating the implementation, in association with lenders, of practices of periodic model validation and revision. Therefore, within credit scoring, the construction of the constitution of risk is thus never taken for granted but must be constantly evaluated, maintained, and recreated in order to preserve the integrity and reliability of such constitution.

In terms of the constitution of risk, however, not only have statistical models been problematized but they have been challenged by alternative epistemologies that have found some application with the domain of consumer credit, including decision tree and neural network systems (Boyle et al. 1992; Thomas 2000; Malhorta and Malhorta 2003). Nevertheless, these competing alternatives do not engender a fundamental challenge to the discourse of risk around which the sanctioning systems of creditors are built. In fact, as Gruenstein suggests, any credit risk evaluation system is implicitly a statistical one (2001: 182). Each technology, in practice, seeks to know better the risk adhering to an individual applicant within the context of a population, to more accurately represent it in order to reduce the overall incidence of default endured by the creditor. In essence, the use of any one of these diverse techniques is assembled around the same ontological conception of what risk means. Although they differ by offering alternative avenues for knowing that risk, they share a common objective which is to more accurately render it as an objectified quality of the individual. Each, too, is concerned with the calculable effects of default, not "causes." In every case, default is conceived as an inherent aspect of the group and individuals are persistently conceived as agglomerations of attributes that are historically, probabilistically associated with a repayment outcome. Like more conventional statistical techniques, all of these alternative methods are predicated on failure. As the occurrence of default is conceived as being integral to the group and all attributes presented by all individuals are integrally related to a greater or lesser effect with default, then default remains inescapably uncertain at an individual level (see Kavanagh, 1993: 15–7).

At the same time, none of these alternatives provide a clearly dominant paradigm for the construction of risk in terms of exhibiting an agreed discriminatory superiority in the practice of making credit decisions (Hand and Henley, 1997: 535–7; Makuch, 2001b: 138–9; Thomas, 2000: 160–1). Not only are they bound to a common conception of risk, none represent an advanced coherent rationalization of the problem of knowing risk for each rival appears to confront its own autonomous technical dilemmas in the process of creating risk. Where as risk technologies are presented as an advance upon traditional judgmental sanctioning processes, assessable through a discourse of efficiency that measures its superiority in terms of greater calculability and accuracy, lower costs and higher revenues, competing risk technologies are locked into a discourse of relativism. For instance, a logistic regression model might be more predictive than a discriminant analysis but it is vastly more difficult to compute and implement in practice (Lee and Jung, 2001: 217). Similarly, a neural network might be good for modeling from a small number of cases but its key strength of mapping hidden relations in data renders it impenetrable to an intuitive explanation as to why a customer was determined to be an excessive risk—a statutory requirement under federal law in the United States (Malhotra and Malhotra, 2003: 93).[8]

Proliferating Risk

Through the strategic deployment of an array of technologies to mine their recorded history of lending to a population of credit consumers, consumer lenders have come to conceive of future default contingencies by new credit customers within a discourse and apparatus of risk. But, with the entrenchment of credit scoring within commercial practices of consumer credit, the idea of risk has also come to colonize aspects and domains of the lending process within and beyond the original problematic of determining the creditworthiness of new customers. In doing so, it extends the scope of risk as well as rearticulating other contingent areas and events of the lending process through its rubric. The development of credit scoring, as a system of risk, has also innovated and facilitated the treatment of conditional losses experienced by a lender across its portfolio of consumers, producing imaginative new connections between the "micro" risk of the individual credit consumer and the "macro" risk of a portfolio of such consumers.

Risk Colonization

With the advent of new technologies of so-called behavioral scoring, the concept of default risk becomes temporally unbounded. Rather than just assessing a defined, fixed notion of risk before the credit agreement commences ("credit scoring" becomes more aptly termed "application scoring"), the deployment of risk comes to be extended within the post-sanctioning phase in order to encompass the ongoing management of the account by the creditor (Coffman and Chandler, 1983; Hopper and Lewis, 1992; Thomas, Ho, and Scherer, 2001). With application scoring, the ascertainment of an applicant's objectified risk is implicated in the decision as to whether to accept them or what interest rate and restrictive conditions they should be assigned. However, with behavioral scoring, the applicant's risk is monitored on an ongoing basis through the systematic incorporation of new information as to how the applicant performs. This serves to frame a lender's contingent decisions on whether to renew a credit card account, adjust credit limits, target marketing efforts for other products, or submit a delinquent account for collection.[9]

A second crucial dimension of credit risk colonization has been the spatial extension of risk through the construction of bureau-based "generic" scoring models (Poon, 2007: 297–300). In 1989, the scoring consultancy firm Fair Isaac developed a risk scoring model based on the consumer credit history data held by the credit bureau Equifax; by the 1990s, it had extended the formulation of the risk model to the two other national credit bureaus, TransUnion and Experian (Chandler, 2001). Whereas such data had been used by lenders within their own "customized" risk models, the creation of the so-called FICO® model transformed risk scores into a commodity. It could be bundled with individual credit reports sold to lenders who were unwilling or unable to formulate risk scoring models of their own, or it could be incorporated as an element within their own customized risk systems. In either case, the marketing of FICO transformed risk from a discontinuous, variable attribution generated within the bounded population of a creditor's customer base into a standardized, continuous measure of risk constructed within the context of the wider national population; FICO became an enduringly standardized measure of risk permanently absorbing the repayment attributes of millions of credit consumers and updated dynamically across the entire field of consumer lenders.[10]

Finally, a third avenue in the colonization by risk has been its transplantation into other functional areas of contingent decision making within commercial consumer finance. Just as credit scoring transforms the uncertainty of repayment into a calculable risk, the application of statistical modeling attempts to transform relative operational uncertainties in such areas as mortgage lending, segmented marketing, debt collection, and fraud avoidance into similarly numerical probabilities. These can be incorporated into a more efficient organization of those domains. Other operational decision processes beyond new consumer credit sanctioning thus become reconfigured through the framework of risk, with expert designed empirically derived models discerning statistical associations between an array of individual variables and observable events modeled in order to reconstruct decisions on the basis of risk eventualities (Gosh and Reilly, 1994; Stanghellini, McConway, and Hand, 1999; Straka, 2000; Jost, 2001: 198; McAllister and Eng, 2001).

From Micro to Macro Risk

Even across a stock of credit agreements, uncertainty is never rendered completely calculable by the application of credit scoring (Jacobson and Roszbach, 2003: 627). The use of statistical modeling by a lender attempts to calculate the future quantified probability of default of an individual consumer, thus rendering the total anticipated costs of default across an array of customers as calculable and predictable. However, inappropriate modeling, the dependence of risk scoring on extrapolation from the past (which as we have seen, can be buffeted by such factors as unaccounted population drift or market specific conditions) and the simple perils of chance, which can impact upon overall default rates in any given year, all conspire to render levels of default imperfectly calculable at a macro level. In consequence, uncertainty appears as a seemingly irreducible aspect of consumer credit.

During the mid-1980s, a process known as "securitization" grew to encompass stocks of consumer loans (Watkins, 2000: 922; Barth, 2002; Johnson, 2002). This involved consumer credit providers packaging their inventories of credit agreements as tradable assets that could be sold at a price discounted on the basis of future revenue flows accruing to the credit agreement. The price would also be reflective of the level of risk underlying these new assets. Although arising initially for stocks of auto installment loans, loans with fixed predictable repayment schedules, the most recent growth within consumer credit has been in tranches of credit card debt. In this, the five major credit card providers—Bank One, MBNA, Citibank, American Express, and Morgan Stanley Dean Witter (Discover Card)— comprise 70 percent of the market for so-called credit card "asset-backed securities" (Johnson, 2002: 288). Although maintaining responsibility for servicing the repayments from consumers, large credit providers such as banks have been able to remove stocks of debt from their balance sheets, raise fresh liquid capital on the basis of such illiquid assets and lower their stock of non-interest bearing reserves required under transnational banking regulations. Employing a battery of instruments known as "credit enhancements," securitizing firms have also been able, independently of their own corporate risk profile, to explicitly isolate and channel the level of risk presented by the portfolio that they are offering in order to minimize the premium needed to attract investors. Particularly in the case of auto loans, lenders have also been able to offload the majority of the macro-level risk presented by this stock of loans to the investing institutions.

It has been argued that the creation of such securities, carefully calibrated for risk in terms of the likelihood of revenue and default losses across the portfolio exceeding a certain anticipated amount, is inherently connected to the proliferation of credit scoring mechanisms within consumer lending (Glassman and Wilkins, 1997: 55; Guseva and Rona-Tas, 2001: 632; Makuch, 2001a: 17–8; Barth, 2002: 311–12). In consequence, the deployment of risk systems that construct risk determinations at the micro level of an individual consumer set within the context of a population become intimately connected to, and a necessary precondition for, the construction of a higher order of macro risk expressed at the level of the portfolio itself. This has enabled stocks of debt to be sold and traded as assets at a price premium tailored to its level of risk exposure.

Deploying Risk

Some authors (Simon 1987, 1988; Feely and Simon, 1992, 1994) have viewed the use of risk and the deployment of statistical techniques as being indicative of a broader shift in the characteristic form of power being exercised at large in society, from discipline to actuarialism. Actuarialism is characterized by the increasing pervasiveness of abstract risk systems concerned with the management of populations. However, as O'Malley (1992, 1996, 2004) argues, risk systems are deployed in particular contexts for the resolution of practical quandaries within which they are enfolded. Within consumer credit, risk is a technology that is deployed in a diversity of ways and settings for a multitude of ends. Scoring systems are not modeled and executed within generalized social conditions encompassing the increasing diffusion of actuarialism, imposing itself as a linear rationalization in the exercise of power. Rather, they are brought into being within the relatively localized environs of specific creditors for the achievement of more or less cognizable goals. This is not to say that the creation of credit risk does not have its own discursive intensity and dynamism but its adoption and the purposes for which it is put are not uniform. The overall strategic objective behind utilizing a risk technology is not to capture more exactly the risk of individual default presented by credit applicants but to make them visible and knowable as risks in particular, variable ways within the context of the population. The purpose ultimately is to govern them toward the achievement of certain objectives. But what are those objectives?

Profit Scoring

The original development of credit scoring systems held likely defaulters as "high risks" whose probable failure to repay constituted a potentially burdensome cost to lenders. Through the hierarchized attribution of risk to credit applicants, the technocratic dreams of efficiency that scoring promised were that the excessively risky could be isolated and managed through the denial of credit. However, the 1980s and 1990s saw significant changes in the market for consumer credit, particularly in the field of credit card lending. These changes involved a greater emphasis on marketing and branding by Visa, MasterCard, and American Express, the emergence of new products like the American Express Optima card and Montgomery Ward's Discover card, the playing out of the effects of deregulation on interest rates and industry structures leading to the arrival of nonfinancial institutions like AT&T and General Electric to credit card provision and the emergence of new "monoline" banks specializing in the targeted marketing of credit cards to different profiles of consumer (Evans and Schmalensee, 1999; Klein, 1999; Manning, 2000; Millman, 2001). Against this backdrop, as we have seen, credit card ownership proliferated over broader swathes of the consuming population with possession among all American households increasing from around one-sixth in 1970 to over two-thirds in 1998. In the same timeframe, although continually stratified by income, card possession increased most markedly for the lowest income groups, from a low base rising fourteenfold to 28 percent (Durkin, 2000).

This "democratization" of revolving credit in the form of the bank credit card helped reorient the way that risk was to be deployed and acted upon. Traditionally, mail-order firms, finance companies and others involved in the sanctioning of credit had experienced risk as loss. However, the evolving form of plastic credit manifested a concern with consumer credit as a profitable enterprise in its own right, divorced from the sale of particular goods bound within fixed locations of time and space. Implicated within the perpetual, fluid, more self-governed consumption of goods, it heralded a shift away from credit as a discrete instrument of purchase to the regularization of debt as a continuous, lived experience of consumption. This, combined with the standardization of an interest-free grace period, displaced how risk could be understood. Whereas consumers who carried balances month-to-month paid interest on their debt, those who paid off their balances in full each month essentially paid nothing—earning the moniker of "deadbeat" within industry parlance due to their lack of profitability, even costliness (Manning, 2000: 294). Crucially now, deadbeats were no longer those who were excessively risky but those who were excessively *safe*. This transformation altered the way risk could be conceived; it might no longer be represented hierarchically, as something to be isolated and minimized. On the contrary, risk might now be embraced in a lateral government of credit users, as something positive and productive, conducive to market share and profitability (Graney and Wynn, 1992).

As a result, the seemingly straightforward prioritization given to the identification and minimization of default risk by credit scoring experts has been distracted by a range of problematizations in the complex contemporary credit market (see Rosenberg and Gleit, 1994: 592–3; Hand and Henley, 1997: 525; Jacobson and Roszbach, 2003: 626–7). For example:

- Although a customer might be deemed an unacceptable risk at a given time period, refusal to grant credit might interfere with potentially profitable credit agreements with that customer in the future.
- Forms of credit such as credit cards may be more profitable for customers who are a higher risk when interest charges, fees, and penalties are taken into account.
- The costs of misclassifying good and bad applicants are not constant; for example, a defaulted loan may be reclaimed through the use of a collection agency or may need to be written-off, with obvious implications for profitability.
- If a lender offers a portfolio of credit products, it may be profitable overall, through cross-product subsidization, to accept a relatively high risk applicant for one product if it opens marketing opportunities

to offer them another although, complicating this, there is no guarantee that the customer will necessarily accept the offering of a future credit product.

If the simple isolation of high risk consumers has become subordinate to a range of more diffuse goals in terms of lender profitability, this does not represent the eclipsing of the role of statistical expertise and scoring technologies within consumer credit. On the contrary, the problematizations outlined above along with advances in computer modeling and electronic data retrieval have incited something of a transformation in the nature of credit scoring itself. As Thomas (2000) charts, there has been a recent shift away from models based on the determination of default toward the introduction of profit scoring models that explicitly aim to calculably optimize profitability independently of the minimization of default risk. Crucially, this increases the complexity of data management, necessitating the regard for a whole array of new factors such as marketing, service-levels, organizational operations, and pricing across the breadth of the creditor's operations. In effect, with the deliberate attempt to target profitability, the risk of default becomes simply one variable to be included within a more diffuse actuarial form of decision making within the lender organization, breeding the development of more complex modeling techniques (for example Carr and Luong, 2005; Crowder, Hand, and Krzanowski, 2005). The systematic determination of default risk continues but under conditions whereby that risk is subsumed and integrated into another, wider and more complex determination of risk—the risk that the credit consumer will be unprofitable to the lender.

Risk Pricing

Although default risk becomes subsumed within new techniques of profit scoring, the development of new risk pricing techniques denotes an alternative avenue for the deployment of risk. We have seen up to now how creditors have come to utilize scoring techniques in order to produce a risk assessment of individual applicants from which a fixed threshold serves as the decision rule of acceptance or rejection.[11] However, the development of "risk pricing" within the consumer credit industry during the 1980s displaced this binary conception of accept/reject with a continuum where interest rates and agreement terms are set according to the particular level of risk attributable to the applicant. The higher the risk presented, in general, the higher the interest rate imposed on the credit product by the creditor, ostensibly, to compensate themselves for the differential costs of default presented by differential categories of risk (Makuch, 2001a; Edelberg, 2003; Chatterjee, Corbae, Ríos-Rull, 2005).

Dean argues that the use of risk in such a form renders it a continuum rather then a break, or in his memorable phrase, it "does not divide populations by a single division so much as follow the warp and weft of risk within the population" (1999b: 146). There are no longer single population demarcations but rather categories of risk—the rejected are no longer the inverse of the accepted but are subdued as a residual category deemed too risky, even with the attribution of high interest rates. Although the population as a whole remains the primary locus of risk, risk now becomes deployed to allow the targeting of sub-populations, the population as such becoming managed not as a mass but as a spectrum. A similar process of what is termed "risk unpooling" or "segmentation" has recently become evident in the domain of private insurance. Rather than the "socializing" of responsibility (Baker 2002), private insurance firms are now motivated toward producing ever-finer discriminations of risk among their populations of policy holders in order to individualize responsibility while maintaining the exclusion of the excessively costly (Ericson, Barry, and Doyle, 2000).

Edelberg (2003) contends that credit risk pricing only became more common in the mid-1990s in the United States as more sophisticated risk modeling techniques and lower computerization storage costs made such a process practicable. He notes that since 1995 risk-defined premia have increased for numerous types of consumer credit, most prominently, automobile loans, and credit cards. The extension of risk based pricing is related to the profit motivated expansion of consumer credit, allowing as it does for market growth in two directions: individuals who were formally excluded for being unacceptably risky are now included at a higher price, even among conservative creditors, while individuals who were formerly included are now offered credit at a lower price and so are given the potential to consume more of it. Risk pricing is thus seen to enhance the general welfare—rewarding the low risk with low rates and allowing the high risk the opportunities of credit formerly denied to them (Johnson, 1992: 28; Edelberg, 2003: 20–1; White, 2004: 503–4; Dynan and Kohn, 2007: 18).

Perhaps one of the most high profile outcomes of risk based pricing for consumer credit within the United States has been the emergence of the so-called subprime market. With the development of more sophisticated scoring models, some creditors, due to the perceived saturation of the mainstream credit market for good risks, began to specialize in differentiating between "bad" risks, offering credit to the more acceptably risky with restrictive terms including high interest rates, low credit limits, collateral deposits, and swingeing penalties and fines (Gilreath, 1999: 150–3). Among the most infamous of the subprime lenders was credit card provider

Providian, one of a new breed of monoline banks that emerged within the United States during the 1990s:

> Providian may not have invented sub-prime lending, but it certainly perfected it. The company's genius was in segmenting people based on financial behavior. Founded in the mid-1980s and originally called First Deposit, Providian created a [scoring] system that made it possible to find the "perfect" credit card customer: someone who cared more about low minimum monthly payments than high interest rates and who would pile up debt but would rarely default. "We found the best of the bad," says a former executive. (Koudsi, 2002: 2)

Providian's rapid expansion in the late 1990s, assisted by favorable economic conditions and low employment, led it to becoming the fifth largest credit card provider in the United States and one of the most revered companies of Wall Street for its uninterrupted earnings growth. This had the effect of spurring more established competitors like Capital One to copy its subprime practices. Here, entrepreneurialism, represented as the development and deployment of a superior scoring technology combined with the foresight, verve, and skill to embrace a particular market segment that more established competitors were too "risk averse" to countenance brought what seemed like just rewards for the company: spectacular increases in earnings, market share, and equity return (Millman, 2001: 105). Its business success was clouded however by accusations of predatory lending, illegal collection practices, and exploitation, leading to class-action suits and company settlements of $300 million. By the end of the 1990s, economic downturn and consequential risk overexposure drastically curtailed the subprime market, almost destroying the acutely risk-exposed Providian. As such, Providian perhaps represents the emblematic cautionary tale of neoliberalism, that taking risks for reward implies the very real possibility of failure and loss without restitution if greed for success overtakes one's capacity to entrepreneurially manage those risks.[12]

A similar "down-market" process is discerned by Ericson et al. (2000) in their analysis of the contemporary insurance industry. They argue that risk segmentation is simultaneously a process of risk assessment and marketing. The more sophisticated deployment of risk does not mean excluding bad risks—on the contrary, the diffusion of a more complex risk assessment is characterized by a greater level of incorporation of individual consumers within its market fold. This occurs through firms either pricing different levels of risk or concentrating on a particular risk niche market. "Substandard" risks may be profitable once they are adequately priced, no alternative exists and the insurance coverage is compelled. They cite the example of a motor insurance firm that deliberately marketed itself to high risk consumers, profiting handsomely from the high premia it charged, a lack of competition, its restriction of coverage payments and the high interest rates it charged on installment payments.

Risk pricing and the emergence of the subprime markets in credit and as well as other markets demonstrate the new ends to which risk is being deployed. Before, the attribution of risk was used to exclude those deemed more likely to add to costs than to revenues, manifesting as a bifurcate division between the acceptably and the unacceptably risky. However, in a competitive consumer market propelled by profit, this simple division gives way under such techniques as risk pricing to an inclusionary impulse. As with profit scoring, rather than the "risky" being suppressed they are actively engaged with the attribution of risk serving not to locate and divide but to define and price. In a sense, there are no longer bad risks, only unentrepreneurial lenders with inferior or badly leveraged risk technologies resigned to the saturated, low-profit prime markets. The expansion of capital thus leads to an increased downward targeting of consumers with more and more being integrated, on differential terms, leaving only a residuum of excluded, nonconsumers. As with the problematizations and potentials presented by the targeting of profitability, risk pricing cannot simply be reduced to some unilinear, rationalizing process of "actuarialism" or even the manifestation of a practical response to a capitalistic profit motive on the part of lenders. Rather, risk pricing coalesces from the articulation of new forms of expertise and profit with new ways within which individuals, as consumers, can be understood and acted upon as risks.

With this new potential, the identification of risk comes to be used to adjust the price of credit to the particular, discrete self-governing potential of all consumers so that the availability of choice wrought by credit is restricted to their calculated ability to uphold the freedom to choose. Risk pricing ensures that the individual is made culpable for the costs of their own risk and those who share it through a segmented pooling of the similarly risky. They are thus made responsible for their own capacity as a consumer, for the consuming costs and horizons of opportunity implicit in their individualized projects of consumption. "Deserving" consumers pay less (Makuch, 2001a: 16) while, by implication, "undeserving" consumers pay more. Like O'Malley's (1992, 1996, 2000, 2004) conception of the "new prudential" individual who, under newly contrived governmental arrangements, must exercise their own careful, individualized choices in defense against "risks" like illness and unemployment that were formerly distributed across the social body, contemporary credit consumers are made responsible for the risk that they themselves represent. Consumers are obliged to take ownership for the condition of their own lives and the choices that they have made in the past determining their credit consuming potential in the present.

* * *

Within the United States during the 1920s and 1930s, the population emerged as a locus of analysis for lenders offering credit for consumption. The development of credit accounts at department stores and mail-order companies became intertwined with new administrative technologies and accounting procedures at the level of the firm, displacing the borrower as an individual subject whose distinctive "character" augured an uncertain potentiality of default, with financial flows, attributes, and rates of default as constitutive elements of the wider customer body.

Against the backdrop of the postwar consumption boom of the 1950s, a new form of mass consumer credit developed in the credit card; unconnected for the first time with any specific form of consumption, its profitability was inherently bound to its own perpetuation within generalized consumption, implying new forms of population management by lenders as well as a greater reliance on the self-governing capabilities of the consumer. Such plastic credit, in expanding the scope and reach of credit within the everyday lives of consumers, regularized a more or less permanent state of indebtedness. At the level of the state, a new economic policy of Keynesianism elevated collective mass consumption over production as the critical lever of economic growth—deficit spending echoing personal indebtedness in the promotion of consumption. At this time statistical techniques began to give a novel articulation to the problem of identifying nonpayers and reducing the costs associated with default across a lender's population of consumers. Credit scoring, the analysis of statistical relationships between variables and default outcomes within a population thus became applied to the governing of sanctioning decisions by these mass lenders, rendering credit applicants visible and governable in new ways as risks.

With the establishment of the Equal Credit Opportunity Act, programs of credit scoring received official state sanction as "objective" instruments for the determination of creditworthiness and were thus encouraged as a means of ending discrimination within lending. Through the idea of risk, the act naturalized creditworthiness as a capacity of the individual, reflecting risk's more general reification of phenomena as "real" properties of the world. Of course, the deployment of risk itself could not lead to the easing of structural inequalities within society—rather, they became depoliticized, divorced from an oppositional identity, hidden and rendered incontestable within the equations of the expert's model. However, the neutralization of the subjective created a disparity between the opportunity to consume and one's lived experience, fostering opposition to the "iron-cage" treatment of individuals and protests as to the reduction of "human qualities to abstract quantities" (Ritzer 1995: 141).

Systems of risk, however, do not simply disperse through the consumer credit industry according to their own interminable logic as more rational, more efficient means of governing consumers. On the contrary, credit scoring technicians have retrospectively portrayed lender managements of the past as Luddites, organizationally wedded to outdated inefficient methods of judgmental decision making before their inevitable submission to the tide of progress offered by credit scoring. More crucially, though, the systematic statistical constitution of default risk is itself perceived by its experts as being beset by a perpetual array of risks that require the constant reappraisal of methods and procedures and the periodic renewal of models within which risk assessments are created. The very success of a risk discourse in conceiving and governing the problem of default has led to the imaginative investment of its technologies in new ways and in new areas within the operations of lenders. This fragmented its cohesiveness by rearticulating it through an unbinding of time, a broader more continuous reach across the population and a penetration into other areas of contingent consumer management such as debt collection, marketing, and fraud detection. In certain specific ways, the calculation of individual default risk has also become interconnected with a higher order of risk conceived and systematized around the governance of uncertainty and loss experienced at the level of an entire portfolio of consumers and their debts.

Not only are systems of risk open to risks and continuous reevaluation and the concept of risk subject to fragmentation through its application to new practices but the risk determinations constructed within models are themselves invoked by experts and lenders in new and shifting ways. Before, risk embodied a negative connotation with lenders identifying the tolerably risky as the threshold for determining whether the individual was to be sanctioned credit. Although varying from lender to lender, the idea of a single risk threshold denoted a simple binary division between the included and the excluded, the (relatively) safe and the intolerably risky. However, against the backdrop of a dynamic market and the increased emphasis on consumption in the formation of identity, risk assumes a positive status as an attribution to be entrepreneurially assumed and profitably exploited.

Within consumer credit, this has taken one form through the incorporation of default risk within a statistical determination of the profitable credit consumer. Here, the subtext of risk changes, from that which is potentially dangerous and to be avoided to that which is too safe and unconducive to financial return. Elsewhere, the centrality of default risk to the government of credit consumers persists but in a form that increasingly responsibilizes the individual for the costs of their own self-government through the adjustment of interest rates and other terms to the specific identification of risk. Here, the idea of a single risk score representing a single checkpoint to an homogenous collective becomes dissolved onto a spectrum of risks enveloping a segmented market. What was avoided before as bad risk becomes sought after as a high return, growth-fuelled dynamic market segment, as distinct from a safe, sclerotic, "middle of the road" market. Costs, formerly socialized by a single, common interest rate are now individualized, turned upon those segments each according to their due.

At the time of writing, the profound dangerousness of governing through risk has become evident. The American mortgage market has been beset in recent years by rampant house price inflation, the growth of credit scoring, and the development of a subprime market—practices developed initially within the consumer credit market. This, combined with the expansion of mortgage debt securitization to the subprime market, has conspired to form a "credit crunch" that has had such a devastating effect on the global economy in 2008 and beyond. For our purposes here, this indicates the profoundly contingent and uncertain nature of using risk to govern and how risk itself moves and mutates. Credit scoring, subprime risk pricing, and securitization are each predicated on the belief that default and loss can be maintained and managed. Yet, the losses from individual default within the subprime market ceased being risks and became reality, bursting the seams of expected, calculable loss. But, thanks to securitization, such unanticipated losses were now no longer the sole preserve of those lenders who had made the loans. While predicated on the isolation of risk, the slicing and dicing of vast portfolios of debt had the opposite effect, channeling the subprime risk—and ultimately the costs of default—everywhere in such a way that it could not be avoided. In consequence, financial institutions savagely curtailed inter-bank lending, financial activity and confidence plummeted, the entire Western financial system faced ruin, and many national economies lurched into recession. In attempting to extend, intensify, and broaden the governing possibilities of risk in the interests of ever-greater and unsustainable levels of profit, a nuclear reaction occurred. In a confluence of events, the risk of a group of uncreditworthy homeowners defaulting on their mortgages transformed into the risk of another Great Depression.

CHAPTER 8

Borrowing on the Fringe: The Fate of the Risky

With the deployment of sophisticated risk technologies, the question arises as to the fate of the "excluded," that risk residuum deemed to lack the responsibility to pay for their own risk; "what to do about those not in a position to aspire (legitimately) to the seductions of commodities—the unemployed, the incompetent, the criminal and the dispossessed?" (O'Malley, 1994: 213). It seems that no matter how risk is drawn, deployed, or acted upon, it creates a permanent bifurcate division between those that are tolerably risky and those that are not. Even with the proliferation of risk-pricing techniques within which the risk of default loss is compensated by higher interest rates and the development of a viable subprime market wherein higher risk consumers may be profitably targeted, the very continuance of risk as a conceptual and technological tool within consumer credit presupposes a residuum. These underclass consumers are, it seems, fated to remain beyond the reaches of a mainstream credit market so dependent for its profitability on the capacity of free consumers to govern the permanent cycle of desire, fulfillment, disillusionment, and new desire so intimated and facilitated by credit. As acutely observed by Valverde (1996: 361), liberalism's claim to universal freedom has always been tempered by its absence in reality, demonstrating not so much its hypocrisy as an essential aspect of its constitution. Similarly, for Bauman (1988), freedom is a permanent relational state, defined against that which is unfree and coerced.

Within consumer credit, the "acceptably risky" are those identified who can be trusted to achieve a stable equilibrium between the ongoing fulfillment of their consumerist desires with the responsibility of timely repayments. As we have already discussed, risk is a relational construct; it embodies no intrinsic meaning except as part of a quantitative hierarchy. A consumer is only more or less risky than any other consumer. Therefore, risk always implies the possibility of excessive risk, those whom are seen to be unable to exert the necessary self-government, those who are conceived as being unable to achieve the necessary balance between the hedonism of credit-enabled purchases and the puritanism of regular, interminable monthly bill payments.

But how is such exclusion achieved? Of course, unstable employment or insufficient income may be obvious attributes that weigh heavily in formulating a low credit score for an individual. But within the contemporary consumer credit market, the ability to self-govern is most clearly and coherently evidenced by one's credit identity, the inscribed history of one's credit use and notable failures in repayment. As we have seen, credit reports create an objectivized history of the consuming subject, a real-time "data-double" dynamically reflecting and determining the possibilities of self-governed credit consumption. Through the assemblage of credit reporting, exclusion manifests two avenues. On the one hand those with no history of credit use, in particular, the poor, the young, and recent immigrants, are unable to fabricate a credit identity and thus, from the general prospective of creditors, are unable to demonstrate a viable potential to govern themselves. Its absence thus embodies their exclusion and becomes a double-bind perpetuating their marginalization within credit markets. On the other, those demonstrating histories inscribed with payment delinquencies, defaults, collection actions, court judgments, or bankruptcies are bound to an identity that actively demonstrates for creditors, through the empirical predictive framework of risk, the incapacity of that consumer to effectively regulate their future selves. These too are fated to remain outside the marketing sphere of mainstream credit providers.

Bankers to the Poor

Despite a general state of exclusion from mainstream consumer finance, however, such consumers are not excluded from the possibilities of credit consumption. Rather, the types that they do consume exhibit a structure and form that make no effective claims to, nor depend for their profitability upon, the self-governing abilities of these consumers. In practice, they do not deploy technologies of credit scoring constituting individuals as risks nor feature as junctures within a national credit reporting assemblage which derive and calibrate the consumer's capacity to self-govern. These lenders are known as "fringe," "second-tier," "high-cost," or "non-status" lenders, such labels explicitly distinguishing them from conventional banks, credit card firms, and finance companies, their perceived presence beyond the mainstream reflecting the persistent exclusion of their clientele as much as the features of their operation.

Within the contemporary American market, there are three main types of fringe-lenders that can be identified: pawnbrokers, payday lenders, and rent to own retailers.

Pawnbrokers

These are the historical successors to the nineteenth-century forms examined in chapter 1 with the general function of the pawn transaction remaining the same—a small amount of money is advanced on the temporary pledge of personal items that are later redeemed on repayment of the amount advanced with interest (Johnson and Johnson, 1998; Karger, 2005: 66–72; Peterson, 2004: 18–21; Caskey, 1991, 1994: 37–54, 2005: 26–30; Caskey and Zikmund, 1990; Oeltjen, 1989, 1990). The most commonly pledged items of value are jewelry, electronic equipment, cameras, musical instruments, and firearms. Traditionally, pawnbrokers have been regulated at a state and municipal level through the statutory specification of such terms such as maximum monthly interest rate and additional fees, licensing and bonding requirements, transaction and forfeiture procedures, oversight authority, and inspection contingencies (Oeltjen, 1990: 234). According to Caskey, effective interest rates, including fees, on an average size loan can vary from between 36 percent to 355 percent per annum (1994: 40) while he estimates that, although pawnshop loans represent significantly less than 1 percent of outstanding consumer debt, around 10 percent of the American population may have recourse to regular pawn transactions as a source of credit (1990: 49).

Following a steep decline since the 1930s, the number of pawnshops has increased dramatically since the 1970s to around twelve thousand nationwide, with such growth concentrated mainly in Southern and Central states (Caskey, 1994: 47–9, 2005: 27). However, in the last few years, pawnshop numbers have declined relative to the increasing popularity of payday lending (Caskey, 2005: 27–8). One significant recent development, though, has been the emergence of so-called car title loans as a variant on pawning (Quester and Fox, 2005; Fox and Guy, 2005). These are high-value loan transactions secured on the basis of title or possession of an individual's car, with principal and interest payable at the end of a single monthly period; in the event of nonpayment, of course, the lender claims ownership of the collateral. According to Fox and Guy, the regulatory system for title lending varies nationally with certain states authorizing high or no interest ceiling title loans in some form, others enforcing lower cost title loans, and the rest regulating the industry under general usury or small loan rate ceilings. Interest rates for these types of loan are believed to average 300 percent per annum including fees (2005: 5–10).

Payday Lenders

Payday lenders tend to be examined as a subset of the check cashing industry, which itself is often framed against the wider problem of access by poor and minority groups to mainstream banking facilities and the relatively expensive commissions charged by check-cashing firms (Caskey, 1994: 54–78, 2005: 31–40; Mullen, Bush, and Weinstein, 1997; Squires and O'Connor, 1998; Manning, 2000: 205). Check cashers, as their name suggests, are essentially commercial offices that offer cash in exchange for government, payroll, or private checks, charging a variable commission to the individual for the service. The rate of commission is often dependent on the perceived risk of the transaction, with higher commission charged for personal checks more susceptible to bouncing. According to a Consumer Federation of America (CFA) survey, commissions for pay checks average 2.34 percent of the check's face value, for Social Security checks, 2.21 percent, and for personal checks, 9.36 percent.[1]

Payday or "deferred deposit" loans, a relatively recent innovation from the latter half of the 1990s, represent an increasingly available additional service offered by check-cashing firms and others. In a payday loan transaction, a customer writes a personal check to the lender held as security or postdated with the individual's date of wage payment. In exchange, the borrower receives the amount agreed for which the check is drawn less a fee representing the loan's interest payment (Squires and O'Connor, 1998; Manning, 2000: 205–8; Wiles and Immergluck, 2000, Peterson, 2004: 10–18; Caskey, 2005: 17–26; Stegman and Farris, 2003; Elliehausen and Lawrence, 2001). On a two-week $100 loan, a 2001 CFA and Public Interest Research Groups (PIRG) report found average equivalent annual interest rates of 470 percent nationally, rising to an average of 780 percent APR in Massachusetts and New York (Fox and Mierwinski, 2001: 12–13). Estimated numbers of payday lenders have risen from insignificant levels in the early 1990s to around 14,000 major offices, lending anywhere between $8 and $14 billion to approximately 15 percent of American households (Stegman and Faris, 2003: 9). Recent variants on such loans include so-called refund anticipation loans where a discounted loan is advanced by a lender, in this case usually one of the main commercial tax preparation service firms such as H & R Block or Jackson Hewitt, for a period of between seven to fourteen days, secured on the basis of an individual's anticipated federal tax refund (Wu, Fox, and Woodall, 2006).

Rent to Own Centers

This form of lending represents a reactivation of the old British concept of *Hire Purchase*, designed to legally mask a consumer credit transaction under the guise of a lease agreement. Rent to owns are essentially specialized retailers that lease goods to consumers over a defined period of time, at the end of which the consumer assumes legal ownership (Manning, 2000: 208–9; Swagler and Wheeler, 1989; Martin and Huckins, 1997; Hill, Ramp, and Silver, 1998; Peterson, 2004: 21–5; Lacko, McKernan, and Hastak, 2000, 2002). However, each payment increment is autonomous so the consumer endures no legal obligation to continue with payments until the end of the agreed period. In the event that payments cease, the rental agreement may be terminated with possession of the good reverting to the retailer. Fulfilled ownership rates from rent to own agreements are uncertain with estimates by the industry itself of 25–30 percent contrasting with alternative findings of between 60–70 percent by independent studies (Lacko et al., 2002: 128).

Goods provided by rent to own are, in the main, home appliances and electrical equipment such as televisions and computers but also includes such items as home furniture and jewelry. At the end of the 1990s, it was estimated that there were around 7,500 such outlets nationwide dealing with some 3.5 million customers and generating industry revenues of $4.5 billion (Martin and Huckins, 1997: 385). In not generally being recognized as forms of credit, rent to own transactions are not specifically governed by federal or state credit laws, such regulation being effected in the vast majority of states through their framing as lease agreements. However, courts in several state jurisdictions have ruled that rent to own transactions are credit sales and thus subject to the requirements of state credit statutes (Lacko et al., 2000: 3). As a rental form, there is no explicit specified interest rate, with the cost of payments embedded within the weekly or monthly charge—in this, a 1997 PIRG survey found that rent to own good prices were between two and five times that of conventional retailers producing implicit annual interest rates of around 100 percent.[2]

Credit Consumption on the Fringe

What is particularly striking from the foregoing description of fringe credit forms is the enormity of the interest rates being charged. Compared with prime mortgage interest rates of 4–6 percent and credit card rates of 15–25 percent, fringe lenders exact enormous annual equivalent interest rates stretching well into triple figures. Industry apologists point to the relative small size and short-term nature of most loans and the relatively high administrative costs, which require lenders to charge high interest rates in order to produce a profit. Detractors accuse the industry of gouging the poorest members of society who, often in desperately perilous financial circumstances, have nowhere else to turn for stop-gap loans and whose lack of education makes them particularly susceptible to questionable lending practices (Caskey, 2005: 18–19). They point also to the continuous exploitation of consumers whose marginal existence means they often cannot repay the amounts owed and must continuously roll-over the principal, paying even more interest to service what they cannot pay off (Karger, 2005). It is obvious that such lenders exert a considerable hold over the poor, profitably extracting large amounts of interest from those least able to pay it. Indeed, it is particularly ironic that banks who themselves exclude risky borrowers have been partnering with payday lenders in order to share in the buoyant revenue streams of the industry (Fox, 2004).

What is interesting, however, is the degree to which fringe borrowing becomes a site for the reactivation of old dilemmas, arguments, and quandaries. We saw previously how the loan sharks and low grade installment lenders of the nineteenth century were similarly accused of exploiting the most needy individuals. Similarly, advocates for the legitimization of consumer borrowing pointed out the necessity of higher usury ceilings for consumer loans relative to general commercial loans given the former's relatively small size, short duration, and high risk. In the 1960s, David Caplovitz's (1963) path-breaking sociological study *The Poor Pay More* revealed the high rates of interest and duplicitous sales practices experienced by individuals and households living in disadvantaged communities. As such, what questions of usury and exploitation expose beyond themselves is the anxiety that society permanently feels toward the poor and the destabilizing effects perceived to be attached to their consumption and credit practices. At the same time, the responses and interventions called forth to alleviate their difficulties indicate much about how the state, and other sites of power, comprehend the task of government.

Pawning, payday lending, and "renting" represent distinctive forms of credit; yet they are bound by common features that collectively both characterize and distinguish them from conventional consumer financing. Numerous studies indicate that the young, low and moderate income earners, renters, the relatively poorly educated, and Black and Hispanic ethnic minority groups are the predominant consumers of pawnbrokers (Caskey, 1994: 68–73; Caskey and Zikmund, 1990: 6–7; Johnson and Johnson, 1998: 37–50), payday lenders (Squires and O'Connor, 1998; Wiles and Immergluck, 2000: 5–7; Fox and Mierzwinski, 2001: 5–6; Elliehausen and Lawrence, 2001: 28–32; Stegman and Faris, 2003: 14–15), and rent to own retailers (Lacko et al., 2000: 31–4, 2002: 132; Hill et al., 1998). Spatially, too, such types of lender are calculated as being generally overrepresented geographically within poor and minority neighborhoods (for example, Graves, 2003; King et al., 2005) as well as in districts with military bases containing ready supplies of low-paid, "vulnerable" military personnel (Graves and Peterson, 2005).

At the same time, though, these lenders do not represent a marginalized form of enterprise commercially. Like the chattel and salary lenders of the late nineteenth century, contemporary fringe lenders have expanded through chain and franchise networks but, unlike these, they have been very heavily capitalized in doing so (Karger, 2005: x). The most striking example has been the success of Cash America Investments, which expanded from a group of four Texas pawnshops to become a publicly quoted company in 1987, later achieving a listing on the New York Stock Exchange in 1990. In 2005, it operated 464 pawnshops across 21 states under the Cash America and Super Pawn brands as well as 286 payday advance offices with total gross revenues of over $594 million.[3] Within the rent to own industry, the NASDAQ listed Rent-A-Center, founded in 1986, has emerged as America's leading rent to own retailer with 2,775 stores and 297 franchises across the United States, Canada, and Puerto Rico and corporate earnings in 2004 of over $2.3 billion.[4] Payday lenders have also forged operational connections with mainstream, nationally chartered banks that allow these lenders to evade state usury and other loan ceilings: by operating legally under the umbrella of the bank, they can lend on the basis of the rate ceiling pertaining to the state in which the bank has its headquarters (Fox and Mierzwinski, 2001; Fox, 2004).

Fringe lending represents not the antithesis of consumer credit, a fading legacy of the past to be eliminated through the colonizing impetus of banks and credit card companies. On the contrary, its form and reach has expanded and developed in concert with the growth of mainstream consumer credit since the 1970s. Pawnshop numbers have expanded significantly, doubling their numbers alone over the course of the 1990s (Johnson and Johnson, 1998: 7). Rent to own stores more than tripled their number between 1982 and 1996 (Manning, 2000: 209) while the payday industry, only in existence in the latter half of the 1990s, has grown to perhaps as many as 14,000 major outlets (Stegman and Faris, 2003: 9–10). These lenders thus represent an inherent part of consumer lending, its logic of exclusion, its necessary dark side specializing in the poor and disenfranchised.

Interestingly, many commentators have pointed to the effects of market liberalization on the upsurge of fringe banking (Manning, 2000: 198–200; Squires and O'Connor, 1998: 7–10, Johnson and Johnson, 1998: 8–9; Dymski, 2005: 124–7). For instance, the Depository Institutions Deregulation and Monetary Control Act of 1980 removed interest rate ceilings on bank deposit accounts. Having previously subsidized artificially low interest rates with low or no account fees and charges, this deregulatory measure raised deposit interest rates but increased annual fees, minimum deposits, check cashing fees, and others costs associated with the operation of checking accounts. In many cases, this puts them beyond the feasible reach of low-income households. The Financial Services Modernization Act of 1999 ended New Deal-era restrictions on financial institution ownership, thus leading to industry consolidation, a pattern of branch closure concentrated in low income and minority communities and a greater orientation toward financial products tailored toward wealthier house-holds, again lowering proportions of poorer and minority families with ties to conventional banking institutions. According to the Federal Reserve, households without some form of bank account tended to be of "low incomes, to be headed by a person younger than thirty-five, to be nonwhite or Hispanic, to be headed by a person who was neither working nor retired, to be renters, or to have relatively low levels of wealth" (Bucks, Kennickell, and Moore, 2006: 12). Without access to conventional banking facilities, such segments of the population may be cut-off from their attendant credit facilities and to be drawn toward high-cost fringe alternatives. Under lib-eralization, then, fringe lending has expanded as the necessary "other" of consumer credit; the alternative commercial domain for the temporary res-olution of material necessity and transient realization of consumerist needs for those existing on the margins.

There is, however, no stark division between the mainstream and the fringe consumer. Jock Young (1999, 2007) argues that the identification of a binary division between an "included" majority and an "excluded" or "underclass" minority simplifies the complex nature of inequality, ignores the functional role played by the poor and underplays wealth and power divisions that exist across the supposedly included. In relation to fringe loans themselves, payday lending, for one, requires that borrowers main-tain a working checking account at a mainstream financial institution, thus blurring the boundaries between mainstream and fringe. The bound-aries are further effaced with the development of new credit forms includ-ing the subprime market discussed earlier and secured or preloaded cards—forms of credit that allude to a multitiered contemporary economy of credit (Burton, 2008: 71). Fringe borrowers themselves may well be members of what Karger (2005) calls the "functionally poor middle class" who possess reasonable incomes but whose excessive accumulation of con-ventional consumer debt and steep repayment schedules expose them to the risk of bankruptcy. As he remarks: "when their credit lines are exhausted, greater numbers will undoubtedly slide into more fringe economy services" (ibid: 36).

Complexity aside, the three main forms that fringe lending takes collec-tively manifest a lack of dependence upon the self-governing capabilities of the individual to maintain repayments. Each, rather, provides an alterna-tive set of external mechanisms that transcend the perceived lack of will of the consumer, coercing repayment or enframing action that alleviates or manages the risk of financial loss to the lender. Pawnbrokers, historically, have been the paradigmatic case whose loans are framed around the physi-cal deposit of valuable collateral that requires repayment with interest by the individual for redemption—or which is liquidated to satisfy the debt. Typically pawn loans are advanced to the value of half of what the item would achieve if it were sold, providing a calculable financial gain to the lender regardless of the contingent outcome. Nonredemption rates are estimated at between 10–30 percent (Caskey, 1994: 41–2). Payday loans are similar to pawn loans except that the form of collateral deposited, a personally drawn check, represents a more abstract, but more readily disposable, form of value in the event of default. Given this lack of intrinsic value, there is a greater marshalling of the actions of the individual upon which the value of the check is dependent. Unlike the other two forms of fringe borrowing, the individual must maintain a conventional checking account in good standing and exhibit a history of paycheck deposits in order to be eligible for a payday loan (Elliehausen and Lawrence, 2001: 54; Fox and Mierzwinski, 2001: 5–6). Finally, rent to own transactions are constituted on the basis of being a sequence of autonomous transactions with an ultimate outcome of ownership or return; such lenders thus always maintain legal ownership of the item until the end of the contracted "rental" period. In the event of default, the lender may at any stage claim repossession of the good to be leased in a new transaction as well as possession over whatever payments had been made (Zikmund-Fisher and Parker, 1999: 200).

Ironically, then, the most "risky" strata of consumers pose little effective risk to fringe lenders in terms of default (Karger, 2005: 11). Axiomatically, in engaging in a coercive government of credit consumers to regulate the risk of financial loss, fringe lenders are characterized by both a general absence of risk assessment technologies and referrals to credit reporting systems. As such, systems designed to assemble and calculate the self-governing potential of the individual are irrelevant when the actions being recorded are not free but, instead, are channeled through external constraints that obviate the risk of financial loss. It is for precisely this reason that Burton refers to these kinds of lenders as "non-status" (Burton, 2008: 76–9). In fact, this freedom from freedom is often the primary marketing line for fringe lenders, for example "everyone is preapproved . . . no credit is needed" (cited in Manning, 2000: 208). Meanwhile, the absence of assessment procedures is cited as a key motivating factor in the consumer's decision to borrow from these sources with such consumers having already been turned down for conventional credit or anticipating that they will be (Swagler and Wheeler, 1989: 152–3; Hill et al., 1998: 4; Elliehausen and Lawrence, 2001: 56; Johnson and Johnson, 1998: 67).

The credit use of fringe consumers is thus not assessed nor recorded and so does not form part of a formalized credit identity enveloping and framing future credit choices. As we have analyzed in chapter 6, objectivized credit identities trace the individual's process of self-narrativization through consumption, forming an accumulated, dynamic, historically constituted picture of the individual's self-governing abilities. In contrast, fringe borrowing is discontinuous and short-term, exhibiting no institutional memory of the individual's actions. Whereas bank loans and home equity lines of credit are measured in months and years, mortgages in decades, and credit cards indefinitely, or at least until the consumer finds a better offer, payday and pawn loans are transacted in fortnightly or monthly bursts. Even rental credit, calculated across contractual periods of 18–24 months, remains discontinuous, the actual obligation for payment extending no longer than the end of that week or month, each period autonomous and independent of the previous and subsequent one. Such discontinuity also describes the engagement of fringe loans. They exist not with a predictable regularity like a monthly credit card bill or a loan statement but at certain times of the years, in response to particular pressing events. As such, "the likelihood that recent [payday] customers will have an advance outstanding at any point in time varies according to seasonal factors" (Elliehausen and Lawrence, 2001: 47). In relation to Rent to Own, around 30 percent of items leased are not carried through to ownership despite the inherent loss of capital (Lacko et al., 2000: 56).

Fringe borrowing is far less about responding to desire within a process of personalized self-fulfillment, of tracing an inner self, a coherent story anchoring the subjectivity of the individual.[5] Rather, it represents a response to external pressures, of needing rather than wanting to borrow (if such a Veblen-esque distinction can defensibly be made). For pawning and payday loans, relatively small amounts of money are contracted at irregular times in response to unforeseen events. In Elliehausen and Lawrence's (2001: 47) study, two-thirds of payday loans were in response to "unplanned expenses" and to tide over a "temporary income reduction," with consumers often becoming ensnared in a continuous "rolling-over" of loans through the individual's inability to pay-off the amount owed in full (Wiles and Immergluck, 2000: 3–5; Stegman and Faris, 2003: 19–25). Caskey (1994: 70) similarly cites a 1990 survey by the New York Provident Loan Society where 81 percent of pawners indicated pressing circumstances or outstanding bills as the reason for borrowing. Even the seemingly discretionary expenditure of rent to own is circumscribed, like payday lending and pawning, by the individual's general lack of access to alternative credit forms.

In the consumerist market where the individual is tasked with the obligation to uphold the continuous, informed exercise of choice between different goods and services, fringe borrowers excluded from conventional credit exhibit no choice, have no alternatives to choose between. Politically and economically marginalized within society through poverty, underemployment and ethnicity, they borrow in order to pay utility bills or furnish their homes, reacting to threatening contingency and poverty of circumstance that disrupts and impinges the possibility of self-determination rather than acting according to the neoliberal virtues of autonomy and choice. Such borrowing manifests the relative unfreedom of attempting to overcome acute and chronic crises, of utilitarian necessity and curtailed resources, rather than the relative freedom of pursuing a flowing aestheticization of the self.

In Bourdieu's framework, the social class position possessed by individuals shapes and molds the level of their economic and cultural capital, their informational and symbolic resources, and the particular habitus or set of internalized dispositions that they demonstrate toward multiple fields of social life (Bourdieu, 1984, 1986; Bourdieu and Wacquant, 1992). However, as he suggests, the means of transmission of cultural capital remain hidden, its exhibition giving the appearance of a natural, unquestioned competence rather than one that is contingent. The position of the fringe borrower, their "choice" to consume various forms of fringe credit, is fundamentally rooted in the economic conditions which render them excessively risky in the bureaucratic assessment procedures of mainstream lenders and without much alternative to pawning and the payday loan for their often pressing needs. At the same time, their lack of economic capital conditions their lack of the specific cultural capital required to negotiate financial transactions with banks and other mainstream lenders. Their dominated economic position also conditions a habitus unconsciously predisposed to, at ease with and at home in the expensive, "irrational" forms of fringe borrowing objectively designed (small loans, short periods, fixed fee, no obligation, etc.) for those of their socioeconomic position (see Aldridge, 1998: 5). In a sense, where one (desperate?) individual sees a manageable $30 fee on an essential two-week $300 payday loan, another sees a horrendous annual equivalent interest rate of 260 percent. Thus not only is the exclusion of the poor accomplished actively, though technologies of risk, but passively, through their lack of informational resources and embodied "taste" for forms of credit that exacerbate and exploit their own poverty.

Transforming the Fringe Consumer: Rationality, Markets and Risk

With a presupposition of rational *homo economicus* attempting to maximize his or her scope to choose, analysts of the fringe borrowing phenomenon have attempted to grapple with the problem of why ostensibly rational individuals would choose to consume such punitively expensive forms of credit. In relation to rent to own leasing, Zikmund-Fisher and Parker (1999: 204–8) hypothesize that such consumers operate with sets of preferences manifested through their restricted choices ("price insensitivity"), a strong preference of present benefits against future costs, a desire for the imposed budget discipline of rental payments, and a high risk aversion that values the payment escapability of a lease contract (see also Swagler and Wheeler, 1989: 148–53; Elliehausen and Lawrence, 2001: 56; Bertrand et al., 2006). The rationality of fringe borrowers is thus shaped by the confluence of circumstances within which they are culturally and economically entrenched, in a fashion that distinguishes it from middle-class forms of rationality. In a similar but more overtly normative vein, Peterson (2004) argues that fringe borrowers, in general, consistently underestimate the problems of fringe debt, excessively value the present over the future, have cultivated a manifestly compulsive "addiction" to high-cost credit and resolutely fail to update their preferences in light of new information. As such, fringe borrowers are seen as individuals who are different from mainstream consumers. Their rationality has been pathologically distorted to the extent that exploitatively expensive forms of credit are chosen over cheaper alternatives (2004: 165–91).

Yet, this micro-economic analysis of a "relativistic" as opposed to an "impaired" rationality is really a discursive sleight of hand. In airily positioning fringe borrowers as making choices that are a function of particular economic, cultural, or social conditions, these conditions are solidified as an overwhelming determining cause of action, which somehow interpolate the individual, are solidified within them and forever after determine what and how they choose. Mark Granovetter (1985) calls this the "oversocialized" conception, which ironically, individualizes and atomizes in its explanation of economic behavior as much as the undersocialized view of the neoclassical economic paradigm. In such a fashion, the choices of fringe borrowers are explained in relation to wider causal factors, but in such a way that reindividualizes the explanation of those choices. Ultimately, then, their conduct persists in being perceived as the product of an inherited, flawed rationality.[6]

This, as we shall see shortly, plays out in the mode of intervention called for to alleviate the financial difficulties of such borrowers. Rather than a political solution concerned with the structures of society and attendant inequalities, it takes as its focus the need to "educate" and "enlighten" the choices made by them in conjunction with the installation of a contrived market mechanism to envelop the realization of those choices. Rather inevitably, the oversocialized account flatters the prejudices of neoliberal government, its preoccupation with the autonomous, enterprising subject, its valorization of the market and its repudiation of acting on poverty through the structures and solidarity of society.

In his analysis of fringe lenders, sociologist Robert Manning (2000) repeatedly emphasizes the vulnerability of fringe consumers. He posits that their poverty and lack of education make them particularly susceptible to the advertising siren calls of the fringe lenders offering opaquely costed credit with easy access terms and no credit check protocols or risk assessment procedures (2000: 209). Despite his sympathetic account of their plight, Manning's narrative of susceptibility similarly treats fringe borrowing as a form of deficient rationality. For instance, in vividly describing the sales strategy of rent to own retailers, he details how:

> The feeding frenzy commences immediately as salespeople befriend potential customers, assess their initial needs and desires, trump them with "special offers" for higher-quality products or models with "premium features," and then swiftly seal the deal with instant credit approval and same-day delivery and installation. *Unsuspecting customers*, especially those who have been frequently rejected for retail credit, *are overwhelmed by the slick sales pitches, personal flattery, and instant fulfillment of their consumer romance.* (2000: 214, my emphasis)

Embedded in the perpetual drudgery of poverty, afflicted with inadequate education and tasked with enduring an almost permanent exclusion from the consummation of a sensuous "consumer romance," the will of fringe consumers toward moderated consumption and deferred gratification is held to be severely compromised. Consequentially, this leads to their engagement of credit use that is not in their own ostensible best interest, either through the lost equity of unsustainable leasing payments or ensnarement within a permanent cycle of rolled-over debt that renders them trapped and helpless. Perhaps the most startling narrative of this absent will attaches to the rent to own industry that has been beset by lurid media reports highlighting the extremes of consumer vulnerability associated with this form of credit. These include harassment and threats, breaking and entering, even the solicitation of sexual favors (so-called couch payments, presumably by female debtors to male collectors) in lieu of payment in cash (Lacko et al., 2002: 128). Thus, steeped in the difficulties of material deprivation compounded by personal failing, resistant cultural values and the cynical ploys of lenders, the individual is seen to be locked into a dependence upon fringe borrowing through which they manifest and reinforce an impaired ability to exercise rational choices (Caskey, 1994: 78–83).

But what is to be done about fringe borrowing as a perceived social problem of exploitation? How are programmatic, ameliorative strategies of intervention framed by policy experts under the rubric of neoliberal government? One approach focuses on bolstering the rationality of the individual subject. In relation to the specific case of rental credit, extension of the Truth in Lending Act is sought. As we have seen earlier, the entrepreneurial autonomy of consumers became acted upon within the conventional credit market through the Truth in Lending Act, which mandated the disclosure by creditors, in a standardized fashion, of the dollar and percentage cost of any proposed credit agreement. The extension of this system of disclosure is advocated for rental consumers (Hill et al., 1998: 8; Swagler and Wheeler, 1989: 158; Martin and Huckins, 1997: 424; Lacko et al.,

2000: 89–97). In relation to fringe borrowing more generally, credit counseling and the promotion of individual financial literacy through targeted educational programs, which nurture and develop the choosing capabilities of consumers are proposed (Martin and Huckins, 1997: 424; Stegman and Farris, 2003: 28; Barr, 2002: 460–1, 2004: 236–7). Payday borrowers are themselves encouraged to shop around and compare costs, seek alternative cheaper forms of credit and enroll in a debt repayment plan with a credit counseling agency (for example, FTC[7]; Fox and Mierzwinski, 2001: 24).

Peterson, while advocating similar disclosure and protection measures, proposes the radical solution of actively testing a consumer's ability to understand simple credit agreement terms and calculations as a precondition for a borrower's receipt of a fringe loan (2004: 300–4). Comparing the "irrational" consumption of high-cost credit to the "irrational" decision to smoke tobacco, Peterson also suggests adding stark "financial health warnings" to credit advertisements and other documents in order to help match the individual's "purchasing preferences with their own best welfare" (p. 309). He sees such emphasis on safety rather than morality as an effective way to avoid the patronizing of borrowers—rather than being told borrowing is "wrong," they must be cautioned to be "cautious." From Peterson's perspective then, irrational, unrestrained borrowers must be heavy-handedly "persuaded" by a benevolent state to properly govern themselves in ways that are known to be in their own interest.

Other proposals focus on the formation of the fringe market itself and call for specific interventions to alter its functioning to ameliorate the conditions experienced by vulnerable consumers. Consumer Federation of America studies, in particular, have advocated the outright legal prohibition of payday lending based on personal check possession. They have also called for the elimination of legal loopholes that allow payday lenders to evade state usury, small loan and consumer protection laws by partnering with nationally chartered banks or by offering services across state lines through the internet (Fox and Mierzwinski, 2001: 24; Fox, 2004: 27–8; Fox and Petrini, 2004: 37). By highlighting a play upon the legal capacities of the state, the market itself can be seen to be directed in a way that protects fringe borrowers susceptible to its exploitative grip.

Beyond the individual and the fringe market itself, the conventional consumer credit market, and mainstream financial services industry more generally, are targeted as a domain through which marginalized, fringe borrowers might be inducted to become mainstream borrowers. Encouraging the opening of bank checking accounts is seen as a key site and locus point where contact can be established between the individual and the financial system through more flexible opening hours, the creation or better advertisement of low-cost checking account services including overdrafts, and the introduction or return of bank branches and ATM services to marginalized and minority communities (Caskey, 1994: 128–38; Mullen et al., 1997: 7; Squires and O'Connor, 1998: 10; Hermanson and Gaberlavage, 2001: 8–9).

The state too is seen to have a role to play through more stringent enforcement and a more effective formulation of the Community Reinvestment Act, which as we saw in chapter 5, attempts to encourage responsiveness by institutions to the financial needs of excluded communities within which they are geographically located (Squires and O'Connor, 1998: 11; Barr, 2004: 233–5). More recently, through a separate initiative in 2001, the Department of the Treasury established the "First Accounts" scheme that sought to provide government funds to financial institutions and organizations to subsidize the cost of providing electronic banking accounts and other services to low income individuals, as well as contributing to the provision of consumer education and counseling services (Barr, 2004: 222–3).

In a similar manner to the Treasury initiative but outside the ambit of the state, the National Community Investment Fund, a semi-philanthropic financial body created to promote investment within community-based financial organizations, fashioned the "Retail Financial Services Initiative" in 2003. This was a pilot scheme designed to promote access to financial services for low-income "unbanked" individuals through a group of participating banks and credit unions (NCIF, 2005). Through the initiative and in strategic partnership with community-based organizations, small emergency loans and forms of credit mirroring the structure of payday and tax refund anticipation loans were offered to consumers. Such rates and terms, however, were significantly less onerous than fringe alternatives. Yet, the provision of access to low-cost forms of credit provided only one side of the solution for these persistently "risky" consumers. Inherent to the scheme was a focus upon permanently changing the behavior, the rationality, of marginalized borrowers by way of lender-based education and counseling plans enveloping and developing the "whole customer":

> Though RFSI institutions work with customers many other institutions would consider high-risk, most would argue that customers who get into trouble with overdrafts or late loan payments rarely do so with fraudulent intent. Rather, they don't understand how financial products work and what the consequences of misusing them are. Or they simply have bad habits, and changing them takes time. Monitoring and early intervention are thus essential tools for both reducing risk and helping customers develop good financial habits. *It's not enough to give customers access to products; institutions have to help the customers use them prudently.* (NCIF, 2005: section 8.2, my emphasis)

Thus, through the actions of specific community and civil society groups, vulnerable fringe borrowers have been inducted into prototype or transitional alternative markets. Rather than being generated within the capitalist sphere for the creation of profit, these have been custom designed to protect and rehabilitate these marginalized consumers with credit forms designed to meet their small loan and credit needs at a significantly lower cost than those offered by the fringe market (see Stegman and Farris, 2003: 27–8 on credit union provided alternatives to payday loans and Hill et al., 1998: 8–9 on an alternative credit scheme offered in place of rent to own). However, with low-cost access comes the quid pro quo of obligatory credit counseling as a precondition of access, an interventionist scheme to permanently change their financial habits.

In initiating consumers constituted as risky into the mainstream market for credit and financial services as an alternative to exploitative, fringe lenders and check cashers, the latter's deployment of punitive interest rates and coercive forms of government are replaced by transitional credit forms. These mimic the functional arrangement of the fringe but are operationalized through mechanisms that improve or rehabilitate the self-governing capacities of the excluded. To make them self-governing requires the fabrication of a market alternative to allow them the continuous possibilities of autonomous choice. But it also necessitates the exertion of a close surveillance and pedagogic instruction that transforms them as subjects so that they might be able to comprehend what it means to regulate the self, or at least be persuaded of the need to exert a routine of good habits in the conduct of their financial affairs (cf. Valverde, 1996; Reith 2007). The possibilities of choice thus require that the right sorts of choices be made.

In an interesting scheme reported by Bertrand, Mullainathan, and Shafir (2006), a North Carolina Credit Union offered a Salary Advance Loan program mimicking the period and size of payday loan provision but secured instead on the deposit of the individual's future salary payment. Built into the scheme was an obligatory "Cash Account," an interest-bearing savings account, into which was forwarded 5 percent of the value of each loan advanced. By despotically enforcing good savings habits through the use of credit, the rationality of the individual is braced in ways that are understood to be ultimately beneficial for them. Like a child being inveighed to eat their greens who grows up to find a meal without a vegetable portion to be wanting, it is hoped the imbuing of good habits will lead to a permanent transformation in the way the individual makes free choices in relation to borrowing and saving.

At the beginning of this chapter, it was argued that technologies such as credit reporting and risk scoring systems calibrate and measure the self-governing abilities of credit consumers. In doing so, they reflect and shape their pattern of access to mainstream credit sources and systematically exclude pools of consumers unable to exhibit such a narrative of disciplined consumption. For these, the discontinuity and coercive regime of fringe borrowing remains the only credit alternative to sustain the household through emergency and fulfill the miraged longings prompted by consumption. However, just as they serve as the locus of exclusion, both the credit reporting assemblage and technologies of credit scoring represent manipulable possibilities for inclusion. Rather than transitioning such manifestly "risky" borrowers to mainstream alternatives or acting to augment their will to promote sustainable credit choices, technologies of surveillance and risk may be deployed in a fashion that alters the constitution of individuals as risks in order to ostensibly recognize their potentially secure, "true" self-governing natures. This has been codified as the problem of "underserved" or "thin file/no file" market segment encompassing the young, immigrants, the poor, and minority groups:

> Those with low income and who are left out of the credit system have a difficult time building assets. To a considerable extent this is because they cannot borrow. They have a hard time borrowing because there is far too little information on their credit history to predict risk. Note that this is true of those consumers with "thin-files" who are credit risky as well as those who are creditworthy. (IPI, 2005: 5)

Therefore, because credit reports inscribe creditworthiness through the surveillance of particular types of information, certain groups (particularly minorities and recent immigrants) are systematically and persistently excluded. This exclusion encompasses not just credit but all those marketed services, including insurance providers, employers, and tenants, which make consumer access dependent on the content of a credit report. In the field of credit reporting, the Information Policy Institute (IPI) advocates the inclusion and reporting of "alternative data sources," such as telecoms, utility, and rental data that have "credit like" characteristics and the assessment of which might be statistically predictive of future credit actions. In such a fashion, the credit bureau Experian has begun collecting an array of just such alternative data from checking accounts, landlords, payday lenders, and money transfer companies. The aim is to assess the logistical feasibility of collecting such information and to empirically test its statistical predictiveness of credit default (Tescher, 2006). Meanwhile, the credit score modeling firm Fair Isaac has developed a scoring product known as the "FICO Expansion score®." This produces risk attributions for credit sanctioning decisions based on alternative and other data sources available to the lender, as opposed to the traditional FICO system's dependence on credit reference bureau data (Horan, 2005).

This is not, though, about providing indiscriminate access to credit for those who are poor or marginalized but, rather, about enhancing the technologies of the market in order to identify the "underserved's" effectively self-governing sections—those who pay their phone and electricity bills as fastidiously as a conventionally creditworthy consumer pays their credit card bill. By technically adjusting how objectivized credit identities are inscribed and readjusting the empirical terrain of risk assessment scoring systems, narratives and calculations of self-governed consumption can be systematically conjured into existence for situating lending decisions. Potentially, underserved "deserving" consumers can be absorbed through the boundaries of the market, promoting not only profitable consumer credit use but the consumption of other services, employment, mortgage credit, and the possibilities of asset-building inherent in homeownership. Thus from the potentialities of market involvement stem directly the promises of a wider inclusivity.

Social Inclusion and Marginalized Consumers

Within Europe, a discourse of "social exclusion" is seen to have become central for framing governmental intervention in the alleviation of poverty and social fragmentation (Levitas, 2005; Byrne, 2005; Young 1999). With a transformation of emphasis from equality to "equality of opportunity" and social rights to "social responsibilities," paid work and education have become the primary malleable programmatic vehicles through which a "multi-dimensional" poverty—cultural, political as well as economic—is to be acted upon and the lowest strata "integrated" into the rest of society. In Britain, the specific effects of exclusion from mainstream financial services whereby poor consumers are reliant upon relatively expensive door-step moneylenders for access to credit has been documented by historians, policy experts, and social scientists (Rowlingson, 1994; Kempson and Whyley, 1999; Taylor, 2002; Leyshon et al., 2004a, 2004b). Here, it has been shown how such strategies as rigorous weekly collections, community familiarity, and the deployment of "friendliness" allow lenders to govern the borrowing and repayments of these consumers.

While the concept of social exclusion currently has much less currency within the United States, the more narrowly focused issue of exclusion from financial services has gained attention (for example, Bradford, 2003; Dymski, 2005). Within the foregoing analysis of the overlapping problems of fringe borrowing and exclusion from mainstream financial services, the usual suspects have persistently appeared: the poor, the young, ethnic minorities, and immigrants, a heterogeneous underclass located within territorialized communities spatially and socially cut adrift from the rest of society. They are, as Bauman describes them, "flawed consumers":

> people unable to respond to the enticements of the consumer market because they lack the required resources, people unable to be "free individuals" according to the sense of "freedom" as defined in terms of

consumer choice. They are the new "impure," who do not fit into the new scheme of purity. Looked at from the now dominant perspective of the consumer market, they are redundant—truly "objects out of place." (1997: 14)

But society does not condone such "objects out of place." The question remains, then, as to how are they to be "tidied" in the framework offered by neoliberal government? Although identified and located as explanatory variables, their social conditions and the structural features of their expropriation do not serve as the site of intervention or amelioration. Rather, expertise articulates the problem as a discrete dimension of social exclusion—the "unbanked," the "credit underserved"—and frames intervention through the relation of these groups to the market for credit and financial services and through the ways that these individuals are understood to make choices. Whether by way of the legislative power of the state, the beneficence and enlightened self-interest of financial organizations or the pragmatic localism of community-based groups, the targeted individual is to be subjectively conditioned; in concert with debt counselors and personal finance advisors, they will be equipped with an augmented capability to exert an autocratic self-regard over the sustainability of their consumption practices and credit choices.

At the same time, the objective conditions and context within which choices are made are deliberately and multifariously engineered through programs of market regulation, "transitionary" credit forms and mechanisms more responsive to the specific conditions of marginal consumers that steer the limits of what can be chosen. Here, the market represents less a site for the mutual fulfillment of interest than a malleable tool, or set of tools, for ensuring maximum personal choice. Yet, what both have at their core is a concern with developing the autonomy of abject consumers so that they can become self-realizing, or more effectively self-realizing, consuming subjects, capable of managing the risk that they represent as consumers and free to entrepreneurially pursue the conduct of their lives as a narrative of their own choosing.

* * *

At the beginning of this chapter, the question was posed: what is to be done about the "excluded," that "risk residuum" of credit consumer deemed to lack the ability or responsibility to pay for their own risk? What is to be the fate of the "flawed consumers" of consumer society (Bauman, 1997)? As we have seen, they are denied access to the easy seductions of the market. They are excluded from circuits of credit consumption through their paltry or blackened credit record and the manifestation of personal attributes—occupation, income, neighborhood—"objectively" indicative of their lack of creditworthiness or, what amounts to the same thing, their inability to manage themselves. For them, the fringe financial service providers await. These are the pawnbroker, the payday lender and the rent to own center that envelop the irrational, un-self-governable within more coercive mechanisms that guarantee governability: the pledge of collateral, the holding of a customer's postdated, guaranteed check or the denial of the transaction as a de jure credit agreement. While such consumers may exist on the fringe, the ever closer relationship between fringe lenders and mainstream financial capital reveals that even the poor, the excluded, the marginalized are not beyond the interest of capital and profit.

CHAPTER 9

Risk, Identity, and the Consumer

Let us all be happy and live within our means, even if we have to borrer the money to do it with.

—Artemus Ward

Monica Greco (1993), in analyzing contemporary conceptions of health, argues that disease is no longer conceived today merely as the opposite of health, the irruption of a normal state of being through the manifestation of a particular set of symptoms. On the contrary, everyday life has become pathologized with the individual perceived to be always potentially "at risk" from illness through the complex interplay of individual disposition and environmental context. Within this, she argues, the individual has become encumbered with the responsibility of ensuring the maintenance of their own health through the making of "healthy choices" in every facet of their life, from exercise to alcohol consumption, from salt intake to workplace stress. However, the exercise of a personal preventative capacity through the making of these prudent, informed choices is not enough. At the same time, the unwillingness or inability to act "healthily" must itself be acknowledged as a form of disease. Illness thus comes to denote a lack of self-mastery while health becomes an expression of enterprise, a personalized project sustained through the ongoing prudent exercise of choice.

The idea of health provides a substantial imaginary whenever individual creditworthiness is discussed:

> Your credit score influences the credit that's available to you, and the terms that lenders offer you. It's a vital part of your credit health. Understanding credit scoring can help you manage your credit health.[1]
>
> Lenders can partner with myFICO® to help their customers improve their credit understanding and health.[2]
>
> The easy to use kit facilitates better financial health by interactively walking consumers step-by-step through the process.[3]

Credit scores are a lot like cholesterol counts—you cannot evaluate a patient's overall health based solely on that one number. Physicians must consider the patient's lifestyle, family history, eating habits, as well as the cholesterol count.[4]

What is revealing about this health metaphor is that it follows the contemporary understanding of psychosomatic health presented by Greco. Health, whether medical or credit, is no longer a *state*, something considered when disease strikes or a loan application is refused by a lender; it becomes, rather, a *personal project* for which the individual is required to manage. In this sense, health is the continuously reproduced outcome of an array of choices that the individual must be persuaded to take in order to be healthy (see also Peterson and Lupton, 1996; Cockerham, Rütten, and Abel, 1997; Bauman, 2000; Vaz and Bruno, 2003). This is the position of the individual under neoliberalism whose operation of freedom, autonomy, and fulfillment become the conduit of government rather than its antithesis.

As we have seen previously, the rise of a mass market for consumer credit was an interweaving process accompanied by the promulgation of written, tabulated records of repayment and the sanctioning of access around relativistic conceptualizations of creditworthiness. Within this emerged a heightened understanding by individuals of themselves as credit users and the realization of a responsibility to manage themselves. With the greater deployment by lenders of statistical scoring systems constituting individual consumers as risks, especially with the rise of the Fair Isaac FICO model based on data held by credit bureaus, a demand for score disclosure became articulated by consumers themselves. This ultimately lead to Fair Isaac and the credit bureaus offering scores to consumers as a marketed product.

However, a credit score exists in the abstract. It represents the data in a credit bureau file in a specific way, creating in numerical form a default risk assessment relative to the mass population of credit users. This bureaucratized technology was created for lenders to calculably determine acceptable default levels and so guide individual sanctioning decisions on all applications for credit. To be incorporated within individual self-governance, it had to be made meaningful and relevant; it had to be articulated as a norm that the autonomous individual could deploy in order to shape their actions toward ends beneficial to a care of the self.

The final three chapters of this book attempt to examine how contemporary American credit consumers have become aligned to a credit identity articulated as risk. In particular, these chapters seek to explore how consumers have come to subjectively understand and govern themselves through such an attribution born from technologies of actuarial government forged by the consumer credit industry. This chapter outlines the significance of the FICO credit scoring system developed by the company

Fair Isaac as a so-called generic form of credit risk analysis based on the information held by the three national credit bureaus. It also examines the events that led to its formalized, marketed disclosure to consumers, even against the initial wishes of the company itself.

Chapter 10 examines the specific mechanics of how an alignment is made between the individual's actions in using credit and the technologies of FICO so that the individual becomes aware of the significance of their FICO score. It is demonstrated that these technologies of risk have become parlayed into "security toolkits" to be purchased and incorporated as consumer goods by the individual in order to defend, enhance and illuminate their personalized lifestyles.

Chapter 11 scrutinizes how these security toolkits, based around the disclosure of the individual's actual score, are used by the individual to reflexively manage their risk-expressed identity and thus their ongoing consuming potential. An attempt is also made to demonstrate the significance of the concept of "uncertainty" and how risk, as a technology for producing a calculable relation to the future, has become an attribution to be understood and acted upon under everyday incalculable conditions.

The Rise of the Generic Credit Score: The Branding of Risk

By the end of the 1980s within the United States, a significant shift occurred in the technology of credit reporting. As detailed in chapter 7, credit scoring technologies had begun to proliferate among lenders from the end of the 1970s as a means of interpreting the creditworthiness of individual consumers based around empirically established conceptualizations of risk. In 1989, Fair Isaac, the leading developer of credit scoring risk systems for creditors, began to develop a standardized generic statistical risk system formulated not on the localized recorded data of individual lenders but on data held by the three national credit bureaus. With this system, any individual with a credit report could be attributed a quantified risk score. By 1991 the systems were in place, individually branded and marketed by the three national bureaus to lenders as a new product for deriving credit risk, integrable within established, customized lender-specific scoring models or functionable as a standalone credit sanctioning tool. These FICO scores extended further the constructed objectivity of credit reports by overlaying a technology of risk.

As we have discussed earlier, interpreting and expressing creditworthiness as a numeric risk helped dislocate a qualitatively rich conception of creditworthiness intimately understood within the moral framework of individual character. In doing so, credit default was established as an empirical phenomenon endemic to the population. It was linked not to fixed causes, explicable in terms of specific individual character, but rather to probability based combinations of variables, exhibited to a greater or lesser degree, by all individuals within a population. Risk is thus the apogee of a relativistic articulation of creditworthiness: its attribution to individuals is dependent upon the specific technology of risk through which they are interpreted and the formation of the population within which they are located.

The emergence of a generic risk technology with respect to consumer credit records provided a common standardized means of conceptualizing and measuring the relative default risk of a new population of consumers inscribed into reality through the burgeoning assemblage of credit reporting. In turn, the idea of a standardized, empirically derived credit risk capable of being attributed to virtually any consumer depended upon the rendering into existence of just such a population. Through what Rose (1999b: 205) labels "the potency of numerical technology," the formulation of FICO scores enabled the specific ordering of consumers within a hierarchy of risk through the computation of data lines on the credit report as relatable variables associated with a commonly defined default outcome. Therefore, different items on a credit report, from types of accounts opened to numbers of delinquencies, could be balanced and merged to form a risk score specific to that individual. In turn, changes to the credit report could result in changes to that attribution over time in terms of a progression to a higher or lower risk. And crucially, individuals could be compared to each other and ranked on a spectrum of risk.

The FICO score thus represents the formation of a new norm across the population of consumers, as simultaneously a rule and a means of producing that rule (Ewald, 1990: 154). In this context, it represents a unified understanding of what kind of default risk a given individual poses. It is a technology for producing a common risk assessment across the whole population of consumers, to which a given level of risk can be compared. However, unlike the norms inherent in disciplinary power, individuals are not coercively *normalized*. FICO scores are only rendered into being within individual transactions for credit; they exist only at particular points in time when autonomous individuals actively seek to enter into a credit agreement. Rather than creating an homogeneous social space as the deployment of discipline sought to do, whereby norms act as standards to be obtained by those so subjected, the deployment of a generic credit scoring system fosters a diverse market space. In a general sense, less risk is preferred to greater risk by lenders within the market, but how the attribution of a risk assessment will be acted upon will vary from lender to lender, depending on the market segment that they seek to profitably exploit. In other words, FICO scores act as a general interpretation of credit risk, but no single cut-off point, no common threshold of exclusion exists for all lenders. Indeed, lenders do not base their decisions exclusively on a FICO score. Therefore, the deployment of a generic risk scoring technology as a new means of assessing creditworthiness only enhances diversity and further segments the market for credit.

By the end of the 1990s, FICO had become firmly established as the standard, generic credit scoring product across the U.S. consumer credit market. This position was further strengthened when Freddie Mac and Fannie Mae, the two congressionally chartered companies responsible for developing secondary markets for home mortgages, directed their use to primary lenders in the mortgage sanctioning process. As the significance of one's bureau-based FICO score for accessing credit began to develop, we see the emergence of a disclosure debate mirroring what had taken place before with regard to credit bureau records in the 1970s. This time disclosure was concerned with the rights of consumers to access their FICO credit scores.

The Politics of Score Disclosure

In September 1999, Representative Cannon introduced a bill to the House of Representatives proposing to amend the Fair Credit Reporting Act by requiring consumer disclosure on demand of all credit scores held by bureaus.[5] As Cannon announced at a press conference:

> Consumers will better know what mortgages and loans they qualify for, and what type of interest rates they can get based upon their credit history. They will be able to shop for the best financial services they can get, and know what to expect.... Giving a consumer this information empowers them to make wise financial decisions.[6]

In early 2000, cosponsored by E-Loan, the Californian Association of Realtors and consumer interest group Consumers Union, Senator Figueroa presented a bill to the Californian legislative assembly that would allow consumers, within the context of a lending decision, to see any score used to help determine the success or failure of a credit application.[7] Later that year, the bill was passed by the assembly and signed into law by the governor. In September 2000, a federal bill modeled on the Figueroa one, requiring lender disclosure, was brought before the Senate by Senators Schumer and Allard.[8] Testifying before a congressional subcommittee, Schumer projected as "sinister" the fact that "lenders have access to all the decision-influencing information and consumers are left in the dark." He advocated the terms of his bill as being necessary to ensure consumer access to their credit scores so that they could make sure that they themselves were able to get the best competitive terms to meet their own credit needs. This was deemed so particularly with respect to mortgage credit access and the realization of "the American Dream of home ownership."[9]

Schumer's statements are further mirrored in how consumer rights advocates Consumers Union interpreted the territory inhabited by credit consumers. In an article published in their journal *Consumer Reports*, they bemoaned the lack of balance present in the consumer credit industry where creditors know the credit scores of consumers but such information is kept from consumers themselves.[10] Due to this lack of self-knowledge and the proliferation of risk pricing whereby interest rates paid for credit are dependent on one's credit score, they argued that consumers were systematically being disadvantaged within credit agreements and inhibited from "shopping around." This was especially true for those consumers with relatively low credit scores tied to the high-interest "subprime" market. However, it is not collective solidarity that is prescribed; indeed, risk pricing and its effect of burdening the individual through specifically tailored interest rates with the costs of the individualized risk that they represent was defended as "only fair." On the contrary, these consumer campaigners sought:

> legislation that requires credit bureaus and lenders to disclose a consumer's credit score, explain deficiencies, and advise how to repair problems . . . [it] should also require that lenders disclose their matrix of rates, credit scores, and credit tiers to anyone who requests this vital comparative-shopping information.[11]

Thus the ability of all consumers, including the marginal, to choose the most adequate and efficient credit product to meet their needs within a free market was posited as being constrained by the profit-oriented interests of the credit industry. This ultimately degraded consumer choice and the fulfillment of the self. Only when consumers can become properly self-calculating as consumers, in turn energizing their ability to choose, can autonomy be assured.

The impulse behind these legislative initiatives was, of course, the protection of consumers but, as with the FCRA, its particular emphasis was on the state providing the means by which individuals as consumers could be rendered autonomous. Within a contemporary political rationality that forges a link between general economic success and the unconstrained productive capacity of autonomous consumers, these political interventions represent an acute concern of the state for the elevation and privileging of the position of the consumer. In other words, the state seeks to intervene, not in the interests of collective solidarity, but to remove self-interested industry imposed distortions. Ultimately, the aim is to provide consumers with the capacity and means by which they could secure their own independence within the market.

Most dramatic, however, was the controversial, highly publicized move by Internet-based lender E-Loan to reveal the score of any consumer logging on to its website, in direct violation of its contract with Equifax.[12] Despite the protests of Equifax representatives, E-Loan persisted in revealing FICO scores until, under pressure from Fair Isaac, Equifax exerted what it was claimed was its contractual right and disconnected its electronic link to E-Loan. This effectively left them without any access to its credit referencing files and thus prevented the continued dissemination of scores (not to mention credit) to consumers. As a consequence of this bruising retaliation, E-Loan backed down but not before numerous emotional outbursts from its CEO about Equifax and Fair Isaac's attempts to deliberately put "him out of business." In the continuing debate about score disclosure, the E-Loan rebellion became the rallying point for angry accusations that the credit reporting industry was engaging in secretive practices harmful to the well-being of consumers. Both Equifax and Fair Isaac defended themselves on the basis that E-Loan had broken the terms of its contract but, more interestingly, it argued that attempts to disclose scores were actually *against* the consumer interest. They suggested that the offering of raw information could confuse consumers and easily lead them to take actions that might actually *harm* their credit score. Thus the centering of consumers within the domain of government conditioned the industry to present its defensive actions as a safeguarding of consumer autonomy. This autonomy, it seems, could be damaged if the knowledge revealed by the score was not accompanied by the inculcation of self-calculability, that is, an appreciation and knowledge of the significance of the score.

E-Loan, although certainly anxious to profit from their attempts at score disclosure in terms of establishing loyalty ties with customers, primarily justified their actions on the basis of autonomizing consumer choice. They emphasized the secretive nature of the credit scoring "black box," the growing consumer demand for information—particularly after having been turned down for a loan on the basis of an unknown score—and their intention to help people understand and manage their own credit.[13] E-Loan's CEO Chris Larsen even interpreted that score disclosure would empower people to "manage their debt in the same way they manage their assets," bringing into sharp relief the contemporary significance of consumers as entrepreneurs of their own lives. Thus with an emphasis on individual self-fulfillment, managing debt could thus become a productive activity through the maximization of one's own consumption potential.[14]

From Actuarial Risk to the Consumption of Risk

Prior to 1999, Fair Isaac's commercial focus was on the provision of statistical credit scoring services to creditors and, with the development of its bureau-based FICO system, came to act as an intermediary between creditors and bureaus. In doing so, it became more implicated within the infrastructure of consumer credit provision. Its purpose as a capitalist firm was not concerned with the management of consumers in the interests of profit but, less directly, with the creation and supply of a technical means of inscription for the actuarial management of populations of credit consumers by lenders. Its refusal to reveal the specific weight of the different factors within its statistical formulations, its claims as to scoring's proprietary nature and the exercise of U.S. trade secret and patent law in its defense were manifest expressions of the firm's protection of its intellectual capital within a competitive marketplace. However, Fair Isaac's persistent repudiation of demands for consumer access and its establishment of nondisclosure contracts with creditors are instances of its protection of its scoring algorithms, not directly from competitors, but from consumers themselves. It saw disclosure as introducing a means whereby consumers would enhance their access to credit by manipulating or "gaming," their own scores—a form of feedback pollution that would deplete the predictive capability of its model. As Fair Isaac representative Pete McCorkell retorted at a Federal Trade Commission conference on consumer credit scoring in 1999:

> And in fact, I'm sorry to tell you this, but Fair Isaac's job is not to tell you how to get a better score. Our job is to produce a score that is the best possible predictor of your credit performance. And so we want to score your behavior.... We don't want to have consumers trying to alter their behavior in short terms ways that.... has nothing to do with their long term credit risk. And we don't want to get into that discussion with consumers.[15]

For the firm, the problem was not so much the release of scores as an identifier so much as attempts to alter it, in particular contexts, that would disrupt default outcomes. In such circumstances, it perceived that risk scores might come to embody the reflexive actions of particular consumers in meeting the specific qualifying criteria of credit agreements rather than the naturally occurring probability of default empirically associated with their demonstrable attributes. As a result, default rates associated with particular score ranges might be distorted, thus diminishing the predictive efficacy of its model in the experience of lenders. What Fair Isaac feared was not their loss of ability to govern consumers, but the loss of profitability resulting from the debilitation of their clients' (that is, lenders) ability to govern consumers.

During 2000, in the aftermath of the E-Loan saga, the state and federal legislative maneuvers described above and increased consumer awareness, a discursive shift appeared in Fair Isaac's articulation of the score disclosure issue. Contrary to its previous dismissal of a consumer right of access, it too began to position itself more within the rubric of promoting consumer autonomy through disclosure. However, Fair Isaac problematized the role of credit scores in consumer self-government. The company argued that consumer knowledge of a single abstract score provided a fractious basis for managing one's credit use given the dynamism of scores and the complexity of a diverse market context where creditors have different risk acceptance thresholds and deploy different mechanisms in sanctioning credit.[16] In fact, it was argued that knowledge of a score might actually lead to it being *lowered* if the consumer attempted to take action to improve it without understanding the significance of their actions. Dropping its contractual consumer nondisclosure terms with lenders, Fair Isaac advocated the release of credit scores within the context of a lending decision:

> Fair, Isaac's view is that consumers need additional information and individual counsel from a lender to truly understand their credit standing and how to improve it in the eyes of the lender. . . . For that reasons, the contracts between Fair, Isaac and credit reporting agencies prohibit the disclosure of credit risk scores to consumers *outside of the context of a lender's explanation of a credit decision.* (my emphasis)[17]

Self-knowledge of credit scores, for Fair Isaac, had to be located within a particular transaction. Where credit consumers were refused, the possibility of score disclosure was permitted but only in a specific time-space where a lender could intervene to firmly direct the self-governing possibilities of the consumer in light of that score. In bowing to the inevitability of consumer self-government, Fair Isaac attempted to shape the form of calculability that this self-government would take.

Fair Isaac, though, soon began to feel pressure from TransUnion who, in light of their established responsibilities to ensure access of consumers to their files, the possibilities of legislative compulsion and the greater demands for self-calculability by consumers, began to develop plans to create their own version of the FICO scoring model. By disseminating approximated scores to consumers, they hoped to side-step the Fair Isaac embargo.[18] Faced with the alternative possibility that its restrictions could now actually degrade or destroy the preeminence of FICO within the consumer credit market, just as it had previously feared that consumer disclosure would have the same effect, Fair Isaac found itself being compelled to directly satisfy the demands of credit consumers. Over a short time period, Fair

Isaac was quickly encumbered with the task of directly governing the self-government of consumers:

> We're...seeing a variety of initiatives to meet the perceived consumer interest in more detailed information about their credit standing. As the developer of the FICO score, we're in the best position to provide the context and explanation for a consumer's credit standing. We still think the lender relationship is the best context for a discussion to help a consumer understand their credit standing. The second best would be a credit explanation from Fair, Isaac based on information in the credit report.[19]

In mid-2000, the company publicly released a list of the factors considered within the FICO model and the relative statistical weight assigned to each one.[20] In November of that year, it unveiled its fee-charging, Web-based service "Ficoguide." Although primarily aimed at lenders in order to allow them to interpret a credit score to a consumer within the context of a credit application, consumers themselves were permitted to access it. In this latter case, however, consumers had to have already secured their score and associated "reason codes" (statutory factors listed on a credit report to explain why a score was not greater) from a lender.[21] Nevertheless, the service helped the consumer interpret their own FICO-based creditworthiness in relative terms against the recorded population of consumers, informed them what their score implied about the possibilities of their defaulting on credit agreements, provided more in-depth analysis of the reason codes as well as advisory actions on how to avoid such score-depleting factors.[22]

By the beginning of 2001, Fair Isaac and Equifax announced an alliance to provide direct consumer access to FICO scores, based on an individual's Equifax credit report, through the internet. Like the Ficoguide before it, planned services to be offered in addition to the score included broad interpretations of how lenders would view the score, explanations of the four most prominent reason codes that prevented the score from being higher, how the individual consumer's score compared across the population and generalized advice on how to improve the score in addition to manned customer advice help-lines.[23] In April of that year, the service was up and running on both companies' websites and, after three months, both companies claimed higher consumer interest with forty million visits to the combined website service. Actual numbers of sales were not revealed, though.[24] Soon, a flurry of companies began to offer so-called FICO "clone" scores, scores generated from models designed to emulate the FICO model, direct to consumers based on their credit reports. Alternatives included iPlace,[25] CreditXpert (in conjunction with E-Loan),[26] and Worthknowing.com,[27] each claiming to be responding to the new-found consumer demand for personal credit information.

In responding to iPlace's action, now rivals within the consumer credit education market, Fair Isaac accepted that such scores might be "educational." However, they were not as useful as the FICO score given that FICO was the only consumer-marketed model actually being used by a majority of lenders; like Oral B advertising that its toothbrushes are the product of personal choice for dentists, Fair Isaac espoused the superiority of its product for self-education on the basis of its real world fidelity. Only Fair Isaac offered the means of credit self-governance based on how consumers were governed in the market. Thus, consumer self-education acquired a commodified form, risk scores becoming marketed for the first time to consumers as well as lenders. However, whereas risk had been deployed exclusively by lenders as part of an actuarial-type management of a population of consumers, for consumers, risk was to be delivered as part of a service for creating and recreating the conditions for a new governance of the self.

Marketing Security Toolkits

If the prudential subject depends on a governmentally contrived arrangement of choice, how is such an arrangement formed for the reflexive credit user? What is the economy of the choices that they are faced with? In what ways has the contemporary credit user become able to align themselves with an objectivized identity with which they are able to calibrate and constrain their actions? How have the market choices that have emerged, developed in form and content? As we have seen, the credit reporting industry and Fair Isaac exhibited a strong defensiveness around the issue of score disclosure to consumers, arguing that its use in consumer self-management was unfeasible given its abstract construction and that such usage would likely deplete its predictive capacity for lenders. Such a defensiveness is indicative of the market to which the credit reporting industry was targeting—their client-base were lenders and other credit providers seeking to manage populations of credit users actuarially through the use of risk. Consumers were the raw material being measured and ordered but were certainly not consumers of scores themselves. Where shareholder profitability was tied to providing services to lenders, any interference with consumers as units to be tested and rendered calculable on behalf of lenders posed a threatening development.

With the agitation for score disclosure, however, not to mention the threat of state regulation, the credit reporting and scoring industry became oriented to the possibility of disclosing scores to consumers for their incorporation as part of a regime of credit self-management. In doing so, however, it approached it as a profitable business venture. Ever since the Fair Credit Reporting Act of 1972, which compelled consumer disclosure of credit files for a "reasonable fee," the self-governing practices of consumers have existed as a revenue stream for the industry. However, it was only in terms of risk scores that it was actively sought, for the first time, to render such practices as an explicit market opportunity:

> In 2001, working with Equifax, we [Fair Isaac] began selling consumers their FICO scores directly, via our myFICO® Web site at www.myfico. com. Now the same scores lenders use as a ubiquitous, affordable measure of credit risk provide credit empowerment to individuals. With the myFICO service, *we have turned score disclosure into a revenue source, extremely positive public response and an expansion of the Fair, Isaac brand.* And we've already given close to 1 million people the understanding they need to improve their credit options. (my emphasis)[28]

From an enterprise viewpoint then, the parlaying of the FICO score and credit bureau information, from an actuarial technology deployed in the objective assessment of applicants for credit into a tool to be incorporated within subjective self-government of one's own credit use, represented a creative exploitation of a business opportunity to realize profit. However, this transformation of purpose did not create but, on the contrary, depended on the emergence of credit users reflexively concerned with their credit identity. Nevertheless, as O'Malley (1996) points out, a prudential risk manager can only exercise risk management within a context of proffered choices; thus the reflexive consumer must be located within the rise of marketized consumer choices for the management of credit identity. What I call here security toolkits are essentially consumer services; translated from technologies marketed to creditors, they form Web-based utilities based around the personalized release of the individual's specific FICO score for which the individual concerned pays a fee. The individual thus comes to partake in the project of self-mastery. This results not just from knowledge as to how scoring works and the significance of having a FICO score but from a *self-knowledge* chosen and consumed within the market, centered on what their actual FICO score is.

This transformation can be seen in the treatment of this new market of consumers—rather than being merely objects of analysis they become implicated directly within the capitalistic orientation of Fair Isaac and the credit bureaus. Equifax, in its analysis of the consumer market, calls it a "new frontier" enabled by the internet. Like target production levels for mass produced consumer goods, it cites the 100,000 consumers purchasing its credit profile service each month.[29] In its 2001 Annual Report, it proudly points to a tripling of revenues and the 2.1 million sales of its combined product suite. It also speaks of "renewal rates" by customers and the continuous levels of profitability inherent in its consumer direct service.[30] Despite the stockholder-impressing context of these pronouncements, the material significance of the consumer market can be seen in the proportion of revenues gleaned from the consumer market over time as a proportion of the total revenues of the whole conglomerate, rising from 2.6 percent to 6.9 percent between 2001 and 2003.[31] Meanwhile, Fair Isaac views an enormous market opportunity in the nearly three-quarters of Americans who have credit records and where "even modest penetration with low-cost services could yield significant results."[32] For its part, it cites an eight million dollar increase in revenues between 2001 and 2002 and an 11.2 million increase in the following period.[33]

CHAPTER 10

"See How Lenders See You": From Actuarial to Subjective Governance

I t has been argued that risk, as a technology, has a "political polyvalence" that can be invested in different political rationalities of government. Within contemporary neoliberal government, socialized risk management exemplified by such programs as social insurance have become dismantled concomitant with the decentering of the social as the crucial space of government. With neoliberalism's concentration upon the individual as the site of rule, the rational choice actor optimizing their interest, these programs recede in favor of what is termed *new prudentialism* (O'Malley, 1996). Instead of risks being calculated and shared socially, prudentialism emphasizes the responsibility of individuals, households, and communities for their own risks; they must minimize exposure to risk and engage in private risk management initiatives, often through the market. For example, in relation to health, along with the rise of private health insurance, we have seen an increased emphasis on personalized, discipline-based risk minimizing practices—from antismoking and weight-loss campaigns to healthy eating initiatives. Therefore, not only are populations targeted as risks but individuals become actively engage in managing their own risks. As O'Malley emphasizes, the individual is rendered both moral and calculating; they are invested with the responsibility of ensuring, through careful strategies of self-protection, that they do not become a burden or a liability to a society no longer sympathetic to the principle of collective welfare.

Within this vein, individual credit users have moved away from being solely agglomerations of risk factors calculated and managed through predictive risk mechanisms. With a clamoring demand for score disclosure to consumers, the same risk technologies which had formally, exclusively, been used to govern the population actuarially became exploited for a new purpose, that of self-governance. Increasingly, consumers have been persuaded of the need to align themselves to a numerically expressed risk identity, as such, to be personally responsible for the risk that they, as credit users and consumers more generally, are constituted to be.

Your Own Personal Risk

Through numerous avenues, the contemporary American consumer is faced with the significance of their credit identity and the importance of understanding its meaning in the living of their lives as consumers. A Federal Trade Commission (FTC) "Facts for Consumers" leaflet prods interest by asking, "ever wonder how a creditor decides whether to grant you credit?"[1] Meanwhile, a brochure from the Consumer Federation of America (CFA) is less oblique in confronting the consumer:

> Think your grade point average is your only score that matters? Think again! There's another score that's important as you go through life. It's called a credit score. And whether you know it or not, someone is already keeping track.[2]

The media too reflect and amplify this insistence on knowing. On a web discussion, *Washington Post* personal finance guru Michelle Singletary remarks, "despite the system's significance, few people know about it, and those that do, little *(sic)* understand it."[3] This theme of consumer ignorance finds expression in surveys as to what consumers actually know about scoring. In one study, for instance, the CFA find that only 34 percent of consumers appreciate that credit scores are a measure of default risk.[4] Similarly, the hosting of an interactive web quiz by Fair Isaac leads the company to authoritatively remark that "the financial literacy of American consumers rates a poor grade of 'D'."[5] In every case, knowledge of how the scoring system works and contextualizing one's ongoing credit use in relation to this knowledge to understand the constitution of one's own identity is presented as critical. It provides a means for acting upon those elements of the self, which the model considers in order to improve one's credit identity and thus maximize one's credit consumption:

> Understanding credit scoring can help you manage your credit health. By knowing how your credit risk is evaluated, you can take actions that will lower your credit risk—and thus raise your score—over time. A better score means better financial options for you.[6]

As scoring becomes ubiquitous within the consumer credit market, as it comes to be used for more products such as mortgage credit and to increasingly determine the interest rate paid by consumers, an enhanced credit identity helps open up the possibility of choosing more credit products, expediting applications for new credit and lowering the effective cost of consuming it.

Through its Web site service, myFICO®, Fair Isaac acts to align the individual with the conception of a credit identity articulated as a risk score—a "calculable personal property" (Poon, 2007: 300). It accomplishes this by inculcating a knowledge within the credit user as to how credit scoring works, how the statistical model is constructed and how it assimilates and articulates information to produce a specific credit identity in terms of risk.[7] As FICO scores are produced through credit bureau data, the individual is firstly familiarized with the content of what a credit report contains, namely:

- *Identifying information* that conjoins the living individual and their actions with their virtual identity
- *Trade line information* that reports types of credit used currently and in the past; the duration of the accounts; balances; current status, and the nature and extent of any delinquencies
- *Inquiries*: date and type of reported applications by the individual for new credit
- *Public record/collection*: publicly recorded court judgments for debts and defaulted amounts referred by lenders to collection agencies[8]

Essentially, for the individual, their credit identity is constructed as an amalgam of their previous use of credit, their attempts to use credit and significant failures to commit to repaying credit accounts outstanding.

Beyond this, the credit user is enlightened with the five categories through which the FICO score model interprets this information in cohering individual scores: payment history, that is, the extent to which the individual is deemed to have repaid amounts on time; amounts owed as well as number, type, and spread across different credit accounts; overall length of credit history as well as the age of specific accounts, the nature of recently acquired credit and requests for new credit and, finally, the balance or "mix" of credit types held by the individual.[9] As well as the categories themselves, Fair Isaac denotes the specific emphasis placed on each category within the FICO model—with payment history at 35 percent being the most important factor and credit mix, at 10 per cent, the least (see fig. 10.1).

Striking a cautionary note, the company attests to the uniqueness of each individual credit user and the fact that this weighting, relevant for the whole population of credit users, may differ depending on the specific credit history of the individual. However, it is not just informing the individual of their characteristics and weightings that is important. Fair Isaac

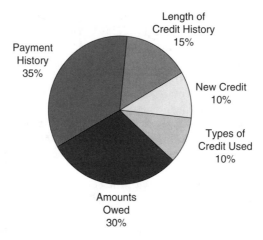

Figure 10.1 FICO components.

Source: Reproduced from "Understanding your credit score," Fair Isaac.

cautions the credit user as to what is *not* considered within the model, including among other things: discriminatory attributes such as race, gender, religion, and other such factors legislatively prohibited under the Equal Credit Opportunity Act; income; specific interest rates on credit accounts held, and "any information that is not *proven* to be predictive of future credit performance."[10]

Although credit identity is positioned as an outcome of individual actions in the past, the interpretation of it through a risk score implies its function as a norm, a relativistic attribution generated within the context of a population. This requires that the individual understand the significance of their credit identity against the group. As Ewald (1990) suggests, the function of a quantified risk as norm attains its meaning not against absolute standards but only as part of a population distribution. Giving expression to an individual as a risk score only makes sense against the expression of other individuals as risk scores and the extent to which it is higher or lower than these. The credit user is thus instructed not just as to how an individualized score is created but the meaningfulness of the scale upon which scores are posited and how a FICO, as an individualized risk attribution, stacks relative to the incidence of risk across the population of American consumers as a whole (see fig. 10.2).

This relativistic understanding of one's own credit identity is central for the process of aligning individuals to it is so that they will come to act upon themselves in order to enhance it, reaping the financial benefits. We saw in chapter 7 how, in recent years, lenders increasingly price their interest rates by credit score. Therefore, through a self-consciousness as to their position within the hierarchy of consumers, the individual can be presented with their current score collegiate and its attendant possibilities for credit consumption, collegiates to aspire to with their greater consuming potentials and ones to avoid with their diminished domains of choice. Figure 10.3, for instance, shows consumers the graded interest rates and repayments on a residential mortgage associated with a hierarchy of FICO scores.[11] Therefore

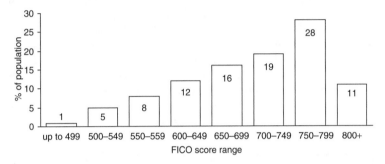

Figure 10.2 National distribution of FICO scores.
Source: "Credit scoring," Fair Isaac.

Save the Smart Way

As you improve your FICO® scores, you pay less when you buy on credit--whether purchasing a home loan, cell phone, a car loan, or signing up for credit cards. For example, on a $150,000 30-year, fixed-rate mortgage:

Your FICO Score	Your Interest Rate	Your Monthly Payment
760–850	5.37%	$840
700–759	5.59%	$861
680–699	5.77%	$877
660–679	5.99%	$898
640–659	6.42%	$940
620–639	6.96%	$994

Figure 10.3 FICO scores and risk pricing.
Source: Fair Isaac.

in a score's function as a norm, the individual is directed to a personalized "ethic of improvement."

In terms of understanding themselves as risks, credit consumers are engendered to acknowledge the scientific rationalism of scoring: its empirical derivation, its reliance on factual credit records, its mathematical formulation, its rigorous testing to ensure "the most accurate picture of credit risk possible using credit report data," and its use of permitted characteristics statistically proven to be predictive of default.[12] In addition to its rationality, scoring is also presented as being "fair," excluding potentially discriminatory attributes, holistically assessing the information in the credit report to ensure an adequate reflection of the individual. It is these very characteristics of scoring that are depicted as having helped make possible the dynamic contemporary market embodying instant credit, where personal feelings and nonrelevant characteristics are excluded, where all information is judiciously balanced and weighed up and where more credit is available at lower rates of interest. All of these facets are presented as making it easier for people to enjoy more liberal credit use. In asserting the scientific credentials of scoring, it implies that the regulation of the self by risk where individuals have not done so before is, in itself, a rational and appropriate practice. More generally, staking its centrality to the credit market and the greater availability of credit to individuals makes one's score understood as a fundamental attribution, one to acknowledge and adhere to in order to maximize ongoing consuming potential.

Disciplining the Self

The alignment of an individual to their credit identity and its articulation as a FICO score implies the disciplining of the self, one's actions in the use of credit, in relation to time. To sustain and to increase the possibility of choice through the improvement of one's score, the credit user is persuaded of the need to keep current on credit payments, to keep balances low on revolving credit accounts like credit cards, to pay-off debt rather than circulate it around; ultimately, against the structuring of time, the credit user is to exert a rigid regimen of the self to ensure their repayments and credit use are smooth, controlled and to term. In disciplining themselves in this manner, the individual is made responsible for their past actions, the consequences of which cannot be evaded—"[n]ote that closing an account doesn't make it go away. A closed account will still show up on your credit report, and may be considered by the score."[13] However, the past is not an albatross around the neck of consumers—the transformation of the self, possible through acting in light of one's credit identity, always implies the possibility of transcendence in the present. The receding past fades in statistical significance to be replaced by the interpretation of more recent "good" behavior in the conduct of credit.

Against this ethic, "base manipulation" through such actions as willfully opening and closing accounts to quickly increase one's score is to be avoided. For instance, the credit user is advised, "don't close unused credit cards as a short term strategy to raise your score" while, almost in the same breath, the advice is "don't open a number of new credit cards that you don't need, just to increase your available credit. This approach could backfire and actually lower your score."[14] Although the credit user is to be calculating, such calculation cannot herald easily exploitable technicalities. Rather, the injunction is almost a puritan one: to pay one's bill on time, to "get current and stay current," not to take on too much or unneeded credit. In the actuarial management of credit default through risk by lenders, various characteristics and attributes are technically perceived to be related to a probabilistic default outcome, which the creditor can deploy to profitably target a certain segment of borrowers.

We have seen how some lenders utilized developments in scoring technologies to actively market high-interest credit facilities to the so-called subprime market of relatively risky consumers. This new market is equally, if not more, profitable than the conventional prime market, with higher interest rates compensating for great levels of default. In this context, no moral claims are made for the "rightness" of "wrongness" of particular attributes, only the exploitation of profitable opportunities. However, in the subjective government of FICO scores, individual conduct is moralized. This occurs not against a universal truth or belief but in relation to the extent that one's score contributes toward depletion or bolstering of one's credit identity and thus an inhibition or enhancement of one's credit consuming potential. Shifting relativized statistical relationships between variables and outcomes thus become immute, moral precepts.

In analyzing what he sees as the critical role of moralization within practices of government, Hunt (1999) argues that morality frequently invokes a utilitarian claim where conduct being deemed bad or unworthy has a wider personal or social harm attached to it. So it is for the contemporary credit user, whose lack of self-mastery invokes a future eroded of opportunities to consume. But there is a wider social implication here too; if economic activity and growth are built around personal consumption, and credit use increasingly facilitates this consumption, then the agglomeration of undisciplined credit use and the shrinking of credit provision might be seen to have wider, far-reaching social consequences for national prosperity. Certainly, its opposite is perceived to be true by credit bureau Equifax: "[t]he more we enlighten, enable and empower individuals to better manage their financial health...the more we foster consumer confidence and economic growth."[15]

Ironically, within this process of moralized governance, the centrality of credit to contemporary economic activity and lived experience casts the traditional suspicion of credit on its head:

Have credit cards—but manage them responsibly. In general, having credit cards and instalment loans (and making timely payments) will raise your score. People with no credit cards, for example, tend to be higher risk than people who have managed credit cards responsibly.[16]

A demonstration of no or limited credit use implies a higher level of individual risk than that by disciplined, well-managed credit use so that morality itself is adjudged not through one's use of credit but one's *conduct* in the use of credit. An interesting example of this understanding is the joint venture between Fair Isaac and a Californian credit counseling organization to incorporate the former's services to help those who "want to rebound from credit problems."[17] In this understanding, it is not credit use that is the problem for the dangerously indebted, nor is prohibition the answer; rather it is a lack of self-mastery, which is problematized and professional guidance through an identity conscious restoration of one's self-mastery, the solution.

In being governed to maximize their personal consuming possibilities, the credit user grapples with uncertainty in the management of their FICO score. Unlike the actuarial deployment of risk, there are no formulas to follow to ensure a calculated outcome in the future. As we saw above, mere calculation alone can, in fact, imply a destructiveness of identity and the degradation of consumer choice. However, such uncertainty does not represent an abandonment of government but rather a particular form for its realization. Guided by expertise in the continuous exercise of foresight, prudence through the calculable exercise of self-discipline and moral responsibility for their credit use, the individual is empowered to adapt themselves to the changing environment of consumer goods and the ever-shifting play of needs and desires. They, in effect, become better equipped to fulfill the obligation of continuously choosing to consume. Thus rather than encouraging endless, hedonistic consumption, consumers are nurtured to be moral in their credit use and consumption more generally in a way that encourages sustainability of choice. In other words, for consumers, the "right way to live" within a consumer society is to be able to maximize consumption over the course of time—requiring strict limits on the credit use of the present.

Identity and the Self

In discussing what he terms the contemporary "reflexivity" of modernity, Giddens (1991) and Beck (1992) argue that social activity, freed from the binding constraints of tradition, is permanently engaged in the exercise of self-questioning as to its nature and purpose. Within this context, the idea of a distinctive individualized identity emerges. Rather then one's existence in the world being fixed, preordained by lineage or class, an individual's sense of identity in late modernity is a fluid construct, sustained and recreated dynamically through the individual's continuous action upon it. In this sense identity is self-referential and reflexive for, with the decline of established sources of meaning, it becomes the product of the individual's observation and analysis of themselves and their accumulated diverse actions. Identity assumes a coherent trajectory spanning a past mined for meaning yet simultaneously to be escaped and a future of possibility and promise to be attained. It becomes the particular responsibility of the individual whose constant endeavors constitute it as a coherent and convincing narrative from which, in turn, the individual draws meaning in an individualized world.

As discussed in chapter 4, such a reflexive project of the self, rather than being merely an effect brought about by late modernity, can be viewed as the means by which the contemporary individual is governed. With individual autonomy being located as the conduit of government, the concept of enterprise, as a mode of activity, comes to pervade the way in which the individual is governed to govern themselves. Through his or her own endeavor, ability, and drive, the individual is to make an enterprise of their own life, to create a fulfilling independent lifestyle for themselves through the free expression of their consumption choices and the choosing of marketed guidance provided through the psy-sciences and their affiliates (Rose, 1996a; see also O'Malley, 2004). Identity is a willed project of the self, etched out through the expression of choice; yet those choices taken exist as a product, the inevitable expression of an inner, authentic self. The conception of enterprise undermines old binary divides between production and consumption for consumption is now no longer the destructive hedonism described by Bell, undermining the ascetic puritan ethic that culturally underpins the capitalist accumulation process. On the contrary, the contemporary individual is directed with the responsibility of producing a worthwhile life for themselves, not simply through what they consume now but through their whole array of consuming choices within and throughout their life. To sustain this obligation, the individual must regulate their own freedom, sustaining and widening their consuming possibilities through a refined, all-embracing self-control (Reith, 2007; Starr, 2007).

In Weber's ([1930] 1976) analysis, he portrayed the Protestant ethic as the key cultural impetus behind the rise of capitalist accumulation where asceticism and deferred gratification impel a maximized accumulation of capital and realization of profit. Elias (1991, 1994) by contrast, countered that rationality should not be understood as the progressive displacement of ideal types but rather as a measure of the degree to which short-term affects are subsumed by longer-term considerations. For him, this process was as a consequence of long-term changes in the structure of society toward greater interdependency. Elias argued that while, for instance, court rationality and bourgeois rationality had differing social dynamics, the former valuing prestige and honor, the latter money and capital, both were united by individuals' transcendence of emotions, desires, and momentary inclinations of the present. Each exhibited greater foresight toward future goals, reflective of particular kinds of social interdependency (1994: 484). From this perspective, credit use and its active self-government represents a "rational" form of action where long-term considerations of maximizing ongoing future credit consumption outweigh short term urges to exploit one's present credit opportunities. We might call this a "credit consumer rationality," where access to money is predicated on formalized reputation. However, such an aptitude is not merely an unintended consequence of a blind process of social change but, as we have seen, is actively grafted within the individual as a desirable way of living one's life. Nevertheless, it effectively makes the contemporary credit user no less foresighted, calculating, dispassionate, and self-disciplined—"rational"—than their forebears.

In line with Giddens's argument, a FICO score is made salient for the individual as a unifying thread, weaving past and current actions into a cohesive sense of self; an attribution that has a dynamism and a sense of movement, and for which the individual is made responsible for. In certain ways, the individual is encouraged to view it as intrinsic to them, as something which can be acted upon to unlock their "true credit potential," an authentic subjective state that must be given expression to. This idea must be sustained against the reality that a FICO score exists externally to the individual, captured within the records of the credit bureau, the formulation of the scoring technology and dynamic shifts within the population of consumers. It also manifests not merely as the outcome of choice but in turn, as a determiner of choice; created through the credit choices of the consumer interpreted through a shifting technological assemblage, such an attribution serves to define the boundaries and limitations of future consumption possibilities.

A FICO score embodies a measurement of the entrepreneurial abilities of the credit user; universal in scope, it embraces potentially all consumers in their instrumental management of credit. As an attribution, it is individual-ized and unique to each credit user. However, it is not sought for its own intrinsic fulfillment, for recognition from the self or from others but rather for the possibility that it can be acted upon through acting on one's current credit use; it is desired for the broader purpose of optimizing ongoing future ability to consume, whatever form that consumption that might take.

Alignment to a credit identity creates the possibility of consumers defining who they are through the operation of a disciplined regime of the self. It gives expression to freedom by empowering them to choose to consume in such a way so as to maximize future freedom to consume. However, paradoxically, consumers cannot escape their dependency on that identity as it becomes essential to the maintenance of freedom. Consumption and the formation of lifestyle are ongoing projects that span individual lives and so such a freedom must be continuously worked on and safeguarded. In consequence, consumers are increasingly conditioned toward the pursuit of a whole panoply of actions—to repay on time, "to get current and stay current," to keep credit card balances low—embodying resistance to the lures of consumer desire and restraint on the urge to self-indulgent credit use.

It is an inherent paradox of neoliberal government that as individuals become governed through their autonomy and freedom to exercise choice they become, as Rose (1999a) remarks, "obliged to be free"; they must evaluate themselves via norms, values, and choices contrived within the market and proffered within the domain of therapeutics. For contemporary American credit consumers, this encompasses an obligation to deploy a calculated self-constraint over their consuming choices for, in pursing an imperative of sustaining or expanding a freedom to choose through credit, the individual is enjoined to an ever greater exercise of *unfreedom* over how they choose. The individual's FICO score reflects the ongoing process of their credit consumption and thus the engagement of their lives as an enterprise of the self. In conditioning future choice, the possibility of more, this score comes to distill the entrepreneurial abilities of the individual to themselves. It is a consumer capital that is possessed and self-consciously invested in new credit through which it can be maintained, augmented, or diminished by an informed self-mastery.

Self-mastery and a Snapshot in Time

In articulating the significance of payment history, amounts owed, length of credit history, new credit applied for, and the mix of credit as being relevant to the construction of a FICO score, such acts are infused with the conception of individual self-mastery in relation to time. Time exists as a structuring agent against which the individual's acts in their inescapable past have taken place and from which the individual's ability to exhibit control over themselves in how they manage credit use can be assessed. In payment history, has the individual repaid their installment loans or met the minimum balance on their credit cards as agreed every month? If not, how late were the repayments and how long ago in time were they? Did this self-management in time disintegrate to the extent that accounts were forwarded for collection or result in court proceedings? Or perhaps the ultimate dissolution in one's responsibility to repay across the full gamut of credit accounts manifested itself in the declaration of bankruptcy? If so, how long ago?

As credit agreements themselves exist as the exchange of funds over time, the measurement of balances owed demonstrates the extent to which the individual can discipline their use of credit over time. The absolute length of credit history is also critical in the evaluation of risk for the longer one's demonstrable use of credit, the more established one is as a credit consumer; in essence, credit history indicates a greater or lesser *history* of self-regulation. New credit explicitly looks at the present and the degree to which one is, in the here and now, responsibly acquiring or encumbering oneself with credit obligations; the degree to which one's current accumulated range of credit agreements is "healthy" is similarly assessed in the present.

Norbert Elias (1998) presented the historical refinement of the measurement of time, its gradual standardization and quantified operation as an endemic characteristic of the intensifying division of social functions and extending web of interdependencies within and between emergent nation-states, particularly with industrialization (see also Thompson, 1967 and Adam, 2004). Concomitantly, the greater time consciousness of individuals in modern societies and their feeling and experience of time as an external compelling force that must be accounted for reflects the tangible reality of their dependency within a web of interdependency. Therefore, the experience of a multilayered compulsion of time by the self-governing credit user demonstrates the degree to which they are dependent upon a greater range of multiple organizations, lenders, retailers, and bureaus in their increasingly credit-realized consumption. Although, as we noted above, contemporary self-governance exists not as an unintended outcome of history but as a contrived aim of government, the responsibilization of the individual within the expansive market for consumer credit encumbers them with the task of managing their actions. This must be accomplished against a tightly woven, all-encompassing, unyielding flow of time.

Time is also significant in that FICO scores are designed to be dynamic. As a marker of a consumer's self-mastery, their ability to sustain a freedom to choose, it responds coherently to the actions of consumer choice. As they attempt to construct a lifestyle based around consumption and as credit becomes integral to their ability to consume, their FICO score is presented as being only ever contingent. During the course of the consumer's engagement with credit, the surveillant assemblage interlocking consumers, lenders, bureaus, courts, and other actors updates their FICO score to account for such instances as new credit sought or a missed credit card payment. This dynamism is reflected, even when the consumer does not actually consume for, as we saw, the model incorporates the passing of time, updating the duration of an individual's credit history or the time elapsed since a repayment delinquency. In choosing not to consume, the consumer still chooses. The flow of time conditioning a FICO score, reflecting ongoing consumption, avoids locking consumers into a static characterization. Past transgressions of consumption self-mastery—late-payments, defaults, even bankruptcies—fade in statistical predictive significance as they grow distant over time and so weigh less on risk attribution. In contrast, recent strict self-management is rewarded more prominently. Therefore, a FICO score in the present is locked into and shaped by the individual's actions of the past from which it is constructed and through which consumer freedom is conditioned. At the same time, however, the past declines in prominence as it fades toward the horizon. Through every action, the consumer experiences the possibility of renewing their credit identity and thus transforming their future through actively taking responsibility for their own autonomy. As Fair Isaac declare:

Fallacy: A poor score will haunt me forever.

Fact: Just the opposite is true. A score is a "snapshot" of your risk at a particular point in time. It changes as new information is added to your bank and credit bureau files. Scores change gradually as you change the way you handle credit. For example, past credit problems impact your score less as time passes. Lenders request a current score when you submit a credit application, so they have the most recent information available. Therefore by taking the time to improve your score, you can qualify for more favorable interest rates.[18]

Loss of the Future

In being governed to manage a FICO score within contemporary consumerism, past, present, and future have no form as discrete states for the consumer. The past always exists in the present, conditioning the permanent ongoing exercise of a choice forever cognizant of the future as a territory of choices to be made. The neoliberal preoccupation with the embedding of choice mediated through nurtured markets creates a merry-go-round, with commodities and experiences as leaping, twirling horses forever conjoined to a spinning but stationary axle of choice. Time exists simply as the regenerated exercise of options, the present resembling the past and the future, the present, differing only in terms of scale and degree of the choice experienced.

Under the welfarist political rationality that located the site of government in society, an optimistic transcendent vision of the future was enjoyed, a future within which mechanisms of security such as redistributive spending and social insurance would help alleviate poverty and inequality, ameliorating the conditions of society. Keynesianism denoted the possibility of national economic intervention and management in the collective interest to ensure a softened business cycle, controlled employment and continual, predictable incremental growth. More generally, a belief in progress and faith in science imbued technological progress with an unproblematic utopianism, beckoning toward the certainty of higher productivity and enhanced living standards. Within such societies as François Ewald (2002) presents it, risk was to be deployed and tamed through the mechanism of solidarity realized through "social contract" and a generalized strategy of "prevention."

Today however all have become, or are in the process of becoming, discredited. Neoliberal strategies have dismantled many state mechanisms and the possibility of governing through the social. In questioning the sustainability of human progress, environmentalism, the new domain of a jaded political left, creates a dystopian vision of a future to be avoided through the doctrine of the precautionary principle (Furedi, 2002; Sunstein, 2005). As the idea of the social as a unified space becomes rejected, the site of rule becomes reoriented toward the government of autonomous individuals, their choices and their ability to imaginatively create their own self-referential narrative of the self. Consequentially there is, in Margaret Thatcher's famous aphorism, no alternative to the market. The state, in conjuring markets through deregulation and the transformation of welfarism, increases the scope of choice for the individual so that the proliferation of choice (and "contestability") becomes the sole end of government. Paradoxically then, choice is both fluid and static: although that which is to be chosen is fluid and changing, the practice of choice itself is an exercise in the monotonous repetition of choosing, a monotony that expands and deepens. We have, as Giddens remarks, no choice but to choose (1991: 81).

Thus, the ever greater availability of consumer credit permits a freedom for the suitably equipped individual to dynamically create their lives through what they choose to consume. However, this freedom entails a perpetual exercise of choice, a variable capacity with which the individual is tasked to uphold and protect to ensure its continuance. The vitality of the individual exhibited through the continual inventiveness of consumption is bound to a flattened experience of time, a reduction to the present that has become ongoing and inescapable (Beck, 1992: 135).

Credit Identity as Risk Score

A FICO score is conceived as a formation that determines access to credit not just in the present but also the future, prejudicing the degree and extent of the whole domain of ongoing consumer choice. In doing so, as the individual credit user comes to acknowledge this attribution, it reveals a clearer relationship of that individual to their future. As we will examine later, such an attribution is actionable in the present. Through enlightenment as to its existence, significance and operation, the consumer is empowered to reflexively consider their own credit use in light of a numerical formation that distills those actions. In doing so, the possibility of ongoing future choice is brought into greater resolution in the present.

A FICO score acts to secure the point of entry to credit consumption. For such an attribution to exist, an individual must have a credit record, an objectivized credit identity, which is contingent on the individual having used credit in the past. In addition, the creation of a score is dependent on minimum criteria: that a credit account exists on record which is at least six months old and that the consumer demonstrates actual use of at least one credit agreement within the same time period.[19] Although risk scores are not absolute and are individually interpreted by different lenders, the pervasiveness among lenders of FICO use demonstrates that the lack of such an identity on the part of the consumer signifies a state of exclusion. Where contemporary freedom becomes articulated through the medium of consumption, and credit increasingly becomes a conduit of consumption, the absence of a FICO score signifies, as we have seen, one's membership among the excluded, the marginal, the fringe. Unable to access mainstream forms of credit, one is unable to consume in the proper sense; unable to give proper vent to a continuous succession of inner wants, one is denied significant participation in the contemporary experience of freedom.

As we analyzed in chapter 6, older notions of creditworthiness were inexorably bound to an absolutist idea of character that intimated a broader sense of moral meaning and understanding about the individual located within their social context. In a certain sense, a FICO score has taken on an aspect of providing for an understanding of the individual within a multitude of contexts beyond credit use. One's credit identity and score thus broaden in scope and their understanding diffuses within society as multiple fields of social engagement become articulated as consumer/provider contractual relationships. Trust or other modes of calculation are replaced with a harmonized, measurable index of consumer capital.

As the inculcation of choice becomes paramount in practices of government, it becomes crucial to contrive an environment wherein the ability to choose between becomes essential. Publicized league tables, for example, allow colleges to be hierarchized and compared in terms of the quality of the educational product they offer, permitting parents as consumers of education for their children to select between different options (Chang and Osborn, 2005). On the other side of the divide, a credit score becomes a standardized index of the consumer, signifying their level of generalized self-discipline. Thus, to avoid tenants who may not pay the rent promptly, landlords access and assess each potential tenant's FICO score. Employers can access the scores of job candidates before hiring them to positions of responsibility. Courts can incorporate the score of a father to help determine likelihood of adherence to child support payments. However, it is in the creation of the insurance bureau score that this diffusion has achieved its most developed form. The "insurance bureau" score was developed by Fair Isaac in the early 1990s as a product for insurers to assess the calculated probability of loss on a premium offered over a specific timeframe. This differs from the FICO score in that it measures not the default risk of an applicant for credit but the future loss ratio relativity of an applicant for insurance; however, it is calculated in a similar manner based on exactly the same data: credit bureau data comprising an individual's credit identity.

In the past, the inculcation of discipline through the monotonous rhythms of the factory, the work ethic, the physical arrangement of public space and architecture, the moralization and sanitization of the family home were crucial for the entrenchment of self-discipline. This was essential to a society that sought to subject the worker to the rigors of the capitalist "free" labor market (Bauman, 1998a; Rose, 1999b; see also Stearns, 1999). Within contemporary society, a credit identity thus rearticulates a certain sense of a polyvalent morality—it exerts a claim not just to an individual's ability to manage credit but to their ability to manage the *self*, to be responsible, to exercise a calculable self-mastery over their actions through time. In attempting to justify why a credit record is relevant to insurance cover, Fair Isaac argue that:

> when a person utilizes one's resources well to maintain a home or a car in safe operating conditions, he or she is probably maintaining his or her finance and credit. For instance, when the car battery, headlights, motor oil level, etc. are maintained regularly, there is less chance for an accident. *Good credit managers are usually good risk managers.* (my emphasis)[20]

The last sentence in particular reveals a clear connection between the conceptions of the self-mastered credit user and the prudential subject as characterized by O'Malley. The prudential subject is both moral and calculating; appalled at the possibility of becoming a burden or having their freedom curtailed, they take measures to guard against risks to their well-being through choosing to be informed and disciplined, through voluntary interaction with like-minded others and the purchasing of commodities and services to offset the possibility or consequences of such events. Against this, those who take no such defensive measures are made responsible for their situation (O'Malley, 2004: 72–3). Likewise, the conscientious credit consumer user is made responsible. They maintain a strict self-control over the repayment of their credit obligations in order to sustain their ability to be a consumer or actively seek to familiarize themselves with, and to reflexively manage, their credit identity. Foreswearance of such a rigor of the self inevitably shrinks the future domain of choice. The insurance bureau score provides an interesting linkage between credit identity and private insurance, this latter being one of the main conduits for personal, prudential protection. To minimize costs, contemporary insurance requires not only the continual renewal of a premium but the continuous maintenance of responsible behavior of those insured, a responsibility indicated through the diffusion of credit identity as a proxy for self-mastery.

With the focus of government centering on the autonomy of the individual, the prudential management of risk becomes a feature of the choices made by individuals and their families as "active citizens" and consumers. Within a context where freedom is conceived as autonomy of the self, any state that compels dependence or inhibits the free exercise of choice in the continual creation of the self through consumption is to be studiously avoided. Risk management in a diversity of spheres—from cholesterol counting to avoid heart attacks to mortgage insurance which pays one's bills in the event of unemployment—becomes a set of critical choices to make in the interests of sustaining an ongoing ability to choose. The prudential subject is thus rational and knowledgeable; exercising the fundamental faculty of choice within a governmentally conceived context of choices, they calculate the contingencies, avoid risky behavior and institute the most effective means to protect against the paralyzing effects of risks. So too is the credit user to be prudential. Conditioned to be acquainted with their credit identity and its specific manifestation as a FICO risk score, they become calculating and knowledgeable as to the consequences of their credit use in the past and the possibilities for action in the present. The strategic objective is the ongoing sustenance of choice within an unfurling future to come, not only in credit but a range of other arenas, from employment to insurance. The risks faced by consumers, however, are not only their own actions in the management of credit but, as we will see, the possibility of misrepresentation and error within the credit reporting process itself.

CHAPTER 11

Securing the Self

W e have seen how individuals are led to appreciate the importance of different elements of their credit identity and how these become articulated through a quantified score on a continuum of scores representing the whole field of consumers. They are also educated as to what their scaled scores denote as to their ability to govern themselves in using credit. But what is the purpose, the consequence of aligning individual consumers with their FICO scores? Within the contemporary credit market where the quality of access to credit is significantly determined through the use of actuarial FICO scoring, the ability to understand the significance and composition of one's own score is presented as being critical. As individual freedom expresses itself through the ability to choose and the capacity to sustain or enhance consumer choice over time, one's FICO score becomes a key technology setting and resetting the boundaries of that choice. Ultimately, self-governing consumers must take on the project of sustaining and optimizing themselves.

In this, they embrace what I call an "ethic of improvement" to incrementally increase their FICO attribution through the use of marketed "security toolkits." As we have seen elsewhere, the autonomous individual is exhorted to live their lives as an enterprise of the self, strategically accumulating happiness and well-being, partially through giving expression to a sense of self from the consumption of meaning-imbued commodities. If the individual is an entrepreneur in such a way, then one's credit identity denotes one's consumer capital, a resource to be carefully invested in through reflexive action, preserved and nurtured to sustain its potency as a key to credit consumption. But what is the method by which this is achieved?

The Paradox of Empowerment

In presenting an understanding of the purpose of security toolkits, the firms concerned discursively relay their operations as one of "empowering" the consumer:

> Consumers not only use our site to become better informed but to become empowered to improve their credit standing.[1]

> These services are the next big step in our continuing push to provide consumers with the knowledge and tools they need to gain true credit empowerment.[2]

> Our Consumer Direct business continued to expand by using Equifax information to enlighten, enable and empower consumers.[3]

As Baistow (1994) discusses, empowerment has become a key term within contemporary health and welfare services where it has been invoked as a key value in the transformation of outdated, patronizing monolithic services. In its place is envisaged a reformed, liberating environment for localized participation and the realization of personal choice. Within this context, empowerment is the prized attribute of the autonomous individual who has the understanding and behavioral skill-set to plot out the course of their own lives. As she acutely notes, "[t]aking control of one's life, or particular aspects of it, is not only seen as being intimately connected with the formation or reformation of the self as empowered, *it is increasingly becoming an ethical obligation of the new citizenry*" [emphasis in original] (1994: 37). Under contemporary practices of government, the individual becomes acted upon as the site of that government, conditioning and creating a market-like context of choice for them to realize their autonomy.

Of course, as Baistow notes, empowerment is not something that is done to oneself but, rather, something which is done to one—individuals are not governed despite their autonomy but through it. In being empowered, consumers are to be rendered more able to choose and thus to enjoy a greater sweep of freedom in the future by getting "the most lucrative return from their credit potential."[4] However, in doing so, the individual becomes dependent on the expertise inherent to security toolkits to make this possible. They become conditioned to act and to conduct their credit use in particular ways that aligns the goals of the consumer credit industry for minimum default and maximum profitability with the ambitions of consumers for more, better, cheaper credit. The proliferation of security toolkits promises the consumer freedom through the enrichment of their available choices to consume but in a way that establishes ever stricter boundaries to, and an ever more finely grained, all-encompassing regulation over how, they choose.

"The One That's Right for You"

FICO security toolkits are supplied as Internet-based services on the specialized website of Fair Isaac—myFICO.com—and also the website of the credit bureau Equifax.[5] Individual consumers access them online by inputting (obviously, but somewhat ironically) a credit card number to which the cost is charged, their social security number and also a specific identifying piece of information relevant to some part of their credit identity that only they can know, for example, the monthly repayment on the individual's mortgage loan. Like any consumer good whose quality or performance varies by price, the array of security toolkits are differentiated by the scale and scope of the service they offer. These vary by:

- *Accessibility*, the number of times or the duration, in days, of access
- *Comprehensivity*, the number of bureaus sources from which scores are produced
- *Detail*, the amount and richness of information relayed
- *Specialism*, some products are specifically tailored for home buying or to protect against fraud
- *Contextuality*, information allowing the individual to take specific measures to improve their score
- *Bolt-ons*, additional services such as "score simulators," current market interest rate provision or debt reduction calculators

Differentially priced security toolkits, selected via market choice, thus facilitate differential levels of security and benefit to the individual. In a very real sense then, securing one's credit identity exists as a form of consumption in and off itself irrespective of the credit consumption it allows the individual to countenance. It not only undergirds the narrativizing of a lifestyle but, in itself, represents an attempt at narrative, creating meaning for the individual in terms of being "enterprising." Fair Isaac's premier product, the Platinum Kit® boasts it will show you "how to get ahead and stay ahead,"[6] presumably of other consumers. The FICO Saver for Homebuyers® "gives you the inside information that mortgage industry professionals use,"[7] again, to get that cheap mortgage that other individuals will not secure. Exclusively through the security toolkits supplied, the consumer is empowered with a new competitive capacity, a more effective way of being enterprising.

Self-knowledge

As we examined earlier, contemporary American consumers are conditioned toward the exertion of self-governance whereby they regulate their credit use according to an understanding of the significance of their FICO scores. More precisely, they come to govern themselves through a specific rearticulation of the means by which they are simultaneously governed by lenders. Security toolkits further develop the possibilities for self-governance through conjoining knowledge of the scoring system, the realization of its significance, with the self-knowledge of the individual's own FICO score at specific points in time. As an abstract, quantified representation, the revelation of the score alone does not constitute self-knowledge alone for self-knowledge depends on a contextualization of the meaningfulness of the score. This meaning is engendered along six dimensions.

Population

The individual's three digit FICO score, drawn from one or more of the national bureaus, is located on the FICO scale running from 300, the highest risk, to 850, the lowest. Overlaid on this scale is an additional measure indicating that score's, and thus the individual's, percentile place within the population of U.S. consumers recorded by the credit bureaus. Within this context, the FICO score becomes a norm to be understood relativistically, a means of understanding who one is now and where one lies against one's peers. It is also a means of seeing where one could be in the future if this self-knowledge is applied to one's credit use. For example, a hypothetical consumer with a FICO score of 707 is shown the illustration in figure 11.1.[8]

Default

The individual's score is also mapped in terms of the average delinquency probability represented by the range their FICO score falls within and how

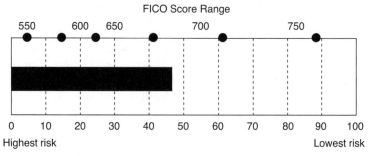

Figure 11.1   FICO ranking.
Source: Fair Isaac.

this compares against the general population of consumers (see fig. 4.5).[9] What "delinquency" means is also defined for the consumer, namely, loan default, bankruptcy or a 90 day late payment on at least one credit account in the following two years.

Reason Codes

The score may also be contextualized according to the individual's own actions through a statement of the "reason codes." These are a specific, limited categorization of factors within the model that most influenced the makeup of the individual's score based on the analysis of the particular attributes presented. These categories are divided into positive factors most enhancing the score, for example no late payments or the demonstration of a relatively long history, and negative ones most impacting, such as too many accounts open.

Financial Opportunities

One's FICO score is also rendered meaningful in financial terms so that one's potentialities and weaknesses as a consumer become plugged into the possibilities of market place choice. On the "myFICO loan savings calculator®," selecting their desired standard loan type, amount required and geographical location, a consumer is presented with FICO score ranges

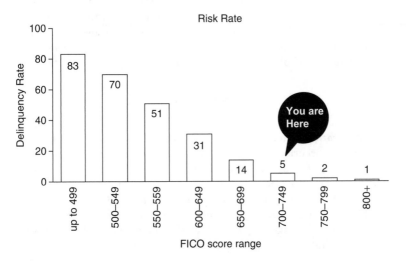

Figure 11.2   FICO risk distribution.
Source: Fair Isaac.

and associated interest rates applicable for such a loan along with the monthly payment and the total interest payable over the life of the credit agreement.[10] A segmented chart demonstrates what the individual, by dint of their risk virtuousness, avoided paying and what in the future, through the application of an ethic of improvement, they could save.

Specialist Information

In relation to planning for a mortgage, for example, the "myFICO Saver for Homebuyers" imparts specialist self-knowledge for the aspiring homeowner.[11] "Andy" the automated mortgage coach, through an analysis of the credit report and through the application of some judicious questions to the individual, weighs up total debts outstanding, FICO score, income, value of home sought, type of mortgage product desired, and preferred down payment to tell the individual how much they are likely to be able to borrow for a home loan, at what interest rate, and for what house price value.

Moral Standards

The consumer is didactically instructed on the ethicality of their FICO score, an attribution indicative of their absolute moral aptitude as a consumer, or even as an individual. For instance, within a brochure for one of their security toolkits, a notional consumer with a low ranking score is described in no uncertain terms as not having "good" scores, as being an "extreme risk" who will be "paying through the nose" on an "enormous interest rate" because of their fallibility and needs to "get their act together big-time."[12] Such a lack of self-mastery damns them as an aberration within the project of personalized entrepreneurialism and consigns them to the outer margins of choice.

Self-action

Beyond the generalized advice for action to improve one's FICO score described earlier such as "pay your bills on time" and "don't max out your credit cards," security toolkits offer possibilities of self-action predicated on self-knowledge for the directing of an ethic of improvement. Knowledge of one's score and one's position within the population demonstrates where one should be in a normative sense. In this, the FICO score as a norm exhibits a duality of meaning. For lower scored individuals, a norm implies the mass of the average-scored to which the individual should aspire while among the higher-scored, it represents an aspiration toward the highest bandwidth of scores attracting the lowest rates and the easiest terms of access.

To these ends "reason codes," in addition to situating self-knowledge in the present, allow the individual to take immediate remedial action on the most critical elements depressing their score while defending those factors, thus directing the continued pursuit of particular actions, which boost and elevate that score. Credit coaching facilities attached to some security toolkits direct the user on a wide array of actions with respect to their credit agreements. Specific action plans can be created and tailored to pay off revolving balances or lower interest rates being paid on credit cards thus raising score levels. Interactive tools allow the individual to see what they would be able to afford in terms of buying a house or car and how to attain these goals in the most cost-effective way. Within the "FICO Saver for Homebuyers" product, aspiring homeowners can extrapolate the consequences of certain actions on their required repayment levels for the mortgage amount they wish or are qualified to secure such as enhancing their FICO score, increasing the down payment percentage they are willing to offer or choosing a particular type of mortgage, such as a fixed or variable interest rate.[13]

However, it is through Fair Isaac's "Score Simulator®" that the specific future consequences of one's actions are rendered most meaningfully in the present.[14] Through this utility, individuals are shown the likely future consequences on their FICO score of certain individual actions they might take. These are divided into:

- *Always improve your score*: pay bills on time, pay down credit card balances, pay down delinquent balances
- *Might improve your score*: seek new credit, transfer credit card balances
- *Always harm your score*: miss payments, max out credit cards

In the example shown below, the consumer is shown how their score would change if they followed various close-ended actions, with everything else remaining the same. To the individual, it demonstrates the possibilities for one's FICO score of following certain courses of self-action in the event that other things stay same. Despite its appearance however, there is no specific future calculability inherent in this projection. Rather than providing an all-encompassing predictive picture of the future, it serves to demonstrate to the individual the inherent *possibilities* of certain, isolated courses of action at certain points in time that might be taken within the ongoing present, giving depth and meaning, but not *predictability*, to the personalized ethic of improvement. In crude terms, the score simulator facility shows what *can* happen, not what will happen[15]:

> See how your FICO Score might change if:
> - You miss payment this month on an account that is currently paid up-to-date.
> - You miss payments this month on all accounts for which a payment is due.
> - You declare bankruptcy.

Therefore, within the use of security toolkits, the individual is oriented toward a state of self-knowledge. Their desires and ambitions to consume through credit are brought into alignment with an understanding of oneself as a credit user in terms of how lenders understand it: one's risk score, one's location within the population of credit users and the consequences of one's FICO score for the possibility and cost of accessing credit. However, in coming to comprehend themselves as individuals with such quantified identities, consumers are infused with a moral awareness of their own position as consumers, understanding themselves as having a "good" or "bad" FICO score. For instance, in letters to a mortgage advice column syndicated within the United States, individual consumers commented:

> My credit report is great, with a 740 FICO score. But my husband's credit report is pretty bad, with only a 594 FICO score.[16]
>
> But my FICO score is 724 so you know my credit is good.[17]
>
> Because he has no income, the mortgage company has contacted me, as co-signer, threatening to ruin my superb 770 FICO credit score if I don't pay my nephew's $8,700 of unpaid mortgage payments.[18]
>
> My FICO score is only 590, and my wife doesn't have much credit. That's pretty bad, isn't it? But we are now current on all our bills.[19]

Each consumer thus makes a value judgment as to their own FICO score and what it proclaims about them as a consumer. As an objective statement of probability within an actuarial strategy of management, risk implies no judgment in and of itself until it enters into the specific context of a decision. However subjectively conceived, where the individual is made responsible for the consequences of their credit actions, it can exist as a definitive means of self-appraisement as to the exertion or the failure to exert a sustained self-mastery over one's actions. In doing so, it allows the individual to judge the extent of their own entrepreneurial aptitude. It is not so much the acts which are judged to be intrinsically moral or immoral but the relationship, evidenced by one's score, which the individual has to themselves.

The imperative of lenders to directly or indirectly maximize profitability through the marketing of consumer credit and to reduce costs through calculation of default risk becomes translated into a way for credit users to understand themselves, and through such understanding to act upon it, in their projects of consuming fulfillment. Individuals, as entrepreneurs of their own lives, become also entrepreneurs of credit consumption, attempting to optimize credit choice through ensuring what access is possible and achievable at the lowest possible cost. A FICO score is thus never fixed in representing and conducting the pursuit of the personalized entrepreneurial project, it is always amenable to change. To these ends, an ethic of improvement toward self-mastery is enjoined through the governing of self-action, a reflexively directed choreographing of one's FICO score through one's credit actions in the ongoing present. From this, it is hoped, the scope of ongoing future credit choice may be enhanced.

The Significance of Uncertainty

A FICO score exists as a probability statement, a quantified calculation of the likelihood that the individual will become delinquent with a certain degree of severity on credit obligations over a certain specific timescale. However, probability only achieves a calculable predictiveness within a large-scale context (Kavanagh, 1993; Reith, 2002, 2004a). For example, probability theory may suggest that tossing a fair coin will produce, on average, 500 heads over 1,000 tosses but it cannot reveal what the next single toss will produce. Uncertainty is irreducible in risk.

Similarly, in deciding on applications for credit facilities, creditors use the FICO score of any given individual only within a framework of dealing with a population of applicants. In a certain sense, the use of risk technologies in such a manner implies the inevitability of failure—a creditor will unavoidably encounter defaulting credit users and experience financial losses as a result. Nevertheless, in doing so, FICO and other risk scoring systems transform such losses into a more or less fixed cost of doing business, like taxes or employee salaries, which, once made calculable, can simply be offset against revenues to ensure the profitability of the firm. In the short term and on a micro level, any given score can never tell a lender how an individual will perform on a credit agreement ("a single toss"); rather, scoring helps produce a calculated assessment of how a population will perform ("1,000 tosses") and generates an assessment of the necessary macro costs of default that must be embraced to realize revenue and thus profit.

As we have analyzed so far, the generation of a FICO score has come to be used as a technique of governing the credit user to govern themselves. However, although it provides a generalized indicator of one's "esteem" or reliability as a credit user compared to the wider population, it cannot tell the individual whether they themselves will default; neither can it demonstrate to them how they will necessarily be treated by lenders given the diversity and niche marketing of the contemporary consumer credit marketplace. Just as for the lender in relation to any single consumer, no certainty applies to the isolated individual in relation to themselves. Therefore, in the parlaying of FICO from a bio-political technology into a technology of subjective self-understanding and self-management, the way in which a FICO score comes to be interpreted and deployed changes. In the former, an abstract actuarial conception locates the individual as an agglomeration of risk factors historically referenced to the empirically documented reality of the population. In the latter, an abstract attribution self-consciously represents the accumulated outcome of an individual's morally weighed and weighted credit conduct; while located and understood in relation to other credit users, it illuminates for the individual their own continuous process of consumption. Paradoxically then, a risk attribution comes to act as a means for the government of the self under conditions of uncertainty.

O'Malley (2000; 2004) argues that, rather then having been progressively eliminated by the diffusion of statistical technologies of risk in practices of government, uncertainty persists as a way of conceiving of the future. Analytically, he locates "uncertainty" and "statistical risk" not as binary opposites, but as opposite ends of a broadly conceived continuum of risk. In fact, not only has uncertainty not been superseded by probabilistic risk but uncertainty has come to be valorized within contemporary neoliberalism as a key attribute of the entrepreneurial spirit. Entrepreneurs in common cultural parlance, are not, as O'Malley suggests, risk minimizers but risk takers, approaching the future not as a source of peril to be quantifiably ascertained and negotiated but as a domain of profitable possibility to be exploited through adaptation and flexibility. Where statistical risk depends on the resemblance of the possible future to the empirical past, the entrepreneur must eschew the past and recognize future opportunities in the dynamic trajectory of the present through reliance on their own experience, reasoned estimation and skill. Thus, for O'Malley, uncertainty as a specific configuration of risk, although not formally calculable, nonetheless provides for a rational approach to the future.

O'Malley's concept of uncertainty provides a useful tool to analyze the actions of the reflexive credit user. Scoring as a technology of risk operates according to a sequential, episodic conception of time. The empirical performance of credit users with regard to repayment provides a known past in light of which a specific decision is taken in the present, generating a calculable outcome with respect to a defined point in the future. Such a technology is also specific in that it refers default outcomes in the past to default probabilities in the future. However, in making use of a specific risk score within subjective self-management, a different conceptualization of time is evident, one that is disorganized and fluctuating. Rather than risk serving to interpret the past, for a decision in the present with respect to an event in the future, risk distills the past into a coherent, ongoing sense of oneself in the present. In doing so, risk does not preempt the future nor refer to a particular future state but provides merely the medium to defend or enhance the self against uncertainties in the interests of securing ongoing autonomy and freedom of choice. In this regard, risk is continual—it refers not to specific decisions taken continuously at specific points in time but rather to a continual, shifting, changing attribution to be diligently acted upon in the unfurling present for the benefit of an ongoing future.

This blurring of time, or perhaps more specifically the disappearance of a transcendent future, is evident in how risk as an attribution exists as both the means and goal—as something to be acted upon for the purpose of maintaining and developing it, in doing so becoming a dynamic to its own continuance in an inescapable present. Thus as an actuarial population-based technology, scoring transforms uncertainty into calculable risk. But in its forming of a subjectively managed attribution, risk is given effect within "technologies of uncertainty": those security toolkits described in the previous section. As O'Malley suggests, uncertainty is closely affiliated with liberty—unlike calculable risk that ties a vision of the future to a repetition of the past, uncertainty implies dynamism and freedom; in contemporary neoliberal terms, the potentialities of creative entrepreneurialism to apply initiative, to innovate and realize the fruits of its own vigor and resourcefulness.

The Uncertainty of the Self

But what is it that is uncertain for the individual credit user? How is uncertainty being managed? Centrally, it is the self that exists as a source of uncertainty. Valverde argues that:

> the persistence of illiberal practices of moral governance is indicative not of a failure to complete the liberal project but rather of a seldom noticed but irreducible despotism in the heart of the paradigmatic liberal subject's relation to himself. (1996: 359)

What she demonstrates in her argument is that, in liberalism's dependence upon the self-governing capacities of subjects, the individual exerts a continuous, sustained reign of control upon themselves, a "despotism" of the self, creating and re-creating the conditions for the victory of reason over the sensuous passions of nature. It is not simply that the individual, with the internalization of control imbued through socialization and education, becomes a free self-governing individual but that a recidivism of unreason, an atavism, constantly threatens in the liberal imagination to destroy that freedom. Similarly Reith (2004b, 2007), in her discussion of the concept of addiction, cites how the collision of the notions of addiction as a subjective loss of control and risk as vulnerability have created addiction as a realist threat inciting a dense, steadfast effort of self-monitoring on the part of prudent individuals as an inescapable obligation of their freedom.

According to Valverde (1996, 1997; 1998), the concept of habit provides for a particular form of self-despotism whereby the routine, monotonous, repeated engagement of specific actions by the individual aspires to a permanent transformation of the self. For her, habit encapsulates both the liberal aspiration to individual autonomy as well as a pessimism as to its possibility, for the promise of self-government by habit resides not in the content of one's conscious actions but in unconscious incorporation through blind repetition.

Within an environment of consumption and the proliferation of the notion of choice, the individual is held to be a locus of intrinsic needs, wants, and desires subsumed in passion and excited by the array of consumption before it. Pricked by such impulses, the contemporary individual is conceived around a core of atavistic hedonism, potentially never ending and unbounded in its desires. Within neoliberalism, consumption exists as a creative device for the sustained continual exercise of autonomous choice by the individual over an extended time, allowing the inscription of a lifestyle as a project of the self. Desire and need are essential but just as essential is the need for them to be channeled, controlled, and managed over time to allow for the reproduction of choice. This balancing act is part of what Stearns interprets to be a much wider cultural dilemma of self-control:

> The contemporary system of self-control blends the pressures of a consumer society, with its multitude of goods and spectacles begging for indulgence, with the needs of a moralistic society whose conscience owes much to Victorian precedent. (1999: 29)

It is not choice per se that demonstrates one's freedom but the ability to sustain and propagate it. Without control, choice can quickly become expended in the short term and the sustenance of a lifestyle break down, thus turning consumption from a creative resource into a destructive one and rendering the individual unfree for its pursuit. As a critical conduit in the service of consumption, the indiscipline or inability to sustain repayments signifies just such a lapse into destructive hedonism and becomes exhibited as the collapse of self-mastery in time over one's credit identity and FICO score. Thus the capricious and aleatoric play of one's needs and desires and the manifestation of one's choices—a new car loan, a mortgage for a bigger home, loans for college tuition fees for one's children—are, over time, uncertainties that must be governed through one's FICO score. These are uncertainties of the self to which one must maintain a constant vigilance.

In many ways the vigilance of the contemporary credit user takes the form of habitual action. In the actual use of one's credit, injunctions to pay your bills on time, keep balances low, and apply for new credit only when needed imply a need for ongoing, time structured good habits as much as consciously considered action. Through the reflexive management of one's score, the consumption of security toolkits to acquire one's score on a regular basis, receive updates whenever one's score changes or renew one's subscription also embody a sense of accustomed action whose effectiveness in instilling self-government derives as much from the ordered repetition of reflexivity as the reflexivity itself engendered.

As I have attempted to demonstrate, however, the process of managing uncertainty is not merely a defensive formation but an active project of maximizing one's credit potential. Through the honoring of one's repayment obligations or careful applications for new credit, one can improve one's score (albeit incalculably) thereby enhancing future freedom of choice as opposed to merely maintaining one's quota of current freedom. Such freedom, though, is not only instrumental but emotional. In plotting out the imagined month-by-month credit tribulations of "Vera, a single mother," a Fair Isaac information leaflet tells us in the ultimate month that:

> Vera has steadily paid down her high credit card balance and monitored her score. When her score has improved, Vera applies and is approved for an excellent rate on an auto loan. She buys a used car and *feels good about how she has managed her credit.* (my emphasis)[20]

It is not simply that "Vera" has reaped the consuming benefits of self-mastery and enjoys the sensuous thrills of automotive freedom but that she is induced to "feel good" about her moral elevation as a consumer and its implication as to her worth as an individual.

Systemic Uncertainty

Uncertainty does not reside only within the individual themselves; it also exists within the technology used to generate a risk attribution. In terms of being assessed as a credit risk, the individual can be located within a complex, shifting three dimensional field of risk. Multiple systems and interpretations of risk are used to actuarially govern the individual credit user therefore, in governing their own actions, the individual must be cognizant of them and their differences. Ultimately, this signifies the relativity of risk as a norm that is generated within a population toward specific ends and does not correspond to anything intrinsic to the individual; nevertheless they are made known to the individual as parallel risk circuits existing within the beneficially competitive diversity of the credit market and which locate the individual in specific, localizable ways.

On the first dimension, as we have analyzed in chapter 7, different types of risk system exist. Most commonly, lenders operate their own specific application risk system constructed on the specific population of their customer base rather than on credit bureau records, allowing the lender to produce a more specialized risk assessment and also incorporate additional information. The reflexive credit user, although not having general access to this specific risk assessment, is instructed as to its specificity and cautioned as to the types of additional information that may be included as well as the fact that such scores often incorporate a FICO score assessment.[21] The individual is thus made aware not just of FICO, but also its limits and boundaries—gaining access to credit is not simply down to the information comprising one's credit identity but other information including income or residential neighborhood. To govern oneself effectively through a FICO score thus requires knowledge of how its actuarial use within lending is distinct from, or articulated with, the attributions generated through alternative, localized risk systems.

On the second dimension, different bureau-based scoring systems exist as alternatives to FICO, which work off the same data yet generate alternative scores on different scales depending on how the model was constructed and how it interprets attributes and characteristics. These may be marketed to and used by lenders to generate risk attributions within the context of credit decisions as well as being FICO "clones" aimed purely at the consumer market. These alternative scores are essentially rivals to Fair Isaac, both as suppliers of scores to lenders and to consumers. In this second case, consumers are alerted to the fact that such devices exist but are cautioned that "when purchasing a credit score for yourself, make sure to get the FICO score, as this is the score most lenders will look at in making credit decisions about you."[22] In redirecting their scoring technology as a security toolkit for credit users, Fair Isaac exploit their preeminence among lenders to define the real world fidelity of their consumer product and competitively differentiate it from others. Consumers are enjoined to be *rational* in defining and acting upon themselves as subjects according to a risk attribution upon which they are most likely to be actuarially defined and acted upon. In fact, reflexively acting on the basis of a non-FICO score to enhance access to credit could actually prove counterproductive. Consumers thus should be educated as to differences between bureau scoring systems.[23]

On the third dimension, there is not simply "one" FICO score. Firstly, given that the relationship between bureaus and lenders within the credit reporting assemblage is a market one, lenders can choose which and how many bureaus they wish to share information with. Secondly, clerical errors between lenders, bureaus, and others in reporting information about the credit conduct of individuals can lead to discrepant information being posted on a consumer's credit record. For instance, a study by the Consumer Federation of America presented evidence of a significant variation in the information being held between the three national credit bureaus.[24] In its sample of consumers, 31 percent experienced disparities of at least 50 FICO points between reports while 5 percent experienced disparities of 100 points or more.[25] Therefore, given that an individual's record of repayments and credit use may not be the same at all bureaus, the FICO model will interpret and distill potentially discrepant information to produce differing FICO risk identities. Such inconsistencies exist, it is argued, not despite the rational objective nature of risk scoring but because of it. Almost like the Christian holy trinity, each credit user is composed of one FICO score with three distinct essences depending on whether or how their actions are recorded.

Discrepant diversity, far from being projected in a negative way, is conceived partially as an asset of the credit reporting assemblage. Different bureaus have different unique "data strengths" to which the FICO model is specifically tailored, increasing its overall predictiveness.[26] In addition, it is suggested that the competition between each of the bureaus drives down costs and promotes innovation so that "[b]oth lenders and consumers benefit from having more than one choice."[27] However, such schizophrenia does not undermine such a project of reflexive self-government; on the contrary, it extends the scope and reach of responsibility for the consumer who becomes conditioned to manage three sub-scores in one. Of course, lenders and credit bureaus act to ensure consistency in the reporting and recording of repayments and other information but the individual themselves must regularly examine for significant inconsistencies in their different FICO scores, scrutinize the content of credit reports from all three bureaus and act to remedy any non- or mis-reporting of their credit actions.[28]

*   *   *

Within a Foucauldian framework of power, individual subjectivity is created through processes of government:

> This form of power applies itself to immediate everyday life which categorizes the individual, marks him by his own individuality, attaches him to his own identity, imposes a law of truth on him which he must

recognize and which others have to recognize in him. It is a form of power which makes individuals subjects. (Foucault, 1983: 212)[29]

As subjects, free individuals come to think about, and act upon themselves, as individuals through the means by which they are governed. In contemporary times, where the individual's faculty of choice, their autonomy and enterprise are the site of government, the individual is steered toward governing their own autonomy and enterprising their own conduct. The legislative impulse since the 1970s has had just that as its aim—for example, the Fair Credit Reporting Act (FCRA) delineated certain rights of the consumer to check their credit record and provided specific remedying procedures for misreporting but, in doing so, established the credit file as the partial responsibility of the individual to uphold, helped define for individuals the difference between legitimate and illegitimate reporting and, more broadly, helped establish a sense of calculation in the minds of consumers as to the constitution of creditworthiness. This was not a process that was imposed but, on the contrary, it met with demands by activists and consumers for a legally enforceable right to know the content of their reports, to determine and shape their own destiny as consumers; demands which ultimately accepted the legitimacy of personal information gathering and dissemination where it facilitated the individual's capacity for enterprising consumption.

The 1970s disclosure debate leading to the FCRA found resonance at the end of the 1990s when consumer groups, media, politicians, and others agitated for score disclosure to consumers. The logic of contemporary individual self-government makes it seem almost impossible that the outcome could have been anything other than such disclosure as demanded. However, what distinguishes it was that it was not legislatively imposed (although this was threatened) and that it took the form of a commodity to be sold to consumers as a product realizing a commercial profit. Rather than a "right" to which the credit bureaus could demand an administrative fee as happened with credit report disclosure, score disclosure took the form of a "good," a good to be branded, marketed, advertised, and sold on the enterprise-inducing potential it offered consumers willing to submit themselves to it.

In light of the process of disclosure, the past three chapters have attempted to set out how consumers have come to govern themselves according to a risk-based FICO score fabricated from and through their individualized credit identities. It has also sought to explore the significance of this process within the contemporary American neoliberal rationality of government. Crucially, as we have seen, consumers are instructed on how their actions in using credit are interpreted to form an individualized FICO score represented as "their" quantified score. In creating such an alignment, this risk score functions as a "rational" norm by which the individual comes to judge themselves as a consumer, becoming a mechanism for regulating their credit conduct in order to expand their consuming potential. In governing themselves in light of their score, the individual is confronted with the morality of their actions, the slow steady uncertain accumulation of "good" actions over time being the path to self-improvement rather than any predictable technical expediency. Morality in this sense refers not to action but conduct, the relationship that the individual exhibits with themselves in using credit. Therefore, as free individuals fulfilling their lives through consumption and the ongoing project of identity creation and personal fulfillment, conducting individuals in the management of their FICO scores becomes a means of empowering them to become more enterprising, to equip them with the means to increase their capacity for future choice by lowering the costs and qualifications of accessing credit. To be enterprising requires the individual to balance the consuming needs and desires of the present with the responsibility of sustaining an ability to consume for the duration of their lives.

A risk score of this kind thus comes to represent, in a certain sense, the consuming capital of the individual, reflecting the outcome of their credit conduct and in turn, delimiting the possibilities of their future choice. As we have seen, this has consequences not just in relation to credit but a multitude of fields where the individual exists as a consumer. In conditioning ongoing consuming freedom, a FICO attribution indexes the degree of discrete "unfreedoms" that the individual has, over time, been able to exert over themselves, becoming a generalized catalog of their prudence. As we noted above, Fair Isaac Corporation and the Equifax credit bureau began, from 2001, to supply consumers their scores as a marketed product. In doing so, scoring became parlayed from an actuarial technology supplied to lenders to calculably manage the default risk exposure of their loan portfolios to a consumer product or product range for individual consumption. This transformation produced significant changes in how consumers were conceived and also in how the broader credit market operated, with new alliances and formations emerging to profitably govern the self-governing capacities of consumers. As goods, they not only promise the possibility of enhanced consumption but represent, within themselves, a manifestation of consumption incorporable within particular kinds of lifestyle.

The use of security toolkits, including the repetitive revelation of an actual score, represent an attempt to move consumers beyond a knowledge of the significance of their FICO scores to the sustained, personalized practice of self-knowledge and self-action in the governing of their credit conduct. To the individual consumer, their score alone is relatively meaningless unless contextualized as an attribution in terms of the broader population of consumers, the most pressing specific categories of variables swaying it, the credit consuming opportunities it represents within the market and the "moral" plateau it is deemed to inhabit. Simultaneous to this self-knowledge, means of self-action to direct improvement are also allotted to the consumer: the function of the score as a population norm inducing the consumer toward a more prosperous category while reason codes, coaching, and the generation of simulated outcomes encourage them to actively pursue particular tactics to attain this. Although a score represents a defined, objective probabilistic risk for a lender, its attribution within subjective self-government sheers it of this calculability—deployed within security toolkits, it guides consumer conduct only by way of uncertainty.

Uncertainty in this sense, however, does not represent a relative fallibility but rather cohabits necessarily with the obligation of the consumer to render their life as an enterprise of the self. Discursively, enterprise implies prudence, dynamism, flair, and adaptability to shifting conditions within which to realize opportunity; therefore, the requirement of the consumer to make an enterprise of their lives cannot grant a calculability or predictability to action but depends fundamentally on their flexibility and spontaneous creativity. Enterprise is about freedom; but this freedom, as we have seen, has as its corollary a more all-round, finely grained management of the self. In their inducement to self-government through risk, the consumer is thus bound between two poles of uncertainty: an "uncertainty from within" residing in the individual's own unending impulses and desires to consume; and a "systemic uncertainty" located within the multiple, shifting technologies of risk. A further uncertainty that potentially threatens consumers and which security toolkits can be deployed against is an "uncertainty from without": the growing hazard of identity theft by other renegade consumers (see Marron, 2008). Against these uncertainties, only a sustained mastery by the individual over themselves, and over their credit identity, provides a counter strategy for ensuring their autonomy and freedom.

Conclusion: Taking Life

In Visa's 2005 television advertising campaign, a child is shown skillfully negotiating a series of handrails at a playground (life takes ambition), a pretty blonde woman clumsily sends a bowling ball down an alley, achieving an unlikely strike in the process much to the delight of her companions (life takes luck); a young man tiredly but stubbornly consumes his way through an enormous hamburger (life takes determination); an athletic young black woman feints a male opponent to score (life takes confidence), which is given the briefest but most significant of hand acknowledgments (life takes respect); a young male office worker warily maneuvers sixteen stacked cups of coffee (life takes talent); a young girl merrily skips and weaves across a concrete landscape (life takes joy); and a young couple walk down the aisle of a Vegas-style "Chapel of Love" (life takes spontaneity). These are the attributes being elicited from the contemporary consumer who must undertake life as a personal journey full of purpose and meaning, a life that both accepts and requires—in a general sense—this particular branded form of credit.

What is intimated is that for the individual, life becomes a function of choices made and alternatives foregone, the cumulative success of which depends on the relative strengths demonstrated, whether inherent, honed, or aleatoric. What we put in, our own "individual wit and muscle" as Bauman (1997: 39) puts it, determines what we produce out, whether alone, against or in conjunction with others—with credit serving as both the infrastructure and medium for exercising those choices. Credit responds not only to our needs and desires but our wants, producing an immediate outlet for their realization within a universalized, globalized marketplace. The credit card, the true fixed global currency, the lingua franca of consumer commerce operates as the incarnation of our choosing potential. Embossed with our name and unique sixteen digit number, emblazoned with our chosen provider, group, or status group, it embodies who we are in the modern consumer marketplace.

Yet, in Bauman's (2000) terminology, credit cards are liquid, always contingent and only ever held until further notice. In the West, consumers play the "surfing game" and the "credit card shuffle," effortlessly slipping from card to card for the latest balance transfer deal and rewards offer as financial institutions covet and cannibalize each other's market share (Manning, 2000). Yet, both Visa and its oligarchic rivals MasterCard and, to a lesser extent American Express, represent perhaps the meta-choice of consumer society with their preeminent payment networks and massive market shares, much like how personal computer manufacturers' market wares run exactly the same Microsoft software. They provide the permanent cybernetic interface of consumerism, plugging us as choosing (and chosen) subjects into the product or experience that is to be purchased, regardless of bank or provider.

From the early days of consumer capitalism, credit has been a personalized contingent resource enabling, often problematically, the fulfillment of certain needs or desires. As that which is chosen within the market has proliferated, so too have the arenas where credit can be used, the providers of credit and the credit alternatives themselves. It seems hard to imagine that it was only in the early 1990s that supermarket chains began to regularly accept credit cards while the successful development of internet shopping would seem an impossibility today without their ubiquity; and in a strange symbiosis, not only do we get our credit cards from banks but branded, too, from the likes of Wal-Mart and Amazon.com. It seem, then, that not only do we choose our credit card but, in doing so, we choose ourselves: credit cards can be customized to reflect our cultural pursuits and interests, our professional occupational group, our alma mater or favorite charity or cause; credit cards also represent our degree of meta-choice with, in the example of American Express, an inflation of green, gold, platinum, and black cards providing a color-coded hierarchy of our income, credit, and "pecuniary potential."

In perhaps a profound cultural turn, the array of credit cards encased within the wallets of the average American seem to have usurped the Social Security card as the new expression of citizenship. Just as the Federal Trade Commission warns consumers not to carry their Social Security cards for fear of identity theft, marketers equally caution the credit card consumer against leaving home without it. In a climate of insecure, short-term job contracts, downsizing, recession, career shifts, and permanent training, credit cards provide an easily accessible resource to smooth the bumps and troughs of income, to maintain an acceptable standard of living and condition the pursuit of a coherent lifestyle (Bernthal, Crockett, and Rose, 2005: 135–6). If the welfarist state provided unemployment assistance grounded in work to sustain the income of the household until it could be reengaged in labor, the credit card prolongs purchasing power and consumption patterns to sustain the lifestyle of the household. Where the former came to be collectively instituted by a corporative union of the state, capital, and labor within the context of a politicized class consciousness, the latter is offered through the logic of the market and competition, data-mining, and segmented marketing practice. It is an object to be "freely" and individually chosen on the basis of income, credit identity, and other qualifying criteria.

The contemporary consumer market is not an exclusive club; although, that is not to say that it does not play out divisions, reinscribe inequalities, and exacerbate exploitation nationally and across the globe. Yet never have authorities, political and economic, been so keen to encompass everyone within its fold. In relation to credit, the Marquette Supreme Court judgment of 1978, which helped liberalize state interest rate ceilings and subsequent statutory deregulation, acted to streamline the market to enhance the depth and scale of choice. In 2004, the then private but congressionally sponsored wholesale mortgage buyer Fannie Mae committed itself in its "American Dream Commitment Plan" to expanding rates of homeownership among minorities and lower income groups, promulgating the entrepreneurial accumulation of real estate equity that could be borrowed and reborrowed against, secured by rising property prices. Individual debt rather than collective redistribution was the governing mantra as lenders, more generally, aligned profitability to new subprime markets for mortgages, loans, and credit cards. But the gravity of value and inequality could not be cheated forever.

Beyond tiered mainstream provision, financial interests have also plumbed the outer "fringe" market of consumption through the revival of pawnshops and salary lenders on a large-scale commercial level. Yet despite the rhetoric of "democratization," market involvement is never equal nor does it ever provide a universal equality of opportunity. Opportunity, rather, depends on the individual's resources and resourcefulness as a consumer, their means, skill, and luck in keeping a particular narrative going, their particular ability to cherish their life as a dynamic project. Through the lender inscription of consumer choices and attributes, the frictionless circulation of such information and the statistical mining of data at the level of a population, what is made available to the individual consumer depends on what they bring. This means everything: the material and cultural resources of class with their attendant possibilities; the relative financial resources of an occupation well or ill-chosen; the institutional reputation of that postcode where one chooses (or can only afford) to live and all the other basic structural divisions that circumscribe every individual within society. More specifically, it also embodies the tactical outcome of every credit-related, market-mediated choice made, from the taking-out of student loans to defaulting on incurred medical bills.

Our scale of choice is dependent on how we manage ourselves in the consumer-rendered living of our lives, how we balance, within ourselves, personal horizons to individual circumstances, how we tailor the ongoing present, in light of our ever present past, in the interest of an extended future with its pronounced uncertainties and engaging opportunities. In short, we are permanently assessed in our project management abilities where that project is the conduct of our own lives. Perhaps even more so in a time of recession.

Liberal government has never assumed the liberal subject; he or she has always had to be made, forged, and fabricated with the potential to endure responsibility. Contemporary government, from numerous sites, articulates the problem and pedagogically inculcates within consumers the careful regulation of personal credit use. Lewis Mandell (2002) bemoans the failure of high school students to grasp the basics of credit use while the not-for-profit Jump$tart Coalition for Personal Financial Literacy (who commissioned Mandell's research) aims to improve the basic skills of children in the management of financial affairs. Sociologist Robert Manning castigates the campus marketing efforts of credit card companies that solicit students into a life of debt while American universities respond by offering modules in personal finance. Or perhaps, as Pinto, Parente, and Mansfield's (2005) research indicates, it is parents who are the best teachers. Meanwhile, various state agencies, lenders, and personal finance experts prompt us to keep a careful running eye on our outgoings and expenditures, to check our credit reports and credit scores and keep a weather eye out for the identity thief who may rummage through our trash cans to infiltrate our lovingly arranged credit identities. Just as workers fought collectively for their rights before the state and capital, equally consumers have fought for and have been grudgingly granted rights to sustain their consuming endeavors. These include, notably, the right to due process in credit decisions, the right to receive copies of credit reports and the opportunity to purchase credit scores. Yet just as capital once endorsed the welfare state as an essential component to its survival, commercial lenders have ultimately come to embrace these consumer rights as self-evident necessities of a modern credit market.

For those who breach the terms of good conduct in credit use, whose enthusiasm for credit and consumption outstrips the disciplined requirement to sustain a regime of repayment, intervention is at hand to bolster or brace the sclerotic will. Personal credit counselors offer subjective self-administered tests for examining and articulating the existence of a problem; techniques are suggested for measuring the extent of the paralyzing debt; tactical advice is presented on how to manage creditors and collectors and strategic guidance proffered on the legal process of bankruptcy; suggestions for consolidating debt are listed; and finally, strategies are proposed for rebuilding a credit identity and getting back on a new, sustainable path. For the same effect, the consumer may turn to the pages of self-help literature promising an elusive means for that longed-for personal transformation. Titles like *Credit Repair to Credit Millionaire, The Guerrilla Guide to Credit Repair,* and *Credit After Bankruptcy: A Step by Step Action Plan* pledge the possibility of revolutionizing the self, from a repressed to a free authentic state, in small, incremental steps.

More profoundly, undisciplined credit use may become interpreted as one of compulsion or addiction, the manifestation of a particular "epidemic of the will" (Sedgwick, 1992). As two consumer researchers claim in an examination of psychologically "compelled" credit users, "[i]t is likely that for these people, the typical credit abuse intervention program involving consumer counseling, education, and good budgeting skills will not be sufficient. Clearly psychological counseling and support groups will be critical in overcoming this problem" (Faber and O'Guinn, 1988: 106). Here, a clear distinction is made between the poorly socialized and the pathological, requiring differing forms of guidance and intervention. Yet, today, the addict suffers not so much from the imposition of a deviant label as engages a voluntary identification with a subjective state that is static and permanent; the embrace of a determined modality that denies the contemporary obligation to choose (Reith, 2004b: 296). This identity is given force and weight through such peer-help groups as Debtors Anonymous, its manual *Currency of Hope* and associated Twelve Step forums. These provide a means by which individuals can express and rationalize their perceived lack of control in relation to credit and habitualize a regime of abstinence. "Eternal vigilance is the price of recovery."

Many analysts, commentators, and others question the sustainability of the national burden of consumer debt or accuse it of helping to precipitate a banking and economic crisis. Others question the alteration of cultural values, criticize the misery of indebtedness and poverty, and the solicitation of individuals to live in the moment. These are crucial issues and, indeed, it remains to be seen how much the current deep recession and rising unemployment levels will transform, in C. Wright Mills's terminology, the "private trouble" of debt into a much wider "public issue" of indebtedness. Yet, as we have seen, fears about credit are not and cannot be disengaged from the historically specific fears that certain groups feel toward others, whether they be other groups or society as a whole. Today, practices of "fringe credit" interlink with concerns about how to govern the practices and will of the poor as much as the market; perhaps also, concern about the growing burden of middle-class debt and the loss of a self-determination express the anxiousness of the middle class toward their own position, status, and purpose or the progress of society more widely. Since the emergence of consumer credit, such fears, manifested in discourses of excess, overindulgence, chaos, temptation, and exploitation, have served as precursors to intervention by state or expert. As we analyzed in chapter 1, early municipal pawnbroking regulations sought to alleviate the position of the impoverished pawner and police the disorder perceived to attach to the business. In the nineteenth century, small loan lending attracted the attentions of philanthropists, and later the partnership of the Russell Sage Foundation and individual state legislatures, concerned with easing the burden on the working poor. Most recently, the 2005 Fair and Accurate Credit Transactions Act has sought to make it easier for consumers to protect themselves, and recover from, the debilitating impact of identity theft perceived to have been released by the dynamism of the contemporary market. Freedom to borrow, it seems, is always warily encountered.

In a more fundamental sense, though, and as this book has attempted to elaborate, governance and control are at the heart of the credit transaction. Within the specific confines of consumer credit transactions, lenders have always attempted to bind the actions of the borrower against some conception of the future, whether through the security of valuable collateral, the channeling of repayment actions within bureaucratic procedures, the alignment of legal coercion, or some form of assessment as to the will of the borrower under material constraints. The future, an abstract temporal conception itself arising from the complexity and interdependency of human action within the world, represents a chancy state to which repayment, and thus profit, is tied. In this, lenders attempt to tame chance through such historically diverse and complex strategies as trusting to the relative strength of will of certain class or ethnic groups; legally, temporally, and bureaucratically binding the actions of consumers; empirically transforming chance into risk through the statistical analysis of a population of consumers or holding an individual's personal postdated check from which repayment can be relatively assured.

The contemporary mainstream credit market of the last several decades, characterized by "democratization" and mass accessibility, fluidity, depth, and diversity of choice—in a word, freedom—has only been made possible by subtle yet extensive and far-reaching mechanisms of government that shape and direct the conduct of consumers. These include the development of a rhizomatic, technologically mediated mechanism of surveillance that creates virtual credit identities reflecting and shaping the possibilities of choice; the uncertain, shifting rolling out of risk technologies allowing distant and unknown consumers to be instantaneously "made known" and assessed; and the inculcation of moralized, temporal habits and practices of reflexive self-government in relation to individual credit use. What is perhaps most characteristic of the contemporary credit system within the United States and elsewhere is the degree to which formal mechanisms of government are embedded in the very "soul" of the consumer. Such control over credit use penetrates deep into the subjective state of the individual; individualized and internalized, it embodies not only the individual's generalized injunction to self-government but an increasing reflexivity over the means by which they are assessed and judged by lenders. Like Cooley's looking-glass self, the individual credit user has come to be governed to think about and act upon their own credit use through the means by which the population of consumers are so governed. Yet, such new forms of governance are not perceived to be an imposition upon the individual and their mode of conduct; on the contrary, they have been achieved under the aspirational rubric of privacy rights, freedom, and consumer empowerment.

If one wishes to see the sheer efficacy of this technological and subjective mode of governance, one need look no further than the growing body of fringe lenders, chains of pawnbrokers, household good rental centers, and payday lenders that act as bankers to the poor, the marginal, and the economically and consumerstically disenfranchised. Here sophisticated, subtle, all-embracing mechanisms of control are deliberately forsaken to target this market. In their stead are eye-watering triple-figure interest rates on small-scale, short-term loans and stiff corralling methods that compel repayment due or act to obviate loss for any single transaction. As Jack Daugherty, the founder of Cash America pawnshops bluntly put it, "I could take my customers and put them on a bus and drive them down to a bank and the bank would laugh at them. That's why they're my customers" (cited in Caskey, 1991: 88). Lacking much institutional recognition as self-governing subjects, the contemporary fringe borrower must seemingly offer up more, in terms of both repayments and freedom, for the privilege of a loan. It is, perhaps, only by examining this dark side of the consumer credit market that we can truly illuminate the crafty genius of government, airy and delicate yet resolute and ubiquitous, embodied within exchanges and flows of the contemporary consumer credit system. Like the heddles of a loom, it helps secure the warp of desire for the weft of profit. Like a latter-day Huxleyan soma, it ensnares us the more it makes us free.

Notes

Introduction

1. See, for example, *Remarks by Chairman Alan Greenspan at the Economic Development Conference of the Greenlining Institute*, 11 October 1997, San Francisco CA. In more recent testimony to Congress, Greenspan admitted that the financial crisis of 2008 instigated by the "credit crunch" had caused him to question his belief in unfettered markets.
2. Mennell (2007) raises the wider point that growing employment within vast organizations during the twentieth century exerted a "civilizing" effect on individual conduct. Through an "increasing social constraint towards self-constraint," individuals could be relied upon more to control and manage their own conduct.
3. A recent exception to this is Burton, 2008.

2 Consuming by Installments: The Rise of Retail Credit

1. Over a century later, Russian banks would use a similar strategy to expand, grow, and develop their nascent credit card programs (Guseva, 2008). Within the British moneylending industry, which focuses on relatively poor households as its primary market, existing customers are often invited to suggest friends, neighbors, and acquaintances as new customers (Leyshon et al., 2006b: 177–8).
2. Rappaport (2000) discusses a similar phenomenon centered on London's West End shopping areas.

4 Mass Credit, Mass Society, and Their Discontents

1. It should be acknowledged that the FHA was, in effect, institutionally racist. It promoted a policy of redlining, or noncoverage, which discriminated against Black American families (Hillier, 2003).
2. Interestingly, the Russell Sage Foundation did develop two uniform laws on installment credit in the 1940s but achieved no success in having a version passed in any state; the organization later withdrew from credit as a field for its activities after the war (Mors, 1950: 206).

5 Plastic Credit, Plastic Lifestyles

1. A marketing analysis of credit cards at the time found that credit cards users could be segmented, yet this was on the basis of "class" rather than "lifestyle" (Mathews and Slocum, 1969). "Middle," "upper middle," and "upper" classes segments who were able to defer gratification were characterized as being convenience users (that is, paid-off balances each month) while "lower" and "lower middle" class segment, where "immediate gratifications and readiness-to-express impulses are observed" (p. 72), were deemed far more likely to revolve credit balances.

2. This is, perhaps, both ironic and inevitable given that the transactional use of credit cards for such relatively banal consumer practices as supermarket shopping and dental checkups has increased.

3. "The MBNA Cash Back Platinum Plus MasterCard Credit Card.". Available online at https://wwwa.applyonlinenow.com/USCCapp/Ctl/entry?sc=C0HH& mc=A000001SSG [accessed 6 February 2006]; "The Motley Fool Cashback Platinum Plus Visa Card." Available online at https://wwwa.applyonlinenow. com/USCCapp/Ctl/entry?sc=HWV2&mc=A000001OMJ [accessed 6 February 2006].

4. "Fidelity Investment Rewards Visa Signature Card." Available online at https:// wwwa.applyonlinenow.com/USCCapp/Ctl/entry?sc=GLA1&mc=A000001TST [accessed 6 February 2006]; "Babymint 529 College Savings Platinum Plus Mastercard Credit Card." Available online at https://www.applyonlinenow. com/USCCapp/Ctl/ entry?sc=L0AJ&mc=A000001VYH [accessed 6 February 2006].

5. Of course, the objection can be raised that this is lender propaganda. The savings being accumulated are vastly outweighed by the potential debts being incurred and that credit cards are merely appealing to a Protestant ethic as they simultaneously encourage a departure from it. This is, of course, true. The point being made here, however, is that consumers are encouraged to widen and nurture their sphere of choice through consuming and saving at the same time. Within neoliberalism, the irrational or inept consumer is the one who, through habit or laziness, does not shop around for these available options.

6. "MBNA Elvis Presley Foundation Worldpoints Platinum Plus Credit Card." Available online at https://wwwn.applyonlinenow.com/USCCapp/Ctl/ entry?sc=LWW8&mc=A000001VLW [accessed 26 January 06].

7. Affinity cards have proven very successful for lenders in attracting a higher rate of applications and exhibiting a higher turnover of transactions relative to conventional offerings (Burton, 2008: 102).

8. Design Week, 27 May 2004: p. 6.

9. "Benefits of the Platinum Card from American Express." Available online at https://www124.americanexpress.com/cards/platinum/benefits.jsp [accessed 4 February 2006].

10. "Visa Signature." Available online at http://www.usa.visa.com/personal/cards/credit/ visa_signature.html?it=R3|/|Visa per cent20Signature [accessed 9 February 2006].

11. "American Express Platinum Card Concierge." Available online at https://www124. americanexpress.com/cards/platinum/concierge.jsp [accessed 4 February 2006].

12. Carter's move should be seen within the wider context of his concern for the decline that he believed had infected the nation in the 1970s, economically in terms of stagflation and the OPEC shocks but also morally and spiritually in terms of the loss of American cultural values, institutional decline, and the growth of a selfish consumerism. Interestingly, Lasch's "culture of narcissism" and Bell's "cultural contradictions of capitalism" were sociological concepts that were extremely influential in shaping the president's famous "malaise" speech (Horowitz, 2004: 225–44).

6   Credit Reporting and Consumer Surveillance

1. For example, according to Experian, "Your Experian credit report does not contain—and Experian does not collect—data about race, religious preference, medical history, personal lifestyle, political preference, friends, criminal record or any other information unrelated to credit." See "Credit report basics FAQs," Experian. Available online at http://www.experian.com/consumer/ credit_report_faqs.html [accessed 2 March 2006].
2. Hier (2003), though, cautions that such rhizomatically structured surveillance does not imply that social hierarchies themselves are necessarily leveled, arguing that the "shoots of the assemblage" can be readily deployed by established authorities for the purposes of social control.

7   Risk and Technologies of Credit Scoring

1. "Consumer FAQs," TransUnion. Available online at http://www.transunion. com/content/page.jsp?id=/personalsolutions/general/data/GeneralFAQ.xml [accessed 25 March 2006].
2. For a brief account of these early studies, see Meyers and Forgy (1963).
3. Of course, risk is not an overarching definition but is created within particular relations with specific lenders for particular types of credit product. It has no stable coherency as an identity for individuals but emerges, discontinuously, at particular access points within circuits of consumption. Nevertheless, the preponderance of risk definitions that encompass the individual through their credit choices, shaping their credit opportunities, do coalesce around the individual over time to determine their general place within, or outside, the margins of consumption.
4. Consider the following quote from score modeling firm Fair Isaac: "*Scoring considers only credit-related information.* Factors like gender, race, nationality and marital status are not included. In fact, the Equal Credit Opportunity Act (ECOA) prohibits lenders from considering this type of information when issuing credit. Independent research has been done to make sure that credit scoring is not unfair to minorities or people with little credit history. Scoring has proven to be an accurate and consistent measure of repayment for all people who have some credit history. In other words, *at a given score, non-minority and minority applicants are equally likely to pay as agreed*" (Fair Isaac, 2005, my emphasis).

5. Either way, racial discrimination persists within the American consumer credit market (Ards and Myers, 2001).

6. However, the constitution of risk is no mere "social construction." The attributions of risk produced by credit scoring come into being within particular social contexts for the organization of individuals in respect of the future; nevertheless, through such production, individuals are materially acted upon as risks, an identification that restricts or enhances their future consuming possibilities which, in turn, influences their future identification as risks. Risk, as a means of intervening within the world, changes the nature of the world within which it is created (Adams, 1995: 19–21). In being acted upon as risks, people *become* risks.

7. Similarly, at the level of the firm, Lawrence (1992) shows that the implementation of a scoring model to replace a judgmental system requires the approval and oversight of management who may call into question the use of certain attributes where there is no intuitive reason for their effect. Without "cause," a variable will often be left out of the design of a credit scoring system, regardless of its statistical predictiveness. Even the fact that the Equal Credit Opportunity Act prohibits the use of the characteristics of gender or race indicates that despite possible statistically significant correlations between such characteristics and default outcomes, political and cultural values of equality specify what "should" determine whether an individual can get access to credit.

8. More generally, the application of a risk technology to the question of how to govern credit consumers is not seen to confront a homogenous problem of how to ascertain risk. In a large and diverse market with lenders of varied size and specialism armed with different priorities and resources, and engaging with a particular array of consumer target markets, different technical means have particular characteristics that make them suitable for different kinds of creditor in different contexts depending on the structure of the data, the characteristics used and the speed of change in the population (Hand and Henley, 1997).

9. Different approaches exist for creating a framework to determine this conception of risk. One simply incorporates new information as it comes on-stream within an existing scoring model. Another approach is to directly model customer behavior—either by a conventional means of relating individual attributes to the experience of the group or through the use of Bayesian methods, which attempt to statistically extrapolate into the future based on the relatively small amount of information inherent in the individual consumer's demonstrable actions.

10. Ironically, though, it is this very standardization and commodification, creating a permanent circuit of risk visibility, that undermines the effect of its hegemony as a measure of default risk. Because it is a generalized measure of risk based on a mass population of consumers and constructed on the limited characteristics of repayment history, it is perceived to be a relatively inaccurate measure of risk when contrasted to models developed on the more particular empirical framework and market profile of individual lenders and which assess and incorporate a wider array of data including income, occupation, and address (Chandler 2001: 50). Similarly, as the profitability and competitive advantage of lenders are seen to be linked to the discriminatory efficacy of the

risk models they deploy, then a generic commodified model, which any lender can access, provides no competitive advantage.

11. Within consumer credit, the development of a scoring model by a lender typically resulted in two forms of decision-rule: either a single risk cut-off point would serve as a threshold or else a double threshold top-and-tail system would be introduced. In this latter, the lender would automatically accept all applicants exceeding the upper threshold and reject all applicants underneath the lower threshold. Intermediate area risks would then be subject to a more intensive review before a final decision would be made as to whether credit would be advanced or not.

12. For an account of "subprime" and "predatory" lending practices in relation to the home mortgage market, see Squires (2004).

8   Borrowing on the Fringe: The Fate of the Risky

1. CFA (1997), "Check cashers charge high rates to cash checks, lend money," Consumer Federation of America Press Release, 21 August 1997.

2. PIRG (1997), "Don't rent to own: the 1997 PIRG rent to own survey," U.S. Public Interest Research Group. Available online at http://www.pirg.org/consumer/rtotext.htm [accessed 21 April 2006].

3. America Annual Report 2005. Available at http://www.cashamerica.com/pdf/2006Narrative.pdf [accessed 7 June 2006].

4. Rent A Center, "Corporate Overview." Available at http://www6.rentacenter.com/site/page/pg5639.html [accessed 7 June 2006].

5. Interestingly, Lehtonen (1999) examined the experiences of Finnish consumers enrolled on a severe, court-mandated controlled debt plan for the heavily indebted. Despite no access to credit and highly constrained disposable incomes, even these consumers "are still able to retain an active relation to the world of consumption and to themselves as consumers" (1999: 260).

6. A similar ambiguity has overshadowed the problematic "culture of poverty" thesis. Individual actions are undoubtedly shaped by material conditions, but it is much more contentious to examine these as engendering autonomous behavioral traits that may be passed down to subsequent generations.

7. "Payday Loans = Costly Cash," FTC Consumer Alert. Available online at http://www.ftc.gov/bcp/conline/pubs/alerts/pdayalrt.pdf [accessed 7 June 2006].

9   Risk, Identity, and the Consumer

1. "Understanding your credit score," Fair Isaac, p. 1.

2. "What the CFA got right—and wrong—about credit score accuracy," Viewpoints, January/February 2003.

3. "myFICO.com terms with personal finance guru Suze Orman to help consumers strengthen their credit," Fair Isaac Press Release, 25 May 2004.

4. "Why is a Credit Checkup so Important?" Physicians' Money Digest: The Practical Guide to Personal Finance, 30 April 2002.

5. "Bill lets consumers see credit scores," National Mortgage News, 17 July 2000; "Shedding light on credit scores," Credit Card Management, August 2000.
6. "Bill lets consumers see credit scores," National Mortgage News.
7. "California banks knock score disclosure bill," American Banker, 10 July 2000; "Credit scores are due to go public," Money, August 2000.
8. "Schumer of N.Y. to fight for credit score access bill," American Banker, 22 September 2000.
9. "Schumer urges house subcommittee to take action against secret credit scores," Press Release by New York Senator Charles Schumer, 21 September 2000.
10. "New Assault on your Credit Rating," Consumer Reports, January 2001.
11. "New Assault on your Credit Rating," Consumer Reports, January 2001, p. 24.
12. "Web lender will report credit scores to customers," American Banker, 22 February 2000; "Equifax pulls plug on E-Loan after FICO row," American Banker, 10 April 2000.
13. "Web lender will report credit scores to customers," American Banker, 22 February 2000.
14. "Bill lets consumers see credit scores," National Mortgage News.
15. "Public forum: the consumer and credit scoring," Federal Trade Commission, 22 July 1999, p. 298. Available online at http://www.ftc.gov/bcp/creditscoring/creditscorexscript.pdf [accessed 2 February 2005].
16. Letter to the editor by William Catucci, executive vice president and group executive Equifax North America Information Services, American Banker, 14 April 2000; "Fair, Isaac to tell people their credit scores," American Banker, 9 June 2000.
17. "Loan Biz Not Playing Fair, Isaac," Wired News, 7 April 2000.
18. "Fair, Isaac to tell people their credit scores," American Banker; "Credit scores are due to go public," Money, August 2000.
19. "FICO next in line to offer access to credit scores," Bankrate.com, 15 July 2000. Available online at http://www.bankrate.com/brm/news/mtg/20000615.asp [accessed 2 February 2005].
20. "Fair, Isaac to tell people their credit scores," American Banker; "Shedding light on credit scores," Credit Card Management.
21. "Fair Isaac site offers credit score details," National Mortgage News, 6 November 2000; "Fair, Isaac web site offering explanations of credit scores," American Banker, 14 November 2000.
22. "Fair, Isaac web site offering explanations of credit scores," American Banker.
23. "Fair, Isaac credit scores: seller beware," American Banker, 31 January 2001; "After you beat'em, join'em," U.S. Banker, February 2001.
24. "Equifax puts credit scores online," Mortgage Servicing News, May 2001.
25. "iPlace tries to make a score by marketing a 'FICO clone'", American Banker, 2 February 2001; "Firms offer access to credit scores," National Mortgage News, 5 March 2001.
26. "E-Loan offers free credit scores as sub for Fair, Isaac," American Banker, 24 April 2001.
27. "Letting consumers know the score," Credit Card Management, May 2001.
28. Fair Isaac Annual Report, 2001.
29. Equifax Annual Report, 2000, p. 3.

30. Equifax Annual Report, 2001, p. 7.
31. Equifax Annual Report, 2003, p. 19.
32. Fair Isaac Annual Report 2001, p. 9.
33. Fair Isaac Annual Report 2003: Form 10K, pp. 19–20.

10 "See How Lenders See You": From Actuarial to Subjective Governance

1. "Credit scoring," FTC Facts for Consumers, p. 1.
2. "Know your score," Consumer Federation of America and Freddie Mac.
3. "Color of money live with Michelle Singletary," 22 June 2000. Available online at http://www.washingtonpost.com/wpsrv/liveonline/00/business/singletary/singletary0620.htm [accessed 27 October 2004].
4. "Most consumers do not understand credit scores according to a new comprehensive survey," Consumer Federation of America / Providian Financial Press Release, 21 September 2004.
5. "American consumers score a 'D' on Fair Isaac's national credit genius quiz," Fair Isaac Press Release, 29 April 2003.
6. "Understanding your credit score," Fair Isaac, p. 1.
7. Fair Isaac is the creator of the generic risk scoring system known as "FICO" which is based exclusively on the data contained in a consumer's credit bureau file. According to the company, FICO scores are used in over 75 percent of credit decisions within the United States. Within this chapter, whenever reference is made to credit risk or a "score," I am explicitly referring to risk scores generated through this system unless otherwise indicated.
8. "Understanding your credit score," Fair Isaac, pp. 4–5.
9. Ibid., pp. 8–13; "Color of money live with Michelle Singletary," 22 June 2000.
10. "Understanding your credit score," Fair Isaac, p. 11.
11. The enjoining of an "ethic of improvement" toward one's score rests somewhat ambiguously with the reality that the development of scoring has diversified and expanded market provision. However, for the individual, it is not merely a matter of accessing credit but the quality of access: how quick and how cheap it is. The scores and interest rates shown below are taken from "FICO scores affect your monthly payments," Fair Isaac. Available online at http://www.myfico.com [accessed 24 May 2005].
12. "Understanding your credit score," Fair Isaac; "Credit scoring," Fair Isaac.
13. "Understanding your credit score," Fair Isaac, p. 13.
14. Ibid., p. 10.
15. Equifax Annual Report, 2003, p. 10.
16. "Understanding your credit score," Fair Isaac, p. 13.
17. "Fair, Isaac and CCCS of Santa Clara and Ventura counties team up to bring credit empowerment to Californians," Fair Isaac Press Release, October 2002.
18. "Credit scoring," Fair Isaac.
19. "Understanding your credit score," Fair Isaac, p. 6; "Credit scoring," Fair Isaac.
20. " Predictiveness of Credit History for Insurance Loss Ratio Relativities," Fair Isaac, October 1999, p. 21.

11   Securing the Self

1. "Fair, Isaac offers consumer award-winning credit monitoring service to help safeguard their credit health," Fair Isaac Press Release, 25 November 2002.
2. "myFICO forum focuses on consumer empowerment," Viewpoints, July/August 2003.
3. Equifax Annual Report, 2001, p. 7.
4. "Fair Isaac announces National Credit Power Week to test consumers' know-how and boost their credit health," Fair Isaac Press Release.
5. Actual FICO scores can only be accessed from Fair Isaac and Equifax. While Experian and TransUnion credit bureaus provide FICO-branded scores to lenders, they supply their own proprietary scores to consumers, scores which Fair Isaac deride as "estimates" of theirs. However, it should be noted that Fair Isaac and each bureau allow the consumer to access data from all bureau sources.
6. "Suze Orman's FICO Kit Platinum," Fair Isaac; "myFICO.com teams with personal finance guru Suze Orman to help consumer strengthen their credit," Fair Isaac Press Release.
7. "FICO Saver for Homebuyers," Fair Isaac. Available online at http://www.myfico.com/Products/FICOSaver/Description/aspx [accessed 29 October 2004]; "Fair Isaac reinvents how consumers prepare for mortgages, introduces powerful new service with insider information," Fair Isaac Press Release.
8. "Understanding your credit score," Fair Isaac,p. 16 (notional consumer).
9. "Suze Orman's FICO Kit Platinum," Fair Isaac (notional consumer).
10. "Loan Savings Calculator," Fair Isaac. Available online at http://www.myfico.com/LoanCenter/?fire=1 [accessed 1 November 2004].
11. "FICO Saver for Homebuyers," Fair Isaac; "Fair Isaac reinvents how consumers prepare for mortgages, introduces powerful new service with insider information," Fair Isaac Press Release.
12. "Suze Orman's FICO Kit Platinum," Fair Isaac (notional consumer).
13. "FICO Saver for Homebuyers," Fair Isaac; "Fair Isaac reinvents how consumers prepare for mortgages, introduces powerful new service with insider information," Fair Isaac Press Release.
14. "Fair, Isaac and Equifax give consumers new score power tools offering greater insights for managing their credit health," Fair Isaac Press Release, 21 May 2002; "FICO Score Simulator," Fair Isaac. Available online at http://www.myfico.com/Products/FICOOne/Sample/Sample_ScoreSimulator.aspx?ProductID=Deluxe [accessed 29 October 2004].
15. "FICO Score Simulator," Fair Isaac.
16. "Robert Bruss letters": "Jessie," Washington Post. Available online at http://www.washingtonpost.com [accessed 26 February 2009].
17. "Robert Bruss letters": "James," Washington Post. Available online at http://www.washingtonpost.com [accessed 28 October 2004].
18. "Robert Bruss letters": "Grace," Washington Post. Available online at http://www.washingtonpost.com [accessed 28 October 2004].
19. "Robert Bruss letters" : "Rico," Washington Post. Available online at http://www.washingtonpost.com [accessed 28 October 2004].

20. "Your credit scores," Fair Isaac, p. 4.
21. "Understanding your credit score," Fair Isaac, p. 2; "Credit scoring," Fair Isaac.
22. "Understanding your credit score," Fair Isaac, p. 7.
23. "Written testimony of Fair Isaac Corporation before the hearing on consumer understanding and awareness of the credit granting process," United States Senate Committee on Banking, Housing, and Urban Affairs, 29 July 2003.
24. "Credit score accuracy and implications for consumers," Consumer Federation of America/National Credit Reporting Association, December 2002.
25. "Credit score accuracy and implications for consumers," Consumer Federation of America/National Credit Reporting Association, p. 37.
26. "What the CFA got right—and wrong—about credit score accuracy," Viewpoints, January/February 2003. Indeed, as Poon (2007) makes clear, the *idea* of a single FICO model had to be forged out of three distinctly different modeling technologies developed by Fair Isaac in partnership with Equifax, Experian, and TransUnion.
27. "Colour of money live with Michelle Singletary."
28. "Understanding your credit score," Fair Isaac, p. 4; "Your credit scores," Fair Isaac, p. 6. Security toolkits provide a useful mechanism for such self-monitoring—see "Suze Orman's FICO Kit Platinum," Fair Isaac.
29. Written as one of his latter works, Foucault here does not seem to be espousing a pessimistic or fatalistic vision of individuals, or subjectivity, held forever in sway of power. Power, as he argues, is an irreducible component of social relations but our conceptions of it must shed their sovereign, legalistic hue. Rather, power should be seen as a process that dynamically plays between individuals endowed with a capacity for action—Elias's (1978) "game models" seem to come very close to what Foucault is attempting to elucidate here. Foucault, for his part, refers explicitly to the resisting capacities of individuals, the need for "us" to cease being the kinds of subjects that power has formed us to be and the possibility for individuals of attaining alternative subjectivities.

References

Abelson, E. (1989) *When Ladies Go A-Thieving: Middle Class Shoplifters in the American Department Store*, Oxford: Oxford University Press.

Achenbaum, W.A. (1986) *Social Security: Visions and Revisions*, Cambridge: Cambridge University Press.

Adam, B. (2004) *Time*, Cambridge: Polity Press.

Adams, J. (1995) *Risk*, London: University College London Press.

Adorno, T. and Horkheimer, M. (1972) *Dialectic of Enlightenment*, New York: Continuum.

Aldridge, A. (1998) "Habitus and cultural capital in the field of personal finance," *Sociological Review* 46(1): 1–23.

Anderson, E. (2005) "Experts, ideas, and social welfare policy: the Russell Sage Foundation and the Uniform Small Loan Law, 1910–1940," Paper presented to the International Sociological Association Research Committee on Poverty, Welfare and Social Policy Annual Conference, 8–10 September 2005, Northwestern University, Chicago.

Anonymous. (1979) "Credit scoring and the ECOA: applying the effects test," *Yale Law Journal* 88(7): 1450–86.

Ards, S., and S. Myers. (2001) "The color of money: bad credit, wealth, and race," *American Behavioral Scientist* 45(2): 223–39.

Avery, R.B., P.S. Calem, and G.B. Canner. (2003) "An overview of consumer data and credit reporting," *Federal Reserve Bulletin*, February 2003: 47–73.

Avery, R.B., R.W. Bostic, P.S. Calem, and G.B. Canner. (2000) "Credit scoring: statistical issues and evidence from credit bureau files," *Real Estate Economics* 28(3): 523–47.

Ayres, M. (1938) "The economic function of the sales finance company," *Journal of the American Statistical Association* 33(201): 59–70.

Bachelor, R. (1994) *Henry Ford, Mass Production, Modernism, and Design*, Manchester: Manchester University Press.

Baistow, K. (1994) "Liberation and regulation? Some paradoxes of empowerment," *Critical Social Policy* 14(3): 34–46.

Baker, T. (2002) "Risk, insurance, and the social construction of responsibility," in T. Baker and J. Simon (eds.) *Embracing Risk: The Changing Culture of Insurance and Responsibility*, Chicago: University of Chicago Press, pp. 33–51.

Baldassare, M. (1992) "Suburban communities," *Annual Review of Sociology* 18: 475–94.

Barnett, C., P. Cloke, N. Clarke, and A. Malpass. (2005) "Consuming ethics: articulating the subjects and spaces of ethical consumption," *Antipode* 37(1): 23–45.

Barr, M. (2002) "Access to financial services in the 21st century: five opportunities for the Bush administration and the 107th Congress," *Notre Dame Journal of Law, Ethics and Public Policy* 16(2): 447–73.

———. (2004) "Banking the poor," *Yale Journal on Regulation* 21(2): 121–37.

Barron, J., and M. Staten. (2001) "The value of comprehensive credit reports: lessons from the U.S. experience," Paper presented to the Annual Social Science Research Conference Credit, *Trust and Calculation*, 16–17 November 2002, San Diego University.

Barth, J. (2002) "Discussion—consumer loan securitization," in T.A. Durkin and M.E. Staten (eds.) *The Impact of Public Policy on Consumer Credit*, Boston: Kluwer, pp. 307–12.

Barton, M. (1989) "The Victorian jeremiad: critics of accumulation and display," in S. Bonner (ed.) *Consuming Visions: Accumulation and Display of Goods in America 1880–1920*. New York: W.W. Norton, pp. 55–71.

Baudrillard, J. (1998) *The Consumer Society: Myths and Structures*, London: Sage.

Bauman, Z. (1988) *Freedom*, Milton Keynes: Open University Press.

———. (1997) *Postmodernity and its Discontents*, Cambridge: Polity Press.

———. (1998a) *Work, Consumerism and the New Poor*, Buckingham: Open University Press.

———. (1998b) *Globalization: The Human Consequences*, Cambridge: Polity Press.

———. (2000) *Liquid Modernity*, Cambridge: Polity Press.

———. (2007) *Consuming Life*, Cambridge: Polity Press.

Beck, U. (1992) *Risk Society: Towards a New Modernity*: London: Sage.

Beck, U., A. Giddens, and S. Lash. (1994) *Reflexive Modernization: Politics, Tradition and Aesthetics in the Modern Social Order*: Cambridge: Polity Press.

Beck, U., W. Bonss, and C. Lau. (2003) "The theory of reflexive modernization: problematic, hypotheses and research programme," *Theory, Culture and Society* 20(2): 1–33.

Belasco, J.W. (1997) *Americans on the Road: From Autocamp to Motel, 1910–1945*, London: Johns Hopkins University Press.

Bell, D. (1996) *The Cultural Contradictions of Capitalism*, 20th Anniversary Edition, New York: Basic Books.

Benson, S. (1986) *Counter Cultures: Saleswomen, Managers and Customers in American Department Stores, 1890–1940*, Urbana, IL: University of Illinois Press.

Berger, M.L. (1979) *The Devil Wagon in God's Country: The Automobile and Social Change in America, 1893–1929*, Hamden, CT: Archon.

Berger, R. (1935) "Usury in instalment sales," *Law and Contemporary Problems* 2(2): 148–72.

Bernthal, M., D. Crockett, and R. Rose. (2005) "Credit cards as lifestyle facilitators," *Journal of Consumer Research* 32(1): 130–45.

Bertrand, M., S. Mullainathan, and E. Shafir. (2006) "Behavioral economics and marketing in aid of decision-making among the poor," *Journal of Public Policy and Marketing* 25(1): 8–23.

Black, H. (1962) *Buy Now, Pay Later*, New York: Giant Cardinal.

Blanke, D. (2000) *Sowing the American Dream: How Consumer Culture Took Root in the Rural Midwest*, Athens, OH: Ohio University Press.

Bogard, W. (1996) *The Simulation of Surveillance: Hypercontrol in Telematic Societies*, Cambridge: Cambridge University Press.

Boorstin, D.J. (1973) *The Americans: The Democratic Experience*, New York: Random House.

Bostic, R. (2002) "Trends in equal access to credit products," in Durkin and Staten (eds.) *The Impact of Public Policy*, pp. 172–208.

Bourdieu, P. (1984) *Distinction: A Social Critique of the Judgement of Taste*, London: Routledge.

———. (1986) "The forms of capital," in J. Richardson (ed.) *Handbook of Theory and Research in the Sociology of Education*, New York: Greenwood Press, pp. 241–58.

Bourdieu, P., and L. Wacquant. (1992) *An Invitation to Reflexive Sociology*, Cambridge: Polity Press.

Bowlby, R. (2001) *Carried Away: The Invention of Modern Shopping*. New York: Columbia University Press.

Boyer, P. (1978) *Urban Masses and Moral Order in America, 1820–1920*, London: Harvard University Press.

Boyle, M., J.N. Crook, R. Hamilton, and L.C. Thomas. (1992) "Methods for credit scoring applied to slow payers," in L.C. Thomas, J.B. Crook, and D.B. Edelman (eds.) *Credit Scoring and Credit Control*, Oxford: Clarendon Press, pp. 75–90.

Bradford, W. (2003) "The savings and credit management of low-income, low-wealth black and white families," *Economic Development Quarterly* 17(1): 53–74.

Brand, D. (2002) "Competition and the New Deal regulatory state," in S. Milkis and J. Milear (eds.) *The New Deal and the Triumph of Liberalism*, Amherst, MA: University of Massachusetts Press, pp. 166–92.

Brandt, W., and G. Day. (1974) "Information disclosure and consumer behaviour: an empirical evaluation of truth-in-lending," *University of Michigan Journal of Law Reform* 7(2): 297–328.

Brinkley, A. (1995) *The End of Reform: New Deal Liberalism in Recession and War*, New York: Vintage.

Brinkley, D. (2004) *Wheels for the World: Henry Ford, His Company, and a Century of Progress*, London: Viking.

Brockman, N. (1966) "The National Bar Association, 1888–1893: the failure of early bar federation," *American Journal of Legal History* 10(2): 122–7.

Bucks, B., A. Kennickell, and K. Moore. (2006) "Recent changes in U.S. family finances: evidence from the 2001 and 2004 survey of consumer finances," *Federal Reserve Bulletin*, 22 March 2006. Available online at http://www.federalreserve.gov/pubs/bulletin/2006/financesurvey.pdf [accessed 15 April 2006].

Buenker, J.D. (1977) "Essay 1" in J. Buenker, J. Burnham, and R. Crunden (eds.) *Progressivism*, Cambridge, MA: Schenkman, pp. 31–70.

Bunn, D., and G. Wright. (1991) "Interaction of judgemental and statistical forecasting methods: issues and analysis," *Management Science* 37(5): 501–18.

Burchell, G. (1993) "Liberal government and techniques of the self," *Economy and Society* 22(3): 267–82.

Burnham, D. (1977) "Essay 2," in Buenker, Burnham, and Crunden (eds.) *Progressivism*, pp. 3–29.

Burton, D. (2008) *Credit and Consumer Society*, Abington: Routledge.

Byrne, D. (2005) *Social Exclusion*, 2nd Edition, Maidenhead: Open University Press.

CFA. (2004) "2003 changes to the Fair Credit Reporting Act: important steps forward at a high cost," *Consumer Federation of America Comments*. Available online at http://www.consumerfed.org/pdfs/credit_reporting_summary_of_final_law.pdf [accessed 3 March 2006].

Calder, L. (1999) *Financing the American Dream: A Cultural History of Consumer Credit*, Princeton: Princeton University Press.

———. (2002) "The evolution of consumer credit in the United States," in Durkin and Staten (eds.) *The Impact of Public Policy*, pp. 23–35.

Camden, B. (1988) "Fair Credit Reporting Act: what you don't know may hurt you," *University of Cincinnati Law Review* 57(1): 267–93.

Campbell, C. (1983) "Romanticism and the consumer ethic: intimations of a Weber-style thesis," *Sociological Analysis* 4(4): 279–96.

———. (1987) *The Romantic Ethic and the Spirit of Modern Consumerism*, Oxford: Blackwell.

———. (1995a) "The sociology of consumption," in D. Miller (ed.) *Acknowledging Consumption*, London: Routledge, pp. 96–126.

———. (1995b) "Conspicuous confusion? A critique of Veblen's theory of conspicuous consumption," *Sociological Theory* 13(1): 37– 47.

Campbell, R., B. Roberts, and K. Rogers. (2008) "An evaluation of lender redlining in the allocation of unsecured credit in the US," *Urban Studies* 45(5 and 6): 1243–54.

Caplovitz, D. (1963) *The Poor Pay More: Consumer Practices of Low-income Families*, London: Collier-Macmillan.

———. (1968) "Consumer credit in the affluent society," *Law and Contemporary Problems* 33(4): 641–55.

Capon, N. (1982) "Credit scoring systems: a critical analysis," *Journal of Marketing* 46(2): 82–91.

Carliner, M. (1998) "Development of federal homeownership 'policy,'" *Housing Policy Debate* 9(2): 299–321.

Carr, V., and D. Luong. (2005) "Strategy optimization for credit: maximise profit while managing risk," Proceedings of the Ninth Conference on Credit Scoring and Credit Control, 7–9 September 2005, University of Edinburgh. Available online at http://www.crc.man.ed.ac.uk/conference/presentations/2005/carr-v-loung-d.pdf [accessed 28 March 2006].

Carruthers, B.G., T.W. Guinnane, and Y. Lee. (2005) "The passage of the Uniform Small Loan Law," Paper presented to the London School of Economics, *Economic History Seminar Series*, March 2005, London School of Economics.

Caskey J.P. (1991) "Pawnbroking in America: the economics of a forgotten credit market," *Journal of Money, Credit and Banking* 23(1): 85–99.

———. (1994) *Fringe Banking: Check-Cashing Outlets, Pawnshops, and the Poor*, New York: Russell Sage.

———. (2005) "Fringe banking and the rise of payday lending," in P. Bolton and H. Rosenthal (eds.) *Credit Markets for the Poor*, New York: Russell Sage, pp. 17–45.

Caskey, J.P., and B. Zikmund. (1990) "Pawnshops: the consumer's lender of last resort," *Federal Reserve Bank of Kansas Economic Review*, March/April 1990, pp. 5–8.

Castel, R. (1991) "From dangerousness to risk," in G. Burchell, C. Gordon, and P. Miller (eds.) *The Foucault Effect: Studies in Governmentality*, Chicago: University of Chicago Press, pp. 281–98.

Cate, F. (2002) "Privacy, consumer credit, and the regulation of personal information," in Durkin and Staten (eds.) *The Impact of Public Policy*, pp. 229–76.

Cavers, D.F. (1935) "The consumer's stake in the finance company code controversy," *Law and Contemporary Problems* 2(2): 200–17.

Caves, R. (1989) "An historical analysis of federal housing policy from the presidential perspective: an intergovernmental focus," *Urban Studies* 26(1): 59–76.

Chambers, J.W. (1980) *The Tyranny of Change: America in the Progressive Era, 1900–1917*, New York: St. Martin's Press.

Chandler, G.C. (2001) "Generic and customized scoring models: a comparison," in E. Mays (ed.) *Handbook of Credit Scoring*, Chicago: Glenlake, pp. 23–55.

Chang, G., and J. Osborn. (2005) "Spectacular colleges and spectacular rankings: the 'US News' rankings of America's best colleges," *Journal of Consumer Culture* 5(3): 338–64.

Chapman, J.M. (1940) *Commercial Banks and Consumer Instalment Credit: Financial Research Program—Studies in Consumer Instalment Financing 3*, New York: National Bureau of Economic Research.

Chatterjee, S., D. Corbae, and J. Ríos-Rull. (2005) "A recursive equilibrium model with credit scoring and competitive pricing of default risk," Working Paper, Federal Reserve Bank of Atlanta Research Department. Available online at http://www.atl-res.com/macro/papers/chatterjee%20paper.pdf [accessed 16 March 2006].

Chutkow, P. (2001) *Visa: The Power of an Idea*, Chicago: Harcourt.

Clark, E. (1930) *Financing the Consumer*, London: Harper.

Cockerham, W.C., T. Rütten, and T. Abel. (1997) "Conceptualizing contemporary health lifestyles: moving beyond Weber," *Sociological Quarterly* 38(2): 321–42.

Coffman, J.Y., and G.G. Chandler. (1983) "Applications of performance scoring to accounts receivable management in consumer credit," Working Paper No. 46, Credit Research Center, Krannert Graduate School of Management, Purdue University.

Cohen, L. (1990) *Making a New Deal: Industrial Workers in Chicago, 1919–1939*, Cambridge: Cambridge University Press.

———. (2001) "Citizens and consumers in the United States in the century of mass consumption," in M. Daunton and M. Hilton (eds.) *The Politics of Consumption: Material Culture and Citizenship in Europe and America*, Oxford: Berg, pp. 203–221.

———. (2003) *A Consumer's Republic: The Politics of Mass Consumption in Postwar America*, New York: Knopf.

Cohn, D.L. (1940) *The Good Old Days: A History of American Morals and Manners as seen through the Sears, Roebuck Catalogs 1905 to the Present*, New York: Simon and Schuster.

Cole, R.H. (1988) *Consumer and Commercial Credit Management*, Scarborough, ON: Irwin.

Coppock, J.D. (1940) *Government Agencies of Consumer Instalment Credit: Financial Research Program, Studies in Consumer Instalment Financing 5*, New York: National Bureau of Economic Research.

Creamer, M. (2006) "Charge it, please, and bring on Michelle Wie," *Advertising Age* 77(3): 3–4.

Cross, G. (2000) *An All-Consuming Century : Why Commercialism Won in Modern America*, New York: Columbia University Press.

Crowder, M.J., D.J. Hand, and W.J. Krzanowski. (2005) "On customer lifetime value," Proceedings of the Ninth Conference on Credit Scoring and Credit Control, 7–9 September 2005, University of Edinburgh. Available online http://www.crc.man.ed.ac.uk/conference/presentations/2005/Crowder%20Hand%20Krzanowski%20talk.pdf [accessed 28 March 2006].

Crowther Committee. (1971) *Consumer Credit: Report of the Committee*, Department of Trade and Industry, London: HMSO.

Davis, J. (1977) "Protecting consumers from overdisclosure and gobbledegook: an empirical look at the simplification of consumer-credit contracts," *Virginia Law Review*: 63(6): 841–920.

Dawes, R.M. (1999) "A message from psychologists to economists: mere predictability doesn't matter like it should (without a good story appended to it)," *Journal of Economic Behavior and Organization* 39(1): 29–40.

Dean, M. (1991) *The Constitution of Poverty: Towards a Genealogy of Liberal Governance*, London: Routledge.

———. (1999a) *Governmentality: Power and Rule in Modern Society*, London: Sage.

———. (1999b) "Risk, calculable and incalculable," in D. Lupton (ed.) *Risk and Sociocultural Theory: New Directions and Perspectives*, Cambridge: Cambridge University Press, pp. 131–59.

Defert, D. (1991) "'Popular life' and insurance technology," in Burchell, Gordon, and Miller (eds.) *The Foucault Effect*, pp. 211–33.

De Long, J.B. (1996) "Keynesianism, Pennsylvania Avenue style: some economic consequences of the employment act of 1946," Working Paper 5611, National Bureau of Economic Research, June 1996.

———. (1998) "Fiscal policy in the shadow of the Great Depression," in M. Bordo, C. Goldin, and E. White (eds.) *The Defining Moment: The Great Depression and the American Economy in the Twentieth Century*, Chicago: University of Chicago Press, pp. 67–85.

Deleuze, G. (1992) "Postscript on societies of control," *October* 59(4): 3–7.

Donzelot, J. (1980) *The Policing of Families*, London: Hutchinson & Co.

———. (1991) "The mobilization of society," in Burchell, Gordon, and Miller (eds.) *The Foucault Effect*, pp. 169–79.

Dresser, R. (1982) "Ulysses and the psychiatrists: a legal and policy analysis of the voluntary commitment contract," *Harvard Civil Rights-Civil Liberties Review* 16(3): 777–854.

Dunkelberg, W., R. Johnson, and R. DeMagistris. (1979) "Consumer perceptions of credit bureaus," Working Paper No. 26, Credit Research Center, Krannert Graduate School of Management, Purdue University.

Durand, D. (1941) *Risk Elements in Consumer Instalment Financing* (Technical Edition), New York: National Bureau of Economic Research.

Durkin, T. (2000) "Credit cards: use and consumer attitudes, 1970–2000," *Federal Reserve Bulletin*, September 2000: 623–34.

Durkin, T., and G. Elliehausen. (2002) "Disclosure as a consumer protection," in Durkin and Staten (eds.) *The Impact of Public Policy*, pp. 109–43.

Dwyer, J. (2000) *To Wire the World: Perry M. Collins and the North Pacific Telegraph Expedition*, Westport, CT: Praeger.

Dymski, G. (1999) *The Bank Merger Wave: The Economic Causes and Social Consequences of Financial Consolidation*, London: M.E. Sharpe.

———. (2005) "Banking strategy and financial exclusion: tracing the pathways of globalization," *Revista de Economica* 31(1): 107–43.

Dymski, G., and J. Veitch. (1996) "Financial transformation and the metropolis: booms, busts, and banking in Los Angeles," *Environment and Planning A* 28(7): 1233–60.

Dynan, K., and D. Kohn. (2007) "The rise in U.S. household indebtedness: causes and consequences," Finance and Economics Discussion Series 2007–37, Federal Reserve Board, Washington DC.

ECOA. (1974) *Equal Credit Opportunity Act*, United States Government Printing Office. Available online at http://ecfr.gpoaccess.gov/cgi/t/text/text-idx?c=ecfr&sid=ee1c3ba7 00283b3b6ca3a35322eb4db5&rgn=div5&view=text&node=12:2.0.1.1.2&idno=12 [accessed 9 September 2005].

Edelberg, W. (2003) "Risk-based pricing of interest rates in household loan markets," Finance and Economics Discussion Series: Staff Working Papers, United States Federal Reserve Board.

Elias, N. (1978) *What is Sociology?* New York: Columbia University Press.

———. (1991) *The Society of Individuals*, Oxford: Blackwell.

———. (1994) *The Civilizing Process: The History of Manners and State Formation and Civilization*, Oxford: Blackwell.

———. (1998) *On Civilization, Power, and Knowledge: Selected Writings*, Chicago: University of Chicago Press.

Elliehausen, G.E., and T.A. Durkin. (1989) "Theory and evidence of the impact of equal credit opportunity: an agnostic review of the literature," Credit Research Center, Monograph No. 28, Krannert Graduate School of Management, Purdue University.

Elliehausen, G.E., and E.C. Lawrence. (2001) "Payday advance credit in America: an analysis of customer demand," Credit Research Center, Monograph No. 35, Georgetown University, Washington DC.

Elster, J. (1984) *Ulysses and the Sirens: Studies in Rationality and Irrationality Revised Edition*, Cambridge: Cambridge University Press.

Emmet, B., and J.E. Jeuck. (1950) *Catalogues and Counters: A History of Sears, Roebuck and Company*, Chicago: University of Chicago Press.

Ericson, R., D. Barry, and A. Doyle. (2000) "The moral hazards of neo-liberalism: lessons from the private insurance industry," *Economy and Society* 29(4): 532–58.

Evans, D.S., and R. Schmalensee. (1999) *Paying with Plastic: The Digital Revolution in Buying and Borrowing*, London: MIT Press.

Ewald, F. (1990) "Norms, discipline and the law," *Representations* 30(1): 138–61.

———. (1991) "Insurance and risk," in Burchell, Gordon, and Miller (eds.) *The Foucault Effect*, pp. 197–210.

———. (2002) "The return of Descartes's Malicious Demon: an outline of a philosophy of precaution," in Baker and Simon (eds.) *Embracing Risk*, pp. 273–301.

Ewen, E. (1985) *Immigrant Women in the Land of Dollars: Life and Culture on the Lower East Side, 1890–1925*, New York: Monthly Review Press.

Ewen, S. (1976) *Captains of Consciousness: Advertising and the Social Roots of Consumer Culture*, New York: McGraw-Hill.

Ewen, S., and E. Ewen. (1992) *Channels of Desire: Mass Images and the Shaping of American Consciousness*, 2nd Edition, London: University of Minnesota Press.

Faber, R., and T. O'Guinn. (1988) "Compulsive consumption and credit abuse," *Journal of Consumer Policy* 11(1): 97–109.

FACTA. (2003) *Fair and Accurate Credit Transactions Act*, United States Government Printing Office. Available online at http://frwebgate.access.gpo.gov/cgi-bin/getdoc. cgi?dbname=108_cong_public_laws&docid=f:publ159.108.pdf [accessed 2 March 2006].

Featherstone, M. (2007) *Consumer Culture and Postmodernism*, 2nd Edition, London: Sage.

Feely, M., and J. Simon. (1992) "The new penology: notes on the emerging strategy of corrections and its implications," *Criminology* 30(4): 449–74.

———. (1994) "Actuarial justice: the emerging new criminal law," in D. Nelken (ed.) *The Futures of Criminology*, New York: Sage, pp. 173–201.

Filene, P. (1970) "An obituary for the "Progressive movement"," *American Quarterly* 22(1): 20–34.

Fisher, G. (1936) "The use of multiple measurements in taxonomic problems," *Annals of Eugenics* 7: 179–88.

Foote, K.E. (2003) *Shadowed Ground: America's Landscapes of Violence and Tragedy*, Austin: University of Texas Press.

Foster, W. (1938) "Public supervision of consumer credit," *Journal of the American Statistical Association* 33(201): 71–80.

Foster, W., and L. Foster. (1935) "Rate aspects of instalment legislation," *Law and Contemporary Problems* 2(2): 189–99.

Foucault, M. (1979) *Discipline and Punish: The Birth of the Prison*, London: Penguin.

———. (1983) "Afterward," in H.L. Dreyfus and P. Rabinow *Michel Foucault: Beyond Structuralism and Hermeneutics*, Chicago: University of Chicago Press, pp. 229–64.

———. (1990) *The Will to Knowledge: The History of Sexuality Volume 1*, London: Penguin.

———. (1991) "Governmentality," in Burchell, Gordon, and Miller (eds.) *The Foucault Effect*, pp. 87–104.

Foulke, R. (1941) *The Sinews of American Commerce*, New York: Dun & Bradstreet.

Fox, J. (2004) *Unsafe and Unsound: Payday Lenders Hide behind FDIC Banks to Peddle Usury,* Report by the Consumer Federation of America, 30 March 2004.

Fox, J., and A. Petrini. (2004) *Internet Payday Lending: How High-priced Lenders Use the Internet to Mire Borrowers in Debt and Evade State Consumer Protections*, Report by the Consumer Federation of America, 30 November 2004.

Fox, J., and E. Guy. (2005) *Driven into Debt: CFA Car Title Loan Store and Online Survey*, Report by the Consumer Federation of America, November 2005.

Fox, J., and E. Mierwinski. (2001) *Rent-a-Bank Payday Lending: How Banks Help Payday Lenders Evade State Consumer Protections*, Survey and Report by the Consumer Federation of America and the U.S. Public Interest Research Group, November 2001.

Frank, T. (1997) *The Conquest of Cool: Business Culture, Counterculture, and the Rise of Hip Consumerism*, Chicago: University of Chicago Press.

Fromm, E. (1942) *The Fear of Freedom*, London: Routledge & Kegan Paul.

Furedi, F. (2002) *Culture of Fear: Risk-taking and the Morality of Low Expectation*, 2nd Edition, London: Continuum.

Galbraith, J.K. (1958) *The Affluent Society,* Cambridge, MA: Riverside.

Gandy, O. (1993) *The Panoptic Sort: A Political Economy of Personal Information*, Boulder CO: Westview.

Gans, H.J. (1967) *The Levittowners: Ways of Life and Politics in a New Suburban Community*, London: Allen Lane.

Garrison, M.L. (1976) "Credit-ability for women," *The Family Coordinator* 25(3): 241–8.

Gartman, D. (1986) *Auto Slavery: The Labor Process in the American Automobile Industry, 1897–1950*, New Brunswick, NJ: Rutgers University Press.

Gelpi, R., and F. Julien-Labruyère. (2000) *The History of Consumer Credit: Doctrines and Practices*, translated by L. Gavin, Basingstoke: Macmillan.

Giddens, A. (1991) *Modernity and Self-Identity: Self and Society in the Late Modern Age*, Cambridge: Polity Press.

Gilreath, E. (1999) "The entrance of banks into subprime lending: First Union and The Money Store," *North Carolina Banking Institute* 3: 149–68.

Glassman, C., and H. Wilkins. (1997) "Credit scoring: probabilities and pitfalls," *Journal of Retail Banking Services* 19(2): 53–6.

Glenn, J.M., L. Brandt, and F.E. Andrews. (1947) *Russell Sage Foundation 1907–1946*, in Two Vols., New York: Russell Sage.

Glennon, D. (2001) "Model design and validation: identifying potential sources of model risk," in Mays (ed.) *Handbook of Credit Scoring*, pp. 243–74.

Gordon, C. (1991) "Governmental rationality: an introduction," in Burchell, Gordon, and Miller (eds.) *The Foucault Effect*, pp. 1–51.

Gosh, S., and D.L. Reilly. (1994) "Credit card fraud detection with a neural-network," Proceedings of the 27th Annual Hawaii International Conference on System Sciences 3, 4–7 January 1994, Maui, HI: 621–30.

Graney, M.F., and A.J. Wynn. (1992) "An optimistic and proactive view of credit assessment?," in Thomas, Crook, and Edelman (eds.) *Credit Scoring*, pp. 209–16.

Granovetter, M. (1985) "Economic action and social structure: the problem of embeddedness," *American Journal of Sociology* 91(3): 481–510.

Grant, J. (1992) *Money of the Mind: Borrowing and Lending in America from the Civil War to Michael Milken*, New York: Noonday Press.

Graves, S. (2003) "Landscapes of predation, landscapes of neglect: a location analysis of payday lenders and banks," *Professional Geographer* 55(3): 303–17.

Graves, S., and C. Peterson. (2005) "Payday lending and the military: the law and geography of "payday" loans in military towns," *Ohio State Law Journal* 66(4): 653–832.

Greco, M. (1993) "Psychosomatic subjects and the 'duty to be well': personal agency within medical rationality," *Economy and Society* 22(3): 357–73.

Greene, E. (1935) "Better Business Bureau activities in aid of the time purchaser," *Law and Contemporary Problems* 2(2): 254–8.

Gruenstein, J. (2001) "Optimal use of statistical techniques," in Mays (ed.) *Handbook of Credit Scoring*, pp. 149–83.

Guseva, A. (2008) *Into the Red: The Birth of the Credit Card Market in Postcommunist Russia*, Stanford, CA: Stanford University Press.

Guseva, A., and A. Rona-Tas. (2001) "Uncertainty, risk and trust: Russian and American credit card markets compared," *American Sociological Review* 66(5): 623–46.

Gutman, H. (1973) "Work, culture, and society in industrializing America, 1815–1919," *American Historical Review* 78(3): 531–88.

Hacking, I. (1986) "Making up people," in T. Heller, M. Sasna, and D. Wellbery (eds.) *Reconstructing Individualism: Autonomy, Individuality and the Self in Western Thought*, Stanford, CA: Stanford University Press, pp. 222–36.

———. (1990) *The Taming of Chance*, Cambridge: Cambridge University Press.

———. (1991) "How should we do the history of statistics?" in Burchell, Gordon, and Miller (eds.) *The Foucault Effect*, pp. 181–95.

Haggerty, K., and R. Ericson. (2000) "The surveillant assemblage," *British Journal of Sociology* 51(4): 605–22.

Hall, P.D. (1982) *The Organization of American Culture, 1700–1900: Private Institutions, Elites, and the Origins of American Nationality*, New York: New York University Press.

Haller, M.H., and J.V. Alviti. (1977) "Loansharking in American cities: historical analysis of a marginal enterprise," *American Journal of Legal History* 21(2): 125–56.

Ham, A. (1909) *The Chattel Loan Business*, New York: Charity Organization Society.

———. (1912) *The Campaign against the Loan Shark*, New York: Russell Sage.

Hamilton, G.G., and J.R. Sutton. (1989) "The problem of control in the weak state: domination in the United States, 1880–1920," *Theory and Society* 18(1): 1–46.

Hand, D.J. (2001) "Reject inference in credit operations," in Mays (ed.) *Handbook of Credit Scoring*, pp. 225–40.

Hand, D.J., and W.E. Henley. (1997) "Statistical classification methods in consumer credit scoring: a review," *Journal of the Royal Statistical Society: Series A* 160(3): 523–41.

Harrison, R. (1997) *State and Society in Twentieth-Century America*, London: Longman.

Haskell, T.L. (2000) *The Emergence of Professional Social Science: The American Social Science Association and the Nineteenth-Century Crisis of Authority*, Baltimore: The Johns Hopkins University Press.

Hays, S.P. (1957) *The Response to Industrialism, 1885–1914*, Chicago: University of Chicago Press.

Hendrickson, R. (1979) *The Grand Emporiums: The Illustrated History of America's Great Department Stores*, New York: Stein and Day.

Hermanson, S., and G. Gaberlavage. (2001) "The alternative financial services industry," Public Policy Institute Issue Brief 51, August 2001.

Hier, S. (2003) "Probing the surveillant assemblage: on the dialectics of surveillance practices as processes of social control," *Surveillance and Society* 1(3): 399–411.

Hill, R., D. Ramp, and L. Silver. (1998) "The rent-to-own industry and pricing disclosure tactics," *Journal of Public Policy and Marketing* 17(1): 3–10.

Hillier, A. (2003) "Redlining and the Home Owners' Loan Corporation," *Journal of Urban History* 29(4): 394–420.

Hilton, M. (2004) "The legacy of luxury: moralities of consumption since the eighteenth century," *Journal of Consumer Culture* 4(1): 101–23.

Hiltz, S.R. (1971) "Black and white in the consumer finance system," *American Journal of Sociology* 76(6): 987–98.

Hofstadter, R. (1955) *The Age of Reform: From Bryan to F.D.R.,* New York: Knopf.

Holt, D. (1997) "Poststructuralist lifestyle analysis: conceptualizing the social patterning of consumption in postmodernity," *Journal of Consumer Research* 23(4): 326–50.

———. (1998) "Does cultural capital structure American consumption?," *Journal of Consumer Research* 25(1): 1–25.

Homer, S. (1963) *A History of Interest Rates*, New Brunswick, NJ: Rutgers University Press.

Hopper, M.A., and E.M. Lewis. (1992) "Behaviour scoring and adaptive control systems," in Thomas, Crook, and Edelman (eds.) *Credit Scoring*, pp. 257–76.

Hoppit, J. (1990) "Attitudes to credit in Britain, 1680–1790," *Historical Journal*, 33(2): 305–22.

Horan, J. (2005) "FICO scores and the credit underserved market," Paper presented to the roundtable Using Alternative Data sources in Credit Scoring: Challenges and

Opportunities, 15 December 2005, Brookings Institution, Washington DC. Available online at http://www.brookings.edu/metro/umi/20051215_JHoran_FairIssac.pdf [accessed 12 April 2006].

Horowitz, D. (1985) *Attitudes towards the Consumer Society in America, 1875–1940*, London: Johns Hopkins University Press.

———. (2004) *The Anxieties of Affluence: Critiques of American Consumer Culture, 1939–1979*, Amherst, MA: University of Massachusetts Press.

Hower, R.M. (1943) *History of Macy's of New York, 1858–1919: Chapters in the Evolution of the Department Store*, Cambridge MA: Harvard University Press.

Hsia, D.C. (1979) "Credit scoring and the equal credit opportunity act," *Hastings Law Journal* 30(2): 371–448.

Hudson, K. (1982) *Pawnbroking: An Aspect of British Social History*, London: Bodley Head.

Hunt, A. (1999) *Governing Morals: A Social History of Moral Regulation*, Cambridge: Cambridge University Press.

Hunt, R.M. (2002) "The development and regulation of consumer credit reporting in America," Working Paper 02–21, Federal Reserve Bank of Philadelphia.

———. (2006) "Development and regulation of consumer credit reporting in the United States," in G. Bertola, R. Disney, and C. Grant (eds.) *The Economics of Consumer Credit*, Cambridge, MA: MIT Press, pp. 301–45.

IPI. (2005) *Giving Underserved Consumers Better Access to the Credit System: The Promise of Non-Traditional Data*, Report by the Information Policy Institute, July 2005.

Jackson, K. (1985) *Crabgrass Frontier: The Suburbanisation of the United States*, Oxford: Oxford University Press.

Jacobs, M. (2001) "The politics of plenty: consumerism in the twentieth-century," in Daunton and Hilton (eds.) *The Politics of Consumption*, pp. 223–39.

Jacobson, T., and K. Roszbach. (2003) "Bank lending policy, credit scoring and value-at-risk," *Journal of Banking and Finance* 27(4): 615–33.

Jeacle, I., and E. Walsh. (2002) "From moral evaluation to rationalization: accounting and the shifting technologies of credit," *Accounting, Organizations and Society* 27(8): 737–61.

Jennings, A. (2001) "The importance of credit information and credit scoring for small business lending decisions," Proceedings from the Global Conference on Credit Scoring, 2–3 April 2001, Washington DC: pp. 5–12.

Jentzsch, N. (2001) "The economics and regulation of financial privacy: a comparative analysis of the United States and Europe," Working Paper 128/2001, John F. Kennedy Institute for North American Studies—Economics Section, Freie Universität Berlin.

Johnson, K.W. (2002) "Consumer loan securitization," in Durkin and Staten (eds.) *The Impact of Public Policy*, pp. 287–306.

Johnson, R.W. (1992) "Legal, social and economic issues in implementing scoring in the US," in Thomas, Crook, and Edelman (eds.) *Credit Scoring*, pp. 19–32.

Johnson, R.W., and D. Johnson. (1998) "Pawnbroking in the U.S.: a profile of customers," Monograph No. 34, Credit Research Center, Georgetown University, Washington DC.

Jones, M.A. (1992) *American Immigration*, 2nd Edition, Chicago: University of Chicago Press.

Jordan, R., and W. Warren. (1966) "Disclosure of finance charges: a rationale," *Michigan Law Review* 64(7): 1285–322.

Jost, A. (2001) "Data mining," in Mays (ed.) *Handbook of Credit Scoring*, pp. 185–213.

Karger, H. (2005) *Short Changed: Life and Debt in the Fringe Economy*, San Francisco: Berrett-Koehler.

Katz, M. (1996) *In the Shadow of the Poorhouse: A Social History of Welfare in America*, 10th Anniversary Edition, New York: Basic Books.

Kavanagh, T. (1993) *Enlightenment and the Shadows of Chance: The Novel and the Culture of Gambling in Eighteenth-century France*, Baltimore: The Johns Hopkins University Press.

Kempson, E., and C. Whyley. (1999) *Extortionate Credit in the UK: A Report to the DTI*, Personal Finance Research Centre, June 1999.

King, U., W. Lee, D. Davis, and K. Ernst. (2005) *Race Matters: The Concentration of Payday Lenders in African American Neighbourhoods in North Carolina*, Report by the Center for Responsible Lending, 22 March 2005.

Klausen, J. (2002) "Did World War II end the New Deal?," in Milkis and Mileur (eds.) *The New Deal and the Triumph of Liberalism*, pp. 193–230.

Klein, D. (2001) "Credit-information reporting: why free speech is vital to social accountability and consumer opportunities," *Independent Review* 5(3): 325–44.

Klein, L. (1999) *"It's in the Cards": Consumer Credit and the American Experience*, Westport, CT: Praeger.

Klein, D., and J. Richner. (1992) "In defence of the credit bureau," *Cato Journal* 12(2): 393–412.

Knight, F.H. (1971) *Risk, Uncertainty and Profit*, Chicago: University of Chicago Press.

Koudsi, S. (2002) "Sleazy Credit," *Fortune* 145(5): 143–6.

Kripke, H. (1968) "Consumer credit regulation: a creditor-oriented viewpoint," *Columbia Law Review* 68(3): 445–87.

———. (1969) "Gesture and reality in consumer credit reform," *New York University Law Review* 44(1): 1–52.

Kubik, P.J. (1996) "Federal Reserve policy during the Great Depression: the impact of interwar attitudes regarding consumption and consumer credit," *Journal of Economic Issues* 30(3): 829–42.

Lacko, J., S. McKernan, and M. Hastak. (2000) *Survey of Rent to Own Customers*, Bureau of Economics Staff Report, Federal Trade Commission, April 2000.

———. (2002) "Customer experience with rent-to-own transactions," *Journal of Public Policy and Marketing* 21(1): 126–38.

Lasch, C. (1979) *Culture of Narcissism: American Life in an Age of Diminishing Expectations*, New York: W.W. Norton.

Lawrence, D. (1992) *Handbook of Consumer Lending*, Englewood Cliffs, NJ: Prentice Hall.

Leach, W. (1993) *Land of Desire: Merchants, Power, and the Rise of a New American Culture*, New York: Pantheon.

Lears, J. (1989) "Beyond Veblen: rethinking consumer culture in America," in S. Bronner (ed.) *Consuming Visions: Accumulation and Display of Goods in America 1880–1920*, New York: W.W. Norton, pp. 73–97.

———. (1994) *Fables of Abundance: A Cultural History of Advertising in America*, New York: Basic Books.

Lee, T. (2001) "Measures for model validation," Mays (ed.) *Handbook of Credit Scoring*, pp. 275–84.

Lee, T., and S.C. Jung. (2001) "A multi-score approach for portfolio management," in Mays (ed.) *Handbook of Credit Scoring*, pp. 215–24.

Lee, W. (2000) "MBNA targets wealthy with quantum card," *American Banker* 165(145): 10.

Lehtonen, T. (1999) "Any room for aesthetics?: Shopping practices of heavily indebted consumers," *Journal of Material Culture* 4(3): 243–62.

Levidow, L. (1994) "Dereifying risk," *Science as Culture* 4(3): 440–56.

Levine, S. (1913) *The Business of Pawnbroking*, New York: D. Halpern.

Levitas, R. (2005) *The Inclusive Society? Social Exclusion and New Labour*, 2nd Edition, Basingstoke: Palgrave.

Lewis, E.M. (1992a) *An Introduction to Credit Scoring*, San Rafael, CA: Fair Isaac.

———. (1992b) "Credit scoring and credit control from four points of view," in Thomas, Crook, and Edelman (eds.) *Credit Scoring*, pp. 3–17.

Leyshon, A., and N. Thrift. (1999) "Lists come alive: electronic systems of knowledge and the rise of credit-scoring in retail banking," *Economy and Society* 28(3): 434–66.

Leyshon, A., D. Burton, D. Knights, C. Alferoff, and P. Signoretta. (2004a) "Towards an ecology of retail financial services: understanding the persistence of door-to-door credit and insurance providers," *Environment and Planning A* 36(4): 625–45.

Leyshon, A., P. Signoretta, D. Knights, C. Alferoff, and D. Burton. (2004b) "Walking with moneylenders: the ecology of the UK home-collected credit industry," *Urban Studies* 43(1): 161–86.

Ling, P.J. (1990) *America and the Automobile: Technology, Reform and Social Change*, Manchester: Manchester University Press.

Lubove, R. (1967) "Workmen's compensation and the prerogatives of voluntarism," *Labor History* 8(3): 254–79.

Lynn, R.A. (1957) "Installment credit before 1870," *Business History Review* 31(4): 414–24.

Lyon, D. (2003) "Surveillance as social sorting: computer codes and mobile bodies," in D. Lyon (ed.) *Surveillance as Social Sorting: Privacy, Risk and Digital Discrimination*, London: Routledge.

Madison, J. (1974) "The evolution of commercial credit reporting agencies in nineteenth-century America," *Business History Review* 48(2): 164–86.

Maki, D. (2002) "The growth of consumer credit and the household debt service burden," in Durkin and Staten (eds.) *The Impact of Public Policy*, pp. 43–63.

Makuch, W.M. (2001a) "Scoring applications," in Mays (ed.) *Handbook of Credit Scoring*, pp. 3–21.

———. (2001b) "The basics of a better applications score," in Mays (ed.) *Handbook of Credit Scoring*, pp. 127–48.

Malhotra, R., and D.K. Malhotra. (2003) "Evaluating consumer loans using neural networks," *Omega* 31(2): 83–96.

Mandell, L. (1990) *The Credit Card Industry: A History*, Boston: Twayne.

———. (2002) "Financial literacy in the U.S. and efforts towards credit education," in Durkin and Staten (eds.) *The Impact of Public Policy*, pp. 149–59.

Manning, R. (2000) *Credit Card Nation: The Consequences of America's Addiction to Credit*, New York: Basic.

Marchand, R. (1985) *Advertising the American Dream: Making Way for Modernity, 1920–1940*, Berkeley: University of California Press.

Marcuse, H. (1964) *One Dimensional Man: Studies in the Ideology of Advanced Industrial Society*, London: Routledge & Kegan Paul.

Maglin, S., and J. Schor. (eds.) (1990) *The Golden Age of Capitalism: Reinterpreting the Postwar Experience*, Oxford: Clarendon Press.

Marron, D. (2008) "'Alter reality': governing the risk of identity theft," *British Journal of Criminology* 48(1): 20–38.

Martin, S., and N. Huckins. (1997) "Consumer advocates vs. the rent-to-own industry: reaching a reasonable accommodation," *American Business Law Journal* 34(3): 385–428.

Marx, K. ([1844a] 1975) "Excerpts from James Mill's Elements of Political Economy," in *Marx: Early Writings*, Harmondsworth: Penguin, pp. 259–78.

———. ([1844b] 1975) "Economic and philosophical manuscripts of 1844," in *Marx: Early Writings*, pp. 279–400.

Mathews, H.L., and J. Slocum. (1969) "Social class and commercial bank credit card usage," *Journal of Marketing* 33(1): 71–8.

May, E.T. (1988) *Homeward Bound: American Families in the Cold War Era*, New York: Basic Books.

McAllister, P., and D. Eng. (2001) "Score-based collection strategies," in Mays (ed.) *Handbook of Credit Scoring*, pp. 303–20.

McCorkell, P.L. (2002) "The impact of credit scoring and automated underwriting on credit availability," in Durkin and Staten (eds.) *The Impact of Public Policy*, pp. 209–20.

McShane, C. (1994) *Down the Asphalt Path: The Automobile and the American City*, New York: Columbia University Press.

Mennell, S. (2007) *The American Civilizing Process*, Cambridge: Polity Press.

Meyer, S. (1981) *The Five Dollar Day: Labor Management and Social Control in the Ford Motor Company, 1908–1921*, Albany: State University of New York Press.

———. (1989) "The persistence of Fordism: workers and technology in the American automobile industry, 1900–1960" in N. Lichtenstein and S. Meyer (eds.) *On the Line: Essays in the History of Auto Work*, Urbana: University of Illinois Press, pp. 73–99.

Meyers, J.H., and E.W. Forgy. (1963) "The development of numerical evaluation systems," *Journal of the American Statistical Association* 58(3): 799–806.

Mill, J.S. (1888) *Principles of Political Economy, with some of their applications to social philosophy*, London: Longmans Green.

Miller, M. (1981) *The Bon Marché: Bourgeois Culture and the Department Store, 1869–1920*, London: Allen and Unwin.

Miller, P., and N. Rose. (1990) "Governing economic life," *Economy and Society* 19(1): 1–31.

———. (1997) "Mobilising the consumer: assembling the subject of consumption," *Theory, Culture and Society* 14(1): 1–36.

Miller, P., and T. O'Leary. (1994) "Governing the calculable person," in G. Hopwood and P. Miller (eds.) *Accounting as Social and Institutional Practice*, Cambridge: Cambridge University Press, pp. 98–115.

Millman, G.J. (2001) "Plastic Meltdown," *Institutional Investor* 35(12): 105–10.

Mills, C.W. (1959) *The Sociological Imagination*, New York: Galaxy Books.

Miron, J., and D. Weil. (1997) "The genesis and evolution of social security," in Bordo, Goldin, and White (eds.) *The Defining Moment*, pp. 297–322.

Mors, W. (1943) "Rate regulation in the field of consumer credit 1," *Journal of Business of the University of Chicago* 16(1): 51–63.

———. (1950) "State regulation of retail instalment financing: progress and problems," *Journal of Business of the University of Chicago* 23(4): 199–218.

Moulton, H.G. (1918) "Commercial banking and capital formation: IV," *Journal of Political Economy* 26(9): 849–81.

Mullen, E., M. Bush, and S. Weinstein. (1997) "Currency exchanges add to poverty surcharge for low-income residents," *Reinvestment Alert* 10, Woodstock Institute, March 1997.

Murphy, S. (1995) "The advertising of installment plans," *Essays in History* 35, Corcoran Department of History at the University of Virginia. Available online at http://etext. virginia.edu/journals/EH/EH37/Murphy.html [accessed 12 December 2005].

Mussey, H.R. (1903) *The Fake Instalment Business*, New York: University Settlement Society.

NCIF. (2005) *From the Margins to the Mainstream*, Report by the National Community Investment Fund, November 2005.

Neifeld, M.R. (1941) "Institutional organization of consumer credit," *Law and Contemporary Problems* 8(1): 23–35.

Nelson, B. (1969) *The Idea of Usury: From Tribal Brotherhood to Universal Otherhood*, 2nd Edition, Chicago: University of Chicago Press.

Nevins, A., and F.E. Hill. (1957) *Ford: Expansion and Challenge*, New York: Scribner's.

Nocera, J. (1994) *A Piece of the Action: How the Middle Class Joined the Money Class*, New York: Simon & Schuster.

Nugent, R. (1933) "Three experiments with small-loan interest rates," *Harvard Business Review* 12(1): 35–46.

———. (1938) "Tendencies in consumer financing," *Journal of the American Statistical Association* 33(201): 42–50.

———. (1939) *Consumer Credit and Economic Stability*, New York: Russell Sage.

———. (1941) "The loan-shark problem," *Law and Contemporary Problems* 8(1): 3–13.

Nye, D (1998) *A Social History of American Energies*, London: MIT Press.

O'Connor, A. (2001) *Poverty Knowledge: Social Science, Social Policy and the Poor in Twentieth-Century U.S. History*, Princeton: Princeton University Press.

O'Malley, P. (1992) "Risk, power and crime prevention," *Economy and Society* 21(3): 252–75.

———. (1994) "Regulating Enterprise Culture," *Canadian Journal of Law and Society* 9(2): 205–15.

———. (1996) "Risk and responsibility," in A. Barry, T. Osbourne, and N. Rose (eds.) *Foucault and Political Reason: Liberalism, Neo-Liberalism and Rationalities of Government*, London: University College London Press, pp. 189–207.

———. (2000) "Uncertain subjects: risk, liberalism and contract," *Economy and Society* 29(4): 460–84.

———. (2004) *Risk, Uncertainty and Government*, London: Glasshouse.

Oeltjen, J.C. (1989) "Pawnbroking on parade," *Buffalo Law Review* 37(3): 751–88.

———. (1990) "Coming to America: observations of statutory non-uniformity and a call for uniform legislation," *Buffalo Law Review* 38(1): 223–87.

———. (1991) "Pawnbroking: an historical, comparative perspective," *Arizona Journal of International and Comparative Law* 8(1): 53–73.

Olegario, R. (2002) "Credit-reporting agencies: their historical roots, current status, and role in market development," World Development Report 2002: Institutions for Markets—Background Papers, World Bank.

Olney, M.L. (1991) *Buy Now, Pay Later: Advertising, Credit, and Consumer Durables in the 1920s*, Chapel Hill: University of North Carolina Press.

———. (1999) "Avoiding default: the role of credit in the consumption collapse of 1930," *Quarterly Journal of Economics* 114(1): 319–35.

———. (2002) "Spendthrift, or sophisticated borrower?: institutional responses to the twentieth century evolution of consumer credit," Proceedings of the Conference on Credit, Trust, and Calculation, 12–14 November, University of California, San Diego.

Packard, V. (1957) *The Hidden Persuaders*, London: Longmans, Green.

Patterson, W.R. (1899) "Pawnbroking in Europe and the United States," *Bulletin of the Department of Labor*, Washington, March 1899.

Peterson, A., and D. Lupton. (1996) *The New Public Health: Discourses, Knowledges, Strategies*, London: Sage.

Peterson, C.L. (2004) *Taming the Sharks: Towards a Cure for the High Cost Credit Market*, Akron, OH: University of Akron Press.

Peterson, R., and R. Kern. (1996) "Changing highbrow taste: from snob to omnivore," *American Sociological Review* 61(5): 900–907.

Phelps, C.W. (1954) *Financing the Instalment Purchases of the American Family: Studies in Consumer Credit No. 3*, Baltimore: Commercial Credit Company.

———. (1955) *Using Instalment Credit: Studies in Consumer Credit No. 4*, Baltimore: Commercial Credit Company.

Pinto, M., D. Parente, and P. Mansfield. (2005) "Information learned from socialization agents: its relationship to credit card use," *Family and Consumer Sciences Research Journal* 33(44): 357–67.

Plummer, W.C., and R.A. Young. (1940) *Sales Finance Companies and their Credit Practices: Financial Research Program, Studies in Consumer Instalment Financing 2*, New York: National Bureau of Economic Research.

Poon, M. (2007) "Scorecards as devices for consumer credit: the case of Fair, Isaac & Company Incorporated," *Sociological Review* 55(2): 284–306.

Porter, G. (1973) *The Rise of Big Business, 1860–1910*, New York: Crowell.

Porter, T.M. (1992) "Quantification and the accounting ideal in science," *Social Studies of Science* 22(4): 633–51.

———. (1995) *Trust in Numbers: The Pursuit of Objectivity in Science and Public Life*, Princeton: Princeton University Press.

Poster, M. (1990) *The Mode of Information: Poststructuralism and Social Context*, Chicago: University of Chicago Press.

———. (1996) "Databases as discourse, or electronic interpellations," in P. Hellas, S. Lash, and P. Morris (eds.) *De-traditionalization: Critical Reflections on Authority and Identity at a Time of Uncertainty*, Oxford: Blackwell.

Power, M. (1997) *The Audit Society: Rituals of Verification*, Oxford: Oxford University Press.

Procacci, G. (1991) "Social economy and the government of poverty," in Burchell, Gordon, and Miller (eds.) *The Foucault Effect*, pp. 151–68.

Quester, A., and J. Fox. (2005) *Car Title Lending: Driving Borrowers to Financial Ruin*, Center for Responsible Lending and the Consumer Federation of America, 14 April 2005.

Raby, C. (1924) *Regulation of Pawnbroking*, New York: Russell Sage.

Rappaport, E. (2000) *Shopping for Pleasure: Women in the Making of London's West End*, Princeton: Princeton University Press.

Recchiuti, J. (2007) *Civic Engagement: Social Science and Progressive-Era Reform in New York City*, Philadelphia: University of Pennsylvania Press.

Reith, G. (2002) *The Age of Chance: Gambling and Western Culture*, 2nd Edition, London: Routledge.

——. (2004a) "Uncertain times: the notion of 'risk' and the development of modernity," *Time and Society* 13(2): 383–402.

——. (2004b) "Consumption and its discontents: addiction, identity and the problems of freedom," *British Journal of Sociology* 55(2): 283–300.

——. (2005) "On the edge: drugs and the consumption of risk in late modernity," in S. Lyng (ed.) *Edgework: The Sociology of Risk Taking*, London: Routledge, pp. 227–45.

——. (2007) "Gambling and the contradictions of consumption: a genealogy of the "pathological" subject," *American Behavioral Scientist* 51(1): 33–55.

Reuss, H.S. (1935) "Legislation: protection the instalment buyer," *Harvard Law Review* 49(1): 128–43.

Riesman, D., N. Glazer, and R. Denney. (1950) *The Lonely Crowd: A Study of the Changing American Character*, New Haven: Yale University Press.

Ritzer, G. (1995) *Expressing America: A Critique of the Global Credit Card Society*, Thousand Oaks: Pine Forge.

Robinson, L., and M. Stearns. (1930) *Ten Thousand Small Loans: Facts about Borrowers in 109 Cities in 17 States*, New York: Russell Sage.

Robinson, L.N., and R. Nugent. (1935) *Regulation of the Small Loan Business*, New York: Russell Sage.

Rock, P. (1973) *Making People Pay*, London: Routledge and Kegan Paul.

Roe, A.L. (1965) "Bankers and thrift in the age of affluence," *American Quarterly* 17(4): 619–33.

Rose, N. (1993) "Government, authority and expertise in advanced liberalism," *Economy and Society* 22(3): 283–99.

——. (1996a) "Psychiatry as a political science: advanced liberalism and the administration of risk," *History of the Human Sciences* 9(2): 1–23.

——. (1996b) *Inventing Our Selves: Psychology, Power and Personhood*, Cambridge: Cambridge University Press.

——. (1999a) *Governing the Soul: Shaping the Private Self, 2ⁿᵈ Edition*, London: Free Association Books.

——. (1999b) *Powers of Freedom: Reframing Political Thought*, Cambridge: Cambridge University Press.

——. (2002) "At risk of madness," in Baker and Simon (eds.) *Embracing Risk*, pp. 209–37.

Rose, N., and P. Miller. (1992) "Political power beyond the state: problematics of government," *British Journal of Sociology* 43 (2): 173–205.

Rosenberg, E., and A. Gleit. (1994) "Quantitative methods in credit management: a survey," *Operations Research* 42(4): 589–613.

Rothstein, H., M. Huber, and G. Gaskell. (2006) "A theory of risk colonization: the spiralling regulatory logics of societal and institutional risk," *Economy and Society* 35(1): 91–112.

Rowlingson, K. (1994) *Moneylenders and their Customers*, London: PSI.

Rowlingson, K., and E. Kempson. (1994) *Paying with Plastic: A Study of Credit Card Debt*, London: PSI.

Rubin, E. (1991) "Legislative methodology: some lessons from the 'Truth-in-Lending' act," *Georgetown Law Journal* 80(2): 233–307.

Rule, J., D. Caplovitz, and P. Barker. (1969) "The dossier in consumer credit," in S. Wheeler (ed.) *On Record: Files and Dossiers in American Life*, New York: Russell Sage, pp. 143–75.

Sandage, S. (2006) *Born Losers: A History of Failure in America*, Cambridge, MA: Harvard University Press.

Santoni, G.J. (1986) "The Employment Act of 1946: some history notes," *Federal Reserve Bank of St. Louis Review*, November 1986: 5–16.

Schelling, T.C. (1980) "The intimate contest for self-command," *Public Interest* 60(Summer): 94–118.

Schill, M., and S. Wachter. (1994) "Borrower and neighbourhood racial and income characteristics and financial institution mortgage application screening," *Journal of Real Estate Finance and Economics* 9(3): 223–39.

Schor, J.B. (1998) *The Overspent American: Upscaling, Downshifting, and the New Consumer*, New York: Basic Books.

Schreft, S.L. (1990) "Credit controls: 1980," *Federal Reserve Bank of Richmond Economic Review*, November/December 1990: 25–55.

Sedgwick, E. (1992) "Epidemics of the will," in J. Crary and S. Kwinter (eds.) *Incorporations: Zone 6*, New York: Urzone, pp. 582–95.

Seligman, E.R.A. (1927) *The Economics of Installment Selling: A Study in Consumers' Credit, with special reference to the automobile*, New York: Harper.

Shay, R.P. (1965) "Major developments in the market for consumer credit since the end of World War II," *Journal of Finance* 21(2): 369–81.

Shergold, Peter. (1978) "The loan shark: the small loan business in early twentieth-century Pittsburgh," *Pennsylvania History* 45(2): 195–223.

Simmel, G. (1978) *The Philosophy of Money*, London: Routledge and Kegan Paul.

Simon, J. (1987) "The emergence of a risk society: insurance, law and the state," *Socialist Review* 95: 61–89.

———. (1988) "The ideological effects of actuarial practices," *Law and Society Review* 22(4): 771–800.

Simpson, W.R., F.K. Simpson, and C. Samuels. (1954) *Hockshop*, New York: Random House.

Sloan, A. ([1963] 1980) *My Years with General Motors*, Geneva: Orbit.

Smalley, O.A., and F. Sturdivant. (1973) *The Credit Merchants: A History of Spiegel, Inc.*, Carbondale and Edwardsville: Southern Illinois University Press.

Smith, A. ([1776] 1910) *The Wealth of Nations, in Two Vols.*, London: J.M. Dent.

Souccar, M. (1999) "Optima, Advantage, and MBNA top survey of card satisfaction," *American Banker* 164(147): 1–2.

Spiekermann, U. (1999) "Theft and thieves in German department stores, 1895–1930: a discourse on morality, crime and gender," in G. Crossick and S. Jaumain (eds.) *Cathedrals of Consumption: The European Department Stores, 1850–1939*, Aldershot: Ashgate, pp. 135–59.

Squires, G. (2004) "The new redlining," in G. Squires (ed.) *Why the Poor Pay More: How to Stop Predatory Lending*, Westport, CT: Praeger, pp. 1–23.

Squires, G., and S. O'Connor. (1998) "Fringe banking in Milwaukee: the rise of check-cashing businesses and emergence of a two-tiered banking system," *Urban Affairs Review* 34(1): 126–50.

St. Clair, D.J. (1986) *The Motorization of American Cities*, London: Praeger.

Stanghellini, E., K.J. McConway, and D.J. Hand. (1999) "A discrete variable chain graph for applicants for credit," *Applied Statistics* 48(2): 239–51.

Starr, M. (2007) "Savings, spending, and self-control: cognition versus consumer culture," *Review of Radical Political Economics* 39(2): 214–29.

Stearns, P. (1999) *Battleground of Desire: The Struggle for Self-Control in Modern America*, New York: New York University Press.

Stegman, M., and R. Faris. (2003) "Payday lending: a business model that encourages chronic borrowing," *Economic Development Quarterly* 17(1): 8–32.

Stover, J.F. (1961) *American Railroads*, Chicago: University of Chicago Press.

Straka, J.W. (2000) "A shift in the mortgage landscape: the 1990s move to automated credit evaluations," *Journal of Housing Research* 11(2): 207–32.

Strasser, S. (1989) *Satisfaction Guaranteed: The Making of the American Mass Market*, London: Smithsonian Institution Press.

Sullivan, T., E. Warren, and J.L. Westbrook. (1989) *As We Forgive Our Debtors: Bankruptcy and Consumer Credit in America*, Oxford: Oxford University Press.

———. (2000) *The Fragile Middle Class: Americans in Debt*, New Haven: Yale University Press.

Sunstein, C. (2005) *Laws of Fear: Beyond the Precautionary Principle*, Cambridge: Cambridge University Press.

Susman, W. (2003) *Culture as History: The Transformation of American Society in the Twentieth Century*, Washington: Smithsonian Institution Press.

Swagler, R., and P. Wheeler. (1989) "Rental-purchase agreements: a preliminary investigation of consumer attitudes and behaviors," *Journal of Consumer Affairs* 23(1): 145–60.

Taylor, A. (2002) *Working Class Credit and Community since 1918*, Basingstoke: Palgrave Macmillan.

TBWA. (2005) *Visa*, TBWA Advertising. Available online at http://www.tbwa.com/index.php/disruptiveideas/1;2 [accessed 13 May 2006].

Tebbutt, M. (1983) *Making Ends Meet: Pawnbroking and Working-Class Credit*, Leicester: Leicester University Press.

Tedlow, R. (1990) *New and Improved: the Story of Mass Marketing in America*, Oxford: Heinemann.

Tescher, J. (2006) "Expanded credit data will help banks, poor," *American Banker* 171(37): 8.

Thomas, L.C. (2000) "A survey of credit and behavioural scoring; forecasting financial risk of lending to consumers," *International Journal of Forecasting* 16(2): 149–72.

Thomas, L.C., J. Ho, and W.T. Scherer. (2001) " 'Time will tell,' behavioural scoring and the dynamics of consumer credit assessment," *IMA Journal of Management Mathematics* 12(1): 89–103.

Thompson, E.P. (1967) "Time, work-discipline, and industrial capitalism," *Past and Present* 38(1): 56–97.

Thompson, R.L. (1947) *Wiring a Continent*, Princeton: Princeton University Press.

Trescott, P.B. (1963) *Financing American Enterprise: The Story of Commercial Banking*, New York: Harper & Row.

Tucker, D. (1991) *The Decline of Thrift in America: Our Cultural Shift from Saving to Spending*, New York: Greenwood Press.

Turow, J. (1997) *Breaking Up America: Advertisers and the New Media World*, Chicago: University of Chicago Press.

Valverde, M. (1996) "'Despotism' and ethical liberal governance," *Economy and Society* 25(3): 357–72.

———. (1997) "'Slavery from within': the invention of alcoholism and the question of free will," *Social History* 22(3): 251–68.

———. (1998) *Diseases of the Will: Alcohol and the Dilemmas of Freedom*, Cambridge: Cambridge University Press.

Vaz, P., and F. Bruno. (2003) "Types of self-surveillance: from abnormality to individuals 'at risk,'" *Surveillance and Society* 1(3): 272–91.

Veblen, T. ([1899] 1925) *The Theory of the Leisure Class: An Economic study of Institutions*, London: Allen and Unwin.

Verstraete, G. (2002) "Railroading America: towards a material study of the nation," *Theory, Culture and Society* 19(5–6): 145–59.

Walsh, E., and I. Jeacle. (2003) "The taming of the buyer: the retail inventory method and the early twentieth century department store," *Accounting, Organizations and Society* 28(7–8): 773–91.

Warde, A. (2005) "Consumption and theories of practice," *Journal of Consumer Culture* 5(2): 131–53.

Wassam, C. (1908) *The Salary Loan Business*, New York: Charity Organization Society.

Watkins, J.P. (2000) "Corporate power and the evolution of consumer credit," *Journal of Economic Issues* 34(4): 909–32.

Weber, M. ([1930] 1976) *The Protestant Ethic and the Spirit of Capitalism*, London: Allen and Unwin.

Weinstein, J. (1967) "Big business and the origins of Workmen's Compensation," *Labor History* 8(3): 156–74.

Weir, M., and T. Skocpol. (1985) "State structures and the possibilities for 'Keynesian' responses to the Great Depression in Sweden, Britain, and the United States," in P. Eveans, D. Rueschemeyer, and T. Skocpol (eds.) *Bringing the State Back In*, Cambridge: Cambridge University Press, pp. 44–77.

Westin, A., and M. Baker. (1972) *Databanks in a Free Society: Computers, Record-keeping and Privacy*, New York: Quadrangle/New York Times Books.

White, A. (2004) "Risk-based mortgage pricing," *Housing Policy Debate* 15(3): 503–31.

Whyte, W.H. (1956) *The Organization Man*, New York: Simon and Schuster.

Wiebe, R.H. (1967) *The Search for Order, 1877–1920*, London: Macmillan.

Wightman, J. (1996) *Contract: A Critical Commentary*, London: Pluto.

Wiles, M., and D. Immergluck. (2000) "Unregulated payday lending pulls vulnerable consumers into spiralling debt," *Reinvestment Alert* 14, Woodstock Institute, March 2000.

Williams, B. (2004) *Debt for Sale: A Social History of the Credit Trap*, Philadelphia: University of Pennsylvania Press.

Williams, R.H. (1982) *Dream Worlds: Mass Consumption in Late Nineteenth-Century France*, Berkeley: University of California Press.

Worden, D., and A.C. Sullivan. (1987) "Shopping for consumer credit: implications for market efficiency," Working Paper No. 54, Credit Research Center, Krannert Graduate School of Management, Purdue University.

Wu, C.C., J. Fox, and P. Woodall. (2006) *Another Year of Losses: High-Priced Refund Anticipation Loans Continue To Take a Chunk Out Of Americans' Tax Refunds*, Report by the National Consumer Law Center and the Consumer Federation of America, January 2006.

Young, J. (1999) *The Exclusive Society: Social Exclusion, Crime and Difference in Late Modernity*, London: Sage.

———. (2007) *The Vertigo of Late Modernity*, London: Sage.

Zelizer, V. (1994) *The Social Meaning of Money*, New York: Basic Books.

Zikmund-Fisher, B., and A. Parker. (1999) "Demand for rent-to-own contracts: a behavioral economic explanation" *Journal of Economic Behavior and Organization* 38(2): 199–216.

Zukin, S. (2004) *Point of Purchase: How Shopping Changed American Culture*, London: Routledge.

Zweig, F. (1934) *The Economics of Consumers' Credit*, London: P.S. King.

Index

Becoming Subjects

Reconstructing the Public Sphere
in Curriculum Studies

Series Editors: William F. Pinar, Marla Morris, and Mary Aswell Doll

Becoming Subjects

Sexualities and Secondary Schooling

MARY LOUISE RASMUSSEN

Routledge
Taylor & Francis Group
New York London

Published in 2006 by
Routledge
Taylor & Francis Group
270 Madison Avenue
New York, NY 10016

Published in Great Britain by
Routledge
Taylor & Francis Group
2 Park Square
Milton Park, Abingdon
Oxon OX14 4RN

© 2006 by Taylor & Francis Group, LLC
Routledge is an imprint of Taylor & Francis Group

Printed in the United States of America on acid-free paper
10 9 8 7 6 5 4 3 2 1

International Standard Book Number-10: 0-415-95161-5 (Hardcover) 0-415-95162-3 (Softcover)
International Standard Book Number-13: 978-0-415-95161-6 (Hardcover) 978-0-415-95162-3 (Softcover)

Library of Congress Cataloging-in-Publication Data

Catalog record is available from the Library of Congress

Taylor & Francis Group
is the Academic Division of Informa plc.

Visit the Taylor & Francis Web site at
http://www.taylorandfrancis.com

and the Routledge Web site at
http://www.routledge-ny.com

Contents

Acknowledgments

In the course of writing this book, I have received generous assistance from diverse people and institutions across several states in Australia and the United States. First and foremost, I wish to express my deepest gratitude to Professor Jane Kenway, who has been and continues to be, a valuable and incisive critic. Dr. Vicki Crowley and Dr. Valerie Harwood have also provided intellectual inspiration and emotional encouragement. I am also appreciative of the generous support for this project provided by Dr. Jane Mitchell and Professor Bill Pinar. I am also grateful to Deakin University, the University of South Australia, and Monash University for providing me with time and financial assistance to complete this manuscript. Thanks are also due to Professor Glorianne Leck and Youngstown State University for being a welcoming sponsor of my research in the United States. Finally, I wish to express my gratitude to the Arndt and Rasmussen families.

This book would not have been possible without those who agreed to be participants in this study. I am most grateful for the time shared by all of these wonderful people. In Australia these participants included Michael Crowhurst, Margaret Edwards, Jacqui Griffin, Ian Hunter, Kenton Miller, Amanda Nickson, Maria Pallota-Chiarolli, and Derek Williams. In the United States participants included Barbara Blinick, Al Ferreira, Jesse Greenman, Joyce Hunter, Kevin Jennings, Jaron Kanegson,

Christopher Rodriguez, and Gail Rolf. I would also like to thank Kevin Gogin from the San Francisco Unified School District; Jerry Battey, the founder of the EAGLES Center in the Los Angeles Unified School District; and representatives of the Bay Area Network of Gay and Lesbian Educators; the Safe Schools Program for Gay and Lesbian Students located in the Massachusetts Department of Education; and the Audre Lorde Project in Brooklyn, New York. I also wish to thank Carrie Moyer, Tina Fiveash, and Deborah Kelly for giving me permission to reproduce their artwork in the production of this manuscript.

Several earlier versions of work that appear in this book have been published elsewhere. I thank the following publishers for permission to revise and reprint my work. Portions of Chapter 1 pertaining to arts of inclusion are a revised version of Rasmussen (2001). Portions of Chapters 3 and 4 are a revised version of Rasmussen (2004c). Portions of Chapters 1 and 6 are a revised version of Rasmussen (2004a). A portion of Chapter 7 pertaining to gender melancholia is a revised version of Rasmussen (2005). Portions of Chapter 7 also appear in a revised version of Rasmussen (2004d). Portions of Chapter 6 are a revised version of Rasmussen (2004b). Excerpts from Chapter 5 previously appeared in Harwood and Rasmussen (2003).

Preface

This book focuses on key contemporary discourses related to sexualities and schooling. Such discourses comprise educational strategies used to support lesbian, gay, bisexual, and transgender (LGBT) students; considerations of how educators might influence students' sexual identity; scientifically authorized narratives of risk and violence often associated with LGBT youth; stories of salvation and protection; as well as debates relating to the "closet" and calls to "come out" in the classroom. People who are often left out of discussions of sexualities and schooling are also incorporated into this text: people such as Krystal Bennett — a prom king in Ferndale, Washington — or a boy-dyke-fag supporting transgender high school students in San Francisco. Heterosexuals are another group often unmarked in sexuality education; here they are examined via a public art project that uses humor, gloss, and parody to educate people about their particular characteristics and privileges. The influence of heroic figures such as Matthew Shepard is also considered alongside less well-known representatives of the LGBT community: people such as Matthew Limon, an 18-year-old who was sentenced to 17 years in prison for having consensual sex with another young man at a high school in Kansas. This analysis is informed by theoretical resources associated with queer theory, feminism, and poststructuralism, as well as interviews conducted with prominent activists for LGBT young people such as Kevin Jennings, executive director of the Gay, Lesbian, Straight Education Network, and Christopher Rodriguez, associate executive director of policy and public information at the Hetrick-Martin Institute in New York City.

Introduction

I think everyone who does gay and lesbian studies is haunted by the
suicides of adolescents. To us, the hard statistics come easily: that
queer young teenagers are two to three times likelier to attempt
suicide, and to accomplish it, than others; that up to 30 percent of
teen suicides are likely to be gay or lesbian; that a third of lesbian
and gay teenagers say they have attempted suicide; that minority
queer adolescents are at even more extreme risk.

This knowledge is indelible, but not astonishing, to anyone with
a reason to be attuned to the profligate way this culture has of
denying and despoiling queer energies and lives. I look at my adult
friends and colleagues doing lesbian and gay work, and I feel that
the survival of each one is a miracle. Everyone who has survived
has stories about how it was done.

(Sedgwick, 1993b, p. 1)

This evocative description of the situation of "queer young
teenagers," and of those who study them, comes from Eve
Kosofsky Sedgwick, a professor located in the South in the
United States. She cites these statistics as part of her motivation in gathering together a collection of her essays informed
by queer theories. More than a decade after it was written, such
statistics still operate as a salient reminder of some of the issues

1

that influenced my decision to focus this book on issues related to lesbian, gay, bisexual, transgender, and intersex[1] (LGBTI) teachers and students in high school settings.

Like Sedgwick, I too am appalled by the "despoiling of queer energies and lives," and I located my research in the field of education so I could play a part in the process of determining how those interested in the schooling of young people might be involved in remedying this situation. Thus, I set out to research programs designed to support LGBTI-identified teachers and students in high school settings in Australia and the United States.

Although I shared Sedgwick's motivation when I began this study, in the course of constructing this book I found myself becoming increasingly ambivalent about the value of such motivations in research related to LGBTI-identified young people. My ambivalence is not linked to the dire statistics Sedgwick quotes relating to the suffering of LGBTI-identified young people, though I do hold some concerns in this regard. Rather, a process of repetition perturbs me — a continuous repetition of the statistics cited by Sedgwick at the beginning of this introduction that has seen these statistics gradually become a part of the canon in research related to sexualities and secondary schooling. These statistics are too often taken as a point of departure when contemplating the lives of LGBTI-identified young people (Benton, 2003; Ferfolja & Robinson, 2004; Page & Liston, 2002; Pinhey & Millman, 2004; Russell, Driscoll, & Truong, 2002; van Wormer & McKinney, 2003).

The deployment of such evocative images of young people within the context of queer theory (see Sedgwick) is somewhat paradoxical according to Lesnik-Oberstein and Thomson (2002). They argue the "whole rhetorical effort is to find a way of affirming gayness as something admissible while refusing to ascribe an essence or a telos. Hence the importance, and the problem, [is] of the proto gay kid, who is strangely destined and yet not destined" (p. 45) in this instance, as in so many others, to become an object of pathos in queer and educational research relating to LGBTI-identified young people.

Although I introduce this book with a quote once again repeating these statistics, I do this in order to interrogate the paradox Lesnik-Oberstein and Thomson (2002) identify in order to explore strategies that "affirm gayness" while refusing the notion that gayness constitutes an unshakeable destiny. Moreover, I want to problematize the point of departure that reinscribes pathos and to keep open the way for alternative approaches to researching "queer young teenagers" (Sedgwick, 1993b, p. 1). In this task I acknowledge the inspiration of other researchers who have initiated a movement away from a focus on abjection and survival in research relating to LGBTI subjects, particularly the work of North American–based researcher William Haver (1997, 1999). In seeking a movement away from the "proto gay kid," this abject poster boy who is so often the foundation of LGBTI research in schools, I draw upon and analyze diverse resources.

My movement away from the wound is informed by queer, feminist, and poststructuralist theoretical frameworks that critique and deconstruct heteronormalizing practices and discourses and draw attention to "those fictions of identity that stabilize all identificatory categories" (Jagose, 1996, p. 125). This notion of identities as fictions emphasizes individuals' agency in the creation of their own subjectivities and identities. This agency intersects with stabilizing forces that work to continuously buttress heteronormalizing processes (Butler, 1997d) and to reinforce the individual's affinity with the familiar.

Queer theories seek to disturb familiar identity categories such as woman, man, lesbian, gay, and straight: categories that are often used unproblematically in educational research. Although queer theories are inextricably tied to poststructuralist and feminist theories, queer theorists tend to focus their gaze upon sexualities. Butler (1998) discusses her decision to focus on the study of sexuality by reference to the notion of rhetorical excess:

> I am probably willing to commit a sort of rhetorical excess in order to keep the question of homosexuality, and lesbianism in particular, alive. Which is not the same as saying that all scholarship ought to do that or that it is the primary oppression, or the key, or whatever. It rather indicates where I enter into critical discourse these days. (p. 284)

This approach does not seek to create a hierarchy of oppression but, rather, signifies a particular entry point into the production of discourses related to sexualities and secondary schooling. This study is also indebted to other researchers in the United States who have also adopted a queer theoretical lens in the study of education (Pinar, 1998; Talburt & Steinberg, 2000).

This queer theoretical analysis is also integrally related to Foucault's (1996g) conceptualization of power. He argues that "[w]e cannot jump *outside* the situation, and there is no point from which you are free of power relations. But ... we are always free ... there is always the possibility of changing" (p. 386, emphasis in original). The benefit of such a conceptualization of power is that it may be used to destabilize normalizing processes that endeavor to compel stable identities. I find this theoretical approach appealing in the context of this book because it incorporates individuals' capacity to alter relations of power. Butler (1990a), in her theory of performativity, has extended Foucault's work on the regulatory practices that compel a particular set of performances relating to sexual and gender identities. She proposes that "[i]n the place of the law of heterosexual coherence, we see sex and gender denaturalized by means of a performance" (p. 175). Within this queer theoretical framework, gender and sexual identities are perceived as unstable performances, constantly mediated by relations of power and open to the possibility of change. Although the work of Foucault and Butler is critical in the production of queer theories, it is not the sole theoretical basis of this book. Theorists working in education, feminism, poststructuralism, and cultural studies also inform this study. All of these bodies of knowledge are interdisciplinary and resistant to definition.

Based on this theoretical framework, this book addresses three central questions. First, what are some of the key discourses relating to sexualities and secondary schooling? Second, how are these discourses manifest in the field of sexualities and secondary schooling, and why do they manifest in these particular ways? And, third, what are some potential alternative directions for the production of theories and practices related to sexualities and schooling? These questions signal some new directions in research related to sexualities and schooling. Together they constitute a process of layering whereby research materials and innovative conceptual devices are integrated to identify, critically examine, and deconstruct some of the key discourses widely deployed in this field of inquiry.

The first question posed pertains to the process of identifying some of the key discourses that inform studies of sexualities and schooling, during which time this question also prompts an exploration of discourses that may be so familiar that identification or elaboration of them seems unnecessary. Moreover, I examine some discourses that may, at first, appear unrelated or unmarked in the area of sexualities and schooling, and I consider how these discourses are significant in the production of debates in this area.

Building on my identification of some of the key discourses that inform this area of inquiry, I consider two interrelated questions: How are these discourses manifest in the field of sexualities and secondary schooling? Why do they manifest in these particular ways? Discourses might manifest in some educational spaces but not in others, or they may be articulated outside formal educational settings and may be constrained within the space of the school. I pose these questions in order to consider how time, space, place, and relations of power mediate these discourses.

The third question focuses on how the theoretical resources and conceptual devices I have deployed in this book might contribute to the process of thinking differently about sexualities and schooling. I also consider pedagogical practices that might inform educational programs related to sexualities located within and outside formal educational settings.

In developing these potential alternative directions for research in the area of sexualities and secondary schooling, I draw on a range of materials, specifically focusing on data pertinent to Australia and the United States, allowing me to draw on personal experiences of political organization in LGBTI communities in both countries. U.S. trends in sexualities and secondary schooling do influence the shape of Australian discourses in this area, and, to a much lesser extent, the reverse is also true. As Epstein and Sears (1999) note, there can be no doubting that the power located in the United States is "a key element in the construction of 'master narratives' of sexuality as of so much else" (p. 3). Although my focus is on data from these two countries, this is not a comparative study, and it is not exclusive to materials from Australia and the United States.

The analysis of a broad range of academic journals and texts pertaining to queer, feminist, and poststructuralist theories, sexualities, genders, and schooling is also fundamental to the development of this research. I have utilized relevant publications on issues related to sexualities and secondary schooling produced by education departments, by LGBTI community groups, and by representatives of various religious organizations.

Research for this book also incorporates extensive analysis of resources drawn from the World Wide Web (WWW), including web zines, an interview with a lesbian prom king from Ferndale High School in Washington State, letters to a nationally syndicated U.S. agony aunt, and web-based promotional material produced by MTV. And I have incorporated photographs taken from an Australian-based visual arts project.

Secondary, rather than tertiary (college) or primary (elementary), settings are the central focus of this study. Unlike programs based on tertiary campuses, those working in secondary and primary settings must negotiate the problems that arise in the discussion of issues related to sexuality involving people under the age of consent.[2] The potential for allegations of recruitment is critical in shaping discussions of sexual and gender identities in educational contexts where students are below the age of consent. People working in secondary and primary settings must also consider the role of parents and carers, increasingly influential players in the development of curricula, school staffing, and students' subject choice.

Given this focus on secondary schooling, interviews with participants working with LGBTI-identified teachers and students in and around high school settings were another valuable source of data. Several of the people interviewed had postgraduate qualifications and were also involved in research, writing, and organizing related to sexualities and schooling. In total I interviewed 17 participants — eight from Australia and nine from the United States. Australian participants had worked in states and territories in mainland southeastern Australia, namely South Australia, Victoria, the Australian Capital Territory, and New South Wales. U.S. participants working in San Francisco, Los Angeles, New York, and Boston were interviewed. In part, I selected participants in these cities because I was already familiar with their work. These cities also lent themselves to such a study, as they all have large LGBTI communities supporting an array of programs related to sexualities and secondary schooling.

The interviews, which were unstructured and fairly informal, took place in 1998 over a period of about 6 months. I interviewed each participant once, and the interviews averaged about 2 hours. All participants were given a transcription of the interview and the chance to amend the transcript as they desired. In addition, publications produced by participants in this study or related organizations contributed to the fashioning of this book. I asked participants about their work in the area of sexualities and secondary schooling, including what motivated them to work in this particular area and how they shaped the programs or strategies with which they were involved. Participants were also asked questions relating to how homophobia and heterosexism shaped their work, and I inquired as to whether they limited their work practices and speech for fear of persecution or harassment. Participants were also asked to talk about their understandings of sexual and gender identities and about how these understandings might shape the programs they develop. Finally, I questioned participants on how different members of the school community reacted to their work on sexualities and schooling and on how these reactions influenced their programs and teaching strategies. These questions were partially inspired by Namaste (1996, pp. 198–99).

With one exception, participants agreed to be identified; all were given the option of remaining anonymous. In reporting on her research with "queer community activists" in Ontario in Canada, Owen (2000) notes that

> ... almost every participant I interviewed did not care about anonymity. In fact, some activists specifically did not want their names left out ... In hindsight this only makes sense ... . Queer political activists are few enough in number in this province that it would be difficult to disguise their identities ... . Secondly, given that I was speaking to "out," high-profile activists in many cases, there is no reason that they would not want credit for the work they have done. (p. 56)

The observations made by Owen resonate with my own experience of the research process. Most of the participants in this study were on public record as working to develop programs in support of LGBTI-identified teachers and students, so preserving anonymity because of fears of being "outed" was generally not an issue.

ABOUT THE CHAPTERS

This diverse range of theoretical resources, research materials, and interviews inform the seven chapters that constitute this study. In the first chapter, I identify key discourses that have been deployed in attempts to be inclusive of LGBTI-identified teachers and students. I analyze the ways in which these discourses manifest around the theme of inclusion and consider how these manifestations might be problematized. Drawing on Foucault and queer theories, I also consider the efficacy of reconceptualizing the notion of inclusion as an art or exercise that takes into account differing styles of existence.

The epistemological and methodological underpinnings of this study are outlined in Chapter 2. I ponder how it is possible to do research related to sexualities and schooling that is informed by queer, feminist, and poststructuralist theories, considering some of the critiques and pitfalls that may adhere to such an approach. I also propose a methodological framework for inspiring alternative ways of thinking about educational research relating to sexualities, and I detail the conceptual devices that support this approach.

Chapter 3 utilizes the theoretical resources outlined in the previous chapter to elaborate on notions of identity and subjectivity and essentialism and constructivism. I also reiterate and expand upon the value of a deconstructive approach in research related to sexualities and schooling. In the latter half of this chapter I detail how Foucault's three modes of objectification of subjects inform this research on sexualities and secondary schooling.

I focus on processes of subjectivization and identification in Chapter 4. I demonstrate how differing conceptualizations of processes of subjectivization and identification influence the manifestation of an array of essentialist and constructivist tropes in discourses related to sexualities and schooling. Scientific classifications and expert knowledges relating to gender and sexual identities and adolescence are the principal focus of Chapter 5. Here I detail some tropes commonly associated with LGBTI adolescence and highlight the dominance of discourses of woundedness. I also consider some of the effects that can ensue from this mode of objectification. Finally, I turn to some of the difficulties of theorizing alternative approaches to sexualities and schooling given the authority of scientific classifications.

The interrelationship between specific discourses and temporal, spatial, and discursive dividing practices is the focal point of my analysis in Chapter 6. I sketch some familiar and some lesser-known discourses that surface in studies of sexualities and secondary schooling. My analysis interrogates how these discourses manifest and attends to some of the implications of their emergence and repetition.

The process of reconfiguring the wound and unsettling passionate attachments to subjection is the principal object of study in Chapter 7. Utilizing the work of Butler, I analyze the persistence of discourses that appear to reinscribe subjection and consider how this relationship to woundedness might be transformed. Here I also turn to the subject of heterosexuality. I analyze some of the difficulties that may arise in attempts to disrupt normative heterosexual identities, and I study a public art project that relies on irony and the mimicry of advertising as a means to underscore some of the privileges associated with some heterosexual identities in Australia. In this brief turn to heterosexual identities, I also consider how public pedagogical practices might inform classroom-based pedagogies. Following from this, I consider the absence of pleasure in official discourses related to sexualities and schooling and posit the efficacy of pleasure as a conceptual device that might refuse wounded interpellations.

1

Queer Trepidations and the
Art of Inclusion

INTRODUCTION

In an interview on "An Aesthetics of Existence," Foucault (1996a)
traces a historical movement from morality conceived as "essentially a search for a personal ethics to a morality as obedience to
a system of rule" (p. 451). He goes on to argue that a morality
based on the former

> ... did not suggest what people ought to be, what they ought to
> do, what they ought to think and believe. It was rather a matter of
> showing how social mechanisms ... have been able to work, how
> forms of repression and constraint have acted, and then, starting
> from there ... one left to the people themselves, knowing all the
> above, the possibility of self-determination and the choice of their
> own existence. (p. 452).

In this passage, Foucault emphasizes individuals' responsibility
and agency in their own processes of self-determination, eschewing analysis or ethics of a didactic bent. The following analysis of
discourses related to sexualities and secondary schooling invokes
the notion of inclusivity as an art or aesthetics in order to analyze
the social mechanisms by which this art operates. Many arts of
inclusion are manifested in these discourses, and I identify these
various arts, tracing some of the constrictions and possibilities that
might ensue from their operation. An art of inclusion designed to

respond to some of these critiques is also put forward, yet my goal is not to perfect the art of inclusion. The *raison d'être* of this approach is that it fosters a reflection on how best to exercise this controversial art. I do not assume any universal agreement about what constitutes inclusion or exclusion.[1]

This concept of art is useful in this analysis of inclusivity. Art may be considered as somehow oppositional to science, thus providing a counternarrative to the scientificity and rationality that are often invoked in discourses related to sexualities and secondary schooling; others consider art as something beyond politics. Adrienne Rich (1986) points to some of the problems of situating art in an apolitical realm:

> There is the falsely mystical view of art that assumes a kind of supernatural inspiration, a possession by universal forces unrelated to questions of power and privilege or the artist's relation to bread and blood. In this view, the channel of art can only become clogged and misdirected by the artist's concern with merely temporary and local disturbances. The song is higher than the struggle. (184)

For Rich art is not created apart from life, and those who insist on the separation of life and art ignore the material, political, and embodied foundations from which art necessarily emerges. Similarly, I argue that inclusivity should not be perceived as "higher than the struggle." There is a tendency to valorize those who struggle (research or teach) in the name of inclusivity. Such a valorization is problematic, it is argued, if it acts as an impediment to a critical consideration of the exercise of the art of inclusivity. Instead, like art, inclusivity might be better understood as an ongoing practice that can never be conceived as outside the political realm or somehow beyond criticism by virtue of its good intentions.

In their analysis of sexualities and schooling in the United Kingdom, Epstein and Johnson (1998) draw attention to the utilization of discourses that construct "… lesbian and gay identities as very different from straight identities and from each other … " (p. 18). These strategies not only divide people who identify themselves as lesbian and gay from people who identify as heterosexual, but they also divide lesbian- and gay-identified people from those who engage in same-sex activities but identify as heterosexual, who identify as queer by choice, and who identify as intersex. The continuing absence of these latter groups in discussions of sexuality and gender in educational contexts is the source of ongoing tension.

Situating the exclusion and inclusion of diverse sexual and gender identities in a broader context, Rubin (1984) traces the historical development of a hierarchy determining the acceptability of a small range of sexual identities and practices and the demonization of other identities and practices. Rubin's "sex hierarchy" illustrates people's need to "draw and maintain an imaginary line between good sex and bad sex" (p. 282). The relations of power that Rubin identifies operate as a process of exclusion of those identities and practices that fall under the rubric of "bad" sex (queer, transgender, intersex, nonmonogamous, sado-masochistic — to name a few). This hierarchy influences the art of inclusion in educational contexts by continuously delimiting the bounds of what might be accommodated within, or constructed as outside, prevailing discourses of inclusion.

Pitted against this tendency to divide people according to acceptable and unacceptable sexual practices and identities are queer theories. As Jagose (1996) notes, these theories are sometimes critiqued because they are "seen as having the potential to work against lesbian and gay specificity and to devalue those analyzes of homophobia and heterocentrism developed largely by lesbian and gay critics" (pp. 112, 113). Proponents of queer theory tend not to be preoccupied with the appropriate nomenclature for people with diverse sexual and gender identities as much as the relations between certain identities and their construction by competing community and political interests. For Duggan (1992), the term *queer* focuses on the "very problematic construction of identities" (p. 18).

The deployment of a deconstructive strategy informed by queer theories enables people to trace "the interconnections of gendered and sexualized categories, stress the instability of these boundaries and seek to transgress boundaries on both gender and sexuality" (Epstein & Johnson, 1998, p. 198). This is not to say that a deconstructive analysis of such definitional knots, however necessary, is at all sufficient to disable them (Sedgwick, 1990, p. 10), though there is a chance this may at least advance a greater understanding of the operation of heteronormative practices within school environs.

The value of deconstructing the interrelationship between heterosexuality and homosexuality is outlined further in Eve

Kosofsky Sedgwick's (1990) *Epistemology of the Closet*. Here
Sedgwick draws on the work of Beaver (1981) to argue that

> The aim must be to reverse the rhetorical opposition of what is
> "transparent" or "natural" and what is "derivative" or "contrived"
> by demonstrating that the qualities predicated of "homosexuality"
> (as a dependent term) are in fact a condition of "heterosexuality";
> that "heterosexuality," far from possessing a privileged status, must
> itself be treated as a dependent term. (p. 10)

For Beaver (1981), the relationship between heterosexuality and
homosexuality constitutes the latter as a deficit. As such, striving
for inclusion through the recognition of "homosexual," "gay,"
or "lesbian" rights may potentially reinscribe this deficit position. Rather than striving for equal recognition for diverse sexual
identities, it might be preferable to continue to problematize the
privileges associated with heterosexual identities and to examine
further their relation to the subjection of homosexual identities.

So the art of inclusion is exercised in a cultural context in
which some artists question the value of identity categories
while others strive to preserve the specificity they attach to their
identity. It is not my desire to resolve this tension but, rather, to
consider how this tension is played out in the production of discourses related to sexualities and schooling.

Following is an analysis of some of the various arts of inclusion
that are interwoven into the production of key discourses related
to sexualities and secondary schooling. This analysis commences
with a consideration of the exercise of the art of inclusion alongside notions of "tolerance of difference" and "equity for all" in
educational discourses.

Art Objects

One art of inclusion found in contemporary research related to
sexualities and secondary schooling focuses on ways to eliminate homophobia and heterosexism. Within this paradigm the
notion of what constitutes sexual and gender identities is often
assumed to be known. One effect of this attitude toward identity
is that the complex social processes that influence subjectivities
and identities tend to become obfuscated.

Often researchers and educators prefer to tell compelling
stories of violence and abjection (Unks, 1995) in order to

garner support for LGBTI (Lesbian, Gay, Bisexual, Transgender, Intersex)-identified young people. Following is a demonstration of how these stories are sometimes complicit in the objectification of LGBTI-identified teachers and students.

In 1997, at age 14, Christopher Tsakalos became the first student in Australia to sue an education department for "failure to protect him against alleged homosexual vilification and violence" (Passey, 1997, p.38). The media's reporting on the Tsakalos case offers one example of the public objectification of young people through the storying of homophobia. Tsakalos took the New South Wales[2] (NSW) Department of School Education to the NSW Supreme Court. He alleged that the department had failed in its duty to provide him with a safe environment in which to attend school. The Tsakalos case was compared in the Australian press to that of Jamie Nabozny (Skotnicki, 1997) in the United States. Nabozny, a young gay man who was subjected to ongoing physical and verbal abuse at school, successfully sued three officials at two Wisconsin schools and was awarded more than a million (US) dollars in damages.

The *Sydney Morning Herald* (*SMH*), one of Australia's more respected broadsheet newspapers, reported Tsakalos's story under the banner heading "Schoolyard victims." Reporter David Passey (1997) wrote that while attending a public school in Sydney's western suburbs, Tsakalos

> ... claims to have been the subject of death threats, of gang-bashing by up to 20 students ... and of having scissors held to his throat as he was attacked for being gay. Most serious of all, perhaps, he claims that the teachers knowingly let the abuse go on. Tsakalos is known to be a difficult child. Even so, he has tried to commit suicide three times and says this was a plea for help.

> "I hated it and I didn't know what to do," Christopher said this week. "I'm gay, I know I'm gay and I can't see why that should make me a victim. Why should I be treated like s ... ? The school has to pay for what it has done. I want to help stop this happening to other gays. (p. 38)

These excerpts set the tone of the *SMH* article on the Tsakalos case. In a photo taken from the *Australian* (another broadsheet newspaper), similar to one accompanying the *SMH* article, Tsakalos is presented to readers as a forlorn and wounded young

Figure 1.1   Christopher Tsakalos with his mother. Copyright 1997, *Australian.*

man, a schoolyard victim, taking a stand to prevent the victimization of other gay students (see Figure 1.1). The image may reinforce his identity as victim. By photographing Tsakalos at his mother's side, relying on her for support, brows furrowed, eyes pleading for sympathy, he may be perceived as a classic representation of the suffering experienced by young people who identify as gay. He is situated as the object of the reader's pity.

However, this victim narrative only represents one version of the media coverage of the Tsakalos story. In the *Daily Telegraph*, a tabloid opposition to the *SMH* and the *Australian*, another narrativization of Tsakalos appears in words and images. The *Daily Telegraph* devoted its entire front page to the Tsakalos story, including a full-length image of Tsakalos and the prominent headline "Walk Like a Man." The photo of Tsakalos (see Figure 1.2) is extremely camp, highlighting the impossibility of him ever walking like a "real" man — he cannot even hold his sign straight. In another report in the *Daily Telegraph*, Miranda Devine (1997) suggests that in order to

> ... protect Christopher and children like him from being ostracized, you would have to make mincing homosexuality the norm in schools. The torment he has suffered has less to do with his homosexuality than the fact he is different from his peers. (p. 10)

Figure 1.2 Christopher Tsakalos protesting gay bashing in school.
Copyright 1997, *Daily Telegraph*.

Reporters from the *Daily Telegraph* also pursued the Tsakalos story in an article titled "Gay boy asked for it — students" (Trute & Angelo, 1997). Situated beside a photo and story about Jamie Nabozny, *Telegraph* reporters imply that Tsakalos's court case is suspect because, as students at the school suggested, "he brought it upon himself and they resented him taking legal action" (Trute & Angelo, 1997, p.3.). Whereas the *SMH* and *Australian* newspapers' reporting of the Tsakalos case evokes readers' sympathy, the reporters from the *Daily Telegraph* emphasize the young man's camp. There is an insinuation that Tsakalos's camp behavior may explain — even justify — the homophobia he experienced at the hands of fellow students and teachers.

Devine (1997) argued that anybody, such as Tsakalos, who is different is an easy target in the schoolyard and that preventing such harassment is an impossibility. Reporters also questioned the authenticity of Tsakalos's camp performance, suggesting it may have been skillfully managed by gay activists in an endeavor to gain financial reward and to make Tsakalos into "an international poster boy for the homosexual movement" (Devine, 1997, p.10.).

What is absent from such reporting is any attempt at a rich engagement with Tsakalos. Readers are not introduced to the complexities of Tsakalos's story. There is no discussion of what motivates his performance of the "sissy boy" (Jennings, 1998) role in a hostile school environment or of how his performance is read by others within the school community beyond the homophobic responses secured by a *Daily Telegraph* reporter's interviews with Tsakalos's peers.[3] Whether Tsakalos is depicted as hapless homosexual or questionable queer, the media reporting of the Tsakalos case highlights the ways in which young people may become objectified in discourses produced in relation to sexualities and secondary schooling. This process of objectification is no doubt heightened by the requirement for reporters to make a good story by inserting necessary doses of human interest, pathos, or demonization. The objectification of young people who choose LGBTI identities is not only to be found in newspaper reporting. It may also be found, in subtler forms, in teacher-education contexts.

Understanding Teaching: Curriculum and the Social Context of Schooling (Hatton, 1998) is a text designed to be used in student-teacher training courses in Australia and Aotearoa/New Zealand and is therefore a potentially quite significant resource in the construction of beginning teachers' knowledge about sexualities and schooling. I used an earlier edition of the same text when studying to become a secondary teacher in Australia in 1996. The revised version of the text still appears on reading lists in education faculties in Australia and Aotearoa/New Zealand. *Understanding Teaching* is designed to provide student-teachers with a "better chance of working for socially just outcomes through the provision of critiques that may ultimately improve teaching practice" (Hatton, 1998, p. xvi). When I began my student-teaching year, I was pleasantly surprised to find a text that actually had dedicated a chapter to the subject of sexuality.

The book also had chapters dealing with social class, gender, multiculturalism, Aboriginal and Maori educational policy, and rural education. In essence, it tried to cover all the bases of oppression in education — to paint us all in the picture.

In *Understanding Teaching* it is also possible to see how efforts to combat homophobia can slip into modes of objectification. In an analysis of the objectification of young people in the production of discourses of protection, Hatton, Maher, and Swinson (1998) write,

> So this chapter is necessarily written for all readers rather than just those who are LGBT [lesbian, gay, bisexual and transgender]. After all, teachers are not simply going to have to create a safe, productive learning environment for heterosexual students, they will need to look after the safety and learning of queer students too. (p. 299)

All students and teachers are included in the right to a safe and productive learning environment, regardless of their sexual orientation. Although the focus is ostensibly the creation of a safe environment for all, the comments of LGBT-identified young people given a voice in Hatton et al.'s (1998) discussion gesture toward a different narrative. They highlight their alienation in educational contexts, talking about their experiences of physical and verbal abuse and suicide attempts, leaving readers with an overwhelming sense of their isolation related to homophobia. One woman writes,

> Before I came out, I was respected by my teachers. But soon after I came out, some of my teachers started to give me dirty looks ... I actually had a teacher, as I walked by his desk whisper under his breath "God forgive her," as if I were sinning just being alive. (Hatton et al., 1998, p. 302).

There is an underlying implication in the presentation of these stories that once readers are exposed to the woes experienced by LGBT-identified young people, they may be inspired to enter into schools and triumph over homophobia and heterosexism.

Discourses that produce narratives encouraging practitioners in the belief that they might somehow "boost the academic performance of subordinated minority youth, black [and queer] students and even help them to pull even with their white [heterosexual] counterparts" (McCarthy, 1990, p. 33) have been problematized. For McCarthy (1990), the liberatory potential of these discourses is often questionable because such frameworks fail to take into account "structural inequalities and differential power relations" (p. 56) within schools, leaving teachers and students with the untenable task of restoring equality within a fundamentally unequal framework.

Assuming that people have the desire or the capacity to construct learning environments safe for all students ignores teachers' and students' investments in sustaining heteronormalizing processes[4] within educational contexts. When the art of inclusion is exercised through the construction of LGBT teachers and young people as objects of pathos or empowerment, it deflects analysis away from the broader social mechanisms invested in these same people's continued objectification. Exhorting these people to reach their potential may also fail to color in those most invested in the ongoing production of heteronormalizing processes and in the subjection of LGBTI-identified teachers and students.

In preference to strategies of inclusion that focus on the objectification of LGBTI people's suffering, Bibby (1998) suggests an approach that enables "students of all orientations to delight in their variety" (p. 26). He writes,

> Homophobia is an unsatisfactory focus for education about sexual orientation, just as anti-racist education cannot be content with violence as its main focus ... Gay, lesbian, bisexual and transgender (GLBT) students should not be seen as victims of a cruel fate. Instead, students of all orientations should learn to delight in the variety of humans. (pp. 25, 26)

Bibby rejects strategies of inclusion that confirm young people who identify as GLBT as victims of homophobia. However, his suggested approach also reinforces the differences between groups rather than seeking a greater understanding of how differences are sustained and operate to privilege particular identities. I want to resist the temptation to construct LGBTI-identified teachers and students as fundamentally different from their heterosexual counterparts or as people who are uniformly abject and in need of protection. Instead, I advocate strategies that support teachers and students in examining the mechanisms that simultaneously sustain and compel marginalization. I now turn to an examination of arts of inclusion associated with "the closet" and "coming out."

Closet Art

Closeted — The experience of living without disclosing one's sexual orientation or gender identity (also referred to as being "in the closet").

Coming Out — Becoming aware one's sexual orientation or gender identity and beginning to disclose it to others. A person may be selectively "out" in some situations or to certain people without generally disclosing his or her sexual orientation or gender identity. "Coming out" is a process that takes place over time, in some cases over many years. (Bochenek and Brown, 2001, p. xiii)

In these definitions, there is a sense that "the closet" and "coming out" are easily understood. People may be closeted if they live without disclosing their sexual orientation or transgender identity. Alternatively, people who declare their sexual orientation or gender identity publicly may be construed as having come out. Such neat definitions inevitably elide the complexities of dealing with these issues in discourses related to sexualities and secondary schooling. Regardless of their sexual or gender identities, teachers and students may have different investments in the in–out binary. Putting aside the issue of different people's motivations in deploying discourses of coming out and the closet, it is important to recognize that these discourses are absolutely fundamental to contemporary understanding of sexualities and secondary schooling, and therefore they warrant closer scrutiny.

This section examines some of the complexities attached to discourses of coming out and the closet — complexities that are inevitably mediated by the particular bodies engaging in these discourses and the spaces they occupy. My principal argument is that rather than urging students and teachers to come out, they may be better served by further consideration of the diverse moral, political, and pedagogical issues that influence the production of discourses of coming out.

Some of these issues are highlighted in a study of gay-identified British university students conducted by Telford (2003a, 2003b). He highlights the difficulties young people may encounter in endeavoring to come out. Drawing on interviews he conducted, Telford highlights the ways in which sexual identity can become compartmentalized in young people's lives due to pressures family and peer groups placed on them (Telford, 2003b). Pressures not to come out might be allied to a young person's racial or ethnic background, family's religious affiliations, or family threats, real or implied, regarding the withdrawal of financial support. As Telford (2003b) notes, "fears about being cut off financially seemed to be an important factor for the young person when deciding to come out" (p. 137). If family members fund a young person's education, then coming out might compromise his or her access to schooling. Such pragmatic considerations are just one factor that may complicate young people's negotiations of the in–out binary.

In an article critiquing the Toronto Board of Education's Triangle Program (an alternative education program specifically targeting lesbian- and gay-identified high school students), Snider (1996) points to the Toronto lesbian and gay communities' failure to account for issues of race in coming-out discourses. She disputes the notion of coming out as a liberatory process for all lesbians and gays and poses the following questions in relation to celebratory discourses on coming out:

> How can the disruptive potential of coming out be actualized for lesbian and gay youth confronting not just homophobia but racism as well? Is the dominant discourse subsuming the speech of lesbians and gays? Moreover, does the dominant discourse within lesbian and gay politics subsume the speech of lesbians and gays of color? Finally, in what ways has the coming out discourse altered underlying systems of domination, and in what ways are these systems being reproduced within this discourse? (p. 300)

The questions posed by Snider offer an important challenge to the construction of heroic tales of coming out while also drawing attention to some of the potentially negative effects of coming-out discourses (e.g., the silencing and shaming of people for whom coming out is not a realistic or preferred option). In her discussion of the process of coming out in Asian communities in the United States, Varney (2001) also critiques celebratory narratives that permeate mainstream "queer youth groups where people are urged to be proud, and out to everyone" (p. 94).

In "Black in the Closet," Akanke (1994) discusses her decision not to come out to peers when she was a university student and to remain closeted in her interactions with school authorities as a lesbian parent in the United Kingdom. Akanke, who identifies herself as a black Jamaican woman, states,

Being "closeted" is not a choice I wish to make. Nevertheless, because of the pervasiveness of racism, it is one that I *choose* to make. Being Black, however, is not a choice. As a black woman my colour is my most obvious feature, not my sexual preferences. (p. 102, italics in original)

Although Akanke expresses a preference for a life lived out of the closet, she goes on to argue that outing herself would be foolhardy, as it may compromise her relations with her black community. She notes further that the support of that community "far outweighs any desire to 'openly' assert my sexuality" (p. 113). Akanke feels that there is no escaping discrimination based on her color, but discrimination based on the grounds of her sexual identity is something she feels she has more agency in trying to control.

In "The Great Down-Low Debate," an article published in the *Village Voice*[5] (Wright, 2001), it is possible to see other constraints that may be associated with coming-out discourses. Below I outline Wright's commentary on men who identity as "down-low" (DL) and then consider how this might inform pedagogical strategies related to sexuality education. Wright (2001) sketches the DL identity through an interview with Tevin, a young man who identifies as DL:

Tevin is a lady's dream. But he's also the Don Juan fantasy of a certain group of men: guys who live "on the down low," or DL ...

"I like girls. I have a girl, ... But every once in a while, cause women can be very stressful, I might chill with a dude."

Tevin won't have anything to do with gay culture, doesn't know anything about it and couldn't care less. By and large, his thoughts on the subject are in lockstep with most of black America's: It's all good if it's your thing, but I ain't no punk ... Nor is Tevin willing to accept a sexual orientation. "I consider myself just sexual," he professes. "A freak!" ... "I think if you're a dude, you should act like a dude, look like a dude, talk like a dude. If you're a chick, you should act like a chick," Tevin explains. "When you start mixing 'em up, that makes me nervous. I wouldn't disrespect people who act like that, but it just turns me off."

It is apparent that Tevin constructs his sexual activities as distinct from those found in gay culture. This construction points to some of the inadequacies of terms such as the closet and coming out. These terms, and their corresponding assumptions about becoming aware of and then disclosing one's sexual orientation, have little meaning for people like Tevin who reject gay identities. Similarly, Wright (2001) notes that some "flamboyantly feminine black men" have "rejected the gay label because of its perceived weakness"[6] and association with whiteness.

Expectedly, people within the African-American community have conflicting views on young men like Tevin and on the value of convincing these men to come out of the closet and to accept a gay identity. Wright (2001) notes that "… unambiguously gay African Americans have responded to the DL and homo-thug trends by declaring these guys nothing more than repackaged closet cases." Others resist efforts to reach these men by deploying the terminology of coming out, opposing

> … "gayified" blacks trying to shove a white concept down the community's throat. "One of the assumptions gay makes is that if you don't call yourself gay then you're in the closet," snaps Cleo Manago, an Oakland area AIDS activist who is a leader in the "Same Gender Loving" movement on the West Coast … . That movement aims to discard pink triangles and rainbow flags — symbols created by and for Europeans — and build a new identity around words and concepts created by and for black people. Among the first to go, Manago says, is the in and out of the closet dichotomy that serves only to emphasize separation from the larger community. "Instead of demanding that people respect you because of how you fuck, do something within the community," Manago rails.

> … Gay activists respond that Manago is peddling a cultural relativism that should stop at the closet door … . Franklin (Gay Men of African Descent) notes that he and others like him live and socialize as open gays in the black community. "It doesn't mean that we have to go out carrying rainbow flags," adds activist Keith Boykin. "But we do have to acknowledge sexual orientation." (Wright 2001)

There is no consensus within African-American communities about the value of coming out and identifying as gay. As just stated, opposition to gay identity may be embedded in broader discourses that link gayness to whiteness and effeminacy. Some African-American men choose to situate themselves outside this equation by identifying as hypermasculine, regardless of their sexual practices. Alternatively, those who embrace gay identities may challenge the association of gayness with Western gay symbols; others may denigrate men who identify as DL as repackaged closet cases.

Wright's reporting of the DL debate is indicative of some of the tensions that underlie people's relationship to the closet and coming out — tensions mediated by race, geographic location, age, ethnicity, and gender. It is evident that people resist coming out for a range of reasons. Implying that those who do not come out are somehow dishonest perpetuates the in–out dichotomy. This approach to coming out also perpetuates a teleological narrativization of gay and lesbian life in which people are constructed as having literally no agency in the adoption of their sexual identity. I am arguing for a more nuanced pedagogical approach to diverse sexual identities, one that makes space for those who choose to identify as gay, those who feel they have no choice, and those who eschew such categorizations altogether.

I am also advocating a rethinking of programs such as National Coming Out Day, which has become an annual event in the United States. Organized by the Human Rights Campaign[7], it runs in hundreds of U.S. schools and colleges each year. The booklet produced to promote National Coming Out Day tells readers that when they come out they will "discover that being true to yourself feels better — more natural — than denying your true self ever did" (HRCF, 2004, p. 4). Readers are also called upon to be "honest and open" (p. 4) about their sexual orientation. Underlying this request that people be "honest and open" is the claim that "Your Sexuality or Gender Identity Is Not a Choice. It Chooses You" (p. 11). When the largest, most influential, and well-resourced lesbian and gay organization in the United States argues that homosexuality is not a choice, people are presented with two choices: come out, or remain in the closet.

The familiarity of this perspective on identity is demonstrated in the movie *In & Out* (Oz, 1997). Kevin Kline plays the role of a clueless gay schoolteacher who is outed by an ex-student before he realizes he really is gay. At no point does the film endeavor to question the in–out binary; rather, the drama rests on the audience's collusion in the notion that one is either "in" or "out." Similarly, the National Coming Out Day booklet relies on students' and teachers' acceptance of the notion that one is "in" or "out" and that there is no in-between (HRCF, 2004).

Akin to the Human Rights Campaign's position on coming out is Babbit's (1999) *But I'm a Cheerleader*, a happy coming-out movie in which true community enables identity (Talburt, 2004, p. 21). In her analysis of this movie, Talburt critiques the tendency of such films to story queer youth in specific ways in which they become intelligible, to themselves and to others, only through the adoption of a particular narrativization of gay identity (pp. 19, 21). This narrativization is similar to that depicted in the Human Rights Campaign's literature on coming out in which one does not choose to become a homosexual but, rather, like the cheerleader or schoolteacher created in Hollywood, homosexuals are chosen.

Although the in–out dichotomy represents a familiar and powerful narrativization of sexual and gender identity, this story is sometimes contested and rejected. Some have rejected this binary because they associate it with whiteness or effeminacy. Others prefer to highlight the complexities associated with the ongoing negotiation of sexual and gender identities. For instance, Evans (1999) emphasizes the difficult terrain that students and teachers navigate in determining how to manage their various identities and their potential coming out within and around school settings. She notes the "interactive nature of identity negotiation" and argues that the construction of divisions between public and private spheres must be "constantly renegotiated" (p. 240). Teachers' and students' ability to renegotiate their identity is necessarily mediated by the varying circulations of power in the community, the classroom, the playground, and the staffroom. In short, not all teachers or students desire to come out of the classroom closet, and, even if they want to, this is not always a realistic option in secondary educational settings.

This section briefly analyzed discourses associated with the closet and coming out as they apply to educational and broader cultural contexts. I have argued that these discourses have become central to some influential applications of the art of inclusion through programs such as National Coming Out Day. I have also problematized this particular art of inclusion because of its tendency to constrain sexual and gender identities that do not conform to this aesthetic and because the imperative to come out fails to adequately consider the exclusions it produces.

Sacred Iconography

Another art form that regularly appears in the production of discourses related to sexualities and secondary schooling is the personal narrative, focusing on the lived experiences of lesbian- and gay-identified teachers and students (Garber, 1994; Jennings, 1994; Kissen, 1996). These narratives provide a pantheon of teachers and students who appear to have mastered the art of inclusion. It should be noted at the outset that transgender, bisexual, queer, and intersex teachers and students rarely enter this discursive terrain. These narratives have emerged from a perceived need for "a forum in which teachers can share their pedagogies and strategies for professional survival and success" (Garber, 1994, p. ix) and "so ... other lesbian and gay teachers ... would know that they were not alone, that they could fight back and win" (Jennings, 1994, p. 12). There is a sense that these texts have the potential to guide and inspire others through the recollections of those who have excelled and for these stories to thereby "challenge homophobic stereotypes and improve the lives of gay and lesbian educators" (Kissen, 1996, book cover) and students. Following is an analysis of these narrativizations of LGBTI "superteachers" (Blinick, 1994, p. 142) and "superstudents" and a consideration of some of the ways they both constrain and contribute to the art of inclusivity.

It is worth noting that these stories do serve as an important counternarrative to those stories produced by conservative religious organizations that seek to present homosexuality as a pathological disorder. The following excerpt, from an article by Lerner (2001) in the *Village Voice*, details this frequent disordering of homosexuality at a conservative conference she attended on homosexuality in youth:

> Workshops focused on identifying threats to straightness first in the home and family and then in the schools, where "a one-sided agenda [is] being seductively pushed on innocent minds," according to conference materials.

> The key, according to Joseph Nicolosi, a psychologist with the National Association of Research and Therapy on Homosexuality, is to "attack early." His idea, which serves as the starting point for Focus on the Family's [2005][8] multitiered campaign, is that an errant sexuality is more easily stopped early than reversed later.

Accordingly, he offered the parents, teachers, and school counselors in the audience a list of the warning signs of "pre-homosexuality," which, for boys, included having a sensitive temperament, being aesthetically inclined, and responding strongly to either well- or badly dressed women. Janelle Hallman, a daintily attired therapist, gave a parallel accounting of tomboy red flags, which included wearing army boots.

The passage above makes clear connections between homosexuality and gender transgression and the need to protect "innocent minds" from "errant sexuality." It is important that Focus on the Family[9] and similar organizations[10] are not the only voices being represented in the production of discourses related to sexualities and schooling. Differing narratives of LGBTI-identified teachers and students will clearly have different foundations and strategic aims. Next I consider the art of inclusivity I call *sacred iconography*, a discourse peopled by exemplary characters — hard-working, competent professionals who have come out in their school communities.

One of the first superteacher narratives to appear in the United States was produced by Rofes (1985). On the cover of his autobiographical text, *Socrates, Plato, and Guys Like Me*, readers learn that "Rofes is not your typical schoolteacher." The text's title aligns Rofes with other icons in education: exceptional figures in Western thought who have inspired others to think and behave differently. In a later publication, Rofes (1999) argues that schools are enhanced when students share the experience of being taught by an openly gay teacher, quoting one of his own students in order to illustrate this point. "Having an openly gay teacher taught me to be receptive to diversity and about the complexity of human beings …. I think it would benefit all children and society if they had openly gay teachers" (p. 92).

In these texts, Rofes (1985, 1999) implies that teachers who openly identify as gay will help promote inclusivity. There is an underlying assumption that people who have the courage to come out will exercise the art of inclusion simply by virtue of publicly declaring their sexual identity. But it is worth asking whether being out in school necessarily equates to a promotion of inclusivity. Surely, people who are openly LGBTI identified can be as homophobic, racist, and sexist as the next person; in that way, at least, "gay teachers are [surely] no different from heterosexual teachers" (Rofes, 1999, p. 91).

Rofes is not alone in the pantheon of LGBTI superteachers. Blinick (1994) also reflects on the superteacher phenomenon. "Recently while discussing my personal strategy for being out in my classroom, a fellow gay teacher remarked, 'You're being a superteacher — having to be extra good, extra dedicated to prove how wonderful lesbian teachers are.' I was a bit taken aback, until I thought about it. He was right" (p. 142). Blinick recognizes her cultivation of the role of superteacher and suggests that her desire to be one is motivated in part by a need to compensate for a perceived lack, a vulnerability that might be located in being situated as less than normal within the school environ. At the time of writing, the superteacher phenomenon has not, to my knowledge, been critically analyzed, but the "superstudent" has been previously identified (see Sears, 1995).

In their handbook designed for lesbian-, gay-, and bisexual-identified young people, Bass and Kaufmann (1996) include the following brief entry about superstudents: "Some gay students feel they need to do perfectly in school as a defense to conceal what they believe is their deeper 'flaw' of being gay. The pressure of this can be overwhelming (p. 209). Bass and Kaufmann link superstudent behavior to feelings of inadequacy resulting from the devaluing of LGBTI identities in the broader culture, whereas Sears (1995) perceives superlative performance as a veil used to conceal gay identity. Jacob, a black high school student who is gay identified in the South in the United States

> ... completed the ninth grade having achieved his goal of making the academic top 10 and graduating as class valedictorian...by virtue of Jacob's school related activities and achievements, Jacob's effeminate mannerisms and lack of interest in girls were rarely questioned by friends or family. "It was like, 'He don't have time for girls. He's smart. He's doing his books.'" (pp. 139,140)

The superteachers and students peopling these narratives just outlined gesture toward the persistence of people's desire to prove themselves equal to, if not better than, heterosexual-identified counterparts in educational settings. In addition, superteacher and superstudent performances may act as a cloak of protection against the potential of exclusion or as a veil to hide a perceived lack associated with LGBTI identity.[11]

Regardless of the motivation for the production of these narratives, their repetition may have adverse consequences. If

LGBTI-identified teachers and students are given role models who are, as a rule, exemplary overachievers leading respectable lives, what happens to lesbian and gay teachers and students who are not respectable, exemplary, or "out" at school? Are such tales of superteachers and superstudents empowering, or, like superheroes in popular culture, do these tales set up fantasies that many people can admire but never really hope to emulate? It is possible that, whatever their motivation, such narratives may impact adversely on other LGBTI-identified students and teachers by establishing unrealistic expectations. These narratives may thus set limits to the efficacy of this particular art of inclusion.

In contrast to these stories, Epstein's (1994) anthology *Challenging Lesbian and Gay Inequalities in Education* comprises a diverse range of narratives including "a story about a teacher arrested for indecency" (Bartell, 1994, p. 78) that details the musings of a man who has lost all semblance of respectability. Epstein's inclusion of this story gives voice to some of the people on the margins of LGBTI cultures. Such stories are a salient reminder that LGBTI cultures are full of "complexities and contradictions" (Epstein, 1994, p. 6) and are not only inhabited by superteachers and superstudents.

Potentially, superteachers and superstudents may be conceived as part of a broader project to mainstream people who identify as LGBTI. This drive toward respectability operates in the broader society and also from within lesbian and gay cultures (Vaid, 1995, p. 203). Vaid (1995) argues that this drive "reflects an increase in opportunities only for members of gay and lesbian communities that already most resemble the mainstream"(pp. 202–203). This underscores the value of continuing the process of self-consciously deconstructing these narratives of superteachers and superstudents.

Stories peopled by diverse students and teachers provide readers with some knowledge of the complex relations of power that accompany students' and teachers' performances of their sexual and gender identities. As indicated at the beginning of this chapter, the art of inclusion provides people with an understanding of how "forms of repression and constraint have acted" (Foucault, 1996a, p. 452). Although well intentioned, celebratory stories of superteachers and superstudents may run somewhat counter to this impulse by providing people with lesbian and gay icons — models for what they might achieve. It may be beneficial to resist the temptation to establish a pantheon of exalted LGBTI teachers and students, encouraging individuals to exercise an art of inclusion that best suits their style of existence.

The Art of Being Gay

> I would say that one must use sexuality
> to discover or invent new relations.
> To be gay is to be in a state of becoming ...
> it is not necessary to be homosexual
> but it is necessary to be set on being gay.
>
> (Foucault, 1996e, p. 370)

From where people depart is particularly salient in determining future directions (Probyn, 1996). When sexuality is seen as culturally produced, a product of human conception, or agency rather than an inherent element or something essential, the art of inclusion may be exercised differently. The following discussion of the art of being gay commences with an analysis of how queer theory can be drawn upon to develop an art of inclusion emphasizing the continual invention and negotiation of identity categories, working against the impulse to divide individuals in accordance with the heterosexual–homosexual binary.

This emphasis on the invention and negotiation of identity is integrally related to the sorts of subjects activists, educators, and researchers might try to create. Fine and Bertram (1999) argue for

> ... work that simply and outrageously changes the subject, that credits not at all the perversions of dominant ideologies, that moves instead into the joys, struggles, plastic subjectivities, the camp of queer lives with a refusal to educate in conversation with homophobic "common sense"? (p. 157)

Inspired by Fine and Bertram (1999), this art of inclusion interrogates the "common sense" foundations of the production of discourses related to sexualities and schooling. Refusing to go along with the tendency to stabilize the subject, I focus on the process of continuously becoming subjects, a process that may involve not only struggle but also creativity in the reinscription of subjectivities and identities.

Crowley (1999) interrogates processes of subjectivization played out in educational contexts in her analysis of "letters she wrote but never intended to send, letters that are drawn from real life scenarios" (p. 213), in which subjectivities are constrained and identity categories performed. Crowley's letters suggest the

> ... impossibility of an embodied politics that is somehow, not always-already more complexly and contradictorily configured than is named and positioned through a single category such as lesbian, gay, bisexual, transgender or heterosexual. The polite terms of sexualities cannot suggest the difficult fissures that fracture the lives of queer identities and subjectivities. (p. 221)

The subjectivities and identities people create in high school settings are configured within the bounds of highly constrained discourses in which single categories such as straight, lesbian, or gay might conceivably be the only options proffered to young people considering how to best identify themselves and their feelings. However, it is possible to argue for an art of inclusion that might engage this "embodied politics" and assist in the navigation of "the difficult fissures" found in the coupling of sexualities and secondary schooling.

As part of his project to queer elementary education, Sears (1999) endeavors to shift the focus of inclusion away from further discussion of subjectivities and identities, turning to the task of deconstructing the "sexual and gender binaries ... that are the linchpins of heteronormativity"(p. 6). Although Sears is dedicated to deconstructing heteronormative practices, he dismisses the question of "what causes homosexuality," preferring to focus on the "factors that contribute to the homophobia and heterosexism that make coping with one's sexual orientation so difficult" (p. 7). But what is the value of distinguishing between these two tasks so neatly? Is it possible to mindfully engage with the process of "being gay" without giving due consideration to "what causes homosexuality"? This is not to imply that people should seek conclusive scientific evidence of the etiology of homosexuality. I do not advocate this approach, and I doubt this is Sears's objective. However, Sears's proposition that "sexual identity is constructed from cultural materials; [and] sexual orientation is conditioned on biological factors" (p. 7) may be problematic in terms of the exercise of the art of inclusion I posit here. Such an analysis reinstates a division between identity and orientation, leaving readers with a sense of unified lesbian, gay, and queer subjects who inhabit educational settings alongside their heterosexual counterparts.

Although Sears focuses on the destabilization of identity categories, the extent to which queer theorists might seek to disturb people's identities is a pivotal tension. Stein and Plummer (1996), offering a North American perspective on queer projects, seek "a rejection of civil rights strategies" in favor of a "problematization of sexual and gender categories, and of identities in general" (p. 134). Epstein's (1987) analysis of the limitations of constructionism and essentialism (p. 48) provides an apt reminder that neither queer theories nor liberal equity discourses are beyond reproach. Arts of inclusion have constraints and limitations regardless of the theoretical ground in which they are embedded.

Queer theories are also utilized by Quinlivan and Town (1999) in order to critique rights-based strategies in the area of schooling and sexualities. They argue these strategies tend to construct "queer youth as a disenfranchised minority" (p. 509) in Aotearoa/New Zealand by situating them within stable identity categories. For Quinlivan and Town, such an approach to the art of inclusion may have the negative effect of increasing young people's feelings of alienation (p. 512). They advocate a movement toward an understanding of schools as heteronormalizing institutions. Although I concur that equity frameworks may be problematic, there still needs to be an ongoing recognition that "human rights regarding sexuality are important and still not respected in many places" (Foucault, 1996g, p. 383). Therefore, it is argued, rights-based discourses are still fundamental elements of this art of inclusion.

ARTFUL OVERTURES

The preceding discussion has acted as an overture for this book. I have sought to problematize and disturb familiar notions of identity that underpin much research and pedagogy designed to be inclusive of teachers and students who identify as lesbian and gay, and, less often, those who identify as bisexual, transgender, and intersex. I will argue that the continuing trend to construct LGBTI students and teachers as unified subjects is often accompanied by an omission of any consideration of the social, spatial, political, and cultural practices that underlie the construction of these sexual and gender identities.

Arts of inclusion are enhanced when they give due consideration not only to how sexual and gender identities are practiced and perpetuated in school settings but also to why people who identify as transgender, intersex, queer, and questioning are often absent in the production of discourses in this area. Interrogating how sexual and gender identities are deployed in school settings also opens up a consideration of how people researching, teaching, and working in this area perceive the "role of, and meaning attached to LGBT communities and identifications" (Dowsett, Bollen, McInnes, Couch, & Edwards, 2001). To this end, this study draws on the work of Dowsett et al. (2001) insofar as it focuses on the

> ... pedagogy of ... community-based gay educators and their educational practices, their self- and programme-evaluation techniques ... or the distinctive vision of "gayness" they bring from their own experiences as gay men living in gay communities and, for many, working in gay communities based organizations. (p. 208)

Participants interviewed in the course of this study identified as gay, lesbian, heterosexual, bisexual, transgender, and queer, and all had distinctive versions of how people become sexual and gendered subjects. This study traces these differing versions and considers how they are threaded through the production of discourses related to sexualities and secondary schooling. It is argued that research in this area has not focused adequately on how people's versions of processes of becoming subjects fundamentally impacts on the construction of programs designed to support LGBTI-identified teachers and students in school settings.

Related to the question of how individuals understand the process of becoming subjects is a consideration of how some identities gain currency in educational discourses whereas others continue to be suppressed. How do certain identities come to be considered authentic, and what constitutes this authenticity? What is elided when these notions of authenticity are produced within and outside LGBTI communities? These questions, influenced by the work of Britzman (1993), point to a further consideration of how "knowledge [is] racialized, sexualized, and made synonymous with the social markers of identity?... Which subject positions emerge from which knowledge" (p. 127)? And if subjectivities and identities are not representative of something "real" but are produced from the continuous interplay of power, "truth games" (Foucault & Martin, 1988, p. 15), and the production of expert knowledge, what are the implications for educational research and pedagogy?

As indicated in the introduction to this study, research in this area has tended to trace the victimization of LGBTI-identified teachers and students. As such, there has been a focus on telling people how LGBTI-identified teachers and students are suffering and on how people might strive to be more inclusive of them. There is a tacit assumption in these discourses that virtually any overtures on behalf of LGBTI teachers and students should be applauded simply by virtue of their rarity and degree of difficulty. Researchers and practitioners in the field of sexualities and secondary schooling are vulnerable to harsh criticism by virtue of their involvement in this controversial art (Bryson, 2002). Such controversy may deter the integral role of art criticism because of concerns that such criticism may be used to prevent further research or pedagogy. Such fears may hamper the art of inclusion. Alternatively, critical considerations of the art of inclusion might be viewed as indispensable contributions to the production of discourses related to sexualities and schooling.

Another aspect of these discourses that I explore concerns the linkages between sex and pleasure in educational contexts. Once again I draw on queer theories as a helpful, though not unproblematic, aid in analyzing the continued focus on the subjection of LGBTI-identified teachers and students. I further consider the potential of affirming the body and pleasure in research on sexualities and secondary schooling. As I will show, the disavowal of sex and absenting of the body within many educational discourses is antithetical to the art of inclusion because of its tendency to exclude diverse bodies, pleasures, and desires from discussions of sexualities and schooling.

This overture has begun a problematization of some familiar arts of inclusion associated with people who identify as LGBTI in high school settings. It also provides an introduction to the extended work of this book, which uses the work of queer, feminist, and poststructuralist theories in order to further consider mainstream, alternative, and imagined arts of inclusion. I resist the temptation to paint us all in the picture. Rather, I am interested in the people who paint the pictures, the types of pictures they paint, the galleries in which their pictures are hung, and the censorship and valorization of particular artists and visions.

2

Queering Epistemologies and Methodologies

... All this emphasis on ourselves simply puts me off.

(Patai, 1994, p. 65)

A postmodern anthropologist and his informant are talking; finally the informant says, "Okay, enough about you, now let's talk about me."

(Newton, 1996, p. 212)

This interrogation of sexualities and secondary schooling moves beyond a desire to paint us all in the picture toward an analysis of the exercise of the art of inclusion. Drawing on queer, feminist, and poststructuralist theories, in this chapter I analyze the implications of these modes of theoretical analysis for reading and writing practices and for the development of epistemological and methodological approaches to this study of sexualities in secondary educational contexts. I introduce each section in this chapter with a brief departure into biomythography.[1] The two epigraphs at the beginning of this chapter "suggest a certain absurdity in the so-called reflexivity discourse" (Newton, 1996, p. 212). I have chosen to revel in this absurdity by using biomythographical vignettes as jumping-off points to my analysis of epistemology, methodology, and method.

These vignettes are designed to underscore aspects of my analysis, for together they point to the fluidity of sexual and gender identities and highlight some of the ramifications of engaging in identity-based politics. Lamphere (1994) argues that the inclusion of personal biographies in research projects enables a discussion of "our own positionality as researchers in our conceptions of research and address(es) the impact of race, class, gender, and sexual orientation on the institutions we analyze and the subjects of our research" (p. 223). Although this biomythography gestures toward a consideration of my positionality, it is simultaneously intent on revealing positionality as chimera. It is motivated by a queer theorist's determination to destabilize unified understandings of identity. This biomythography is also designed to reflect upon "the interplay between individual agency and social dynamics" (Kehily, 1995, p. 30) in the shaping of my own and others' sexual and gender identities. There is a plethora of ways of narrativizing identities related to sexualities and genders, and these identities are in turn mediated by shifting educational and other contexts.

The ensuing section constitutes a queering of the epistemological foundations of this book and a consideration of the efficacy of this approach in research related to sexualities and secondary schooling. This is followed by a study of some existing approaches to research methodologies and methods in the area of genders and sexualities and an elaboration on the process of queerly fashions of fieldwork.

QUEERING EPISTEMOLOGY

I was only a Lesbian Avenger for a while, which made sense, really. You can only wear a cape for so long before the novelty fades. In the first place, the Avengers attracted me because they are fierce, loud, and political. The group organizes itself similarly to Queer Nation and the AIDS Coalition to Unleash Power (ACT UP) — organizations whose direct action politics and imaginative street theater had already made them familiar in Australia. On a more immediate level, the Avengers were attractive because they appeared to be a fairly sexy crowd who felt that throwing wild parties (see Figure 2.1) was an important political organizing strategy.

The Avengers' motto, "We Recruit," was printed on the back of their T-shirts. On the front was an anarchist bomb encircled by

Figure 2.1 Party invitation (From *Lesbian Avengers' Handbook*, 2nd ed., 1993). With permission of Carrie Moyer.

the words "Lesbian Avengers" (see Figure 2.2). Initially based in New York City, the Avengers are a nonviolent, direct-action group focused on issues vital to lesbian survival and visibility. Although mission statements are fairly consistent across chapters of the Avengers, there are differences between chapters regarding who qualifies for lesbian "superhero" status. For instance, the Chicago Avengers were open to all lesbian- and bisexual-identified women, whereas the Washington, D.C., Avengers welcomed lesbians, bisexual women, and transgender people.

For some Avengers, the group's explicit focus on issues relevant to lesbians attracted them to the organization; to them it was a refreshing change from a queer politics that often perpetuates lesbian invisibility. For others in the group, the name was catchy but not representative of an essentialist politic within the organization; many Avengers' actions involve working with broad queer coalitions (Schulman, 1993). When I joined, these political nuances were not foremost in my mind — I just wanted to be a Lesbian Avenger.

Figure 2.2   Lesbian Avengers' logo. (From *Lesbian Avengers' Handbook*, 2nd ed., 1993). With permission of Carrie Moyer.

This vignette gestures toward some of the complexities of representation attached to the use of lesbian identities in political organizing. How does political organizing, linked to sexual and gender identities, adjust to the continuous contestation of these identities? Is it possible to define any issue as a lesbian issue? Does an issue qualify as a lesbian issue if it supports fag visibility as well? If the Lesbian Avengers were to organize a protest related to homophobic hate crime, can they only talk about hate crimes perpetrated against dykes? What about Brandon Teena?[2] What was an appropriate Avengers response to this senseless murder? It is not clear whether Brandon identified as a lesbian, but part of the reason he was killed was because he was read as a biological woman who loved women. It is difficult to predict the fate of identity-based movements in the midst of the queer turn, yet there is a growing recognition of how people's identities are mediated by the spaces and places in which they are contextualized and described and by the bodies they inhabit.

As indicated in the introduction, the epistemological framework of this study draws on queer, feminist, and poststructuralist theories to interrogate sexual and gender identities. Queer theories have existed under several guises[3] but were not named as such until the early 1990s (Duggan, 1992). They have emerged, largely in the United States, out of dissatisfaction with feminist and socialist theorizing about gender and the attendant undertheorizing of sexualities. Queer theorists have addressed these concerns by making sexualities the central focus of their analysis, though it is recognized that the study of genders is indivisible from the study of sexualities.

Queer theories are a useful device for analyzing sexualities and genders, and they work in concert with feminist theories. Gayle Rubin, in an interview with Judith Butler (Rubin & Butler, 1998), argues that in her foundational essay "Thinking Sex" (Rubin, 1984)[4] she was trying to envision "better scholarship on sexuality, and a richer set of ideas about it than were readily available. She was striving to articulate a sexual politics that did not assume that feminism was the last word and holy writ on the subject" (p. 62). In short, Rubin (1998) argues feminist theorizing about gender should not be seen as the privileged site for work on sexuality (p. 45). She neither perceives feminism as having the last word on sexuality nor advocates that queer theories should be the sole vehicle for productive research in the area of sexualities.

Sedgwick (1990), another influential scholar in the field of queer theory, argues that gender and sex are inextricable but they "are nonetheless not the same question" (p. 30). Over the past 20 years, there has been an abundance of educational research related to gender and schooling, girls and schooling, and, more recently, boys and schooling (e.g., Kenway, Willis, Blackmore, & Rennie, 1997; Mac An Ghaill, 1994). This research has often touched on issues related to sexuality but has not taken sexuality as the central subject of study. Another level of understanding may be developed within educational research if sexuality, and not gender, becomes central. As sexuality and gender are not synonymous, theorizing about them distinctly is useful. Although it is instructive to address gender and sexuality separately, it is also necessary to consider their various linkages. Analyzing sexualities independently of other aspects of identity may reify sexual identities and may diminish the importance of other elements that constitute the self.

Butler (1998) discusses her decision to focus on the study of sexuality by reference to the notion of rhetorical excess:

> I am probably willing to commit a sort of rhetorical excess in order to keep the question of homosexuality, and lesbianism in particular, alive. Which is not the same as saying that all scholarship ought to do that or that it is the primary oppression, or the key, or whatever. It rather indicates where I enter into critical discourse these days. (p. 284)

By adopting Butler's notion of excess, I enter into this discussion of schooling through a focus on the production of diverse sexualities. This approach does not seek to create a hierarchy of oppression but, rather, signifies a particular entry point into discourses related to sexualities and secondary schooling. This study is indebted to other researchers in the United States who have also adopted a queer theoretical lens in the study of education (Pinar, 1998; Talburt & Steinberg, 2000).

Queer theoretical analysis is also strongly influenced by post-structuralism, although as Pinar (1998), drawing on the work of Seidman (1993), notes, "Queer theory is ... simultaneously modernist and postmodernist, structuralist and poststructuralist. It straddles, as it were, the divide. It shares with both defenders of identity politics and its poststructural critics a preoccupation with the self and the politics of its representation" (p. 10). Namaste (1999) analyzed poststructuralism's relation to queer theory in order to postulate a "sociological queer theory" that "offers a specifically historicized understanding of sexual identities, politics and communities" (p. 205).

Although Namaste's (1998) analysis of queer theory fails to make explicit the necessity of considering intersections among sex, gender, class, race, and sexualities, it remains instructive in the framing of this book. Namaste (1996) defines some of the key questions of queer theory as follows:

> How do categories such as "gay," "lesbian," and "queer" emerge? From what do they differentiate themselves, and what kinds of identities do they exclude? How are these borders demarcated, and how can they become contested? What are the relations between the naming of sexuality and political organization it adopts, between identity and community? Why is a focus on the discursive production of social identities useful? How do we make sense of the dialectical movement between inside and outside, heterosexuality and homosexuality? (pp. 198–199)

Attending to the way identities are produced causes researchers to concentrate on what Sears (1992) calls "the rules of the game of homosexuality" (p. 154). This represents a movement away from research questions interested in " ... the representation of gay and lesbian subjects and experience to analysis of practices as they are constructed in social and institutional locations" (Talburt, 1999, p. 526). Following from this outline of how queer theories are conceptualized in this study, I now turn to a consideration of their relationship to the study of sexualities and secondary schooling.

This queer theoretical approach opens up an interrogation of how people's conceptions of the formation of sexual and gender identities intersect with assumptions made about research and teaching on sexualities, genders, and schooling. It enables a consideration of how some researchers and research projects come to be constructed as risky or inappropriate in educational contexts while others are valorized. This approach also facilitates an exploration of how researchers' and participants' shifting racial, ethnic, gender, and sexual identities intersect with the construction of methodologies of inclusion in educational research. Implicit here is a critique of educational research that shrinks from problematizing and/or essentializing identities. The process of critiquing the exclusionary aspects of identity politics "is crucial to the democratization of queer politics" (Butler, 1997a, p. 14).

Foucault (1996e) points to the contradictory role of identity categories in the production and pathologization of desire:

> These [identity] categories were used, it is true, to pathologize homosexuality, but they were equally categories of defense, in the name of which one could claim rights. The problem is still very current: between the affirmation "I am homosexual" and the refusal to say it, lies a very ambiguous dialectic. It's a necessary affirmation since it is the affirmation of a right, but at the same time it's a cage and a trap .... One can never stabilize oneself in a position; one must define the use that one makes of it according to the moment. (p. 369)

Foucault (1996h) reconfigures the notion of homosexuality in order to negotiate this trap of affirming oneself in this "finally inadequate category" (p. 326). For Foucault (1996e), homosexuality is inadequate as a descriptor because it refuses ambiguity and fixes one's sexual identity through the affirmation "I am homosexual." When identities are conceived as unavoidable, yet in a constant state of process, they might provide the basis for "creative ways of life" (pp. 369, 370) and for creative research related to sexualities and secondary schooling. Such an approach prioritizes people's agency in the representation and performance of their sexual and gender identities.

Conversely, research relating to sexual and gender identities invested in the maintenance of stable identity categories may reproduce truths that have previously been commandeered as a justification for the ultimate act of exclusion. Hughes (1999) cites the vast numbers of people (including homosexuals) who perished in the holocaust as testimony to the "appalling intolerance of modernity, to the ways in which 'mythic truths' about the moral order of bodies can be pressed into the service of genocide" (p. 169). Hence, research epistemologies anchored in essentializing notions of sexual and gender identity may succeed in the struggle for the affirmation of equal rights, but they may also be deployed for more sinister ends.

I have just outlined the efficacy of queering the epistemological framework of this study. Before proceeding further, I will briefly consider some of the criticisms that have been lodged against this theoretical approach. Martin (1994) has argued that although she remains

> ... convinced of the potential of "Queer Studies" to provoke more complex accounts of gender and sexuality ... I am worried about the occasions when antifoundationalist celebrations of queerness rely on their own projections of fixity, constraint, or subjection onto a fixed ground, often onto feminism or the female body, in relation to which queer sexualities become figural, performative, playful, and fun. (p. 104)

Martin is sympathetic to queer projects but is critical of the tendency of queer theorists, such as Butler and Sedgwick, to situate feminism or the female body as somehow less transgressive and sexy than their queer counterparts. I am mindful of Martin's warnings about unthinking "celebrations of queerness" and recognize the capacity of queer theories to be a force for subjection.

In developing an understanding of transgression within a queer theoretical framework, I also draw on Grosz's (1995a) reminder that transgression is not always transgressive. She argues that we should resist

> ... too ready a generalization of straights as the crippled emotional slaves and gays, lesbians, and other queers as the transgressive sexual radicals. In each of us there are elements and impulses that strive for conformity and elements that seek instability and change ... . Simply being straight or being gay, in itself, provides

no guarantee of an individual's position as sexually radical: it depends on how one lives one's queerness or how one renders one's straightness as queer. (p. 223)

It is not my aim to valorize all things queer or to equate all acts of transgression within an emancipatory framework.

Following the work of Hammonds (1997), I am also mindful of the importance of considering questions of race in the context of a queer theoretical analysis of the production of discourses related to sexualities and secondary schooling. Hammonds notes that discussions of sexualities often translate into discussions of white sexualities, silencing discussions of the production of sexualities of women and men of color. She asks

... if the sexualities of black women have been shaped by silence, erasure, and invisibility in dominant discourses, then are black lesbian sexualities doubly silenced? What methodologies are available to read and understand this void and its effects on that which is visible? Conversely, how does the structure of what is visible, namely white female sexualities, shape those not-absent-though-not-present black female sexualities ...? (p. 141)

In response to this silence and invisibility, Hammonds argues that it is not enough to make black women visible to white women and to each other. She argues for a queer theoretical analysis that recognizes the structures that sustain racism, homophobia, and misogyny — not as analogous oppressions but as "discursive and material terrains where there exists the possibility for the active production of speech, desire, and agency" (p. 152). Sex, gender, sexual, racial, ethnic, and class identity categories inform one another: Ignoring these intersections continues the erasure of individuals' lived experiences and obfuscates the power relations that underpin discourses related to sexualities and secondary schooling.

The foregoing discussion has suggested how queer, feminist, and poststructuralist theories inform the epistemological foundations of research related to sexualities, genders, and schooling. I have argued for the value of taking sexualities as a central focus of analysis while simultaneously emphasizing the interconnectedness of sexualities with other biographical fragments. I have also gestured toward the importance of continuously critiquing identity politics, and I have highlighted some of the problematics associated with the political mobilization of sexual identity categories. The tendency to reify queer theory as a transgressive point of departure has also been challenged.

METHODOLOGIES OF INCLUSION: ARTFUL CONTRIVANCES

The issue of bisexuality was much debated during my time in the Avengers. Though lesbianism was not a requirement of membership in the Avengers, it was rife in the organization. Cathy was one exception — she identified as bisexual. Many of us suspected that Cathy really was a lesbian, despite her frequent declarations to the contrary. It was monotonous having to listen to her drone on about bisexuals at every meeting, even if she was one herself.

Is an organization dedicated to lesbian visibility and survival the appropriate place for such a dialogue? If Lesbian Avengers want to fight for bisexual visibility and survival, should they consider a name change? Maybe they should consider becoming the "Lesbian and Bisexual Avengers" or the "Transgender, Bisexual, Lesbian, and Intersex Avengers" or maybe just the "Avengers." Even though I like the idea of coalition building, I do not know if I would have joined a coalition group. There was something about the specificity of becoming a Lesbian Avenger that I found quite enticing.

Some conflicts peculiar to identity-based groups emerge in the vignette just presented. The agenda of identity-based groups may appear straightforward, but just whom these groups represent is often an ongoing point of tension. Similarly, methodologies of inclusion inescapably produce their own exclusions. As Slee (2001) noted, inclusive education is an oxymoronic organizing concept (p. 172). Consequently, methodologies of inclusion may be conceived as artful contrivances, ostensibly devised to be inclusive but often obfuscating their own exclusions. In order to consider these artful contrivances in more detail, I now turn to study notions of empathy, insider relationships, and researcher biographies in relation to the exercise of the art of inclusivity in educational research methodologies.

One artful contrivance in the research process, it is suggested, may be found in how researchers conceive of the relationship with participants involved in their study. Identifying as "not straight" or "straight" in the context of an interview does have repercussions for the conduct of an interview. However, it does not follow that researchers and participants will be involved in an empathetic process on the basis of a shared identity. Kennedy and Davis (1996) observed that a shared lesbian identity only accounts for one aspect of the researcher–participant relationship. In their own research experiences, these authors note "the common bond of lesbianism and familiarity with the social context did not make positioning ourselves in relation to the complex and powerful forces of class, race, and gender oppression — not to mention homophobia — easy" (p. 173). A shared biographical fragment (whether it be sex, sexual or gender identity, racial identity, ethnicity, nationality, class, or all of these) does not necessarily translate to shared interests and a greater possibility of empathetic understanding or sensitivity between researcher and participant.

Others have attested to the advantages of being gay when doing research in gay communities. Herdt and Boxer (1993) argued that, in their research with gay and lesbian teens, "being gay made it possible for us, both by social identity and by sensitivity to the issues, to gain entry into the gay and lesbian community" (pp. xvii–xviii). A shared sexual identity does not automatically make researchers more sensitive. Sexual and gender identities are only one factor mediating relationships between researchers and participants, and if these are shared, they do not necessarily produce more empathetic or inclusive effects. Other elements of researchers' and participants' biographies will inevitably influence the research process; therefore, it may be prudent not to assume shared knowledge or interests, regardless of the biography of those involved.

In their research on nonheterosexual-identified couples, Heaphy, Weeks, and Donovan (1998) called attention to the problem of overemphasizing the commonalities between researchers and participants. They observed that some participants in their project

> ... assumed that the respondent and researcher may have some shared political agenda; and the implications this might have in terms of the 'pressure' on the respondent to tell a 'good' story or 'appropriate' story ... some respondents may have a picture in mind not only of the aims, but the *results* of the research. (pp. 456–457, italics in original)

Problems may arise if too much is taken for granted based on shared identity between researchers and their participants.

Participants and researchers cannot assume shared aims in the representation of homosexuality in research, because, as King (1999) argues, there are many ways of representing homosexuality but "none is itself a stable category," and there is not a need for a "comprehensive framework for homosexuality" (p. 478).

The process of research illustrates that, irrespective of people's identities, individuals produce and envisage different questions, aims, and outcomes depending on their various, shifting standpoints. As a consequence, inclusivity in research is not necessarily enhanced by an emphasis on empathy or on the value of insider relationships. Indeed, it may have the potential to be enhanced by the disruption of these methodological assumptions.

This discussion of people's identities, biographies, and standpoints should not be understood as suggesting that these features are inconsequential in the development of a research methodology; clearly, they do influence the research process. However, this influence then should neither be construed as making individuals somehow representative of a broader community standpoint nor be associated with essentialist notions regarding greater clarity of perspective or instantaneous inclusivity through shared and/or empathetic identities. Researchers might also interrogate their individual investments in maintaining insider–outsider binaries in the development of research methodologies in projects inquiring into people's sexual and gender identities.

RESEARCH SENSIBILITIES[5]

> I do not imagine I would have become a Lesbian Avenger unless I had become a lesbian first. I decided to go native, so I moved into a lesbian group house where I was instructed in butch dyke fashion. Apparently, white taffeta was not conducive to the development of a butch aesthetic, but almost anything black was okay. I purchased lesbian music, an Indigo Girls CD. And I purchased a pair of hair clippers to ensure that my hair would always be suitably spiky.

Whether a person comes out as a debutante or as a lesbian, a certain sensibility is required — though, as my story suggests, not the same sensibility. My observations of some of the identities and aesthetics I have observed and performed highlight the fluidity of sensibility. As the following definition suggests, the notion of sensibility is ambiguous.

SENSIBILITY 1: ability to receive sensations: SENSITIVENESS <tactile sensibility> 2: peculiar susceptibility to a pleasurable or painful impression (as from praise or a slight) — often used in plural 3: awareness of and responsiveness toward something (as emotion in another) 4: refined or excessive sensitiveness in emotion and taste with especial responsiveness to the pathetic (i.e. having a capacity to move one to either compassionate or contemptuous pity). (Merriam-Webster, Inc., 2005c)

Sensibilities change within individuals and within communities; they can be pleasurable and painful, peculiar and pathetic. A sensibility might also be construed as the ability to perform in a manner sensitive to the emotions and tastes of one's surroundings, whatever they may be. The sensibility being advocated here is particularly focused on the development of a research methodology that is aware of and responsive to the research environment.

The research environment in this study constitutes secondary schools. I envisage a sensibility that is "aware of and responsive to" the LGBTI-identified teachers and students who inhabit these schools. These people are often characterized as worthy of pathos. However, the sensibility cultivated here endeavors to disrupt the comfort of such familiar associations. It is argued such associations are founded, in part, on the "peculiar susceptibility" of educational research to draw on

... the language of rationality ... rationality weaves paths to justification, and in so doing, allows both methodologies and practices and readings of sexuality to settle in rationalized comfort ... .(Rasmussen & Harwood, 2000, p. 2)

Rasmussen and Harwood (2000) argue for a turning away from the comfort of rationality and scientificity that incites educational research to reify claims of truth. This antipathy toward rationality draws on Foucault's (1998) theorizing regarding the "conditions of possibility of a science"(p. 326) to ask what are the "conditions of possibility" for fashioning sexuality research in education not embedded in the language of rationality.

The notion of "truth" is something with which the researcher is necessarily entwined: Truth is present in and permeates through the research within which the researcher is situated. In particular, truth is an enticing ally for the "scientification" of inclusivity.

It is therefore vital that truths be sought after and interrogated in inclusive educational research. The research sensibility advocated by Harwood and Rasmussen (2002) thus incites a form of methodological provocation that demands suspicion of the "language of rationality" and requires researchers to develop strategies for managing the complexities and paradoxes of working within and against truth.

Other researchers in education have also drawn on a queer theoretical perspective to argue the value of cultivating the notion of sensibility in developing research methods and methodologies. Specifically, Morris (1998) argues for the development of a "queer sensibility." According to her, "[a] queer sensibility concerns the reception and reading of a text … . The text is a site of interpretation. Thus there is nothing inherently queer about a text, even if one may read a text queerly … . For me a queer reading of a text uncovers the possibility of the text's radical political potential" (pp. 276–277). Morris's notion of a queer sensibility emphasizes the importance of how a text is read and recognizes the possibility that any text may be read using a queer theoretical analysis. Thus, sensibility is not limited to readings related to sexualities and schooling but also has applications for other aspects of educational research.

Although I find Morris's (1998) notion of queer reading instructive, I am less persuaded by the definition of queerness she elaborates in order to shape her conception of a queer sensibility:

> (a) Queerness as a subject position digresses from the normalized, rigid identities that adhere to the sex = gender paradigm; (b) Queerness as a politic challenges the status quo, does not simply tolerate it, and does not stand for assimilation into the mainstream; (c) Queerness as an aesthetic or sensibility reads and interprets texts (art, music, literature) as potentially politically radical. A radical politic moves to the left, challenging norms. (p. 277)

By defining queer as not normalized or mainstream, Morris reinforces the notion that queer = not normal. In her definition a queer sensibility becomes aligned with an unspecified place on the "left," challenging norms. It is Morris's (1998) hope that a queer sensibility will aid "queer curriculum workers" (p. 284), whom she contrasts to "anti-queer curriculum workers" (p. 284). In her analysis, the latter may ultimately produce "students not unlike the students featured in Pink Floyd's *The Wall*, whereby students are pushed through a meat grinder (the schoolhouse) only to become worms (fascists)" (p. 284). Morris's argument is clearly hyperbolic. However, she constructs another binary whereby a queer sensibility is equated to something progressive and radical, whereas a nonqueer sensibility is associated with a conservative, fascistic, and normalizing stance. However, presumably there are other methodological positions beyond those informed by a queer sensibility, from which to enter critical discourse and to disturb the notion of schoolhouse as meat grinder.

DISCOURSE, TROPES, AND CATACHRESES

I have indicated that queer, feminist, and poststructuralist theories have been influential in the fashioning of this study. Influenced by these theoretical traditions, I use discourse, tropes, and catachreses as conceptual devices in order to discomfort the familiar.

Discourse

Hall (1992) notes that the term *discourse* is often associated with the linguistic concept related to writing or speech. Hall contrasts this usage of the term discourse with Foucault's deployment of the term to argue for an understanding of the term that is not purely linguistic:

> By "discourse," Foucault meant "a group of statements which provide a language for talking about — a way of representing the knowledge about — a particular topic at a particular historical moment …. Discourse is about the production of knowledge through language. But … since all social practices entail *meaning*, and meanings shape and influence what we do — our conduct — all practices have a discursive aspect." (p. 291 in Hall, 2001, p. 72)

This comment on the way in which Foucault's use of the term *discourse* differs from linguistic applications of the term is critical here because, as Hall (2001) goes on to note, it accentuates the historicity of discourse (p. 74) and simultaneously exposes the malleability and cultural specificities of discursive regimes.

In *The History of Sexuality, Volume 1: An Introduction*, Foucault (1990) elaborates on his use of the term discourse.

Indeed, it is in discourse that power and knowledge are joined together. And for this very reason, we must conceive discourse as a series of discontinuous segments whose tactical function is neither uniform nor stable — we must not imagine a world of discourse divided between accepted discourse and excluded discourse, or between the dominant discourse and the dominated one; but as a multiplicity of discursive elements that can come into play in various strategies. (p. 100)

By emphasizing the various "discursive elements" influencing, constituting, and reproducing power and knowledge, Foucault facilitates a study in which discourses are situated as competing knowledges of sexual subjects produced by continuously shifting relations of power.

In his discussion of discourses on sex, Foucault (1990) recommends further that they be questioned on "the two levels of their *tactical productivity* (what reciprocal effects of power and knowledge they ensure) and their *strategical integration* (what conjunction and what force relationship make their utilization necessary in a given episode of the various confrontations that occur)" (p. 102, italics added for emphasis). Thus, I consider how discourses related to sexualities and secondary schooling intersect, how they are deployed, how they gain authority, and how they are de-authorized in given contexts. I also attend to "reciprocal effects of power" and "force relationships" via an analysis of the various ways that researchers and participants conceive of and speak about sexual and gender identities. Allied to this Foucaultian-inspired discourse analysis is a study of the relationship between discourse and tropes.

Tropes

Tropic is the shadow from which all realistic discourse tries to flee. This flight, however, is futile; for tropics is the process by which all discourse *constitutes* the objects which it pretends only to describe realistically and to analyze objectively. (White, 1978, p. 2, italics in original)

It is evident from White's words that tropes cast a shadow upon claims to rationality. In rhetoric, tropes are understood as "the use of a word or expression in a different sense from that which properly belongs to it" (Merriam-Webster, 2005d). This definition brings forth the question of what might constitute a *proper* definition of any word or expression. In this analysis of tropes, the emphasis will be on the study of customary understandings of words and expressions and how these customary understandings might take hold and shroud their tropological status.

In *Tropics of Discourse*, White (1978) notes that there are four kinds of tropes within rhetoric (pp. 254, 255):

1. *metonymy*: "[a] trope in which one word is put for another that suggests it; as, we say, a man keeps a good table instead of good provisions" (Merriam-Webster, 2005b) (e.g., straight; used to mean heterosexual)
2. *synecdoche*: "a figure or trope by which a part of a thing is put for the whole ... or the whole for a part ... " (Merriam-Webster, 2005e) (e.g., queers; for all sexual minorities) or vice versa
3. *irony*: "[a] sort of humor, ridicule, or light sarcasm which adopts a mode of speech the meaning of which is contrary to the literal sense of the words" (Merriam-Webster, 2005a) (e.g., She was a bitter old tart, but we loved him anyway)
4. *metaphor*: "a figure of speech in which a term or phrase is applied to something to which it is not literally applicable, in order to suggest a resemblance" (Macquarie Dictionary, 2001, p.1201) (e.g., She might have been a lemon, but she still liked other fruit).

The metaphor used in the example "necessitates knowledge of a specific extra-linguistic context in order to be understood" (Klein-Lataud, 1991, p. 74 in Namaste, 1999, p. 214), though not all metaphors require such detailed knowledge.

In contrast to these rhetorical definitions of tropes, White (1978), drawing partially on Foucault's (1970) *The Order of Things: An Archaeology of the Human Sciences* and Vico's (1968)[6] classical discussion of tropes, suggests that all discourse is "more tropical than logical" (p. 1). Discourses may be conceived as somehow holding the truth or reality regarding a particular issue or subject. However, the extent to which a discourse is known to be authentic may provide some indication of how deeply it has been set on our horizon. White's reconfiguration of the trope emphasizes the uncertainty that underlies all discourse and thus disturbs notions of the familiar, regardless of how authentic a discourse may appear. When a discourse is conceived as tropological, it must always be understood as constitutive of truth, even if it may appear to describe reality.

Building on White's (1978) analysis of the tropical tendencies of language, Butler (1997d) notes further that "a trope cannot operate, that is, generate new meanings or connections, if its departure from custom and logic is not recognized as such a departure. In this sense a trope presupposes an accepted version of reality for its operation" (p. 201). Given this understanding of tropes, for people to understand what it means to identify as straight, it is necessary for them to have some conception of what it might mean to be "not straight."

Although tropes presuppose a certain reality, they also represent "a deviation *toward* another meaning, conception, or ideal of what is right and proper *and true* 'in reality.' Thus considered, troping is both a movement *from* one notion of the way things are related to another notion ... " (White, 1978, p. 2, italics in original). Butler (1997d) argues this tropical tendency toward movement means tropes are "not restricted to accepted versions of reality" (p. 201). Thus, following Butler's analysis, tropes may operate not only to reinforce the familiar but also to create new versions of reality.

But what is the value in determining that such familiar discourses are tropological? White (1978) proposes a tropological typology of discourse in part to

> ... recognize that it is not a matter of choosing between objectivity and distortion, but rather between different strategies for constituting "reality" in thought so as to deal with it in different ways, each of which has its own ethical implications. (p. 22)

By focusing on the way that discourses are "hardened into ideologies" (White, 1978, p. 22) and are made familiar, White's theorization of the trope underscores the different strategies used to constitute different versions of reality through discourse. White also invites readers to consider the ethical implications of these competing strategies of truth creation. White's tropical typology facilitates an analysis of some of the terms central to this book. When these terms are perceived as tropes, they may be viewed as strategies that some people deploy and call upon in specific circumstances to construct familiar and identifiable narratives of people and their sexual and gendered selves. Related to this notion of tropes is the idea of catachreses.

Catachreses

In discussions of rhetoric, catachreses are sometimes distinguished from tropes because the latter extend existing meanings of terms while the former "mark a reality for which our language is inadequate" (Namaste, 1999, p. 226)

Whereas Namaste distinguishes catachreses from other tropes, for Shiff, catachresis "applies a figurative sense as a literal one, while retaining the look or feel of figurality" (Shiff, 1991, p. 84 in Sobchack, 2000, para. 33.) For Sobchack (2000), catachresis points to the gaps between the figures of language and literal lived-body experiences. She goes on to characterize the relationship between catachresis and lived-body experience as having a precise task within rhetoric: This task is not only to point to but also to fill gaps in speech — gaps that are presumably provoked by people's experience (Sobchack, 2000, para. 34).

Catachreses are also conceptualized "as a way by which one adapts existing terms to applications where a proper term does not exist … " (Silva Rhetoricae, 2005). Thus, people may talk about the eye of a storm, "words which mark a reality for which our language is inadequate" (Namaste, 1999, p. 226). Catachresis may also be taken to mean the misuse or strained use of words (e.g., She wept a mountain). In *Bodies That Matter*, Butler (1993) perceives catachreses "in those figures that function improperly, as an improper transfer of sense, the use of a proper name to describe that which does not properly belong to it" (p. 37).

In terms of this book, I rely primarily on Butler's (1993) notion of catachresis regarding "figures that function improperly." More specifically, I use this notion to explore some of the gaps apparent in the production of educational discourses related to sexual and gender identities and to ponder the methods people have used to fill these gaps. The fillers people use, and their reasons for using them, may be as redolent as the gaps themselves.

Given such a schema, terms such as *lesbian, gay, transsexual, drag king, boy-dyke fag,* and *sissy-fag* might be understood as catachreses rather than tropes; these terms seek to create a signifier for an individual performance or experience that previously had no descriptor. All of these terms rely on existing ideas within language to convey meaning, but they are also more readily understood as constructions; therefore, their proper meanings may be more open to contestation. Finally, catachreses are deployed as a means to consider how identity categories are constructed in order to suit particular performances.

Following this elaboration of the epistemological and methodological foundations of this study is an outline of the theoretical basis that structures most of the second half of this book.

3

Identities, Sexual Subjectivities, and Three Modes of Objectification of Subjects

How do you become a homosexual?
Well, first there's the talent competition,
then evening wear, then the
all-important swimsuit competition.

(Orleans, 1994, p. 20)

If people's conceptions of subjectivities and identities are integral to the production of discourses related to sexualities, then it is important for me to deploy these terms precisely within the context of this book. *Identity* and *subjectivity* are terms used with gay abandon in queer theory and poststructuralist discourse. These terms are often used interchangeably, yet like the term *gay* they clearly have different meanings across place, time, and space. This chapter commences with an analysis of the matter of identity, after which I consider how tropes of essentialism and constructivism play a role in the production of identity. I also analyze the efficacy of using deconstruction in analyzing tropes of identity.

Subsequent to this is an analysis focused primarily on Foucault, as his work is pivotal in the developmental of queer theoretical perspectives on the question of the subject. I introduce Foucault's "Three Modes of Objectification of Subjects" as a device for considering how people are categorized, produced, and constrained by processes of subjectivization and identification, scientific classification, and dividing practices. This analysis of modes of objectification structures the second half of the book. In the penultimate chapter, attention turns to the study of melancholy, grief, and pleasure.

THE MATTER OF IDENTITY

There is no doubt that "*identity matters* both in terms of social and political concerns within the contemporary world and within academic discourses" (Woodward, 1997, p. 2, italics added for emphasis). Society tends to be organized around identities: identities as cultural constructions, identities as difference, identities as duties and ethics, identities as knowledge, identities as performative acts, identities as relational, identities as representational[1] (Talburt & Steinberg, 2000, p. 233), and identities as essential. The identities people adopt are often thought to be related to their subjectivities. How these two terms are conceived is integral to the ways people shape the production of discourses related to sexualities and secondary schooling.

Writing on the relationship between identity and subjectivity, Woodward (1997) notes that these terms are "occasionally used in ways which suggest they may be interchangeable" (p. 2). When they are conceived as interchangeable, the notion of identity may be perceived as representative of people's sense of self, though this connection is often contested, as indicated by Hall (1996). In response to the question "Who needs identity?" Hall states that identity may be conceived as a

> ... meeting point, the point of *suture*, between on one hand the discourses and practices which attempt to "interpellate," speak to us or hail us into place as the social subjects of particular discourses, and on the other hand, the processes which produce subjectivities, which construct us as subjects which can be "spoken." Identities are thus points of temporary attachment to the subject positions which discursive practices construct for us. (p. 5, italics in original)

This conception of identity perceives the development of identities as a process of "articulation" (Hall, 1996, p. 6). The evocative notion of suturing together — or interweaving interpellation of — subjectivity and identity constitutes the process of articulation. Throughout this book I conceive of notions of identity through such discursive theories of the production and regulation of subjects. Echoing the work of Hall and Butler, I also interweave psychoanalytic and discursive theories of the subject in analyzing people's attachments to specific identities.

However people are labeled or may choose to identify, individuals and groups are exposed to various influences as they move through their worlds. When these contacts occur, different individuals adopt various positions, and for the purposes of this book, "[t]he positions which we take up and identify with" (Woodward, 1997, p. 2) are understood to constitute identity. Identity may also operate to give people an "... idea of who we are and of how we relate to others and to the world in which we live. Identity marks the ways in which we are the same as others who share that position, and the ways in which we are different from those who do not" (Woodward, 1997, p. 2). Although identities may act as a marker, their ink is by no means indelible, and people's identities may change. Identities may also have the effect of causing trouble, because certain individuals may be prohibited from adopting identities that align with their perception of how they relate to others. Then again, individuals may feel that no available identities represent their perception of how they relate to others or of how they desire to be perceived by others.

As Britzman (1998) notes, drawing on the work of Sedgwick (1992), identities are not limited to those positions people occupy; they also include "identification of, ... identification against, over-identification" (p. 83) and, I would add, underidentification. Though identifications are sometimes deployed to suggest uniformity among groups, Crimp (1992) points out that "[i]dentification is ... identification with another, which means that identity is never identical to itself ... identity is always a relation, never simply a positivity" (p. 12, in Britzman, 1998, p. 83; see also Britzman, 1992). If identities are relational and are part of an ongoing process of articulation, then it is possible to argue that they are subject to the characteristics of relationships: the misunderstandings, the long partnerships, the torrid affairs, the brief flings, the constant negotiations, the cultural and temporal variations.

Identities are not only subject to the vagaries of relationships and articulations, but they are also profoundly political. I consider people's attachments to specific sexual and gender identities

59

and examine the ways these attachments provide a foundation for programs related to sexualities and secondary schooling. What is interesting about identities in terms of this book is not discerning their truth but rather seeking a greater understanding of how identities are articulated in relation to sexualities and genders in educational contexts. In short, this is in part a study of how sexual and gender identities are deployed, rationalized, negotiated, and prohibited at different moments in different educational spaces and places.

As indicated in the previous chapter, Foucault (1996e) conceives of identities, or what he terms *categories*,[2] as instrumental in the production and pathologization of desire (p. 369). In order to negotiate the trap of affirming oneself as a homosexual, Foucault reconfigures the notion of what a homosexual is. Identity politics and identities can be used for the affirmation of rights, but they can be deployed for more sinister ends. It is understood that some identities are unavoidable, but if these identities or categories are perceived to be in a constant state of process, they might provide the basis for "creative ways of life" and for "refusing existing lifestyles" (p. 369) in the continuous process of becoming subjects.

A different approach to "refusing existing lifestyles" has emerged in Jagose & Halberstam (1999). This work argues the value of proliferating sexual and gender identities as a strategy to disrupt regulatory heteronormative practices and "reimagine[s] the complex set of relations between sexuality, gender, race and class" (para. 7). Drawing on the work of Foucault in an interview with Jagose, Halberstam states, "Resistance has to go beyond the taking of a name ('I am a lesbian') and must produce creative new forms of resistance by assuming and empowering a marginal positionality" (para. 11). She argues,

> Unlike a theorist like Butler who sees categories as perpetually suspect, I embrace categorization as a way of creating places for acts, identities and modes of being which otherwise remain unnameable. I also think that the proliferation of categories offers an alternative to the mundane humanist claim that categories inhibit the unique self ... . I try to offer some new names for formerly uninhabitable locations. (para. 7)

Setting for herself the task of reclaiming the value of activities such as coming out, organizing, and producing new identity categories, Halberstam argues that it is limiting to think of these processes as end points (Jagose & Halberstam, 1999). Halberstam contends further that coming out and the like have been too maligned by a queer politics intent on "working against identificatory taxonomies" (para. 8). Rather than perceiving categorizations as "perpetually suspect" (para. 7) or as potentially creative of new ways of life, it may be more instructive to consider what reading of a particular categorization or identity is most appropriate within a given context.

Butler (1994) is skeptical of the strategic value to be gained in a proliferation of "identificatory taxonomies." For example, she argues that drag (and presumably identities related to drag such as drag kings and drag queens) is not a "paradigm for the subversion of gender. I don't think if we were all dragged out gender life would become more expansive and less restrictive. There are restrictions in drag" (p. 33). Although Butler is careful not to overemphasize the potential of drag in processes of resignification, she does favor the development of subversive practices that "challenge conventions of reading, and demand new possibilities of reading" (p. 38). Although I agree that the subversive potential of drag is limited, I will later show that certain performances of drag in educational contexts can "demand new possibilities of reading." Thus, I explore the conventions of reading that are challenged by the materialization of the Lesbian Avengers and lesbian prom kings in school settings.

Akin to Butler (1994), Grosz (1995b) also resists a proliferation of identities as a strategy to reinvent relations. She prefers to consider the possibilities that exist for resistance and pleasure that operate within existing identities. She is particularly unconvinced of the value of new identity categories such as queer. Grosz argues that the usefulness of queer is questionable, as it is a reactive category insofar as it defines itself as somehow oppositional to "a straight norm" (p. 219). In arguing that *queer* is reactive, Grosz adopts a narrow definition of the term; presumably a similarly narrow definition could be applied to the term *lesbian* in terms of its subordinate relationship to the category *gay*. I show throughout that either definition oversimplifies the complex significations that now attach themselves to both categories. As indicated by Grosz, the choices people make regarding the deployment of identities are inevitably fraught, and sometimes a queer identity may be more strategic than that of lesbian and vice versa. Although I am keenly aware of the limitations of identity, I am also inspired by the moments of subversion and disruption that sometimes burst out in the suturing together of identities.

In writing against the proliferation of new words and concepts for women's sexual desire and relations, Grosz (1995b) prefers the tactic of working with and within the term lesbian. She argues that the undertheorization and lack of specificity accompanying lesbian desire open it up to many possibilities, enabling it to be productive or reactive depending on how individuals imagine it. The refusal to efface the specificity of the term lesbian entails its own exclusions, but so too the impulse toward generality or universality means "no particular form of oppression can be adequately accounted for in its concrete articulations" (p. 251). Thus, no mode of identity should be conceived as somehow liberating. Instead of seeking liberation through attachment to identity, Grosz suggests a "need to experiment with [sexuality], to enjoy its various modalities, to seek its moments of heightened intensity, its moments of self-loss where reflection no longer has a place" (p. 227).

In the context of this present study, identities are conceived of as persistent, disruptive, and sometimes contagious; simultaneously, they are not reified, pathologized, or abandoned. I strive to explain their role in the production and circulation of key discourses related to sexualities and secondary schooling. Building on this analysis of the matter of identity, I now turn to a discussion of the related notions of essentialism, constructivism, and deconstruction.

ESSENTIALISM, CONSTRUCTIVISM, AND DECONSTRUCTION

Identities are often interpreted within the bounds of essentialism and constructivism.[3] As such, these broad frameworks of thought are integral to this study. This section briefly analyzes some of the theoretical debates that circulate in relation to essentialism and constructivism and also considers the value of deconstructing essentialist and constructivist representations of the subject. Before proceeding with this analysis, it is worth noting that, in the context of this book, constructivism and essentialism are perceived as tropes. These terms, and the theories that inform them, are often called upon in the construction of familiar and identifiable narratives of young people and their sexual and gender identities, but neither trope is understood to hold the truth of identity. However, insofar as these terms structure relations of power, their various deployments do have ethical and strategic implications for the production of discourses related to sexualities and secondary schooling. I begin with the trope of essentialism and then move to a consideration of constructivism and deconstruction.

Essentialism

Many popular understandings of identity are linked to essentializing discourses, which tend to establish causal links between identities and a person's social experience or behavior. In her influential study of essentialism and feminism, Fuss (1989) defines *essentialism* "as a belief in a true essence — that which is most irreducible, unchanging, and therefore constitutive of a given person or thing" (p. 2). McWhorter (1999) notes that "for most essentialists, the process of developing self-awareness is the process of learning about something already present, a self who is already homosexual, lesbian, or gay" (p. 82). In this sense, the search for a self is motivated by the desire to understand one's essence.

In his study of the operation of essentializing discourses and related assumptions people might make about the working class, Grossberg (1992) remarks that " ... if you occupy a particular social experience [working class, lesbian, gay] you are already locked into its necessary consequences, consequences defined by virtue of it being what it already is" (p. 30). This characterization of essentialism highlights the assumptions that tie a person's identity to an array of "necessary consequences" and performances. In such a process, evidence of the authenticity of identity may be provided through the performance of the necessary consequences attributed to that identity. Thus, for people who adopt LGBTI identities, the process of coming out may serve as a marker of authenticity, signifying the essential nature of that identity. In the following chapter, I consider an array of necessary consequences that LGBTI-identified teachers and students may feel locked into by virtue of essentializing discourses.

Essentialism linked to social experience and related performances represents only one brand. Fuss (1989), drawing on the work of Spivak (1987),[4] advocates the efficacy of a politics of "strategic essentialism." Fuss argues that essentialism is not intrinsically good or bad *per se*; rather,

> ... the radicality or conservatism of essentialism, depends, to a significant degree, on *who* is utilizing it, *how* it is deployed, and *where* its effects are concentrated ... . To insist that essentialism is always and everywhere reactionary is, for the constructionist, to buy into essentialism in the very act of making the charge; *it is to act as if essentialism has an essence.* (p. 20, italics in original)

Although Fuss (1989) is adamant that the political nature of essentialism is linked to the way it is deployed as a political tool, Butler (1990a) is more cautious about the strategic value of utilizing essentialist positions,[5] at least in relation to gender and sexual identities. She contends such discourses may be problematic because they run counter to the notion that these identities are constructs produced by relations of power (p. 30).

In an interview with Cheah and Grosz (1998), Butler further clarifies her position relating to the value of strategic essentialism. Butler distinguishes an essentialism focused on philosophical understandings of essence from an essentialism that seeks to locate people in particular categories for strategic purposes. Elaborating on this point, she argues there are some categories

> ... without which one cannot move .... So if someone were to ask me if the category of woman is something without which we cannot do, I would say, absolutely, it is a category without which we cannot do. (p. 22)

Given this conception of categories "without which one cannot move," which acknowledges the continuing importance of some identity categories in contemporary political cultures, Butler (1993) points to the necessity of a double movement where it becomes possible to invoke

> ... the category and, hence, provisionally to institute an identity and at the same time to open the category as a site of permanent political contest ... . [We] do this precisely in order to learn how to live the contingency of the political signifier in a culture of democratic contestation. (p. 222)

Importantly, the double movement Butler conceives of does not celebrate the intrinsic value of contestation but, rather, links contestation to the sustenance of democratic cultures. The value of this double movement may be interrogated in the context of a letter written to *LGNY*[6] titled "Identity speech: It's who we are, not what we say" (Sheil, 2000). In the letter Sheil encapsulates some essentialist arguments that are often deployed in Australia and the United States in struggles for the civil rights of lesbian and gay communities. The ensuing discussion of Sheil's letter is thus designed to inform my analysis of the operation of essentializing tropes in educational contexts.

Critiquing a decision of the U.S. Supreme Court relating to the exclusion of the Irish Lesbian and Gay Organization from participating in the St. Patrick's Day Parade in Boston, Sheil (2000) writes that in their judgment the Supreme Court held "that sexual orientation is a form of free speech" (para. 2). In objecting to this finding, Sheil writes, "Only when courts recognize sexual orientation as status rather than message, essence rather than expression, will gay civil rights gains be secure from discriminatory 'editing out'" (para. 19). Sheil suggests that gay, and presumably lesbian, civil rights will never be secure until the courts stop treating "sexual orientation as speech rather than identity" (para. 19). Building on the equation that sexual orientation equates to identity, he argues that an individual's presumably innate sexual orientation should afford them equal protection alongside other individuals who are protected because of their race or gender. In the context of Butler's (1993) double movement, it is apparent that Sheil invokes the category of essentialism, but he evokes it with the idea of "essence rather than expression" (para. 19). His strategy, if successful, may have the deleterious effect of closing down sexual identity categories as a site of permanent political contest. It is just such a movement Butler cautions against because she argues it is antidemocratic.

In *Excitable Speech*, Butler (1997b) develops another argument against the use of essentializing discourses. For her, the state "represents one of the great threats to the discursive operation of lesbian and gay politics" (p. 22). As such, any extension of state power must take into account the notion that often the state is more interested in supporting the status quo than in upholding the rights of minorities. Therefore, claiming recognition of sexual and gender identity as "status rather than message" (Shiel, 2000, para 19) may be problematic. Such an approach may not secure hoped-for civil rights protections, and it may even make the situation of minorities more precarious because the state is no guarantor of the rights of minority groups (pp. 23–24). Although identities remain within the double movement, the way is left open for resistance and opposition not predicated on the recognition of an essential identity — one that may be deployed to a minority's detriment by an often-hostile state apparatus.

After Butler (1997b), I argue that there are identity categories "without which one cannot move" (Cheah & Grosz, 1998) in the production of discourses related to sexualities and secondary schooling. These categories may be conceived as essential — distinct from essentializing. Discerning the identity categories people can, and cannot, do without is a continually evolving task critical to the process of democratic contestation, a task that may be closed down by the movement from strategic essentialism to philosophical notions of essence.

To this point I have focused on notions of strategic essentialism and on ontological essentialism. However, the last decade has seen the strong development of another thread of essentialism: that which seeks to reclaim the idea that sexual identities have a biological basis. Although the essence of heterosexual identities remains a largely unexplored phenomenon in science and social science, the search for a biological source for a gay identity has continued to gain momentum, especially in the wake of the Human Genome Project. As Terry (1995) notes,

> We [lesbians and gay men], as deviant subjects, have had to account for ourselves as anomalies. We are compelled to ask certain questions of the self, beyond the generic question of "Who am I?" In addition we ask "How did I come to be this way?" "How and why am I different?" "Is there something wrong with me?" "Is there something in my background that would explain my homosexuality?" "Is there something different about my body?" "Am I a danger to myself or others?" Deviant subjectivity is produced in these questions.[7] (pp. 137–138)

There is a variety of motivations behind the search for a gay gene,[8] and some of these motivations are no doubt inspired by questions such as those posed by Terry (1995). Rixecker (2000) notes one of these motivations in her discussion of genetic research related to sexualities. She argues that "with the advent of molecular biology and genetic mapping … it is assumed that the molecular level, through the genotype, will be able to reveal who one is — be it heterosexual, bisexual, homosexual, or some other hybrid" (p. 266). Behind such a desire to reveal "who one is" lies an assumption that people's authentic identities are there to be found, as long as researchers dig deep enough. This search for who one is might also reveal something about the comfort of essentializing tropes of identity, a comfort affirmed by the prospect that "merely cultural" (Butler, 1997c) descriptors might somehow be validated through biological research. However, those who subscribe to the notion that sexual identities rest on contingent foundations may question the value of scientific research predicated on biological essentialism that seeks to locate the elusive gay gene (Rixecker, 2000; Terry, 1999).

Essentializing tropes of sexual identity have many foundations. They may be produced through recourse to transhistorical narratives that tend to attribute equivalent meanings to same-sex practices in all times and in all cultures. Alternatively, or simultaneously, essentializing tropes may be ascribed scientific underpinnings. People may also utilize essentializing tropes of identity primarily for strategic reasons. This discussion of tropes of essentialism supports McWhorter's (1999) and Fuss's (1989) arguments that constructivism and essentialism are not dualistic; there are many varieties of each (Fuss, 1989; McWhorter, 1999, p. 80). Regardless of the theoretical underpinnings of essentialist positions, essentialism and constructivism are often defined in opposition to one another.

Constructivism and Deconstruction

This section commences with an outline of some broad theoretical propositions relating to constructivism rather than endeavoring to categorize various forms of constructivism. Subsequent to this is a discussion of constructivism and deconstruction. This latter discussion draws primarily on Butler's (1993, 1997c, 1998) theorizing of these concepts in relation to sex, gender, and sexuality. In the following chapter I discuss notions of constructivism under the rubric of "choice," as participants in this study tend to adopt the language of choice when considering people's capacity to choose sexual and gender identity categories. Discourses of choice are underpinned by diverse theories of constructivism.

In the context of a discussion of representation, Hall (1997) deploys the term *constructivism* in such a manner as to suggest that constructivist and constructionist approaches to the development of meaning in language are synonymous (p. 25). Following Hall and Butler (1997c), I employ the term *constructivist*. Hall argues that constructivists

... do not deny the existence of the material world. However, it is not the material world which conveys meaning: it is the language system or whatever system we are using to represent our concepts. It is social actors who use the conceptual systems of their culture and the linguistic and other representational systems to construct meaning, to make the world meaningful and to communicate about that world meaningfully to others. (p. 25)

Although Hall's (1997) description of constructivism provides a useful entrée to this concept, it may also gesture toward some agreement on the notion of constructivism, though, as indicated already, there are many varieties of constructivism. Constructivist theories of the homosexual self have been formulated in the work of Mary McIntosh (1997), Jeffrey Weeks (1986), and Kenneth Plummer (1992) (Epstein, 1987).[9] Epstein characterizes these constructivist positions on "homosexual" identity formation as follows:

... Constructionists demonstrated that the notion of "the homosexual" is a sociohistorical product, not universally applicable ... [They] focused attention on identity as a complex developmental outcome, the consequence of an interactive process of social labeling and self-identification. (p. 17)

Following in this tradition, in the introduction to *Bodies That Matter*, Butler (1993) outlines some basic propositions regarding constructivism.[10] Her propositions can be read in the context of a broader project in which she conceives "sex" not as a "bodily given on which the construct of gender is artificially imposed, but as a cultural norm which governs the materialization of bodies" (p. 3). She argues that

... construction is neither a single act nor a causal process initiated by a subject and culminating in a set of fixed effects. Construction not only takes place *in* time, but is itself a temporal process which operates through the reiteration of norms; sex is both produced and destabilized in the course of this iteration. As a sedimented effect of a reiterative or ritual practice, sex acquires its naturalized effect, and, yet, it is also by virtue of this reiteration that gaps and fissures are opened up as the constitutive instabilities in such constructions, as that which escapes or exceeds the norm, as that which cannot be wholly defined or fixed by the repetitive labor of that norm. (p. 10, italics in original)

Drawing partially on Foucaultian insights into shifts in historically produced knowledges of sex, Butler (1993) asserts that "[t]he concept of 'sex' is itself troubled terrain" (p. 5). She is critical of constructivist models that persist in maintaining distinctions between the "social" (gender) and the "natural" (sex), especially when a natural or biological sex is counterposed to a socially constructed gender (p. 5) and the former becomes somehow fixed and uninhabited by the social. Thus, in Butler's schema sex, gender, and sexuality are conceived as constructs that might be defined by their "constitutive instability"; therefore, none of these categories represents the truth of one's body or provide the ground for the authenticity of one's sex, gender, or sexuality.

In seeking a movement beyond essentialism and constructivism, Butler (1993) places an emphasis on the value of deconstruction. *Deconstruction* is a term most closely associated with the work of Derrida. Barker (2000) defines Derridean (1984) deconstruction as the " ... 'undoing' of binaries of western philosophy .... In particular, deconstruction involves the dismantling of hierarchical conceptual oppositions ... which serve to guarantee truth by excluding and devaluing the 'inferior' part of the binary." (p. 33)

In *Epistemology of the Closet*, Sedgwick (1990) makes use of this notion of deconstruction to

> ... demonstrate that categories presented in a culture as symmetrical binary oppositions — heterosexual/homosexual, in this case — actually subsist in a more unsettled and dynamic tacit relation according to which, first, term B is not symmetrical with but subordinated to term A; but, second, the ontologically valorized term A actually depends for its meaning on the simultaneous subsumption and exclusion of term B; hence, third, the question of priority between the supposed marginal category of each dyad is irresolvably unstable, an instability caused by the fact that term B is constituted as at once internal and external to term A. (p. 10)

Sedgwick's (1990) deconstructive study of the heterosexual–homosexual binary is not an endeavor to disable this dyad; rather, she suggests "contests for discursive power can be specified as competitions for the material or rhetorical leverage required to set the terms of, and to profit in some way from, the operations of such incoherence of definition" (p. 11). Although Sedgwick reworks Derridean notions of deconstruction to analyze contests for discursive power relating to the heterosexual–homosexual binary, Butler (1993) draws more heavily on Foucault in order to deconstruct the notion of sexed bodies.

By conceiving of bodies as "matter, not as site or surface, but as *a process of materialization that stabilizes over time to produce the effect of boundary, fixity, surface that we call matter*" (Butler, 1993, pp. 8–9, italics in original), Butler is able to analyze the materialization of sexed bodies through regulatory norms (p. 10). This deconstructive analysis relies on a Foucaultian formulation of regulatory power whereby power not only subjects but also inaugurates subjectivities. I argue that the value of the deconstruction of sexual and gender identity categories is also fundamental in the production of discourse related to sexualities and secondary schooling. This ongoing project of deconstructing categories might also be seen as intrinsic to the process of inventing or creating a gay or heterosexual, bisexual, intersex, or transgender life. To "become" (Foucault, 1996g, p. 382) rather than being focused on producing a liberated gay man, lesbian, intersexual, bisexual, transsexual, or heterosexual deconstruction is conceived as a means to constructing a way of life that can yield a culture and an ethics (Foucault, 1996d, p. 310).

In writing about the value of deconstructing categories relating to lesbian and gay identity, Epstein (1993) expresses her ambivalence regarding such an approach. Although agreeing with this movement in theory, she argues,

> I find myself in a certain amount of difficulty in practice. Since lesbian and gay images are virtually absent from the school curriculum (see Epstein, 1994) *any* positive mention seems better than none. It somehow seems a bit 'previous' to start to deconstruct the categories 'lesbian' and 'gay' before they have even been acknowledged within the school context (except, possibly, in the context of AIDS and death) and while invisibility remains a major problem for young lesbians and gays, but especially for young lesbians. (p. 281, italics in original)

Representations of LGBTI-identified people in secondary educational contexts are often still severely constrained (Gard & Meyenn, 2000; MacGillivray & Kozik-Rosabal, 2000). Potentially, the continued invisibility of LGBTI-identified people and related subjects within school curricula might provoke continued caution around strategies of deconstruction. Alternatively, the introduction of deconstructive strategies might provide the means for teachers to engage students in ongoing critical analysis of sexual and gender identities.

In educational contexts and beyond, people who identify as transgender, queer, lesbian, gay, bisexual, intersex, and heterosexual and those who seek to pathologize "perverse" forms of desire deploy varieties of essentialism and constructivism. Sometimes "combinations of the two positions are often held simultaneously by both homophobic and anti-homophobic groups" (Jagose, 1996, p. 9). Tropes of identity are fundamental to people's conceptions of individuals and groups within their culture. Moreover, the tropes people use to describe sexual and gender identities in educational contexts are not neutral; instead, they work to reinscribe particular essentializing or constructivist positions. The ongoing deconstruction of categories is useful because this process facilitates an interrogation of the strategic deployment of particular tropes of identity. Deconstruction also has ethical implications, insofar as the practice of deconstruction avoids the dangerous intellectual paralysis that results from the labeling of such interrogations as redundant or beside the point. I now turn to a consideration of Foucault's theorization of the subject.

FOUCAULT AND THE CONSTRUCTION OF SEXUAL SUBJECTS

Before proceeding with this discussion, it is worthwhile to clarify why I have decided to examine the notion of the subject: How is it relevant to my study of the interrelations between people's conception of sexual and gender identity and the production of discourses related to sexualities and secondary schooling?

In the study of identity, I argue that processes of identification are not synonymous with processes of subjectivization. Although identities are tied to subjectivities, Nixon (1997) argues that subjectivities are not tied to identities. Drawing on Foucaultian theorizing of the subject, Nixon notes, "Subjectivization does not require individuals to be interpellated through mechanisms of identification to secure the working of power knowledge over them … specific discourses can work upon you — can subject you — without necessarily winning you over in your head" (p. 316). Consequently, a study of the subject and subjectivization is important because processes of subjectivization are not the same as processes of identification. However, both are fundamental to the production of discourses related to sexualities and secondary schooling. Next I consider Foucault's contribution to theorizing the subject and related notions of agency and resistance.

Foucault's theorizing of the subject, relations of power, and the circulation of knowledges has been instrumental in the development of major shifts in the way some people comprehend sex, sexualities, and genders. In his earlier work, Foucault (1988) states he focused too much on the regulation of subjects and "on the technology of domination and power" (p. 19). He subsequently becomes more interested "in the interaction between oneself and others and in the technologies of individual domination, the history of how an individual acts upon himself, the technology of the self" (p. 19).

Foucault describes technologies of the self as those

> ... which permit individuals to effect by their own means or with the help of others a certain number of operations on their own bodies and souls, thoughts, conduct, and way of being, so as to transform themselves in order to attain a certain state of happiness, purity, wisdom, perfection, or immortality. (p. 18)

Technologies of domination and power, which were prominent in Foucault's (1988) earlier work, are outlined as follows:

> (1) technologies of production, which permit us to produce, transform or manipulate things; (2) technologies of sign systems, which permit us to use signs, meanings, symbols, or signification; (3) technologies of power, which determine the conduct of individuals and submit them to certain ends or domination, an objectivizing of the subject. (p. 18)

All of these technologies inform this analysis of the production of discourses related to sexualities and secondary schooling. However, Foucault's (1982) formulation of technologies of the self and the processes through which "men have learned to recognize themselves as subjects of 'sexuality'" (p. 208) are the primary focus of this study.

In one of his last interviews, Foucault (1996f) defines processes of subjectivization by saying, "I would call subjectivization the process through which results the constitution of a subject, or more exactly, of a subjectivity which is obviously only one of the given possibilities of organizing a consciousness of the self" (p. 472). Foucault (1988) does not conceive of processes of subjectivization as finite processes with a beginning, middle, and end but as continuous processes driven by the "the interaction between oneself and others" (p. 19). From now on I rely on this term *processes of subjectivization.* The shortened version, *subjectivization*, may be less clumsy, but it fails to adequately convey the proposition of continuing motion inherent in the coupling of *processes* and *subjectivization.*

Foucault's (1982) conceptualization of the processes by which people recognize themselves as sexual subjects is also integral to this study because in this formulation sexual subjectivities are not produced prior to discourse; rather, they are conceived as powerful productions of historically specific regulatory discourses. These discourses come to be understood as truths through repetition, time, and the intersections of power and knowledge.

In linking the production of sexual subjectivities to regulatory discourses, Foucault is also writing against the notion that people have the ability to be straight or gay subjects. In Foucaultian terms no one can ever be the quintessential homosexual. For this reason, Foucault's theorizing of the subject works against the notion that subjects are created via some essence. If people are always in a state of "becoming," then the subjectivities they adopt are necessarily provisional and the question of how individuals might transform the relation of the self to the self becomes more salient. However, the possibilities for organizing a consciousness of the self are not infinite; processes of subjectivization are mediated by points of resistance that are present everywhere in, but not exterior to, relations of power (Foucault, 1990, p. 95).

This question of how much agency Foucault's theorizing allows individuals in processes of subjectivization is addressed by Butler and Connolly (2000), where, in a discussion with Connolly, Butler argues that in Foucaultian terms

> ... the self forms itself, but it forms itself within a set of formative practices that are characterized as modes of subjectivations. That the range of its possible forms is delimited in advance by such modes of subjectivations does not mean that the self fails to form itself .... On the contrary, it is compelled to form itself, but to form itself within forms that are already more or less in place. (p. 22)

Subjectivities are partially formed by external influences, and these influences work to produce agency in processes of subjectivization.

Consequently, agency is socially produced; it is not entirely voluntary or somehow outside relations of power. It is also worth noting that the amount of agency individuals have to form themselves is by no means uniform.

Butler (1997d) conceives of agency as

> ... the assumption of a purpose unintended by power, one that could not have been derived logically or historically, that operates in a relation to contingency and reversal to the power that it makes possible, to which it nevertheless belongs. This is, as it were, the ambivalent scene of agency, constrained by no teleological necessity. (p. 15)

In Butler's formulation, individual subjects have access to a variety of subjectivities through this "ambivalent scene of agency" (p. 15). Agency should not only be conceived of in relation to its constraints, but the notion of agency also speaks to the possibilities of transformation of the self. As such, I consider the constraints placed upon processes of subjectivization in addition to some of the moments when these processes are not constrained by teleological necessity.

Foucault's (1996b) theorizing on processes of subjectivization does enable the development of techniques and strategies that allow for the exercise of agency. However, he does not advocate that agency should be associated with the task of liberation. He asks,

> ... does it make any sense to say, "Let's liberate our sexuality"? Isn't the problem rather that of defining the practices of freedom[11] by which one could define what is sexual pleasure and erotic, amorous and passionate relationships with others? This ethical problem of the definition of practices of freedom, it seems to me, is much more important than the rather repetitive affirmation that sexuality or desire must be liberated ... liberation does not give rise to the happy human being imbued with a sexuality to which the subject could achieve a complete and satisfying relationship. Liberation paves the way for new power relationships, which must be controlled by practices of freedom. (pp. 433, 434)

Producing a manifesto for the liberation of sexual desire in education is not the goal of this book. I strive to disturb the quest for liberation in the production of discourses related to sexuality and schooling. Such quests, as Foucault suggests, inevitably pave "the way for new power relationships" (1996b, p.434) involving new compromises and new inclusions and exclusions.

Though the subject's ability to exercise agency is not discounted in Foucault's (1990) theorizing, I do not wish to overstate the subject's power to resist subjection. Resistance here is understood in the Foucaultian sense, in relation to power, though "never in a position of exteriority in relation to power" (p. 95). Resistance is neither exterior to power nor always linked to intention. Warner (1999) argues resistance has many variations; it "can be either conscious or unconscious: it can be manifest in bodily realms of pleasure or abjection that are not explicitly theorized as norms, but it can just as easily take the form of explicit norms and, indeed, of demands to inhabit a coherent identity" (p. 156). Notions of agency and resistance are critical in Foucault's discussion of ethics. If the subject has no agency and no power to determine its relationship with itself or others, it cannot undertake to invent new relations or modify existing ones in an ethical manner.

I now turn to a study of three modes of objectification of subjects Foucault (1982) outlines in his essay "The Subject and Power." These three modes of objectification are intertwined, and considered together I use them as a theoretical device to interrogate the production of discourses pertaining to LGBTI-identified students and teachers situated in high school settings in Australia and the United States.

THREE MODES OF SUBJECT OBJECTIFICATION

In the course of his scholarship, Foucault (1982) outlines three modes of objectification that "transform human beings into subjects" (p. 208): (1) dividing practices, (2) scientific classification (Foucault, 1965), and processes of subjectivization (Foucault, 1982, p. 208). As indicated already, Foucault's later work focused primarily on processes of subjectivization. Rabinow (1984) describes these three modes of objectification of the subject as follows:

> ... those that categorize, distribute and manipulate (dividing practices); those through which we have come to understand ourselves scientifically (scientific classification); those that we have used to form ourselves into meaning-giving selves (processes of subjectivization). (p. 12)

This theoretical framework for examining the transformation of human beings into subjects provides the scaffolding for the next three chapters of this book. It thus organizes the ensuing analysis of how people in educational contexts are categorized and manipulated by privileged knowledges bounded by relations of power. Although this scaffold is organized around modes of objectification, it also allows for a study of the "ambivalent scene of agency" (Butler, 1993, p. 15), as objectification is not absolute but is a series of processes that must be continuously renegotiated.

For the purposes of this study, these modes of objectification are analyzed primarily in relation to the production of discourses related to LGBTI-identified teachers and students in high school settings. However, these modes of objectification are by no means limited to people who are LGBTI identified; they profoundly influence the lives of all members of school communities, regardless of their sexual and gender identities. As such, these modes of objectification organize this analysis of key discourses related to sexualities and secondary schooling, and they do not preclude a consideration of heterosexual-identified teachers and students.

Though I am critical of some modes of objectification, this is not a treatise against all modes of objectification, at all time, in all places. There can be no denying the frisson of objectification, both in objectifying others and, in turn, in being objectified. Nor should processes of subjectivization and identification be conceived as somehow the antithesis of modes of objectification; rather, processes of subjectivization and identification are both integral aspects of modes of objectification.

I now turn to an analysis of how each of these three modes of objectification is instrumental to this book. Although for the purposes of this study, one chapter focuses primarily on one mode of objectification, it is apparent that these modes are not easily separated one from the other; rather, they all continuously inform and sustain one another. I begin with an analysis of processes of subjectivization and identification, because, as indicated earlier, this mode of objectification is most influential in Foucault's later theorizing on sexuality. I utilize the term *identification* to underscore the instability of identity and the ongoing interrelationship between subjectivity and identity.

Processes of Subjectivization and Identification

Foucault's theorization of processes of subjectivization is predicated on his understanding of disciplinary power. In *Discipline and Punish*, Foucault (1979) defines disciplinary power as a power that is

> ... exercised through its invisibility; at the same time it imposes on those whom it subjects a principle of compulsory visibility. In discipline, it is the subjects who have to be seen .... It is the fact of being constantly seen, of being always able to be seen, that maintains the disciplined individual in his subjection. (p. 187)

Foucault notes that normalization is one of the great instruments of disciplinary power and that the power of normalization imposes homogeneity, but it also individualizes by making it possible to measure gaps (p. 184). For the purposes of this study of processes of subjectivization and identification, what is critical in Foucault's formulation of disciplinary power is his formulation of how normalization

> ... extends power from the sovereignty of the king into micropractices of the self relations, and the body. Thus, much that other conceptions of identity take for granted as natural substrates are, in Foucault's view, highly infused with power and have increasingly become the object of knowledge. The more power infuses everything, the deeper the knowledge of the subject about itself becomes. He argues that an increased emphasis on sovereignty is not the antidote to this normalizing power. Both sovereignty and normalizing power are closely related to one another. (Mayo, 1997, para. 6)

Mayo (1997), in her paper titled "Foucauldian Cautions on the Subject and the Educative Implications of Contingent Identity," contends that Foucault's conceptualization of disciplinary power facilitates a critique of the concept of the individual subject as independent agent. This view of the subject encourages an analysis of the uses and disjunctures of identity, prompting questions about the relationship of identity to exclusion and limitation. Although I concur with Mayo's desire to question identity, I also contemplate people's reluctance to interrogate the contingent foundations of identity.

I also analyze the interrelationship between disciplinary power, normalization, and processes of subjectivization and identification in order to consider how they intersect to produce and compel certain "micropractices of the self." Pursuant to this, it is apparent that if processes of normalization are integrally related to ways of being, they are also integrally related to people's conceptualizations of sexual and gendered identities. In other words, the micropractices of the sexual and gendered self are thus, in part, shaped by "heteronormalizing practices."

In the introduction to *Fear of a Queer Planet,* Warner (1993) employs the term *heteronormalizing practices* to denote practices that privilege heterosexual culture and take heterosexuality as the norm — simultaneously devaluing sexual practices — and sexual and gender identifications deemed to be outside the heterosexual mainstream (p. xxi). In a Foucaultian-inspired analysis, these heteronormalizing practices are not conceived as something imposed from above but, rather, as imperatives to codify sexual relations and to normalize sexual and gender identities. The pressures to marry (someone of the opposite sex) and to have children (with someone of the opposite sex) — to be "normal" — are just two examples of obligations to conform to heteronormalizing "principles of compulsory visibility" (Foucault, 1979, p. 187).

The power relations that shore up these imperatives are often invisible. At this point in time, heteronormalizing practices are all-encompassing. Like the air we breathe (Town, 1998, in Quinlivan & Town, 1999, p. 510), these heteronormalizing practices are difficult to see, yet they are so pervasive they are also a primary source of knowledge about the self. These heteronormalizing practices also can appear elemental (Warner, 1993, p. xxi). Over time, certain understandings of the self can seem so elemental they require no further interrogation; they just are. It is this sense of certainty, this deep knowledge of the subject brought about by the effective operation of heteronormalizing practices, that provides a cloak of invisibility so aptly described by Rich (1993) as "compulsory heterosexuality" (1993). Even as heterosexuality may appear compulsory, however, this compulsion is resisted and disrupted.

The search for "gaps and fissures" (Butler, 1993, p. 10) in normalizing processes is a critical element of queer theorizing. In an interview with Jagose on the subject of "Queer World Making," Warner argues that although resistance to heteronormalization might be considered an integral aspect of queering, this is not the same as saying that "queerness resists all norms" (Jagose & Warner, 2000, para. 23), which is a somewhat reductionist view of queer theorizing.[12] Rather, it is to recognize that a critical part of queer world making is an acknowledgement that "[j]ust because something is statistically normal doesn't mean it should be normative" (para. 22). For instance, a Foucaultian and queer theoretical analysis of processes of subjectivization and identification informs this inquiry; thus, it is invested in a proliferation of its own "normative insights" (para. 24).

My analysis of processes of subjectivization and identification is also informed by Britzman's (1998) version of queer pedagogy. Acknowledging the significance of Foucault in the development of the modes of questioning that inform queer theories (p. 151), Britzman describes her queer pedagogy as that which attends to "what it is that structures the ways in which feelings are imagined and read" (p. 84). Processes of subjectivization and identification are evident in the ways people talk about themselves, their expressions of feelings, and their behaviors and identities. I am not seeking to discern the meaning behind these stories but, rather, to look at what stories are told. I am looking for recurring themes in people's stories, and I am looking for differences, for new departures, for gaps and fissures, and for silences. I undertake this analysis through an exploration of the production of essentializing tropes and tropes of choice. I also highlight the contingency of identities that circulate in educational contexts via a consideration of gender and sexual identities as catachrestic conversions.

Scientific Classification

The second step in this study of the modes of objectification of subjects focuses on "modes of inquiry which try to give themselves the status of sciences" (Foucault, 1982, p. 208) and on the implications of deploying particular scientific classifications in educational discourses relating to genders and sexualities. Foucault's analysis of scientific classification is prompted in part by the following question: "What are the relations we have to truth through scientific knowledge, to those 'truth games' which are so important in civilization and in which we are both subject and object?" (Foucault & Martin, 1988, p. 15)

Offering a counterpoint to the idea that the rigorous production of a specific knowledge equates to truth, Foucault (1980a) defines truth as "the ensemble of rules according to which the true and the false are separated and specific effects of power attached to the true" (pp. 132–133). If truth is an assemblage, produced by a game, then it is possible to have many rules "according to which the true and the false are separated and specific effects of power attached to the true" (pp. 132–133). Following from this understanding of truth in its relation to power, Foucault poses the question, "What rules of right are implemented by the relations of power in the production of discourses of truth?" (p. 93) Drawing on this Foucaultian formulation of truth, I am not prompted to seek the truth regarding the etiology of sexuality but, rather, to consider "the ensemble of rules" that produce truths relating to sexual and gender identities within and around educational contexts. More specifically, I consider how particular scientific classifications come to produce certain authoritative "truths" related specifically to young people, sexualities, and schooling.

Particular knowledges do not only gain currency via their attachment to scientificity, however. Warner (1999) has argued a particular story (or knowledge) may "become dominant both because it is what many people want to hear and because it is *all* they hear" (p. 132, italics in original). In order to further examine the interplay between relations of power-knowledge, objectification, and competing "games of truth" (Foucault, 1996b, pp. 445, 446), Foucault turns his attention to the study of what he calls "disqualified" or "subjugated knowledges."

In seeking to distinguish between subjugated and authoritative knowledges, Foucault (1980b) contends "subjugated knowledges" might be characterized as "naive knowledges, located low down on the hierarchy, beneath the required level of cognition or scientificity" (p. 82). Hence, knowledges may be "disqualified as inadequate to their task" (p. 82) by virtue of their lack of scientificity. Foucault undertakes to study subjugated knowledges in order to consider their "claims to attention ... against the claims of a unitary body of theory which would filter, hierarchize and order them in the name of some true knowledge and some arbitrary idea of what constitutes a science and its objects" (p. 82). In such a formulation, subjugated knowledges are studied as a means to recognize how knowledges are hierarchized and ordered. Conversely, by studying everyday truths that prevail in discourses related to sexualities and secondary schooling, it may be possible to ascertain how other knowledges become subjugated.

Related to this analysis of truth is a consideration of the creation of what Foucault (1990) terms "reverse" discourses. Disqualified knowledges may be seen as part of a reverse discourse (p. 101). A reverse discourse is "in no way the 'same' as the discourse it reverses. Indeed its desire for reversal is a desire for transformation" (Jagose & Halberstam, 1999, para. 10). Thus, as the name suggests, reverse discourses are inextricably tied to the discourses they desire to transform and to their associated truths and knowledges.

In writing about reverse discourses in relation to homosexuality, Foucault (1990) argues that although the appearance of psychiatric and legal discourses on homosexuality and other "perversions" increased the regulation of particular groups of individuals, these discourses also enabled

> ... homosexuality to speak in its own behalf, to demand that its legitimacy or "naturality" be acknowledged, often in the same vocabulary, using the same categories by which it was medically disqualified. (p. 101)

These reverse discourses pose an ongoing problem within identity politics and queer theorizing relating to how it is possible to promote agency when relying on problematic identities for legitimacy. Butler (1997d) asks, "If subordination is the condition of possibility for agency, how might agency be thought in opposition to the forces of subordination?" (p. 10). In *Excitable Speech*, Butler (1997b) partially responds to this question by arguing that "agency begins where sovereignty wanes. The one who acts (who is not the same as a sovereign subject) acts precisely to the extent that he or she is constituted as an actor and, hence, operating within a linguistic field of enabling constraints from the outset" (p. 16). Given this conception of agency, it is possible to see how reverse discourses might describe the potential for "homosexuality to speak on its own behalf," but only within the constraints of the heterosexual/homosexual binary.

I consider how an assortment of religious, educational, and medical institutions; students; teachers; and participants in this study is implicated in the ongoing construction of tropes associated with scientificity. In addition to identifying particular tropes that have become authoritative through recourse to scientificity, I also consider the political climates that help to sustain these tropes and some of the ethical implications that ensue from their continued production.

Dividing Practices

A third mode of inquiry Foucault (1982) employs in order to study the objectification of subjects involves an analysis of "dividing practices." It is through the use of these practices that "[t]he subject is either divided inside himself or divided from others. This process objectivizes him. Examples are the mad and the sane, the sick and the healthy, the criminals and the 'good boys'" (p. 208). One could easily add heterosexuals and homosexuals to this list — and maybe gays and queers. Rabinow (1984) writes that these dividing practices might be understood as "modes of manipulation that combine the mediation of a science (or pseudo-science) and the practices of exclusion, usually in a spatial sense, but always in a social one" (p. 8).

In *Foucault and Education,* Ball (1990) argues that dividing practices saturate the major disciplines within education:

> ... Dividing practices are critically interconnected with the formation, and increasingly sophisticated elaboration, of the educational sciences: educational psychology, pedagogics, the sociology of education, cognitive and developmental psychology ... . Knowledge and practices drawn from the educational sciences provided ... modes of classification, control and containment. (p. 4)

It might also be argued that these "educational sciences," which produce a range of dividing practices, are generally focused on seeking to improve the school climate for all students. Accordingly, dividing practices interrelated with these sciences, including various modes of classification and containment, may appear to be developed as a result of struggles to protect the rights of individuals (such as LGBTI-identified teachers and students) who are objectified by educational institutions. And people may develop passionate attachments to these dividing practices.

Although dividing practices are perceptible in education, the central question pertaining to these and other modes of objectification may not be apparent. In discussing the three modes of objectification of subjects, Foucault (1982) argues that

> ... all these present struggles [related to modes of objectification] revolve around the question: Who are we? ... the main objective of these struggles is to attack not so much "such or such" an institution or form of power, or group, or elite, or class, but rather a technique, a form of power. (p. 212)

As such, " ... these struggles are not exactly for or against the 'individual,' but rather they are struggles against the 'government of individualization'" (p. 212). However, sometimes this notion that these struggles pertain to techniques of power is lost; instead, these struggles are characterized as reflecting the individual's particular desires or intentions.

Butler's (1993) theory of performativity is useful in considering these struggles Foucault refers to in relation to modes of objectification. For Butler, a performative such as queer works to the extent that it *"draws on and covers over* the constitutive conventions by which it is mobilized" (p. 227, italics in original). Thus, performativity "has a history that not only precedes but conditions its contemporary usages, and that this history effectively decenters the presentist view of the subject as the exclusive origin or owner of what is said" (p. 227). Butler's (1997b) notion of performativity makes it possible to see how struggles related to modes of objectification, such as dividing practices, are not specifically related to individuals but instead to techniques of power that endeavor to control or classify individuals through interpellations such as queer, lesbian, gay, and straight. These techniques or forms of power shift through the continuous performance of speech acts produced within broader historical contexts, not by virtue of a "singular act used by an already established subject" (p. 160).

For instance, a performative such as queer may be effectively deployed as a dividing practice in the schoolyard, but it might also incite insurrectionary acts revolving around the question "Who are we?" These dividing practices and insurrectionary acts may have material effects upon individual bodies. The insurrectionary acts referred to here are understood to take place in "[t]hat moment in which a speech act without prior authorization nevertheless assumes authorization [and] in the course of its performance may anticipate and instate altered contexts for its future reception" (Butler, 1997b, p. 160). As a consequence, I explore moments when dividing practices might be disrupted by a speech act that unexpectedly "assumes authorization" and, in so doing, alters the contexts of its future reception, notwithstanding the dividing practices that constrain such insurrectionary acts.

In clarifying one of his purposes in studying dividing practices, Foucault (1982) writes that in order "[t]o find out what our society means by sanity perhaps we should investigate what is happening in the field of insanity" (p. 211). In keeping with this mode of thought, I consider dividing practices deployed in relation to LGBTI-identified teachers and students in order to find out what is happening in the broader field of sexualities, genders, and schooling. In particular, I turn my attention to the production of discursive, spatializing, and temporizing dividing practices and consider the techniques of power imbricated in these struggles of objectification of subjects. I also interrogate how dividing practices operate to create internal divisions, divisions between the self and others, and external divisions, differentiating between groups.

Conclusion

Identity, subjectivity, constructivism, and essentialism are all integral to the production of discourses related to sexualities and secondary schooling. Thus, in this chapter I considered the notion of identity and analyzed some of the problems of identity politics, and I considered different approaches people have proposed in dealing with these problems. Building on this study of identity, I turned to an analysis of essentialism and constructivism and explored the efficacy of using deconstruction as an analytical tool in the study of identity.

Moving on from the matter of identity, I turned to theories of the subject. More specifically, I discussed Foucault's theorizing on "technologies of the self" and related notions of agency and resistance, and I introduced his three modes of objectification of subjects. Processes of subjectivization and identification are my principal focus in the following chapter. As indicated previously, I prioritize the study of this mode of objectification because of the significance it plays in Foucault's later theorizing. More specifically, I analyze the production of essentializing tropes and tropes of choice in secondary educational contexts. I also consider how a process of interrogating sexual and gender identities as catachrestic conversions might disturb these tropological formations.

4

Processes of
Subjectivization and Identification

... Everything perceived is only evident
when surrounded by a familiar
and poorly known horizon.

(Foucault, 1997, p. 144)

The sense that something can be familiar yet poorly known inspires Foucault's (1997) "ethics of discomfort." Often things we hold dear appear so well known they seem axiomatic. This study of processes of subjectivization and identification in educational contexts is inspired by this "ethics of discomfort" (Foucault, 1997). By surveying the undistinguished horizons of the sexual and gender identities people hold familiar in the area of sexualities and secondary schooling, it is possible to question the established and the everyday. I adapt rhetorical tools in order to conduct this study of some familiar tropical formations and to suggest alternative ways of thinking about identity categories.

In the previous chapter, I argued that certain understandings of sexual and gender identities can seem so elemental that they require no further interrogation. My task in this chapter is to challenge such cocksureness in the production of discourses related to sexualities and secondary schooling. To this end, I consider how tropes of essentialism and constructivism,[1] or what I term *choice*, operate as instruments of heteronormalization. I employ the term choice in my analysis of constructivist notions of identity because it is widely used in discourses related to sexualities and secondary schooling. In my selection of the word, I also recognize that the notion of choice is problematic because of its tendency to imply an easy voluntarism in the assumption of sexual and gender identities.

Troping describes "the process by which all discourse *constitutes* the objects which it pretends only to describe realistically and to analyze objectively" (White, 1978, p. 2, italics in original). As such, tropes are part of the "complex machinery for producing true discourses on sex" (Foucault, 1990, p. 68) and "true discourses" on sexualities and secondary schooling. I will demonstrate how tropes structure the stories we tell ourselves and the stories we tell others. I also explore tropes of essentialism and choice with a view to determining their strategic value and their shortcomings. Inspired by White (1978), I also consider some of the ethical implications that may ensue from the strategies people use to produce different versions of reality through discourse.

In addition to analyzing tropical formations of essentialism and choice, I explore the efficacy of conceiving of sexual and gender identities as catachreses. Some catachreses gradually become familiar, whereas others remain on the borders of discourses relating to sexualities and schooling. This study points to the role catachreses play in the sustenance and disruption of heteronormalizing processes that objectify the subject, beginning with an analysis of essentializing tropes of identity.

THE TROPE OF SEXUAL AND GENDER IDENTITY AS SOMEHOW ESSENTIAL

The notion that people's sexual and gender identities are in some way essential often emerged in interviews with participants. As indicated in the previous chapter, there is no definitive brand of essentialism, but it is often associated with the idea that identities are somehow fundamental and therefore are incapable of change. Essentializing tropes are manifest in various ways in the production of discourses related to sexualities and secondary schooling, and this section considers some of these variations and some of their potential consequences.

Born That Way

I now turn to an analysis of some of the implications of deploying essentializing tropes and unitary identity categories in an effort to secure rights and protections for LGBTI teachers and students. I commence with excerpts from my interview with Gail Rolf, a teacher and coordinator of Project 10² in the Los Angeles Unified School District (LAUSD). In this interview Rolf draws on one prominent trope of essentialism, insofar as she situates sexual and gender identities as transhistorical manifestations of a biological essence.

Rolf calls on familiar narratives of growing up "queer" in the United States as evidence of her essential lesbian identity. She indicates she was "born that way," saying, "I swear that while I was in the womb I knew I was a baby queer and there was no question about it [laughs]." One implication of this trope of identity is that if one is born a lesbian, one will always be a lesbian. Such narratives of sexual and gender identity are well known; many people express the belief that such identities are biologically based.

Responding to my inquiry about what motivates her to work on issues related to lesbian and gay teachers and students, Rolf notes her inspirations as follows:

> Well that probably comes from my own experience, being lesbian and knowing from early on … . So I was one of those children who grew up with my own terrible emotional struggle over it. It was my secret, my burden — I never told anybody. I was fearful of being found out all of my life, even through adulthood, and it was a terrible, terrible emotional price to pay.

> I went through the *typical* struggles with depression and thoughts about suicide. I fortunately never got into drug abuse, or running away, or other destructive behaviors … . Ultimately I had to get into my own process of getting okay with myself and being accepting of who I am as a lesbian woman. (italics added for emphasis)

Rolf's narrative of growing up as a lesbian interprets this identity as something intrinsic — something that may be revealed and accepted but probably not easily denied without causing harm to the self and others. She appears comfortable in relating her own narrative about "getting okay with" herself and triumphing over the "typical" struggles with the closet.

In the previous chapter, I drew on the work of Grossberg (1992) to argue that essentialism "can operate to tie a person's identity to an array of 'necessary consequences' and performances"

(p. 30). This characterization of essentialism is apparent in Rolf's perception of depression and suicide as typically connected to the process of coming to terms with one's sexual identity. In Rolf's narrative it is possible to see how depression and suicide might act as markers of authenticity, reinforcing the truth of her identity.

Although Rolf does not consider herself "an expert in the area of human sexuality," she feels she knows about the nature of sexual identities. She states,

> ... What I do know is that homosexuals exist, always have, always will, unless of course we have genetic engineering in the future that might eliminate our population altogether. Secondly, bisexuality has always existed, always will. And heterosexuality has always existed. And now we are looking at things such as pansexuality,[3] and transsexuality, and transgenderism, and a whole host of things. What concerns me most is that we simply acknowledge that we all exist and what's important to me is that we all learn to coexist and be mutually accepting of one another and to be affirming and validating and loving and nurturing and to break down any barriers that might exist because of our sexuality.

In this excerpt, Rolf expresses her belief that people "learn to coexist" when they can accept one another's intrinsic sexual differences. Tolerance of difference thus becomes part of a broader discourse that situates homosexuality as biologically essential. "Deviant subjectivities" (Terry, 1995, pp. 137–138) such as homosexuality and transexuality are thus continuously reproduced by means of these powerful and familiar connections.

Although Rolf appears to link peaceful coexistence to acceptance of the transhistorical[4] and biological nature of sexual identities, she also argues against the notion that coexistence and mutual acceptance should be predicated on essential notions of identity. She says, "Whether it's a choice or whether it's genetic really should be of no consequence; it is *who you are*" (italics added for emphasis). Regardless of how individuals come to define themselves (using tropes of choice or essentializing tropes), Rolf argues that individuals' sexual or gender identity is fundamental to their sense of self and therefore is worthy of protection. On these grounds Rolf advocates for the " ... right to be who *we* are. And as long *we* are not hurting ourselves, *we* are not hurting children and *we* are not hurting others, whose business is it? (italics added for emphasis)" The "right to be who we are" is not founded upon an essence but on people's right to be left alone as long as they are not harming others. At face value the desire to "be who we are" appears defensible and desirable. Do not students and teachers routinely labeled as the "we" of gay and lesbian in educational discourses deserve protection in schoolyards and in staffrooms?

However, invoking this "we" may be problematic for a number of reasons. If the State is no guarantor of the rights of minority groups (Butler, 1997b, pp. 23–24), then organizing around minority identities may result in the erosion of rights rather than the protection of them. According to Phelan (1997), "conceptualizing gays and lesbians as distinct people" (p. 65) also raises the critical question of just who is represented by organizations that claim to speak for the "we" of gays and lesbians. When Rolf speaks of the "right to be who we are," who does this we represent? In his analysis of the notion of race, Gilroy (2000) argues that the perilous pronoun "we" forces us to reckon with the patterns of inclusion and exclusion it cannot help creating (p. 99).

For Gilroy (2000), the "we" of identity is most perilous "once it has been engaged tactically or in manipulative, deliberately oversimple ways ... and when the idea of a fundamentally shared identity becomes a platform for the reverie of absolute and eternal division" (p. 101). These platforms of absolute and eternal division may be created by the tendency to analogize the experiences of gays and lesbians with other minorities in order to secure the right to be who we are. This strategy may place the experiences of both groups outside the realm of "permanent political contest" (Butler, 1993, p. 222). Phelan (1997) argues that if we are to avoid sloppy theory and bad politics, such analogies should be avoided in favor of strategies that pay careful attention to the various dimensions of, and forms of, oppression (p. 65). Although the "we" of identity is sometimes perilous, this is not to say there is no value in strategic essentialism. However, those who organize using essentializing tropes should be wary of their limitations and should remember the importance of Butler's (1993) double movement when utilizing "categories without which we cannot do" (Cheah & Grosz, 1998).

Fantasy, Behavior, Identity

Fantasy, behavior, and identity (FBI) are three categories some of the people interviewed for this study use to account for differences within LGBTI communities without displacing the authority of essentializing tropes of identity. In the framework provided by these categories, it is possible for individuals to make choices about their behaviors and identities. However, generally these choices are perceived to be founded on the rejection or acceptance of fantasies that represent the truth of one's identity. In this section, I consider the role of the FBI trio in sustaining essentializing identities and then turn to a study of the comfort of identity.

Rolf makes a clear distinction between behavior and orientation. For Rolf, sexual orientation, like fantasy, is situated as an inherent and reliable indicator of who or what you are. Although orientation may be something essential, Rolf also states that people's sexual orientation is not always a reliable indicator of their behavior. She states,

> In talking with psychiatrists and psychologists who have worked in the field and looking at studies and readings they will say that people are all over the place in terms of sexual behavior. And I think we have to separate sexual behavior from sexual orientation or sexual identity. Sexual orientation is who or what you are, it's your sexuality; it's how you perceive yourself as male or as female, and how you see yourself in the world in terms of relationships, in terms of heterosexual, homosexual, bisexual … . How we act out sexually is sometimes different … .

Concurring with psychiatric and psychological studies that portray sexual orientation as somehow essential and distinct from sexual behavior, Rolf is comfortable drawing a distinction between behavior and orientation. People might behave inconsistently (e.g., women might have sex with men when they are lesbian identified), but this inconsistency in behavior does not change someone's orientation. Implicit within this perspective is a belief in an underlying pattern of consistent behavior at least theoretically associated with particular sexual orientations.

Several participants shared variations of Rolf's understanding of sexual orientation as somehow essential. For instance, Derek Williams, a co-convenor of GaLTaS (Gay and Lesbian Teachers' and Students' group),[5] draws on the insights of Amanda Nickson, another Australian participant in this study, in order to elaborate on his understanding of the formation of sexual identities.

Mary Lou: Can you discuss how you understand the nature of sexual identities? I am trying to get people to talk about how they think we become lesbian or gay or straight or whatever.

Derek: Well I heard Amanda Nickson give a talk one day, and I just really thought it crystallized things so well and I have remembered it ever since. FBI (Fantasy, Behavior, Identity) ... . I think that covers the whole gamut of sexual identities, behaviors, and fantasies. Many people have a fantasy about some sexual behavior with a person of the same gender. They might go through their whole life and never do anything. They would identify as heterosexual, and one day when they are in their fifties they may go from F to B, fantasy to behavior, ... This has happened to many people that I know, *that they always were homosexual and they were just playing the identity game.* They were being straight because mum and dad, 2.2 kids, and a dog called Spot all said that you had to be straight ... . That's why we have people who have the fantasy, who might have the covert behavior, but who won't have the identity ... this fantasy, identity thing, *I think it's something that every homosexual person comes to terms with.* (italics added for emphasis)

The FBI formula, as related by Williams, is founded on the idea that people have essential sexual fantasies or orientations; sometimes people may choose not to fulfill their fantasies because this fulfillment would involve behavior that would be socially frowned upon. However, for Williams, individuals' behavior is somehow beside the point. Regardless of their behavior, if they have the fantasies, "they always were homosexual and they were just playing the identity game."

The underpinnings of the FBI notion are problematized by Phelan (1997). According to Phelan, such notions allow for the construction of discourses, such as Williams's, in which people who exhibit behavior later in life may only be understood as "'late bloomers': people who were 'really' homosexual but didn't recognize it (or admit it to themselves) until later in life" (p. 64). Thus, essentializing tropes attached to the FBI equation may operate to characterize people as suppressing their identity (possibly to their own detriment) or, alternatively, the FBI equation may be situated as "something that every homosexual person comes to terms with." Thus, people who come out of the closet and come to terms with their fantasies will move to action and eventually to identification.

The FBI equation to which Williams alludes is manifest in the strategies he uses to demand access to educational services for students with a broad range of sexual and gender identities. In his capacity as a co-convener of GaLTaS, Williams assisted Christopher Tsakalos in his court case against the New South Wales Department of School Education.[6] In response to allegations that "teachers had told Tsakalos to 'walk like a man,'" Williams is reported to have said "there's no way he can straighten up his image" (Angelo, 1997, p. 4). Williams thus seeks protection for Tsakalos at least partially on the grounds that this young man has no agency in regard to the performance of his identity. The value of confirming people's agency in determining their own identities was touched on in the previous chapter (Butler, 1997d, p. 15; McWhorter, 1999, p. 75). Deploying essentializing notions of identity could have the deleterious effect of closing down political contest of a particular identification, and it may also be invoked to a minority's detriment by an unsympathetic state or school district (Butler, 1997b, p. 22).

In a similar vein to Williams, Tsakalos is reported as saying, "How can someone change a black man to a white man? … I like the way I am and I can't change the way I walk, the way I act, the way I talk because I've tried it before and I don't feel me" (Angelo, 1997, p. 1). Although the value of deploying such essentializing analogies in order to garner rights is questionable (Phelan, 1997, p. 65), Tsakalos's and Williams's comments might still be interpreted as a principled act of resistance. In a school culture that demonizes effeminacy, these men embrace this young man's camp walk and talk and do not shy away from the palpable discomfort it causes himself and others. His refusal to "walk like a man" thus challenges heteronormalizing orthodoxies about what is and is not appropriate for young men. His "sissy boy"[7] performance may thus read be as a declaration that nontraditional masculinities are legitimate and worthy of respect, within and outside the space of the school.

The Tsakalos case underscores the problems and possibilities of strategic essentialism. His insistence that his sexual identity and camp behavior are intrinsic might be employed as a justification for homophobic assault, or, equally, they might be called upon as a strategy to garner rights. Tropes of choice may be just as problematic. If people choose to identify as gay, this may be considered a justification for violence or for a greater recognition of the contingent foundations of all sexual and gender identities. The exercise of homophobic violence is therefore not dependent on the sustenance of a particular trope of identity. However, when essentializing tropes come unhinged from the double movement Butler (1993) describes in the previous chapter, people's capacity to deconstruct heteronormalizing discourses is constrained.

Essentialism and Comfort

Various essentializing tropes of identity remain popular in the production of discourses related to sexualities and secondary schooling. These tropes are called upon by participants in this study: people who work in programs designed to support LGBTI-identified teachers and students in high school settings. Young people also deploy essentializing tropes, as is the case with Tsakalos. Consequently, it is worth considering further people's attachments to essentializing tropes.

In her study of the politics of gay and lesbian identities, Whisman (1996) is critical of essentializing tropes. She argues that "predicating the legitimacy of homosexuality on its not being a choice is profoundly heterosexist ... to the extent that homosexuality is acceptable only if it is not chosen it remains stigmatized, illegitimate, deviant" (p. 6). Whisman goes on to argue that the persistence of tropes of essentialism may be explained by people's need for self-preservation in a homophobic climate. Phelan (1997) suggests that such tropes are popular because they "may perhaps offer some hope for equality in a liberal pluralist society" (p. 64). In my mind, the suggestion that essentializing tropes are "devices which individuals select and use because of what they can do for one in the negotiation of a hostile world" (Whisman, 1996, p. 7) only partially explains people's investments in these particular tropes of identity.

Processes of subjectivization and identification are produced through relations of power, as Whisman (1996) and Phelan (1997) suggest, but particular identities are not just a response to hostility or political efficacy. This section looks briefly at Holliday's (1999) discussion of Freudian psychoanalytic theorizing on the formation of identities in order to consider the comfort to be found in essentialism. Drawing on the work of Lewis and Rolly (1997) and Probyn (1995), Holliday proposes that

> [u]nlike popular notions of narcissism (defined as self-love), Freud's position is not about desire for one's own reflection but for what the self would like to be: an idealized self, but also an identification *with* the object — a desire to be it and to be desired by it. Thus, narcissistic desire is both desire *for* and desire *to be* one's idealized self. (p. 488, italics in original)

Adding to this interpretation of Freud's concept of narcissism, Holliday (1999) states, " ... Queer subjects both desire the objects of their gaze (others whom one identifies with an idealized version of oneself) and want to be their desired object, to be objectified by them. This scenario explains how shared cultural codes ... circulate in queer subcultures" (pp. 488, 489).

Holliday's (1999) theorizing of the narcissistic tendencies of desire provides another level of understanding regarding people's investments in essentializing tropes. These tropes help sustain an economy of desire — an economy that continuously forms idealized versions of the gay and lesbian self, contemporaneously forming a loosely recognizable group of subjects to be objectified by and, in turn, to objectify. Hence, this economy of desire may be another compelling factor in explaining people's sustenance of essentializing tropes.

Subsequent to her theorization of "the comfort of identity," Holliday (1999) goes on to argue that comfort with one's identity

> ... is an easy, unthinking state ... . The comfort of a more liberal state and some protection from discrimination in the workplace have all produced a more comfortable (lesbian and gay) identity and politics. But perhaps comfort is to be feared since it is discomfort, displacement, disruption which moves (queer) politics (and selves) forward into a more complex and less exclusive or complacent place. (p. 489)

An "ethics of discomfort" might be conceived as an appropriate theoretical response to essentializing tropes of sexual and gender identities, which is not to suggest a strategy that advocates a constant state of discomfort. The notion that people might benefit from a state of disruption and displacement all of the time would be politically naive. A balance is required between the comfort (material, sexual, personal, and political) provided by identities and the complex questioning of the very foundations of those same identities. As discussed in the next section, however, the manifold ways people navigate the tropics of choice in educational contexts are often resistant to an ethics of discomfort.

THE TROPE OF CHOICE

The notion that people might have some agency in the construction of their sexual and gender identities was discussed in the previous chapter. Foucault's (1996e) notion that "[t]o be gay is to be in a state of becoming" (p. 370) rests in part on the understanding that the development of identities is an ongoing task and is contrary to the idea that identities are somehow essential, insofar as essentialism refers to ontological or transhistorical stability. Rather than talking about becoming gay, participants in this study invoke the trope of choice; they talk about people choosing their identities. This trope of choice is sometimes used to imply that sexual and gender identities are easily selected and easily discarded. If identities are merely chosen, it is sometimes suggested, then this means that those who hold them are somehow less worthy of protection than those whose identities may seem immutable, such as those whose identities may be based on skin color or ethnicity.

Although tropes of choice may imply voluntarism, the tropology of choice is devilishly confusing. As indicated in the previous chapter, Butler and Connolly (2000) suggest the self "is compelled to form itself, but to form itself within forms that are already more or less in place" (p. 22). Those who use the language of choice may concur with Butler and Connolly and may argue that processes of subjectivization and identification imply varying degrees of individual agency, but not free will. Equally, some people might argue that tropes of choice are synonymous with free will.

This section considers some of the issues participants identified in relation to the deployment of tropes of choice in the production of discourses related to sexual and gender identities in high school settings. This discussion draws on my analysis of constructivism in the previous chapter to consider how sexual and gender identities are produced, destabilized, and affirmed under the rubric of choice and its various contestations and political attachments. However, like constructivism and essentialism, there is no agreement among participants in this study about how choice might be constituted or deployed. Furthermore, it is apparent that choice is not conceived as the binary opposite of essentialism or as synonymous with constructivism.

Putting Choice in the Closet?

Tropes of choice were often raised in my interviews with participants, only to be quickly discounted. Here I consider examples of the concerns participants expressed about the deployment of choice and our related discussions of why tropes of choice often become closeted in secondary educational contexts. In these discussions I encouraged participants to elaborate on their ambivalence toward choice and to talk about how tropes of choice featured in their conversations with different members of the school community, including students, teachers, parents, and executive staff.[8]

Barbara Blinick, a history teacher in a San Francisco high school and a long-time activist with regard to sexualities and schooling, generally relies on essentializing tropes in school settings in spite of her belief that "maybe it is a choice." Here she offers an explanation of her deployment of essentializing tropes in specific locations:

> I often argue that sexuality isn't a choice to parents (of students) because it is just so much easier. People understand it better that way. But I've been around Linda[9] too long, and I've started saying things like well maybe it is a choice. And the kids get really freaked out by that, and really relieved too, in a weird way. But it makes it much more complicated because then it's sort of all up to them. It's not about what is innate in them anymore. And it gets really confusing for young people. Although I think it's so confusing anyway when they are teenagers I'm not really sure if it does really matter. I think that the work that I have done and the curriculum I have written and taught tends to be much more conservative about sexual identity, you know it talks about it in many ways that could be conceived as an essentialist identity.

> ... But the problem with parents is they are really ready to take on blame. They are not blaming the kid, but they are asking, "Why is my kid gay?" I don't really want them to go there yet, but it's immediately where they go if I tell them it's societal. So I don't emphasize it for that reason.

Blinick raises several issues in this extract. There is a sense that she has made a deliberate decision not to talk to parents about choice because of her expectation that many parents would have difficulty accepting a narrative in which a student expresses a choice to be gay. Allied to this is the concern that parents might potentially hold their child, or their child's teacher, accountable for their child's choice of identity. If parents are dissatisfied with their child's choice, this could have serious negative repercussions for their teacher or the child, or both. In short, the probability of blame's becoming a factor may increase when the trope of choice is introduced into the equation.

Although Blinick is reluctant to talk to parents using tropes of choice, her relationship with students is less straightforward. She observes that students she works with "get really freaked out ... and really relieved too, in a weird way" when she discusses tropes of choice because this means their sexuality is not something beyond their control but is "up to them." Given that so much of contemporary U.S. and Australian culture is deeply predicated on essentializing tropes of identity, a combination of relief and discomfort is an understandable response to the suggestion that sexual identities are not permanently fixed. However, as indicated in the previous chapter, the notion that young people's sexual identities are simply "up to them" is somewhat misleading. Schools and the broader society produce sexual and gender identities, and students are compelled to mold themselves into forms already more or less in place (Butler & Connolly, 2000; Epstein & Johnson, 1998, p. 194).

In the same way as with parents, Blinick is reluctant to deploy tropes of choice with executive staff within her school "because then I become subversive as a teacher, as an out gay teacher, and that becomes really complicated." In response to a query about why tropes of choice are subversive in the mouths of gay teachers, Blinick responds as follows:

> Because I am a visible role model ... . That's the whole argument of the conservatives — why there shouldn't be gay teachers in the classroom — because we are influencing kids. And the fact is we might be influencing kids ... . The biggest fear is that we are influencing kids to be gay, and that's why it is really dangerous for me to talk about it in that way. I do it more among friends and colleagues that I like and trust, if I have to do it. But I don't tend to do it. I haven't really thought about it, but I think that that's probably the biggest issue — it is that I don't want to be perceived as a threat for that reason.

Rather than refute the notion that teachers can influence kids to be gay, Blinick acknowledges that discussion of tropes of choice in educational contexts may have some bearing on students' identities. A student who thinks she cannot possibly be transgender or lesbian because she was not born that way might be more apt to consider these identities if they are not presented by teachers as somehow essential. Recognition of the possibility that young people might choose nonheterosexual identities based on exposure to tropes of choice is extremely politically contentious. People working on issues related to sexuality and young people may therefore rely, intentionally or unintentionally, on essentializing tropes to refute allegations (Cahill & Theilheimer, 1999; Taylor, 1994) such as the one authored by Crick (2001) of the Culture and Family Institute:

> Under the rubric of "safety," "tolerance" and "eliminating homophobia," homosexuality is being normalized in our nation's schools ... . Such programs are now reaching even into the elementary level, where children have a hard time distinguishing between "tolerance" and "acceptance." In older grade levels, "gay–straight" alliances are being formed to recruit sexually confused kids. Often members are steered toward off-campus activities with older homosexuals. (para. 15, 16)

It is apparent that Blinick's concerns about being targeted for influencing kids to be gay are by no means unfounded. Such an admission could expose her to criticism from allies and homophobes alike. This criticism links programs to support LGBTI-identified young people with notions of recruitment into the homosexual lifestyle and exposure to older homosexuals.

Blinick's cognizance of these "truth games" (Foucault & Martin, 1988, p. 15) relating to the production of tropes of choice and essentializing tropes is not apparent in the *Almanac of Gay and Lesbian America* (Witt, Thomas, & Marcus, 1995). The authors express their frustration that "despite all the science and research that has been done, myths about lesbians and gay men persist" (p. 357). Witt et al.'s frustration may stem from the belief that scientific knowledges might somehow act as a suppressant to the perpetuation of specific discourses that strive to denigrate people who identify as gay or lesbian. There is no account here of the "tactical productivity" or "strategic integration" (Foucault, 1990, p. 102) of essentializing tropes complicit in perpetuating the truth games that ensure the ongoing persistence of competing myths about lesbians and gay men.

Those who would seek to malign gays and lesbians are aware of the "tactical productivity" of using media airtime to reproduce discourses of gays and lesbians as child molesters.

> ... On a recent television talk show addressing gay parenting, ... a homophobic fundamentalist was placed on the panel ... . Instead of being able to discuss the complex legal, moral, and social issues surrounding gay parenting, the lesbian and gay panelists spent almost the entire hour debating with the fundamentalist panelist about whether gay people are child molesters and want to have kids to "turn" them gay. (Witt et al., 1995, p. 357)

Scientific facts or statistics relating to child molestation are no bar to the perpetuation of such discourses. Rather than express frustration at the perpetuation of homophobic discourses, Blinick strives to operate within these force relations.

As indicated in the previous excerpt, people who identify as gay and lesbian are often the subject of vilification — those in education are included in this campaign. A highly influential conservative religious group based in the United States, the Family Research Council (FRC, 2005),[10] is vociferous in its protests against the alleged promotion of homosexuality[11] in U.S. public schools. The FRC uses its well-funded and organized resources to target organizations such as Gay Lesbian Straight Education Network (GLSEN),[12] which, according to the FRC, "aggressively promotes instruction about the homosexual lifestyle in elementary schools ... . Children will be encouraged to enter a lifestyle associated with disease and early death" (Dailey & Roberts, 1999, para. 3).

Dailey and Roberts (1999) also state that "GLSEN proposes that elementary schools assume children are sexually ambiguous, and would have teachers encourage their presumed innate tendency towards homosexuality" (para. 7). The rhetoric of the FRC is skillfully designed to promote "traditional family values" over which the organization sees itself as having some guardianship. This rhetoric also raises the specter of recruitment, which, as evidenced already, may operate to silence teachers such as Blinick from discussing tropes of choice for fear they will be accused by the likes of the Dailey and Roberts of "promoting instruction about the homosexual lifestyle" for the purposes of conversion.

Like Blinick, Kevin Jennings, executive director of GLSEN, recognizes the dilemmas related to the deployment of tropes of choice in the construction of public discourses related to sexualities and secondary schooling. He states,

> This whole debate [relating to the etiology of sexual identity] does present real problems in terms of advancing the gay and lesbian field because if someone like me was to get up there and say "I do believe that some people choose to be gay," that opens the door to the Right-wing to say, "See, they do choose to be gay; therefore we should, you know, encourage them to be straight." That is so fundamentally rooted in homophobia that it is hard to even unpack ... . That's why my response to it has been to attack the very legitimacy of the question because I do not believe that it is a legitimate question. And I believe that the more we get caught up in arguing the question the more we lose.
>
> ... The Right-wing brings up the idea of choice for a very different reason than I think you're raising it. The Right-wing wants us to say, "Yes, it's a choice" because their next step is, if it's a choice, then we need to cure all these people. Where the Left-wing is saying well you know it's a very Western male way of thinking to divide the world into gay and straight, we should be more polymorphous. In the end Left and Right come back round in a circle and always meet in the same place. It's just where they jump off once they reach that conclusion that's very different.

Whether or not sexual and gender identities are somehow essential, Jennings is critical of those on the so-called Left and Right who persist in posing questions relating to the etiology of sexual identity. Regardless of one's motivation in posing such questions, Jennings states that the "more we get caught up in arguing the question the more we lose." Jennings's position here appears vindicated by Witt et al.'s (1995) prior description of the television talk show. One controversial issue can dominate discourse, thereby preventing discussion of what Jennings may perceive as more pressing issues relating to LGBTI young people than theoretical musings on processes of subjectivization and identification.

Concerns about debating the etiology of homosexuality or the notion of queer, voiced by Jennings, are also echoed by

Pallota-Chiarolli. She argues that Catholic schools[13] in Australia can only countenance homosexuality if it is not constructed as a choice. As such, Pallota-Chiarolli suggests adopting the position that people are intrinsically gay may be the only viable way of combating the silence around homosexuality in the formal curriculum of these schools. Given the contentiousness of choice, she argues that

> ... to make that leap "from I don't want to know about homosexualities, to all sexualities are constructed and your very own heterosexuality is a construction" ... is just too much for some people to face. And it actually might backfire because it might actually feed the very prejudices. Because a lot of stuff that is coming from particularly religious schools is you can be converted. If "you have a choice" then you don't have to go down that path. And a lot of the social construction stuff is also saying that there are options and agencies and that we can actually resist and manipulate the kind of institutional frameworks that we are living within. So I am just worried that we might backfire that way at this stage.

The backfire Pallota-Chiarolli refers to may manifest in the possible fallout that ensues from invoking the trope of choice in Catholic schools (though this same argument could be easily applied in many other private, religious, and state schools in Australia and the United States). Tropes of choice, once raised, may be used to legitimate claims that young people can be converted to the homosexual lifestyle if overexposed to constructivist discourses. Moreover, tropes of choice may be invoked as a rationale for convincing young people who do choose to identify as LGBTI to question such a choice. On these grounds, it is argued that tropes of choice should not yet be deployed in Catholic schools. If discourses on the subject of homosexuality are somehow connected to an escalation of LGBTI sexual and gender identities, such discourses may be erased from the curriculum, except in the instance of prohibition.

The study participants quoted in this section are, to different extents, convinced by tropes of choice. They are also extremely wary of the potentially negative political implications associated with discussing, in secondary educational contexts, the notion that individuals have some agency in the construction of their sexual and gender identities. Rather than utilize tropes of choice in the production of discourses related to sexualities, these people opt for the language of strategic essentialism, at least in certain educational contexts.

In considering further the notion of strategic essentialism, Fuss (1989) argues,

> There is an important distinction to be made, I would submit, between "deploying" or "activating" essentialism and "falling into" or "lapsing into" essentialism. "Falling into" or "lapsing into" implies that essentialism is inherently reactionary — inevitably and inescapably a problem or a mistake. "Deploying" or "activating," on the other hand, implies that essentialism may have some strategic or interventionary value. (p. 20)

Among the participants in this study, some call upon essentializing tropes because of a belief in some form of homosexual essence. This is not so much a falling into; instead, essentializing tropes appear so familiar they remain unquestioned. Other participants, such as Jennings, Blinick, and Pallota-Chiarolli, deploy or activate essentialism in discussing sexualities because they believe this is the most politically effective approach in educational settings at this historical moment.

Some reasons behind this deployment of essentialism are expanded upon in the following passage, in which Pallota-Chiarolli reflects further on the difficulties of deploying tropes of choice in Australian schools:

> I found that in some settings, like Catholic school settings, having that kind of pseudo-ethnic, "you are born that way" [argument], actually made it easier to make inroads into the school. Because if you are "born that way" then you can't go ahead and be awful to people that are "born that way." That has been a real dilemma for me. Because [of] the queer theory stuff that I do and the social construction stuff …. But at the same time, to be politically useful, to get stuff done in schools, sometimes I had to come at it from this very basic fixed, essentialist stuff. You know, biological determinism: "If a young boy in our school is gay then that is what he 'is.'" I'd hear myself saying this stuff and then think I really want to launch into a discussion of how sexual identity is constructed, but I knew that as soon as I'd start that I'd alienate the very people that I was edging on alienating anyway.

Jacqui Griffin, a teacher in Sydney, Australia, and former co-convener of GaLTaS, notes other benefits in favoring essentializing tropes in Catholic school settings:

> ... Even Catholicism is saying now that [homosexuality] is an objective disorder. You are born with it, so therefore you are no longer responsible for it, so don't hassle me. "I was born like that." So in some ways I think that born versus made fits more comfortably with people ... from a religious background.

> It can suit [advocates for LBGTI-identified teachers and students] politically too. Because if you are saying you are born that way ... you can't discriminate against us because we are like that. But as soon as ... you say, "Well there's an element of choice," well then it's like you choose to do it that way so you accept the consequences. So, politically, I think it's advantageous, the born rather than the made argument. I don't have a really clear position on that.

Griffin and Pallota-Chiarolli both express some ambivalence about the deployment of essentializing tropes. However, in the Australian Catholic school settings with which they are familiar, both are confident that the "born that way" argument is more politically advantageous. Essentializing tropes are not perceived as being as vulnerable to criticism as tropes of choice, which are constructed as potentially alienating to school communities because people will find them too confronting or too disturbing to their own sense of self or to their religious beliefs. Griffin and Pallota-Chiarolli also see essentializing tropes as more efficacious in defending the rights of students and teachers because if someone is "born that way," then their right to adopt a nonheterosexual identity is less assailable.

The political problems associated with tropes of choice are echoed in conversations with Australian and U.S. participants. However, persisting in the deployment of essentializing tropes is also problematic, because when people predicate tolerance on the possession of innate characteristics, it does set up boundaries about who is and is not worthy of protection. Where does this leave people who adopt gender and sexual identities that are not perceived as somehow fundamental? Whose identities are defined as illegitimate or somehow deviant? And whose business does it become to determine which identities are worthy of protection?

Choice and Discomfort

Somewhere between the comfort of essentialism and the strategic decision to put choice in the closet lies the realm of choice and discomfort. Here, tropes of choice are rejected, not for political reasons but because of their tendency to cause uneasiness, worry, and anxiety — even embarrassment. Here, I consider participants' discussions of various discomforts with tropes of choice, beginning with Nickson, an Australian participant who worked for the New South Wales (NSW) Lesbian and Gay Anti-Violence Project. She was responsible for the development of an antihomophobia program that operated within and outside schools in NSW. There is no direct reference to tropes of choice in the following excerpts, but I take Nickson's discussions of "queer" identity to resonate with other participants' discussions of "choice." For Nickson, who identifies as a lesbian, queer notions cause discomfort at a visceral level.

> Mary Lou: You said you felt a little bit uncomfortable about the notion of queer for you. Could you talk about why?

> Nickson: Because I don't understand what it is. I am a person who likes a fairly clear label to work with, and I don't understand what queer identity is … . No, I understand what people define it as, I don't understand how it feels in your body, and so because I can't relate to how that would feel in my body I find it very difficult to explain to anyone else about what it is … . I don't think that queer is a bad thing. I don't disagree with the notion of it. I just don't understand how it feels.

For Nickson, discussions of queer identity, and the accompanying tropes of choice they may entail, are rejected because they are viscerally unfamiliar or foreign. Instead, Nickson voices her desire for the comfort of a "fairly clear label." The comfort she takes in working with clear labels is also perceptible in her reluctance to deploy queer notions in trainings.

> … I don't know and understand queer so I don't know that I could do it justice in my training, and I don't know that anyone in that training would feel like they understood what in the hell I was on about, or that they could work with that as a concept. And I suppose I feel like I have a responsibility in my training to

not leave people worse off than they started, to challenge them, yes, to make them a bit uncomfortable, yes, but not to leave them with a bigger bag of worms than they started with because they trusted me to move them through that.

It is evident that Nickson appreciates the value of causing some discomfort through her training sessions, but she is also loath to extend this discomfort too far. She implies that discussions of queer notions would potentially be too confusing and discomforting. In Nickson's formulation queer notions become conflated with the abrogation of trust, a disruption of her mission to "move people from A to B." There is an implication that people who attend her trainings deserve and require a degree of certitude at the end of a session, and queer notions might disrupt this certitude. Unspoken here is the idea that other tropes of sexual and gender identity will not be so discomforting. Such an approach to the notion of queer is contrary to the exercise of an "ethics of discomfort," in which Foucault (1997) suggests that one should never consent to being completely comfortable with their own certainties (p. 144).[14]

Blinick notes that tropes of choice may also cause discomfort in the minds of sympathetic colleagues, such as the cosponsor of her school's Gay–Straight Alliances (GSA).[15]

I have a really good friend I teach with who identifies as straight, and she is the straight person who is the other sponsor of the GSA. She's the one who teaches psychology. And she goes nuts when I say things like that, "What if it's really fluid?" She says, "What do you mean?" [relates disturbed tone of her colleague] And now I just do it to bother her, but she really doesn't believe that's true.

In this excerpt, the statement "What if it's really fluid?" represents the trope of choice. Blinick recognizes her colleague's desire to be extremely supportive of the GSA, but she is also aware of her need to maintain solid borders around her heterosexual identity. Knowing her colleague is extremely disturbed by any challenge to these borders, Blinick is able to disturb her colleague by positing the idea that identities are fluid. There is a sense that people who maintain heterosexual identities may be invested in the notion that they can be supportive of gay people, but they can't be gay — so they find tropes of choice discomforting, though discomfort with choice is not the sole province of people who are heterosexual identified.

People who adopt lesbian and gay identities can be disturbed by tropes of choice, as observed by Pallota-Chiarolli.

> ... I've tried to use words like bisexuality a lot more, and I find that some people are resistant to that. Even gay teachers and lesbian teachers onside are really resistant to the fact that you are "muddying the waters." "You're either gay, lesbian, or straight," and bisexuality is "muddying the waters" and it's "too much for kids." And yet kids can handle a lot of this stuff, and it's often the adults themselves who really have problems.

The discomfort experienced, even by gay teachers and lesbian teachers, might be because they share Blinick's concerns expressed in the previous section regarding associations made between choice and the specter of homosexual recruitment. However, as indicated by Holliday (1999), homophobia is not the only motivation behind people's commitment to essentializing tropes; there are also material, sexual, personal, and political imperatives that may discourage the adoption of tropes of choice in school settings. It appears that there are many grounds upon which to find discomfort with tropes of choice. This complex relationship between discomfort and choice is further explored in the following section, which focuses on debates about deferring discussions of choice and on associations between choice and equity.

CHOICE, TIME, AND JUSTICE

To this point I have focused on various expressions of comfort and discomfort associated with the production of essentializing tropes and tropes of choice in educational contexts. Time and justice are two more factors nominated by participants as justifications for their discomfort in deploying tropes of choice. In this section I consider how the introduction of tropes of choice into educational contexts is deferred by the invocation of time and justice and also ponder some of the ethical implications of this strategy in the context of the broader discussion of processes of subjectivization and identification.

In the subsequent excerpt, Pallota-Chiarolli elaborates on her reluctance to deploy tropes of choice in Australian school settings at this historical moment.

... I think at this point in time we are just beginning to do something in schools. We are just beginning to make an inroad, and at this stage I think we just have to focus on the issues ... . The fact that there are kids and teachers who are really being harassed and are not being able to be open and discuss their lives and have some role models ... — now if what it takes to make that kind of inroad is to almost [groan] use essentialist notions of sexuality then I am prepared to do that ... . My bigger aim at this stage is to get the stuff onto the curriculum, is to get the stuff into policies and to have the gay and lesbian teachers be able to say, "This is who I am" ... . Once that's established, and as it's becoming more established, then I would be one of the first people to actually introduce a queerifying and a more deconstructive approach to these issues. And I have done it with some year 12 students and they love it ... .

Pallota-Chiarolli expresses her desire to introduce a "queerifying and a more deconstructive approach" to conversations around sexuality and schooling, even as she resists such an approach because she feels school communities in Australia are not, at this point in time, ready to move away from the comfort of essentializing tropes. Predicating the introduction of a more queerifying approach on the achievement of a bigger aim of policy and curriculum change is not without its liabilities.

Reliance on essentializing tropes in the hope of gaining advantage in the short term may be "profoundly disempowering and deceptive" (Phelan, 1997, p. 64) because such an approach does not adequately represent the complexity of people's sexual and gender identities. Once the notion of discrete categories of lesbian, gay, bisexual, and straight subjects becomes enshrined in the curriculum, it may become more difficult to disturb people's investments in being able to say, "This is who I am." Nevertheless, although some of the participants in this study acknowledge problems in the deployment of essentializing tropes, most believe that the costs of pursuing a queerifying and deconstructive approach outweigh the potential benefits.

Rather than question the timing of introducing tropes of choice in educational contexts, Al Ferreira[16] poses an alternative argument against too much emphasis on tropes of choice, though he is not averse to the notion of choice.

The longer I work in this field the more I understand the complexity of the continuum from heterosexual to homosexual ... .

It's a much more complex process than I ever thought it was, and that we in fact are very complex human beings when it comes to both our gender identity and our sexual orientation.

... For some people I think it would be helpful for them to know that it is a genetic, predetermined, reality. To me it doesn't matter. I have gone past that point, mostly because I have met women who because of negative experiences with men have nurtured lesbian relationships ... . I never thought of that as a possibility until I met with some very articulate women who explained what they had been through and why they felt the way they did ... . I suddenly realized that just as I want heterosexual people who don't understand homosexuality to believe that I am telling the truth about my experiences, I also have to accept the truth of other people's realities.

Ferreira's understanding of tropes of choice is expressed in relation to the notion that some women choose lesbian identities on the basis of negative experiences with men.

Building on this conception of identity, Ferreira asserts that equity and justice should be the prime concerns of people working to support LGBTI-identified teachers and students. He argues that issues related to sexuality and schooling are, fundamentally, " ... civil rights issues and an issue of equity and justice for all people. I am less concerned about labels and boxes and definitions than I am about equity and justice for all." Thus, Ferreira seeks a movement away from a discussion related to the value of tropes of choice and essentializing tropes. Ferreira's desire to focus on "equity and justice" in favor of "labels and boxes and definitions" evidences something of a theoretical separation of these two issues. The interrelationship between processes of subjectivization and identification and issues of equity and justice thus becomes obscured.

A commitment to equity and justice over and above processes of subjectivization and identification may thus operate to veil the ongoing production of essentializing tropes and accompanying sets of material practices that are produced historically and work to differentiate, normalize, and effect subjection (Britzman, 1993, p. 125). Hence, it may be problematic when processes of subjectivization and identification somehow become removed from the discourse of equity and justice.

No Choice?

In the analysis of preceding interview excerpts, it is clear that tropes of choice may be seen as a source of possible conflict and discomfort. In educational settings and in the discourses of teachers who are "out" at school, the notion of choice is often perceived to be something of a political liability. Regardless of people's private affinities with tropes of choice, they may have cause to perceive such tropes as problematic, especially when spoken in front of specific groups of people. As indicated, Blinick refrains from using tropes of choice in conversations with parents and executive staff; Nickson eschews tropes of choice in training sessions with "straight audiences"; and Pallota-Chiarolli advises against the deployment of tropes of choice in Australian Catholic schools.

Tropes of choice are also seen as subversive in school settings, because they promote students' agency in the construction of their sexual and gender identities. Once students are recognized as having agency, it follows that they may be at risk of becoming gay. Potentially, this gives some credence to the Religious Right's assertion that lesbian- and gay-identified teachers use schools as recruiting grounds insofar as talking about LGBTI identities in educational contexts may increase the repertoire of options by which young people might choose to define themselves. Tropes of choice have a tendency to cause discomfort, whereas tropes of essentialism are sometimes perceived as more politically saleable.

A continuing examination of how tropes of choice and essentializing tropes are deployed in educational contexts acts as a means to better understand the practices — some of which are described in preceding sections — that regulate the tactical productivity of particular knowledges of the subject. In *Gender Trouble*, Butler (1990a) elaborates further on why it is important to study "subjects." She argues that "the question of 'the subject' is crucial for politics, and for feminist politics in particular, because juridical subjects are invariably produced through certain exclusionary practices that do not 'show' once the juridical structure of politics has been established" (p. 2).

The exclusionary practices that regulate the use of essentializing tropes and tropes of choice are often difficult to see. I have sought to analyze competing processes of subjectivization and identification in order to reveal some of the exclusionary practices that sometimes do not show. Thus, the question of the subject is crucial not only for feminist politics (Butler, 1990a, p. 2) but also in analyzing the production of discourses related to sexualities and secondary schooling.

A critical examination of the question of the subject brings about a consideration of people's varied and changing conceptions of processes of subjectivization and identification and the relations of power that influence their "strategical integration" (Foucault, 1990, p. 102). It is problematic when such considerations are marginalized or delayed because they are inseparable from broader discourses relating to equity and justice for all students. As such, I find it difficult to concur with those who defer the crucial question of the subject from the production of discourses related to sexualities and secondary schooling, even in spite of the discomforts this may sometimes cause.

FINDING A VOICE FOR CHOICE?

Having explored various participants' concerns with the deployment of tropes of choice in school settings, I now turn to a brief analysis of how tropes of choice enter into the production of discourses related to sexualities, genders, and schooling. As Jennings notes, the reluctance to draw on tropes of choice only represents one aspect of the storying of sexualities and genders in schooling.

> ... The fundamental premise of the GSA is that no one has to label their sexuality to come into the room. So we have tried, wherever possible, to create places where labels are not so predominant, that the only qualification you need for being in that room is because you feel the need to be in that room. You don't have to explain to anyone else why you are there. So there are some ways in which we try to embody what we really feel is more accurate.

Despite its name, the informal structure of the GSA appears to offer members a chance to question labels and recognize their own agency in processes of subjectivization and identification. Mayo (2004) argues that because GSAs "require difference, they maintain their ties through ethical curiosity, not only of what others who are different might be like, but what it might mean to be different than one is at present" (p. 28). Thus, the student groups that organizations such as GLSEN support may deploy tropes of choice, whereas, simultaneously, members of GLSEN such as Jennings, may use essentializing tropes for the sake of political expediency. This strategy reinforces Jagose's (1996) contention (p. 9) that varieties of constructivism and essentialism are often espoused simultaneously by individuals and groups.

Jaron Kanegson, the youngest participant interviewed for this study, is also influenced by tropes of choice in her/his work at Lavender Youth Recreation and Information Centre (LYRIC),[17] located in the heart of the Castro, San Francisco's "very" gay district. Kanegson identifies as a boy-dyke-fag,[18] and in the following excerpts s/he reflects on the construction of sexual and gender identities.

> … I think that identities totally grow and change and every differ-
> ent culture has its own different types of identity, what gender is,
> and what it means to be a certain gender. And the roles of what
> men do and women do are different in different cultures … so
> each culture in each time period does construct its own idea of
> what gender is and what appropriate norms are around sexuality
> and sexual expression and gender expression.

> That said, it has a sort of created reality. Everyone believes that
> women should be this way, so it is expected in our society that
> women will be this way, and men will be that way, and this gender
> group will date that gender group, and so on … . I know people
> personally with a very wide range of gender identities. I mean,
> first of all people who are women and men, then people who are
> transsexual — they were born as women, and now they are men.
> Or they were born as men, and now they are women … . My gen-
> der identity is still something that I am exploring a bit. It's sort of
> changed over the last few years… .

Kanegson is receptive to the idea that people's gender and sexual identities are not fixed but that they are "created realities" that work to normalize specific behaviors and desires at different moments in different cultures. As a consequence, in working at LYRIC, Kanegson may not be focused on affirming the authenticity of young people's identities as much as affirming their right to construct and reconstruct their own identities within the constraints of available options.

Certain identity categories are necessary for processes of community building according to Kanegson, who is also involved in challenging essentializing tropes that underpin these same categories, particularly those pertaining to people's gender identities.

> ... I think people need identities to bind communities around and organize around, but I also think that when the borders of a community are patrolled kind of, which perhaps inevitably happens, it doesn't work very well. So I am in favor of a much broader range of gender identities. And when you start to have a broader range of gender identities, then words like *dyke* or *fag* or *bisexual* or *poly* start to lose their meaning a bit. You know, I'm a dyke fag because I am kind of a man and a woman, who dates people who are men and women. So I think we need a lot more language, and the words we have for gender need to grow and change a lot.

Here, Kanegson's conception of the construction of sex, gender, and sexuality is reminiscent of Halberstam's advocacy of a proliferation of categories that disrupt heteronormalizing processes and "offer some new names for formerly uninhabitable locations" (Jagose & Halberstam, 1999, para. 7). For Kanegson, it appears that the complexities of choice are already apparent in the fluidity of existing identities s/he perceives in her/his own community.

The production of discourses of choice in secondary schooling is also apparent in Kanegson's formal dealings with the San Francisco Unified School District (SFUSD). Here, Kanegson is conscious of visibly performing a transgender identity.

> I think that there are many people who just perceive me as a lesbian or a dyke, and I don't necessarily correct them if it is not relevant. However, when I went to a school to meet with teachers where a student who was transsexual was having a lot of problems, I dressed up to go. So naturally[19] I dressed up in a button-down shirt and a tie. It was interesting because I was partially curious to see how they would react to me, because I figured that there might be some parallels to how they reacted to the student... .

Kanegson not only strives to find a voice for choice; s/he finds a matching outfit as well. Schools, like many other institutions, are almost exclusively organized around the notion that there are only two gender identities: male and female. Teachers, students, and other members of school communities who do not fit these categories are reminded of their failure to conform on a daily basis when they negotiate toilets, dressing rooms, name-calling, school socials, parent–teacher interviews, and invisibility within most formal school curricula. The conscious performance of a transgender identity by Kanegson not only supports a young person who identifies as transsexual; this performance also disrupts the heteronormalizing constraints placed on the visual performance of sexual and gender identities in school settings. *Cross-dressing*, for lack of a better word, may thus in certain circumstances be read as a corporeal enactment of support for the production of tropes of choice in educational contexts.

In GSA meetings, in performances such as that described by Kanegson, and in conversations in school grounds and in classrooms, tropes of choice are evidenced in high school settings. These tropes of choice color unusual and sometimes uneasy hues on the familiar and poorly known horizons of sexualities and schooling. Tropes of choice are neither invisible nor as prominent as essentializing tropes of identity. It appears that the comforts of identity are many, and finding a voice for choice in school settings is considered to be difficult for various reasons at time of writing. Kanegson's discussion of queer identities and Pallota-Chiarolli's discussion of bisexuality (see "Choice and Discomfort") are salient reminders that identity categories associated with tropes of choice continue to be controversial within and outside LGBTI communities. I now consider the efficacy of using the rhetorical tool of catachresis as a means to further draw attention to the malleability of sexual and gender identities.

INTERROGATING SEXUAL AND GENDER IDENTITIES AS CATACHRESTIC CONVERSIONS

In discussions of rhetoric, catachreses are distinguished from tropes because the latter extend existing meanings of terms whereas the former "mark a reality for which our language is inadequate" (Namaste, 1999, p. 226). Catachreses highlight and fill gaps in speech, thereby extending meaning and creating new versions of reality. Here, I consider how some new and some more familiar sexual (lesbian, gay, and bisexual, or LGB) and gender (transgender and intersex, or TI) identities might be conceived as catachreses. This process of conceiving of sexual and gender identities as catachrestic conversions is intended as a device to disrupt the comfort of identity.

Identities such as lesbian, gay, bisexual, and, increasingly, transgender are well-known elements in the construction of discourses related to sexualities and secondary schooling. Cohen (2001) traces the historical development of the narrativization of lesbian and gay identities in countries such as Australia and the United States:

> Over the last century or so, as some men and women sought to affirm ... the possibilities for establishing sexual and emotional intimacies with people of the "same" sex, they were challenged to develop new ways of imagining and representing these possibilities as part of a life story ... . In so far as our current notions of lesbian and gay "identity" are organized through and around the trope of "coming out," they are explicitly predicated upon the effects of such a (re)narrativization ... . To some extent the "coming out" story becomes the basis for the production of an identity to which the narrating individual lays claim precisely by pronouncing this story to be his or her own ... the conventional understanding of "coming out" as an event precipitated by an emergent sexual identity is a metaleptic[20] representation of such transitional moments: that the "event" of "coming out" per se is only (re)cognizable within a story which retrospectively fixes a narrative identification, producing what I'd call an "identity effect" by constituting it as the position from which the story both makes sense and gives pleasure. (para. 1)

This conception of sexual identity categories as "identity effects" makes it possible to see how terms such as *lesbian* and *gay* have been designed to simultaneously create and describe particular sexual and gender identities. Practices of repetition operate to make certain identities appear natural and familiar, so, as Cohen indicates, people may come to identify themselves as being lesbian or gay. However, because practices of repetition that sustain ongoing processes of becoming are always incomplete, they are also malleable, and people may create new identity categories when existing ones appear inadequate.

People's sense of attachment to people of the same sex, people's desire for people of both sexes, and people's urge to change their dress or their body in order to suit particular performances of gender have all resulted, and will continue to result, in the development of new words that fill gaps in language. As a consequence, less familiar sexual and gender identities emerge as existing practices of repetition fail to compel adherence to their particular narrativizations. It is in these gaps "between the figures of language and literal lived-body experience" (Sobchack, 2000, para. 34) that catachrestic conversions materialize. And as new catachreses emerge, older identity categories such as straight, lesbian, gay, and bisexual may come to be perceived as more authentic.

By considering terms associated with sexual and gender identities as catachreses, I propose a way for educational researchers to recognize the capacity of these terms both to extend meaning and to draw on existing terms in order to accrue new meanings. For instance, de Lauretis (1999) notes the ways that *transgender*[21] is related to but is different from the term *transsexual*:

> ... Although modeled on transsexual, and thus carrying the sexual reference, transgender seems to refer to a transformation that is not, or not only, the bodily transformation from one anatomical sex to another (as the term transsexual is usually, if simplistically, understood), but a transformation into a being who is beyond the two traditional genders (masculine and feminine), beyond the two traditional sexes (male and female), and beyond the two allegedly "traditional" forms of sexual organization (heterosexual and homosexual) ... . [T]ransgender is a trope that fully realizes the nature of the signifier; that is to say, it is meaningful only as a sign, it signifies "I am a signifier," and bears no reference to a gender, a sex, a sexuality, or a body. No reference to anything but its own discursive nature. (p. 261)

Terms such as *transgender* emerge as people continually search for more truthful descriptors of themselves. As such, this category can be seen to resemble other sexual and gender identity categories. All such categories are meaningful only as a sign; intrinsically, they bear no reference to a gender, a sex, a sexuality, or a body. For instance, any body can conceivably adopt the signifier of lesbian, but how that particular body is read in correspondence to that signifier will vary according to the context in which that particular body is located. Thus, a man who dons the popular T-shirt with the words "Nobody knows I'm a lesbian!" effects different readings in different times, spaces, and places. Conceivably, some people may read this declaration as authentic; others may perceive it is as ironic; and some may wonder just what a lesbian is and why this man thinks he is one. Similar to a transgender identity, a lesbian identity entails no inherent reference to a gender, sex, or sexuality, though there are familiar connections people in Australia and the United States might be expected to make with each of these signifiers.

These catachrestic identities evoke shared understandings, enable some people to be identified by others within and outside their communities, and also play a role in individual processes of subjectivization and identification as people nominate themselves as somehow being LGBTI (to name but a few options). As terms such as *lesbian, gay,* and *bisexual* have become more familiar, there may even appear to be a sense of agreement pertaining to educational researchers' understanding of what a lesbian is, or what a gay man is. Processes of repetition and unquestioning certitude may thus obscure the contingent foundations underlying these terms.

Identities such as *transgender, intersex, boy-dyke-fag, sissyfag,* and *drag king* remind us of these contingent foundations. They are still unfamiliar in many educational contexts; subsequently, they may still provoke discomfort and debate. The cues to how these terms might be interpreted are already there. For instance, coupling the term *drag* with the term *king* resonates with the more familiar *drag queen.* However, these terms may never achieve the familiar status of *gay, lesbian,* and *bisexual.*

I am not advocating that researchers, students, and educators need to familiarize themselves with the ever-increasing lexicon of sexual and gender identities. Rather, drawing on Butler (1994), I want to "challenge conventions of reading, and demand new possibilities of reading" (p. 33). Akin to the horizons evoked in the epigraph to this chapter, identities may appear to provide certitude, but they are, in effect, compelling yet poorly known. Identities may come to represent dominant knowledges or experiences of sexualities and genders, but these knowledges and experiences are not evidence of authenticity; rather, they are part of the processes through which people learn "to recognize themselves as subjects of 'sexuality'" (Foucault, 1982, p. 208).

Although this strategy of conceiving sexual and gender identities as catachrestic conversions is linked to some constructivist theories of the self, its primary focus is not, fundamentally, to prove that tropes of choice are more efficacious than essentializing tropes. This strategy is inspired by the possibilities of deconstruction and is a means to continue the task of questioning categories that are integral to the production of key discourse related to sexualities and schooling. When the contingent foundations of discourses related to sexual and gender identities are more apparent, the heterosexual–homosexual binary and its attendant exclusions may also be more easily interrogated. This interrogation is not designed to displace the heterosexual–homosexual binary with something else or to do away with essentializing tropes of identity. As indicated in the previous chapter, this process of deconstruction facilitates an analysis of the strategic deployment of particular identities. This deconstructive analysis is predicated, in part, on the pliability of these same identities, a pliability that is manifest when they are perceived as catachrestic conversions.

CONCLUSION

The analysis in this chapter reflects the ambivalence that runs through participants' production of public and private discourses relating to sexualities and secondary schooling. In short, what these participants think about the etiology of identity may not be reflected in how they talk about sexual and gender identities. Moreover, participants disagree on how they conceive of sexual and gender identities, and this in itself is a significant point. When discussing sexualities and schooling, even within a small sample of people who share a focus of supporting LGBTI-identified teachers and students in high school settings, there is no consensus about the operation of processes of subjectivization and identification.

If people's understandings of sexual and gender identities differ, then their visions for how to support LGBTI-identified teachers and students may also vary. Thus, Rolf's struggle for the "right to be who we are" differs markedly from Kanegson's focus on testing the limits of existing identities and on her/his call for "a lot more language" to better represent people's diverse sexual and gender identities. At this historical moment, there is a belief that tropes of choice are often too controversial to be useful in contemporary educational contexts. However, essentializing tropes are widely utilized not only because of their perceived strategic usefulness; they may also be used because people are intellectually and emotionally invested in the comfort of essentializing tropes. Whatever their motivation, participants in this study have complex discursive repertoires upon which they draw in order to construct and to rationalize their discussions of sexualities and secondary schooling. Following from this, it is possible to debate some of the ethical consequences that ensue from the deployment of competing tropes relating to processes of subjectivization and identification in educational contexts.

5

Scientific Classification

W/e speak out knowing w/e continue to
come to terms with our dislocatedness
in a society where our queer youth

(Grace & Benson, 2000, p. 107)

"belong to two groups at high risk of suicide:
youth and homosexuals."

(Gibson, 1994, p. 15, in Grace & Benson, 2000, p. 107)

I now turn to an analysis of some of the ways in which gender
and sexual identities have become objects of scientific classifications, and I study the relationship between these "scientific"
knowledges and intermingling of notions of adolescence and risk.
I also consider some potential impacts of these knowledges on
the rhetoric of educational programs designed to support young
people who adopt LGBTI identities. Finally, I analyze some of
the complications that may be associated with the reinscription
of risk in the production of expert knowledges pertaining to
LGBTI adolescence. In short, my aim in this chapter is to trace
some of the connections among scientific classifications, the
construction of adolescence, and expert knowledges pertaining to
LGBTI-identified young people in high school settings. In tracing
these connections, I draw on relevant academic research, interviews with participants, and resources from the Internet, which

is an increasingly important source of information for students, teachers, academics, and others researching issues relating to LGBTI-identified young people.

For the purposes of this book, scientific classification is conceived as a mode of objectification integrally linked to the production of truth and relations of power. As indicated in the previous chapter, Foucault (1991) conceives of scientific classifications, or discourses, "as an ensemble of regulated practices" (p. 69). He then considers how scientific discourses can become objects of a political practice and in what system of dependence they can exist in relation to a political practice (p. 69). I argue here that "expert" knowledges, girded by scientific discourses, are a familiar element in the production of key discourses related to sexualities and secondary schooling. However, the foundations of these expert knowledges, and their relations to particular political practices, often go unchallenged, as they may come to be perceived as irrefutable. Theorizing about the status, conditions of exercise, functioning, and institutionalization of these scientific discourses is fundamental to furthering the goals of progressive politics (p. 65) in the construction of programs related to sexualities and schooling.

Foucault (1991) expects his approach to the consideration of scientific discourses not to be enthusiastically received because of the uncertainties it provokes and because of "how irritating it is to approach discourses not by way of the gentle, silent and intimate consciousness which expresses itself through them, but through an obscure set of anonymous rules" (p. 70). The path to uncertainty Foucault would have people follow is more desirable than the refusal to analyze discourses in their conditions of existence and rules of formation (p. 70). This refusal, which leaves the power relations underpinning the interplay of scientific discourses uninterrogated, is anathema to Foucault's theorization of a progressive politics.

I am interested not in the certitude offered by scientific classifications but in the underpinnings of these classifications and their impact on the production of truths and knowledges about young people who adopt LGBTI identities. These scientific classifications are produced, exercised, and given status by those experts enticed by the language of rationality. Foucault (1996g) is critical of scientific classifications regarding sexuality. He states, "...What the gay movement needs now is much more the art of life than a science or scientific knowledge (or pseudo-scientific knowledge) of what sexuality is ... . Sex is not a fatality ... ." (p. 382).

In moving away from the comfort of scientificity and rationality, I seek to distinguish those experts who are critical of scientific classifications relating to sexuality from those who develop, promote, and support such knowledges. In this chapter, I thus utilize the term *expert* to refer to those who draw on scientific discourses to construct sex as a fatality.

These particular experts, and their associated knowledges, come to be perceived as authoritative and therefore integral to the reinscription of scientific classifications relating to sexualities and schooling. In his studies of the conditions of existence and rules of formation (Foucault, 1991, p. 70) influencing the continuous production of powerful scientific discourses, Rose (1998) traces the emergence of

> ... a range of *new social authorities*, ... such as clinical, [and] educational ... psychologists ... [who] claim social powers and status on account of their possession of psychological truths and their mastery of psychological techniques ... . Psychology has been bound up with the constitution of a range of *new objects and problems* over which social authority can be legitimately exercised, and this legitimacy is grounded in beliefs about knowledge, objectivity and scientificity. Notable here are the emergence of *normality* as itself the product of management under the tutelage of experts, and the emergence of *risk* as danger *in potentia* to be diagnosed [and managed] by experts ... . (p. 63, italics in original)

It is possible to see in this excerpt the methods by which individuals and institutions, through their attachments to expert knowledges and scientificity, become authorized (and authorize one another) to produce powerful ideas and associated diagnoses. These ideas and diagnoses may determine what is and is not normal, what constitutes risk, and how best to guide people who are defined as "at risk" or somehow "abnormal" on the path to safety and normality.

Prior to discussing experts and expert knowledges produced in relation to LGBTI-identified subjects, it is apposite to consider how these LGBTI subjects are produced so as to become identifiable objects of expert knowledge. Hence, I commence my analysis of expert knowledges with a focus on some of the conditions of existence and rules of formation (Foucault, 1991, p. 70) that produce contemporary knowledges certifying the truths of sexual and gender identities. I argue that these knowledges and their reiteration and reification are integral to the development of programs related to sexualities and secondary schooling because they sustain the belief that people are straight, or gay, or lesbian, or transgender and that they should therefore be understood as such and treated accordingly.

GENDERS AND SEXUALITIES AS OBJECTS OF SCIENTIFIC CLASSIFICATIONS

Psychiatrists' ability to determine a medical diagnosis based on expert knowledge has, in the past (at least in Australia and the United States) (Jagose, 1996, pp. 37, 38), resulted in the diagnosis of people who identified as lesbian, gay, and bisexual as perverse and abnormal. Only in 1973 did the American Psychiatric Association make the decision to remove homosexuality as a diagnostic category from their *Diagnostic and Statistical Manual of Mental Disorders* (*DSM*). At present, the DSM's fourth edition (*DSM-IV*) continues to be accepted as an authoritative classificatory authority on "mental disorders." It is used not only by psychiatrists and psychologists but also increasingly by general practitioners and postgraduates (Bower, 2001, p. 2).

There has been a discursive shift in Australian history from the classification of homosexuality as a criminal offense to its treatment as a medical condition. According to Reynolds (1996), who has traced this shift, in Australia in the 1960s and 1970s treatments to cure homosexuals of their pathology included aversion therapy whereby "homosexuals ... are shown projected still pictures of nude men. Just before this the patient is given an injection of apomorphine, a morphia derivative, which produces deep nausea, and is timed to produce a feeling of sickness just after the picture is screened" (p. 29).

As Reynolds (1996) notes, medical experts' official prognosis "often deployed strategies of surveillance and regulation which were brutally invasive ... neatly encapsulat[ing] the constraints of a medical discourse" (p. 43). The practice of constructing homosexuality as an aberration has been officially halted within the discipline of psychiatry (at least in Australia and the United States).

Notwithstanding these discursive shifts in official psychiatric discourse, there are many who still argue that homosexuality can be "changed." For instance, Muehlenberg (2003), the National Secretary of the Australian Family Association, notes that

> in America ... there are around 200 centres which help gays to go straight, and there are thousands of former gays who now are straight, many of them happily married with children. And it is not just "religious" organisations that are involved in helping gays go straight. The decidedly non-religious Masters and Johnson Clinic in St. Louis has treated hundreds of homosexuals and bisexuals. Masters reports that they have successfully "changed" more than half of their homosexual clients, and higher than 75 percent of bisexuals ... . A two year study involving nearly 860 individuals and 200 therapists found that change is clearly possible. The study found that "before counseling or therapy, 68% of the respondents perceived themselves as exclusively or almost entirely homosexual, with another 22% stating they were more homosexual than heterosexual. After treatment, only 13% perceived themselves as exclusively or almost entirely homosexual, while 33% described themselves as either exclusively or almost entirely heterosexual. (p. 35)

In order to argue the value of changing homosexuality, it must first be characterized as something undesirable that needs changing. This notion of homosexuality as undesirable may be linked to the historical reading of homosexuality referred to by Reynolds (1996). It would appear that expert knowledges regarding the deficiency of homosexual identities continue to influence contemporary discourses relating to sexualities.

Anti-gay groups such as the Australian Family Association also advise readers on their website to be watchful of the young, as they are at risk of being recruited into the gay lifestyle.

> There are very real dangers of homosexuals seeking to recruit impressionable youth. The promotion of homosexuality, in the schools for example, will result in a number of young people being enticed to experiment with anal intercourse and other practices endemic in the gay community. Public policy should seek to discourage this kind of promotion of the homosexual lifestyle. The health and well-being of our children is at stake. Indeed, a war is waging over the minds and hearts of our young people. (Muehlenberg, 2003, p. 35)

In this excerpt homosexuality is clearly constructed as infectious, dangerous, and unhealthy. This demonization of homosexuals draws on an array of assumptions about the innocence of youth and the predatory nature of the gay community. Here the scientific discourse is reversed, and the gay movement is vested with the power to entice and recruit unsuspecting adolescents.

Even if people who identify as lesbian, gay, and bisexual have not been removed from the unofficial annals of pathology, they are no longer officially disorders in the DSM. However, people who identify as transgender, transsexual, and intersex[1] are still commonly pathologized within medical discourse. In a study on how "technologies of gender"[2] work to produce sexual and gender identities, Spurlin (1998) draws on Sedgwick's (1993a) analysis of the " ... revisionary psychoanalytic developments ... that depathologize *atypical sexual object-choice* (homosexuals) while in the same move, through the inclusion of gender identity disorder in the DSM, pathologizing *atypical gender identification* (trans)" (Sedgwick, 1993a, p. 158 in Spurlin, 1998, p. 77).

The material power of knowledges, authorized by their scientificity, to pronounce disease and disorder is apparent in these shifting diagnoses relating to people's sexual and gender identities. This movement from the pathologization of sexual identity disorders to the pathologization of gender identity disorders (GID) reflects how certain conditions of existence underpin such diagnoses. These conditions of existence underscore the shifting assumptions that underlie the classification of "normal" sexual and gender identities; those that do not conform to these norms may, at different historical moments, be classified as pathological.

By way of demonstrating the continuing power of experts to produce heteronormalizing sexual and gender identities, I briefly outline some contemporary debates regarding the construction of GID. Young people who are thought to exhibit atypical gender identifications may now be diagnosed with GID in childhood. The criteria for the development of such a diagnosis in childhood include " ... a repeated desire to be the other sex, a strong preference for cross-dressing, strong and persistent preferences for cross-sex roles in make-believe play, an intense desire to participate in the games and pastimes of the other sex, and a strong preference for playmates of the other sex" (APA, 1994, p. 537 in Spurlin, 1998, p. 81).

Embedded in this diagnosis is experts' investment in conditions of existence that support the maintenance of a distinct gender binary. For this diagnosis to exist, it is necessary for practitioners to assume that there is some general agreement about what constitutes appropriate masculine and feminine attire, games, and pastimes. This delineation of masculine and feminine attire and behaviors must then be accompanied by the knowledge that the consistent desire to cross is somehow reflective of psychopathology.

A bigendered therapist from Norway, Esben Benestad/Esther Pirelli (Benestad, 2001), is critical of the construction of the GID diagnosis, arguing that the

> ... major proportion of children who have been diagnosed with GID grow into lesbian women and homosexual men with no transgender identity: a smaller proportion become heterosexual women and men with no transgender identity; a very small proportion[3] become transgendered..

As a medical expert, Benestad draws on statistics regarding how children diagnosed with GID choose to construct their sexual and gender identities in adulthood in order to point to some of the problematics that may be associated with such a classification. These statistics imply strong links between GID diagnosis and the construction of lesbian and gay sexual identities.

In his study "Sissies and Sisters," Spurlin (1998) makes the case that GID diagnosis has homophobic and gender phobic underpinnings, arguing that

> ... not only is the clinical domain not disembodied from heteronormativity .... Little attention is given to how what is proffered in the name of "clinical common sense" may have social and political consequences insofar as "treatment" of GID, usually at the behest of "concerned" parents, is often aimed at the prevention of gay outcome. (p. 83)

For Spurlin and Benestad (2001), the diagnosis of GID appears inextricably tied to parental and medical anxieties about children's sexual identities. The links to previous diagnoses of atypical sexual object choice resonate in the formation of GID diagnoses; both are underpinned by the privileging of heterosexuality as the elemental form of sexual identity.

Another element of contestation surrounding GID diagnosis is articulated in a report on the *Third International Congress of*

Sex and Gender, held in Oxford, England, in 1998. Written by norrie mAy-welby (1998), an Australian transactivist, the report underscores some of the tensions that may arise between medical and nonmedical discourses on trans issues:

> Herbert Bower, from Melbourne's gender dysphoria clinic, wailed about the "widening gap between the medical model and the non-medical model." However, what he failed to grasp was obviously well understood by the majority of (transgender and non-transgender) doctors and therapists present: That there are more than two models for transgender people to choose from. They talked not about "the medical model", but about plural and diverse models that allowed for combinations of selections from the full range of medical and other options ... .

In this report, Bower (2001), an Australian medical expert on gender dysphoria, is characterized as anxious about shifting knowledges pertaining to transgender identities. It implies that there are tensions within and around the medical and trans communities regarding whose knowledge should prevail in the determination of treatments for people who self-identify as trans.

In an article on GID diagnosis, Bower (2001) cites Murray (1998) to highlight his belief that such diagnoses are "'inescapably subjective, relating to private experiences such as thoughts, feelings, impulses' ... . We would like the procedure to be accepted as objective and scientific. It is not" (p. 1). Seemingly contrary to the former reference to GID's contingent foundations, Bower's discussion of this condition is firmly embedded in scientific discourses of rationality. He argues

> The *DSM-IV* does not ... stress sufficiently the fact that cross gender identification of the adult primary transsexual almost invariably starts prior to puberty, and cross-dressing first practised in adolescence or adulthood makes the diagnosis at least questionable ... . Anal intercourse, in the preoperative phase of the male-to-female transsexual is at times practised and explained as a wish for penetration and therefore femininity, and occasionally enjoyed. (p. 2)

According to Bower (2001), transsexuals need to establish a long history of cross-dressing in order to be legitimated in their classification. He notes further that too much enjoyment of anal sex may be associated with a homosexual proclivity, canceling out the validity of the transsexual identity. A thorough contestation of Bower's construction of GID is beyond the scope of this study. Rather, I want to highlight Bower's reliance on scientific and psychiatric knowledges. He endeavors to scientifically authenticate a GID diagnosis through recourse to quantifiable data such as the longevity of an individual's experience of cross-dressing and their narrativization of the motivation behind their participation in anal sex. The use of such indicators for the authentication of a GID diagnosis underscores the contingent foundations that bind expert knowledges such as Bower's to authoritative discourses regarding the production of sexual and gender identities.

In contrast to Bower (2001), other medical experts such as Benestad (1998) have voiced their opposition to developing medical treatments for young people who do not conform to normal expectations of gender appropriate behavior:

> The quest is not for the possibly transgendered child or adolescent to understand or take care of the world, but for the world to understand and take care of the transgendered ... . [T]ransgenderedness is not a disease (and can thus not be treated) ... . The main source of pain and trouble for transgendered young people is the way they are met and perceived by the world. The main therapeutic route to a better situation for the identified transgendered is to treat their world of significant others: parents, teachers, siblings, and so on. (para.5)

Advocating a movement away from the medical treatment of transgendered young people, Benestad suggests that these young people's families and school communities should become the focus of attention. In a similar vein, May (2002), a practicing psychosexual therapist from the United Kingdom, argues that

> in order to really hear individual realities and begin to create incentives for their more widespread expression, it seems important for therapists who feel able to, to attempt to bridge cultures and sub-cultures: different worlds. This will require the courage to not 'pass' as perpetuators of the medical system, the preparedness to abandon familiar therapeutic tools, and the capacity to tolerate murkiness: to cope with not knowing and linguistic approximation. (p. 462)

The approaches advocated by Benestad (1998) and May (2002) are motivated by a different understanding of the status, conditions of exercise, functioning, and institutionalization of these scientific discourses (Foucault, 1991, p. 65). Benestad strives to disturb the notion of GID as pathology by focusing on the social norms that regard those who do not conform to hegemonic masculine and feminine identities as requiring treatment. May urges therapists to tolerate the "murkiness" that accompanies people's lived experience of gender identity.

This analysis of the irruption of GID diagnoses and the deletion of "atypical sexual object-choice" from the DSM provides contemporary examples of the processes by which scientific classifications may be used to exercise control over the lives of individuals through the development of medical diagnoses. These diagnoses, such as GID, are borne from the circulation of powerful knowledges and through the production of scientific discourses that are highly contested and inextricably connected to heteronormativity.

The ensuing discussion of tropes of adolescence and risk sets out to rupture persuasive truths purveyed about young people — truths often supported by expert knowledges. It is an exploration of how these truths emerge and how, through the deployment of scientific discourses, some knowledges are valorized whereas others are disqualified in discussions of sexualities and schooling. It is also an interrogation of how hetero- and homonormalizing processes work to make particular knowledges more persuasive. I also consider some of the adverse consequences of producing knowledges about young people, sexualities, and schooling that are embedded in discourses of scientificity.

ADOLESCENCE/QUEERING ADOLESCENCE

Adolescence is a familiar and contested term in studies of sexuality and schooling. As such, it is important to clarify my usage of this term. In the context of this book, adolescence does not refer to "ontological or transhistorical reality" (Gordon, 1999, p. 3). Drawing on the work of Gordon, adolescence is conceived as "a discursive field that in the twentieth century has been the dominant mode of knowledge of a certain cohort of subjects, loosely defined by age" (p. 3). This conception of adolescence is deployed as a counterpoint to theories that posit adolescence as a scientifically produced field of study.

In effect, I am arguing the value of conceiving of adolescence as a trope, as constantly in production. As such, the focus here is not upon finding the essence of, or the real, "queer" adolescence. Alternatively, I focus on tracing the power relations and expert knowledges that produce familiar tropes of young people's experiences, as I believe these tropes are influential in the construction of young people's subjectivities and sexual and gender identities. In this task I am influenced by Lesko's (2000, 2001) efforts to highlight the sociohistorical context of adolescence while simultaneously critiquing various assumptions that have underpinned common contemporary understandings of young people. As Lesko has shown, tropes of adolescence are authorized in part by the expert knowledges produced in fields of study such as youth studies and educational and developmental psychology. These tropes are also increasingly produced at the behest of adults who inhabit lesbian, gay, bisexual, trans, and intersex communities.

Within gay and lesbian communities and, I would argue, similarly within trans communities,

> ... the meaning of adolescence is always understood to become apparent only in hindsight; it is structured by a foreshadowed denouement, which is the subject's arrival at adulthood ... [and because] this denouement must never occur too soon; the narrative must be allowed to run its course ... . [Therefore] the gay and lesbian account of adolescence ... is itself, irreducibly narrativistic.[4] (Gordon, 1999, p. 3)

Gordon's analysis points to people's reiteration of familiar stories of gay and lesbian adolescence, stories that necessarily involve a period of turmoil prior to the calm of adulthood. This conception of adolescence as trope and gay and lesbian adolescence as "structured by a foreshadowed denouement" (p. 3) may be useful in determining how certain tropes of LGBTI adolescence come to dominate whereas others are rendered unqualified or unfit.

Like the adults to whom Gordon (1999) refers, experts may become invested in certain narratives or tropes relating to high school students, variously known as *teens, adolescents, youths,* and *young people*. These labels are often seen as one and the same, but, according to Patton (1996), each has its own specific connotations and consequences. Each reinforces particular understandings of adolescence and is predicated on powerful truths that circulate about the "nature" of young people. The power of these labels is analyzed by Patton in her study of the provision of sexuality education to differing groups of young people. Patton turns her attention to

> … the two most common views of adolescence: the raging hormones (or storm and stress) theory and the youth as subculture theory … [Both assume] the existence of a stage between a natural and innocent childhood and an accomplished, knowing adulthood.

> Dominant class youth were described as the "adolescents" of storm and stress theory, while gay teenagers were treated as a subculture anxiously linked to both heterosexual peers and to adult homosexuals …. Understood as premodern, and therefore, outside either model of adolescence, youth of color were outside the discourse of innocence that veiled and protected their white, heterosexual age-peers. (p. 37)

What is apparent from Patton's (1996) analysis is that terms used to describe young people are not neutral. They are often inflected by the sexuality and race of the "age-peers" they seek to describe. This variance in terminology indicates that young people may not be equal within the context of sexuality education; some are considered innocent, some potentially dangerous, whereas young people of color may be conceived as already, always abject and therefore incapable of ever belonging to the innocent world of adolescence. In the context of this study, what is useful about Patton's analysis is the supposition that all young people are not equal in the eyes of sexuality educators; perceived differences between groups of young people may be found in the terms people use to describe them.

Next, I analyze expert discourses related to sexualities and secondary schooling that objectify LGBTI-identified young people as at risk. Such an examination may assist in the disruption of established truths pertaining to risk in adolescence.

Before proceeding further with this analysis, I want to affirm that my objective here is not to discount the existence of violence, homophobic abuse, and self-harm. I am convinced that the effects of homophobia profoundly mark the lives of many people, young and old. Whether living in rural Idaho, suburban Adelaide, or metropolitan New York, I am palpably aware of the constraints I place on myself and that are placed on others due to real fear of violence. However, inspired by Foucault (1991), I am also convinced of the need to reflect on "the conditions of existence and rules of formation" (p. 70) that sustain contemporary tropes associated with adolescence and risk. The repetition and reiteration of these tropes, I argue, is a critical mode of objectification of young people.

At Risk of Being Gay

There is an overwhelming sense in discourses related to adolescence that this period is a risky time. Here I consider how the trope of risk is constructed and sustained through an analysis of research relating to adolescence and through interviews conducted with participants in this study who are people working in programs to support LGBTI-identified young people. I also consider how this trope of LGBTI adolescence as risky has been problematized.

The association of *adolescence* with the notion of *risk* is not confined to discourses related to sexualities and schooling. Sometimes it appears that notions of adolescence are incomplete without the idea of risk. In a study of journal articles related to the subject of adolescence, the sense of gloom and doom that prevails in literature on young people was carefully documented, and Ayman-Nolley and Taira (2000) found " ... a persistent bias towards research on the negative aspects of adolescence such as risk-taking and adolescent turmoil, especially in the case of Black and Hispanic youth ... . [T]he prevailing force within the field of psychology continues to be the view of adolescence as a 'stage of storm and stress... '" (p. 35). Research focused on the "dark side of adolescence" (Ayman-Nolley and Taira, 2000, p. 35), it is argued, inevitably provides a skewed and dim perspective of young people.

Not surprisingly, young people of color, who are not middle-class, and who are not heterosexual identified were the most highly endangered groups in Ayman-Nolley and Taira's (2000) findings on research pertaining to adolescence (pp. 42, 43). In research relating to African-American middle school students, Davis (1999) also observed an overemphasis on what he terms "at-riskness" (p. 50) and a related absence of " ... how black males construct personal meaning for lives in and out of school. Particularly, discussions about how black males make sense of their own masculinity and sexuality and others around them has been noticeably absent" (p. 50). This focus on at-riskness and the lack of research on how

131

young people make sense of gender and sexuality has resonances in research conducted on LGBTI-identified young people. These findings provoke further consideration of how such an emphasis might contribute to and potentially confirm the pathologization of particular groups of young people.

In research related to sexualities and schooling, LGB young people are often depicted as an acutely endangered minority (Bochenek & Brown, 2001; MacGillivray & Kozik-Rosabal, 2000; Rogers, 1998). One source of this sense of endangerment might be located in the expert knowledges produced by authoritative organizations such as the American Academy of Pediatrics (AAP). In a policy statement titled "Sexual Orientation and Adolescents," Frankowski and the Committee on Adolescence (2004) observe that

> although only representing a portion of youth who someday will self-identify as gay, lesbian, or bisexual, school-based studies have found that these adolescents, compared with heterosexual peers, are 2 to 7 times more likely to attempt suicide, are 2 to 4 times more likely to be threatened with a weapon at school, and are more likely to engage in frequent and heavy use of alcohol, marijuana, and cocaine. It is important to note that these psychosocial problems and suicide attempts in nonheterosexual youth are neither universal nor attributable to homosexuality per se, but they are significantly associated with stigmatization of gender nonconformity, stress, violence, lack of support, dropping out of school, family problems, acquaintances' suicide attempts, homelessness, and substance abuse. (p. 1829)

This statement is used by the AAP in advising their 60,000 members on the treatment of young people. In the academy's statement, it appears that young people who identify as gay, lesbian, or bisexual are at heightened risk of many psychosocial problems. Happiness may be deferred until young people have navigated the turmoil of adolescence.

These scientifically authorized statements about the riskiness of lesbian and gay adolescence inform, and in turn are informed by, expert knowledges relating to sexualities and schooling produced by adults who provide support to LGBTI-identified young people. This cross-fertilization is apparent in interviews conducted as part of this study in which the belief that LGBTI-identified young people represent a population at risk is ubiquitous.

For instance, Christopher Rodriguez, who worked at the Hetrick-Martin Institute (HMI)[5] in New York when he was interviewed for this study, describes himself as "an advocate for young people, for high-risk youth." For Rodriguez, it appears that LGBTI-identified young people and high-risk youth are synonymous. Rodriguez goes on to state, "It's common knowledge that GLBT youth are more at risk of depression and suicide. More so than just about any other population of young people." But how does such knowledge become both common and authoritative?

One way in which this "common knowledge" becomes authoritative is through repetition. A cofounder of HMI and another participant in this study, Joyce Hunter, states, " ... Young person after young person told stories about how they had been discriminated against by students and staff in the public schools in the communities in which they lived." For Hunter, these repeated narratives of vulnerability were the rationale for founding HMI.

This familiar knowledge of the riskiness of LGBTI adolescence is also authorized through recourse to statistics. In this vein, Rolf, the co-coordinator of Project 10 in the LAUSD, states,

> We know just looking at the statistics that kids are killing themselves in drugs, numbing themselves out as a way of avoiding the pain they are feeling. They are getting themselves pregnant as a way of hiding. They are subject now to HIV infection and other STDs. They are having high-risk sex and are engaging in tremendously risky behaviors and I am very concerned about that.

Many studies[6] support the production of these widely produced knowledges that LGBTI-identified young people are at risk. The difficulties and risks already identified are corroborated in Australian research. For instance, Nicholas and Howard (1998) suggest that gay youth are 3.7 times more likely to attempt suicide than their straight male counterparts (p. 2). Drawing partially on research conducted in the United States and Canada, the NSW Gay and Lesbian Rights Lobby (GLRL, 2000) also reiterates such dire statistics in its *Gay and Lesbian Youth Fact Sheet*:

> Research, mostly done in the US and Canada, indicates 25% to 45% of young lesbians, gay men and bisexuals have attempted suicide, with up to 85% feeling suicidal. The few Australasian studies confirm the extent of the problem here. For example,

a 1996 Western Australian study of young gay men found over half had attempted suicide … . The more in-depth research has shown that suicide risk for young gays, lesbians and bisexuals is related to isolation and loneliness; rejection and lack of support structures; coming out and difficulty in accepting one's sexual orientation. (para. 5)

As indicated already, I do not question the notion that some LGBTI-identified students experience profound alienation and discrimination. However, I am disturbed by the continuous reproduction of the "common knowledge" that being young and dealing with sexuality and identity problems effectively doubles people's troubles. Margaret Edwards, one of the Australian participants in this study, was a co-convener of the Gay and Lesbian and Teachers' and Students' group in Sydney, NSW, prior to moving to Wagga Wagga in rural NSW, where, at the time of interview, she worked as a high school teacher. Edwards also reiterates this idea of double jeopardy, noting that

… kids who are dealing with sexuality and identity problems have got a double whammy, because not only are they dealing with adolescence and what that means and puberty and growth changes and emotional ups and downs, but they are also dealing with "Heh, I am different to other people." They are scared. They are frightened. They are dealing with two parallel things happening, and it's very confusing.

In Edwards's words, the chain of signification that entwines adolescence, (homo)sexual identity, and unspecified problems is manifest. Over time, the process of developing LGBTI identities has come to be perceived as a confusing and frightening process that puts young people at risk.

In seeking an explanation for the proliferation of notions of risk in research on adolescence, Ayman-Nolley and Taira (2000) posit several explanations, including the following: "Our lack of knowledge about many areas of *normal development* during adolescence may have at times sent us astray with respect to the kind of environments, schedules and activities which are conducive to positive outcomes for this age group and which activities highlight their weaknesses" (p. 44, italics added for emphasis).

There is a sense in this explanation that there is a normal developmental path adolescents tread — a path that might be better mapped if researchers turned their attention to research "conducive to positive outcomes." Drawing on Foucault's (1991) reading of scientific discourse, it is possible to argue that such an explanation for the proliferation of risk in research on adolescence is blind to the "truth games" underlying such research. Ayman-Nolley and Taira (2000) fail to account for "an obscure set of anonymous rules" (Foucault, 1991, p. 70) that guide researchers and other experts in constructing adolescence and queer adolescence as risky and violent. When expert knowledges are construed as political practices linked to relations of power, it is apparent that what passes for normal is, and will always be, contested.

Like me, Kevin Jennings, executive director of GLSEN (Gay, Lesbian and Straight Education Network) in the United States, has also noted the tendency to characterize LGBTI-identified young people as potential victims:

> And here's another thing that's very disturbing to me. We have been cornered for a long time into portraying gay students as victims ... . We had to hammer home the suicide statistics, the violence statistics, the drop-outs, the drug addiction, as a way of generating sympathy for gay youth. And I think that's a very problematic strategy, that it pathologizes gay youth, it victimizes them and portrays them as deserving of pity, and I personally try as hard as I can not to do that anymore. But then you get that other kind of problem which is that when I start to talk about the many wonderful gay youth I know that work in this office right now, people start saying, "Oh, we are all better now, we don't need to do anything."

The reiteration of the trope of LGBTI adolescence as synonymous with risk is worrying to Jennings because this practice can have the negative effect of pathologizing all gay youth. However, Jennings is also worried about the consequences of experts such as himself admitting that there are "many wonderful gay youth." Paradoxically, it appears that by affirming gayness and questioning the repetition of tropes of risk, adults who work to support LGBTI-identified young people may breed apathy among the donors who support their work.

Tropes of risk are a key discourse related to sexualities and schooling. They have an important strategic role and are part of the conditions of existence and rules of formation (Foucault, 1991,

p. 70) that authorize and legitimize the work of organizations such as GLSEN and HMI. At the same time that Jennings worries about the deployment of tropes of risk, Kenton Miller, one of the Australian participants in this study, laments the lack of authoritative Australian data characterizing LGBTI young people as at risk. Miller, who has undertaken research and has developed education programs relating to LGBTI adolescence in various Australian states, argues this lack of data is contradicted by

> ... those that provide services to homeless young people ... [who are] willing to say off the record, "Oh yes, a tremendous amount of the people I see are actually young people who are homeless because their parents couldn't handle them and they got thrown out because of their sexuality." But the statistics were never there, and the statistics weren't kept around it.

According to Miller, this lack[7] of statistics is of particular concern for those seeking to provide services specific to young people, because "we had to actually prove that young gay and lesbian people were at risk" before schools and service providers would fund services within their existing frameworks. Discourses of risk are not only instrumental in attracting donations; they are also pivotal to the provision of funding for support services for LGBTI-identified young people. It appears that groups identified by experts as being most at risk are more likely to receive donations and funding for support services. In such an economy, tropes of risk flourish.

Even as Miller is concerned by the dearth of data recording the abjection of LGBTI-identified young people, the current momentum behind youth suicide research and policy in Australia also perturbs him. He argues,

> ... the government response, the health response to youth suicide (is) already being hijacked by the mental health/mental illness lobby. At one of the conferences, one of the people there ... suggested, strongly, that about 95% of youth suicide cases could be traced back to people with a history of mental disorders ... and I suggested ... that these were in fact *symptomatic*, not causative, *symptomatic* of a deeper seated problem.

In characterizing the mental health/mental illness lobby as "hijacking" responses to youth suicide, Miller is cognizant of the power of these scientific discourses to construct persuasive truths. In the production of discourses related to sexualities and secondary schooling, these truths are potentially more powerful than those put forward by Miller:

> I think the major problem with that whole thing is that, if we argue for the recognition of gays and lesbians as part of suicide prevention programs, we run the risk of repathologizing ourselves … and becoming seen as mentally unstable … . It's still being made into an individual pathological medical condition … . They want to make it the victim's problem, or what they call the survivors of suicide, the close family and friends who outlived the person who killed themselves. And they don't want to see that there might actually be a significant societal shift that might actually need to take place, for example, in greater support around gay and lesbian issues — that would make a big difference.

As he does not have scientific credentials, Miller's objection to the narrative that constructs youth suicide as a mental disorder may be disqualified as it lacks the authority of expert critique, at least within the specialist field of mental health.

For Miller, government-supported youth suicide prevention programs' tendency to focus on individual pathology obfuscates a need for broader societal change. The heteronormalizing processes that pathologize LGBTI-identified young people will not be disrupted by the official discourse of individual pathology.

This interrelationship of "risk" and LGBTI youth is also sustained, according to Jennings, by the powerful influence of the media and the Religious Right in the United States:

> … They [the Religious Right and the media] have reduced the debate to the lowest common denominator. It's not thoughtful. It's not educative. It's not enlightened. As a result of their tactics … we kind of get pushed in a corner. They have their horror stories about us recruiting children and we have our horror stories about the kids who blew their brains out. And I don't think that it's a very enlightened discourse for anyone, frankly.

Pathological and pathologizing tales are the stuff of headlines, and Jennings feels that if he consents to do a television interview, he is required to tell these tales. However, this performance is variable.

Keep in mind that we are talking about different settings. Like if I am doing a teacher training for an hour and a half then I'll have a much more enlightened, thoughtful, discussion than I will if I am on television debating Ralph Reed[8] in a three minute evening news segment.

MLR: So you are conscious of performing your identity differently in different situations?

Yeah … if you are on *Nightline*[9] or something, then you really need to be focused more on advocacy because, frankly, I don't need to be enlightened versus Ralph Reed, I need to beat him. I need to be better than he is on television.

Although Jennings may be skeptical about the educative value of such public debate, he must perceive benefits in endeavoring to beat Reed, or he would not participate. Appearing on television has a number of advantages for organizations dependent on fundraising: It provides advertising for the cause, provides the opportunity to be seen to be doing something, and, probably most importantly, potentially increases an organization's reach and therefore its ability to raise funds and continue its mission. Consequently, there may be some strategic and economic value in the very public construction of tropes that position LGBTI young people as victims of homophobic violence.

The construction of what Edwards terms the "double whammy" of being young and gay is produced by tropes of risk authorized by medical and LGBTI-identified experts, the media, statistics, and processes of repetition. I have also pointed to some of the concomitant difficulties that arise in publicly affirming the lives of young people who are LGBTI identified. Having focused on "apocalyptic" descriptions produced in relation to LGBTI-identified young people, I now turn to a consideration of the production of discourses relating to the salvation of purportedly vulnerable gay teenagers or kids.

At Risk of Salvation

This analysis of discourses of salvation is influenced by Race's (2001) study of risk associated with HIV/AIDS and his observation that the "technological optimism so characteristic of scientific narratives… promises both impending apocalypse and salvation" (p. 180).

An example of one discourse of salvation is provided in a description by Melloy (1999), a reporter for the *Wigglefish* webzine,[10] of Jennings as a savior for LGBTI-identified young people — "playing David to the Religious Right's Goliath" (para. 1):

> ... Hardened cynics from the religious conservatives' quarter declare that GLSEN's citation of the statistics relating to gay teenagers who commit suicide amount to nothing more than an attempt to gain sympathy from the broader culture, and they are correct: when kids are killing themselves because they have been told they are "inherently evil" (as the Vatican recently branded homosexuality), someone needs to take a stand on their behalf and try to explain why compassion, not violence and intimidation, is called for when helping young people come to terms with the confusions and fears surrounding emergent human sexuality. In this regard, Jennings' organization is in the business of offering life-saving hope for young people across America. (para. 1)

By portraying GLSEN as a "life-saving hope for young people across America," Melloy endeavors to situate adults such as Jennings as enlightened guardians of at-risk young people. These guardians cite statistics as a means to refute the Vatican's evil rhetoric and to defend young people coming to terms with their emergent sexual identities. Implicit within this emotive reportage is that without the help of enlightened adults, young people will continue to kill themselves as a result of religious bigotry. Such a characterization vests these adults with the power to literally save young people. It also infantilizes young people; there is an insinuation that unless young people are protected by more knowledgeable adults, they may be susceptible to suicide upon hearing homophobic religious rhetoric.

In a similar vein of salvation, Verna Eggleston, executive director of HMI, can be found looking after New York's "throwaway teens" in a story developed by Connie Chung[11] for *20/20* in the United States (Richter, 1999). The following is part of a transcript of the program including Eggleston:

VERNA EGGLESTON (VE): Hey. How you doing baby? How you been? You taking care of yourself?

TEEN BOY: Yeah.

VE: All right. Then you know what to do, right?

CONNIE CHUNG (voiceover): For Verna Eggleston, going out on the street to check on her kids, as she thinks of them, is part of her job. In New York City, the hangout for gay teens with nowhere to go is the Greenwich Village pier, but she worries about where they'll go after the sun goes down.

VE: That's 8:15. When I come back this way, you better be heading towards your home. I'm not joking with you … .

VE: Many teenagers leave home at 18, you know? It's OK. It's very different when you're forced out of your home. And you're pushed out of your home and you're not ready and you have nowhere to go. Then you become a victim of the streets, and the streets begin to eat away at your life.

In the medium of current affairs (where pseudo-scientific data lend stories appropriate gravitas), Eggleston is portrayed as a concerned parent, providing support where others, as the title of the story indicates, have failed. Through media reporting, the executive directors of GLSEN and HMI are associated with highly evocative images and statistics of young people in need of protection. They step in when these "throwaway teens" are rejected by religion, by their parents, or both. Jennings is seen combating the fear and confusion "surrounding emergent human sexuality," and Eggleston worries about what might happen to young men on the streets after dark. Such tropes produce and sustain the ties that bind notions of risk to "vulnerable" LGBTI-identified young people: young people who need to be saved from their families, the streets, and homophobic religious rhetoric.

In her study of safer sex education in the United States, Patton (1996) argues that adults in organizations such as HMI and GLSEN find themselves in a paradoxical situation in which "they are trying to protect youth from an adult culture of which they are members" (p. 52). These adults, who may be indistinguishable from their predatory counterparts, are on the streets and on television telling tales of young people who are unable to care for themselves because of adults who cannot be trusted to have their best interests at heart — a representation that "leaves the adult in the position of interpreting the youth's development toward a state in which he … can make a good decision about sexuality" (Patton, 1996, p. 52) or, in this case, about where to sleep or how to reject the urge to commit suicide.

It appears that certain adults, preferably ones with expert knowledge and parental instincts, are situated as the saviors of young people who are unable to look after themselves in a homophobic world. If these adults are not there for young people, providing support, counsel, and resources, then young people may find themselves in serious trouble; they might even pay the ultimate price because adults did not care enough. This reinforces the belief that young people are dependent on adults as protectors and, as indicated next, this may consequently diminish the agency of young people. In short, young people who are LGBTI identified may sometimes be characterized as being in need of salvation.

The situation of adults in the role of enlightened protectors of young people's best interests is underpinned by "psycho-physiologically based theories of adolescence, ... [theories that] view these years as a liminal phase during which young people attempt to acquire the knowledge necessary to becoming adults" (Patton, 1996, p. 52). By virtue of their age, young people are situated as unenlightened, vulnerable, and capable of jeopardizing their own futures without appropriate guidance. I have sought to argue that LGBTI-identified young people may be situated as objects of a political practice that characterizes adolescence as liminal and risky. I have also outlined the system of dependence that may exist in relation to political practices (Foucault, 1991, p. 69) that situate young people's sexual and gender identities as emergent, fearful, and confusing. It is these political practices that underpin this mode of objectification, allowing it to manifest as a familiar horizon of adolescence and sexuality.

These tropes of risk and salvation are also supported by the production of heteronormalizing sexual and gender identity categories outlined in the first section of this chapter. Thus, young people may become disordered, and therefore at risk and in need of salvation, simply by adopting an LGBTI identity. Scientific classifications thus perpetuate the infantilization and abjection of LGBTI-identified young people, providing a rationale for adults to act in their best interests rather than to work with them. This process may consequently have the effect of reducing young people's agency under cover of providing them assistance. The repetition of tropes of adolescence as a stage of turmoil and stress also obfuscates people's economic, scientific, strategic, and psychoanalytic investments in the abjection of young people who are LGBTI identified.

WHERE ARE THE HAPPY YOUNG HOMOSEXUALS?

The previous section considered some of the strategic foundations and relations of power that underpin expert knowledges produced in relation to sexualities and secondary schooling. Another layer to this analysis is provided by Gordon's (1999) writings on adolescence and queer theory. Gordon posits a different explanation for the reiteration of abject images and statistics pertaining to LGBTI-identified young people. According to him, the proliferation of representations of unhappy homosexuals in contemporary narratives of gay or lesbian adolescence

> ... is structured by a double bind: either one refused interpellation as queer, which has rendered adolescence a site of shame, or one accepted interpellation as queer and its consequences, which has rendered adolescence a site of abjection. Hence, perhaps, the ubiquitous invocation of an unhappy childhood in gay and lesbian narratives. (p. 19)

The element of shame that structures tropes of gay or lesbian adolescence is, in Gordon's (1999) analysis, manufactured at least in part by the melancholia of lesbian and gay communities. Lesbian and gay adolescence is constituted "almost pietistically, as the territory of an inevitable martyrdom, the reward for which is postponed until adulthood" (p. 19), supporting the reproduction of teleological narratives of suffering adolescence followed by liberated adulthood.

This tendency to constitute lesbian and gay young people as at risk is, Gordon (1999) argues, itself a risky business. When tropes of risk become pervasive in narratives of adolescence, tales of a risk-free adolescence, especially a risk-free LGBTI adolescence, may become devalued or perceived as somehow less important or less credible than those of an adolescence associated with risk and violence.

Whereas Gordon's (1999) explanation of the focus on abjection in the narrativization of LGBTI adolescence takes a psychoanalytic turn, other researchers provide different explanations for the repetition of tales of violence and risk (MacGillivray, 2000). Several commentators[12] have pointed to the dangers of rehearsing statistics that seem to reinforce the prevalence of risk within communities of LGBTI-identified young people. For example, MacGillivray (2000), in the conclusion to his article on LGBTI queer and questioning students in America's schools, writes that

> ... although many GLBTQ (Gay, Lesbian, Bisexual, Transgender, Queer) students suffer horrific abuse in the schools, not all GLBTQ youth have the same experience. In fact, there are many happy and well-adjusted GLBTQ youth who are loved and supported by their families, schools, and communities. Focusing narrowly on the horror stories does have its consequences. The director of a local support group for GLBTQ youth explains that some of her group members, who are otherwise healthy and well-adjusted, seem to get caught up in the drama and pathology created around being GLBTQ and develop self-destructive behaviors because it is expected of them. They report feeling like there's something wrong with them if they do not also have horror stories about being GLBTQ to share. (pp. 320–321)

Although MacGillivray (2000) is cognizant of the downsides of reiterating stories of abuse, he is also aware of the persuasive value of presenting "horror stories" of GLBTQ adolescence. He goes on to provide justification for the reiteration of these stories, stating

> ... We as a society are in a crisis situation. Ending the antigay violence that leads youth to kill themselves or others should be our first priority. I know of no better way to do this than making all people, but especially educators, aware of the horror stories that many GLBTQ students live through. We do risk misrepresenting GLBTQ youth and sending the message that if one is GLBTQ, then these horror stories should be his or her own experience. However, it may be worth the risk at this time. (p. 321)

If the GLBTQ young people identified here as "otherwise healthy and well-adjusted" present with pathologies in order to fit the trope purveyed by the likes of MacGillivray, is it possible that well-intentioned researchers are somehow contributing to levels of risk, unintentionally helping to fulfill their own dire predictions?

Akin to Race's (2001) analysis of the castigation of positive gay men in the construction of discourses on HIV/AIDS in Australia, it is apparent that "the mechanisms we use to convey knowledge have a field of operation that is immanent to them. Indeed, they produce subjects" (p. 186), and it is salient to inquire as to what sorts of subjects tend to be produced by discourses of risk and violence. Greater consideration needs to be given to the question of how continuous exposure to tropes of risk insinuates itself into young people's processes of subjectivization and identification.

The notion that horror stories may play an educative role, as suggested by MacGillivray (2000), is worth interrogating further. Robins (1996), in his study of people's emotional and imaginary investments in visual culture and experience, points to "our contradictory condition of engagement and disengagement" (p. 77) with the world through media images. He notes,

> Increasingly we confront moral issues through the screen ... . At the same time, however, it screens us from those dilemmas: it is through the screen that we disavow or deny our human implications in moral realities ... . Yet through the distancing force of images, frozen registrations of remote calamities, we have learned to manage our relationship with suffering; it does not and cannot, in and of itself implicate us in the real and reciprocal relations necessary to sustain moral and compassionate existence ... . It may no longer be a question of whether this strengthens conscience and compassion, but of whether it is actually undermining and eroding them. (p. 77)

Drawing on Robins's (1996) analysis of media images, I argue that continuously reiterating the horrors many GLBTQ students live through may be problematic for two reasons. First, the repetition of these statistics can produce a distancing effect, whereby readers and viewers may come to "disavow and deny our human implications in moral realities" (p. 77). Expert knowledges that situate large numbers of LGBTI-identified young people as in crisis and at risk may become another layer of calamity frozen into people's brains amidst many other snapshots of devastation and despair.

Second, reiterating these horror stories may be problematic because doing so perpetuates the belief that such stories will somehow ameliorate the perceived crisis of violence and risk currently pervading discourses related to sexualities and secondary schooling. It could equally be argued that the ubiquity of these horror stories sustains a perceived state of crisis within these same discourses, slanting the construction of programs related to sexualities and secondary schooling toward the continued management of violence and risk. These stories also work to deflect research and pedagogy away from a consideration of the operations of heteronormativity in schooling toward a focus on individual/group pathology.

In the context of this broader discussion of the power of scientific discourses to produce authoritative knowledge, it is possible to see how research may confirm particular stories. Hence, the liminality of adolescence coalesces with tropes of risk and the notion that there are discrete groups of young people who are LGBTI identified and in need of salvation. This coalition of scientific classifications, when uninterrogated, gradually provides the justification for its own reiteration.

Conclusion

Remembering that there are happy young LGBTI-identified people may be one way of combating the persistence of the "Dark Side," but this is not an argument for the celebration of happy endings or the simple deployment of a pride agenda. It is recognized that shared stories and experiences of violence and risk can allow us to enact connections (Probyn, 2000), not only with other members of LGBTI communities but also with other individuals and groups. However, at the time of writing, the notion of LGBTI adolescence as a turbulent period is such a familiar horizon that the value of these interconnected tropes is rarely questioned. Participants in this study and researchers on adolescence and sexuality tend to paint more hues on this familiar horizon rather than to interrogate the horizon's usefulness or its conditions of existence.

6

Dividing Practices

... Identity is constructed in the temporal and linguistic mobilisa-
tion of space, as we move through space we imprint utopian and
dystopian moments upon urban life. Our bodies are vital signs
of this temporality and intersubjective location. In an instant, a
freeze-frame, a lesbian is occupying a space as it occupies her.

(Munt, 1995, p. 125)

INTRODUCTION

The Foucaultian notion of dividing practices is the focal point
of the present chapter. I explore the intersections of time, space,
and discourse in relation to the objectification of subjects in
educational contexts. More specifically, I consider temporal
dividing practices in the milieu of debates about coming out
and the closet.[1] Spatial dividing practices are discussed through
an analysis of the regulation of sexualities in school spaces and
the production of *safe space*. Finally, I analyze the production
of discursive dividing practices in two brief case studies relating
to sexualities and schooling in rural Washington and New York
City. My aim is to interrogate some of the implications that may
ensue from attempts to construct sexual and gender identities in
various temporal, spatial, and discursive educational contexts.
I commence this analysis by elaborating upon an earlier discussion of Foucaultian dividing practices.

Dividing practices are one of three modes of objectification of subjects identified by Foucault (1982) in his essay "The Subject and Power." Foucault writes that these dividing practices might cause subjects to be divided inside themselves or divided from others. This process objectivizes subjects (p. 208). For the purposes of this chapter, I analyze both of these aspects of dividing practices, focusing on the ways in which they are interiorized and the ways that individuals are divided from others.

This analysis of the interior and exterior workings of dividing practices could adopt many different lenses to consider their production in the area of sexualities and schooling. However, as indicated, I have determined three lenses through which to examine the area of sexualities and schooling: temporal, spatial, and discursive. As indicated in the epigraph, these lenses are not clearly defined one from the other. In the course of this chapter, some of the amalgamations of these various modes of objectification of the subject become apparent.

The decision to focus on these particular dividing practices is informed by the work of Foucault and Grosz (1995b), who writes,

> If bodies are to be reconceived, not only must their matter and form be rethought, but so too must their environment and spatio-temporal location .... [B]odies are always understood within a spatial and temporal context, and space and time remain conceivable only insofar as corporeality provides the basis for our perception and representation of them. (p. 84)

The interconnectedness of space and time points to the value of considering these two modalities in unison. Grosz's (1995b) analysis also suggests the reciprocity inherent in the relations of corporeality, processes of subjectivization and identification, and spatio-temporal contexts. The understandings of space and time put forward by Grosz complement Rabinow's (1984) discussion of dividing practices in the introduction to *The Foucault Reader*.

Rabinow (1984) argues that Foucault conceives of dividing practices as operating to produce social and personal identities through spatial and discursive manipulation, including modes of classification such as sexual and gender identities (p. 8). In addition, his discussion of Foucaultian dividing practices draws attention to the relationship of dividing practices: " ... to a distinctive tradition of humanitarian rhetoric on reform and progress; and the increasingly efficient and diverse applications of these combined procedures of power and knowledge mainly, although not exclusively, to dominated groups or to groups formed and given an identity through dividing practices" (p. 8).

Proceeding from this conception of dividing practices, the LGBTI-identified young people who form the central focus of this chapter may be understood as a group "given an identity through dividing practices" who thus become the object of "diverse applications" of power and knowledge. Through this conception of the productive role of dividing practices, it is possible to interrogate how this group forms relations within and around this mode of objectification and how these dividing practices are utilized in the name of reform, salvation, and domination.

Before I discuss these discursive and spatial dividing practices, I provide an analysis of temporal dividing practices. As indicated, temporal dividing practices are inseparable from discursive and spatial dividing practices, and bodies must be interpreted within the context of these fluid spatio-temporal locations (Grosz, 1995b, p. 84). To be more precise, this analysis considers how temporal dividing practices are given histories, presents, and futures, allowing individuals and communities to create (shared and contested) narratives of their own and others' gender and sexual identities.

TEMPORAL

If all that we think today may be thought differently tomorrow, then the philosophical task is to "tell the present" (Morey in Armstrong, 1992, p. 122), to problematize the production of the normal and investigate "the weight of the normal on the present" (Bell, 1994, p. 162).

In discussing his use of genealogy, Foucault (1984a) is critical of the assumption that words keep their meaning, that desires still point in a single direction, and that ideas retain their logic (p. 76). Foucaultian genealogical strategy "rejects the metahistorical deployment of ideal significations and indefinite teleologies. It opposes itself to the search for 'origins'" (p. 76). This analysis of temporal dividing practices is underpinned by an understanding of the discontinuities of history and language; thus, it continues the process of challenging continuities and the temporal identities upon which these continuities rely (Deleuze in Bell, 1994, p. 159). In contrast to a teleological understanding of the present, Bell (1994) argues that "Foucault wanted his work to act like a dream in the sense that it would 'jarr' [sic] readers into an experience of their temporality" (p. 159).

This analysis of temporal dividing practices is focused on disturbing the teleological flights of identity politics. Following Probyn (1996), it is positioned

> against a trend to posit childhood as a point of departure in the construction of queer being, a manoeuvre which indicates a bare-ly hidden yearning within some formations of identity politics for something that would ground difference ineluctably, I want to consider childhood as the point from which we "laugh at the solemnities of origin" … . Far from treating childhood as an origi-nary moment from which we might emerge as proud grownup queers, we need to remake childhood into evidence of the neces-sary absence of any primary ground in queer politics. (p. 96)

Drawing on Probyn's problematization of this search for "an originary moment," I use this theoretical point of departure to cast a shadow over the ongoing centrality of debates focused on how and when people might emerge from the educational closet. Simultaneously, I endeavor to jar familiar notions of the teleological development of LGBTI identities.

Repetition is another keyword in the analysis of temporal dividing practices. Schwartz (1999), in his discussion of repeti-tion in the later work of Foucault, argues that "Foucault was aware of the productive role of repetition … but he also severs the event of historical repetition from one's becoming 'authentic' or not" (p. 122, 124). In a similar vein, Butler (1993) writes,

> … Performativity cannot be understood outside of a process of iterability, a regularized and constrained repetition of norms. And this repetition is not performed *by* a subject; this repetition is what enables a subject and constitutes the temporal conditions for the subject. This iterability implies that "performance" is not a singular "act" or event, but a ritualized production, a ritual reiterated under and through constraint, under and through the force of prohibition and taboo, with the threat of ostracism and even death controlling and compelling the shape of the production, but not, I will insist, determining it fully in advance. (p. 95, italics in original)

Both Foucault (1996b) and Butler (1993) perceive the con-nection often made between continuous repetition of norms and authenticity.[2] If repetition constitutes "the temporal conditions for the subject," it is possible to see how the repetition of norms relating to sexuality may appear to create unified sexual subjects; "however, this productive capacity of discourse is derivative, a form of cultural iterability or rearticulation, a practice of *resig*-nification, not creation ex nihilo[3]" (p. 107). Intertwined with these notions of discontinuity, performativity, and repetition, the following examination of temporal dividing practices is mindful of their productivity and their inherent instability.

COMING OUT IN TIME

To advance this discussion of temporal dividing practices, I draw on three articles on coming out published in the same issue of *GLQ* in 1999. Two of these articles deal specifically with some of the problems posed by coming out in educational spaces (Khayatt, 1999; Silin, 1999), whereas the other (Gordon, 1999) conceives of coming out in terms of its temporality. Gordon's analysis provides a useful way of revisiting the debate between Silin and Khayatt in relation to coming out in educational contexts.

In interrogating the temporal qualities of the coming out process, Gordon (1999) questions narratives of identity in which "the intelligibility of the subject is in part constituted as the effect of a diachronic interval between the assumption of sex and gender, on the one hand, and that of sexual orientation on the other" (p. 4). Expanding on this temporal explication of processes of subjectivization and identification, Gordon goes on to argue, "... [T]he perpetually foreshadowed fixity of adult sexual identity informs the purported liminality of adolescent sexuality at every point of its discursive articulation" (p. 6, italics in original).

Gordon's (1999) articulation of the "purported liminality of adolescent sexuality" in relation to the supposed denouement of sexual identity in adulthood concurs with Cohen's (2001) tracing of the narrativization of coming out. For Cohen, "coming out" is a metaleptic representation ... only (re)cognizable within a story which retrospectively fixes a narrative identification" (para. 1). For both Gordon and Cohen, coming-out narratives serve to create a teleological stability borne from various desires and investments. In the context of this critique of the temporality of coming-out processes, I now turn to a discussion of Silin's (1999) and Khayatt (1999)'s articles on coming out in educational settings.

Displacing Coming Out

The question of whether to come out of the closet in educational settings, as indicated in the introduction to this chapter, is a key discourse in educational research related to sexualities and schooling. Following an analysis of two articles that critically engage with this discourse, I consider the value of displacing questions related to coming out with a new set of related questions informed by the preceding discussion of temporal dividing practices.

In his article "Teaching as a Gay Man," Silin (1999) poses questions such as "How is pedagogy changed when we dismantle the wall between private and professional experience? What risks do we take? What goals do we achieve when we open our lives for public inspection?" (p. 96). Silin, a teacher educator who works in New York City, partially responds to these questions by stating "being gay" in the classroom "encourages the authentic voices I hoped my students would assume in their own classrooms" (p. 96), though he also points out that his coming out "will surely alienate rather than engage certain students" (p. 97).

Silin (1999) also observes that the stories he tells his students regarding his sexual identity "change over time and are transformed by the times" (p. 99). I wonder if his awareness of the relationship between time and the stories he tells his students about himself and his sexuality is somewhat at odds with his desire to encourage the assumption of authentic voices in his students. I wonder how he or his students would determine which voices relating to their sexual identity are authentic, given the propensity of these stories to continue to change over time. Perhaps teacher educators would do better to focus conversations on how sexual identities "change over time and are transformed by the times." Such a focus on the differences, discontinuities, and similarities between and within people's sexual stories may alert students and teachers to the idea that people's sense of self does not develop and then stagnate; rather, it continues to change and transform over time. Students may come to consider the notion that sexual identities are not imposed on them; they change over time, and students have some agency in negotiating these changes.

Later in the same article, Silin (1999) argues that confessing the personal in the classroom involves an exchange in which "we give up being like our students or even liked by them in order to foster authentic dialogue with them" (p. 99). There is no doubt that coming out in the classroom does dismantle taboos about what is and is not pedagogically appropriate in educational spaces, enabling Silin to shift "some of his discomfort about teaching onto the students" (p. 96). I, too, am an advocate of the provocative abilities of discomfort in the pedagogical process (Harwood & Rasmussen, 2003), but I question the methods Silin deploys to provoke discomfort. I wonder if he could strive to be more discomforting by refusing not only to occupy "the position [students and institutions often require of their teachers] of objective purveyor of truth" (p. 105) but also to make connections between statements about identity and authenticity. Such a position would enable him to challenge the role of teacher as truth teller about all subjects, including gayness.

In a response to Silin's (1999) article, Khayatt (1999) interrogates the "pedagogical benefit of coming out in the classroom, particularly through a declarative statement" (p. 108). She argues that the process of coming out to students through the use of a declarative statement is "pedagogically unsound,"

> ... not least because one's identity is *continually in flux*, and the act of freezing one's identity in place to render the declarative statement true, even for a moment, does not do justice to the teacher presenting herself or himself in class. What it does is to define the teacher as standing for an entire group. Furthermore, there is nothing to guarantee how the statement will be heard by the individual student. (p. 108, italics added for emphasis)

Khayatt argues against coming out using declarative statements through recourse to the temporality of one's identities. If identities are continuously in a state of flux, then how is it possible to state one's outness in the classroom without "freezing one's identity"? Besides, what happens if or when your identity does change?

As Telford (2003a) observes, Khayatt's (1999) motive in questioning the pedagogical value of coming out "is not advocating living a closeted life .... Her point is that unsettling heterosexuality may be as well, or better, achieved through the curriculum and by refusing to behave as if queer sexuality were a secret requiring a declaration" (p. 106). This argument is compelling insofar as it makes a valuable distinction between pedagogical discussions that unsettle heterosexuality and the act of coming out. Clearly, these differing pedagogical strategies may have different effects. For example, the act of coming out may have the reverse effect of reinforcing heterosexuality because of its tendency to underpin the heterosexual–homosexual binary.

However, I am concerned that Khayatt's (1999) argument could also have the effect of implying that coming out is always pedagogically unsound in classroom settings. To me, this is an untenable position. Within and outside educational spaces, people will continue to choose to come out, and others will refuse to disclose their sexual identity. The pedagogical implications of the decision to come out in the classroom will surely vary according to the teacher, school, parents, and community who are all drawn into and impact from this act of coming out. From a pedagogical perspective, coming out is not inherently good or bad. It does not necessarily equate to unsettling heterosexuality, and it does not necessarily define the teacher as standing for an entire group.

As Khayatt (1999) goes on to observe, the telling of one's identity is not restricted to the form of speech acts. She notes, "Telling may occur through the ways in which our bodies are inevitably read by students and/or through what we include in and leave out of syllabi" (p. 110), and "some of us are perceived as queer regardless of what we say, while for others the act of announcing one's queerness does not ensure this perception" (p. 112). In clarifying her particular objection to the use of declarative statements, Khayatt notes,

> ... Whenever I use a declarative statement to proclaim my sexuality unequivocally to friends and colleagues, it seems to end the exchange ... . We move onto another subject, *closing this one forever.* I find that by assuming instead that they are aware of my sexual orientation, it does not focus *menacing* attention on itself but remains a *natural* part of the conversation and continues to come up whenever relevant. (p. 110, italics added for emphasis)

Khayatt's (1999) position is somewhat contradictory. She is particularly critical of declarative statements about coming out but recognizes that these statements take many forms. Thus, there is a distinction made in her argument between teachers who are outed by their tone of speech or body language and teachers who are outed because of their speech content. Given such a distinction, is it then plausible to suggest that one method of outing will attract menacing attention and foreclose speech forever, whereas the other will allow sexual orientation to remain a natural part of conversation? This prompts further questions. How does a discussion of sexuality becomes naturalized in conversation? Is it only possible to discuss sexual orientation naturally if one has not made a prior declarative statement? And do these guidelines regarding declarative statements also hold true for people who choose to identify as heterosexual?

Regardless of how teachers tell about their queerness, it is also worth remembering that in practice educators cannot prevent their "students forc[ing] our polymorphous perversities into their prefabricated boxes of limited understanding" (Khayatt, 1999, p. 112). Consequently, I argue the value of engaging students and teachers in conversations about how the coming-out process is constructed differently, depending on the individual (and his or her gender, sexuality class, ethnicity, nationality, and so forth) and the time, place, and space in which that individual is located. Such a change in direction not only would be productive on its own merits; it also would enable a movement away from the problematic and largely unsolvable questions relating to when, how, and if teachers should come out in the classroom.

Spatial

> Any sexual identity can assume
> space and space can assume
> any sexual identity ...
> space is *produced*,
> and it has both material
> and symbolic components
>
> (Bell & Valentine, 1995, p. 18, italics in original)

> I think it is somewhat arbitrary to try to dissociate the effective practice of freedom by people, the practice of social relations, and the spatial distributions in which they find themselves. If they are separated, they become impossible to understand. Each can only be understood through the other. (Foucault, 1984b, p. 247)

These epigraphs both emphasize the relational temperament of space and how this intersects with people's ability to construct identities. The following discussion of spatial dividing practices is underpinned by the notion of space as a relational production, shifting according to the places, times, and bodies with which it interacts. In a brief essay titled "Of Other Spaces," Foucault (1986) elaborates on this notion of space as relational.

> The space in which we live, which draws us out of ourselves, in which the erosion of our lives, our time, our history occurs, the space that claws and gnaws at us, is also, in itself, a heterogeneous space. In other words, we do not live in a kind of void, inside of which we could place individuals and things. We do not live inside a void that could be colored with diverse shades of light, we live inside a set of relations that delineates sites which are irreducible to one another and absolutely not superimposable on one another. (p. 23)

If space is considered to be relational, then inevitably schools and the communities that inhabit and interact with them will be the site of complex tensions — tensions that are irreducible to other spaces.

Foucault (1986) also introduces the notion of *heterotopia* and provides six principles that may be used to provide a "systematic description" (p. 24). Following, I briefly introduce three of the principles of heterotopia and point to the efficacy of using this Foucaultian notion in analyzing the production of other spaces (or spaces that other) in key discourses relating to sexualities and secondary schooling.

In the first principle, Foucault (1986) describes heterotopias of deviation as "those in which individuals whose behavior is deviant in relation to the required mean or norm are placed. Cases of this are rest homes and psychiatric hospitals, and of course prisons" (p. 25). In his third principle, "the heterotopia is capable of juxtaposing in a single real place several spaces that are in themselves incompatible" (p. 25). In describing his fifth principle of heterotopia, Foucault writes that

> heterotopias always presuppose a system of opening and closing that both isolates them and makes them penetrable. In general the heterotopic space is not freely accessible like a public space. Either the entry is compulsory ... or else the individual has to submit to rites and purifications ... . There are others, on the contrary, that seem to be pure and simple openings, but that generally hide curious exclusions. Everyone can enter into these heterotopic

sites, but in fact this is only an illusion: We think we enter where we are, by the very fact that we enter, excluded. (p. 26)

In the "safe spaces" and "queer spaces" analyzed next, various strategies are deployed, ostensibly to offer spatial protections to LGBTI-identified secondary students. I consider the protections these spaces purport to provide and pose the question of whether these spaces may be conceived as heterotopic — merely creating the illusion of protection and inclusion. The following discussion also analyzes the juxtaposition of competing and often incompatible interests (interests proximally located within and around schools) relating to the production of spaces, genders, and sexualities in educational contexts.

This discussion of sexuality and space in schools reflects a trend within queer theories toward a focus on sexual spaces that are not " ... easily produced as transgressive ... creating a forum in which those spaces not commonly considered 'sexual' might be discussed as productive of queer selves ... working from the premise that all spaces have queers in them, and all actions are performed by queers" (Hemmings & Grace, 1999, p. 391). Members of school communities possess a variety of sexual and gender identities. They are compelled to rub up against one another within and around school settings; thus, they are all complicit in the production of all manner of sexed and gendered selves.

The Invention of Sexualities and Genders in the Spaces of Schooling

Because space is relational, it has the capacity to produce certain practices of freedom and certain exclusions, thereby influencing the invention of sexualities and genders. This section considers the school as a heterotopic space where, at least for some students, "entry is compulsory" (Foucault, 1986, p. 26) and where all members of school communities are required to negotiate the problematics of a heteronormalizing school environment. This "struggle for space" (Armstrong, 1999, p. 76) inspires the following analysis of students' and teachers' negotiation of an environment imbued with "values and meanings which ... sustain differences and exclusions" (p. 76).

Ian Hunter, a study participant and a teacher at a Year 11 and 12 public secondary college[4] in Canberra, Australia, at the time of the interview, points to some of the ways in which processes of heteronormalization create spatial tensions on his campus.

> ... I rang up the Sydney Gay and Lesbian Mardi Gras[5] and asked them to send down some posters of Mardi Gras, and I put a few of those around the school, behind glass, to try and prevent them from being ripped down as much as possible.

> The way that the school is laid out is in a very sort of seventies architecture. You have offices that have glass as dividers in the interior of the building. So I could go into a staff member's office and put this poster up behind the glass for display into the corridors. And that was interesting because the posters were being ripped down, and I really thought it was staff, not students, because of the very difficult nature of having to get into a staff member's office to rip them down. So I was running a battle with whoever it was for about a week. They would rip it down, and I would go in the next morning and stick it back up again. I literally found one in pieces, and I literally stuck all the pieces together on the glass to deliberately make the point that I wasn't going to let them get away with it, and, of course, I didn't have very many of the posters so I couldn't keep replacing them. I had to keep sticking them back together again. (Both laugh.)

This response to Hunter's attempt to construct a space that reflects gay and lesbian identities within the school's interior may be read as a concerted attempt to heteronormalize the school through a very literal dividing practice: ripping up a poster. The removal of the poster may also be symbolic of the attempted removal of a queering presence in the school, so it may be interpreted as a method of preserving the school space as compulsorily heterosexual (Rich, 1993). Hunter's strategy of repairing rather than replacing the posters operates to underscore the precarious place of lesbian and gay identities within the school space.

Although Hunter has spoken to teachers and students at his schools about homophobia, he senses certain limitations on how far he can go in supporting students at the school.

> For example, if you wanted to organize an afternoon group of young gays and lesbians who were going through the coming-out process, like some of those instances in America, I really think

that what is stopping me from doing that is those forces.[6] Because I know that I would be putting myself on the line and would probably have to go the full gamut from individual parents complaining right through to press coverage or whatever that might mean. And that I suppose is too daunting. Even though there is that part of me eating away that would really like to be doing that. Because, as I say, there's that feeling that you need to be helping, to know just what a benefit that would be to those young people who are dealing with that, and maybe have no one.

Whether the constraints Hunter points to here are real or imagined, they are effective in preventing him from constructing a space where he might comfortably join in conversations with students about sexuality and identity. At the time of writing, to my knowledge, Australia has no national- or state-based lobby group (such as GLSEN) focused specifically on organizing around issues pertinent to education and LGBTI issues.[7] One potential effect of this absence is that few discussion groups, akin to the Gay–Straight Alliances (GSA)[8] that have flourished in the United States, have arisen within the bounds of Australia's secondary schools.

Safe Space?

Kanegson: … I think schools have a long way to go still and that they are not the safe environments that they need to be. And I think it's really sad because I think one of the major ways that homophobia still has a huge impact, and transphobia especially has a huge impact on people's lives, is that youth who are GLB or have nontraditional gender identities or whatever — they basically are denied access to an education because they are not safe in schools, and they don't feel welcome in schools.

Kanegson's characterization of schools as unsafe places for students and teachers due to the homophobia and transphobia occurring within their surrounds is a sentiment echoed by all of the participants in my research and is also reflected in educational research that has characterized schools as unsafe places for LGBTI-identified students and teachers due to the homophobia and transphobia that occurs within their environs (Bochenek & Brown, 2001; Ferfolja & Robinson, 2004; Page & Liston, 2002).

In response to the notion that schools may be unsafe, there has been a trend toward the development of discourses that promote safe spaces within and outside schools for LGBTI-identified teachers and students (Benton, 2003; Griffin & Ouellett, 2002; Reis, 1997). Given this trend, it is worth examining further this increasingly familiar trope of the *safe space*. It may be useful to consider how it intersects with discourses related to sexualities and schooling: What does a safe school look like? How might a school be made safe for LGBTI-identified young people? From whom is a school being made safe? Alternatively, from whom does the school need to be protected? Is there such a thing as a safe space? Finally, who gets to decide what is safe and what is not?

I consider some of these questions in the context of a brief analysis of two Safe Schools Resource Guides and of comments made by a participant regarding the use of "safety transfers"[9] in New York City (NYC) public schools. The Maine *Safe Schools Resource Guide* (Maine Safe Schools Resource Collaborative, 1999) is partially based on a similar document (Reis, 1997) produced for the Safe Schools Coalition of Washington (SSCW).[10] The first recommendation of both guides commences with a definitive classification of the persons for whom they are seeking protection:

> … The misunderstanding that one's sexual orientation or gender identity is solely a behavior. First, it is important to address the misunderstanding that one's sexual orientation or gender identity is solely a *behavior*. A person can be celibate for his or her entire life and still have a *sexual orientation*. One's *sexual orientation* reflects the gender of people toward whom one feels romantically, emotionally, spiritually and sexually attracted. If a person's most frequent or intense crushes or loves are of the other gender, the person may call him or herself *heterosexual*. If he or she mostly falls in love with people of the same gender, he or she may consider him or herself *gay* or *lesbian*; if they are of both genders, he or she may identify as *bisexual*. A *transgender* person challenges widely accepted notions of gender identity. (Maine Safe Schools Resource Collaborative, 1999, p. 5, italics in original)

At the outset, these guides seek safer schools via recourse to essentializing tropes of identity — a movement that potentially produces its own spatial exclusions. People allowed into the safe spaces supposedly provided by these safe schools frameworks are those who conceive of their gender or sexual identity as somehow fundamental. As such, these safe spaces might be described as heterotopic, insofar as they "presuppose a system of opening and closing that both isolates them and makes them penetrable" (Foucault, 1986, p. 26). It is arguable that the safety of schools may be diminished by the rhetoric that calls for the creation of safe spaces. Students who defy sexual and gender norms but eschew LGBT identities may not be deemed worthy of protection within the confines of such spaces, as it appears that behavior must be perceived as nonvolitional before it is protected.

In her analysis of safe sex education, Patton (1996) considers the problems inherent in creating spaces that inevitably reinforce the heterosexual–homosexual binary:

> Heterosexism demands that we name partners and limit sexuality to a narrow range of cross-gender behaviors. To demand a narrow gay identity — even implicitly ... runs the risk of duplicating this form of oppression. To refuse to claim that everyone any of us has ever had sex with is thereby "gay" is not to degay our community: rather, it is to complicate and confound heterosexuality, to create more space for sexual alliances, not less. (p. 154)

Patton's analysis of safe sex discourse is pertinent to this analysis of the trope of safe space because she allows for a more complex envisioning of the notion of safe space in school settings. By refusing to claim everyone who has ever had gay sex is gay, Patton gestures toward a school space that encompasses a broader range of people who exercise a wider range of behaviors and identities — a strategy that may have the effect of broadening the support base of the safe schools movement.

Although the trope of safe space is ostensibly designed for the protection of the rights of the individual, it has also been deployed as a means to remove troublesome students. In the following, one of the U.S. participants in this study describes the way schools may use the notion of safety to remove a transitioning transgender student from the school space:

> ... There was an enormous amount of pressure put on the student, an MTF [male-to-female], to not cross dress, and transition publicly at school ... even though the student was not a problem, like to the school environment so much. What they did was safety

transfer the student ... . Instead of dealing with the issue, bringing in people to do education or trying to change the environment, they just safety transfer the student out.

The guidance counselor that the student had was, like telling the student that you need to go to Hetrick-Martin and not be here ... . [T]he student did not want to leave the school and had no plans to leave that school ... . It's really not what the Hetrick-Martin Institute or Harvey Milk High School (HMHS) has done ... . It's what the Board of Education or certain schools perceive it (HMHS) as. That is, anytime they have a lesbian, gay, or transgender student ... they cannot deal with that student, and [they] stick them in an all gay school.

For Foucault (1984b), "(s)pace is fundamental in any form of communal life; space is fundamental in any exercise of power" (p. 252), exemplified previously where the safety transfer reflects an "exercise of power" to preserve the public space of the school within the confines of a heteronormalizing framework. Thus, tropes of safe space can be used as a mechanism to remove students that trouble the heterosexual–homosexual binary under the guise of providing for their safety.

In this instance, as in the case of the safe schools program, there is a sense that everyone can enter into a safe space, but these heterotopic spaces may only offer the illusion of inclusivity. In practice, it appears that acts of entry into these safe spaces can be predicated on a process of exclusion from the hetero norm. As Skeggs (1999) notes in her study of visibility and sexuality in leisure spaces, the production of safe gay spaces is an impossibility, and such a vision represents a failure to challenge the legitimacy of those who create the desire for safety in the first place (p. 228). Similarly, the safety transfer just described may be read as indicative of a failure to interrogate the heteronormalizing behaviors that make the school unsafe for transitioning students.

On the surface, tropes of safe space, like notions of inclusion, are difficult to critique. However, on closer scrutiny, it is apparent that this trope may operate as a dividing practice, producing material and symbolic exclusions of particular individuals from the imaginary realm of safe space. As the preceding example indicates, it is also necessary to take into account the relations of power that underlie the invocation of safe space in educational contexts and to determine whose interests are served by the construction of such spaces.

Queering Safe Space

Another form of safe space manifest in the United States[11] comes in the form of high schools specifically catering to the needs of LGBTI-identified young people. In the subsequent analysis, I am not focused on determining whether these schools provide a positive educational experience for their students; rather, I analyze the rhetoric that supports and opposes the construction of high schools that spatially divide young people based on their sexual and gender identities.

One such school, Harvey Milk High School (HMHS), is located in NYC. Initially, HMHS was one of numerous services provided by the Hetrick-Martin Institute (HMI). The institute, according to its website, is "a leading professional provider of social support and programming for all at-risk youth, particularly lesbian, gay, bisexual, transgender or questioning ('LGBTQ') youth" (HMI, 2005a). Founded in 1985, HMHS is administered by the NYC Department of Education and is branded as "the first and largest of its kind in the world — a public school devoted to fulfilling the specific needs of at-risk youth" (HMI, 2005a).

There is some ambivalence within HMI about the existence of schools like HMHS.[12] Rodriguez[13] argues that schools such as HMHS exist because of failures in the school system, situations where students are

> ... not getting the resources and support they need in their communities or their community schools ... . Ideally, one of the things we are going to do is transform the public schools of NYC, but that is a long time in coming. So until those schools are transformed and able to support all of the young people there in all of the ways they need to be supported, we are going to continue to support alternative programming like this that is going to meet specific needs.

Here is a sense that HMHS, by its very existence, is indicative of the failure to accommodate all students within the mainstream space of the NYC Board of Education. Such spaces are thus portrayed as ongoing testaments to the spatial exclusions produced by homophobia and transphobia in educational settings.

Programs such as HMHS have also received criticism from within and outside LGBTI communities.[14] One of the biggest ongoing criticisms of HMHS, according to Hunter (one of the school's founders), is

> ... this whole issue of isolating the kids. In fact, people said we were ghettoizing them ... . They said, Why would you isolate this group of kids? ... Why are you not going for integration? ... People have to understand that these young people have isolated and ghettoized themselves to the streets ... . There are a group of kids who have been so traumatized by the school system that they are just not going to go back. And so this school provided a place for them to get a safe education.

HMHS has also been criticized by people who have religious objections to the spatial division of students based on their sexual and gender identities. At time of writing, HMHS's future was under threat by a lawsuit brought by Democratic state senator Ruben Diaz (Ables, 2004). The Walt Whitman Community School (WWCS)[15] in Dallas was another school that catered primarily to young people who identify as LGBTI, but it closed in 2003. The educational spaces created by these schools are the subject of much emotive debate — for and against their existence.

Partially in response to various critiques, these schools have developed a discourse that seeks to produce the educational spaces they create as necessary havens in an alienating world. An example of the production of such a discourse appears in the following extract. A teacher at WWCS in Dallas, Wally Linebarger, in the course of an interview with Martin (2001), notes,

> Few people criticize hospitals, for example, for segregating the sick in order to best treat them. Similarly, some students who are living in gay or lesbian environments and struggling with their sexual identity need special attention in order to best function in the larger, mainstream society. We're kind of like an educational hospice along the way to college and life. (p. 1)

The series of medical metaphors alluded to by Linebarger construct sexual identity as akin to a sickness in need of treatment prior to the restoration of students to mainstream society. The associations Linebarger draws between LGBTI-identified students and their need for "special attention" are also evident in the comments of Sandy Miller, a teacher at the Out Adolescents

Staying in School (O.A.S.I.S.) program in Long Beach, California: "The students at O.A.S.I.S. 'have already been segregated,' Miller said, explaining that the kids wouldn't be in the program if things were OK in their traditional schools. 'We're trying to make them whole again so that when they leave here they can feel comfortable dealing with what's out there'" (Ables, 2004).

Returning once again to Foucault's (1986) notion of heterotopia, I argue that these educational spaces may be conceived as "heterotopias of deviation," working to reinscribe categories of deviant and normal students. Almost inevitably, students who attend these schools appear damaged, less than whole, classified as deficit by virtue of the struggles associated with LGBTI adolescence. The production of such spaces might also reinforce Gordon's (1999) suggestion that adults who identify as LGBTI have a tendency "to reduce adolescence to a stable site of either shame or abjection in gay and lesbian narrative" (p. 20).

Although I argue that the rhetoric of abjection referred to here is problematic, there is also no doubt that many of the young people who attend HMHS and WWCS are thankful to receive support services that go beyond those provided in mainstream high school settings. In the paradox of endeavoring to affirm gayness as something admissible while refusing to ascribe an essence or a telos (see Introduction) (Lesnik-Oberstein & Thomson, 2002, p. 45), it is apparent that these programs are intent on affirming gayness. As Colapinto (2005) argues in the conclusion to his article on HMHS, coming out does open up students to hostility and violence and it is understandable that students would seek sanctuary from such bigotry.

David Mensah, executive director of the Hetrick-Martin Institute, is critical of detractors like Colapinto who

> ... stand on the sidelines, filing lawsuits and engaging in solipsistic hand-wringing about the constitutionality of our existence. We are providing some of the city's most marginalized and underserved youth with an education and, in many cases, hot meals, counseling and referrals to homeless shelters and medical care. Day in and day out, as our agency has for the past 25 years, we are working against the odds to provide these kids and young adults with a future that holds more than prostitution, homelessness and death ... . We at HMI look forward to the day when our services are no longer necessary; when at-risk youth live and flourish in the world; when their survival is not in jeopardy but instead the world embraces them fully and unequivocally. (Mensah, 2005, para. 3,4)

At the risk of engaging in the act of "solipsistic hand-wringing," it is difficult to escape the conclusion that educational spaces such as HMHS do affirm LGBTI-identified youth as simultaneously essential and pathetic. This affirmation has potentially become more apparent in the information HMI publicly disseminates in relation to HMHS.

Although HMHS is widely known as a gay high school, the webpage for questions and answers (Q&As) on HMHS no longer makes mention of students' sexual or gender orientation, except to ensure readers that being heterosexual does not bar a student from entry into the school. The exclusion of any mention of LGBTI youth from the school's webpage may have been executed to ensure that the school complies with anti-discrimination guidelines; whatever the motivation, it has the effect of confirming that the gay high school is the school for students who are at risk.

Q: What's the Harvey Milk High School?

A: The Harvey Milk High School is an inclusive voluntary public high school focusing on the educational needs of children who are in crisis or at risk of physical violence and/or emotional harm in a traditional educational environment. (HMI, 2005b)

The Hetrick-Martin Institute, collocated with HMHS, also offers students access to "counseling services, and socialization activities, and training opportunities, and case management" (HMI, 2005b). According to Rodriguez, these services are fundamental in enabling the young people attending HMHS to complete their studies and to graduate from the program. Such a model of comprehensive support services has clear associations with the case management of other groups of people depicted as abject by the broader society.

As indicated in the previous chapter, these discourses of protection are, in part, strategically motivated. Portraying these young people as vulnerable reinforces these schools' requests for continued financial support, apparent in the following comments made by Eggleston (2001) in the *HMI Reporter*.

It bears repeating that these and other initiatives can only be realized with donor support. Homophobia, unfortunately, is not going away. Young people are coming out at earlier ages than ever before, and many continue to face ostracism in their schools and in their homes. Places like HMI are still necessary in the year 2001 and, as far as we can tell, will continue to be necessary in the years to come ... . We here at HMI remain committed to this vulnerable population ... . (p. 2)

Although Eggleston and her peers emphasize the problems caused by homophobia in mainstream educational spaces, it is apparent that the factors driving students into requiring the services provided by these safe spaces go beyond discrimination based on sexual and gender identities. The young people who use these services in NYC are, as Rodriguez states, mostly

... from working poor backgrounds. It is ... roughly 80–85%, a population of young people of color, the largest numbers of which are Latino and African American. We have almost equal numbers of young men and women in the program now, who are coming ... from families in crisis, or communities in crisis ... .

Considering that the young people who use these services are racially or ethnically and economically marginalized, it appears that their sexual and gender identities are but one factor contributing to their level of risk. Violence and harassment based on gender and sexual identification are married with poverty and racial discrimination to create a particularly vulnerable group of young people.

In her analysis of the ways in which safe sex education works to construct young people of color as "already lost," Patton (1996) argues that, unlike their white counterparts, young people of color are often considered to be "geographically situated 'where the trouble is.' [T]he risk faced by youth of color becomes a public, collective phenomenon, rather than a private, individual one. Viewed as hard-to-reach, potentially already lost ..." (p. 61). However, Patton's analysis of safe sex education does not resonate with the rhetoric behind the development of schools designed to provide safe spaces for LGBTI-identified young people. Within the rhetoric of these programs, rather than being characterized as already lost, the preponderance of young people of color may not be widely advertised. Homophobia and the oppression of young people are two elements that can be woven into a narrative that will appeal to a broad range of donors within and outside LGBTI-identified communities. Bell

(1999b), drawing on the work of Butler (1990a, 1997b), argues "one site of the construction of difference can act as the 'unmarked background' for another" (p. 5). In this instance, the exclusion from the public rhetoric of these programs of the economic and racial dividing practices imbricated in young people's need for their services effectively elides the complexities that sustain young people of color's ongoing need for the services they provide. Thus, race and class may become the unmarked background in discussions of sexuality and schooling.

This analysis of some of the spatial dividing practices that operate within these programs is not intended as an argument in favor of their dissolution. It is a call to reexamine the factors that contribute to the spatial division of young people of color in educational programs cast under the rubric of providing services to LGBTI-identified young people. My hope is also that this analysis will prompt further consideration of the role these programs must inevitably play in reinscribing these young people's status as potentially already lost, while simultaneously struggling to provide these same young people with essential services and educational opportunities.

The spatial dividing practices that reinforce the marginal position of programs such as these, and the young people who utilize them, are not just found in the rhetoric they produce or the physical relocation of students. The EAGLES Center in LA is spatially and symbolically isolated from the Los Angeles Unified School District (LAUSD). Of the two centers I visited in 1998, one was located in the basement of a high-rise building in Hollywood, California, that had been abandoned by all other tenants, and the other was located in the rooms of a shop front. The O.A.S.I.S. program in Long Beach, California, is located within the grounds of the First Methodist Church.

In contrast to O.A.S.I.S., HMHS occupies more well-resourced premises, including traditional school spaces such as classrooms and a cafeteria. The physical layout of HMHS reflects Rodriguez's following statements about what the young people want from the school.

> They want a high school with teachers that they can develop relationships with, they want a school bell, they want a lunch period, they want books, folders and homework to take home and bring back everyday. What they really seek is to have an experience like every young person has during the high school years.

Rodriguez's description of students' expectations of HMHS speaks to their desire for a normalizing school experience. On some levels it appears that standard temporal dividing practices such as those imposed by school timetables and bells, which may operate to constrain discussions of identity in some traditional school environs, take on a different meaning in these "other spaces." At HMHS, the timetable and bell may signify a temporal compensation for the students' spatial division from the mainstream school system.

All of the schools described in this chapter strive to provide safe spaces to young people who, for a variety of reasons, have rejected or been rejected by mainstream high schools. They deploy and produce a range of spatial dividing practices in an effort to provide students with another route to educational qualifications that may enable them to move out of these liminal spaces and into mainstream high schools, colleges, or jobs. There is an awareness among those involved in these schools that physical, social, and curricular space is reproductive of social relationships and values in society, but there is also a sense that the transmission of these relationships is susceptible to mediation and contest (Armstrong, 1999, p. 83). As indicated by Rodriguez already, by virtue of their existence, these schools create spaces that illuminate the exclusions produced by wider social and educational relations of power. These relations of power continue to be simultaneously contested and reinscribed by the people who construct the heterotopic spaces outlined here.

Discursive

Drawing upon Foucaultian formulations of discourse, the following section traces the "tactical productivity" and "strategical integration" of discourses on sexuality and gender in education. This study involves a consideration of how knowledge intersects with relations of power in two particular instances to valorize and deauthorize specific knowledges relating to people's sexual and gender identities. This analysis pays attention not only to what is said but also to who is speaking and to the spatial, institutional, and sexual locations these people inhabit. It also recognizes the role of discourse in producing and prohibiting certain discursive practices in educational contexts.

Mills (1997) argues that in Foucaultian terms "a discourse is something which produces something else (an utterance, a concept, an effect), rather than something which exists in and of itself and which can be analyzed in isolation" (p. 17). Implicit within this notion of discourse is the understanding that no objective position can be adopted that is outside discourse; thus, this discussion of discourse inevitably forms part of competing contemporaneous notions of discourse. Butler, in an interview with Bell (1999a), draws upon and extends this Foucaultian understanding of discourse. Elaborating on the question of whether or not "everything can be reduced to discourse" (Bell, 1999a, p. 165), she notes,

> ... the subject in speech is always both more than itself and less than itself in any given speech act, that what it speaks is not simply its own speech but it speaks a life of discourse and it is installed, as it were, in a life of discourse that exceeds the subject's own temporality.... It's actually about being, as it were, always already lost to or always already expropriated by a past of discourse that I do not control, and a future of discourse that I do not control. (pp. 165, 166)

For Butler, discourse is beyond the control of any one individual, but it is also beyond the control of any institution or nation state. Given this conception of discourse, it becomes possible to question the past and the present of discourses and to argue that discourses are fluid and therefore capable of change.

In an analysis of the term *discourse*, Bove (1995) responds to those who would conceive of discourse analysis as apolitical or as an exercise in intellectual abstraction. Emphasizing the materiality of discourses, he notes that "discourses are linked to social institutions which 'have power' in the very ordinary sense we mean when we use that phrase: such institutions [like schools] can control bodies and actions" (p. 57). This analysis of discursive dividing practices similarly recognizes that discourses have power to control bodies and actions in schools, but although this power "exceeds the subjects own temporality," it is also this temporal instability of discourse that is the "condition of autonomy" (Bell, 1999a, p. 166) for the subjects that constitute school communities. If discourses are unstable, they allow the possibility for change in schools, even when particular discourses may seem fixed. More specifically, this analysis focuses on the ways forbidden knowledges, actions, and words not only operate to silence or negate but also

... to figure out how a subject who is constituted in and by discourse then recites that very same discourse but perhaps to another purpose ... . That's always been the question of how to find agency, the moment of that recitation or replay of that discourse that is the condition of one's own emergence. (p. 165)

Butler, in an interview with Vikki Bell (1999a), expresses an interest in how the study of discourse may enable a study of the fundamental "question of how to find agency." Making a distinction between agency and intention, Mills (2000) notes that individuals' intentions to perform certain actions are not equivalent to their capacity to control and fix the effects of those actions. This suggests that despite best intentions, certain intentions are made possible whereas others are not (p. 276), or, in Foucaultian terms, "[p]eople know what they do, they frequently know why they do what they do, but what they don't know is what what they do does" (Foucault in Dreyfus & Rabinow, 1982, p. 187 cited in Mills, 2000, p. 276).

Moreover, although the reiteration of discursive dividing practices may promote agency in processes of subjectivization and identification, this agency is not bound to intentionality and thus can, and often does, produce unintended consequences.

As indicated already, the foregoing analysis of the term *discourse* focuses on two discursive acts performed in two separate schools in the United States — one in 2001 in Ferndale, Washington, and the other in 1992 in Queens, New York — which are only made possible by the discursive dividing practices that endeavor to produce subjects with discrete sexual and gender identities. My decision to focus on these discursive acts is also informed by Talburt's (1999) following discussion of the directions of ethnographic inquiry relating to people who are LGBTI identified. Talburt argues, " ... Ethnographic inquiry into gay and lesbian subjects has been limited by its disciplinary and sociocultural locations and must move beyond the production of realist representations that voice and make visible identity and experience ... ." (p. 529).

The ensuing analysis of these discursive acts constitutes an attempt to move beyond the desire to merely make LGBTI-identified people visible in research. I focus on two unconventional educational acts and the ways they intersect with relations of power in schools. In this analysis I am also mindful of the intersections of space, bodies, and texts and their relations to the "making of the material spaces we inhabit" (Threadgold, 2000, p. 58).

I Was a Lesbian Child [16]

I undertake this analysis chronologically, beginning in New York City in 1992. Schulman (1994), a New-York based journalist, writer, and activist, was overcome by the public levels of homophobia she saw broadcast on television, particularly at the Republican National Convention. Schulman also was motivated to act by the dispute over multicultural education, in which "conservative districts like Board 24 [17] in Queens [18] object[ed] to any mention of homosexuality in the public school curriculum" (p. 256).

In response to this dispute, Schulman (1994) argued that "lesbian and gay adults must take a strong, insistent stand for the inclusion of homosexual life in the public school curriculum" (p. 257). The strong, insistent stand Schulman speaks of was scheduled to begin on the opening day of the 1992 school year at an elementary school in Middle Village [19] in Queens. The action, the first performed by the Lesbian Avengers [20] of which Schulman was a founding member, involved 300 helium-filled balloons emblazoned with the words "Ask about lesbian lives," 50 Avengers wearing T-shirts printed with "I Was a Lesbian Child," and a kilt-clad marching band playing "We Are Family" (an anthem of the lesbian and gay movement in the United States). After the parade reached the school grounds, members of the Avengers handed out balloons to arriving students.

> Some parents let their kids keep the balloons. Some refused. But every child who attended school that day heard the word "lesbian," and for some, it just might have been the most important day of their lives. It certainly forced the teachers to discuss the existence of lesbians, regardless of what restrictions had been placed on them by Mary Cummins, the bigoted chair of the local school board. (p. 256).

Schulman (1994) goes on to characterize the Lesbian Avengers' action as having confronted "the greatest taboo in the culture — homosexuals in the school yard. And we did it in a creative, imaginative, and constructive way. It was a strong, radical, confrontational action. But it was friendly" (pp. 281, 282). In the production just described, it is apparent that activist groups such as the Lesbian Avengers have the potential to be "key players in the formation of relationships between bodies and social/political institutions" (Bell & Valentine, 1995, p. 9).

The Lesbian Avengers' action sought to intervene in the formation of students' relationships to their school by focusing their attention on the exclusions produced by the school board's prohibition of any discussion of lesbian and gay sexualities in the school's curriculum. The performance Schulman (1994) describes might be read as a discursive provocation related to the silencing of lesbian identities. It is a provocation to teachers, students, and parents to think about lesbians and about some of the material consequences of the board's prohibition on discussion of anything to do with lesbians.

The space inhabited by the Lesbian Avengers is crucial to this provocation, because as Probyn (1995) notes, lesbian desire may change structures of spatiality and may be changed within different spatial structures (p. 79). When lesbian desire parades on the perimeter of an elementary school, handing out balloons and singing, it will be heard, despite prohibitions. Locating lesbian desire in this particular space is also significant because, as Schulman (1994) notes, it challenges taboos on homosexual recruitment — taboos that produce and sustain prohibitions on the discussion of LGBTI identities in school settings. Such an action may "begin to skewer the lines of force that seek to constitute" (Probyn, 1995, p. 81) all students as straight. When the desire of one woman for another is publicly displayed, it produces a small opening (p. 81) in heteronormalized and heteronormalizing school spaces, "a crack through which ... [students] may see the possibility of sexed space" (p. 81).

Although the Lesbian Avengers momentarily succeeded in inhabiting the perimeter of the school, potentially destabilizing its heteronormalizing spatial and discursive dividing practices, they were also physically unable to enter the school except through the messages stamped on the balloons handed to students. The Lesbian Avengers' intervention also was fleeting: just one morning in the lives of these young people who may spend their entire school years in discursive spaces that otherwise seek to erase or negate lesbian desire. Sumara & Davis (1999) argue that by creating an event in which things not usually associated with one another are juxtaposed, language will be allowed to become more elastic, more able to collect new interpretations, and more able to announce new possibilities (p. 205). However, equally such an event may be utilized to reinforce prohibitions or to create new ones, exposing students to parents' and teachers' hostilities toward the Avengers. As Skeggs (1999) notes, "If public visibility and spatialization are mechanisms for the construction of oppositional gay identity, they also become the instigation for attack … . Struggles for visible identities will often incite danger, for visibility can threaten the normalized landscape" (p. 221).

The results of visibility are not predictable, and they cannot necessarily be guaranteed to promote safety. For such reasons, this action was controversial, even within the Lesbian Avengers:

> A number of people objected to our first action being planned at a public school because they felt we were endangering the children. A furious discussion ensued about whether or not school and family were neutral, safe places for children and whether or not introducing children to the *Lesbian Avengers* was to the kids' advantage or disadvantage. We lost some people, but gained many more. But the debate clarified that this was not going to be a movement for everyone. (Schulman, 1994, p. 281, italics in original)

There was no agreement within the Avengers that the effects of the action would be totally positive. Some members argued that the school, which they constructed as a safe or neutral space, might become hostile as a result of the action. Invoking this language of safety or neutrality provokes the question of whether schools are currently safe and neutral spaces. When LGBTI-identified activists demur from encroaching on school space, they implicitly reinforce the discursive dividing practices that produce schools as somehow neutral and safe. Like other educational institutions,[21] schools are not neutral or safe in relation to the production of discourses related to sexuality; there is no outside to this discourse, and silence may be as powerful a discursive dividing practice as prohibition (Rofes, 2000).

In addition to the mixed reaction of members of the Avengers to the planning of this action, members of the school community no doubt experienced an array of responses to the action. If students entered the school and chose to identify with the Avengers, this gesture of allegiance potentially may have reinforced their discursive isolation due to negative remarks by teachers, parents, or school administrators. LGBTI-identified members of the school community who preferred to defer discussion of sexual identities within the space of the school may have been dismayed at the promotion of lesbian visibility because, as Skeggs (1999) notes, "visibility may foreclose the possibility of invisibility, which for some is a necessity, a desire, a strategy. There is a real power to remaining unmarked (if it is possible); to be marked is often to carry pathology" (p. 228).

It is also possible to imagine that some members of the school community may have been heartened by the action and felt that it represented an important intervention against existing prohibitions on discourse. In short, as a result of the action, a lesbian-identified teacher attending the school might have been prompted to join the Lesbian Avengers or to disavow them entirely. Although the organizers of this action focused on the potential positive implications of proliferating discourse on lesbian identities in the face of school board prohibitions, the group also had to bear responsibility for the potential negative implications that may have ensued from such actions.

This study of a Lesbian Avengers' action outside an elementary school in Queens, New York, suggests the multiplicity of discursive elements that may emerge in relation to the public performance of lesbian identities in school settings where such performances have been expressly prohibited. Somewhat ironically, it is likely that such a performance would never have taken place outside a Queens school without the motivation provided by the prohibition. I have not sought to demonstrate the efficacy or inadequacy of the Avengers action; rather, I have considered some of the "enunciations required and those forbidden" (Foucault, 1990, p. 100) within and outside a lesbian-identified community relating to the discursive performance of lesbian identities in a specific educational context.

Krystal Bennett[22] — *Prom King*

This year, in Ferndale, Washington, students elected a woman prom king. And not just any woman, but a big, butch, out dyke who brought her girlfriend to the prom. The openly gay senior, Krystal Bennett, saw it as a great political statement. Parents got on the phone and complained, and now the principal says there will be clearer guidelines about who can and cannot be nominated; I am sure it will be based on gender (like only boys can be kings — well, tell that to Murray Hill).[23] This system will work for a while to squash the gay kids from reigning as queens, and the butch dykes from flagrantly waving their scepters; however, the administrative bigots will get tripped up again when the first openly transgendered student wants to be nominated. It'll happen, and I can't wait to chaperone that prom. (Taormino, 2001)

In the spring of 2001, Krystal Bennett[24] was nominated as prom king by her senior class at Ferndale High School in Washington. Bennett's reign as king provides an opportunity to trace the discourses that emerge when a ritual designed to reinforce heteronormalizing discourses in the school environment is subverted.

In this analysis of Bennett's reign as king, I am also informed by Foucault's (1986) contention that

> ... despite all the techniques for appropriating space, despite the whole network of knowledge that enables us to delimit or to formalize it, contemporary space is perhaps still not entirely desanctified ... . To be sure a certain theoretical desanctification of space ... has occurred, but we may still have not reached the point of a practical desanctification of space. And perhaps our life is still governed by a certain number of oppositions that remain inviolable, that our institutions and practices have not yet dared break down. These are oppositions that we regard as simple givens ... . All these are still nurtured by the hidden presence of the sacred. (p. 23)

I argue that the proliferation of discourses that emerged around Bennett's election as king may be read as a vindication of Foucault's contention regarding "the hidden presence of the sacred" in the production of space. It is possible that Bennett's election provoked so much debate because it disturbed one of the most sacred spaces of U.S. secondary school cultures: the school prom. This space is where heteronormalizing discourses that permeate school cultures are ritually reproduced and exemplified in the selection of a prom king and queen. In this section, I examine media coverage of the Ferndale prom, the reaction of Ferndale High School's principal, and some of Bennett's own comments on her reign as king. I also consider some of the possible consequences of Bennett's reign in the context of this discussion of discursive dividing practices.

Esteban (2001), a local television news reporter who broadcast a story about the Ferndale prom, reports, "There was nothing unusual about the voting process, but who (the students) picked for their prom king was very unusual. Ferndale's prom king is Krystal Bennett, an openly gay senior." In a videotaped interview with Esteban, Bennett states, "I really wanted to win and was excited about it ... but because it didn't seem realistic, I didn't take it as seriously as I felt about it." Although Bennett is clear about her desire to be prom king, some of her other desires may be less evident. Although Esteban does remark that "Krystal has always been open about her sexual orientation," she never states what Bennett's sexual orientation might be; instead, viewers are left to fill in the gaps. The final shot in the video broadcast is of Bennett dancing intimately with a girl. Viewers of the interview must rely on these visual images rather than on spoken words to perceive Bennett's identity. The absence of speech relating to Bennett's sexual identity points to the operation of discursive dividing practices that operate to marginalize people with LGBTI identities through the production of gaps in speech.

In contrast to Esteban's (2001) speech, which appears somewhat constrained, Bennett is eager to discuss the prom, showing Esteban photos of the prom queen posing alongside her. Bennett is aware that a woman being crowned king has wider ramifications and notes that this event is "one the entire school is going to hear about, one everybody is going to have to address, one that's really going to directly affect the administration and the staff." This interview, broadcast on the local news channel, evidences Bennett's claim that this discursive performance does have potential ramifications beyond the school grounds, and the principal reports receiving various types of feedback from community members about Bennett's reign as king. Esteban goes on to note, "The school says it got about 10 calls from the community, a few complaining, but most callers were just curious" (Esteban, 2001).

There is no sense in Esteban's (2001) report of a community decrying the immorality of Bennett's reign. However, the student body president at Ferndale, Landin Fusman, is reported in the Associated Press as saying, "I guarantee the vast majority of our school thinks there is something a little bit disgusting or very wrong about homosexuality ... . [But] if you think it's wrong, try to change them in a loving fashion."[25] Asked about Bennett's nomination, the principal of Ferndale High School, David Hutchinson, says, "It was okay. They're [the students] telling Krystal that we support you" (Esteban, 2001). Somewhat contradictorily, Esteban reports, "Krystal thinks most of the students voted for her as a joke, but she says she is going to get the last laugh" (Esteban, 2001). Bennett was harassed by classmates after the vote and was reported to have been considering leaving Ferndale afterward because she says, "I'm not sure if I want to surround myself with negativity."[26] Students' reaction to Bennett's election was by no means uniform; other students were reported as saying the vote to elect Bennett was sincere and that "when they announced who the king was, there was a distinct group of people cheering ... . I'm glad she came out and that she was accepted like that in our school."[27]

There is no sense in the reporting of this event of a consensus at the school regarding students' motives for electing Bennett king or about how students' received her election. However, the discursive explosion surrounding Bennett's election is indicative of the provocative nature of this event, taking place in this space, at this particular moment in the United States. Bennett's reign as king also garnered national media interest (it was featured, via a story in the Associated Press (2001), in *USA Today* and the story was also covered by numerous LGBTI community newspapers and websites). Gay and lesbian proms may still attract some local media coverage, but they no longer warrant the degree of national attention that Bennett's election provoked. Why should the election of a woman as prom king be so newsworthy? Bennett's story has such currency because it challenges not only discursive dividing practices relating to sexual identities but also divisions relating to gender identities. Effectively, Bennett's election momentarily reconfigures the sacred space of the prom and exposes its contingent foundations.

It appears that Bennett's reign as king produced multiple effects within Ferndale High School. Bennett's performance was not one school authorities were eager to have repeated. Hutchinson appeared in the final section of the report by Esteban (2001), headed "Unlikely It'll Ever Happen Again." Hutchinson states that Bennett's reign as king "is one way to deal with homosexuality, but it may not be the best way ... . In this venue it wasn't as appropriate" (Esteban, 2001). The principal goes on to note that "based on student input, the school will more clearly define who can and can not be nominated for king and queen" (Esteban, 2001). There is no discussion in the interview of why Hutchinson believes Bennett's election was inappropriate.

Maybe Esteban perceived Hutchinson's objections would be so obvious that such a question did not even bear asking. Through such a discursive mechanism, it appears natural that the hetero-normalizing prerogative traditionally attached to the venue of the prom requires protection from future disruptions akin to that produced by Bennett's election as king. Paradoxically, the need to establish guidelines determining who is fit to be king and queen bears testimony to the vulnerability of the supposedly natural relations produced within the space of the school prom. By associating Bennett's reign with a strategy for dealing with homosexuality, Hutchinson also assumes that lesbians are the only women who desire the king's crown — though, presumably, a woman could desire to be king without desiring other women just as a man who is straight identified might fancy himself as a prom queen.

Bennett's election and the discourses it produces operate to reinforce and disrupt heteronormalizing processes in educational contexts. In the epigraph to this section, Taormino (2001) suggests that Bennett's election points the way to the disruption of other purportedly stable identities such as "when the first openly transgendered students wants to be nominated" king or queen. However, the school's official response to Bennett's election, and the lack of reported opposition to this strategy of prohibiting women from being elected kings and men queens, also reveals the unquestioning reinscription of discursive dividing practices in many secondary educational settings at this particular moment in the United States.

In the context of this book, Bennett's reign as king is also significant because it is not defined by discourses of risk, safety, or protection. Thus, by studying Bennett's subversion of heteronormalizing discourses, it is possible to momentarily disrupt narratives of oppression that are too often associated with LGBTI-identified young people. These narratives are apparent in my analysis of discourses relating to the production of safe spaces and queer spaces in educational contexts. Although these narratives of risk may serve some strategic purposes, they may also serve to reinforce the heterosexual–homosexual binary and thereby to limit people's agency in the production of sexual and gender identities. This study of Bennett is also informed by Friedrich Nietzsche's assertion of the "importance of 'little deviant acts' in a life where accumulated tensions are always becoming naturalized and moralized" (Connolly, 1998, p. 114):

> For nothing *matters more* than that an already mighty, anciently
> established and irrationally recognized custom should be once
> more confirmed by a person recognized as rational ... . All
> respect to your opinions! But *little deviant acts are worth more.*
> (Nietzsche, in Connolly, 1998, pp. 114–115, italics in original)

Sumara and Davis (1999) ponder "how curriculum might
begin to insert itself into the tangled web of ignorance that
currently exists in and around discourses about sexuality"
(p. 200). The actions of people like Bennett and the Lesbian
Avengers do challenge the heteronormative underpinnings of
existing educational discourses. And because these actions
challenge normative conventions of sexuality and gender,
they may also act as a conduit for a conversation that might
fleetingly be inserted into school curricula, destabilizing
the "tangled web of ignorance that currently exists." But the
actions described here are short-lived, and as Hutchinson's
remarks indicate, they may be closed down as quickly as they
are opened. However, as Nietzsche suggests in his reference
to "little deviant acts," the transitory nature of such actions
does not diminish their ability to underscore the contingent
foundations of identities and the potential of subversion to
trouble the production of heteronormativity, even in some of
schooling's most sacred spaces.

Confirming Nietzsche's suggestion, Bennett (2005) argues in
retrospect that his election as king was a positive community-
building event. In the four years he was at Bellingham High,
no students at the school, himself excluded, were out at school.
Following his election, Bennett says that several students at the
school outed themselves. Bennett also reports that although he
identified himself as a male-to-female (MTF) transsexual while
at high school, he never declared this publicly to teachers or
peers. He felt unable to enter this discursive terrain within the
space of secondary schooling; it was just too difficult. Thus,
Bennett was the trans king foreshadowed by Taomorino (2001)
but felt unable to declare himself as such in a space he felt was
already hostile toward lesbian- and gay-identified youth. There
is a sense that, at least at Bellingham High in 2001, a trans
identification represented an opposition people dared not yet
break down, an opposition "still nurtured by the hidden presence of the sacred" (Foucault, 1986, p. 23).

CONCLUSION

Throughout this chapter I have drawn on the Foucaultian notion of dividing practices in order to analyze some temporal, spatial, and discursive modes of objectification of subjects in diverse educational contexts in Australia and the United States. I argued that these dividing practices are integral to the ongoing production of sexual subjects and to the process of heteronormalizing the spaces and places of schooling. Following an elaboration of how I conceive of temporal dividing practices, I also analyzed debates relating to the notion of coming out and argued the efficacy of promoting an interrogation of the narrativization of the coming-out process, as opposed to debating questions relating to the appropriateness of being in or out.

I utilized the Foucaultian notion of heterotopia in order to analyze the production of some spatial dividing practices and to consider how relations of power operate to produce educational spaces in which people who adopt LGBTI identities may be othered, or symbolically divided from their heterosexual-identified counterparts. I also sought to problematize some of the rhetoric that underpins the production of high schools in the United States catering to LGBTI-identified students and critiqued a tendency in the rhetoric of some of these schools to confirm, once more, the abjection of LGBTI-identified young people. Finally, I turned my attention to the production of discursive dividing practices and considered how they work to silence, to negate, and to produce particular kinds of sexual subjects.

Moving on from these three modes of objectification of subjects, I now turn to a study of melancholy, grief, and pleasure and consider how they might be deployed to unsettle the passionate attachments to subjection so prevalent in key discourses related to sexualities and schooling.

7

Melancholy, Grief, and Pleasure: Unsettling Passionate Attachments to Subjection

Following Chapter 6's analysis of three modes of sexual subject objectification, here I consider a different, but not unrelated, explanation for the persistence of constraining categorizations of heterosexuality and homosexuality in educational contexts. In this task I draw on Butler (1997d) to consider the question of "how the subjection of desire requires and institutes the desire *for* subjection" (p. 19, italics in original) — that is, "gender melancholy" (p. 140). In particular, I consider how Butler's theorization of subjection might contribute to the reproduction of what Haver (1997) terms *wounded identities*. I utilize this notion of gender melancholy in the deconstruction of an Australian public art project titled "Hey, hetero!" Following this melancholic departure, I turn to the related notion of grief. In the context of contemporary U.S. discourses related to sexualities and schooling, I ponder Butler's (2002) question, "What makes for a grievable life?" (p. 3).

Subsequent to this analysis of gender melancholy and grief, I explore Foucault's (1996b) concept of governmentality as a possible means to continuously revisit the relationship of the self to the self and the relationship of the self to others (p. 448), which provides one alternative to research focused on abjection. Hence, I turn to a consideration of how an ethics of pleasure might serve as a timely intervention into the relationships people might form with themselves, and with others, in educational settings.

Pleasure may operate to rupture the connections between the wound and subjection, occasionally allowing the possibility of practices of freedom to emerge. As Probyn (2000) notes, the "freedom that Foucault sought was only to be found in the bone-crunching, ligament twisting limits of thought and action" (p. 25).

WOUNDED IDENTITIES

The notion of *wounded identities* here comes from the work of Haver (1997) in the context of his analysis of contemporary "queer research" in the United States. Haver asks,

> What if queer research were to be something other than the hermeneutic recuperation of a history, a sociology, an economics, or a philosophy of homosexual subjectivity? What if, ... queer research were something more essentially disturbing than the stories we tell ourselves of our oppressions in order precisely to confirm, yet once more, our abjection, our victimized subjectivity, our wounded identity? (p. 278)

Haver is clearly critical of queer research that reinscribes rather than disrupts and disturbs "our wounded identity." Here, I interpret wounded identity as conveying the notion that LGBTI-identified people are abject by virtue of their identity. However, I am unconvinced that the modes of objectification I have already analyzed tell a sufficiently nuanced story regarding the production of wounded identities.

In developing her notion of subjection, Butler (1997d) draws on Foucault's (1979) "formative dimension of power" and Freudian psychoanalytic theory. Some, for instance, Dean (2000), consider marrying Foucaultian and psychoanalytic theories is antinomic.[1] For Dean, the process of "assimilating the category of sexuality to imaginary and symbolic formations ... produce[s] queer bodies ... [who are] subjects of the signifier, not subjects of desire" (p. 187), a problematic digression from a Lacanian psychoanalytic perspective. de Lauretis (1998) argues for the feasibility of considering how Freudian psychoanalytic theory might inform Foucaultian analysis, arguing that "Freud's and Foucault's conceptions of sexuality are not as incompatible or mutually exclusive as they are generally taken to be" (p. 2). She reasons that these two theories may have some common ground, at least insofar as neither Freud nor Foucault considers sexuality to be innate.

de Lauretis (1998) asserts that "what is innate for Freud is the drive, the psychic mechanisms that implant a socially constructed sexuality by articulating the drives to the body and the psyche through particular representations or fantasies" (p. 4). Like de Lauretis, Butler (1997d) seeks out the complementarity "between Freud and Foucault."[2] She undertakes this project in order to circumvent the limitations she perceives in Freudian psychoanalytic theory and Foucaultian analysis. At the same time Butler (1996) is indebted to Foucault's theorizing of the subject, she also argues that Foucault elides any theorization of the ways that power relations work "not merely through the mechanism of regulation and production but by foreclosing the very possibility of articulation" (p. 68).[3] For Butler, Foucault's failure to account for foreclosure also results in his failure to theorize the exclusions and erasures continually produced by regulatory practices. Here Butler (1997d) relies on a Freudian understanding of foreclosure as a "desire that is rigorously barred, constituting the subject through a certain kind of preemptive loss" (p. 23). She argues that desires such as same-sex or interracial relations might be understood as foreclosed desires.

Foucault's reluctance to embrace psychoanalytic theories of the subject has also been criticized by Hall (1996), who argues that this refusal to engage with "*the unconscious*" leaves Foucault's theorization of the self "overwhelmed by an overemphasis on intentionality" (p. 14, italics in original). To insist that psychoanalysis is "simply another network of disciplinary power relations" (p. 14) is problematic, Hall argues, because it bars any meaningful engagement with psychoanalytic theories. de Lauretis (1998) attributes Foucault's reluctance to engage with psychoanalytic theory to the historical conditions within which his work was produced and claims that he is writing in opposition to conceptions of the subject "in which consciousness and self-representation are aligned with ideology, on the one hand, and ego-psychology, on the other" (p. 5).

Although Butler (1993) clearly sees value in elements of psychoanalytic theorizing, she also distances herself from aspects of the psychoanalytic project. She argues that

> ... psychoanalytic perspectives locate the constitution of "sex" at a developmental moment or as an effect of a quasi permanent symbolic structure, I understand this constituting effect of regulatory power as reiterated and reiterable .... It is crucial to add that power also works through the foreclosure of effects, the production of an "outside," a domain of unlivability and unintelligibility that bounds the domain of intelligible effects. (p. 22)

However, when Butler (1997d) talks about an outside, she does not conceive of an outside to power "but rather something like the unconscious of power itself, in its traumatic and productive iterabililty" (p. 104).

Provocatively, Butler (1997d) reconfigures both Foucaultian and psychoanalytic theorizations of the subject. She remains indebted to Foucault's theorization of the subject, insofar as she understands subjects to be constituted through operations of power. However, Butler argues that Foucault's theory of the subject is inadequate unless enjoined by a theorization of the effects of foreclosure. She goes on to consider how Foucault's notion of a "regulatory ideal, an ideal according to which certain forms of love become possible and others, impossible" (p. 25) might be reconfigured in the light of foreclosure. She proposes that these social sanctions should not be understood as prohibition — as in Foucault's critique of the repressive hypothesis — but, rather, as a "mechanism of production that can operate on the basis of an originary violence" (p. 25).[4] Reworking the Foucaultian reading of prohibition in this way is integral to this discussion of people's attachments to subjection. To elaborate further, for Butler, " ... any mobilization against subjection will take subjection as its resource, and that attachment to injurious interpellation will, by way of a necessarily alienated narcissism, become the condition under which resignifying that interpellation becomes possible" (p. 104).

Configuring the interpellation of the subject, as detailed by Butler (1997d), does not perceive the resignification of attachments to subjection as inevitable. Rather, readers of Butler's work are invited to constantly consider the value of "assuming and stating a 'subject position'" (p. 29) and to consider the role they play in their own subjection.

It is important to clarify that the notion of attachment referred to here is not intended to imply intentionality in the process of disavowal. As Butler (1997d) notes, "we cannot simply throw off the identities we have become" (p. 102). For Butler, the passionate attachment to subjection is a critical aspect of identity formation. In short, identities are constituted via injurious interpellations, and the price of identification is some complicity in the process of disavowing some subjects as other. Given such a theory of subject formation, it is possible to better conceive people's attachments to coherent identities. Thus, the work of Butler helps to theorize the depths of people's "passionate attachments to subjection" (p. 105) and to seek out moments of resignification that disrupt injurious interpellations and unsettle stable identities.

Insofar as Butler's (1997d) project emphasizes the centrality of subordination in processes of subjectivization, she foregrounds the possibilities of conceiving foreclosure as a mechanism of production. Thus, Butler posits what for me is a convincing explanation of people's investments in essential notions of the sexual subject. No doubt there is happiness to be derived from an investment in stasis, but the cost of continuously maintaining the chimera of stability is the foreclosures and disavowals Butler aptly details. Butler concedes that her formulation of processes of subjectivization is not optimistic, yet she does not conceive of the process of becoming as predetermined.

By taking into account this theorization of the subject, researchers and educators might be prompted to recognize that choices can be made that allow for resignification and reworking of passionate attachments while simultaneously recognizing their instrumental role in the constitution of the subjectivities (Butler, 1997d, p. 105). As Albury (2002) notes in her book about heterosex, in *Gender Trouble*, and in subsequent texts (Butler, 1993; Butler, 1997b),

> ... Butler suggests that even though women are expected to repeat certain feminine roles: wife, nurturer, virgin, slut, etc., the *way* we repeat different behaviours can completely change the meanings of these labels ... . [W]hen biological women knowingly behave "like women" in order to *be* women, they can stretch the boundaries of femininity. When we know we're playing a game, it becomes a lot easier to understand (and bend) the rules. (pp. 104–105, italics in original)

This reading of Butler's earlier work speaks to the possibilities of disrupting heteronormalizing techniques and discourses through processes such as deconstruction. However, given Butler's (1997d) analysis of foreclosure and gender melancholy in *The Psychic Life of Power*, the possibilities for disruption appear to be constrained not only by ignorance of the game we are playing but also via the consolidation of heteronormativity through the persistent disavowal of homosexuality. As such, the possibilities for the disruption and deconstruction of heteronormativity in research and pedagogy, although still apparent, may be less straightforward.

In the next section I consider how this desire for subjection influences the production of educational research on sexualities and schooling, after which I consider how attachments to grief and the wound might be reconfigured for the purposes of community building.

Gender Melancholy

The continuing reproduction of heteronormative discourses in educational research demonstrates the pervasiveness of passionate attachments to subjection. Sexuality research in education tends to be divided into two camps: those who research lesbian- and gay-identified teachers and students, and those who research sexuality and schooling. Within each of these camps, heterosexuality often remains unmarked. Some studies have tended to focus on lesbian- and gay-identified teachers and students. A search in January 2005 using the terms "(homosexual or gay or lesbian) AND school NOT heterosexual" in databases such as Educational Resources Information Center (ERIC) yielded 379 results, whereas the search "(heterosexual) AND school NOT homosexual or gay or lesbian" yielded only 26 results.[5] When compared to lesbian- and gay-related issues, it appears that heterosexuality registers as a mere dot on the landscape of educational research.

Clearly, research in education does focus on young people who identify as heterosexual. What this brief search of the literature suggests is that the practice of labeling the objects of research is often not deemed necessary when the research is being conducted in relation to young people perceived to be heterosexual identified. This observation is not made in an effort to provoke theorizing on methods that might be deployed to categorize all of the groups of people who may possibly be represented within the scope of educational research projects (though such an exercise may be useful in exposing the problematics of identity categories). Rather, I make this observation about the absence of heterosexuality as an explicit marker in educational research as an indication of a continuing tendency to differently classify subjects of sexuality research.

This system of classification may be predicated on the ongoing production of what Butler (1997d) terms "a class of persons for whom it would be unthinkable for me to love" (Bell, 1999a, p. 170). Butler argues that

> ... the prohibition on homosexuality operates throughout a largely heterosexual culture as one of its defining operations, the loss of homosexual objects and aims (not simply this person of the same gender but *any* person of the same gender) would appear to be foreclosed from the start. I say "foreclosed" to suggest that this is a preemptive loss, a mourning for unlived possibilities ... . In this sense we might understand both "masculinity" and "femininity" as formed and consolidated through identifications which are in part composed of disavowed grief. (p. 139, italics and brackets in original)

For Butler, heteronormative idealizations of *masculinity* and *femininity* are predicated on the foreclosure of homosexual desire — a foreclosure sustained through constant disavowal whereby cultural institutions, such as schools and universities, dictate that "there are certain kinds of love that are held not to be love, loss that is held not to be loss, that remain within this kind of unthinkable domain" (Bell, 1999a, p. 170). The sustenance of heteronormative discourses within educational research may be sustained due to "the unthinkability and ungrievability of homosexual attachment" (Bell, 1999a, p. 170).

When heterosexuality does gain a mention in educational research, some researchers — even with the best intentions — may effectively reinscribe the homosexual as other. One example of such an approach may be found in Reiss's (1997) article titled "Teaching about Homosexuality and Heterosexuality." He begins with a commentary on the difficulty of discussing sexual orientation in classroom settings; at the outset sexual orientation becomes convoluted with homosexuality, and the notion that heterosexuality also qualifies as a sexual orientation is obfuscated. Reiss then turns his attention to a discussion of the question, "Should schools teach about homosexuality?" (p. 344) No subsequent section ensues debating the validity of teaching about heterosexuality. Overall, Reiss appears to be in favor of "teaching about sexuality orientation" (p. 351) in secondary schools, and the tone of his article suggests that this means he condones teaching about homosexuality.

There is also a presumption in Reiss's (1997) article that teaching about sexual orientation happens only when teachers explicitly discuss sexual orientation; there is no indication here of the centrality of heteronormalizing practices in the production of educational discourses relating to citizenship, popular culture, families, and community. Such awareness might entail an appreciation of the irony of the subheading "Treating Homosexuality and Heterosexuality Even-handedly" (p. 348). Although Reiss's agenda is ostensibly to argue the value of teaching about homosexuality in educational research, his article reinscribes the homosexual–heterosexual binary and implicitly confirms the status of heterosexuality as the only legitimate sexual identity.

This unmarked status may result in the observation that heterosexuality is absent in discourses pertaining to sexuality and schooling. However, heterosexuality is clearly not absent in educational discourses. Rather, the ongoing production of heteronormative discourses that endeavor to produce discrete heterosexual and homosexual subjects is a critical element of sexuality education in schools, and this production is often sustained in educational discourses regardless of whether heterosexual subjects are marked or unmarked.

Educational discourses that reinforce the notion of unified gay and lesbian subjects are also complicit in the production of heterosexual subjects. Butler (1997d) argues that

> ... within the formation of gay and lesbian identity, there may be an effort to disavow a constitutive relationship to heterosexuality. When this disavowal is understood as a political necessity in order to *specify* gay and lesbian identity over and against its ostensible opposite, heterosexuality, that cultural practice paradoxically culminates in a weakening of the very constituency it is meant to unite ... . For a gay or lesbian identity position to sustain its appearance as coherent, heterosexuality must remain in that rejected and repudiated place. Paradoxically, its heterosexual *remains* must be *sustained* precisely through insisting on the seamless coherence of a specifically gay identity. (pp. 148, 149, italics in original)

As such, discrete gay or lesbian identities, like heterosexual identities, are necessarily sustained through a continuous process of disavowal. In the case of gay and lesbian identities, this disavowal forecloses the possibility that the homosexual may ever become heterosexual, thus sustaining the heterosexual–homosexual dichotomy. Hence, it is possible to see how educational discourses that persist in the production of unified gay and lesbian subjects are also complicit in the production of gender melancholy.

HEY, HETERO!

I can no longer remember exactly when I first saw the "Hey, Hetero!" pictures, but I quickly became passionately attached. I thought they could be a fabulous addition to the introduction to the gender studies course I was then teaching. These pictures had the elements of a useful pedagogical device: They were engaging as well as provocative, fun, and ironic. Moreover, they suggested an effective pathway to introducing the often-discomforting topic of queer theory to my students. Later, I endeavored to theorize the types of resistance I encountered when I sought to introduce these images into the classroom. Why did students not seem to share my enthusiasm for the broader project of unpacking the heterosexual–homosexual binary? How could such a fabulous device fail to involve students in a sophisticated discussion of sexual subjectivity? I contemplate these questions through a consideration of the "desire for subjection" (Butler, 1997d, p. 140). I consider how this theorization of the subject might be instructive in understanding some of the processes that underpin pedagogy related to, and necessarily involving, sexual subjects.[6]

Devised for the Sydney Gay and Lesbian Mardi Gras (SGLMG) in 2001, the "Hey, Hetero!" project involved six photos with text. They appeared in 30 illuminated public advertising spaces in Sydney streets, a city station billboard, magazines, 40,000 Avant postcards (distributed freely through cafes and restaurants), two formal exhibition spaces, and online in February–March 2001 (Kelly & Fiveash, 2001).[7] The interpellation "Hey, Hetero!" introduces each piece, specifically hailing people who, as Kelly notes in a webcast interview, "don't usually think of themselves as a group with their own particular attributes, culture and rituals" (Kelly, 2001).

In developing the "Hey, Hetero!" project, Kelly and Fiveash (2001) state that they deliberately mimicked genres of advertising in an attempt to access

> ... the public attention accorded to commercial messages and denied to "Art"... . The project uses production values which replicate the standards of advertising: gleaming, stylised photography; sophisticated typography, copy writing and design. In this way the familiar, ubiquitous cultural artefact of advertising is invested with new agency: to participate in and broaden the discourses around sexuality which currently preoccupy urban centres around the world. (p. 1)

In effect, the artists endeavor to use humor, gloss, color, and parody to create artworks specifically designed to act as a catalyst for discussion of important cultural issues. As such, these pieces, which resonate with other images that may be familiar to students through their reproduction in magazines and billboards, might entice students to study the reproduction or disruption of certain types of cultural values and norms through the medium of advertising.

In her analysis of the "Hey, Hetero!" project, Sullivan (2003) evokes an Althusserian reading, seeing it as an attempt to subvert the influence of advertising — a mechanism traditionally relied upon by capitalist society to reproduce itself, its values, beliefs, and forms of knowledge in and through the creation of subjects who are its agents and its effects (p. 133). By hailing heterosexuals as subjects, this art project strives to "queer the subject in/of heterosexuality and all that supports and is supported by it" (p. 134). It calls on viewers to question the familiar via the medium of visual art.

By bringing this public visual art project into the classroom, I had hoped to use it as a starting point for an analysis of the construction of normative heterosexuality and a consideration of how heteronormalizing identities may operate as techniques of subjection. It appeared to have the potential to inform a richer pedagogy in the area of sexuality education. In introducing these pictures to students, I had hoped the students would be somehow moved to talk about heteronormalization. The mode of address was direct: "Hey, Hetero!" How could a room, supposedly cluttered with heterosexuals, fail to engage?

Of course, the students did engage, but not in the way I had envisioned. Like many past, present, and future pedagogical exchanges, this episode threw into relief what Felman (1987) defines as the "impossibility of teaching" — an impossibility brought about in this case by the "active refusal of information" (p. 79, in Ellsworth, 1997, p. 57). Faced with these images, students demonstrated their own "passion for ignorance" (Ellsworth, 1997, p. 57), a passion that might be better understood through Butler's (1997d) gender melancholia.

However, prior to a consideration of why "Hey, Hetero!" was met with passionate ignorance, at least by some of my students, it is first necessary to give a more detailed account of these images that encourage viewers to reflect on the heteronormative privileges so familiar that, for many, they do not bear thinking about. The tendency for normative heterosexuality and its associated privileges to remain unmarked helps, in part, to sustain its reified status. For me, this focus on the unmarked and often uninterrogated status of hetero privilege was one of the principle attractions of this art project.

As Albury (2002) notes in her discussion of heterosex, the privileges afforded by heteronormativity do not only preclude people who are LGBTI identified:

> ... While heterosexuality is *supposed* to make straight women normal, in practice this privilege is accorded only to *some* heterosexual women — those in very specific kinds of one-to-one, monogamous relationships ... . Only good, monogamous straights have the "right" to reproduce and raise children without question or censure ... . (pp. 190, 191, italics in original)

Here Albury underscores just some of the boundaries placed around people's access to heterosexual privilege. This privilege also plays out differently according to a person's gender identity, as well as socioeconomic status, geographic location, race, and ethnicity. I had imagined that many students might feel alienated from the privileges of heteronormativity and thus might delight in the opportunity to interrogate the relations of power that sustain this privilege.

Rather than to perceive normative heterosexuality as something essential, located in specific bodies, I had desired students to construe it as a powerful chimera, a worthy object of analysis.

Figure 7.1

In short, rather than attach normative heterosexuality to specific bodies, it might be more usefully construed as a powerful chimera, sometimes accompanied by lots of whitegoods (see toasters, kettles, and irons in Figure 7.1).

The figures in this chapter underscore how activities as basic as constructing a family, having a baby, or getting married are all coded in particular ways. Thus, at least in legal terms,[8] people who are heterosexual identified may enjoy an array of protections and benefits exclusive to the confines of monogamous heterosexual relationships.

On the contrary, people who do not identify as normatively heterosexual do not enjoy similar rights to construct families of

Figure 7.2

choice, to access reproductive technologies, or to get married if they so desire (see Figure 7.1 and Figure 7.2). The privileges afforded heterosexuality are, in Butler's (1997d) terms, foreclosed to those who identity as lesbian or gay; affording such privileges to those who are nonheterosexual would unsettle the originary basis of discrete heterosexual identities. The "Hey, Hetero!" project might thus be used as a mechanism for considering how particular types of sexual identities are produced as unthinkable in contemporary Australian society.

In the "Get married because you can" piece (see Figure 7.4), the combination of traditional values (in the form of confetti, white dress, veil, and flowers), self-satisfied snarl, and defiantly

Figure 7.3

raised finger might provoke a classroom discussion regarding how different members of the public may interact with these images. Debate may also ensue over who produces the advertisements people consume and on how these advertisements operate to reinscribe particular performances of gender and sexuality.

Although Figure 7.1 to Figure 7.4 focus on prohibitions pertaining to access to particular rights, the next images take the campaign to a more personal level and contemplate the production of prohibitions pertaining to same-sex desire. Featuring the text "You can do it with your eyes closed — no fear, no danger, no worries," Figure 7.5 speaks to how one's desire to kiss may become the subject of prohibition. Students might also note

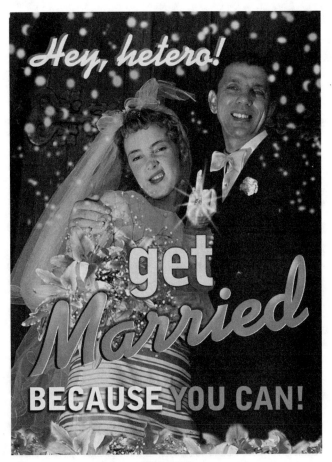

Figure 7.4

(as mine have done before) that a performance such as the one depicted in Figure 7.5 might provoke its own censures if it took place in a "gay space."[9] In one reading, these prohibitions might be attributed to homophobia, and their resolution might consequently be sought through the education of a particular individual or group. For Butler (1997d), these prohibitions on the performance of same-sex desire are not merely an expression of cultural intolerance but, rather, are an example of the defining operations of heterosexual culture.

In Aotearoa/New Zealand, the Young Women's Christian Association (YWCA)[10] used the artwork featuring the kissing couple in what it described as the "Controversial 'Hey, Hetero!'

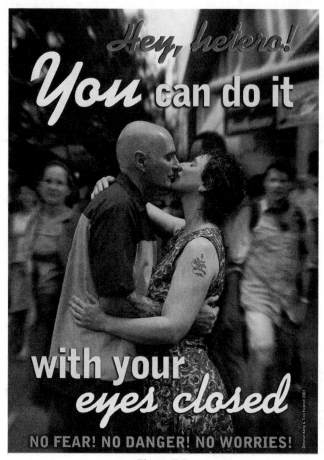

Figure 7.5

Campaign," which had an "anti-gay bashing focus." Robyn
Paterson (Paterson, 2001), YWCA's National Young Women's
coordinator, says she chose to use the posters in the campaign because

> ... the posters are actively challenging. They are fun and
> aesthetically attractive, but the message is serious. According to
> the 1997 Lesbian and Bisexual Women's Discrimination Survey,
> 41% of lesbian and bisexual women have experienced verbal
> abuse, 32% have been threatened with violence because of
> their sexuality, and 13% been physically assulted [sic] ... .
> Violence against gay men also remains disturbingly high in New

Zealand. There have been two murders in New Zealand in 2001 where the sexual orientation of the victim has been reported as a factor in motivation .... (p. 1)

The intention of endeavoring to deliver a serious message in an aesthetically attractive manner is commendable pedagogically, although the connection of the poster to the YWCA campaign's stated focus of anti-gay-bashing seems potentially problematic. In the context of an anti-gay bashing campaign, the poster operates to foreclose any rendering of gayness while simultaneously challenging people who are heterosexual identified to remember that unspecified others may not be quite so lucky when they participate in public displays of affection. This linking of heterosexual privilege and homophobia, within the context of an anti-gay bashing campaign, may operate

... as a caution against two forms of theoretical desire: one in which assuming and stating a "subject position" is a consummate moment of politics; and another in which the dismissal of the subject as a philosophical trope underestimates the linguistic requirements for entering sociality at all. (Butler, 1997a, p. 29)

Marking heterosexuality as a subject position is not, in and of itself, a great leap forward, theoretically speaking. When an anti-gay-bashing campaign places the subject of homosexuality under erasure, the intended desire of protecting homosexuals from bashing might unintentionally have the effect of barring the entry of the homosexual into linguistic sociality, which is the very condition of agency. Whereas the kissing couple in Figure 7.5 is somewhat tenuously linked to the subject of gay bashing, Figure 7.6 focuses on such violence while it deliberately turns the gaze away from the wounded gay identity.

Kelly and Fiveash (2001) make effective use of humor to engage people in the sometimes tragically corporeal effects of homophobia. Figure 7.6 features a crime scene, depicted by a police officer analyzing the chalk outline of a straight couple holding hands — she is the one with pigtails, clasping a handbag. The image in this figure calls upon its audience to empathize with the familiar (a heterosexual couple involved in a public display of affection) in the unfamiliar situation of having been assaulted; it endeavors to illustrate, through a blurring of experiences of the familiar and the other, the potential

Figure 7.6

hazards of nonheterosexual identity. This piece, featured on a billboard at one of Sydney's central railway stations (among other locations), raises the specter of anti-gay violence but also deliberately refuses the temptation to once again perpetuate the "victimized subjectivity" (Haver, 1997, p. 278) so closely associated with LGBTI communities.

The location of this artwork on billboards, in bus shelters, in magazines, in cafes, and on illuminated street posters points to the pedagogical possibilities that exist outside formal classroom settings. Projects such as "Hey, Hetero!" exemplify the ability of art to generate discourse and provide the catalyst for public acts of deconstruction. Such images, accessible to all, might also incite students to develop similar visual art projects extending the themes addressed here or to travel these ideas, using their own art to turn the gaze upon other normalizing stereotypes. Either way, the "Hey, Hetero!" campaign provides an innovative example of how people within and outside the classroom might be encouraged to apply deconstructive techniques to destabilize normative heterosexuality through analysis or creation of posters that are actively challenging, fun, and aesthetically attractive (Paterson, 2001).

As the previous analysis suggests, however, whether heterosexuality is marked or unmarked, the production of unified heterosexual subjects and the concomitant disavowal of homosexual subjects are integral to the production of heteronormalizing discourses. The Butlerian notion of gender melancholy provides some insight into the difficulties of destabilizing our culture's passionate attachments to unified sexual identity categories. And this analysis does not erase the productive possibilities of attempts to deconstruct the heterosexual–homosexual binary and to call attention to the operations of heteronormative discourses. This reading of "Hey, Hetero!" provides an indication of the possibilities and limitations attached to one educational campaign that endeavors to underscore the production of heterosexual privilege in contemporary Australian culture.

In the present analysis of gender melancholy and the "Hey, Hetero!" project, I focused on how particular types of sexual identities are foreclosed and may become unliveable and ungrievable. Next, I consider how particular expressions of grief have come to be configured in the production of U.S. discourses relating to sexualities and schooling.

ON GRIEF AND TRANSFORMATION: RECONFIGURING THE WOUND

In endeavoring to reconfigure the wound, I am inspired by a question posed by Halberstam (2002) regarding whom we select to commemorate in the area of sexualities and schooling, or, to return to Butler (2002), "What makes for a grievable life?" (p. 3). At first glance, such questions may appear to signify a return to the wound. However, Butler steers such inquiries in an alternate direction in the context of a consideration of the transformative potential of loss in furnishing "a sense of political community of a complex order" (p. 3).

For Butler (2002), the transformative potential of grief is predicated on the

> ... understanding that lives are supported and maintained differentially, that there are radically different ways in which human physical vulnerability is distributed across the globe. Certain lives will be highly protected, and the abrogation of their claims to sanctity will be sufficient to mobilize the forces of war. And other lives will not find such fast and furious support and will not even qualify as "grievable." (p. 6)

Although Butler's discussion pertains to September 11, 2001, and the rhetoric surrounding the "war on terror," her analysis is also salient in the area of education. Her musings on grief prompt me to interrogate the conditions of existence that sustain the tendency to focus on the martyrdom of LGBTI-identified young people. I analyze this foundation story of LGBTI adolescence to consider how certain lives come to "qualify as 'grievable'" (p. 6) in educational contexts.

Grief is multifaceted; it is an integral part of people's everyday lived experiences and is something with which all of us must reckon at some point. Drawing on Halberstam (2002) and Butler (2002), I argue for a grieving process that is focused on transformation rather than on the repetition of abjection. In order to make this point, I turn to the story of two young American students, Matthew Shepard and Matthew Limon.

Shepard represents a familiar horizon of grief in LGBTI communities. The following text is from an MTV website, which provided educators with lesson plans relating to a movie about the death of Shepard:

> In 1998, college student Matthew Shepard was brutally murdered outside of Laramie, Wyoming. Today, Matthew Shepard's death stands as a symbol of discrimination and hate crimes taking place all over the country, including those based on race, religion, ethnicity, gender, sexual orientation, and physical and/or mental ability ... . *Anatomy of a Hate Crime* is an original movie for television which explores and documents the different sides of the vicious attack and murder of Matthew Shepard ... . Use *Anatomy of a Hate Crime* to supplement your health or social studies curriculum ... or as part of a larger unit on discrimination, tolerance and/or diversity. (MTV, 2002a)

Here, it is apparent that the tragic death of Shepard is symbolic of all manner of hate crimes "taking place all over the country." It appears that Shepard's life and death, like the lives and deaths of those killed on September 11, has won "fast and furious support" (Butler, 2002, p. 6).

In one of the three lesson plans that accompanied[11] the MTV documentary, the following questions were posed to students: "Why do you think people embraced Matthew's memory so strongly? What was it about this particular hate crime that made people react with such passion and emotion?" (MTV, 2002b) These questions were accompanied by the following quote:

> After the media began reporting the story on a national level, Russell and Aaron's[12] attorneys began to realize the shockwaves Matthew Shepard's murder had caused. One lawyer said, "People don't think he's some gay kid — they think he's their kid." (MTV, 2002b)

Together, these questions and the related quotation point to some of the universalizing processes contiguous with the death of Shepard: processes that purportedly enabled him to become "everyone's child." But Shepard's murder did not cause shockwaves merely on the grounds of its brutality. Shepard was white, male, middle class, handsome, and respectable; altogether, he was considered a suitable candidate for *Time* magazine's 1998 "Man of the Year." Unlike many others who have been murdered because of their sexual or gender identity, it appears that Shepard was a politically saleable icon for the gay movement in the United States.

Given the prominence accorded Shepard's death and the silence that has greeted the slaying of so many others, this disjuncture in grief might provoke a consideration of how "the contours that we accept as the cultural frame for the human limit the extent to which we can avow loss as loss?" (Butler, 2002, p. 6). The mourning surrounding the death of Shepard appears to place him within the bounds of the frame of avowable loss. But what of those who do not fit inside the frame?

Two years after the death of Shepard, Matthew Limon was sentenced to 17 years and 2 months in prison for committing a consensual sexual act with another young man. After two unsuccessful appeals to the Kansas Supreme Court, Limon is still in prison and will not be released until 2017, when he is 36 years old. When the sex act occurred, Limon had just turned 18, and the other young man was 14, nearly 15 — 3 years, 1 month, and a few days younger than Limon. Both young men were residents and students of the Lakemary Center, "a school for developmentally disabled young people in Paola,"[13] Kansas. Limon was convicted under the sodomy laws of the state of Kansas. If he had engaged in consensual sex with a young woman from the school of the same age, he "would have been sentenced to a maximum of 15 months" (ACLU, 2003, para. 2).[14]

In discourses related to sexualities and secondary schooling, there has been a reticence about speaking out on behalf of Limon that stands in stark contrast to the partnership fostered by the Gay Lesbian Straight Education Network (GLSEN) with Judy Shepard, Matthew Shepard's mother. The limits of the cultural frame for avowing loss appear not to encompass Limon. His transgression may be too close to the bone: Educational organizations may resist championing Limon's cause because they "don't want to be accused of pedophilic sympathies, since the boy Limon had oral sex with was 14" (Pursley, 2002, p. 1). In secondary educational contexts, people working with LGBTI-identified students do feel constrained by the notion of recruitment. This constraint, together with the nature of Limon's predicament, culminated in a loss educators seem unwilling or unable to avow.

Rather than perceive Limon as an untouchable political liability, consider the efficacy of grieving the loss of Limon's freedom. How might such an extension of the cultural frame of grieving be conceived as a transformative process? Limon's case has the potential to be construed as

> ... the basis of a profound affinity between movements revolving around gender and sexuality with efforts to counter the normative human morphologies and capacities that condemn or efface those who are physically challenged. And it must also be part of the affinity with anti-racist struggles, given the racial differential that undergirds the culturally viable notions of the human, ones that we see acted out in dramatic and terrifying ways in the global arena at the present time. (Butler, 2002, p. 6)

Ultimately, I argue that cases such as Limon's offer up the possibility of an expansion of grief and a broadening of what constitutes "a normative notion of the human" (Butler, 2002, p. 6) within and outside educational contexts.

Moving on from this study of gender melancholy and grief, I turn now to governmentality, ethics, and pleasure. Like grief, pleasure is multifaceted and an integral part of people's everyday lived experiences. Inspired by Foucault (1990) and Haver (1997), I consider the efficacy of an *ethics of pleasure*, a practice whereby the relations we have with ourselves and others are continuously interrogated.

AN ETHICS OF PLEASURE

As a means of unsettling passionate attachments to subjection, I now turn to the intermingling of sexualities and pleasures. This discussion is not a protest against the documentation and investigation of homophobia and heteronormativity; I do not advocate the abandonment of research that underscores discrimination experienced by diverse LGBTI communities. Rather, I argue that pleasure or subjection may be problematic when they constitute the sole basis of research related to sexualities and schooling.

More than a decade ago, Fine (1988) famously noted the absence of desire in educational discourses. More recently, other researchers in education advise that "any event suggestive of sexuality is problematic and even potentially dangerous" (Tobin, 1997, p. 1) within the context of schooling. Harrison, Hillier, and Walsh (1996) assert that there is not an adequate articulation of pleasure in Australian school-based sexuality education, and they argue that this has negative consequences for young women's safer sex practices and for their sense of identity (p. 75). Other researchers on pleasure in education contend that "schools tend not to be places where bodily pleasure is a legitimate topic of discussion ... . Pleasure exists below the surface, unstated, lacking socially sanctioned vocabularies" (Gard & Meyenn, 2000, p. 32). Such contentions inevitably influence the type of research people take on and leave untouched in schools.

Gard and Meyenn (2000) conducted interviews with boys about pleasure and pain in contact sports. However, they felt it was improper to ask the boys questions about

> ... the pleasure they received when touching or being touched by other boys while playing sport ... . It seemed inappropriate in the context of the research to ask students to explain the

contradictions and slippages implied in their reported actions and words, especially as we suspected that fundamental issues pertaining to gender and sexuality were at stake. The dilemma took on even greater significance given the current climate of fear and suspicion regarding the sexual abuse of children in Australian schools. (p. 23).

Gard and Meyenn raise several issues. First, they suggest a relationship between discussions of physical pleasure in educational settings and the specter of child abuse. Implicit within this excerpt is also a sense that the researchers feel a risk of being construed as predatory if they ask the boys being interviewed about physical pleasure "in the current climate of fear." A sense also exists that such questioning might raise the stakes of the interviews to "fundamental issues pertaining to gender and sexuality."

It is important to acknowledge the problems and prohibitions faced by educators, researchers, and students working in this area. Although some are enthusiastic to consider pleasure, many may be reluctant to discuss sexuality and pleasure in educational contexts (Harrison et al., 1996; Wright, 1999). Related to this is the question of how much agency teachers may exercise in constructing their own curricula relating to discussions of sexuality within the bounds of the classroom. Students' right to challenge teachers who persist in homophobic and heterosexist behavior within the context of sexuality education is also highly constrained. As Epstein and Johnson (1994) observe, sex education, like education in general, ... occurs within the context of grossly unequal power relations (p. 219). The relations of power that exist within schools and in educational research often work to exclude, prohibit, and silence discussions of sex and pleasure in the school's formal curricula.

Because discussions of sex and pleasure are often still taboo in schools and other locations in broader society in Australia and the United States,[15] it may be considered premature to consider the value of pleasure the production of discourses related to sexualities and schooling. However, the liminal and controversial place of sex and pleasure in education should not be used as a justification for the "disavowal of particular forms of sexual pleasure" (Britzman, 1998, p. 69) and the absenting of the body within educational discourses related to sexualities and schooling. Rather, existing gaps may be better conceived of as potential

openings for a consideration of how discourse on diverse pleasures might work to highlight discontinuities and may create
ruptures and eruptions in existing discourses that constitute
sexualities and secondary schooling.

Sex and pleasure are fundamental aspects of students' lives and
school cultures. They are also integral to students' sense of well-
being and can determine their propensity to engage or disengage
with the desire to love, learn, and transform themselves. This would
suggest that the proliferation of practices related to the intensification of pleasure is of great use in educational research and practice, as it is crucial to individuals' ongoing process of becoming.

In responding to this disavowal of pleasure in queer research,
Haver (1997) suggests an alternative: "What if thereby queer
research actively refused to forget that perversity, that chaos of
pleasures and affects, that anonymic existential exigency which
has been the occasion of its emergence?" (p. 278) This movement
toward an exploration of the perversities and pleasures that have
occasioned the emergence of queer theory underpins my exploration of a Foucaultian-inspired ethics of pleasure (Foucault,
1996c) — how it might provide an efficacious departure from
educational research that too often reinscribes pathological
stereotypes of LGBTI-identified young people.

Before proceeding to elaborate on the ethics of pleasure, it
is necessary to clarify the notion of the term *ethics*, which here
does not relate to a traditional understanding of the term tied
to the formulation of codes and principles of moral behavior.
Rather, it is a Foucaultian-inspired ethics perceived as a way of
being and behaving. Implicit within this work one does on the
self, this care for the self, are complex relationships with others
(Foucault, 1996b, pp. 436, 437).

Given this understanding of ethics, a Foucaultian ethics of
pleasure focuses on the modes of being and behaving "by which
one could define what is sexual pleasure" (Foucault, 1996b,
p. 433). Thus, pleasure may be conceived as part of the process
of caring for the self and others, insofar as it enables us to
create new relationships, new ways of seeing, and new ways
of life (Foucault, 1996d, p. 310). In the context of this book,
I relate ethics of pleasure to broader questions of how pleasures — sexual and otherwise — might be related to working
toward greater freedoms for the self and others within educational contexts.

Rabinow (1997) argues that Foucault "is seeking to break open the equation of the forms of pleasure one enjoys and one's supposed identity" (p. xxxvii). Foucault (1990) first sought a movement toward bodies and pleasures and away from sex and desire in the conclusion to his first history of sexuality.[16] He writes,

> We must not think that by saying yes to sex, one says no to power; on the contrary, one tracks along the course laid out by the general deployment of sexuality. It is the agency of sex that we must break away from, if we aim — through a tactical reversal of the various mechanisms of sexuality — to counter the grips of power with the claims of bodies, pleasures, and knowledges, in their multiplicity and their possibility of resistance. The rallying point for the counterattack against the deployment of sexuality ought not to be sex-desire, but bodies and pleasures. (p. 157)

Foucault's counterattack has been the subject of much debate.[17] In an article titled "Revisiting Bodies and Pleasures," Butler (1990b) argues that if "the pleasure of this utopian break is derived in part from the disavowal and repudiation of sex, and, correspondingly, with sexual difference, then feminism remains the disparaged object with which no queer theoretical pleasures can be sustained" (p. 18). This move toward pleasure is not conceived as a repudiation of sex or feminism; on the contrary, I recognize that sex and gender are inextricable from discussions of sexuality and pleasure.

Rather than conceive of bodies and pleasures as a movement away from sex and desire, Bernauer (1992) provides a broader definition of Foucault's thesis in the "Right of Death and Power over Life." He asserts that Foucault's counterattack is not against sexual difference but against the obligation to know ourselves and behave as unreflexive subjects of various modes of objectification (pp. 261–262). Working from this understanding of ethics and pleasure, I consider pedagogical strategies that claim bodies and pleasures as a way of exploring the relations of power that restrict, expand, and prohibit pleasure in educational contexts.

In mobilizing an ethics of pleasure, it is also necessary to be mindful that pleasures are exercised through bodies. These bodies are inextricably connected to a historically produced gender and sex. At different moments, in different locations, and with different degrees of success, these bodies might turn to the intensification of pleasure. However, — and this caveat is critical — bodies and pleasures are continuously mediated by cultural, historical, racial, and economic prohibitions. These prohibitions constrain the practices of freedom that allow for the intensification of diverse pleasures, by diverse bodies, in diverse places.

Tighter prohibitions on bodies and pleasures are apparent in legislation introduced in the State of Victoria in 2004 that bars all people convicted of sex offenses from working with children. This law classifies all sex offenders as equally dangerous. Andrew Phillips, a teacher at Orbost Secondary College, was the first person suspended from teaching under the new law. It was discovered that he had committed a sex offense.

> The offence, involving a 15-year-old girl, occurred in 1992 when Mr. Phillips was 20 and before he became a teacher. Although Mr. Phillips was in a relationship with the girl, she was not 16 and therefore considered a minor. It has been reported that Mr. Phillips, in a consensual act, had touched her breasts. He pleaded guilty to a charge of indecent assault. The magistrate did not record a conviction. (Haywood, 2005, para. 1)

Under this legislation people convicted of sexual indecency for consensual sexual relations with someone a few years their junior (and under the age of consent) are classified as equally dangerous to convicted pedophiles. Such laws run counter to Foucault's ethics of pleasure, reinforcing blanket prohibitions. Telling individuals how to act sets up certain relations among what we do, what we are permitted to do, and what we are forbidden to do. Such prohibitions, which instruct us how to act, also work against the development of an ethics of sexual behavior, insofar as they require certain behaviors rather than foster ethical relations focused on care of the self and others.

Next I consider how this ethics of pleasure manifests in two educational contexts: *Young, Gay and Proud* (MGTSG, 1978), a text written for lesbian and gay young people by an autonomous collective of the Melbourne Gay Teachers' and Students' Group (MGTSG); and a letter written to Dan Savage, a nationally syndicated agony aunt[18] in the United States. It is acknowledged that the introduction of sexual pleasure into the formal curricula of schooling is a fraught process, but as Beckett and Denborough (1995) note, " ... although schools, adults, and our broader culture do a great deal to reduce the possibilities for pleasure and intimacy for young people many of them boys and girls, lesbian, gay and straight — experience great pleasure, intimacy and excitement in their sexual explorations while at school" (p. 403).

Thus, even if discourses of sex and pleasure are often not explicit in research or sanctioned in the formal curriculum, discussions and explorations of sex and pleasure are by no means absent in schools, and they are not entirely absent in educational discourses.

YOUNG, GAY AND PROUD

As the coupling of sex and pleasure seems to be hard to find nowadays in schools' official curricula, I turn to a study of *Young, Gay and Proud (YGP)* (MGTSG, 1978). I analyze this publication in order to interrogate how sex and pleasure came together in educational discourses produced nearly 30 years ago in Australia. Articles relating to sexuality and pleasure in the field of education also appeared in the United States and in Europe in the 1970s (see Bertolus, 1973; Fogel, 1977; and Howell, 1976), when some teachers and students seemed willing to engage with students' desire to know more about sex and pleasure. This was noticeable in material on this topic such as *YGP*, produced by organizations such as MGTSG.

Alongside discussions of pleasure, *YGP*'s authors also touch on the incidence of homophobia within schools, but the text's focus is not to provide statistical or qualitative evidence of discrimination against LGBTI-identified young people. The authors of *YGP* state in their rationale for writing the text that it is intended as an "anti-dote [sic] to the countless number of sex ed. guides that assume everyone is or should be heterosexual" (MGTSG, 1978, p. 3). In addition to sections on sexual identity, sexual health, and coming out, *YGP* has two fairly explicit sections on the logistics of gay and lesbian sex, pointedly titled "Doing It."

The "Doing It" section for lesbians begins with instruction on masturbation, because "one of the ways you can get to know your own body is by masturbating" (MGTSG, 1978, p. 3), and then proceeds with some of the following explicit directions for (no doubt) eager readers:

BUT YOU STILL WANT US TO TELL YOU HOW TO DO IT, RIGHT?

... Using your fingers, try caressing the labia, running them around the whole area, inside the vagina, out again and up to the clitoris until sexual excitation or orgasm happens. You can do this to each other at the same time or take it in turns ... . (p. 3)

The section for boys states that

because mouths are soft and warm, having your penis sucked feels really good. If you are doing the sucking, hold the other person's penis with one hand, and put it gently into your mouth. It feels nice and smooth. Run your tongue up and down it toward the tip, and try and watch out your teeth don't get in the way too much ... they're hard. Don't worry about swallowing the semen. It just tastes salty. And it's perfectly harmless. (p. 40)

These "Doing It" sections on the mechanics of lesbian and gay sexual practices are problematic in many respects. I do not advocate that they be used as a blueprint for contemporary resources, not least because of their total lack of awareness regarding the transmission of sexually transmittable diseases. However, the inclusion of a section in this text acknowledging that young readers (who are the text's intended audience) want to know some explicit mechanics about "how to do it" is an important recognition of the role of pleasure in the lives of young people. Although the authors of *YGP* are open to talking about the mechanics and pleasures of sex, they also advise readers that "you must always remember that you are making love to another person like yourself, not just another penis or anus (arse-hole)" (MGTSG, 1978, p. 3). The authors of *YGP* thus encourage students to think of themselves and others when they engage in sexual pleasures.

In the introduction to *YGP*, the MGTSG (1978) states that it is seeking to counter a society that is "anti-sex (except in so far as sex can be exploited for money-making, or contained within heterosexual marriage for the purposes of procreation)" (p. 3). In a similar vein, Britzman (1998) notes that within contemporary educational discourses pleasure is confined to utility rather than a range of perverse sexual practices (p. 69). Though 20 years apart, there appear to be some connections between the observations of Britzman and the MGTSG about the ways in which sex and pleasure are constructed and bypassed in educational and popular discourse. Britzman rightly points out that "nothing about sex education is easy" (p. 76). Given this comparison, the MGSTG's incorporation of issues related to sexual health, pleasure, and consent within the one text appears to be a prescient endeavor.

In contemplating how discourses relating to sexuality materialize, Patton (1996) notes,

> sexuality emerges in action — participation in and observation of prohibitions and pleasures — and through "reading" — other bodies, medical texts, popular press accounts, how-to-books, pornography ... creat[ing] for each person a set of interpretive strategies that in turn position them in networks of policing, advice, possibilities, styles, erotic preferences, closets. (p. 142)

As a "how-to-book," *YGP* has its own suggestions to make about the meanings attributed to erotic preferences and the rights and wrongs of sexual exchanges. Regardless of how one interprets the text and the value of its content, it may broaden the options of its readers through contributing to and complicating the readings available to young people in relation to sexuality. This is not to say that any how-to book should be granted a place on library shelves or in school curricula, though there is some value to be gained from a proliferation of readings available to young people relating to sex and pleasure. Such a collection may help students of all sexual and gender identities develop creative ways of life that enable them to better care for themselves and others. Hence, an ethics of pleasure might be applied through a proliferation of reading materials and via related discussions of sex and pleasure.

In the following section, I analyze discussions of sex and pleasure outside traditional educational contexts and consider pleasure's relationship to sexual and gender identities. I take this departure in support of the notion that people doing sexuality education within schools may enliven their own pedagogical techniques by further study of the strategies utilized by sex educators working in the broader community.

IDENTIFYING WITH PLEASURE

YGP explicitly ties the information it provides on sexual practices to particular ways of identifying, so the text is geared specifically toward students who choose gay and lesbian identities. This association of particular sexual practices and pleasures with specific sexual identities is problematic if educators strive to disturb the notion that sexual practices are somehow indicative of the truth of one's sexual identity. This is why Foucault's (1996c) ethics of pleasure is not "dominated by the problem of the deep truth of the reality of our sex life" (p. 380). Patton (1996) makes the point that a "[s]exual insurrection must work to open up sexual possibilities regardless of the names people choose for their pleasures" (p. 144). Following Foucault and Patton, I am advocating that discussions of pleasure in research related to sexualities and secondary schooling not be tied to identities or a preoccupation with "the names people choose for their pleasures."

Another strategy for broadening people's knowledges of sexualities, genders, and related pleasures is the advice column. The *Savage Love* column and others offering advice on love, sex, relationships, and pleasure are familiar instruments for structuring discussions relating to sexuality in magazines, newspapers, and online (Currie, 2001). Kehily (1999) notes that popular cultural forms such as agony aunt columns have also been used effectively in schools as a tool to discuss "themes which are generally underdeveloped within sex education programmes such as: sexual abuse, pleasure and danger in sexual relations; constancy and betrayal; homosexuality" (p. 127). It is worth reiterating that discussions that result from such interactions will always be constrained by the relations of power that infuse interactions among students, teachers, and broader school communities.

Kehily (1999) also observes that students in the United Kingdom may be asked to pen their own problems or questions and then to view a video that uses the agony aunt format (p. 128) to respond to sexual queries. Next, I consider further the possibilities of introducing pleasure into school curricula through analysis of advice columns that already exist online and in community newspapers and magazines. Though there may be some pedagogical merit in the introduction of such columns into sex education classrooms, I also argue the necessity of encouraging students to question the expert advice of "sexperts."[19] As Albury (2002) notes, "At best, sex advice provides educational information and a bit of support. At worst, sex advice is narrow and restricts our sexual options into limiting 'one-size-fits-all' rules and checklists" (p. 19).

I analyze just one of these columns in the context of this broader discussion of the application of a Foucaultian ethics of pleasure in secondary educational settings. The *Savage Love* column, which touches explicitly on the relationship between pleasure and identity, gives weekly advice and is written by Dan Savage (1999). His column appears online and in print in various locations across the United States. In the following excerpt, Savage draws on expert knowledges related to transgender issues, enlisting the services of trans theorist Kate Bornstein in responding to a heterosexual-identified man's identification anxieties.

In reading this particular column, provocatively titled "Chicks with Dicks" (Savage, 1999), it is possible to explore how pleasure and identity become entwined in discussions of sex and pleasure. How someone chooses to identify and how they behave or derive pleasure is by no means straightforward, as illustrated by the following.

If a guy intentionally has sex with a "chick with a dick," does that make him gay? Or does this fall under the umbrella of harmless hetero "experimentation"? By the way, I am straight. Honest!

[Signed], "Messed Around"

[Savage's response]

"No, 'intentionally' having sex with a 'chick with a dick' doesn't make you gay," said Kate Bornstein, a male-to-female transsexual and author of the terrific books *Gender Outlaw: On Men, Women, and the Rest of Us* and ... *My Gender Workbook: How to Become a Real Man, a Real Woman, the Real You, or Something Else Entirely* ... . "It means he has a leaning toward people who have a mix going on, gender-wise, and he leans toward a very specific mix. It might make him a transhag or a transfag, but not a gay man."

Bornstein felt that you should worry less about how you're perceived by others, and more about your own happiness. "Gay men want to fuck other gay men, period," Bornstein added. "Is a chick with a dick a gay man? No." What is a guy into chicks with dicks? "He might be a queer het man. That's a good category for straight men who want to explore their options. That's what queer is all about: it allows room for exploration of desire and identity.

If this man is attracted to a chick with a dick, does it make him a gay man? No. Does it make him queer? Yes. Is he any less het? No. Am I speaking in contradictions? Yes." (p. 1)

In responding to "Messed Around," Savage draws on Bornstein to emphasize the contradictions that revolve around sexual desires, sexual practices, and the classifications people attribute to them. Bornstein suggests a focus on the happiness of the letter writer, urging him not to be preoccupied with how others might perceive his behavior. Still, Bornstein goes on to proffer several identity categories that might best describe "Messed Around," thereby giving him a label other than the straight one he uses to identify himself. As such, the advice proffered by Savage and Bornstein indicates that the pleasures a person chooses can call into question the truth of his identity or, somewhat contradictorily, can confirm it. Either way, there seems to be an underlying assumption that pleasure and desire are able to reveal someone's deep identity (Foucault, 1996c, p. 377).

Although I question the impulse to help "Messed Around" define his true sexual or gender identity, I argue that the material covered by such a letter may serve as a platform for the application of an ethics of pleasure within and outside the classroom. First, the letter potentially proliferates sexual pleasures available to readers by introducing them to practices that may be unfamiliar. Second, the letter may induce pleasure in the classroom by virtue of the debates it might provoke. And third, the letter gestures toward the intrinsic value of pleasure.

Rather than equate sexual pleasures or practices with identity categories that represent the deep truths of sex lives or with liberation from homophobia, misogyny, or patriarchy, Grosz (1995b) elaborates on the importance of pleasure for pleasure's sake. She argues for a

> ... refusal to link sexual pleasure with the struggle for freedom, a refusal to validate sexuality in terms of a greater cause or a higher purpose, the desire to enjoy, to experience, to make pleasure for its own sake, for where it takes us, for how it changes and makes us, to see it as one but not the only trajectory in the lives of sexed bodies. (p. 228)

Another approach to sex education that may be more in line with Grosz's theory is found in Albury's (2002) alter ego,

"Nurse Nancy" (Nancy wears a rather short uniform and fishnet stockings and loves talking explicitly about sex).

In an interview with Lizz Kopecny (2003), Albury says she uses Nancy in order "to promote sexual pleasure, and mock scientific/ educational pomposity." (2003, para. 7) She goes on to make explicit connections between sex education and sexual ethics

> ... particularly in regard to negotiating sexual practice, and dis-closing STIs, HIV and other things as part of a sexual encoun-ter. I think contemporary school-based sex education is way too focussed on reproduction, and absolutely under-emphasises sexual communication, and an appreciation of sexual experimentation and sexual diversity. Young people need to learn how to negotiate honestly and respectfully — saying "yes" to the things they want, as well as "no" to the things they don't want. They also need more resources where they can get help if they get hurt, or things go wrong. And sex education needs to be sexy and entertaining! Channel 10[20] should be producing sex education — with my help, of course. (Kopecny, 2003, para. 9)

By placing her emphasis on how young people might negotiate sexual encounters "honestly and respectfully," Albury advocates a significant shift in school-based sexuality education away from the mechanics of reproduction and prevention. She wants sex education to focus on helping young people to communicate more effectively about sex. This focus on being and behaving as sexual subjects is instructive in thinking about how Foucault's ethics of pleasure might effectively translate into classroom practice.

Pleasure should not be construed as the linchpin in the "struggle for freedom" or liberation from some oppressive power. However, when pleasure is considered in the light of the "relationship you have to yourself when you act" (Foucault, 1996c, p. 380), it is an integral element of the technologies of the self. It is these technologies that "permit individuals to effect by their own means or with the help of others a certain number of operations on their own souls, thoughts, conduct, and ways of being, so as to transform themselves in order to attain a state of happiness, purity, wisdom, or immortality" (Foucault, 1988, p. 18). Thus, the application of an ethics of pleasure does not bind pleasure to notions of resistance or liberation; instead, plea-sure is situated as part of ongoing practices of becoming — prac-tices that might be intensified by the insertion of how-to books and advice columns into the realm of schooling and sexuality.

CONCLUSION

I used Butler's (1997d) theorizing of gender melancholy to consider the difficulties of endeavoring to destabilize hetero-normalizing discourses. I also argued the transformative potential of expanding our understandings of grief and of what constitutes "a grievable life" in educational contexts. I also argued that an ethics of pleasure may be of value because it provides a crucial counternarrative to people's investments in wounded identities and the concomitant tendency to narrativize the abjection of LGBTI-identified teachers and students.

An ethics of pleasure allows for the recognition of individuals' agency in their own conduct and pursuit of pleasure while concurrently acknowledging the relations of power that operate to constrain discourses of pleasure and to reinforce coherent identity categories within and around educational contexts. Within such constraints, individuals cannot pursue pleasure however or whenever they please. And not all constraints are negative; some may be effective in assisting the individual in caring for the self and others, whereas others appear to serve no other purpose than to reinscribe hetero-normativity. Researchers, teachers, and students cannot situate themselves outside this web of power relations in which they are always, already, a part.

Conclusion

... [W]e have arrived at the point where we expect our intelligibility to come from what was for many centuries thought of as madness; the plenitude of our body from what was long considered its stigma and likened to a wound;
our identity from what was perceived
as an obscure and nameless urge.

(Foucault, 1990, p. 156)

SCHEMATIZING THE RESEARCH PROCESS

The Foucaultian notion that the familiar is often poorly known (Foucault, 1997, p. 144) resonates throughout this book. The central questions I have devised provide the means for an interrogation of the familiar and also point to some alternative ways of thinking about key discourses related to sexualities and secondary schooling. I restate each of these questions here and detail how each question contributes to the design of this book.

1. What are some of the key discourses relating to sexualities and secondary schooling?
2. How are these discourses manifest in the field of sexualities and secondary schooling and why do they manifest in these particular ways?

3. What are some potential alternative directions for the production of theories and practices related to sexualities and schooling?

At first glance, the identification and examination of key discourses relating to sexualities and secondary schooling may appear an odd point of departure for a study titled *Becoming Subjects*. However, as I argue throughout, the process of becoming subjects is inseparable from the discursive production of sexual and gender identities in research and pedagogy related to sexualities and secondary schooling. The theoretical frameworks upon which I have drawn highlight the significance of this interrelationship.

Key discourses I identified include arts of inclusion, tropes of essentialism and constructivism, and interrelated notions of identity and subjectivity. I also categorized various manifestations of tropes of risk and violence associated with young people who identify as LGBTI. Related tropes pertaining to the production of "safe spaces" and to the salvation of young people at risk also were studied. Diverse narrativizations of the closet and coming out also were identified, both as arts of inclusion and as temporal dividing practices.

Certain subjects are unmarked or foreclosed within formal educational discourses, and these also were identified. As a consequence, I analyzed the performance of drag and trans identities in secondary school settings and detailed the performance of *little deviant acts* (Nietzsche, in Connolly, 1998, pp. 114–115, italics in original) such as the Lesbian Avengers' protest in a conservative U.S. school district that had prohibited any discussion of homosexuality in its curriculum. In this vein, I also identified some differing discursive representations of grief in U.S. educational discourses. In considering how particular types of lives remain unmarked within educational discourses, I also identified pedagogical attempts that reinscribe and disrupt representations of normative heterosexual subjects. I also pointed to the continuing deficit of discourses of sexual pleasure in educational settings and considered some of the consequences of this lack.

How and why these key discourses manifest in particular ways is the focus of the second question posed. In responding to this question, I detailed some of the underlying theories and relations of power that sustain these interrelated discourses. To this end, I considered how discourses of inclusion are often predicated on the production of teachers and students with discrete sexual and gender identities and also detailed different arguments that support diverse manifestations of essentializing tropes and tropes of choice. In addition, I considered how, through processes of repetition and through association with expert knowledges, certain discourses manifest as authoritative and work in conjunction with tales of woundedness.

A primary theoretical resource has been Foucault's notion of subjectivity and his three modes of objectification of subjects. I also drew extensively on the work of Butler to study subjection, gender melancholy, and grief in relation to sexualities and schooling. Butler's more recent writings on the conceptualization of the subject and subjection also were important in my analysis of the continual recourse to wounded identities threaded throughout the key discourses I identified.

The final of the three central questions I posed in this study pertains to some potential alternative directions regarding theories and pedagogical practices related to sexualities and secondary schooling. Details of these suggested alternative and future directions are provided next.

I offered different ways of thinking about the production of sexual identities through my study of debates regarding the question of whether or not it is appropriate or desirable to come out in the classroom. Countering the emphasis often placed on the importance of the coming-out process, I proposed that greater consideration be given to how the coming-out process is constructed through the operation of dividing practices associated with particular bodies, narrativizations, and performances.

Different ways of thinking about discourses related to sexualities and secondary schooling also were stimulated by theorizing the intersections of sexuality and space. As such, my analysis of the production of spaces ostensibly designed to support LGBTI-identified young people in high school settings points to the obfuscation of racial and economic factors that may be imbricated in attempts to make schools "safe spaces." Conceiving of educational spaces as heterotopic assemblages produced by relations of power has facilitated an analysis of the role of these spaces in molding people's sexual and gender identities. Thus, it becomes possible to consider how these spaces have, even with the best of intentions, been co-opted to the task of reinforcing the heteronormalizing function of the school.

In endeavoring to enliven discourses related to sexualities and secondary schooling, I also focused on pleasure and, somewhat curiously, grief. I contemplated the Butlerian question of what makes a grievable life and argued the importance of mourning the loss of people who are perceived as somehow outside normative notions of the human. This expansion of conceptions of what constitutes a grievable life was proffered as a means to cultivate affinities across diverse groups who may be constituted as other in secondary school settings. Also underlying this analysis of grief was a consideration of how people might better care for themselves and others; a similar motivation underscores my use of Foucault's ethics of pleasure, which focused on how individuals become subjects, continuously transforming themselves through processes of becoming. It is hoped that this turn toward pleasure will help to inspire an ongoing struggle for greater freedoms for the self and others within educational contexts. This ethics of pleasure also has the potential to motivate the creation of new relationships, new ways of seeing, and new ways of life.

Some Questions and Future Directions

A number of questions and strategies emerged in the course of this project that may prove as useful points of departure for future research in the area of sexualities and secondary schooling. One such question pertains to the intersections between this work — focusing principally on sexual identities — and existing research focused on questions of gender. Queer, feminist, and poststructuralist theories already inform both of these fields of research. However, many educational researchers studying gender have been relatively slow to engage with queer theories. Thus, the potential value of further analyzing the intersections between feminist, queer, and poststructuralist theorizing in studies of gender and education has yet to be fully explored. The intermingling of the theoretical positions described here might also be particularly effective in theorizing the spaces and places occupied by transgender- and intersex-identified teachers and students.

Although I briefly studied the pedagogical possibilities associated with the construction and deconstruction of heterosexual identities, there is still much more to be done. Educational research would benefit by working against the trend of utilizing the insights of queer theories principally in the study of LGBTI-identified subjects. Queer theoretical analysis has the potential for much broader applications within the discipline of education.

Throughout this study I tended to concentrate on how adults' conceptions of sexual identities influence the production of discourses related to sexualities and secondary schooling. A similar study concentrating on young people's conceptions of sexual and gender identities would be a valuable addition to research in this area. Such a project could provide further insight into how young people respond to, and are influenced by, the tropes of wounded identities currently so persuasive in educational research. In addition, this research could inform the provision of sexuality education in school settings and could potentially enhance an individual's ongoing processes of becoming by interrogating the relations of power that constrain and produce pleasure within and outside the confines of formal curricula.

In Closing

In this book I have ventured to contribute to the ongoing process of developing "a sense of political community of a complex order" (Butler, 2002, p. 3). I have done this through an interrogation of a paradox set out in the introduction to this book: a paradox that seeks to affirm LGBTI identities while concurrently refusing the notion that they are somehow essential or predestined. The epigraph to this conclusion aptly gestures toward the problems inherent in affirming identities associated with madness, the wound and obscure and nameless urges (Foucault, 1990, p. 156). However, the necessity of affirming identities is not diminished by this paradox. It is possible to abhor acts of violence committed against people perceived to be LGBTI identified while simultaneously critiquing such violence and essentializing identities. This paradoxical approach counters educational discourses in which *gayness* is essentialized and becomes synonymous with *risk*.

I also sought to imagine how relations to the wound may be thought differently and argued the value of perceiving subjects as entwined in processes of becoming inspired by an ethics of pleasure. This theorization of grief and pleasure has been seen as fundamental to the task of creating political communities that can engage multiple axes of difference and can foster ethical ways of *becoming subjects*. Juxtaposed to this study of grief and pleasure have been a consideration of people's attachments to the wound and a theorization of the difficulties that may adhere in unsettling passionate attachments to subjection.

223

Engaging these strategies will not provide a way out of the paradox of concurrently avowing and disavowing sexual and gender identities. The discourses analyzed in this study are all entangled in these contradictions, all marked by "the impossibility of *self*-definition as well as the unavoidability of the self as *position*" (Colebrook, 2000, p. 27, italics in original). While not seeking a way out of this paradox, I sought to demonstrate its fundamental significance in the production and analysis of key discourses related to sexualities and secondary schooling.

References

Abelove, H., Barale, M. A., & Halperin, D. M. (Eds.). (1993). *Lesbian and gay studies reader.* New York: Routledge.

Ables, R. (2004). Alternative education offers acceptance. *On-line Forty-Niner,* 24(119), 1. Retrieved February 3, 2005, from http://www.csulb.edu/~d49er/archives/2004/spring/news/volLIVno119-alter.shtml

Akanke. (1994). Black in the closet. In D. Epstein (Ed.), *Challenging lesbian and gay inequalities in education* (pp. 101–113). Buckingham, UK: Open University Press.

Albury, K. (2002). *Yes means yes: Getting explicit about heterosex.* Sydney: Allen & Unwin.

American Psychiatric Association (APA). (1994). *Diagnostic and statistical manual of mental disorders.* Washington, DC: American Psychiatric Association.

American Civil Liberties Union (ACLU). (2003). *Gay and Lesbian Rights: ACLU brief in Limon v. Kansas.* Retrieved March 18, 2005, from http://www.aclu.org/LesbianGayRights/LesbianGayRights.cfm?ID=10858&c=41

Angelo, J. (1997, April 2). Walk like a man: What teachers are accused of telling vilified gay student. *Daily Telegraph,* pp. 1, 4.

Armstrong, F. (1999). Inclusion, curriculum and the struggle for space in school. *International Journal of Inclusive Education,* 3, 75–87.

Armstrong, T. J. (Ed.). (1992). *Michel Foucault: Philosopher.* London: Harvester Wheatsheaf.

Associated Press. (2001). Lesbian's election as prom king causes turmoil. Retrieved June 13, 2005, from http://www.worldnetdaily.com/frame/direct.asp?SITE=www.usatoday.com/news/nation/2001-05-20-prom-king.htm

AVERT. (2005). Worldwide ages of consent. Retrieved February 9, 2005, from http://www.avert.org/aofconsent.htm

Ayman-Nolley, S., & Taira, L. L. (2000). Obsession with the dark side of adolescence: A decade of psychological studies. *Journal of Youth Studies, 3,* 35–48.

Babbitt, J. (1999). *But I'm a cheerleader.* United States: Lions Gate Films.

Ball, S. J. (1990). Introducing Monsieur Foucault. In S. J. Ball (Ed.), *Foucault and education: Disciplines and knowledge* (pp. 1–11). London: Routledge.

Barker, C. (2000). *Cultural studies: Theory and practice.* London: Sage.

Bartell, R. (1994). Victim of a victimless crime: Ritual and resistance. In D. Epstein (Ed.), *Challenging lesbian and gay inequalities in education* (pp. 78–100). Buckingham, UK: Open University Press.

Bass, E., & Kaufman, K. (1996). *Free your mind: The book for gay, lesbian, bisexual youth and their allies.* New York: HarperPerennial.

Beaver, H. (1981). Homosexual signs (In memory of Roland Barthes). *Critical Inquiry, 8,* 99–120.

Beck, J. (1999). Should homosexuality be taught as an acceptable alternative lifestyle? A Muslim perspective: A response to Halstead and Lewicka. *Cambridge Journal of Education, 29,* 121–131.

Beckett, L., & Denborough, D. (1995). Homophobia: Implications for mainstream policy and practice. *Promoting Gender Equity Conference Proceedings* (pp. 391–406). Canberra: Gender Equity Taskforce of the Ministerial Council for Education, Employment, Training and Youth Affairs.

Bell, D., & Valentine, G. (1995). Introduction. In D. Bell & G. Valentine (Eds.), *Mapping desire: Geographies of sexualities* (pp. 1–27). London: Routledge.

Bell, V. (1994). Dreaming and time in Foucault's philosophy. *Theory, Culture and Society, 11,* 151–163.

Bell, V. (1999a). On speech, race and melancholia: An interview with Judith Butler. *Theory, Culture and Society, 16*(2), 163–174.

Bell, V. (1999b). Perfomativity and belonging: An introduction. *Theory, Culture and Society, 16*(2), 1–10.

Benestad, E. E. P. (1998). *Third international congress of sex and gender.* Congress report, Oxford, UK. Retrieved January 2, 2005, from http://www.cat.org.au/ultra/congress.html

Benestad, E. E. P. (2001). *Options of gender belonging* [Live video link]. Viewed July 26, 2001.

Bennett, K. (2005). Personal correspondence with author, March 1, 2005.

Benton, J. (2003). Making schools safer and healthier for lesbian, gay, bisexual, and questioning students. *Journal of School Nursing, 19,* 251–259.

Bernauer, J. (1992). Beyond life and death: On Foucault's post-Auschwitz ethic. In T. J. Armstrong (Ed.), *Michel Foucault: Philosopher* (pp. 260–279). Brighton, UK: Harvester Wheatsheaf.

Bertolus, R. (1973). Le plaisir, parent pauvre (Pleasure: To be frowned upon)? *Pedagogie, 28*(9), 911–4, Nov.

Bibby, M. (1998). Inclusion of gay male, lesbian and other queer issues in pre-service teacher education. In L. Beckett (Ed.), *Everyone is special: A handbook for teachers on sexuality education* (pp. 23–26). Sandgate, Queensland: Association of Women Educators.

Blinick, B. (1994). Out in the curriculum, out in the classroom: Teaching history and organising for social change. In L. Garber (Ed.), *Tilting the tower: Lesbians, teaching, queer subjects* (pp. 142–149). New York, Routledge.

Bochenek, M., & Brown, A.W. (2001). *Hatred in the hallways: Violence and discrimination against lesbian, gay, bisexual, and transgender students in U.S. schools.* New York, Human Rights Watch.

Bove, P. A. (1995). Discourse. In F. Lentricchia & T. McLaughlin (Eds.), *Critical terms for literary study* (pp. 50–65). Chicago: University of Chicago Press.

Bower, H. (2001). The gender identity disorder in the DSM-IV classification: A critical evaluation. *Australian and New Zealand Journal of Psychiatry, 35*, 1–8.

Britzman, D. P. (1993). The ordeal of knowledge: Rethinking the possibilities of multicultural education. *Review of Education, 15*, 123–135.

Britzman, D. P. (1998). *Lost subjects, contested objects: Toward a psychoanalytic inquiry of learning.* Albany: State University of New York Press.

Bryson, M. (2002). Me/no lesbian: The trouble with "troubling lesbian identities." *International Journal of Qualitative Studies in Education, 15*(3), 373–380.

Burton, G. O. (1996–2003). *Silva Rhetoricae.* Retrieved March 14, 2005, from http://humanities.byu.edu/rhetoric/silva.htm.

Butler, J. (1990a). *Gender trouble: Feminism and the subversion of identity.* New York: Routledge.

Butler, J. (1990b). The pleasures of repetition. In R.A. Glick & S. Bone (Eds.), *Pleasure beyond the pleasure principle* (pp. 259–275). New Haven, CT: Yale University Press.

Butler, J. (1992). Sexual inversions: Rereading the end of Foucault's *History of Sexuality,* vol. 1. In Donna C. Stanton (ed.), *Discourses of sexuality: From Aristotle to AIDS* (pp. 344–361). Ann Arbor, MI: University of Michigan Press.

Butler, J. (1993). *Bodies that matter: On the discursive limits of "sex."* New York: Routledge.

Butler, J. (1994, Summer). Gender as performance. *Radical Philosophy, 67*, 32–39.

Butler, J. (1996). Sexual inversions. In S. J. Hekman (Ed.), *Feminist interpretations of Michel Foucault* (pp. 59–76). University Park: Pennsylvania State University Press.

Butler, J. (1997a). Critically queer. In S. Phelan (Ed.), *Playing with fire: Queer politics, queer theories* (pp. 11–29). New York: Routledge.

Butler, J. (1997b). *Excitable speech: A politics of the performative.* New York, Routledge.

Butler, J. (1997c, Fall–Winter). Merely cultural, *Social Text, 52–53,* 265–277.

Butler, J. (1997d). *The psychic life of power: Theories in subjection.* Stanford, CA: Stanford University Press.

Butler, J. (1998). How bodies come to matter: An interview with Judith Butler. *Signs: Journal of women in culture and society, 23*(2), 275–286.

Butler, J. (2002). Violence, mourning, politics (Kessler Lecture Excerpt). *Center for Lesbian and Gay Studies News, 12*(1), 3–6.

Butler, J., & Connolly, W. (2000). Politics, power and ethics: A discussion between Judith Butler and William Connolly. *Theory and Event, 4*(2), 1–40.

Cahill, B. J., & Theilheimer, R. (1999). Stonewall in the housekeeping area: Gay and lesbian issues in the early childhood classroom. In W. J. Letts & J. T. Sears (Eds.), *Queering elementary education: Advancing the dialogue about sexualities and schooling* (pp. 39–48). Lanham, MD: Rowman & Littlefield.

Callalillie (2003, July 29). *The nation's 1st gay high school.* Retrieved March 25, 2005, from http://www.callalillie.com/archives/2003/07/index.html

Campbell, J. (2000). *Arguing with the phallus — feminist, queer and post-colonial theory: A psychoanalytic contribution.* London: Zed Books.

Cheah, P., & Grosz, E. (1998). The future of sexual difference: An interview with Judith Butler and Drucilla Cornell. *Diacritics, 28*(1), 19–42.

Christian Coalition of America (2005). *About Christian Coalition of America.* Retrieved April 20, 2005, from http://cc.org/about.cfm

Cohen, E. (2001). Identity F/X: Identification and narration in "lesbian" and "gay" writing, 1880s–1930s. Retrieved January 9, 2001, from http://english.rutgers.edu/graduate/COURSESsp01.htm#des20

Colapinto, J. (2005, February 7). The Harvey Milk High School has no right to exist. Discuss, *New York Magazine.* Retrieved March 3, 2005, from http://www.newyorkmetro.com/nymetro/news/features/10970/

Colebrook, C. (2000). The meaning of irony. *Textual Practice, 14*(1), 5–30.

Coleman, A., Ehrenworth, M., & Lesko, N. (2004). Scout's honor: Duty, citizenship, and the homoerotic in the Boy Scouts of America. In M. L. Rasmussen, E. Rofes, & S. Talburt (Eds.), *Youth and sexualities: Pleasure, subversion and insubordination in and out of schools* (pp. 153–176). New York: Palgrave.

Community Media, LLC. (2005). *Gay City News.* Retrieved March 7, 2005, from http://www.gaycitynews.com/

Connolly, W. (1998). Beyond good and evil: The ethical sensibility of Michel Foucault. In J. Moss (Ed.), *The later Foucault: Politics and philosophy.* London: Sage.

Crick, A. (2001, November 8). "Hate crimes" curricula are unhealthy. *The culture and family report.* Retrieved March 14, 2005, from http://www.cultureandfamily.org/articledisplay.asp?id=291&department=CFI&categoryid=cfreport

Crimp, D. (1992). "Hey, girlfriend!" *Social Text, 33,* 2–18.

Crowley, V. (1999). Witches, faggots, dykes and poofters: Moments of danger and the realm of subjectivity. In D. Epstein & J. T. Sears (Eds.), *A dangerous knowing: Sexuality, pedagogy and popular culture* (pp. 210–225). London: Cassell.

Currie, D. (2001). Dear Abby: Advice pages as a site for the operation of power. *Feminist Theory, 2*(3), 259–281.

Dailey, T. J., & Roberts, C. (1999). The facts about "just the facts." *Insight*, Family Research Council. Retrieved March 14, 2005, from http://www.frc.org/file.cfm?f=SEARCH_RESULTS&auth=3828973& row=11&&end_date=CURRARCH

Davis, J. E. (1999). Forbidden fruit: Black males' constructions of transgressive sexualities in middle school. In W. J. Letts & J. T. Sears (Eds.), *Queering elementary education: Advancing the dialogue about sexualities and schooling* (pp. 49–59). Lanham, MD: Rowman & Littlefield.

de Lauretis, T. (1991). Queer theory: Lesbian and gay sexualities. *Differences: A journal of feminist cultural studies, 3*(2), iii–xviii.

de Lauretis, T. (1994). Habit changes. *Differences: A journal of feminist cultural studies, 6*(2–3), 296–313.

de Lauretis, T. (1998). The stubborn drive. *Critical Inquiry, 24*(4), 851–858.

de Lauretis, T. (1999). Gender symptoms, or, peeing like a man. *Social Semiotics, 9*(2), 257–270.

Dean, T. (2000). *Beyond sexuality*. Chicago: University of Chicago Press.

Derrida, J. (1984). *Of Grammatology*. London: Johns Hopkins University Press.

Devine, M. (1997). What price to be different? *Daily Telegraph*, p. 10.

Dowsett, G. W., Bollen, J., McInnes, D., Couch, M., & Edwards, B. (2001). HIV/AIDS and constructs of gay community: Researching educational practice within community-based health promotion for gay men. *International Journal of Social Research Methodology, 4*(3), 205–223.

Dreyfus, H. L. & Rabinow, P. (Eds.). (1982). *Michel Foucault: Beyond structuralism and hermeneutics*. New York: Harvester Wheatsheaf.

Duggan, L. (1992). Making it perfectly queer. *Socialist Review, 22*(1), 11–30.

Education Resources Information Center (ERIC). (2004). *About Eric. Overview*. Retrieved January 4, 2005, from http://www.eric.ed.gov/ERICWebPortal/resources/html/about/about_eric.html?logoutLink=false

Eggleston, V. (2001, Spring). Executive director's comments. *HMI Reporter*, p. 1.

Ellsworth, E. (1997). *Teaching positions: Difference, pedagogy, and the power of address*. New York: Teachers College Press.

Epstein, D. (1993). Practising heterosexuality. *Curriculum Studies, 1*(2), 275–286.

Epstein, D. (Ed.) (1994). *Challenging lesbian and gay inequalities in education*. Buckingham, UK: Open University Press.

Epstein, D., & Johnson, R. (1994). On the straight and narrow: The heterosexual presumption, homophobias and schools. In D. Epstein (Ed.), *Challenging lesbian and gay inequalities in education* (pp. 197–230). Buckingham, UK: Open University Press.

Epstein, D., & Johnson, R. (1998). *Schooling sexualities*. Buckingham, UK: Open University Press.

Epstein, D., & Sears, J. T. (Eds.). (1999). *A dangerous knowing: Sexuality, pedagogy and popular culture*. London: Cassell.

Epstein, S. (1987). Gay politics, ethnic identity: The limits of social constructionism. *Socialist Review, 93*(4), 9–54.

Esteban, M. (2001). Ferndale high school elects female prom king. *KOMO4 News.* Retrieved March 07, 2005, from http://www.komotv.com/news/story_m.asp?ID=10882

Evans, K. (1999). When *queer* and *teacher* meet. In W. J. Letts & J. T. Sears (Eds.), *Queering elementary education: Advancing the dialogue about sexualities and schooling* (p. 237–246). Lanham, MD: Rowman & Littlefield.

Family Research Council (FRC). (2005). About FRC. Retrieved March 14, 2005, from http://www.frc.org/get.cfm?c=ABOUT_FRC

Fausto-Sterling, A. (2000). *Sexing the body: Gender politics and the construction of sexuality.* New York: Basic Books.

Felman, S. (1987). *Jacques Lacan and the adventure of insight: Psychoanalysis in contemporary culture.* Cambridge, MA: Harvard University Press.

Female-to-Male International (FTMI) (1995–2002). Our history — Brandon Teena. Retrieved March 1, 2005, from http://www.ftmi.org/Hist/Bran/

Ferfolja, T., & Robinson, K. H. (2004). Why anti-homophobia education in teacher education: Perspectives from teacher educators. *Teaching Education, 15*(1), 9–25.

Ferreira, A. (2004). *Beyond diversity day: A Q & A on gay and lesbian issues in schools.* New York: Rowman & Littlefield.

Fine, M. (1988). Sexuality, schooling and adolescent females: The missing discourse of desire. *Harvard Educational Review, 58*(1), 29–53.

Fine, M., & Bertram, C. (1999). Sexing the globe. In D. Epstein & J. T. Sears (Eds.), *A dangerous knowing: Sexuality, pedagogy and popular culture* (pp. 153–163). London: Cassell.

Focus on the Family. (2005). Family.org. Our mission. Retrieved February 28, 2005, from http://www.family.org/welcome/aboutfof/a0005554.cfm

Fogel, A. (1977). *Beyond sex education: How adults relate to children's sensuality.* Indiana: ERIC Clearinghouse on Elementary and Childhood Education.

Ford, M. (1996). Opening the closet door: Sexualities education and "active ignorance." Retrieved March 02, 2005, from http://www.ed.uiuc.edu/eps/pes-yearbook/96_docs/ford.html

Foucault, M. (1965). *Madness and civilization: A history of insanity in the age of reason.* New York: Random House.

Foucault, M. (1970). The Order of Things: An Archaeology of the Human Sciences. London: Tavistock.

Foucault, M. (1979). *Discipline and punish: The birth of the prison.* New York: Vintage.

Foucault, M. (1980a). Truth and power. In C. Gordon (Ed.), *Power/knowledge: Selected interviews and other writings 1972–1977* (pp. 109–133). Brighton, UK: Harvester Press.

Foucault, M. (1980b). Two lectures. In C. Gordon (Ed.), *Power/knowledge: Selected interviews and other writings 1972–1977* (pp. 78–108). Brighton: Harvester Press.

Foucault, M. (1982). The subject and power. In H. L. Dreyfus & P. Rabinow (Eds.), *Michel Foucault: Beyond structuralism and hermeneutics* (pp. 208–226). New York: Harvester Wheatsheaf.

Foucault, M. (1984a). Nietzsche, genealogy, history. In P. Rabinow (Ed.), *The Foucault reader* (pp. 76–100). London: Penguin.

Foucault, M. (1984b). Space, knowledge, and power. In P. Rabinow (Ed.), *The Foucault reader* (pp. 239–256). London: Penguin.

Foucault, M. (1986, Spring). Of other spaces. *Diacritics*, 22–27.

Foucault, M. (1988). Technologies of the self. In L. Martin, H. Gutman, & P. H. Hutton (Eds.), *Technologies of the self: A seminar with Michel Foucault* (pp. 16–49). Amherst: University of Massachusetts Press.

Foucault, M. (1990). *The history of sexuality, volume 1: An introduction.* New York: Vintage Books.

Foucault, M. (1991). Politics and the study of discourse. In G. Burchell, C. Gordon, & P. Miller (Eds.), *The Foucault effect: Studies in governmentality* (pp. 53–72). London: Harvester Wheatsheaf.

Foucault, M. (1996a). An aesthetics of existence. In S. Lotringer (Ed.), *Foucault live (Interviews, 1961–1984)* (pp. 450–454). New York: Semiotext(E).

Foucault, M. (1996b). Ethics of concern for the self as a practice of freedom. In S. Lotringer (Ed.), *Foucault live (Interviews, 1961–1984)* (pp. 432–449). New York: Semiotext(E).

Foucault, M. (1996c). Ethics of pleasure. In S. Lotringer (Ed.), *Foucault live (Interviews, 1961–1984)* (pp. 371–381). New York: Semiotext(E).

Foucault, M. (1996d). Friendship as a way of life. In S. Lotringer (Ed.), *Foucault live: (Interviews, 1961–1984)* (pp. 308–312). New York, Semiotext(E).

Foucault, M. (1996e). History and homosexuality. In S. Lotringer (Ed.), *Foucault live: (Interviews, 1961–1984)* (pp. 363–370). New York, Semiotext(E).

Foucault, M. (1996f). The return of morality. In S. Lotringer (Ed.), *Foucault live (Interviews, 1961–1984)* (pp. 465–473). New York, Semiotext(E).

Foucault, M. (1996g). Sex, power, and politics of identity. In S. Lotringer (Ed.), *Foucault live: (Interviews, 1961–1984)* (pp. 382–390). New York, Semiotext(E).

Foucault, M. (1996h). Sexual choice, sexual act. In S. Lotringer (Ed.), *Foucault live: (Interviews, 1961–1984)* (pp. 322–334). New York, Semiotext(E).

Foucault, M. (1997). For an ethics of discomfort. In S. Lotringer & L. Hochroth (Eds.), *The politics of truth: Michel Foucault* (pp. 135–146). New York, Semiotext(E).

Foucault, M. (1998). On the archaeology of the sciences. In J. D. Fabion (Ed.), *Michel Foucault, aesthetics, method, and epistemology: The essential works of Michel Foucault, volume 2* (pp. 297–334). New York, Penguin.

Foucault, M., & Martin, R. (1988). Truth, power, self: An interview with Michel Foucault. In L. Martin, H. Gutman, & P. H. Hutton (Eds.), *Technologies of the self: A seminar with Michel Foucault* (pp. 9–15). Amherst: University of Massachusetts Press.

Frankham, J. (2001). The "open secret": Limitations on the expression of same-sex desire. *International Journal of Qualitative Studies in Education, 14*(4), 457–469.

Frankowski, B. L., & the Committee on Adolescence (2004). Sexual orientation and adolescents. *Pediatrics, 113*(6), 1827–1832.

Fuss, D. (1989). *Essentially speaking: Feminism, nature and difference.* New York: Routledge.

Garber, L. (Ed.). (1994). *Tilting the tower: Lesbians, teaching, queer subjects.* New York: Routledge.

Gard, M., & Meyenn, R. (2000). Boys, bodies, pleasure and pain: Interrogating contact sports in schools. *Sport, Education and Society, 5*(1), 19–34.

Gardner Honeychurch, K. (2000). Staying straight: Wanting in the academy. *Discourse: Studies in the Cultural Politics of Education, 21*(2), 175–192.

Gay and Lesbian Rights Lobby (GLRL). (2000). *Gay and Lesbian Youth Fact Sheet.* Retrieved March 20, 2005, from http://www.glrl.org.au/pdf/Gay%20and%20Lesbian%20Youth%20Sept%202004.pdf

Gay, Lesbian and Straight Education Network (GLSEN). (2000). *Gay–straight alliance handbook.* Retrieved March 14, 2005, from http://www.glsen.org/binary-data/GLSEN_ATTACHMENTS/file/32-1.pdf

Gay, Lesbian and Straight Education Network (GLSEN). (2004). *About GLSEN.* Retrieved March 14, 2005, from http://www.glsen.org/cgi-bin/iowa/all/about/index.html

Gibson, P. (1994). Gay male and lesbian youth suicide. In G. Remafedi (Ed.), *Death by denial: Studies of suicide in gay and lesbian teenagers* (pp. 15–68). Boston: Alyson.

Gilroy, P. (2000). *Against race: Imagining political culture beyond the color line.* Cambridge, MA: The Belknap Press of Harvard University Press.

Gordon, A. (1999). Turning back: Adolescence, narrative, and queer theory. *GLQ: A Journal of Lesbian and Gay Studies, 5*(1), 1–24.

Grace, A. P., & Benson, F. J. (2000). Using autobiographical queer life narratives of teachers to connect personal, political and pedagogical spaces. *International Journal of Inclusive Education, 4*(2), 89–109.

Griffin, P., & Ouellett, M. L. (2002). Going beyond gay–straight alliances to make schools safe for lesbian, gay, bisexual, and transgender students. *Angles: The Policy Journal of The Institute for Gay and Lesbian Strategic Studies, 6*(1).

Grossberg, L. (1992). *We gotta get out of this place: Popular conservatism and postmodern culture.* New York: Routledge.

Grosz, E. (1995a). Bodies and pleasures in queer theory. In J. Roof & R. Wiegman (Eds.), *Who can speak?: Authority and critical identity* (pp. 221–230). Urbana: University of Illinois Press.

Grosz, E. (1995b). *Space, time, and perversion: Essays on the politics of bodies.* New York: Routledge.

Halberstam, J. (2002, April 2). *Presentation on the Brandon Teen archive,* South Australia: Mercury Cinema.

Hall, S. (1992). The West and the rest. In S. Hall & B. Gieben (Eds.), *Formations of modernity* (pp. 275–320). Cambridge, UK: Polity Press.

Hall, S. (1996). Introduction: Who needs identity? In S. Hall & P. Du Guy (Eds.), *Questions of cultural identity* (pp. 1–17). London: Sage.

Hall, S. (1997). The work of representation. In S. Hall (Ed.), *Representation: Cultural representations and signifying practices* (pp. 13–64). London: Sage.

Hall, S. (2001). Foucault: Power, knowledge and discourse. In M. Wetherell, S. Taylor, & S. J. Yates (Eds.), *Discourse theory and practice: A reader* (pp. 72–81). London: Sage.

Halstead, J. M. (1999). Teaching about homosexuality: A response to John Beck. *Cambridge Journal of Education, 29*(1), 131–136.

Halstead, J. M., & Lewick, K. (1998). Should homosexuality be taught as an acceptable alternative lifestyle? A Muslim perspective. *Cambridge Journal of Education, 28*(1), 149–155.

Hammonds, E. (1997). Black (w)holes and the geometry of black female sexuality. In E. Weed & N. Schor (Eds.), *Feminism meets queer theory* (pp. 136–156). Bloomington: Indiana University Press.

Harbeck, K. (Ed.). (1992). *Coming out of the classroom closet: Gay and lesbian students, teachers and curricula*. Binghamton, NY: Haworth Press.

Harrison, L., Hillier, L., & Walsh, J. (1996). Teaching for a positive sexuality: Sounds good, but what about fear, embarrassment, risk and the "forbidden" discourse of desire. In L. Laskey & C. Beavis (Eds.), *Schooling and sexualities: Teaching for a positive sexuality* (pp. 69–82). Geelong, Victoria: Deakin Centre for Education and Change, Deakin University.

Harwood, V., & Rasmussen, M. L. (2002a, December). *Sensibility and educational research: Fashioning queer textures*. Paper presented at the annual conference of the Australian Association for Research in Education, Brisbane, Queensland, December 1–5.

Harwood, V., & Rasmussen, M. L. (2002b). *Inspiring methodological provocateurs in inclusive educational research*. Paper presented for Foucault and Education special interest group at the annual conference of the American Educational Research Association, New Orleans, LA. Abstract retrieved February 1, 2005, from http://edtech.connect.msu.edu/searchaera2002/viewproposaltext. asp?propID=2791

Harwood, V., & Rasmussen, M. L. (2003). Studying schools with an ethic of discomfort. In B. Baker & K. Heyning (Eds.), *Dangerous coagulations? The uses of Foucault in the study of education* (pp. 305–321). New York: Peter Lang.

Hatton, E. (Ed.). (1998). *Understanding teaching: Curriculum and the social context of schooling*. Sydney: Harcourt Brace.

Hatton, E., Maher, K., & Swinson, S. (1998). Sexuality, policy and teaching. In E. Hatton (Ed.), *Understanding teaching: Curriculum and the social context of schooling* (pp. 299–317). Sydney: Harcourt Brace.

Haver, W. (1997). Queer research; or, how to practise invention to the brink of intelligibility. In S. Golding (Ed.), *The eight technologies of otherness* (pp. 277–292). New York: Routledge.

Haver, W. (1999). Really bad infinities: Queer's honour and the pornographic life. *Parallax, 5*(4), 9–21.

Haywood, B. (2005, March 29). The letter of the law. *The Age.* Retrieved March 29, 2005, from http://education.theage.com.au/pagedetail. asp?intpageid=1450&strsection=students&intsectionid=0

Heaphy, B., Weeks, J., & Donovan, S. (1998). "That's like my life": Researching stories of non-heterosexual relationships. *Sexualities*, 1(4), 453–470.

Hemmings, C., & Grace, F. (1999). Stretching queer boundaries: An introduction. *Sexualities*, 2(4), 387–396.

Henley, P. (2004, November 19). *When most of your school is gay.* Retrieved March 25, 2005, from http://news.bbc.co.uk/1/hi/magazine/4023335.stm

Herdt, G., & Boxer, A. (1993). *Children of horizons: How gay and lesbian teens are leading a new way out of the closet.* Boston: Beacon Press.

Hetrick-Martin Institute (HMI) (2005a). The Hetrick-Martin Institute: The Past, Present and Future. Retrieved February 13, 2005, from http://www.hmi.org/HOME/Article/Params/articles/1393/pathlist/s1036_o1222/default.aspx

Hetrick-Martin Institute (HMI) (2005b). FAQs. Retrieved February 13, 2005, Hetrick-Martin Institute (HMI) (2005). Retrieved February 13, 2005, from http://www.hmi.org/HOME/Article/Params/articles/1311/pathlist/s1036_o1222/default.aspx#item1311

Hill, M. (2005) Meet Murray Hill. Retrieved June 13, 2005, from http://www.pipeline.com/~jordinyc/kmhill.htm

Holland, S. P. (1988). "Which me will survive": Audre Lorde and the development of a black feminist ideology. *Critical Matrix*, 1 (Spring), 1–30.

Holliday, R. (1999). The comfort of identity. *Sexualities*, 2(4), 475–491.

hooks, B. (2001). *Salvation: Black people and love.* New York: HarperCollins.

Howell, K. (1976). *Sex education for handicapped students.* Paper presented at the Conference on Breaking Affective Barriers for the Handicapped, Virginia Council on Health and Medical Care, Roanoke, Virginia, November, 1.

Hughes, B. (1999). The constitution of impairment: Modernity and the aesthetic of oppression. *Disability and Society*, 14(2), 155–172.

Human Rights Campaign (2004). Human rights campaign: Working for lesbian, gay, bisexual and transgender rights. Retrieved February 14, 2005, from http://www.hrc.org/Template.cfm?Section=About_HRC

Human Rights Campaign Foundation (HRCF). (2004). *Resource guide to coming out.* Washington, DC: Human Rights Campaign Foundation.

Intersex Society of North America (ISNA) (1993). Frequently Asked Questions. Retrieved February 9, 2005, from http://www.isna.org/faq/faq-medical.html#what

Jagose, A. (1996). *Queer theory: An introduction.* Washington Square: New York University Press.

Jagose, A., & Halberstam, J. (1999). Masculinity without men: Annamarie Jagose interviews Judith Halberstam. *Genders.* Retrieved February 2, 2005, from http://www.genders.org/g29/g29_halberstam.html

Jagose, A., & Warner, M. (2000). Queer world making: Annamarie Jagose interviews Michael Warner. *Genders.* Retrieved February 20, 2005, from http://www.genders.org/g31/g31_jagose.html

Jennings, K. (1994). *One teacher in 10: Gay and lesbian educators tell their stories*. Boston: Alyson Publications.

Jennings, K. (1998). *Telling tales out of school: Gays, lesbians, and bisexuals revisit their school days*. Los Angeles: Alyson Books.

Johnson, C. C., & Johnson, K. A. (2000). High-risk behavior among gay adolescents: Implications for treatment and support. *Adolescence, 35*(140), 619–638.

Kehily, M. J. (1995). Self-narration, autobiography and identity construction. *Gender and Education, 7*(1), 23–31.

Kehily, M. (1999). Agony aunts and absences: An analysis of a sex education class. *Melbourne Studies in Education, 40*(2), 127–148.

Kelly, D. (2001). Taking a dead stare at heterosexuality. *Sydney Gay and Lesbian Mardi Gras*. Webcast retrieved November 2, 2001, from http://www.mardigras.com.au/webcast/events.asp?genre=look

Kelly, D., & Fiveash, T. (2001). Hey, hetero! *Sydney Gay and Lesbian Mardi Gras*. Mixed media, photos with text.

Kennedy, E. L., & Davis, M. D. (1996). Constructing an ethnohistory of the Buffalo lesbian community: Reflexivity, dialogue, and politics. In E. Lewin & W. Leap (Eds.), *Out in the field: Reflections of lesbian and gay anthropolgists* (pp. 171–199). Urbana: University of Illinois Press.

Kenway, J., Willis, S., Blackmore, J., & Rennie, L. (1997). *Answering back: Girls, boys and feminism in schools*. St. Leonards, NSW, Australia: Allen & Unwin.

Kessler, S. (1998). *Lessons from the intersexed*. New Brunswick, NJ: Rutgers University Press.

Khayatt, D. (1997). Sex and the teacher: Should we come out in class? *Harvard Educational Review, 67*(1), 126–143.

Khayatt, D. (1999). Sex and pedagogy: Performing sexualities in the classroom. *GLQ: A Journal of Lesbian and Gay Studies, 1*, 107–113.

King, J. R. (1999). Am not! Are too! Using queer standpoint in postmodern critical ethnography, *International Journal of Qualitative Studies in Education, 12*(5), pp. 473–490.

Kissen, R. M. (1996). *The last closet: The real lives of lesbian and gay teachers*. Portsmouth, NH: Heinemann.

Klein-Lataud, C. (1991). *Precis des figures de style*. Toronto: Editions du GREF.

Kopecny, L. (2003). Interview with Kath Albury for bi.org.au. Retrieved June 14, 2005, from http://www.bi.org.au/culture/think/kathalbury.htm

Lakemary Center (2003). *Who we are*. Retrieved March 18, 2002, from http://www.lakemaryctr.org/Who%20We%20Are.htm

Lamphere, L. (1994). Expanding our notions of "critical qualitative methodology": Bringing race, class, and gender into the discussion (response). In A. D. Gitlin (Ed.), *Power and method: Political activism and educational research* (pp. 217–223). New York: Routledge.

Lerner, S. (2001). Straightness 101: Christian conservatives take their antigay campaign to the schools. *Village Voice*. Retrieved February 10, 2005, from http://www.villagevoice.com/issues/0118/lerner.php

Lesko, N. (2000). Making adolescence at the turn of the century: Discourse and the exclusion of girls. *Current Issues in Comparative Education, 2*(2).

Lesko, N. (2001). *Act your age!: A cultural construction of adolescence.* New York: Routledge.

Lesnik-Oberstein, K., & Thomson, S. (2002). What is queer theory doing with the child? *Parallax, 8*(1), 35–46.

Lewis, R., & Rolly, K. (1997). (Ad)dressing the dyke: Lesbian looks and lesbians looking. In M. Nava, A. Blake, I. MacRury, & B. Richards (Eds.), *Buy this book: Studies in advertising and consumption* (pp. 291–308). London: Routledge.

Lipkin, A. (1999). *Understanding homosexuality, changing schools: A text for teachers, counselors, and administrators.* Boulder, CO: Westview Press.

Mac An Ghaill, M. (1994). *The making of men: Masculinities, sexualities and schooling.* Buckingham, UK: Open University Press.

MacGillivray, I. K. (2000). Educational equity for gay, lesbian, bisexual, transgendered, and queer/questioning students. *Education and Urban Society, 32*(3), 303–323.

MacGillivray, I. K., & Kozik-Rosabal, G. (2000). Introduction. *Education and Urban Society, 32*(3), 287–302.

Macquarie Dictionary. (2001). Metaphor, Rev. 3rd ed. NSW: Macquarie Library Pty Ltd.

Maine Safe Schools Resource Collaborative (1999). *Maine Safe Schools Resource Guide.* Portland, ME: Safe Schools Resource Collaborative.

Martin, B. (1994, Summer–Fall). Sexualities without genders and other queer utopias. *Diacritics, 24,* 104–121.

Martin, T. (2001). To be gay, and happy, at school. *Student.com.* Retrieved February 22, 2001, from http://www.student.com/article/gayschool/2001

Matthew Shepard Foundation (1998–2004).

May, K. (2002). Becoming women: Transgendered identities, psychosexual therapy and the challenge of metamorphosis. *Sexualities, 5*(4), 449–464.

mAy-welby, norrie. (1998). *Third International Congress of Sex and Gender.* Retrieved March 14, 2005, from http://www.cat.org.au/ultra/congress.html

Mayo, C. (1996). Performance anxiety: Sexuality and school controversy. Retrieved February 1, 2005, from http://www.ed.uiuc.edu/eps/pes-yearbook/96_docs/mayo.html

Mayo, C. (1997). Foucauldian cautions on the subject and the educative implications of contingent identity. Retrieved February 6, 2005, from http://www.ed.uiuc.edu/eps/pes-yearbook/97_docs/mayo.html

Mayo, C. (2004). Queering school communities: Ethical curiosity and gay–straight alliances. *Journal of Gay and Lesbian Issues in Education, 1*(3), 23–36.

McCarthy, C. (1990). *Race and curriculum: Social inequality and theories and politics of difference in contemporary research on schooling.* Bristol, PA: Falmer Press.

McInnes, D., & Couch, M. (2004). Quiet please! There's a lady on the stage: Boys, gender and sexuality non-conformity and class. *Discourse: Studies in the Cultural Politics of Education, Special Issue Wounded Identities and the Promise of Pleasure,* 24(4), 431–43.

McIntosh, M. (1997). Seeing the world from a lesbian and gay standpoint. In L. Segal (Ed.), *New sexual agendas.* New York: New York University Press.

McWhorter, L. (1999). *Bodies and pleasures: Foucault and the politics of sexual normalization.* Bloomington: Indiana University Press.

Melbourne Gay Teachers' and Students' Group (MGTSG). (1978). *Young, gay and proud.* Melbourne: An autonomous collective of the Melbourne Gay Teachers' and Students' Group.

Melloy, K. (1999). Twenty questions: With Kevin Jennings, August 21, 1999. *Wigglefish zine.* Retrieved June 10, 2005, from http://stories.wigglefish.com/zine/twentyquestions/jennings/

Mensah, J. (2005). Letter to the editor-in-chief of *New York Magazine,* Mr. Adam Moss from David Mensah, Executive Director, The Hetrick-Martin Institute. *Hetrick Martin-Institute Home Page.* Retrieved March 27, 2005, from www.hmi.org

Merriam-Webster, Inc. (2005a). Irony. Retrieved February 2, 2005, from http://www.webster-dictionary.org/definition/irony

Merriam-Webster, Inc. (2005b). Metonymy. Retrieved February 2, 2005, from http://www.webster-dictionary.org/definition/metonymy

Merriam-Webster, Inc. (2005c). Sensibility. Retrieved June 10, 2005, from http://www.merriamwebster.com/cgi-bin/dictionary?book=Dictionary&va=sensibility&x=0&y=0

Merriam-Webster, Inc. (2005d). Trope. Retrieved February 2, 2005, from http://www.webster-dictionary.org/definition/trope

Merriam-Webster, Inc. (2005e). Synecdoche. Retrieved June 10, 2005, from http://www.merriamwebster.com/cgi-bin/dictionary?book=Dictionary&va=synecdoche&x=0&y=0

Merriam-Webster, Inc. (2005f). Pansexual. Retrieved, June 13, 2005, from http://www.merriamwebster.com/cgi-bin/dictionary?book=Dictionary&va=pansexual

Miller, K. (1994). *Ignore them and they'll go away: Gay, bisexual, and lesbian young people and suicide.* Paper presented at the annual conference of the Public Health Association, Adelaide, Australia, September 25–28.

Mills, C. (2000). Efficacy and vulnerability: Judith Butler on reiteration and resistance. *Australian Feminist Studies,* 15(32), 265–279.

Mills, S. (1997). *Discourse.* London: Routledge.

Misson, R. (1999). The closet and the classroom: Strategies of heterosexist discourse. *Melbourne Studies in Education,* 40(2), 75–89.

Moran, L., Skeggs, B., Tyrer, P., & Corteen, K. (2001). Property, boundary, exclusion: Making sense of hetero-violence in safer spaces. *Social and Cultural Geography,* 2(4), 407–420.

Morris, M. (1998). Unresting the curriculum: Queer projects, queer imaginings. In W. Pinar (Ed.), *Queer theory in education* (pp. 275–286). Mahwah, NJ: Erlbaum.

MTV. (2002a). Anatomy of a hate crime. Retrieved May 15, 2002 from http://www.mtvn.com/cic/mtv_hate_crimes.html

MTV. (2002b). Anatomy of a hate crime — Lesson plans. Retrieved May 15, 2002 from http://www.mtvn.com/cic/documents/anatomy_of_hate_crime3.doc

Muehlenberg, B. (2003, July). The challenge of homosexuality. *The Australian Family Association Journal*, July, p. 35.

Munt, S. (1995). The lesbian *flaneur*. In D. Bell & G. Valentine (Eds.), *Mapping desire: Geographies of sexualities* (pp. 114–125). London: Routledge.

Murray, A. S. (1998). Objectively, subjectively, psychiatry and politics. *Australasian Psychiatry, 1*, 59–60.

Namaste, K. (1996). The politics of inside/out: Queer theory, poststructuralism, and a sociological approach to sexuality. In S. Seidman (Ed.), *Queer theorys/sociology* (pp. 194–212). Cambridge, MA: Blackwell.

Namaste, V. K. (1999). The use and abuse of queer tropes: Metaphor and catachresis in queer theory and politics. *Social Semiotics, 9*(2), 213–234.

Newton, E. (1996). My best informant's dress: The erotic equation in fieldwork. In E. Lewin & W. Leap (Eds.), *Out in the field: Reflections of lesbian and gay anthropolgists* (pp. 212–235). Urbana: University of Illinois Press.

Nicholas, J., & Howard, J. (1998, December). Better to be dead than gay? Depression, suicide ideation and attempt among a sample of gay and straight-identified males aged 18 to 24. *Youth Studies Australia*, 28–33.

Nixon, S. (1997). Exhibiting masculinity. In S. Hall (Ed.), *Representation: Cultural representations and signifying practices* (pp. 291–330). London: Sage.

Ontario Consultants on Religious Tolerance (2000–2003). *Religious tolerance.org*. Retrieved March 14, 2005, from http://www.religioustolerance.org/hom_psgr.htm

Orleans, E. (1994). *Who cares if it's a choice?* Bala Cynwyd, PA: Laughlines Press.

Owen, M. K. (2000). "Not the same story": Conducting interviews with queer community activists. *Resources for Feminist Research, 28*(1–2), 49–60.

Oz, F. (1997). *In & Out*. United States: Paramount Pictures.

Page, J. A., & Liston, D. D. (2002). Homophobia in schools: Student teachers' perceptions and preparation to respond. In R. M. Kissen (Ed.), *Getting ready for Benjamin: Preparing teachers for sexual diversity in the classroom* (pp. 71–80). New York: Rowman & Littlefield.

Passey, D. (1997, April 5). Schoolyard victims. *Sydney Morning Herald*, Sydney, p. 38.

Patai, D. (1994). When method becomes power. In A. D. Gitlin (Ed.), *Power and method: Political activism and educational research.* (pp. 61–73). New York: Routledge.

Paterson, R. (2001). Controversial "Hey, hetero!" campaign launched by YWCA. *Young Women's Christian Association website.* Retrieved February 14, 2002, from http://www.ywca.org.nz/hetero.htm

Patton, C. (1996). *Fatal advice: How safe-sex education went wrong.* Durham, NC: Duke University Press.

Phelan, S. (1997). The shape of queer: Assimilation and articulation. *Women and Politics, 18*(2), 55–73.

Pinar, W. (1998). *Queer theory in education.* Mahwah, N.J.: Erlbaum.

Pinhey, T. K., & Millman, S. R. (2004). Asian/Pacific Islander adolescent sexual orientation and suicide risk in Guam. *American Journal of Public Health, 94*(7), 1204–1207.

Plummer, K. (Ed.). (1992). *Modern homosexualities: Fragments of lesbian and gay experience.* London: Routledge.

Probyn, E. (1995). Lesbians in space: Gender and the structure of missing. *Gender, Place and Culture, 2*(1), 77–84.

Probyn, E. (1996). *Outside belongings.* New York: Routledge.

Probyn, E. (2000). Sporting bodies: Dynamics of shame and pride. *Body and Society, 6*(1), 13–28.

Pursley, S. (2002). Free Matthew Limon? *LGNY: The newspaper for lesbian and gay New York.* Retrieved March 27, 2002, from http://www.lgny.com/0179web/Pursley179.html

Quinlivan, K., & Town, S. (1999). Queer pedagogy, educational practice and lesbian and gay youth. *International Journal of Qualitative Studies in Education, 12*(5), 509–524.

Rabinow, P. (Ed.) (1984). *The Foucault reader.* London: Penguin.

Rabinow, P. (1997). Introduction: The history of systems of thought. In P. Rabinow (Ed.), *Ethics: Subjectivity and truth,* Vol. 1 (pp. xi–xliii). New York: The New York Press.

Race, K. (2001). The undetectable crisis: Changing technologies of risk. *Sexualities, 4*(2), 167–189.

Rasmussen, M. L. (2001). Queer trepidations and the art of inclusion. *Melbourne Studies in Education, 44,* 87–108.

Rasmussen, M. L. (2004a). Coming out of "coming out." *Theory into Practice, 43,* 144–151.

Rasmussen, M. L. (2004b). Safety and subversion: The production of genders and sexualities in school spaces. In M. L. Rasmussen, E. Rofes, & S. Talburt (Eds.), *Youth and sexualities: Pleasure, subversion and insubordination in and out of schools* (pp. 131–152). New York: Palgrave.

Rasmussen, M. L. (2004c). "That's so gay": A study of the deployment of signifiers of sexual and gender identity in secondary school settings in Australia and the United States. *Social Semiotics, 14,* 298–308.

Rasmussen, M. L. (2004d). Wounded identities, sex and pleasure: "Doing it" at school. NOT! *Discourse: Studies in the Cultural Politics of Education, 24,* 445–458.

Rasmussen, M. L. (2005, Summer). Melancholy, grief and pleasure: Unsettling passionate attachments to subjection. *Journal of Curriculum Theorizing,* pp. 25–44.

Rasmussen, M. L., & Harwood, V. (2000). *Sensibility and educational research: Fashioning queer textures*. Paper presented at the annual conference for the Australian Association for Research in Education, Sydney, Australia, December 5–9.

Reis, B. (1997). *Safe schools resource guide*. Seattle: Safe Schools Coalition of Washington.

Reiss, M. J. (1997). Teaching about homosexuality and heterosexuality. *Journal of Moral Education, 26*(3), 343–352.

Reynolds, R. H. (1996). *Sexuality, citizenship and subjectivity: A textual history of the Australian gay movement 1970–1974*. Unpublished doctoral dissertation, Department of History, The University of Melbourne.

Rich, A. (1986). Blood, bread and poetry: The location of the poet. In A. Rich (Ed.), *Blood, Bread and Poetry: Selected Prose 1979–1985* (pp. 167–187). New York: W.W. Norton & Co.

Rich, A. (1993). Compulsory heterosexuality and lesbian existence. In H. Abelove, M. A. Barale, & D. M. Halperin (Eds.), *Lesbian and gay studies reader* (pp. 227–254). New York: Routledge.

Richter, J. (1999). *Throwaway Teens. Interview on 20/20 with Connie Chung*. Retrieved March 20, 2005, from http://www.youth.org/loco/PERSONProject/Alerts/Old/1999/20-20-2.html

Rixecker, S. S. (2000). Exposing queer biotechnology via queer archaeology: The quest to (re)construct the human body from inside out. *World Archaeology, 32*(2), 263–274.

Robins, K. (1996). *Into the image: Culture and politics in the field of vision*. London: Routledge.

Rofes, E. (1985). *Socrates, Plato, and guys like me: Confessions of a gay school teacher*. Boston: Alyson.

Rofes, E. (1999). What happens when the kids grow up? The long term impact of an openly gay teacher on eight students' lives. In W. J. Letts & J. T. Sears (Eds.), *Queering elementary education: Advancing the dialogue about sexualities and schooling* (pp. 83–93). Lanham, MD: Rowman & Littlefield.

Rofes, E. (2000). Bound and gagged: Sexual silences, gender conformity and the gay male teacher. *Sexualities, 3*(4), 439–462.

Rogers, M. (1998). *Breaking the silence: A study of lesbian youth in the current, social and South Australian educational context*. Unpublished master's dissertation, Faculty of Education, University of South Australia.

Rose, N. (1998). *Inventing ourselves: Psychology, power, and personhood*. Cambridge, UK: Cambridge University Press.

Rubin, G. (1984). Thinking sex: Notes for a radical theory of the politics of sexuality. In C. Vance (Ed.), *Pleasure and danger: Exploring female sexuality* (pp. 267–319). Boston: Routledge & Kegan Paul.

Rubin, G., & Butler, J. (1998). Sexual traffic. In M. Merck, N. Segal, & E. Wright (Eds.), *Coming out of feminism?* (pp. 36–73). Oxford: Blackwell.

Russell, S. T., Driscoll, A. K., & Truong, N. (2002). Adolescent same-sex romantic attractions and relationships: Implications for substance use and abuse. *American Journal of Public Health, 92*(2), 198–203.

Safe Schools Coalition. (2004). *About us*. Retrieved March 24, 2005, from http://www.safeschoolscoalition.org/about_us.html#OurMission

Savage, D. (1999). Chicks with dicks. *Stranger*. Retrieved February 2, 2005, from http://www.thestranger.com/seattle/SavageLove?oid=998/

Schulman, S. (1993). *The Lesbian Avengers handbook: A handy guide to homemade revolution* (2nd ed.), with contributions by Marlene Colburn, Phyllis Lutsky, Maxine Wolfe, Amy Parker, Sue Schaffner, Carrie Moyer, and Ana Maria Simo. New York: Lesbian Avengers.

Schulman, S. (1994). *My American history: Lesbian and gay life during the Reagan/Bush years*. New York: Routledge.

Schwartz, M. (1999). Repetition and ethics in late Foucault. *Telos, 117*, 113–132.

Sears, J. T. (1992). *Sexuality and the curriculum: The politics and practices of sexuality education*. New York: Teachers College Press.

Sears, J. T. (1995). Black gay or gay black? Choosing identities and identifying choices. In G. Unks (Ed.), *The gay teen: Educational practice and theory for lesbian, gay, and bisexual adolescents* (pp. 135–157). New York: Routledge.

Sears, J. T. (1999). Teaching queerly: Some elementary propositions. In W. J. Letts & J. T. Sears (Eds.), *Queering elementary education: Advancing the dialogue about sexualities and schooling* (pp. 3–14). Lanham, MD: Rowman & Littlefield.

Sedgwick, E. K. (1990). *Epistemology of the closet*. Berkeley: University of California Press.

Sedgwick, E. K. (1992). White glasses. *Yale Journal of Criticism, 53*(3), 193–208.

Sedgwick, E. K. (1993a). *Tendencies*. Durham, NC: Duke University Press.

Sedgwick, E. K. (1993b). Queer and now. In E. K. Sedgwick (Ed.), *Tendencies* (pp. 1–20). Durham, NC: Duke University Press.

Seidman, S. (1993). Identity and politics in a "postmodern" gay culture: Some historical and conceptual notes. In M. Warner (Ed.), *Fear of a queer planet: Queer politics and social theory* (pp. 105–142). Minneapolis: University of Minnesota Press.

Sheil, J. (2000). Identity speech: It's who we are, not what we say. *LGNY: Lesbian and Gay New York*. Retrieved March 15, 2000, from http://lgny.com/issue_128/pages_128/letters_128.html

Shiel, F. (1999). Homosexuality a health risk: Pell. *Age*. Retrieved January 2, 2001, from http://www.theage.com.au/daily/990524/news/news15.html

Shiff, R. (1991). Cézanne's physicality: The politics of touch. In S. Kemal & I. Gaskell (Eds.), *The language of art history* (p. 129–180). Cambridge, UK: Cambridge University Press.

Silin, J. (1999). Teaching as a gay man: Pedagogical resistance or public spectacle? *GLQ: A Journal of Lesbian and Gay Studies, 5*(1), 95–106.

Silva Rhetoricae (2005) Catachresis. Retrieved June 10, 2005 from http://humanities.byu.edu/rhetoric/Figures/C/catachresis.htm

Skeggs, B. (1999). Matter out of place: Visibility and sexualities in leisure spaces. *Leisure Studies, 18*, 213–232.

Skotnicki, T. (1997, April 3). After four years of abuse, Jamie beat the system. *Daily Telegraph*, p. 7.

Slee, R. (2001). Social justice and the changing directions in educational research: The case of inclusive education. *International Journal of Inclusive Education, 5*(2–3), 167–177.

Snider, K. (1996). Race and sexual orientation: The impossibility of these intersections in educational policy. *Harvard Educational Review, 66*(2), 294–302.

Sobchack, V. (2000). What my fingers knew: The cinesthetic subject, or vision in the flesh. *Senses of Cinema*. Retrieved January 2, 2005, from http://www.sensesofcinema.com/contents/00/5/fingers.html

Spivak, G. C. (1987). *In other worlds: Essays in cultural politics.* New York: Methuen.

Spivak, G. C. (1993). More on power/knowledge. In G.C. Spivak, (Ed.), *Outside in the teaching machine* (p. 25–52). New York: Routledge.

Spurlin, W. J. (1998). Sissies and sisters: Gender, sexuality and the possibilities of coalition. In M. Merck, N. Segal, & E. Wright (Eds.), *Coming out of feminism?* (pp. 74–101). Oxford: Blackwell.

Stein, A., & Plummer, K. (1996). I can't even think straight. In S. Seidman (Ed.), *Queer theory/sociology* (pp. 129–144). Cambridge, MA: Blackwell.

Sullivan, N. (2001). *Tattooed bodies: Subjectivity, textuality, ethics, and pleasure.* Westport, CT: Praeger.

Sullivan, N. (2003). *A critical introduction to queer theory.* Melbourne, Australia: Circa Books.

Sumara, D., & Davis, B. (1999). Interrupting heteronormativity: Toward a queer curriculum theory. *Curriculum Inquiry, 29*(2), 191–208.

Sykes, H. (2001). *Teaching bodies, learning desires.* Paper presented at the annual conference of the American Educational Research Association, Seattle, WA, April 9–13.

Talburt, S. (1999). Open secrets and problems of queer ethnography: Readings from a religious studies classroom. *International Journal of Qualitative Studies in Education, 12*(5), 525–539.

Talburt, S. (2004). Intelligibility and narrating queer youth. In M. L. Rasmussen, E. Rofes, & S. Talburt (Eds.), *Youth and sexualities: Pleasure, subversion, and insubordination in and out of schools.* New York: Palgrave.

Talburt, S., & Steinberg, S. R. (2000). *Thinking queer: Sexuality, culture, and education.* New York: Counterpoints.

Taormino, T. (2001). Porn queens and prom kings. *Village Voice*. Retrieved February 5, 2005, from http://www.villagevoice.com/people/0121,taormino,24901,24.html

Taylor, N. (1994). Gay and lesbian youth: Challenging the policy of denial. In T. De Crescenzo (Ed.), *Helping gay and lesbian youth* (pp. 39–74). New York: Harrington Park Press.

Telford, D. (2003a). Post-compulsory heterosexuality: Silences and tensions in curricula and pedagogy at university. In D. Epstein, S. O'Flynn, & D. Telford (Eds.), *Silenced sexualities in schools and universities* (pp. 101–120). Staffordshire, UK: Trentham Books.

Telford, D. (2003b). The university challenge: Transition to university. In D. Epstein, S. O'Flynn, & D. Telford (Eds.). *Silenced sexualities in schools and universities* (pp. 121–140). Staffordshire, UK: Trentham Books.

Terry, J. (1995). The seductive power of science in the making of deviant subjectivity. In J. Halberstam & I. Livingston (Eds.), *Posthuman bodies*. Bloomington: Indiana University Press.

Terry, J. (1999). *An American obsession: Science, medicine, and homosexuality in modern society* (pp. 135–161). Chicago: University of Chicago Press.

Threadgold, T. (2000). Poststructuralism and discourse analysis. In A. Lee & C. Poynton (Eds.), *Culture and text: Discourse and methodology in social research and cultural studies* (pp. 40–58). St. Leonards, NSW, Australia: Allen & Unwin.

Tierney, W. G. (1997). *Academic outlaws: Queer theory and cultural studies in the academy*. Thousand Oaks, CA: Sage.

Tobin, J. (1997). The missing discourse of pleasure and desire. In J. Tobin (Ed.), *Making a place for pleasure in early childhood education* (pp. 1–37). New Haven, CT: Yale University Press.

Town, S. (1998). Queer(y)ing masculinities: Faggots, fairies and the first fifteen. In R. Law, H. Campbell, & J. Dolan (Eds.), *Masculinities in Aotearoa/New Zealand*. Palmerston North, New Zealand: Dunmore Press.

Trute, P., & Angelo, J. (1997, April 3). Gay boy asked for it! — Students. *Daily Telegraph*, p. 3.

Turner, W. B. (2000). *A genealogy of queer theory*. Philadelphia: Temple University Press.

Unks, G. (1995). Thinking about the gay teen. In G. Unks (Ed.), *The gay teen: Educational practice and theory for lesbian, gay, and bisexual adolescents* (pp. 3–12). New York: Routledge.

Vaid, U. (1995). *Virtual equality: The mainstreaming of gay and lesbian liberation*. New York: Anchor Books.

van Wormer, C., & McKinney, R. (2003). What schools can do to help gay/lesbian/bisexual youth: A harm reduction approach. *Adolescence, 38*(151), 409–420.

Varney, J. A. (2001). Undressing the normal: Community efforts for queer Asian and Asian American youth. In K. K. Kumashiro (Ed.), *Troubling intersections of race and sexuality* (pp. 87–104). New York: Rowman and Littlefield.

Vico, G. (1968). *The new science*. Ithaca, NY: Cornell University Press.

Warner, M. (Ed.) (1993). *Fear of a queer planet: Queer politics and social theory*. Minneapolis: University of Minnesota Press.

Warner, M. (1999). *The trouble with normal: Sex, politics and the ethics of queer life*. New York: Free Press.

Weeks, J. (1986) *Sexualities*. New York: Routledge.

Whisman, V. (1996). *Queer by choice: Lesbians, gay men, and the politics of identity*. New York: Routledge.

White, H. (1978). *Tropics of discourse: Essays in cultural criticism*. Baltimore: Johns Hopkins University Press.

Witt, L., Thomas, S., & Marcus, E. (Eds.). (1995). *Out in all directions: The almanac of gay and lesbian America.* New York: Warner Books.

Woodward, K. (Ed.). (1997). *Identities and difference.* London: Sage.

Wright, K. (2001). The great down-low debate. *Village Voice.* Retrieved February 7, 2005, from http://www.villagevoice.com/issues/0123/wright.php

Wright, S. (1999). *Sexuality education: What Australian parents and teachers are saying.* Paper presented at the annual conference on Sexualities: The Australian Kaleidoscope Conference on Sexology, University of Adelaide, Adelaide, October 22–23.

Zine, J. (2001). "Negotiating equity": The dynamics of minority community engagement in constructing inclusive educational policy. *Cambridge Journal of Education, 31*(2), 239–269.

Endnotes

Introduction

1. The website of the Intersex Society of North America (2005) defines intersexuality as "a set of medical conditions that feature congenital anomaly of the reproductive system. That is, intersex people are born with 'sex chromosomes,' external genitalia, or internal reproductive system that are not considered 'standard' for either male or female."
2. For details of age of consent in Australian and U.S. states and territories, see AVERT (2005).

Chapter 1

1. For a discussion of some of the ways inclusivity is contested in the production of discourses related to sexualities and schooling, see Beck (1999), Halstead (1999), Halstead and Lewick (1998), and Zine (2001).
2. New South Wales (capital: Sydney) is located in Australia.
3. For further discussion of the "sissy boy" experience within school settings, see McInnes and Couch (2004).
4. Warner (1993) defines heteronormalization as the " ... normalizing processes which support heterosexuality as the elemental form of human association, as the very model of inter-gender relations, as the indivisible basis of all community, and as the means of reproduction without which society wouldn't exist." (p.xxi)
5. One of the largest alternative weekly newspapers in the United States.
6. In order to explain some African American men's refusal of gay identities, Wright draws on hooks's (2001) research. hooks argues that the African-American community has a history of devaluing gay identities, situating them as a condition of whiteness. According to hooks, discomfort is not just found in

African-American communities' conversations about gay sex; discomfort also permeates most conversations about sex in African-American communities.

7. On its webpage, the Human Rights Campaign's (2004) mission is described as follows:

> As America's largest gay and lesbian organization, the Human Rights Campaign provides a national voice on gay and lesbian issues …. HRC is a bipartisan organization that works to advance equality based on sexual orientation and gender expression and identity, to ensure that gay, lesbian, bisexual and transgender Americans can be open, honest and safe at home, at work and in the community.

8. Focus on the Family's (2005) mission is "to cooperate with the Holy Spirit in disseminating the Gospel of Jesus Christ to as many people as possible, and, specifically, to accomplish that objective by helping to preserve traditional values and the institution of the family."
9. The Christian Coalition and the Traditional Values Coalition (TVC) have also been outspoken in their opposition to homosexuality. For details of these two organizations' attacks on lesbian and gay individuals and communities in the United States, see Vaid (1995).
10. In Australia, organizations opposed to homosexuality include the Festival of Light; Focus on the Family, Australia; and the Australian Family Association.
11. For a discussion of the potential constraints associated with avowedly heterosexual-identified superstudents advocating for their LGBTI peers, see Coleman, Ehrenworth, and Lesko (2004).

CHAPTER 2

1. Audre Lorde developed the notion of biomythography, a form of writing drawing on "history, biography and myth to unfold her personal history" (Holland, 1988).
2. Born female, Teena Brandon moved to Falls City, Nebraska, in 1993 and passed as Brandon Teena. When Brandon's friends learned that he was passing they murdered him, along with two other individuals. For a comprehensive history of the life and death of Brandon Teena, see FTMI (1995–2002). Teena's life was dramatized in the film *Boys Don't Cry*.
3. An extended discussion of the origins of queer theories is beyond the scope of this book. It should be noted, however, that the roots of queer theories reach beyond their entry into academic discourses in the United States at the beginning of the 1990s. For a detailed discussion of the origins of queer theory from a U.S. perspective, see de Lauretis (1991) and Turner (2000).
4. "Thinking Sex" was chosen as the introductory article for Abelove, Barale, and Halperin (1993).

5. The notion of sensibility, discussed throughout this section, was the subject of a conference paper presented by Harwood and Rasmussen (2002a). This chapter also draws extensively on Harwood and Rasmussen (2002b).
6. Vico (1668–1744) was an Italian philosopher who wrote extensively on the subject of rhetoric.

CHAPTER 3

1. These categories are drawn from the index of Talburt and Steinberg (2000) under the heading "Identity."
2. As indicated already by Hall (1996), Foucault had disdain for the term identity because of its associations with essential notions of the subject.
3. I deploy the term constructivism to describe an array of theories that draw on notions of social construction while recognizing that, like essentialism, there is no one definitive brand of constructivism.
4. In writing on the state of subaltern studies, Spivak endorses "a strategic use of positivist essentialism in a scrupulously visible political interest" (Spivak, 1987, p. 205, quoted in Fuss, 1989, p. 6).
5. It is worth noting that Fuss (1989), Spivak (1987), and Butler (1990a) address essentialism in particular and disparate contexts. Fuss's study of essentialism focuses on feminism; Spivak's on subaltern studies, and Butler's on the sex–gender distinction.
6. *LGNY* was a newspaper devoted to the discussion of lesbian and gay issues in New York and the rest of the United States. It has been renamed *Gay City News* (Community Media, 2005). URLs for articles in *LGNY* are no longer active.
7. Terry (1995) proposes that deviant identities are often actively produced in order to account for difference from perceived norms. Those who are said to inhabit deviant identities may come to rejoice in their classification as deviant, taking pleasure in their perversity and seeking out other transgressive bodies. Simultaneously, the label of deviance might produce anxiety, fear, and danger in those classified as deviant and in those who desire to exclude deviant subjectivities from the realm of the normal.
8. These are well detailed in Terry (1995).
9. Another useful overview of the development of social constructivism can be found in Fuss (1989, esp. ch. 6).
10. Under the heading "From construction to materialization," Butler provides a detailed study of some competing notions of constructivism and she responds to some key questions often posed of constructivist theories of the self; see Butler (1993).
11. Foucault (1996b) understands freedom as "the ontological condition of ethics. But ethics is the form that freedom takes when it is informed by reflection" (p. 435).
12. For an example of this (in my opinion, misguided) notion that queerness equates to resistance against all norms, see Dean (2000), who also provides an interesting discussion of the ways normalization is critiqued from a Lacanian perspective.

CHAPTER 4

1. As indicated in the previous chapter, I recognize that the distinctions drawn between essentializing and constructivist notions of the subject are often arbitrary and contested. However, for the purposes of this discussion, I have chosen to work within the tensions of this problematic binary because of its broad application in existing discourses related to sexualities and schooling.
2. Project 10 is described by Rolf as an onsite support program, situated on high and middle school campuses in the LAUSD, for gay, lesbian, bisexual, transgendered, and questioning youth. The program started in 1984 at Fairfax High school. The number 10 represents the 10% of the population believed to be gay or lesbian identified.
3. Pansexuality has been defined as "exhibiting or implying many forms of sexual expression" (Merriam-Webster Inc., 2005f).
4. Sexual identities are understood as transhistorical when they are perceived as having always existed.
5. GaLTaS was located in Sydney, Australia, and is now defunct.
6. For further details of the Tsakalos case, see Chapter 1.
7. Thanks to David McInnes for conversations on Christopher Tsakalos, sissy boys, and resistance.
8. Executive staff in schools are defined here as principals, vice principals, and department heads.
9. Linda Garber, editor of *Tilting the Tower: Lesbians, Teaching, Queer Subjects* (1994).
10. The FRC's (2005) mission statement reads as follows: "The Family Research Council champions marriage and family as the foundation of civilization, the seedbed of virtue, and the wellspring of society. We shape public debate and formulate public policy that values human life and upholds the institutions of marriage and the family. Believing that God is the author of life, liberty, and the family, we promote the Judeo-Christian worldview as the basis for a just, free, and stable society" (para. 1).
11. The term is used here because it is often deployed in the rhetoric of the Religious Right.
12. According to the organization's website, " ... the Gay, Lesbian and Straight Education Network (GLSEN) envisions a future in which every child learns to respect and accept all people, regardless of sexual orientation or gender identity/expression" (para. 1).
13. The difficulty of bringing tropes of choice into the discourses of Australia's Catholic schools is exacerbated by comments such as those made by Archbishop George Pell (now a cardinal and the most senior member of the Catholic Church in Australia). Pell has been outspoken in his opposition to homosexuality and is reported to have said that he would "resist the spread of the 'gay agenda' in schools because homosexuality is a more dire health risk than cigarette smoking" (Shiel, 1999, para. 1).
14. For further discussion of Foucault's "ethics of discomfort," see Harwood and Rasmussen (2003).

15. Gay–Straight Alliances are probably the most prolific and fertile vehicle for organizing around sexuality and gender in high schools in the United States. In 2003 there were more than 1,700 gay and lesbian clubs meeting at high schools in the United States (see Ontario Consultants on Religious Tolerance, 2000–2003). They are described as follows on the GLSEN website: "A Gay–Straight Alliance (GSA) is a student-led, non-curricular school club orga-nized (sic) that aims to create a safe, welcoming and accepting environment for all youth, regardless of one's sexual orientation or gender identity. GSAs bring together LGBTQ and Straight students to address issues that affect us all, including harassment, discrimi-nation and bias. A GSA allows these youth to build coalitions and community that can work towards making safer school environ-ments for all people. Most importantly, GSAs provide support for lesbian, gay, bisexual, transgender, or questioning (LGBTQ) identi-fied students" (GLSEN, 2000, p. 2).

16. Ferreira was founder and coordinator of Gender Equity and Issues of Sexual Orientation for the Cambridge, Massachusetts, Public Schools and has since authored *Beyond Diversity Day: A Q & A on Gay and Lesbian Issues in Schools* (Ferreira, 2004).

17. Lavender Youth Recreation and Information Centre (LYRIC) is a community centre for lesbian, gay, bisexual, transgender, and ques-tioning young people aged 23 and under.

18. Kanegson describes the boy-dyke-fag identity as follows: "A boy-dyke, gosh ... a variation on butch, somebody who is a more effeminate butch, sort of like a gay butch. So boy-dyke-fag is a more effeminate type of masculinity ... often butches who date butches, that kind of thing .... But I also identify with the FTM [female-to-male] community because I identify in some ways with male, you know, I don't fit neatly into male or female .... "

19. I perceive the use of the word naturally to be somewhat ironic, as Kanegson's performance of masculinity would probably be perceived as anything but natural in a school setting.

20. "Reference to something by means of another thing that is remotely related to it, either through a farfetched causal relation-ship, or through an implied intermediate substitution of terms. Often used for comic effect through its preposterous exaggeration. A metonymical substitution of one word for another which is itself figurative" (Burton, 1996–2003, click on metalepsis).

21. Transgender is a widely used descriptor in queer communities in Australia and the United States, but its currency is still not as broad as that of the signifiers lesbian and gay. In March 2005 the Education Resources Information Center (ERIC, 2004) contained more than 1,820 articles with the keyword gay and 1,007 with the keyword lesbian, whereas only 130 articles included the term transgender.

CHAPTER 5

1. For an in-depth discussion of the medical treatment of people who identify as intersex, see Fausto-Sterling (2000) and Kessler (1998).

2. Spurlin (1998) borrows this term from de Lauretis (1994).
3. Benestad (2001) quotes the figure of 4%.
4. Gordon (1999) uses the term narrativistic in relation to adolescence, as he argues that tropes of adolescence are "analogous to the discourse of fictional narrative" (p. 3).
5. "In 1979, a 15 year-old boy living in a New York City group home was beaten and sexually assaulted by fellow residents. Group home staff members responded to the incident by blaming the victim — he was discharged and told that he would not have been attacked had he not been gay. When local community activists Emery S. Hetrick, a psychiatrist, and A. Damien Martin, a New York University professor, read about this tragedy, they realized there was a critical vacancy in the network of available social services. There existed a gap between this group of young people who desperately needed support and the services that should have been available to them. Hetrick and Martin marshaled support from concerned community members and youth servicing professionals, founding the Institute for Protection of Lesbian and Gay Youth, renamed The Hetrick-Martin Institute (HMI) in their honor after their deaths" (Hetrick-Martin Institute, 2005a, para. 2).
6. For a list of the oft-quoted risk factors associated with LGBT-identified young people, see HMI (2005b).
7. In the face of this lack of data, Miller ended up producing his own, writing a paper on gay and lesbian youth suicide in South Australia based on a survey he conducted of suicide files in the State Coroner's Court (see Miller, 1994).
8. Reed was the former executive director of the Christian Coalition of America (2005), an organization formed by Pat Robertson. According to its website, the Christian Coalition is the "largest and most active conservative grassroots political organization in America" (para. 1).
9. *Nightline* is a current affairs show broadcast on U.S. free-to-air television.
10. The link to this excerpt taken from the introduction to an interview Melloy conducted with Jennings is no longer active.
11. The following is a synopsis of Chung's story: "There is a disturbing new trend of homeless gay and lesbian teenagers who say they have been thrown out of their homes by their parents. From the smallest towns of America's heartland, they say they were disowned and left to fend for themselves because of their sexual orientation. Nearly 63,000 gay teens are kicked out of their homes each year by their parents. *20/20*'s Connie Chung follows these teens to learn how they struggle to survive without the security of home" (Richter, 1999).
12. For example, see Johnson and Johnson (2000), Lipkin (1999), and MacGillivray (2000).

Chapter 6

1. Debates about coming out and the closet have constituted a key discourse related to sexualities and schooling in Australia and the

United States over the last decade. For a brief history, see Ford (1996), Harbeck (1992), Khayatt (1997), Misson (1999), and Talburt (2004).

2. Gordon (1999) argues against Butler's theorization of identity because of her "assumption that the logically prior and the temporally prior are neither identical nor ontologically inseparable but, rather, that their inseparability is a corollary of their discursive production" (p. 7).

3. *Ex nihilo* means "out of nothing."

4. Students in these colleges are predominantly 16–18 years old.

5. The Sydney Gay and Lesbian Mardi Gras is a month-long festival, culminating in a street parade and party. It is held in February each year and attracts huge crowds from around Australia and internationally.

6. This may refer to people in the community who equate homosexuality with pedophilia or to those in his college who oppose his work.

7. Several organizations advocating for LGBTI-identified students and teachers in K–12 schools (e.g., Context, GaLTaS, Same-Sex Attracted Friendly Environments in Schools [SSAFE]) have been formed, but at the time of writing, all of these groups have disbanded or been defunded.

8. It is not presumed that a proliferation of these groups within Australian schools would necessarily produce a desirable outcome.

9. The safety transfer is used in several U.S. states and allows for public school students to move to another school on the grounds that their safety is compromised at their existing school.

10. The SSCW changed its name in 2001 to the Safe Schools Coalition (2004): "In recognition of our growing e-services and training on an international scale, the coalition launched this new web site, dropped the 'of Washington' from our name and changed our mission. Our mission became, 'A Public–Private Partnership in Support of Gay, Lesbian, Bisexual and Transgender Youth is to help schools — at home and all over the world — become safe places where every family can belong, where every educator can teach, and where every child can learn, regardless of gender identity or sexual orientation'" (para. 1).

11. To my knowledge, no equivalent programs exist in Australia at the time of writing.

12. There are several alternative schools catering to the interests of specific groups of students operating under the auspices of the NYC Board of Education.

13. At time of interview, Rodriguez was associate executive director of policy and public information at HMI.

14. See Henley (2004). For a list of positive and negative public responses to the opening of the school's new campus, see Callalillie (2003).

15. WWCS operated as a private school when it opened in 1997.

16. Schulman (1994) uses this heading to describe the events I analyze in this section.

17. For a discussion of the events surrounding Board 24's prohibition on the discussion of homosexuality, see Mayo (1996).

18. Queens is one of five boroughs that together constitute New York City.
19. Schulman characterizes Middle Village as "an Irish, working class, right to life district" (p. 252).
20. A direct-action group dedicated to lesbian visibility and survival.
21. For an analysis of the role of universities in producing and policing discourses related to sexuality see Tierney (1997) and Gardner Honeychurch (2000).
22. After completing school Bennett renamed himself Krys and began the process of transitioning from female to male. Accordingly, he now uses the male pronoun.
23. Murray Hill is a drag king based in NYC. In 1997 he ran for mayor as a write-in candidate; see http://www.pipeline.com/~jordinyc/kmhill.htm accessed 03/07/05.
24. To see an interview with Bennett about her reign as king, go to http://www.komotv.com/news/story/0,2933,25235,00.htm accessed 21.11.01.
25. See http://www.foxnews.com/story/0,2933,25235,00.htm accessed 21/11/01.
26. See http://www.foxnews.com/story/0,2933,25235,00.htm accessed 21/11/01.
27. According to a news report in the *Bellingham Herald* by Jim Donaldson and Kari Thorene Shaw. This report was posted on the GLSEN website, see http://www.glsen.org/templates/news/record.html?section+12&record+737 accesseed 21/11/2001.

CHAPTER 7

1. For a vigorous debate on the compatibility of psychoanalytic and Foucaultian theories of the subject, see Campbell (2000) and Britzman (1998).
2. Subheading of Chapter 3.
3. Originally published in 1992 (see reference list) as "Sexual Inversions: Rereading the End of Foucault's History of Sexuality, Volume I." Pp. 344–361 in *Discourses of Sexuality: From Aristotle to AIDS*, ed. Donna C. Stanton. RATIO: Institute for the Humanities. Ann Arbor: University of Michigan Press.
4. Butler draws on Spivak (1993) in her discussion "of the lack of originary violence in Foucauldian notions of discursive productivity" (p. 33).
5. ERIC is a digital library of education-related resources sponsored by the Institute of Education Sciences of the U.S. Department of Education. Recent changes brought about by the Education Sciences Reform Act may further influence the character of sexuality research in education in the United States. Future research projects may be required to conform to specific scientific criteria of validity in order to qualify for funding and dissemination.
6. Following Foucault, for Butler (1997d) subjection is a twofold process signifying an ongoing process of becoming a subject, as well as being subordinated (p. 14, 15).

7. I want to thank Deborah Kelly and Tina Fiveash for granting permission to use this work for academic purposes.
8. The recognition of families of choice varies among states in Australia and the United States, though neither country legally recognizes same-sex marriages or awards equivalent benefits across the board to people in same-sex relationships.
9. For a discussion of the production of heterosexualities in gay spaces, see Moran, Skeggs, Tyrer, and Corteen (2001) and Skeggs (1999).
10. For more information, see the YWCA Aotearoa/New Zealand website. Retrieved June 13, 2005, from http://www.ywca.org.nz/about.html.
11. These lesson plans are no longer accessible on the MTV website.
12. Aaron McKinney and Russell Henderson were the two men convicted of murdering Shepard.
13. The Lakemary Center website (Lakemary Center, 2003) states the center's function as follows: "To learn, to grow, to reach for the stars … . These are the goals and dreams of the people served by LAKEMARY — children and adults with developmental disabilities. Founded in 1969 by the cooperative efforts of parent advocates, community leaders, and the Ursuline Community of Sisters, LAKEMARY … is headquartered on a beautiful 32-acre campus … . In this inspiring setting, youngsters reap the many benefits of our unique children's center, featuring a residential school and treatment program" (para. 1). See http://www.lakemaryctr.org/Who%20We%20Are.htm, accessed 18/03/02.
14. The American Civil Liberties Union filed an Amicus brief relating to Limon's case, available via the ACLU website.
15. For a discussion of the absence of pleasure and desire in the production of contemporary U.S. discourses related to sexualities and schooling, see Frankham (2001), Harrison et al. (1996), Sykes (2001), and Tobin (1997).
16. He named the concluding section to volume 1 of *The History of Sexuality* the "Right of Death and Power over Life."
17. See especially Grosz (1995a), McWhorter (1999), and Sullivan (2001).
18. An agony aunt is someone who publicly responds to questions about sex, love, and relationships posed by anonymous readers.
19. Experts on sex.
20. A commercial television station in Australia.

Index

255

SUBJECT INDEX